REMEMBER *the* DISTANCE *that* DIVIDES US

Elizabeth Margaret Chandler. *Courtesy of the Michigan Department of History, Arts, and Libraries, Michigan Historical Center, State Archives of Michigan.*

REMEMBER *the* DISTANCE *that* DIVIDES US

The Family Letters of
Philadelphia Quaker Abolitionist
and Michigan Pioneer
Elizabeth Margaret Chandler,
1830–1842

Edited by
MARCIA J. HERINGA MASON

Michigan State University Press • *East Lansing*

♾ The paper used in this publication meets the minimum requirements
of ANSI/NISO Z39.48-1992 (R 1997) (Permanence of Paper).

Michigan State University Press
East Lansing, Michigan 48823-5245

Printed and bound in the United States of America.

10 09 08 07 06 05 04   1 2 3 4 5 6 7 8 9 10

LIBRARY OF CONGRESS CATALOGING-IN-PUBLICATION DATA
Chandler, Elizabeth Margaret, 1807–1834.
Remember the distance that divides us : the family letters of Philadelphia Quaker abolitionist and
Michigan pioneer Elizabeth Margaret Chandler, 1830–1842 / edited by Marcia J. Heringa Mason.
p. cm.
Includes bibliographical references and index.
ISBN 0-87013-713-1 (alk. paper)
1. Chandler, Elizabeth Margaret, 1807–1834—Correspondence. 2. Women abolitionists—United States—
Correspondence. 3. Abolitionists—United States—Correspondence. 4. Quaker women—Pennsylvania—
Philadelphia—Correspondence. 5. Women pioneers—Michigan—Correspondence. 6. Women social
reformers—Michigan—Correspondence. 7. Frontier and pioneer life—Michigan. 8. Michigan—Social life
and customs—19th century. 9. Antislavery movements—United States—History—19th century.
10. Women's rights—United States—History—19th century. I. Mason, Marcia J. Heringa. II. Title.
E449.C445 2004
326'.8'092—dc22
2004012330

Cover design by Heather Truelove Aiston
Book design by Sharp Des!gns, Inc.

Michigan State University Press is a member of the Green Press Initiative and is committed to developing
and encouraging ecologically responsible publishing practices. For more information about the Green
Press Initiative and the use of recycled paper in book publishing, please visit *www.greenpressinitiative.org.*

Visit Michigan State University Press on the World Wide Web at: *www.msupress.msu.edu*

For John Heringa (1917–2003)
who gave me his curiosity
and can-do spirit

CONTENTS

ACKNOWLEDGMENTS

When I first met Elizabeth Margaret Chandler through her letters almost ten years ago, I knew immediately that others should meet her, too. This book introduces a remarkable woman, and it has taken many remarkable people to help me create it.

I am very grateful for the professional staff and user-friendly atmosphere at the Bentley Library of the University of Michigan in Ann Arbor, where the Elizabeth Margaret Chandler and Minnie Fay Collections are carefully preserved. Director Francis Blouin, Assistant Director William Wallach, Reference Archivist Nancy Bartlett, Reference Assistants Karen Jania and Malgorzata Myc, and the student pages, who provided prompt service, made my research work a pleasant experience.

The staff at Clements Library of the University of Michigan helped me identify names, places, and events and assisted in deciphering nineteenth-century medical and social language for me. Director John Dann shared with me his personal and professional knowledge of Philadelphia, the Brandywine Valley, and the Chandlers. Don Wilcox looked up the medical information for me. John Harriman also willingly offered his assistance with various inquiries, often above and beyond the call of duty.

I gleaned much information from Charles N. Lindquist, director of the Lenawee County Historical Society in Adrian, Michigan, and author of *Lenawee County: A Harvest of Pride and Promise*. He has preserved valuable historical documents about early settlers and written a succinct history of the county. I was also encouraged by his enthusiasm for my project. I am grateful to the family that lives on the former Chandler farm in Adrian for creating a public easement on the property to allow visitors to the Chandler graves.

The Pennsylvania Historical Society made available important background documentation on the Evans/Chandler families. The Society of Friends' excellent record-keeping methods have made it possible to locate individual Quaker names.

Professors Stanley Solvick and Marc Kruman of Wayne State University were my advisers for my master's thesis on Elizabeth Margaret Chandler, and they said this project was worth pursuing. Without their encouragement, I probably would not have gone forward. Alberta Asmar at Wayne State University received and sent faxes for me. Also at Wayne State, Kathy Mutch used her amazing skills at Internet research to find some of the obscure bits of information that haunted me to the end.

The daunting task of transcribing the letters in the Elizabeth Margaret Chandler Collection was made much more pleasant by Carol Quinn, who rented me her Scottsdale, Arizona, condominium for a winter month, where I spent quiet, uninterrupted time enjoying warm sunshine, exotic bird songs, and spectacular mountain views. Scottsdale neighbor Joannie Kopfensteiner rented me two rooms in her charming condo for a second month so I could finish the transcription. She served me delicious Italian meals and helped me unwind by shopping with me, making me laugh, and offering all sorts of personal advice.

Just when I was getting discouraged about the overwhelming task at hand, I received a phone call and letter from Louanne Lasdon, a Chandler family descendant, who gave me new incentive to keep going, if only for her. Her passion and interest in Elizabeth Margaret Chandler and other distant relatives put new meaning into the project.

Evan Burkholder is my hero. He rescued me when I lost my floppy disks and when the hard drive on my old computer died. Spending untold hours while managing a busy law profession, he scanned the entire manuscript so I could reinvent it. Cathy Phillips provided invaluable help on several obscure items for the endnotes and made my final days on the project easier, especially while I was trying to move a household.

Michigan State University Press has a warm, patient, and delightful staff. Director Fred Bohm, Acquisitions Editor Martha Bates, Assistant Director and Editor-in-Chief Julie Loehr, Production Manager Annette Tanner, Project Editor Kristine Blakeslee, and others have spent hours on the production of this book and put up with my delays and questions with grace and encouragement. They have made my efforts presentable. Editor Ellen D. Goldlust-Gingrich made my words readable and attended to those myriad details that I had overlooked.

I appreciate the time Lynn Bonfield, John Dann, William H. Mulligan, Virginia Bailey Parker, and Patricia Van Pelt spent in reading my manuscript and endorsing the book.

My friend Cynthia Korolov has journeyed with me the whole way on this project, including joining me on a trip to Adrian, where we located Elizabeth Chandler's grave and found treasures in the Lenawee County Historical Society's archives. Cynthia also continues to write to me detailed and fascinating longhand letters in an age of e-mail and phone calls.

My family, John and Lucile Heringa, Heather Leigh DeVries Briody, Cori Jo DeVries Vander Ley, and Rachel Suzanne DeVries Sterner have patiently listened to me talk about Elizabeth Margaret Chandler ad infinitum. Devin DeVries Fisher, Samuel McRae Sterner, Sofia Louise Briody, and Natalie Rae Vander Ley are my sunshine and gave their grandmother reasons to carry on.

Finally, Philip Parker Mason provided the incentive I needed to undertake this project and has supported me in countless ways. He suggested that I write a paper on Michigan pioneer women, the endeavor that first brought me to Elizabeth Margaret Chandler. He read the introduction and offered sage advice. He encouraged me on those occasions when I was ready to quit. He became my research assistant when I needed help. And, finally, he kept me focused, made me feel loved, and gave me reasons to laugh when I wanted to cry.

EDITOR'S NOTES

In an effort to maintain the writer's voice in each letter, I have made minimal changes to the original text. The spellings remain as they appear in the originals, with the exception of an occasional oversight that I am convinced the writer would also have corrected (e.g., adding a *d* to *and* or adding the second *e* to *thee*).

I did, however, intervene to create a more readable sentence and paragraph structure. Because of an absence of nineteenth-century American standards for spelling, grammar, and punctuation, some of the correspondents used dashes and others used commas to separate sentences. At times writers did not begin sentences with capital letters. In their efforts to fit as much content as possible on a page they often separated paragraphs with dashes or simply a space between trains of thought. To facilitate a smoother flow, I have inserted periods and paragraph divisions, and I have regularized capitalization where appropriate. I did not, however, change the use of commas within sentences. I heartily recommend that readers interested in analyzing early-nineteenth-century writing styles examine these letters in their original form. It is indeed a visual treat to see firsthand the writer's ability to write such tiny and dense letters with a quill pen. Elizabeth in particular had a marvelous skill for writing minutely.

In the instances where I was unable to read a word or phrase because the paper was torn, the wax seal obscured the text, or I simply could not decipher the handwriting, I have inserted brackets to show that something is missing. I have added letters or words in brackets to clarify the writer's meaning. All words that are underlined in the originals appear here in italics. All postscripts—additions written after the main body of the letter was finished—appear after the writer's signature, regardless of their original location. Address lines and other material before salutations have not been reproduced; each letter is preceded by a headnote indicating writer, recipient, writer's location, and date on which letter was begun. Some letters were composed over several months; other completed letters waited lengthy periods before being sent; in still other cases writers recopied several letters onto a single sheet of paper before sending them. With the exception of the excerpt from Elizabeth Chandler's letter to Hannah Townsend in chapter 2, all letters appear in chronological order based on when composition began.

I have included in this volume most of the letters from the Elizabeth Margaret Chandler Collection. I did not include a group of letters written from 1793 to 1808 by Elizabeth's grandmother, parents, and aunts because they do not pertain to the story told here. I also left out most of the irrelevant correspondence between Elizabeth Chandler and Anna Coe and a few short notes written by various correspondents in the 1840s. Any other letters to which correspondents refer but that do not appear in this volume are not in the collection.

Where possible I have identified places, events, and unusual phrases in the endnotes and names in the biographical directory.

The introduction provides background and an understanding of the correspondents' religion and cultural setting. It does not constitute a definitive statement on Quakerism, feminism, or pioneer life. The bibliography lists many titles that address these subjects more thoroughly.

INTRODUCTION

———•◆•———

Elizabeth Margaret Chandler, along with her brother, Thomas Chandler, and her aunt, Ruth Evans, migrated to the Michigan Territory in 1830, when it was still a frontier. They left a comfortable urban setting in Philadelphia to settle an eighty-acre homestead, which Elizabeth named Hazelbank, near the banks of the River Raisin in Lenawee County, midway between the towns of Tecumseh and Adrian. Elizabeth wrote many detailed and eloquent letters from Hazelbank to relatives in Philadelphia. Her letters, along with letters written by Thomas and Ruth and by Aunt Jane Howell and others in Philadelphia, reveal important historical information about the family, about the settling of Michigan, and about life in Philadelphia during the early 1800s. A great-niece of Elizabeth's, Minnie Chandler Merritt Fay, donated the collection of family letters and genealogical information to the Bentley Library at the University of Michigan in 1941.

Minnie Chandler Merritt Fay was born on November 14, 1859, in Battle Creek, Michigan, to Charles Merritt and Elizabeth Margaret Chandler Merritt. Charles Merritt, of Battle Creek, was the younger brother of Jane Merritt Chandler, who had married Thomas Chandler in 1843 and joined him at Hazelbank, where they raised their four children. While visiting his sister and brother-in-law at Hazelbank one day in 1856, Charles met Thomas's twenty-one-year-old niece, Elizabeth Margaret Chandler, who was named after her pioneer aunt and who had come from Philadelphia to visit her Uncle Thomas and Aunt Jane. Charles and Elizabeth fell in love and married two years later, establishing their home and a sterling reputation in Battle Creek.

Elizabeth Margaret Chandler Merritt was born on March 20, 1835, in Lancaster, Pennsylvania, to William and Sarah Chandler, brother and sister-in-law of pioneers Thomas and Elizabeth. She was their third child and only daughter. When her aunt, Elizabeth Margaret Chandler, heard in 1834 that William and Sarah were expecting their third child, she apparently expressed the hope that they would add a daughter to their family of two boys. However, she never learned that her hopes had been realized, because she became ill during this time and died on November 2, 1834, before her niece was born. Prior to her death, she had bequeathed her name, a few personal possessions, and a small sum of money to her hoped-for niece.

Because of her aunt's respected reputation, Elizabeth Margaret Chandler Merritt took a special interest in her aunt's legacy. After Sarah Chandler died, her daughter inherited the family letters, which had been gathered together by Thomas and William from Michigan and Philadelphia. In 1909, at age seventy-four, Elizabeth Merritt began investigating her ancestry and requested genealogical information from the Friends' Library in Philadelphia. When she died in 1923 the letters went to her daughter, Minnie Chandler Merritt Fay, who continued the genealogical research.

In 1925, Minnie Fay, with the assistance of her lawyers, Mechem and Mechem of Battle Creek, Michigan, approached the *Yale Review* and the *Saturday Evening Post* to suggest that they publish the entire set of family letters in book form. The *Battle Creek Enquirer and Evening News* and the *Adrian Daily Telegram* had already agreed to secure local publication rights for the entire set. The *Saturday Evening Post* declined the offer, but the *Yale Review* agreed at least to read the group of letters. At the journal's request, Minnie Fay permitted the publication of a few letters in the magazine before having the entire set put into a book form. In March of 1926 nine of the letters appeared in the *Yale Review* and subsequently in the *Battle Creek Enquirer and Evening News* and in the *Adrian Telegram,* but the book was never published.

In 1941, when the entire collection was donated to the Bentley Library, Minnie Fay turned over not only the collection of family letters, which became the Elizabeth Margaret Chandler Collection, but also a considerable amount of genealogical and personal information about the family, which became the Minnie Fay Collection. The material subsequently has seen the light of day only when a researcher has brought the papers out of their boxes in the library. This book will give to these two collections the public attention they have long deserved because they tell an engaging story about an extraordinary woman and her family.

Elizabeth Margaret Chandler was born on December 24, 1807, in Centreville, Delaware (in the Brandywine Valley) to Margaret Evans Chandler and Thomas Chandler. Elizabeth was the youngest of three children. Her brother William had been born on December 6, 1804, and her brother Thomas joined the family on

March 4, 1806. Elizabeth never knew her mother, who died two days after giving birth. Whether Margaret's death was caused by difficulties related to childbirth or by a protracted illness is unclear. A November 1807 letter from her husband, Thomas, to her family in Philadelphia indicates that approximately six weeks prior to Elizabeth's birth Margaret was suffering from abdominal pain. According to Thomas, the "illness attacked her in meeting." Two weeks later Thomas reported that Margaret was "much better." Eleven days later he stated, "Margaret continues poorly," and by December 20 she was "but middling." Margaret's mother, Elizabeth Guest Evans, had traveled from Philadelphia to Centreville to help Margaret during her illness and through the last stage of her pregnancy. After her daughter's death, Elizabeth Evans remained in the Brandywine Valley to help Thomas with the children.[1]

Margaret Chandler's situation was not unlike what her daughter, Elizabeth Margaret, experienced more than twenty years later when she exchanged city life for country life. Margaret had grown up in Philadelphia, but after she and Thomas married, they moved to the Brandywine Valley, where Thomas took up farming. Although Thomas had been educated in Philadelphia and had studied medicine, he chose to take over the family farm, which he inherited from his father, who had received it from his uncle, also named Thomas Chandler. The 167-acre farm was located in the bend of the Brandywine River in Centre Township, Chester County, Pennsylvania. From her farmhouse, Margaret wrote letters to her family in Philadelphia, describing her difficult farm life.[2]

After Margaret died, Thomas remained on the farm for two more years. During this time, he apparently decided that caring for all three of his children while managing the home and the farm was more than he and his mother-in-law could handle, so the three motherless Chandler children took turns visiting Philadelphia, where they were cared for by Ruth Evans and Jane Evans Howell, Margaret's sisters. By October 15, 1808, Elizabeth Evans had returned to Philadelphia with her granddaughter, and Thomas wrote from Delaware, "I should like to see little Elizabeth Margaret—I hope she is a good girl."[3]

A survey of the farm in Centreville was conducted in 1810, and at this time Thomas Chandler left farming and returned to Philadelphia to pursue the medical career for which he had trained.[4] Thomas apparently had no difficulty being accepted as a doctor, in spite of the seven-year gap between the end of his education and the beginning of his practice. Because there were no examining boards for licensure at this time, a school diploma was accepted as qualification to practice medicine.

Medical training in the late eighteenth and early nineteenth centuries could be characterized as rustic and experimental. With the exception of its few key cities, America remained primarily a frontier nation. The first American medical college, founded in Philadelphia in 1765, had originally patterned its curriculum after the medical school at the University of Edinburgh, where early prominent American physicians such as Benjamin Rush had received their medical degrees. The course of study at this time required students to know Latin and Greek; to understand the branches of mathematics and natural and experimental philosophy that would relate to medical issues; to take at least one course each in anatomy, materia medica, and chemistry; and to attend physic and clinical lectures. The student then practiced at the Pennsylvania Hospital for one year, apprenticed under some respectable practitioner, and was required to demonstrate a general knowledge of pharmacy. By 1777, however, these requirements had been relaxed. Latin and Greek were no longer required, and the college course eventually shortened to between twelve and sixteen weeks. Apprenticeships also lost their emphasis because of a lack of qualified instructors. Thomas Chandler received his education during this more relaxed period of medical training and could, therefore, make the transition from farming to medicine with relative ease. He served as a physician at 341 Market Street in Philadelphia for five years, until his death in 1815.

The three Chandler children, orphaned at ages eleven, nine, and eight, were subsequently cared for by their maternal grandmother and aunts. At the time of Thomas Chandler's death in 1815, Elizabeth Guest Evans and her daughters, Amelia and Ruth, were living at 14 South Second Street in Philadelphia; another daughter, Jane Evans Howell, lived with her husband, Lemuel, at 477 North Second Street. The women kept a "little shop of notions" on Second Street, and they appeared to be financially comfortable. Elizabeth Guest Evans's father had been a successful merchant and, in addition to the income from her dry-goods business, she had a considerable inheritance. Lemuel Howell was also a successful businessman who ran a busy construction firm in the city.[5]

Despite the loss of both mother and father at young ages, the three Chandler children never lacked for love or for a sense of family. The surrogate parenting they received from their grandmother and from their aunts and uncle adequately compensated for the loss of their parents. Elizabeth Evans, the children's beloved grandmother, died in 1826, when the three children were young adults living in Philadelphia.

The city of Philadelphia, which had been founded by William Penn in 1682 and incorporated in 1701, was a thriving metropolis during the early years of the republic, and the children grew up within an urban environment that provided them with ample goods and services as well as strong social and religious ties. Philadelphia's 1806 directory described the city in glowing terms. It was the capital of Pennsylvania and considered a chief city of the United States in "size and Splendour." It stood second in "commercial importance" behind New York. According to the directory, "the streets of Philadelphia are paved with pebble stones and bordered with ample footways, raised one foot above the carriage way,

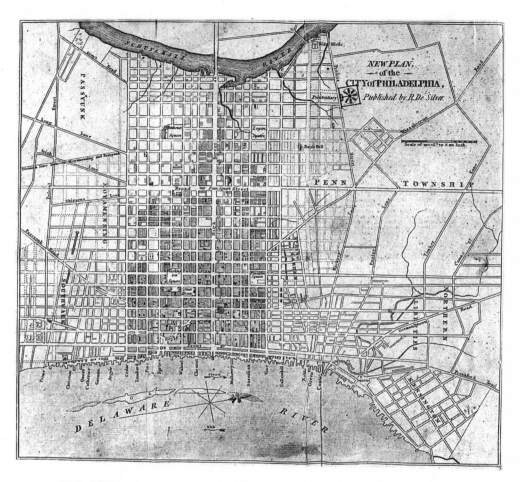

Philadelphia, ca. 1830. *Courtesy of the Clements Library, University of Michigan.*

for the ease and safety of passengers. They are kept cleaner than those of any city in Europe, excepting the towns of Holland, where trade is carried on by canals; and London is the only capital in the world that is better lighted at night." Many of the private buildings were three stories high, built of "clear red brick, ornamented with facings, keystones and flights of white marble."[6]

In 1806 the city contained thirteen thousand homes, eighty thousand people, and thirty churches and meetinghouses. The directory also listed Philadelphia's many public institutions, which only added to its character of refinement. This long list included a university, free schools (public and private), a philosophical society, a museum, a public library, hospital and dispensary, almshouses, and a college of physicians. The city boasted many societies organized to promote agriculture, encourage arts and manufacture, advocate the abolition of slavery, and alleviate the miseries of public prisons. Philadelphia had four chartered banks, six marine insurance companies, two fire insurance companies, and forty-one printing offices, seven of which published daily papers. There was a U.S. mint located in the city, a type foundry, and many manufactories. The directory also proudly declared that births exceeded deaths by five to three, but it admitted to having excessive heat in the summer months, which led to the propagation of the yellow fever of the West Indies, "which of late so frequently introduced in the U.S., through perpetual intercourse, feebly restrained by the inadequate operations of local and temporary health laws."[7]

During this period, the Chandler and Evans families were part of Philadelphia's large Quaker community, and the Chandler children were raised in this embracing and liberal environment, which advocated education for girls as well as boys. All three children received their education in Quaker schools, and Quakerism's influences made Elizabeth Margaret Chandler acutely aware of the social ills of the day, about which she became concerned at a very young age and wrote assionately until her death.

The Quaker movement began in England during an age of tremendous upheaval that followed the Reformation in the late 1600s.[8] During this free-thinking period in England's history, new sectarian movements emerged, among them the Quakers, a derogatory name attributed to group members by those outside the faith. The beliefs and practices of Quakers, officially called the Society of Friends, set them apart as leaders of the concept of spiritual equality, and historians regard them as at the far left of the radical Puritan movement.

Unique to the Quakers was their view of women as spiritual equals to men and their approach to spirituality as being an individual rather than a collective experience. Each society member, man or woman, maintained a private relationship with God and relied for inspiration on "inner light" rather than on leadership from ordained ministers.[9] The emphasis on individualism was later supplanted by appointed ministers in an attempt by Quaker leaders to instill some order in what, through the eighteenth and nineteenth centuries, had become a breeding ground for chaos and schisms within the movement.

These early Quakers rejected social customs prescribed by class status. They used the familiar *thee* and *thou* terms when addressing superiors to indicate a belief in an egalitarian society. The Quakers chose to dress in plain clothes to repudiate the conspicuous style of traditional and elitist culture and the conventions of social distinction. Quakers were bent on removing the traditional landmarks and barriers of social life. George Fox, the Society of Friends' most noted founder, preached that "that of God" existed in all men and women everywhere, no matter their skin color or country of origin. In 1648 he defended the right of women to speak in church and argued that men and women were "helpmeet," or equal.[10]

Within this framework of attempted social disruption, Quaker women in seventeenth-century England became preachers and prophets during a time when public expression was denied to any woman outside the royal line. Quakerism cut across the lines of gender and class and allowed women to engage in a public role such as ministry, encouraging them—as the Church of England had not—to use their gifts and to be active outside of the domestic sphere. Women took advantage of this freedom through the avenues of preaching, prophesying, and publishing, all of which affected society and politics in some way.[11]

Despite this framework of spiritual equality, however, women remained socially subjugated to a patriarchal gender structure in which men believed that women were not capable of exercising real authority in their own right. In addition, as British Friends grew wealthy and conservative toward the end of the seventeenth century, they began to adopt some of the Puritans' concepts of male authority in the household and in the church. Still, between 1648 and 1725 the movement was basically a positive, apostolic, and catholic effort that forged new territories of religion with energy and drive.

Quakerism established itself in America between 1650 and 1800, when traveling women ministers preached and prophesied to colonists in New England, but these women were often misunderstood and characterized as "dangerous heretics and unsubmissive." Their unusual behavior resulted in accusations of witchcraft that led to their imprisonment, deportation, banishment, persecution, and execution. Powerful women threatened Puritan values, especially the role of male authority in the household, which had come to dominate American culture.[12]

In 1658 New York passed an anti-Quaker act. As a result, Quakers felt the need for a colony of their own to ensure protection from widespread persecution. By 1681 William Penn, a Quaker from England, secured land from his friend, Charles II, and established Pennsylvania as a colony, which he called a "Holy Experiment." The Quakers settled in and around Philadelphia, finding comfort and security within homogeneous communities.

Philadelphia's Friends developed a sophisticated system of organization that allowed both men and women active roles in participation and decision making. The organizational structure functioned through preparative meetings, monthly business meetings, and quarterly and yearly meetings in addition to weekly or semiweekly meetings for worship. The monthly meetings served as a monitor to determine if one person's sense of a holy leading met a corresponding answer in the soul of his or her peers. No hierarchy existed among the members. Women held monthly meetings separate from the men and served as the moral monitors, watching over the conversation and behavior of members, particularly the young; speaking to those who strayed; and providing for the poor and the ill and for the education of children. The women also determined a young couple's "clearness" or readiness for marriage. Men's monthly meetings handled the business matters and the political issues that related to Quaker ideology.[13]

The radical flavor of the early Quaker movement eventually stagnated. For almost one hundred years, beginning in the early eighteenth century, the Society of Friends concentrated on a timid exclusivity in which its leaders no longer broke new ground but rather cultivated existing dogma and encouraged the creation of a "peculiar people" set off from the world. However, a disruption in the movement occurred in 1827 and 1828, creating a schism between two factions—the Orthodox and Hicksite Quakers—that has been characterized by some of its members as the "darkest and saddest" period in the history of American Quakerism.[14]

The division began when Elias Hicks, a Long Island farmer and Quaker minister, promoted a radicalism that Orthodox Quakers labeled heresy. He encouraged Friends to embrace a new form of expression that echoed the social and political challenges of the movement's early formation in seventeenth-century England. He returned to the emphasis on the revelatory power of "inner light" over any laws or principles provided in "external aids," including the Bible, and within this belief system he became a strong opponent of slavery. He wore unbleached linen to avoid the use of slave products. Those who followed Hicks's teachings were more likely to be recent immigrants from rural areas or families with old wealth who resented the commercialism of rising entrepreneurs. Hicksites continued to share responsibilities between husband and wife on the farm or in the small shop, were less influenced by the new nineteenth-century roles for men and women, and were more loyal to the older Quaker tradition.[15]

Philadelphia's Orthodox Friends comprised a small, socially cohesive, business-oriented community. They were comfortable with the status quo and did not want their lives disrupted by this new ideology. They also chose to adhere to a gender ideology that promoted patriarchy.

The Evans and Chandler families embraced the Hicksite philosophy, yet their letters reveal an openness to and acceptance of some of the Orthodox Quakers' views. Jane Howell expressed just such an acceptance in one of her letters: "The Orthodox friends are now raising several thousand dollars by subscription for the purpose of liberating and sending to Lyberia a number of slaves in Carolina, and have nearly all subscribed. When they call on me I shall do so with the greatest pleasure."[16]

Elizabeth Margaret Chandler, therefore, viewed life through the lens of a religion that taught her openness, egalitarianism, and concern for humanity of both genders and of every race and color. Her upbringing allowed and even encouraged her to write and publish her views on women, education, and slavery. Before she turned sixteen, she was entering poetry contests and her humanitarian poems and essays began appearing in print in such popular publications as the *Atlantic Souvenir,* the *Pearl,* the *Liberator,* and the *Genius of Universal Emancipation* as well as in abolitionist journals.

When Thomas and Elizabeth Chandler and Ruth Evans removed to Michigan in 1830, it is not immediately apparent that they chose their land, because Quakers were already settled there. The Chandlers and Evans did, however, "find comfort in being situated one mile from Friends Meeting," in spite of the fact that most of those already in the area were Orthodox. In her first letter "beneath our own roof and by our own fireside," written approximately four months after their arrival in Michigan, Elizabeth indicated that "most of the members of our meeting are orthodox" and "among the others there is some division of sentiment, but very little of feeling is at least obvious." To Elizabeth and her family it made "no difference nor do I think it does towards us," though she later mentioned the establishment of the monthly meeting "in our settlement" under the direction of the Orthodox Friends, "so that we, of course, shall be excluded." Nevertheless, the Chandlers intended to continue attending meetings of worship "as usual." She also anticipated "another meeting—Hicksite—established before a very great while" as soon as there were enough "solid members."[17]

By June 1832 Elizabeth indicated that a significant increase had occurred in the number of Friends who had settled in the area. The meetinghouse had at first been "amply sufficient for both men and women in its ends." However, just one year later, even after an addition was built, "a fresh supply of benches to accommodate all its attendants [is needed], and I do not know of one discontented person in all the neighborhood." Two months later she mentioned the arrival "in the neighborhood, [of] Smith Laing and family. . . . The Wife, Abigail, is a preacher, *high proof orthodox.*" By 1833 the Quaker settlement had grown considerably, and on May 25, 1833, Elizabeth observed in a letter to her aunt, Jane, that "we begin to find it quite difficult to keep up our recognition of all the faces at meeting even on the women's side."[18]

The fact that a newcomer into the Michigan Territory was either Hicksite or Orthodox was apparently not as important as whether or not a marriage took place between a Quaker and an "outsider." Even then, the Chandler/Evans family approached the issue with relative acceptance. Although many Friends were migrating into the new territory, there was still the danger of a mixed marriage between a Quaker and an outsider. Ruth Evans relayed her concern about a friend of Elizabeth's, Julia Webb, who "will be married before long to a lawyer in Adrian. I should think it a more suitable connection if he had belonged to the Society of Friends, however, I hope he may prove deserving of her." Elizabeth expressed a similar attitude when she wrote about the wedding. "The bride was an acquaintance of mine. . . . With her chosen I was not acquainted. . . . She was a Friend by birthright, but as he was a Baptist she humored him by having the ceremony performed in Baptist meeting." Elizabeth found this wedding unusual enough to detail in that same letter: "It is quite common here to have marriages performed on first day at the place of worship, or rather it is not uncommon. I was not invited nor anybody else from here." She added a detail about what the bride wore: "In case of thy feeling any curiosity as to the dress of the 'back woods' bride, I can tell thee that she was to wear watered silk dress and white satin shoes, etc., etc."[19]

The subject of marriage rarely appeared in Elizabeth's letters. Elizabeth had been raised mostly by her unmarried aunt, Ruth Evans, but had also been very much attended to by her married aunt, Jane Evans Howell, and was influenced by both lifestyles. The reasons for her decision to remain single cannot be determined from the material available, but some Quaker women's attitudes toward marriage in general may shed light on her comfort with her unmarried status. For example, in 1806 Ruth Evans, who never married, received a letter from a friend, Lydia Logue, extolling the value of celibacy.[20]

Writing about Julia's wedding, Elizabeth Chandler did not reveal any envy about the marriage, only regret that Julia would be moving to Adrian and that they would not be seeing each other as often. There was also little interchange between Elizabeth and Jane Howell regarding the prospects of marriage for Elizabeth—only two mentions by Aunt Jane during their four years of correspondence. In 1831 Jane quoted a conversation between two of Jane's cousins: Betsey Guest said of Chandler, "I think that Elizabeth will become one of the first women in Michigan. And I have hardly a doubt but that she will settle to advantage there." Replied Anna Guest, "But the only husband she could take would be an Indian." In a letter written two years later, Jane Howell asked Elizabeth about the status of marriages "in your settlement . . . or is matrimony quite out of vogue? This is a subject which thee has never touched upon, although it is so universally interesting. I should think young men would be a mere drug there, it must make the girls very saucy in selecting husbands."[21]

The two-year span between these letters reflects the population changes transpiring in the Michigan Territory. Westward migration had increased dramatically, and Jane speculated that the pool of available men had grown. Elizabeth never responded directly to her aunt's query, but in October 1833 Elizabeth wrote about the weddings taking place in the Michigan Territory noting, "As to myself I still keep true in allegiance to the single sisterhood." She also dispelled the theory about the abundance of available men when she added, "The Society here has much improved since we first came on; there is a much larger circle, particularly of females, who seem to maintain the majority with us, though I believe it is not very customary for them to do so in new countries."[22]

Many Quaker women did not see marriage as essential for personal fulfillment, and Quaker women who never married still retained a respected position among fellow Quakers. Their ministry and teaching provided them with means of support that prevented them from being seen as a burden on the households of their male relatives. Elizabeth Chandler died unmarried at age twenty-six. While it is of course impossible to know whether she would eventually have married had she lived longer, marriage clearly was not one of her immediate aspirations.[23]

While the subject of marriage received little attention in Elizabeth's private letters, the matters of women's conduct and education appeared often in her public writings. She had been influenced by Hicksite beliefs and Quaker attitudes toward the spiritual equality of men and women, endowing her with a freedom to express herself publicly. The Quakers in general were also influential in pioneering social reform issues during the early decades of the republic, and education was one of their important causes. In fact, between 1750 and 1850 the Society of Friends established elementary and secondary education for young girls and women in southeastern Pennsylvania and northern Delaware. This emphasis on education did not as such challenge the national ideology of republican motherhood but instead represented a declaration of the value Quakers placed on both females and males as being "of God." They viewed children as members of the Society of Friends at birth rather than as a result of baptism or conversion, as other churches practiced, and charged parents with a responsibility to teach their children to read and write. In 1790 Quakers began a movement to establish schools for themselves and for the poor.[24]

Most of Elizabeth Chandler's essays on education appeared first in Benjamin Lundy's *Genius of Universal Emancipation* and later in other periodicals. She believed that all people should be instructed and that universal education was the "main pillar that must eventually support the temple of our liberty." An important element of female education, in her view, was for the woman "to discharge her duties, not to exalt her till she despises them; to make it her ambition to merit and display the character of the most amiable and intelligent of her sex, rather than aspire to emulate the conduct and capacity of men." While Chandler relegated women to a position of subordination when she suggested that "women may hope to take their true, their most dignified stations, as the helpers, the companions, of education and independent men," she nevertheless promoted intelligence rather than "feminine wiles" as an admirable quality for women to attain. She suggested, too, that while women are "readily and willingly" regarded as having influence on manners, "might not their influence on the *mind* be made quite as irresistible, and far more beneficial?" In her poem "Woman," Chandler advocated a greater degree of education for women and prophesied eventual equality for them when she wrote,

> Such woman is — and shall proud man forbear
> The converse of the mind with her to share?

> No! she with him shall knowledge's pages scan,
> And be the partner, not the toy of man.[25]

In addition to promoting female education, Chandler also championed women as educators. Out of the Quaker movement to educate male and female children came the first open advocacy for young women to become teachers. In 1832 Elizabeth Chandler was faced with an opportunity to teach. She had received "several invitations to keep school" since her arrival in the Michigan Territory and "a week or two since a very pressing one." The request came from a neighbor who lived "about three or four miles distant" and who was "anxious for me to go there and take charge of her daughter and some other girls for a few months." Chandler was attracted to the offer but felt compelled to decline because it would mean leaving Ruth alone with all the domestic duties: "Such a distance" meant that she could not "return at night" and, therefore, could not "extend a care over home." Nevertheless, the appeal swayed her enough to request that Jane send her a math textbook so that she could "furbish up in arithmetic if I should undertake to play teacher, and in case of having an offer made me that I could accept." Chandler thought this would be an opportune time to "fit myself to become a teacher, if at any time it should be necessary or advisable for me to follow that occupation." She was aware of a possible impending need to be self-supporting when she added, "I wish to feel that if I am blessed with health, I can always depend upon myself and my resources for support, and besides, even if no other end is attained, I shall have the satisfaction of improving myself."[26]

The trend during this period was for women teachers to teach reading, spelling, and sewing, while men taught reading, writing, and arithmetic. In studying Quakers in the mid-Atlantic between 1790 and 1850, Joan Jensen found no records of schoolmistresses teaching arithmetic to girls.[27] When Elizabeth requested an arithmetic book to prepare herself to teach the subject to girls, she did not fit the typical pattern that existed back east. Frontier Michigan afforded uncharted opportunities and challenges for women teachers.

Jane Howell's response to Elizabeth's teaching offers is notable. Howell apparently solicited the opinions of her Philadelphia friends and relatives regarding Elizabeth's offers and felt compelled to advise Elizabeth on the matter. Jane assured her niece that her "friends all approve of thy keeping a school providing thee can have one at home." She added, "It will be the means of beguiling many a tedious hour if there is no other advantage arising from it." Aunt Jane also described the idea of Elizabeth teaching at a school any distance from home as "unpleasant to my feelings." In August of the same year Elizabeth "walked over to the school house, to pay a visit to the 'rising hope' of our settlement." It was her first visit to a "country school," and she "felt much interest," but no evidence exists to indicate that she ever accepted a teaching job. She did, however, tutor the farm's servant girl, Emily, who learned to read and write.[28]

The move to solicit female teachers grew out of necessity. Although Quakers considered males to be the proper teachers, the scarcity of teachers gave young women opportunities for public occupation. Because Quaker women in the nineteenth century generally married later than their mothers had, and because responsibilities at home were changing, a longer period between maturity and the establishment of their own homes made women available for such a profession. In spite of the tensions between the potential for liberating change and the potential for culture conformity, literacy, education, and teaching seemed to offer some amount of liberation for women. Literacy carried women beyond the confines of home to a place in the public sphere that they occupied proudly and from which they were able to engage in battles to extend the rights claimed by men. Teaching enabled these women to interact socially and intellectually in ways that previously had been afforded only to men.[29]

Elizabeth Chandler publicly advocated female "school-keeping" and argued in her essays that a shortage of male instructors was a result of many "pursuits, more lucrative and agreeable to active and ambitious young men." She did not stop at the supply-and-demand argument, however. She also believed that women were "by temper and habit admirably qualified for the task" and that they inherently had "patience, fondness for children, are accustomed to seclusion, and inured to self-government." Elizabeth and perhaps other female advocates of education did not consciously view teaching as an open door to the public sphere but rather as an extension of their "natural gifts," which were normally utilized in the home. Yet Elizabeth felt a need to argue for a credible female public voice when she stated that if women were afforded opportunities for improvement and motives for "exertions," they would and could "converse sensibly without the charge of pedantry" and that when women were "expected to be rational, and required to be useful . . . they will not disappoint public expectations."[30]

Although Chandler's views on women's roles did not embody a modern feminist attitude, she can be credited with holding a view that could easily lead to advocacy for women's rights. Quakerism's early roots also deserve some of the credit. Although Fox is not labeled a feminist, since to do so would be anachronistic, his respect for women, his appreciation of their buried talents, and his willingness to battle for their rights certainly led the Society toward a gender equality in the centuries that followed.[31] The advent of Quaker women's business meetings gave women opportunities to develop public leadership skills, to learn to rely on their own strength and wisdom, and to encourage and support each other's talents. The early steps taken by women in the Society of Friends—traveling ministry, business meetings, and the concept of equal education—laid the groundwork for the strides female Quakers would make in the decades ahead.

During the early years of the republic and the formation of cult of true womanhood, Elizabeth Chandler stepped into the public sphere through her published writings. She wrote against feminine superficiality and encouraged women to develop their intellect through education. She challenged women to think for themselves and to resist societal pressures that relegated a woman to a private role in which her primary focus should be on home and family within a patriarchal marital structure. Instead, Chandler asked women to reach beyond the care and concern for their immediate family and step out into the world—specifically, into the world of the slave.

Abolitionism was one of the major reform movements that Quaker women felt comfortable embracing. Abolition fit into their convictions of care and concern for others, and they used the injustices of slavery as a forum for public outcry and activism. Egalitarian views about the value of all humans equipped Quaker women with the necessary arguments for advocating the abolition of slavery and the courage to move into the public sphere for the cause. Through her writings, Chandler chose the abolitionist movement as her primary platform, and she is best known for her antislavery activity. She has been credited as "perhaps the most widely read female writer in the antislavery ranks." In a memoir and tribute following Elizabeth's death, Benjamin Lundy, an abolitionist who hired her to take charge of the Ladies' Department of his weekly paper, the *Genius of Universal Emancipation,* wrote, "No one of her sex, in America, has hitherto contributed as much to the enlightenment of the public mind, relative to this momentous question, as she has done." For almost a decade, from her mid-teens until her death in 1834, Elizabeth crusaded against slavery by writing and publishing, establishing an antislavery society, and joining and promoting the free-produce movement, which advocated that consumers refuse to purchase products grown with slave labor.[32]

Elizabeth Chandler's Quaker background influenced her antislavery passion and gave her the impetus to crusade against slavery. The very early New World Quakers had responded to the antislavery sentiments of George Fox, whose first reference to slavery appeared in 1657. Fox's egalitarian ideas of humanity challenged the spirituality of anyone involved in a master-slave relationship. Following a trip to Barbados, Fox, although he did not condemn slaveholding as such, expounded the idea of the equality of men in the eyes of God.[33]

Thirty years later, on February 18, 1688, Friends in Germantown, Pennsylvania, drew up a very outspoken and clear-cut protest against slavery. These German, Swiss, and Dutch immigrants hated the idea of slavery in the same land to which they had come to find freedom, and they were the first citizens of this land to promote antislavery sentiments. They labeled slave owning "a moral abomination identical to theft" because it promoted adultery as a result of the separation of wives and husbands.[34]

John Woolman, a Quaker minister born in 1720, has been credited as being the most influential Quaker of the eighteenth century and perhaps the most Christlike individual that Quakerism has ever produced. In 1754 Woolman wrote an essay, endorsed by the Philadelphia yearly meeting, stating that the Golden Rule applied equally to all men. In spite of the endorsement, however, many Quakers openly refused to follow the yearly meeting's advice. A deliberate act of defiance was exhibited in the summer of 1758 when several Philadelphia Friends purchased blacks and asked to have the statement prohibiting slave buying removed. Instead, participants at the next yearly meeting decided to remove the slave buyers from positions of authority. This definitive action paved the way for the eventual elimination of slavery first from Philadelphia Quakerism and later from all Quakerism. In fact, as a result of Woolman's and schoolmaster Anthony Benezet's antislavery speeches and writings, the 1776 Philadelphia Yearly Meeting disowned members who refused to free their slaves. Elizabeth Chandler later honored these two influential abolitionists in her poems.[35]

Once the act of buying slaves had officially been banned, slavery itself took its place as the issue to address. By 1778 Quakers began manumitting their slaves. As Fox had advocated a century earlier, the slaves received a start in life at the time of their manumission, with Friends compensating their freed slaves for work done while in slavery. The 1778 and 1779 Philadelphia Yearly Meetings urged local meetings to look after the temporal and spiritual welfare of their former slaves. By the time the colonies achieved their independence from Britain, the Quakers' slaves had likewise received their freedom.[36]

Important to the effectiveness of the early antislavery movement was the formation of organized societies. Either local or traveling agents organized these societies, using predominantly religious arguments and with church and antislavery newspapers as their arena. In 1775 Philadelphia Quakers organized the first association in the New World devoted exclusively to abolition, the Society for the Relief of Free Negroes Unlawfully Held in Bondage. By 1820 more than 140 abolition societies existed in the United States, most of them meeting biennially. They heard reports of local activity on behalf of free blacks and slaves, issued memorials on the slave trade and slavery, and discussed the pros and cons of colonization of African Americans The American Colonization Society, which was founded in 1816 and peaked during the 1820s, encouraged voluntary emancipation (also known as gradual emancipation) and proposed resettling American free blacks in Liberia.[37]

Lundy was one of those traveling agents who supported gradual emancipation. Born to a Quaker saddler from New Jersey, he was converted to abolitionism as a young man by the sight of coffles of slaves winding their way through the streets of Wheeling, Virginia. Lundy began his writing career by contributing articles on slavery to Charles Osborne's *Philanthropist* magazine. Lundy later set up his own paper, the *Genius of Universal Emancipation,* a weekly publication measuring nine inches by thirteen inches and consisting of eight four-column pages decorated at the top with an eagle and the motto "E Pluribus Unum." In 1815 he organized the first abolition society in Ohio, the Union Humane Society.[38]

Lundy's views of abolitionism reflected the general flavor of other Quakers, but their moderate approach to gradual emancipation was soon upstaged by a zealous twenty-two-year-old man from Newburyport, Massachusetts, named William Lloyd Garrison. Lundy met Garrison in Boston in March 1828, when the two men stayed in the same boardinghouse. Garrison had already made a name for himself among abolitionists while serving as editor of the *Journal of the Times* in Bennington, Vermont, a position he left after only six months as a result of ideological differences with the paper's owner. Garrison decided that immediate emancipation was more logical than gradual emancipation because if slavery were considered "right for a single moment, then it might be justified for weeks or months or even years." In spite of their differing views, however, Lundy invited Garrison to become coeditor of Lundy's new paper, and Garrison accepted in July 1829. The two editors handled their differences of opinion by signing individual editorials. The paper's debut issue on September 2, 1829, also contained an announcement of another new assistant, Elizabeth Margaret Chandler, "an amiable and highly talented female writer," who was to be in charge of a "Ladies' Department, to be devoted, as her motto expressed it, to 'philanthropy and literature.'"[39]

The partnership between Lundy and Garrison, however, lasted only six months, and the weekly *Genius* failed as a result of Garrison's personal attacks on individuals who supported slavery, especially Francis Todd, whose vessel transported large numbers of slaves bound in chains. Todd sued the two editors for libel; Garrison was indicted (although Lundy was not); and the paper lost most of its subscribers. In its final issue, Lundy announced the termination of the weekly, commending Garrison for "strict integrity, amiable deportment, and virtuous conduct" in spite of Lundy's disapproval of a few of Garrison's articles.[40] Lundy later published the *Genius* on a monthly basis and restricted its content to the subject of emancipation.

After Garrison left the *Genius* he debuted his own paper, the *Liberator,* on January 1, 1831. Each issue of the new publication consisted of four pages measuring nine by fourteen-and-one-quarter inches, with four columns per page. A salutation to the public in verse, probably by Elizabeth Margaret Chandler, appeared immediately below the heading of the first column. According to Garrison, he wanted to reach several categories of readers: "the religious; the philanthropic; the patriotic; the ignorant, cold-hearted, base, and tyrannical; and the free colored."[41]

Garrison's radical views on antislavery had been influenced by an August 1830 debate conducted in the British Parliament about the abolition of slavery in the colonies. The debate spurred more vigorous action by American opponents of slavery. Garrison responded to this challenge by verbally attacking all slaveholders, distorting facts, and demanding immediate action without regard to consequences. He bitterly denounced all laws that provided a legal basis for slavery, challenged the U.S. Constitution, and opposed any use of political action to accomplish the goal of emancipation.[42] This left little room for any peaceful solutions.

Garrison's forceful approach made some Quakers uncomfortable, and his views eventually replaced the Quaker voice in the abolition movement. The Quaker Abolition Society in Baltimore had disbanded in 1829, and many Quakers began to concentrate on the Orthodox-Hicksite schism occurring at this time. However, some Quakers agreed with Garrison's views of immediatism. In December 1833 the American Anti-Slavery Society was formed in Philadelphia, "devoted exclusively to promoting immediate emancipation." Of the sixty-two supporters in attendance, twenty-one were Quakers, four were women (all Quakers), and three were black men. They all signed the Declaration of Sentiments drawn up by Garrison.[43]

The Chandler/Evans family did not share their fellow Quakers' general concerns about Garrison's fanaticism. By the time Garrison started his new paper, Thomas and Elizabeth Chandler and Ruth Evans had migrated to Michigan, and in a September 8, 1830, letter Jane Howell informed them of Garrison's appearance in Philadelphia:

> William Lloyd Garrison delivered three lectures in this city on the subject of Slavery. He proposes to publish a weekly paper in Washington City to be called the "Liberator" or "Journal of the Times." He says in his prospectus "I shall exercise a strict supervision over the proceedings of Congress and the conduct of its members. The representatives of a moral and religious people 'should walk circumspectly, not as fools, but as wise men' lest they be brought to public shame. This paper will be a terror to evil doers, but a praise to them that do well."[44]

Nine months later, Ruth Evans wrote, "William Lloyd Garrison publishes a paper called the 'Liberator.' . . . [Elizabeth] had two duplicate numbers which she has sent to Anna Coe. He has sent [Elizabeth] the paper regularly since the commencement. . . . It is a very good paper." Two months later, Howell noted that "William Garrison is now in the city attending a convention of the colored people. It occupied nearly the whole of last week. I was invited by Benjamin [Lundy] to attend one of their meetings and I should have done so but for the distance and want of company."[45]

Three and a half years went by before Garrison was mentioned again in the Chandler/Evans/Howell correspondence: just after Elizabeth's death, Howell responded to the publication of an obituary notice "from the pen of William

Lloyd Garrison . . . in words that pleased me much." However, when Garrison indicated that he wanted to write Elizabeth's biographical memoir, Jane wrote,

> I applied to three of the editors of our city papers, but they all made one objection, and that was to the name of William Lloyd Garrison. They said that he had sunk so low in the estimation of the citizens since he has espoused the cause of the colored people in the way that he has, by approving of the intermarrying with whites, etc., etc., that they thought it would be a great disadvantage to the memory of the departed to have his name in any manner connected with it. Would it then be proper, my dear sister for him to publish her biography? Seeing how unpopular he is here, and what part of the Union would it be more eagerly sought after, than in this, our city, where she was so well known, and so dearly beloved? Let nothing be done that can in the smallest degree tarnish the luster of her unspotted character.[46]

By the time the antislavery crusade began in earnest in 1831, when Garrison first published the *Liberator* and formed the New England Antislavery Society, which welcomed women, Elizabeth Chandler had long been an active participant in the crusade. The inclusion of women in this public debate over slavery during the early 1830s challenged the patriarchal codes of that period, which restricted "true women" to the domestic sphere. By 1838 more than one hundred female antislavery societies had been created, and a significant number of their members were Quakers.[47]

During the 1820s, before she moved to the remote Michigan wilderness, Elizabeth had been an active member of the Philadelphia Female Antislavery Society. On April 2, 1831, Lundy expressed his concern that the move to the frontier would cause her to contract "such an affection for the woods" that she would forget "the holy cause." Melodramatically he asked, "Ah, what enticement—what prospect of gratification, fame or usefulness could be held out to thy view, to dispel thy charm and draw thee from a deep seclusion that almost hides thee from the world? My valued friend if thee knew but half the good thee is doing in the holy cause to which thee has so nobly devoted thy attention for years, I am sure thee would see the propriety of placing thyself in a situation where thee might have every advantage that the most extensive and early information of passing events would give thee." Lundy's concern was unfounded, and Elizabeth's zeal for the cause never flagged. In a poem written to the Ladies' Free Produce Society of Philadelphia, after she moved to Michigan, Elizabeth stated, "even from this distant spot, / my thoughts are with you yet." She encouraged them to

> Go, press unwearied on,
> Till when your task is done,

The franchised negro's grateful tear
Proclaims your victory won.

She admonished the Philadelphia female abolitionists to "Yet never your high task forget, / Till they are chainless—free!" and asked the women to remember that "sometimes when you thus are set, / One heart may turn to me."[48]

Within two years of her arrival in the territory, Elizabeth Chandler initiated the formation of Michigan's first antislavery group, the Logan Female Antislavery Society. She enlisted the help of abolitionist and former Quaker Laura Haviland, who had migrated to Michigan from Ontario in September 1829. Haviland, who lived a long life and went on to become a well-known and outspoken advocate for education of African American children, establishing the River Raisin Institute in 1837, has often been credited by historians with initiating the Michigan antislavery society. By Haviland's own admission, however, Chandler clearly served as the impetus behind the group. Haviland wrote in her autobiography, "Our family, with others, united with Elizabeth Margaret Chandler, who organized in our neighborhood the first anti-slavery society in our state." Ruth Evans also credited her niece with founding the society: "Through Elizabeth's influence we have established an Antislavery Society here. Our first meeting was held at the meeting house two weeks ago. They are to be monthly. We suppose there will be about twelve new members at our next meeting. They heartily meet with it, though many have seldom heretofore, thought much on the subject. I trust they will endeavour to abstain from slave raised articles as much as practicable."[49] As a result of Elizabeth's initiative, Lenawee County in southern Michigan became a major center of antislavery opinion before 1833, remaining strongly abolitionist throughout the years of the controversy.

According to Haviland, Chandler did not receive immediate and full support from other Friends. Haviland's autobiography stated that the organizing of the antislavery society "was unsatisfactory to the ruling portion of our Society, as it had cleared its skirts many years ago by emancipating all slaves within its pale. Elizabeth Margaret Chandler was of the Hicksite division of Friends, and as Presbyterians and other religious denominations came into our antislavery society, meetings were frequently opened with prayer, and that was thought to be 'letting down the principles of ancient Friends.' And the subject of slavery was considered too exciting for Friends to engage in, by many Friends of that day."[50] This new antislavery society embraced the cause of immediate emancipation as its initial public expression of sympathy and agreed to organize a free-produce society as part of its program.

When the idea of boycotting slave-produced goods was introduced, many Quakers found it easy to embrace. Prominent Quaker men and women such as Woolman, Benjamin Lay, Sarah Harrison, and Patience Brayton first introduced the idea in the late 1700s. By 1806, when Alice Jackson Lewis of Chester County, Pennsylvania, spoke on the subject at the Philadelphia Quakers' Yearly Women's Meeting, the idea was beginning to germinate into a movement. Elias Hicks expanded and revised the idea in 1807, following his extended trips through Maryland and Virginia, where he had observed slavery firsthand. He argued that if Friends abstained from the use of slave products, they would weaken slavery where it still existed as well as free themselves from complicity in the sin. Slave products became known as prize goods, and the main boycott items were sugar, rice, and cotton.[51]

The Quakers developed an organized campaign to eliminate the consumption of goods produced by slave labor, based on the theory that people who used such items were in some sense responsible for the perpetuation of slavery. The arguments particularly appealed to women, who could make their influence felt in a very real way, since they generally controlled the purchasing of food, cloth, and household supplies. A free-produce society was organized in Pennsylvania in 1827, and a Ladies' Free Produce Society subsequently was established there; Elizabeth Chandler joined the group.

Hicks's free-produce cause never gained much credibility among conservative Quakers, who associated him solely with the Separation of 1827–28 and, therefore, attached his free-produce ideas to his theological views. His opponents eventually completely discredited the free-produce movement because it had been initiated by Hicks. In 1853 even Quaker abolitionist Lydia Maria Child equated the Hicksite separation with the free-produce issue rather than with religious differences.[52]

Both Lundy and Garrison adhered to and publicized the free-produce movement, although Garrison saw it as having only indirect value. Garrison nevertheless advocated a boycott of slave labor in both the *Genius* and the *Liberator.* He printed articles urging the purchase of free goods and included an advertisement for a free-produce store in Philadelphia that specialized in sugars, tea, coffee, chocolate, molasses, tobacco, lamp wick, and cotton goods. He even offered his office's services to take orders for these goods.[53]

Elizabeth Chandler passionately joined these men and others in embracing the free-produce cause. She wrote poems and essays to advocate the crusade, usually appealing to women. In the poem "Slave Produce," Chandler made a plea for the "lady" to "turn aside, / With a loathing heart, from the feat of pride" and to refrain from eating food produced by slaves or using cloth made from cotton grown by slaves. In her essay "Opposition to Slavery," she argued that to "revel in the luxuries" produced by the slave's labor and to be "partakers of its fruits" was to be an "active supporter of the system of slavery." She furthered her argument by stating that unwillingly purchasing slave-produced items did not exempt one from guilt, and using the excuse that it is "impossible to obtain all the articles needed or wanted" meant only that it then rests with one "to relax not your endeavors until it is *no longer* impossible." In "Excuses" she assured her readers that "the voice of conscience is at all times audible, unless we turn a dull ear to her monitions."[54]

Chandler's personal actions supported the admonitions in her public writing. Elizabeth touched on the subject of free produce in several letters to family members: in a June 28, 1831, letter to her sister-in-law, Sarah Chandler, Elizabeth referred to the last weekly volume of the *Genius of Universal Emancipation* and "the first that contains the Ladies Department." She encouraged Sarah "to take it" because

> it would give thee particularly a better opportunity of becoming acquainted with my sentiments, and besides, I should have an opportunity of lecturing you now and then, along with the rest of the folks about making use of slave produce. It is possible, for we have been such strangers that I cannot certainly tell that you may give the preference to goods of the other class, but when I was acquainted with brother Will, he was quite indifferent about it. If he is so still, tell him, dear Sarah, that it is his sisters earnest request that both he and his wife will become better Abolitionists; and will promote the use of free produce as much as it is in their power.[55]

In one letter Elizabeth wanted to know "whether Java coffee is the product of free labor." She later received an affirmative answer from Jane Howell. Continuing to advocate the free-produce cause more than a year later, Elizabeth wrote, "I should like to have sent thy patchwork by this opportunity, but have not yet got it finished, as sewing cotton runs low with us, and I felt unwilling, unless compelled by actual necessity to purchase any of the slave manufacture."[56]

When the Michigan Friends met in October 1832 in their new meetinghouse in Lenawee County, Elizabeth Chandler appealed for support for abolition and for the free-produce movement. The attendees agreed during that meeting to organize a free-produce society, seeking to bring economic and moral pressure into the antislavery movement. They believed that a demand for products of free labor would enhance its significance and that a concurrent decline in the demand for products of slave labor would make slavery inconvenient and expensive. The desired result would be emancipation.[57]

The effectiveness of the free-produce movement has been difficult to determine, and historians tend to dismiss it as a marginal effort. From 1840 on, the free-produce movement lost its universal appeal and became linked solely to the Society of Friends' approach to abolitionism. Attacks on slavery moved into other areas of activism. Yet Margaret Bacon believes that the boycott involved "a movement, incidentally, of greater importance than the notable lack of treatment of the matter in historical literature would indicate."[58]

In addition to the antislavery societies and the free-produce movement, early-nineteenth-century Quaker abolitionists turned to journalism and poetry. The first American Quaker poets were antislavery writers Joseph Sansom and Refine Weekes. Beginning in 1821, periodicals replaced the pamphlets of colonial and early republican times. Weekly or monthly journals served as vehicles of propaganda, and the abolition message could be disseminated much more effectively than through the occasional pamphlet.

Elizabeth Chandler began writing poems and essays flavored with compassion and philanthropy when she was only sixteen. By the 1820s Chandler had already chosen to focus her writings on the subjects of universal education, women's equality, and antislavery, becoming, according to Mary Jones, "America's first poet to concentrate her creative activity on the theme of anti-slavery." Although John Greenleaf Whittier is usually considered America's first antislavery poet, Chandler's writings appeared in print almost a decade before Whittier's.[59]

Chandler's writings challenged her female readers to "strive to experience the brutalities inflicted on slave women." In "The Slave's Appeal," for example, she appealed to the power of mother love, asking women to "Think of those who wildly mourn / For the loved ones from them torn!" In "What Is a Slave Mother?" she created a dialogue between a child's innocent questions about the brutality of slavery and the mother's sorrowful admissions of the truth. The child asks, "May children as young as I be sold / And torn away from their mother's hold—" to which the mother replies, "Alas, yes, my child." When the child says, "Ah, then must the tales I have heard be true, / Of the cruel things that masters do," the mother concurs, "It is so, my child." The child concludes, "Oh surely the land where such deeds are done, / Must be a most savage and wicked one!" and the mother agrees, "It is this, my child."[60] Chandler hoped that no mother reading this dialogue could remain insulated from the realities and brutalities of slavery.

Chandler also asserted a gender identification in her writings, suggesting that an identical womanhood and sisterhood was shared by the genteel white female, whom she called *lady,* and the enslaved black female subject. The theme of sisterhood between slave and free women comes through clearly in "To the Stranger." The voice is that of a female slave pleading with a "young maiden" whose life is apparently filled with filial affection and security. The slave asks her listener to "Then blame me not, that I should seek, although I know not thee, / To waken in thy heart its chords of holiest sympathy." She then pleads,

> Oh lady! when a sister's cry is ringing on the air,
> When woman's pleading eye is raised in agonized despair,
> When the woman's limbs are scourged and sold 'midst rude and brutal mirth,
> And all affection's holiest ties are trampled to earth,
> May female hearts be still unstirr'd, and 'midst their wretched lot,
> The victims of unmeasured wrongs be carelessly forgot?[61]

Chandler encouraged female readers to bridge the distance between whites and blacks by looking at slaves as fellow women. Chandler also hinted at the reader's humanity and conjectured about whether the lady had become dehumanized by her easy life and would pass on unmoved by the sight of the kneeling slave.

While some scholars have questioned the effectiveness of Chandler's writings, which were filled with melodrama, flowery imagery, and moral instruction, they were nevertheless effective as propaganda and were influential in instigating antislavery activities. Women wrote to Lundy in response to Chandler's writings, reporting on abolitionist projects that resulted from reading her material. Lundy credited Chandler's writings as being "directly responsible for the manumission of six slaves upon one occasion."[62]

Chandler's poem "The Kneeling Slave" specifically moved Sarah Mapps Douglass, a young African American woman, to write a poignant March 1, 1833, letter to Benjamin Lundy, requesting that he pass it on to the poet. Douglass wanted to "thank her for her beautiful writings on behalf of my enslaved brethren and sisters" and expressed "gratitude to God for having touched the heart of one so gifted." Enclosed in the letter was a sketch that, according to Douglass, "as a drawing . . . has no merit" but "I beg you will accept . . . as a token of my gratitude and respect." The drawing showed a chained female slave, kneeling on one knee and clothed only from the waist down. British abolitionists first used the female slave image in their literature in 1828, adapting it from the original allegorical figure of a kneeling male slave. The female adaptation caught on quickly because it deeply touched the sympathetic hearts of women abolitionists. Lundy adopted the symbol in his May 1830 issue of the *Genius of Universal Emancipation,* and Garrison used it in 1832 as a heading for the "Ladies' Department" of the *Liberator.* It eventually became a much-used emblem, appearing in later abolitionist literature and on handicraft goods and manufactured items such as chinaware, tokens, linen, and silk goods sold by antislavery women at fund-raising fairs. Lundy also included the figure in his published memoir and tribute to Chandler following her death.[63]

Historian Jean Fagan Yellin has suggested that Chandler's early writings directly influenced later female abolitionists such as Angelina Grimké by blazing "a trail from abolitionism to feminism along which other women could proceed." Chandler's writings challenged her readers to make the leap from intellectualizing about slavery to sensually experiencing the "weight of the chains" through imagination. She asked the free white female to identify with her sister, the enslaved black female, and to transform herself from the observer to the slave. Grimké used the same approach years later by extending it from a pure abolitionism to an abolitionist feminism in which she saw herself not only "as a victimized slave" but also as someone who characterized the condition of all women. She thus envisioned herself as "imprisoned, weighted with chains, able only to weep." Chandler led the way in the creation of a new, independent, and original culture among antislavery feminists.[64]

Elizabeth Chandler began her career as a published author early in her life, but her identity was concealed for some time. Prior to her appointment as editor of the *Genius of Universal Emancipation*'s Ladies' Department, she had submitted many of her writings under pseudonyms, some of them male. Perhaps her motivation was a Quaker effort to guard against vanity and pride, or perhaps she initially chose to accept her role as a submissive female. Whatever the reasons for this concealment, Chandler eventually altered her tactic and took credit for her own writings, pioneering in a field that few women had entered. For example, although Sarah Josephus Hale had published her first issue of the *Ladies' Magazine* in 1828, this publication by design was not a crusading journal but rather a guidebook for woman's proper sphere.[65] Elizabeth Chandler's writings did not defy a woman's sphere as such. In fact, in "Influence of Slavery on the Female Character," she accepted woman's domestic role while encouraging her to go beyond its boundaries: "It is on all sides acknowledged, that the domestic circle is the proper sphere of woman. We do not say that her talents and influence should be confined within these boundaries, but however beneficially they may be felt abroad, if homebred usefulness forms no part of her character, be her claims on our respect and admiration what they may, she fails of one half of her perfection." In the same essay, however, Chandler also challenged a woman, within her proper sphere, to avoid the tendencies that result from slavery, which leads to wealth and causes a woman to "strive for showy accomplishments rather than cultivated minds and well-regulated tempers, [to] wish to shine rather than . . . to be useful, [to] desire wealth and expensive pleasures rather than intellectual advancement, [to] possess an uneasy excitement of a crowd rather than quiet enjoyment of books, retirement, and rational conversation, [to] long for flattery and admiration of many rather than sober approbation of few, [to] follow fancy or caprice rather than reflective judgment."[66] Beginning in 1829 Elizabeth's essays, poems, and editorial work as director of the Ladies' Department of the *Genius* exhibited a boldness and defiance of conventional gender structures.

Again, Chandler's public writing reflected the influence of her Quaker upbringing. As early as the mid–seventeenth century, English Quaker women were breaking conventional gender rules. As women became increasingly literate, they began publishing their prose and poetry writings, which not only proclaimed prophesies but also challenged political ideology. Margaret Fell, who is credited as the female founder of Quakerism alongside George Fox, published a 1666 pamphlet, *Womens Speaking Justified, Proved, and Allowed of by the Scriptures*, that defended female rights to public preaching. Although Fell's pamphlet referred to spiritual speaking within the confines of Quaker meetings, her boldness in publishing provided an impetus for other women who shared a passion to be heard through the printed word. Yet Quaker women in seventeenth-century England faced the same dilemmas as their sisters in eighteenth- and nineteenth-century America. They had the opportunity to participate in radical religious activity and to express ideas individually and collectively with greater freedom than ever before but were still viewed as inferior, passive, and dependent. Therefore, although this religious freedom had questionable value as a means of female emancipation, it did imbue an element of courage that carried over for future generations of Quaker women.[67]

Chandler's public writings cannot by today's definition be called feminist, but she can be legitimately credited with pioneering some of the ideas that eventually led to feminism and the women's rights movement. The movement was led by a network of women formed within the framework of abolitionism in which women could participate at a variety of levels, depending on their degree of comfort and courage. By far the greatest number restricted themselves to promoting antislavery views among family members. But other women joined antislavery societies and became propagandists, fund-raisers, and petitioners. Those who supported Garrison's platform went even further and raised new questions about women's rights in public life. Women's status in society became a focus of attention even before a formal women's rights movement emerged.[68]

Although the Seneca Falls Convention of 1848 usually marks the beginning of organized feminism in the United States, feminist voices had risen in the antislavery movement as early as the late 1830s. Sisters Sarah and Angelina Grimké have been noted as "pioneers for woman's rights and abolition." Angelina E. Grimké's first public appearance occurred on February 2, 1838, when she addressed the Committee of the Legislature of the State of Massachusetts and stated, "We Abolition Women are turning the world upside down."[69] Yet Chandler had publicly written to an audience of thousands more than a decade earlier and, in 1830, when she removed herself from the center of abolitionist activity to the wilderness of Michigan, she carried her zeal and enthusiasm with her. Although her remote situation precluded a personal and public participation at national conventions or meetings of legislatures and her early death precluded her future involvement in such actions, her accomplishments should not be underestimated. Elizabeth Margaret Chandler was a pioneer for women's rights and slavery's abolition as well as a pioneer on the Michigan frontier.

Michigan was still a territory in 1830 when Thomas and Elizabeth Chandler and their aunt, Ruth Evans, migrated to the River Raisin area of Lenawee County.

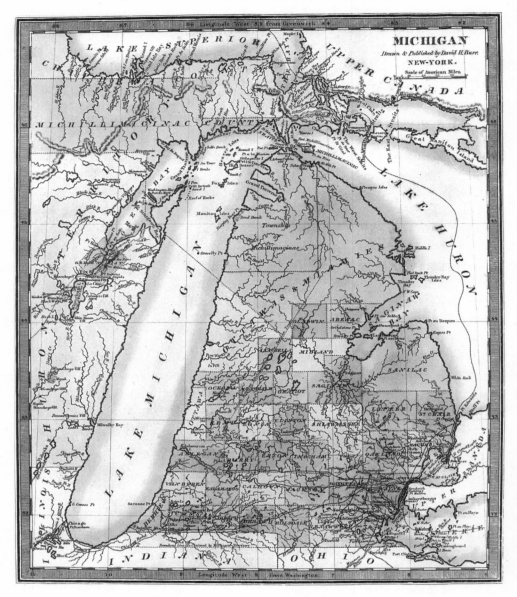

Michigan, 1831. *Courtesy of the Clements Library, University of Michigan.*

The Upper Great Lakes region of the Northwest Territory consisted of what later became the states of Michigan and Wisconsin and parts of Iowa and Minnesota. Settlement and statehood had already reached Ohio in 1803, Indiana in 1816, and Illinois in 1818, but limited transportation routes, fear of hostile Indians with ties to England and Canada, and negative reports about the health of the area delayed the settling of Michigan.

Soon after the War of 1812 Michigan's reputation improved, and easterners learned that the territory was not just swampland but rather possessed some of the finest agricultural lands in the Northwest. The U.S. Land Act of 1820 provided that minimum parcels of eighty acres could be purchased from the government for cash at $1.25 per acre, or a total of $100. The advent of steamboat travel on the Great Lakes, inaugurated by the *Walk-in-the-Water* in 1818, and the completion of the Erie Canal in 1825 opened a new gateway to Michigan, offering a much more comfortable and expedient means of transportation to the west. Travelers from the east could come almost entirely by water until they reached the port in Detroit. These factors enhanced Michigan's appeal, where settlers could start anew, become independent, and even possibly get rich, and the population of the Michigan Territory began to burgeon. In 1826 pioneers could purchase land at one of two Michigan land offices, in Monroe or Detroit; by 1836 there were five land offices.[70]

Elizabeth Chandler summed up her family's attitudes (and perhaps those of other Michigan settlers) in her letter to her brother and sister-in-law dated June 14, 1830, just before moving to the territory: "We still continue of the opinion that Michigan combines the greatest number of advantages and holds out the greatest inducements for us to settle there. In Ohio, the best of the Government lands are taken up, to continue further west what a tremendous tract of country would separate us from our friends, while even there we should not find half the facilities for transforming the wealth of the ground into available cash."[71]

New York and New England spawned most of these immigrants in the 1830s. Indeed, so popular was this area among New Englanders that the press popularized the term "Michigan Fever" as a description of the urge to move west. The U.S. census reflected this rush of settlers. Michigan's 1820 population of 8,675 grew to 31,640 in 1839, 212,267 in 1840, and 341,591 in 1850.[72]

During the planning stages of their move to Michigan, both Thomas and Elizabeth Chandler wrote letters to other family members about their decision to leave Philadelphia and migrate west. Thomas's reason for wanting to move, as he admitted to his brother, William, was that he was "heartily sick of storekeeping." He saw the growing West as offering a new beginning. He felt that "though this may not be profitable in a pecuniary point of view I am inclined to think that it will be more advantageous in the end than anything else which I know of at present as soon as we have fully determined what course to pursue by way of 'making a living.'"[73]

While it is apparent that Thomas was the impetus behind the move, Ruth Evans and Elizabeth each had a role in the decision. Thomas wrote of "we," clearly indicating the two women's involvement in the decision. In February 1830 Thomas explained a delay in the group's planned departure: "We have almost concluded to postpone our purposed emigration until fall or possibly the next

spring. . . . Many reasons might be given for our not going so soon as we anticipated . . . perhaps a sufficient one will be that Aunt Ruth thinks she will be better prepared—and Elizabeth is engaged in a little work which will probably
bring her something handsome."[74]

Originally, according to Thomas, the three had contemplated "removing
to the coal region," considering it "only a temporary arrangement with the expectation of deriving considerable profit as it could not have been otherwise than disagreeable to all of us." The resulting delay gave Thomas an opportunity to
examine other possibilities and to finally settle on Michigan. He would have
gathered information about various westward settlements from the local papers
and from friends who returned from the west with reports of what they had
found. The fact that many Quakers had already settled in the Michigan Territory
also influenced Elizabeth, Thomas, and Ruth's decision to choose Michigan. A
recent study of early Michigan settlements has found that most were "covenanted
communities" of likeminded people organized around a covenant based on religion or ethnicity.[75]

Thomas prepared for the move by living "with some farmer during the ensuing summer, as by that means, besides the information acquired," he wrote, "I
shall become in a measure inured to the labor which would devolve upon me in
our new mode of life." Thomas chose farming because he had "every reason to
suppose that I should like the life of a farmer better than any other which I could
adopt and feel certain that it will yeild something more than a competency in the
western country."[76]

Elizabeth initially admitted to having some reservations about going west
when she wrote to her sister-in-law, Sarah Chandler, "I am very glad to find that if
we remain here until next year there may be some hope of your accompanying us
in our emigration to the 'Western World.' It would tend more than almost anything to obviate my own objections, and reconcile me to the prospect and the reality of going." In June 1830 Elizabeth reported on the progress of Thomas's farm
training, and she, Thomas, and Ruth set out for the territory on August 7, 1830.[77]

Elizabeth described the trip west and her initial reaction to the territory in a
letter to her best friend, Hannah Townsend, back in Philadelphia. The landscape
that Elizabeth described in her letter comprised the two towns of Tecumseh and
Adrian and the open land between them, along the River Raisin, in Lenawee
County. The county, established by Lewis Cass on September 10, 1822, was the
seventh county in the Michigan Territory. The first settler in Lenawee County was
Musgrove Evans, a Quaker native of Pennsylvania and a resident of Jefferson City,
New York. He and his brother-in-law, General Joseph W. Brown, had explored
the area in 1823 and returned in 1824 with ten or twelve others on a schooner
from Buffalo to Detroit. They left their families in Detroit and traveled on foot
approximately sixty miles to Tecumseh, to again look over the farmland and

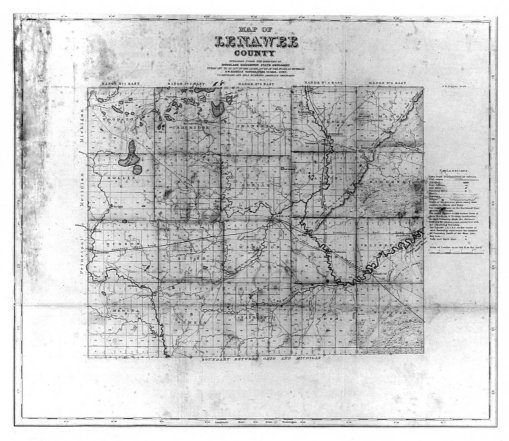

Lenawee County, Michigan, ca. 1830. *Courtesy of the Clements Library, University of Michigan.*

decide where to settle. The area's major asset was the River Raisin, which offered hydraulic power for milling. Brown and Evans erected the first sawmill in 1824, and Evans built a log house that during 1825 and 1826 "furnished shelter for the white settlers of the county, numbering 16." Evans also laid out the plat for the village of Tecumseh, and Brown built the village's first frame house in 1826, operating a tavern or "public house."[78]

Darius Comstock, a Quaker from New York, and his son, Addison, followed Evans and his group in 1825, locating a "beautiful plantation at the valley four miles south of Tecumseh." Comstock bought 480 acres and erected a sawmill on the River Raisin near his residence. General Brown built Comstock's house and described in a memoir his delight at the prospects of a Friends' settlement in the area: "The Darius Comstock that I mentioned is a Friend, of a large fortune, and much of a gentleman; he has been living with me for several weeks this winter. His place he called 'Pleasant Valley,' it is four miles south of us, through an open country, where you may drive a post coach without cutting a tree. . . . A Friend has bought near him, who will be here in the spring; and they bid fair to have a large Friend's settlement, and we anticipate much from the society of such neighbors." Area residents held Comstock in high regard, characterizing him as a "plain-spoken pioneer, . . . founder and main builder of the Friends' meeting house, the first built in the county, and the only one between Detroit and the Pacific ocean, if we except a few Indian missions. His house was always open for the poor and needy, also for hundreds of social friends." Addison Comstock laid out the plat for the village of Adrian in 1828.[79]

When Thomas and Elizabeth Chandler and Ruth Evans arrived in the area in 1830, they stayed with Darius Comstock until their house could be built, and Thomas wrote about their visit on September 8, 1830. On October 10, 1830, "about six weeks . . . since we have been inhabitants in the western country," Thomas described the "society" as "much more like that in the eastern states, though it can not be expected it should equal in refinement some neighborhoods in Pennsylvania." He added a detailed description of their "location in this land of promise" and assured those back home, "We like it very much." He included information about the types of trees growing, "principally white oak," and described in detail the building of their new house, which "is said to be the best log house in this part of the country." He "endeavored in speaking of this country to be strictly candid" and did not wish to "use one word in its favor more than it deserves." He added, "There is hardly a person who is not well satisfied with the country and all seem anxious to add to the improvement of it." Elizabeth echoed the sentiment when she added a postscript to Thomas's letter: "People are crowding very fast into the territory, and there appears to be fewer inconveniences and hardships to sustain than might reasonably be expected in so new a settlement. . . . I am glad we came, and that we came here. Brother seems so happy and satisfied that I could scarcely be otherwise if I were disposed to be." Ruth Evans agreed, writing six months after arriving in Michigan, "How often I wish thee could see how snuggly we are fixed."[80]

Elizabeth explained to Jane Howell on December 23, 1830, that the Chandler/Evans trio had stayed with the Comstocks until November 2, "being delayed considerably longer than . . . expected at the commencement of the building, and for the last two or three weeks, principally on account of the well which had to be sunk much deeper than . . . expected." Neighbors considered the house "a real slick one" and "the *snuggest log house in Michigan*." She proudly described the dwelling in detail, including all the "dimentions" and information about the "doors of walnut" and the "partition boards as well as the chamber floors . . . planed and fitted together by grooving, a thing unknown in any other log house about." She depicted the placement of windows, which were "neatly framed and glazed, which latter operation was performed by aunt Ruth and myself." She explained how the main room was "conjointly parlor, kitchen and hall," and she located each piece of furniture in it:

> The first conspicuous object is a large flour bin, situated by way of sideboard at the parlor end over which from a wooden pin depends the looking glass. On either end of it stands aunt Ruth's walnut box and my cabinet. Against the wall lengthwise of the room on one side of the window stands the dough trough; on the other a long box covered by a walnut board and answering the purpose of a shelf or table; between them and behind the stove, is placed an oaken bench, which with another of somewhat better manufacture, and aunt Ruth's rocking chair compose our whole wealth of seats. A whisk broom, brushes are not in vogue, our kitchen utensils, and the red chest placed on one of its ends against the partition, and covered with a green cloth, to support my desk, with Benjamin Rush and thy landscape picture hanging over it about complete the catalogue of our furniture in the room.

Elizabeth and Ruth's sleeping apartment was about ten feet square, with "brother's somewhat smaller." Thomas had made the bedstead and straw mattress, "on which I assure thee we sleep very comfortably." Each chamber included "a looking glass, a toilet table (that is a covered box) and a couple of pictures." Books were arranged "on shelves against the partition," and the floors were covered with "rag carpeting, curtains at the windows, and chests containing our clothes to sit on if needful." According to Elizabeth, the trio had made for themselves a "very comfortable" home, however primitive it was compared to the refined urban setting from which they had emigrated. She assured Aunt Jane that "very little is actually necessary to supply our wants if we can but think so, and in our case we have so much, so very much to be thankful for, that we can not regard at a straws value such trivial discomfort."[81]

It is apparent from this list of household items that the emigrants had taken quite a few items with them from their previous home, and the inventory taken when Minnie Fay died indicates that several of those items were heirlooms from Thomas and Elizabeth's mother and grandmother. Elizabeth's detailed descriptions exemplify what historians have found in other female pioneers' writings. Artifacts and the material culture that women brought with them from their former homes were important. However, what pioneer women brought with them often was not appropriate or useful. Caroline Kirkland wrote in her novel-like account of Michigan's frontier, *A New Home: Who Will Follow?*, that although she had left home with "a nest of delicate japanned tables" and "great glass dishes," she now found her "ideas of comfort narrowed down to a well-swept room with a bed in one corner, and cooking aparatus in another." She had also brought a "tall cupboard" that remained outside for lack of space inside and eventually became a corn crib. Her chief lesson, she concluded, was that "no settlers are so uncomfortable as those who, coming with abundant means as they suppose, to be comfortable, set out with a determination to live as they have been accustomed to live."[82]

Regardless of the spare housing conditions in these pioneer settlements, historians have found that most women did not find high standards of domesticity to be an insurmountable problem. Such standards were often more ideal than real. Although women's magazines extolled the virtues of planned kitchens, professionalized homemaking, and the latest training in the domestic arts, not many women, eastern or western, achieved these goals. In addition, their Hicksite Quaker beliefs had prepared the Chandlers and Evans to accept physical and material deprivations. The Hicksites believed that simplicity was more admirable than ostentatious living.[83]

The Chandlers and Evans experienced fewer deprivations than did many other settlers, and their home was more accommodating than many of the log homes being built in the Michigan Territory during this time, with the notable exception of Darius Comstock's home. Thomas, Elizabeth, and Ruth also brought with them a young girl, Emily Johnston, a ward or bond servant, who performed many of the household's menial tasks. Very little mention is made of Johnston in the letters, and it is difficult to draw conclusions from what is mentioned. However, the three females in this household certainly shared the domestic load, a situation that allowed Elizabeth more time to write not only her essays and poems but also the lengthy letters she sent back east.[84]

As three unmarried relatives, the Chandler/Evans household did not typify the frontier family unit, which usually consisted of a husband, wife, and children, and Thomas, Elizabeth, and Ruth did not handle their new situation in entirely the same manner as a traditional family unit might have. Although Elizabeth's letters often focused on Thomas, she was not completely dependent on him, as a nineteenth-century wife would have been on her husband. She was not his helpmeet but rather a younger sister who had already created a reputation through her published writings and had become more visible than her brother in Philadelphia's public arena. She had an income of sorts from her publications and could have insisted on remaining in Philadelphia rather than migrating west. Instead, she accompanied her brother and aunt to the wilderness. She was a public female figure who had chosen "deep seclusion," as Benjamin Lundy put it, rather than the "prospect of gratification, fame or usefulness" with which Lundy was trying to entice her to return to Philadelphia.[85] Lundy's assumption was melodramatic and exaggerated, and Elizabeth's life in the Michigan Territory remained fruitful and useful. One can argue that living in the territory provided an opportunity for her to play an even more vital role in the antislavery cause. Whereas in Philadelphia she was one of many advocates for abolitionism, in the Michigan Territory she was a vital lone voice in the wilderness.

Although Ruth Evans, the surrogate matriarch of the family unit, remained a less prominent figure in the letters, she too participated actively in the settling of the homestead. In fact, her lack of readiness initially delayed their departure. The Chandlers and Evans made mutual decisions that did not reflect the usual nineteenth-century setting of male domination. Thomas deliberately delayed the group's departure from Philadelphia because the women were not ready to go. A spirit of equality and mutual respect prevailed between the male and female components of this family unit, as it did in other Quaker families. The dominant theme of gender relations in nineteenth-century American women's history—that is, "separate spheres"—was constantly being challenged by the Quakers' belief system and by the rural male-female construct of interdependency. Not only in the decision-making process but also in the division of labor, the Chandler/Evans household created a mutually cooperative unit to serve the needs of frontier life.[86]

Creating a homestead on the frontier did, however, involve daunting and seemingly endless work. Men and women had to decide how to divide the work to get it all done. While perhaps initially attempting to adhere to the traditional divisions of labor carried from their original homes, pioneers found it necessary to adapt as needed. The Chandler/Evans family established a cooperative system of labor division that worked for them. They shared the responsibilities on the homestead and engaged in a community exchange system of labor common in rural areas.

Historians of the westward movement do not agree on how these systems developed and manifested themselves. Some scholars have concluded that these early pioneers preserved conventional sex roles and maintained the value systems that had been formulated through the patriarchal lifestyle common to rural Midwestern America in the mid–nineteenth century. Other historians have found that those conventional sex roles were set aside and that western migration and frontier conditions seriously threatened to undermine the carefully constructed separation of the sexes. Women had to assume new roles, undertaking tasks outside the prescribed woman's place. Elizabeth and Ruth exemplified this flux when they glazed their windows.[87]

In the urban setting of the nineteenth century, the "separate spheres" paradigm operated efficiently. Men's and women's work, place, and character were clearly defined. The rural—especially frontier—setting broke down some of that hierarchy and disjunction between men and women. The distribution of tasks became flexible and varied within and between households. Workplace and household were not separate income-producing and non-income-producing entities. Pioneer men's and women's responsibilities instead implied a mutual dependency and greater equality. For women, heading to the West required a return to the need for self-sufficiency, which limited the appeal of "true womanhood" ideals.[88]

Yet women on the frontier remained chiefly responsible for domestic affairs, including cooking, cleaning, doing laundry, gardening, milking, churning, tending poultry, making candles, carding, spinning, weaving, and sewing. These women's identities revolved around their work, and they listed their accomplishments in diaries, letters, and reminiscences as evidence of their worth. This was a positive dynamic in which, unlike urban women, whose work was devalued, rural women's labor remained integral to the farm family's economy, and the women focused on their legitimate status through these contributions.

Drudgery and routine characterized frontier women's work, however, and change was slow. Because new technology appeared more slowly in the home than in the field or the place of business, women's work showed a wearying sameness, whether it was in the early or the late nineteenth century. Elizabeth Chandler and Ruth Evans often mentioned work in their letters and included the tasks they and Emily performed in and near the house and the work Thomas accomplished in the fields. Elizabeth's letters were filled with the details of day-to-day tasks, and she admitted to life at times being routine and uninteresting.

Jane Howell initially reacted to the prospects of farm labor with much concern and even some disdain. In an October 10, 1830, letter filled with her typical expressions of concern, she wrote to Ruth, "If you are now occupants of your new log house your domestic duties must nearly fill up your time for where there are cows to milk butter to churn bread to bake etc. etc. etc. there will be but little time for sedentary employment."[89] The work must have appeared especially daunting to Aunt Jane, whose urban life in Philadelphia, where she had hired help and ample goods and services available for purchase, did not place the same demands on her time as the frontier life did on her sister, niece, and nephew.

Ruth Evans' and Elizabeth Chandler's transition to farm work could not have been altogether easy. While Thomas had spent a summer apprenticing with a farmer, the women had not. They left city life and entered that of rural subsistence and interdependency with little prior training. They moved from a nineteenth-century urban setting to a rural one where everyday activity seemed more reminiscent of that of their eighteenth-century ancestors. Yet their letters offer little indication that they viewed this work as insurmountable. For example, on February 5, 1831, six months after leaving Philadelphia, Ruth Evans wrote a letter to her sister, describing with obvious pride some of their recent labor and accomplishments: "Our stock at present consists of one cow and calf and two pigs, expect an addition soon of a pair of oxen and another cow. . . . We made from one hog weighing two hundred and twenty pounds forty pounds of lard and as much sausage meat and scrapple, better I never ate. It was made by Elizabeth."[90]

Jane Howell, however, could not be convinced that her relatives were completely content in their new surroundings. She wrote to Elizabeth on April 4, 1831, "You wrote to me in a very satisfactory manner, and the picture looks pleasant to a superficial observer, but I fancy I can see sometimes a little too much shading to make it altogether what I would have it to be." In the same letter, Howell expressed amazement at the hog butchering: "I think thee and thy aunt Ruth must have been up to your eyes in business when the Big Hog was killed. You must have appeared like farmers indeed, chopping raw suet and trying the lard—I am glad to know that you have been providing meat for the summer."[91]

Eleven days later, Elizabeth reported, "Neighbor Comstock has offered to teach me to spin this summer. I feel some ambition to make brother a coat of my own spinning; but we shall not I expect keep sheep for a year or two." Elizabeth subsequently bragged about what she and Ruth had accomplished: "In doors, we have been pretty busy today making candles. Aunt Ruth has been the principal in the manufacture. She has dipped all of them, near two hundred in number; enough to last a long time. . . . Aunt Ruth and brother have just been up stairs weighing the candles, which muster twenty-seven pounds strong."[92]

Butter churning was an essential and regular task on the farm. Elizabeth wrote on May 5, 1832, "Aunt Ruth is about churning; she wishes thee could have some of the buttermilk, but I with an eye more to the main point propose her opening negosiatins with thee for the sale of a pound or two of fresh butter." Churning again came up in an August letter: "As to our domestic affairs, we have had reasonable good luck with our poultry, and have not had our churning 'bewitched' more than once this season."[93] On October 11, 1833, Ruth Evans mentioned that "Emily . . . wishes me to inform thee that she does all the milking, which consists of two cows, each giving a considerable quantity of milk."[94]

The responsibility for dairying in the Chandler/Evans home fell to the women. Historians have found that throughout the country dairy responsibilities were in flux during this period. New England men took over the dairying as it became commercialized. New York and Pennsylvania women did the dairying, and Mid-Atlantic men and women shared the responsibility.[95] Because the Chandler/Evans household consisted of three females and only one male, practicality dictated that one of the females would take principal responsibility for the dairying.

Females on the frontier also readily accepted the task of gardening. Raising vegetables for food and flowers for pleasure consumed a good deal of their time during the growing season. Frontier women typically admired the wilderness and sometimes feared it but invariably attempted as quickly as possible to domesticate their surroundings into cultivated gardens. Kirkland praised Michigan's flora, including grapevines, flowers, ferns, and "wild straw-berries," and she looked for the "familiar features of earlier gardens." She emphasized that the garden was achieved "all by female effort": "as women feel sensibly the deficiencies of the 'savage' state, so they are the first to attempt the refining process."[96]

Elizabeth Chandler assumed the responsibility for most of the gardening at Hazelbank. She proudly described her fruits and vegetables—"monstrous" onions, potatoes, turnips, and "watermellons"—and she took pleasure in planning for "a pretty garden" that would be "in perfection about the time" Jane Howell came for her expected but never realized visit. Elizabeth requested honeysuckle slips or roots from Philadelphia, and she transplanted from the river "hands full of wildflowers" such as Johnny-jump-ups and "blue star shaped flowers." She also planted strawberries, rose bush shoots, and currant bushes. On April 24, 1833, she wrote to Aunt Jane, "Gardening now occupies several hours of our time almost daily, and will, I suppose, keep me pretty busy for some time longer, even more than at present. It is a business I am not very skillful in, but think I shall grow fond of it as I improve in it. So please do not forget me when thee has a chance of getting seeds, whether flowers or vegetables, if the latter are not very common ones."[97]

Elizabeth's most consuming garden passion was the mulberry seeds she requested and received from Jane Howell. Elizabeth wrote on March 27, 1832, "I am very much obliged to thee for the trouble thee has in procuring my mulberry seed." Her goal in planting these seeds was to use the resulting trees to house silkworms so that "I may in the course of two or three years have the pleasure of furnishing thee with a pair of silk stockings of my own raising and manufacture." Elizabeth chronicled the growth of the mulberry seeds in subsequent letters. On May 5, 1832, she reported having "all my mulberry seeds planted and I expect some of them will shortly peep above ground. It was not a very trifling job I assure thee to drop them all separately in the earth at proper distances from each other, and they occupy quite a respectable portion of our garden." In a portion of the same letter written a few days later, she added, "I have just been out to look at my mulberry seeds. . . . They are I believe about coming up but are so small that I can scarcely distinguish them." By June 20, 1832, the seeds had been "so long coming up that I almost began to despair of seeing them, and to feel a sort of growing enmity towards the whole tribe, but the plants now look very well. I think I shall have a respectable number of trees." The progress of the mulberry trees was not further relayed in later letters, and Elizabeth died before she could provide silk stockings for her aunt.[98]

While the women labored indoors and in their gardens at routine daily and weekly tasks, pioneer men cleared and fenced the land, constructed buildings, tended the livestock, and traded in the market. The men's work involved more variety and opportunity to mingle with others. Men met with other settlers in the course of their work, while women had to create social occasions. Men's work took place in the public domain; women's was private.

Elizabeth and Ruth frequently mentioned Thomas's work. He broke up the land, plowed, harrowed, mowed, and threshed. He planted corn and sowed wheat. He cut the corn, brought cornstalks for fencing the cattle in the pasture, and hauled pumpkins. He tended livestock, chased wayward livestock into the woods, and took his grain to the mill. He made fences, tapped maple trees for sugar, built outbuildings, grafted apple trees, and transplanted ornamental trees. He did carpentry work indoors on days when the weather was bad. On March 27, 1832, Elizabeth explained, "Thomas goes on the principle of exchange with his neighbors, both for cattle and assistance."[99]

In the spring of 1833, Elizabeth listed all the tasks Thomas needed to accomplish:

> Spring is a very busy season in the country, and this spring to us more than any we have yet had in Michigan. There is sowing oats, fence making, plowing, harrowing, planting corn, and I know not what all. Part of it is done and part is yet to do. Brother put in, this spring, between four and five acres of oats. He is now putting up the rails that he split last winter, around about twenty acres, which he wishes to break up during the summer. He has also a big gate to make part of his oats ground yet to enclose in the way of fence making. Corn planting time has not come yet.[100]

In March 1834 Elizabeth reported that Thomas had hired as a helper a fifteen-year-old Comstock boy, paying between $6 and $6.50 per month, and, in anticipation of building a new barn, Thomas had planned to get assistance from a new settler named James Gamble, but he was "engaged elsewhere" and could not help. Elizabeth assured Aunt Jane that "frame barnes and buildings do not require so much work and so many labourers as the substantial stone ones of Pennsylvania."[101]

Barn raisings went on the principle of exchange as well, serving two purposes: much-needed help for the farmer and an opportunity for a social gathering. In August 1832 Elizabeth voiced her opinion that this exchange principle was for Thomas "often rather inconvenient for him to leave his business to attend them, but as it usually requires as many hands as can be raised, he thinks it no more than right to make some sacrifice of his own time to assist a neighbor." She later wrote that "raisings have been going on quite briskly in our own neighborhood this spring. Brother was invited last week to four, two of which he attended, and one the week before." When the Chandler barn was finally raised in May 1834, Elizabeth described the event in what is her last extant letter.[102]

The frontier was not "a product of individualism," as early historian Frederick Jackson Turner concluded. He believed that the "immemorial custom of tribe or village community fell victim to the American pioneer experience" and that "individualism was more pronounced than community life." This view was a product of an American popular culture that fit into the mystique that people wanted to believe about frontier life rather than a factual characterization of it. The Chandler/Evans situation was never one of individualism but rather immediately became one of community and cooperation. A "borrowing system" as well as a labor-exchange system was intact on the frontier. Kirkland also determined this to be true, warning her readers, "Your wheel-barrows, your shovels, your utensils of all sorts, belong not to yourself, but to the public, who do not think it necessary even to ask a loan, but take it for granted."[103]

Thomas, Elizabeth, and Ruth had settled into a system of cooperative labor that enabled them to complete tasks, and Thomas engaged in an exchange agreement with the neighbors for assistance with larger tasks requiring more hands. This internal and external system not only provided settlers with the satisfaction of completed tasks but also gave them an opportunity for social interaction with others in the community.

"Bees," as collective labor exchanges were often called, included a social dimension that featured eating and drinking, which Elizabeth noted in her letters. However, men had more access than women did to these opportunities for social exchange. Elizabeth wrote of the many raisings Thomas attended, while she and Ruth stayed home. Only when the raising occurred on their own homestead did Elizabeth and Ruth become involved with the work of preparing and serving food and drink. Yet Elizabeth Chandler and Ruth Evans had the companionship of each other, which meant their solitude or loneliness was less acute than that of many pioneer wives who were the only women in their households and who faced many days alone. When Elizabeth died in 1834, an alarming change came over Ruth, who not only grieved the loss of her beloved niece but also lost her household companion. Ruth's subsequent letters reflect a chronic sadness or depression, which may have contributed to her death a year later.

Historians who have studied the lives of settlers have consistently found loneliness a prevalent theme in women's writings. Kirkland suggested that a "sense of isolation [was] experienced by the wife that her husband will never know, spending long, solitary 'wordless' days waiting for her husband to return for the evening meal." No matter who else was there, women's writings reflected feelings of being "all alone." Pioneer women's letters and diaries are filled with strikingly frequent comments about new friends and new delights in Western life, juxtaposed with sad yearnings for home and family.[104]

Letters were the primary means of maintaining contact between the settlers and the world outside their log cabins. The exchange of letters between Elizabeth and Ruth Evans in Michigan and Jane Howell in Philadelphia reflects the significance of this correspondence. Although Elizabeth and Ruth had each other and were situated within a welcoming community of like-minded pioneers, they also expressed a longing to receive more frequent letters. Elizabeth described her happiness at receiving a packet of letters from home: "with what pleasure I need not tell thee, for I dare say thee can fancy how triumphantly I sat in the midst of my treasures, scanning hand-writing, breaking seals, and peeping first into one thing to read a line and then into another, as if I feared they might elude my grasp unless secured by the spell of my eyesight."[105]

In Philadelphia, Jane Howell missed her Michigan family, and on October 10, 1830, just weeks after they had arrived in Michigan, she wrote, "When I for a moment think of the distance which divides us I feel amazed, and when I dwell upon it My heart almost sickens at the thought; but as it must be so, I strive to conquer those feelings by thinking as seldom as I can on the subject." Later in the month she wrote to "beg" Ruth "to relieve my anxiety by letting me hear from you." Two more months passed with no letter, so Jane wrote again in December 1830: "I have been waiting these four months past and looking day after day for a letter from you but have not yet received one line—have you forgotten us."[106]

While Elizabeth and Ruth regularly anticipated visits from Jane and Lemuel Howell and from William and Sarah Chandler (none of which ever materialized), the women also placed high value on visits with the local residents. On February 12, 1832, Elizabeth experienced that delicate balance between delight at new friends and loneliness for family and friends back home: "We have had company every first day for this six or seven weeks until the last one, as the spell is broken now I suppose we may look to be oftener alone for a while. The people in our settlement are sociable, but I do not think it can be called a visiting neighborhood." She had earlier expressed a longing for her family, "I hardly knew while I was with . . . you all, how dearly I did love you all. Oh! how I sometimes long to be with you again for a few days."[107]

On May 5, 1832, Elizabeth wrote about "quite a gathering of Pennsylvanians at John Lovetts, as they had other visitors from that state as well as the three from here." The next month, Elizabeth wrote extensively about social activities: "I was at a 'quilting' last week; there were about twenty girls besides myself, and in the evening about the same number of young men. . . . We have paid and received several visits since I wrote last; and are engaged next first day to dine to Samuel Saterthwaite's. . . . We were at John Lovetts not long since." In September 1833 she again wrote about the quilting parties she had attended.[108]

Visiting provided opportunities to share news and gossip as well as to break up the lonely monotony of domestic life. Socializing helped to maintain community life and honored the individuals visited and confirmed their inclusion in the community. Elizabeth expressed a sense of pride whenever she mentioned visitors to the Chandler/Evans household. In fact, a visit from Darius Comstock warranted detailed attention in her March 27, 1832, letter:

> I entirely forgot to tell thee when I wrote last that we had the honor of a second visit from uncle Darius Comstock in company with his wife and aunt Sally. A visit from him is no small compliment, I assure thee, for even his own children consider it a great favor to receive one from him, and one of his sons, when he

first heard of his comming here was quite incredulous upon the subject. Uncle Darius says he has already visited us oftener than he has any body else in Michigan. So that thee sees such a circumstance forms quite an event in our chronology.[109]

In addition to providing physical assistance and opportunities for socialization, Michigan's homogeneous Quaker community embraced the Chandler/Evans family members by utilizing their intellectual talents. Elizabeth participated actively in the establishment and promotion of a local antislavery society, and Thomas was later considered as the anti-Masonic party's congressional candidate, was appointed a local delegate to a convention in Detroit, and was asked to be a magistrate (a position he declined). This reciprocal arrangement provided assistance for the Chandlers and Evans and in turn gave them a sense of their central role in the vitality of the community. Neighbors' actions confirmed to the family members that their presence within the territory was not considered merely marginal.[110]

Thomas and Elizabeth Chandler and Ruth Evans relied primarily on each other for companionship and care. Therefore, when Elizabeth became seriously ill in 1834, anxiety filled the household and rippled through the letters to Philadelphia. The subject of illness and death had appeared in the majority of their previous letters, and the sentence "We are well" was the most important in each letter. Jane, Ruth, and Elizabeth developed the ritual of including those words at the end of each letter, and they were the first words sought when a letter arrived. If a letter contained information about someone feeling unwell, alarm bells resonated in the recipient's mind.

Even almost twenty years after Elizabeth and Thomas's father, Dr. Thomas Chandler, had practiced medicine, illnesses and medical treatments remained fraught with guesswork and fear. Diagnosis and treatment represented an ongoing process of trial and error. Regular doctors during this period still held to the medieval theory that imbalances in the body's humors, or fluids, caused disease. For almost every illness, physicians prescribed bleeding and powerful cathartic or emetic drugs, which they hoped would reestablish the balance.[111] The consequences, of course, were always painful, mostly unsuccessful, and often life altering.

While most settlers welcomed a doctor's presence in the community, some people remained skeptical about the "regulars" and continued to rely on folk medicine, which had its origins in the herbal pharmacopoeia of both Native Americans and Europeans.[112] The letters in the Chandler collection show that the family relied on the regular physicians when serious illness occurred but also used time-honored home remedies acquired from relatives and friends and most often collected and administered by the women of the household. Jane Howell frequently included medical advice in her letters to her Michigan family.

Epidemics such as Asiatic cholera, which plagued the entire country in the early 1830s, terrorized the population. Asiatic cholera was a new disease that had originated in the Indian subcontinent and was making its way west. Ironically, cholera's spread was greatly facilitated by one of the nineteenth-century's greatest achievements, improved ocean and overland transportation. The disease initially erupted in the eastern part of the United States, affecting densely populated urban areas where sanitation and cleanliness were sorely lacking. Philadelphia was hit hard.[113]

The territory of Michigan was also hit. In April 1832 a vessel carrying troops sent to fight in the Black Hawk War arrived in the port of Detroit. Sixteen men on board were sick with cholera, and by the following morning, eleven of them had died. The boat, the *Henry Clay,* was not allowed to land, although some of the stricken men were brought ashore for treatment. By August the epidemic had run its course through the city, and its citizens breathed a sigh of relief. The relief was short-lived, however, because a second epidemic arose in 1834. Although theories of antisepsis and the activity of the microbe were still unknown, some people understood the value of scrupulous cleanliness. Therefore, on June 26, 1834, after cholera had already appeared in other parts of the country, the *Detroit Courier* advised that the city should be thoroughly cleaned in the hope that the scrubbing would ward off the disease. However, by August 13, 1834, the epidemic reached Detroit in full force, and by September 6, 222 cases of cholera were cited in a city of 4,973.[114]

Cholera was a virulent bacterial disease of the intestinal tract with symptoms including depression, sleepiness, lack of appetite, diarrhea, and dehydration. The more severe cholera morbus resembled dysentery. Treatment involved bleeding and administering calomel, a purgative or laxative made from mercurous chloride.[115] None of the extant letters directly state Elizabeth Chandler's symptoms during the summer of 1834 or named her disease. Because the cholera epidemic was raging in Detroit at the time, it is quite possible that she had contracted that disease. The treatments she received, however, seem to suggest that she could have had either cholera or the malarial disease known as ague, which had symptoms including recurrent chills, fever (called the "shakes"), and extreme weakness. On October 28, 1834, Jane Howell recommended that if Elizabeth's "stomach should be irritable so that it will not retain food a little wheat flour put before the fire and slowly scorched until [it] is a fine brown colour, and then made into a thin gruel is the best thing to stay on the stomach and at the same time very nourishing." Aunt Jane went on to say that this remedy had "saved John Childs life at the time he had the cholera," which suggests that she thought

Elizabeth had that illness. After Elizabeth died on November 2, 1834, however, her obituaries and Benjamin Lundy's memoir stated her cause of death as a "protracted remittent fever," another name for the advanced stages of ague.[116]

During the nineteenth century, physicians attributed ague to heat, moisture, and vegetable decomposition. Not until the early twentieth century did scientists discover that the debilitating disease was caused by the bite of the anopheles mosquito. Because nineteenth-century treatments were largely ineffective, pioneers came to expect and perhaps even accept the disease as a normal part of life. The Michigan Territory was known for its problems with mosquitoes, especially in moist or swampy areas. Reports came out of Michigan stating that "flies, gnats and mosquitoes were so numerous that the sky completely darkened," and early explorers composed an unflattering slogan: "Don't go to Michigan, that land of ills; / The word means ague, fever and chills."[117]

On September 29, 1834, Ruth Evans mentioned that the doctors had recommended using mercury, or the "blue pill," as the "safest and most shure course." The hoped-for result would be salivation. The blue pill (or "blue mass") was, along with quinine, the medicine of choice for ague. It contained 33 percent metallic mercury mixed with glycerin and honey and acted as a "sialagogue," which meant it increased the flow of saliva, and a "purgative," which operated more powerfully than a laxative. Mercury is now known to be deadly if ingested, but even then, doctors began to suspect its ill effects. In fact, after Elizabeth's death, Jane cautioned Ruth to avoid mercury as a treatment.[118]

Elizabeth Margaret Chandler died on November 2, 1834, just one month shy of her twenty-seventh birthday, after having been ill for several months. Her death affected more than just her immediate family. Her antislavery efforts had reached across many miles and even across the ocean, and her death was a great loss to the cause of abolitionism. Benjamin Lundy, William Lloyd Garrison, and Lucretia Mott, among others, acutely felt the void. She was quietly buried at Hazelbank on a rise of ground under the trees, just as she had wished for in her poem "The Sylvan Grave":

> Lay me not, when I die, in the place of the dead,
> With the dwellings of men round my resting place spread,
> But amidst the still forest, unseen and alone,
> Where the waters go by with a murmuring tone;
> Where the wild bird above me may wave its dark wing,
> And the flowers I have loved from my ashes may spring;
> Where affection's own blossom may lift its blue eye,
> With an eloquent glance from the place where I lie,
> Let the rose and the woodbine be there, to enwreath
> A bright chaplet of bloom for the pale brow of death;

And the clover's red blossom be seen, that the hum
Of the honey-bee's wing, may for requiem come;
And when those I have loved, 'midst the changes of earth,
The clouds of its sorrow, its sunshine of mirth,
Shall visit the spot where my cold relics lie,
And gaze on its flowers with a tear-moisten'd eye—
Let them think that my spirit still sometimes is there,
My breath the light zephyr that twines in their hair,
And these flowers, in their fragrance, a memory be,
To tell them thus sweet was their friendship to me.[119]

The gravesite at Hazelbank grew through the years as the graves of Ruth Evans, Thomas Chandler, and his wife, Jane, were added to Elizabeth's. In the Quaker tradition, the graves were not marked, though they were enclosed by a picket fence. The passing decades took their toll, and the graves were eventually forgotten amid the overgrown vegetation. However, in the summer of 1928, the Lenawee County Historical Society recognized the significance of this forgotten hillside and placed a marker at the site, dedicating it as a location of "outstanding local historical interest." At the ceremony, Elizabeth's great-niece, Minnie Chandler Merritt Fay, spoke:

I wish to thank the Historical Society of Lenawee County for granting me this privilege to pay tribute to the memory of my great Aunt Elizabeth Margaret Chandler.

I visited very frequently at this Hazelbank home, playing as a child, wandering and dreaming as a young girl and woman, and grew to a very deep admiration and respect for my dear Uncle Thomas and his memory of his departed sister Elizabeth and their Aunt Ruth.

This early association has made a very beautiful background for the more intimate acquaintance that I have gained from reading the letters that were so carefully preserved in the one locked drawer into which the little girl was just once allowed to peep.

I have read and re-read these letters many times, and always with wonder and joy at the clearness and literary finesse with which they led me into their lives as pioneers, of their devotion to truth and justice, and only between the lines do I read of the sister's self-sacrifice, her courage, and fortitude more rare.

She was a brave, good, beautiful woman. *Brave* to undertake and endure the hardships and privations of a pioneer, in the day when even the Governor's mansion was a white-washed log building. *Braver* as a leader in the cause of temperance when it had few advocates. *Bravest* when, as a personal friend of William Lloyd Garrison and Benjamin Lundy, she contributed to their publications, helped by her poems and articles to advance the anti-slavery cause. *Beautiful* because the inward light and love of service of the Quaker faith were reflected in her face and character.

May our faith be like hers and our work as well done.[120]

In 1978, after another fifty years had passed and the graves had again become overgrown and forgotten, Eagle Scout Steve Sommer of Adrian, Michigan, restored the cemetery to its 1928 condition. It now lies behind a row of small houses with large backyards and garden plots along a short gravel road, three miles northeast of Adrian. A 150-yard pathway on private property leads to the graveyard, and large trees still shade the "sylvan grave."

The letters in this volume bring us back almost 175 years. The story begins in 1830 and ends in 1842. Its central character is Elizabeth Margaret Chandler, an extraordinary pioneer of early abolitionism, early feminism, and early Michigan.

CHAPTER I

PREPARING TO REMOVE, 1830

*By early 1830 Thomas and Elizabeth Chandler and Ruth Evans
began planning to move to the Michigan Territory.*

———◆———

THOMAS *and* ELIZABETH CHANDLER *to* WILLIAM *and* SARAH CHANDLER
Philadelphia, February 12, 1830

My dear brother

A few days since thy last letter was received, and thee may suppose was very
acceptable after being anxiously looked for during the space of the last three or
four weeks and without delay, I went to the office for that addressed to Aunt Ruth
which we might have sooner received had I not overlooked the name in the list
of advertised letters though the cause of the oversight was that it was not placed
in the regular alphabetical order. The other came to hand a few days after my last
and my reason for not replying to it was the expectation of receiving a speedy
answer to mine?[1]

Thee wishes to be apprized of our prospects relative to business—of this I can
yet hardly give thee any definite information as we have almost concluded to
postpone our purposed emigration until fall or possibly the next spring though
our resolution to remove west is not altered or abated. To have your company on
such a journey would indeed be an inducement to remain a few months longer.
Although we would have to undergo many difficulties on such a tour I cannot but
think that we should find it a pleasant journey. Many reasons might be given for
our not going so soon as we anticipated. Perhaps a sufficient one will be that Aunt
Ruth thinks she will be better prepared—and Elizabeth is engaged in a little

work which will probably bring her something handsome.[2] Our friends to whom we have mentioned our prospect seem very averse to it—but this we expected and are willing to overcome. But I myself although very opposed to the delay on my own account am willing to think it may be advantageous.

Mature deliberation on the advantages likely to result from our removing to the coal region induced us to decline it. Had we concluded to adopt that plan it would have been only a temporary arrangement with the expectation of deriving considerable profit as it could not have been otherwise than disagreeable to all of us. At the time I wrote to Jos. Taylor we were considering the subject and I requested him to notify thee respecting it that thee might [be] advised of all our plans.[3]

I think it most probable that I shall live with some farmer during the ensuing summer, as by that means, besides the information acquired, I shall become in a measure inured to the labor which would devolve upon me in our new mode of life. And though this may not be profitable in a pecuniary point of view I am inclined to think that it will be more advantageous in the end than any thing else which I know of at present. As soon as we have fully determined what course to pursue by way of "making a living" &c we will endeavor to give thee information of all our plans as soon as practicable. As yet we have not fully resolved upon any plan though. As respects myself I think I shall adopt the last mentioned—unless I should receive an advantageous offer in the city.

We were pleased to hear of thy success in thy present occupation which although more laborious must be much freer from anxiety and perplexity than store keeping.[4] Thee inquired whether Aunt Ruth provided for a release.[5] She did not. Aaron Lippincott wished her to do so but she objected on account of its being contrary to friends' discipline and left it with him to have the article drawn without instructing him to make any reserve. He however excluded all household furniture. Aunt Ruth and I drank tea at Aaron's on first day last and they appeared very much pleased with our having visited them. He offered me a berth in his store which he seemed anxious I should accept. I did not give him a positive answer respecting it but mentioned my plan of devoting my time to farming previous to our removal west. Of farming with regard to profit he does not entertain a very favorable opinion—and for the purpose of inuring myself to labor advised me rather to devote the same time to *carpentering* at which he thought a fortune might be made in the "wild-woods." If that be the case thy newly adopted trade may be of advantage to thee, if you should conclude to accompany us. But the profit of farming would not be the inducement for me to adopt it. I am heartily sick of store keeping and have every reason to suppose that I should like the life of a farmer better than any other which I could adopt and feel certain that it will yeild something more than a competency in the western country. I feel anxious for the arrival of spring that I may be doing something and yet in some points my time passes pleasantly enough. Reading is now my principle employment and although very agreeable I feel a longing to be engaged in some more active pursuit.

Elizabeth wishes me to leave part of this sheet blank for her use and with the hope that thee will not delay writing to some of us a *very long* time I subscribe my self

> thy affectionate brother
> Thomas Chandler

Dear Sally,

I have delayed my intentions of writing to thee from time to time for these six months past, till I should have leisure to send thee a very long letter, and at last find myself limited to a single page. This however, though insufficient for all the manifold things I have to say, may be sufficient to tell thee how often thee has been and is still in our thoughts and (at the risk of repeating what Tom has perhaps already said) how anxiously we have waited to hear from "Penn Hill," waiting the hours of every day with impatience, till the reception of brother Will's letters calmed our uneasiness.[6]

I need scarcely tell thee how much we regret the loss of your little boy. I am sure I should have loved it with an affection scarcely inferior to your own—or how sincerely we sympathise with your feelings; but thy own health, as an object of much greater importance has occasioned us to much solicitude, that the knowledge of its perfect restoration, cannot but almost reconcile us to the loss of our young relative. We received information of this in a letter from J. Taylor to brother T. and thee may imagine with what anxiety we waited for more particular intelligence and to be assured of thy restoration to health. That Will had written I was almost confident, though some unknown cause prevented the letter from reaching us, and to write ourselves appeared useless, while we were in daily expectation of hearing from you. I am glad that it was so, for I should not like to think that even all his multifarious occupations, should make him so far forget us.

I am very glad to find that if we remain here until next year there may be some hope of your accompanying us in our emigration to the "western world." It would tend more than almost any thing to obviate my own objections, and reconcile me to the prospect and—*reality* of going, for, though, if circumstances had rendered our removal next spring the most advisable course, I should not have made any opposition to it. It would have been a severe trial to part from my brother, and a sister whom, though I have not yet had the pleasure of seeing her

I assure thee I love very much.[7] It is true, I suppose that your plans are yet as they must be of course at such a distance of time, undecided. Still it is pleasure [to] think that we may not be separated—not at least by a distance, to which that which now divides us, is comparatively trifling. T. is waiting to go to the post office, so I have only time to say that Aunt Ruth desires to be affectionately remembered to both of you, and to subscribe myself, dear Sarah,

> thy affectionate sister
> Elizabeth

ELIZABETH CHANDLER *to* WILLIAM *and* SARAH CHANDLER
Philadelphia, June 14, 1830

My dear Brother and Sister

I was much gratified by the reciept of your letter on last seventh day, and am much obliged to Sarah for writing to us. I had intended to reply to the last letter almost immediately on its reception, but a press of business at the time and a visit in the country to Aunt Amelia [Evans], since, has occasioned so long a defer of any intentions; though as a further apology I may add that I have now in my desk an unfinished reply to brother Will's letter.

Thomas is much pleased with his situation and with farming; he does not appear to be in the least frightened by the hard work, of which he is now able to endure a pretty tolerable portion, and remains, as much as ever pleased with the idea of becoming a "backwoodsman." He says he feels much better and stronger since his residence in the country which besides the practical knowledge he has acquired of farming, will be a great advantage to him. He appears convinced that such an apprenticeship as he is serving to the business, is the best plan for disposing of his time that he could have adopted.

We still continue of the opinion that Michigan combines the greatest number of advantages and holds out the greatest inducements for us to settle there. In the first place the circumstance of not having to clear off a heavy growth of timber strikes at once the most formidable difficulty from the settlers list of hardships. Then in Ohio the best of the Government lands are already taken up and for an improved farm, in a good neighborhood, a price must be paid which renders it scarcely a sufficient object for removal; and to continue onward still further west, what a tremendous tract of country would separate us from our friends, while even there we should not find half the facility for transforming the wealth of the ground into *available cash* as that which is offered by lake Erie and the New York canal. A late Buffaloe Gazette, after describing the various advantages of lake Erie, its central situation and the readiness with which it may be made a meeting point for vessels from different parts of the Union, or North America rather, adds, that there is probably not a sheet of water in the known world, inland at least, possessed of so decided a superiority of situation &c as that lake.[8] By the Welland canal boats have already ascended to the St. Lawrence; from Buffaloe to Baltimore it is said a barrel of flour may be transported for 50 cts. The completion of the Ohio canal will open an easy passage to New Orleans, while one which it is contemplated to cut across the country, will connect Erie with lake Michigan and Superior.[9]

I do not wonder at your having considered the Territory "an out-of-the-world kind of place" for it has been not much spoken of, or indeed settled in the interior until within the last few years. It is now populating very rapidly and numbers, I believe, about 40,000 persons. In the Saginaw district near the center of the territory the land is said to be so fertile that it will bear farming for 15 or 20 years without [ ]. Game is plenty and cheap—ducks 3 cts per pair, and a fat deer 50 cts—so that there would at least be no danger of starving, and "an industrious man who is able to purchase one or two lots of 80 acres may in five years acquire wealth." So says one of the Michigan papers. We have thought most of Mengwe Co.[10] (where brother Ts friend purchased land) which [is] situated on, or watered by the river Raisin, near the south east corner of the territory. But we cannot entirely determine until we get there and look about us a little. Even if we should conclude to go into Ohio, the canal route would be most advisable, so that if we fix in Michigan, it will be like shortening our journey. The circumstance of no land being sold either by private individuals or Government except for cash (as is said to be the case) almost insures an industrious and respectable population; while the absence of the necessity and the desire of "*making an appearance*" gives us full room for the exercise of hospitality, and where so many persons are convened from different quarters, it is almost impossible that we should not meet with some pleasant associates. Near the county town, Tecumseh, is a small lake abounding with fine fish,[11] and in the same county there is a settlement composed of Friends, who have a meeting house in their town or village; the name of this place is Adrian, it is about 5 or 6 miles from Tecumseh. In this district also the ground is said to be very fertile, and the timber astonishingly fine.

But let us be settled as comfortably and advantageously as we will, there will be still something wanting to complete our happiness, if we are not soon to enjoy the pleasure of having you as well fixed beside us. It will not be half as formidable an undertaking for you to come out after we have performed the office of Pioneers and given you an accurate account of all that is to be done, and of the country itself, and have prepared for your reception. We shall be "strangers in a strange land"[12] verily! However there is nothing like a good hope and a steady heart, to meet difficulties. Our friends appear to think we are doing very right to emigrate. Aunt Rebecca Guest says that had her sons manifested any inclination for farming she would have gone "back" with them willingly and cheerfully. I was rather surprised at such a sentiment *from* her, educated in the manner she has been.

You may depend upon our sending you a plain and unvarnished account of the country and our opinions respecting it. However much pleasure your society might afford us, we should be very sorry that you should follow us, unless we were convinced it would be for your own advantage. At present I am decidedly of the opinion that it would. I will candidly confess that I hate this business of tavern keeping most cordially; besides throwing an undue portion of care and fatigue upon my sister, it is not half as manly and independent and respectable as farming—nor though it may be more profitable, is it so *certain* a method of acquiring a fortune, and you cannot I am sure be near as comfortable. I like Wills "trade"[13] a great deal better, and I dare say he does, than the "hostel," however well my good sister may play the part of lady hostess. I feel half inclined to abuse it a great deal more; but I will however intermit for the present for the purpose of saying while I have room enough, how very much I, or we rather should like to come and spend a little time with you before we go, if it was any how practicable.

The supposition that I am going to spend a month at Brandywine[14] has originated I know not how. I certainly do not expect to do any such thing. Even to go down for a few days to bid Aunt Mary [Chandler] and my other friends farewell, will I fear be out of my power. It would be a great, a very great gratification both to Aunt Ruth and myself to see you before we go, especially if any circumstances should occur to prevent your joining us. But I will not suppose that. It spoils my beau[tiful] ideal landscape entirely to have your house left out of it. But I believe it will be entirely improbable for us to pay you a visit before we go. Our time now is limited and we have much to do. We have not exactly fixed upon a time for our departure, but I suppose it will be some time next month, probably not before the middle or latter part of it. It will be a severe trial to part from our friends, and we shall probably at first have many unaccustomed difficulties and hardships to encounter; but we are not unprepared for them and shall not therefore be liable to be readily discouraged, as if we expected to find only a smooth path.

It is really wonderful what a number of persons have emigrated to the West this spring. I do not know whether either Tom or myself mentioned that Jeremiah Warden intended removing his family to Ohio. He has done so and some of his friends have recieved letters from him expressing his perfect satisfaction with the course he has adopted, and the entire confirmation of his conviction that [he] has acted rightly. He too speaks of the immense number of persons who are removing Westward. The paper states that upward of 1200 pass through Buffaloe during one week.

Aunt Guests are in their usual health and frequently enquire about you. John Merrefield's health has been delicate lately, but he is now much better. Aunt Jane also is rather better, but she has not yet entirely recovered. Of News I believe there is but little stirring. Things go on pretty much after their old fashion. George Guest has, or is about going into the Apothecary business near Pottsville [Pennsylvania]. James Coe has quit there and gone into business for himself in the city.

Brother Tom will probably write soon. He has been talking of doing so. I am sorry Hannah Peirce mends so slowly. Please give Aunt R's love to her, and my own, when you see her. We have been thinking a great deal about her.

You will hear from us again before a great while, and as soon as the time for our departure is decisively fixed, we shall let you know. Do not I pray you think of taking a tavern next spring—even if you should not come out—for if you do I do not know when we shall ever see you, or you can get rid of it again. You are now comparatively "freefooted"—and I do not want you to fasten yourselves here—especially not with such a business as *that*. So says Aunt Ruth also—and she writes too in love now and the hope that we may speedily be united in the West, with

your affectionate sister
Elizabeth

Aunt Jane also desires her love. Hetty Chesnut, the other day when I was writing, bid me remember her to thee, and I have fulfilled my promise by doing so now. Let us hear from you again—as we are so soon to be separated we ought to make good use of our time now and exchange letters frequently.

CHAPTER 2

ARRIVAL AND ADJUSTMENT, 1830

The three pioneers, Thomas and Elizabeth Chandler and Ruth Evans, set out
for the Michigan Territory in early August 1830. The August 6 letter from
Anna Coe, Elizabeth's cousin and friend, which mentioned their leaving "tomor-
row," is the only document that provides a specific date of their departure. These
first letters from Michigan describe in vivid detail the pioneers' new situation,
and Jane Howell's responses exhibit a characteristic anxiety about their safety.

ANNA COE *to* ELIZABETH CHANDLER
{Philadelphia,} August 6, 1830

My Dear Coz

So my doom is fixed it seems, I *must* write though I have not a single idea to
begin with. Indeed I believe I never felt less like it than I do at this moment (stop
a minute—I am going out to eat some preserved plumbs. Maybe in *dabbling*
among them I may find a *new idea*). As Mother is preserving them possibly she
might have lost one.

Just returned—not a whit wiser than when I started for the neighbourhood
of Plum Town. If somebody would be kind enough to hit me a thump on the
knowledge box it might be of some service (*parents consenting of course*). Tom tells
me *we* start tomorrow and I suppose it must be so. I can hardly any how reconcile your going so far. It will put a complete stop to all adventures, frolics, &
togethers, though it cannot to our friendship. I can hardly in this instance make
use of our favorite adage—*"All is for the best."* Can thee Liz just now? Perhaps
though when we meet again we may think so. I shall have nobody to tell my troubles to or fly to when I have the Blues, or at least nobody that will put on a long

face and sympathise with me and now and then put in a little wholesome advice. However I must take to my pen and scribble all I have to unburthen though as to perplexity I hope I have done with all my former ones, and the principal one now is the distance of a *thousand miles.*

However dont let'us think of it now—but look forward to this fall one year. Thee will come *crawling* and *limping* up to the door leaning on *old pine log* for a crutch, plain drab bonnet to hide the *"first gray hair," long waist snuff box* in *thy left hand,* gout in thy right foot and out of thy pocket five or six rolls of—of—of—of—poetry. A knock at the door—thee hears somebody come, *clump* clump, clump down stairs. I step to the door with a *smooth quaker face* look through my *specs,* over them under them, raise them up with a *scientific touch.* Why Liz—Why Nancy. Down goes the specs in the entry, away goes the crutch to the *second story*—down we'll squat in the middle of the entry and begin to talk over old times. Bec [Rebecca Coe] in her hurry to what is going forward tumbles over us both and rolls gracefully out at the front door singing at the same time the tune of Old Hundred[1] to which she keeps time admirably as she *bounces* along. But first I must mention Mother, who in expectation of thy coming, is in the kitchen making some free sugar[2] pies, hearing the general uproar, steps into the entry with a pie in one hand (on the top of which she has just picked with a fork a beautiful image of a young blackmason (by way of improving the task,) ejaculating at the sight, there I told you so. I knew they would be back in a year. We sit there for the space of three minutes, all talking at the same time in great glee, when we are alarmed at a noise behind us. It is Amelia [Coe] who in the act of leaning over the banisters to see the new corner has let her *spectacles* fall & seeing who it is hurrying down as fast as the *rheumatism will let her.* It's Liz, its Liz. There wont be a lamp left whole in the house in two days, if they talk over old times—while Father says never mind let them break forty if they chuse.

How does thee like my picture, Coz? Will it do? Perhaps we may have many merry meetings yet happier than ever we have had. At any rate we will hope so and if sad now recollect I have written this to cheer you up—and thee must not give up too much to trouble. Time will reconcile thee more and more to absence from thy friends, but do if thee can gather sufficient to come on and spend some months with us. Donot forget if we remain single, we shall still all of us remain together I hope, and if I should ever marry I shall *still be Annette,* with a house open always for my *friends.*

I have just come [upon] a sweet little piece I think well worth copying. Thee must give me thy opinion of it some day or other.

THE LAND OF THE LEAVE
Theres a land that we dream of when fancy is free
Distant and dim enough the vision may be—

Where the faithful in *time,* after sorrowful years,
Shall meet in delight, though they parted in tears
This love when 'tis brightest, is shaded with care
But distrust and despondence can never come there
And 'tis sweet to believe of the absent we love
If we miss them below, we shall meet them above
Can you fail, with a land of such promise in view!
Will you leave for the evil the good and the true?
To reach that far country, Oh! will you not strive
Where never the feet of the slothful arrive?
Oh! for that region, that home of the blest
Where the wretched are glad, the weary at rest
Where sorrow finds balm, and innocence bliss
Oh! for that world—I am weary of this

ANNA COE *to* ELIZABETH CHANDLER
{Philadelphia,} August 30, 1830

I have just been watching the Sunset Coz till my eyes are almost *dimmed.* 'Tis like a lovely autumnal evening, though summer is scarce over, and the clouds are displaying their rich and varied hues; my eyes have been fixed on them, till they have changed from the brightest richest tints, and are lost in a dull gloomy colour, still beautiful, though they sadden the thoughts. I have been recalling former times and pleasures, and dwelt so long on by-past hours, that I feel quite *melancholy* almost dull, and I do not know but what my letter would have been quite an interesting one, but unfortunately a few minutes ago all my sentiments was put to flight, by my *dipping my sleeve in butter.* And I begin to think if N P Willis was here he might imagine, I was a boarding school miss and still retained the odors of *bread and butter.*

But to return to the clouds Lizzy—they remind me of those lines of Norma's, that I think so beautiful. Does thee recollect them?

Like the fair rainbow found we trace, around the setting Sun,
In which we gaze until each tint of loveliness is gone,
Thus came the day dreams of my youth, but brighter, lovelier far
Than ever could the gold cloud, around that sinking star!

SEPTEMBER 2ND

A few evenings since that most destructive of all elements, Fire, waged war with *Abraham Lower,* his shop, Maghogany and even made free *with a portion* of his scales (I observed as I passed there the other day) but I do not know wether he lost much by it. I know they made a most tremendous racket; they could not have made more had it been *Cherry Street Meeting.*[3] *Beg you pardon Liz!!!!*

W L Garrison was here some days before he could secure a room for lecturing. He succeeded at last, and has, invited the citizens there this evening, to hear what he might have to *unburthen.* I should have gone myself to hear him, but Amelia has been kind enough to have a *return* of *Chills* and *Fever.* Rebecca has been taking *care of Mother and Father;* so you see my duty called me at home—among the *pots, kettles* and *Dutch Ovens.* There was also mentioned in the paper his proposals for publishing a paper in Washington called The Liberator. I tried for several days to get the paper that had the proposals in for thee, but I believe John [Coe] has torn it up. If I can get it at any future time though I will send it on to—the—the—*Lands End*—in search of a friend of mine called EMC for her perusal.

SEPTEMBER 6TH

We have just been reading thy letter,[4] and are delighted to hear of your safe arrival in the land of *milk and prairies.* We have been very uneasy about you, and longed to hear of the many adventures that befel you on the way, and how you bore up during the fatiguing journey you have had. Just imagine the ridiculous figure I *should* have cut crossing Lake Erie (poor I that can hardly stand a journey of forty miles). Mind Lizzy write to me once a month, and do not write any formal letter to me, but let it be as though we were conversing, and thee was by my side. Oh how many little trifles, I could tell if thee was here.

Caroline Morris I have just heard has been engaged this year past to young Dupont, Victor Duponts nephew or cousin I believe. She has been very sly about it. Do you envy her Liz? I suppose she will reside near *old Brandywine.* George Guest returned from Pottsville very ill, and has been so much worse since that he had his head shaved and they were obliged to apply ice to it constantly but he is now convalescent.

Since I have been writing there has been a *spider* crawling twice across this paper. Some folks would say, it denoted good, some a disappointment, but notwithstanding I have had the blues for some days. I *feel willing to hope* there is no evil impending over me. If there should be a few inconsistencies in what I have this evening written, make my apology for me for there is no less than *eight human beings* gabbing round me as hard as their tongues can go. Uncle T[homas] Guest is one, WRH [William R. Hall] another, Uncle S[amuel] E Coe. Thee may guess the rest.

SEPTEMBER 7TH

Ring all the *bells,* and get all the *frying pans, tongs &c* in the neighbourhood of Tecumseh, or any thing else that will assist in making a pretty loud noise. There is great joy in our neighbourhood. Anna [Merrefield] has ushered this evening a fine little boy into this troublesome world, whom they call after his Father John Guest Merrefield! She sent for Mother about twelve, & the youngster was *introduced* about ½ of six. Anna is now improving very fast. She is quite brave.

Why does thee not write to me Lizzy. I am looking day after day for a letter, and every day am disappointed. I think I shall attack the *letter carrier* some of these days, out of *pure spite,* so if thee has any regard for a fellow being, hunt till thee finds a goose quill, and fill a sheet immediately. I am sure if nothing has occurred worth writing since thee might have had a thought or two, I will not be positive though as to that. I think if these letters should fall into the hands of strangers instead of their destined port, the finder would immediately make his way on to Philadelphia, to have thee conveyed to the Hospital as a fit asylum for such a *rattlecap.*

I received the last number of the Genius[5] the other day. *My gentleman* did not think proper to bring it in but just gave it a twirl across the store. It lodged I do not exactly know where. I remember it did not go beyond the ceiling. Liz write one of thy prettiest pieces in the next or rather in every number unless thee wishes to merit my *displeasure.* I have not heard from Brandywine since thee left. How lovely it must look there now. Let us imagine Aunt Rachel and Hayes [Chandler] gathering chesnuts, and wishing the *girls* were there to assist and partake of them. Maybe we will sometime Liz! Though there will perhaps be some painful changes before then. However, do not let my *croaking* make thee feel dull, particularly when I tell thee the girls have been singing hymns, till I feel *black* and *blue.* What a poetical idea!!!! Eliza Terry was here this evening. I told her we had heard from you. She seemed very much pleased at your prospects and I believe sincerely hopes you will do well (as well as myself).

11TH

Elizabeth Field went into a neighbours house to day, where she found a child weltering in its blood. It had been left in a high chair with a saucer in its hand; had fallen and its head was nearly separated from its body—it lived about a half hour.

16TH

I have had the mantua maker[6] here for several days and have been unable to write to thee but thee will have to excuse my delinquency as we are busy as bees preparing for the wedding of which I will inform thee after a while. This evening we have been spending an hour or so next door with Anna. Her little boy is a fine little fellow—takes a great deal of notice. I was very much divested this evening with John, who is already tired of his *own name* for the child, and seriously wishes to call it *Peter.* He says he is tired of family names, and wants to bring up something *new. Do admire his taste.*

19TH

Went to day (which is Sunday) to meeting in this morning. At eleven they rang all the bells I believe in town and kept up a pretty great clamour till meeting broke, when R and I seeing the smoke, concluded it might be near home. It turned out to be the board yard, just back of us on the wharf. There has been no less than four fires to day in different parts of the City all supposed to be set on fire.[7]

22ND

Last Monday night I dreamed thee was coming on to see us and I do wish there was some likelihood of my dream being realized. What sport we might have this winter. If I thought there was a possibility of it, I would go round the family, and give them each a complete licking a piece, and box their ears to boot. Do not be surprised at my *generosity.* It is *perfectly natural* I can assure thee (to me).

What is the reason thee does not write. The letter carrier goes by so often, and my heart bounces as well as my body off the chair—but no letters. Down I sit chop fallen. But I intend to be *revenged*—for *I'll write a sheet or two more than I intended to.*

Tuesday evening went with Guests girls and AGM [Amelia Guest Merrefield] to Bedells lecture room, to see the magic lantern.[8] It was very interesting as well as instructive. What I was most pleased with in his addressing the children, was his extreme anxiety to explain the vanity of setting their hearts so much upon dress as some of the little creatures appeared to have done. He showed them the finest looking birds such as the parrot, pea fowl, &c, & asked them if they admired the colours and wether they were not beautiful. They seemed delighted with them, thought them elegant. He then told them the little lark and many other plain coloured birds sang far the sweetest, while the voices of those gaudy coloured ones were grating to the ears. He said he thought it was the same with some of the little girls that were there present and were exceedingly fond of gay attire, while the little plain dressed girls were the best very frequently. Many of the pieces were very good (scriptural altogether and the remarks contained a good deal of instruction).

Wednesday evening—*Will* came up to tell us he had got tickets for the Lyceum—and away we posted to the Franklin Institute.[9] As I stepped up the steps I thought it could hardly be possible I could go there *without thee* and felt almost convinced thee must be somewhere behind me, but I looked in vain. Liz its too bad, I do not know what I would give if thee was here. I have *cords* to tell thee and to think I shall have to keep it all treasured up for a year or two. No— I'll *forget it all on purpose,* now. But to return to the evening. The address was delivered (by I know not who). It was very short and pretty good. The principal remark *that I noticed* was that we should not fail in the pursuit of knowledge &c &c &c. But instead of Dr. Backs and the Spirits that used to attend might be seen the heads of five or six of the Coloucall brethren who were performing their best on a number of different instruments, or another making as much noise as possible. There was one who particularly attracted my attention. He had been playing quite a melancholy sort of a slow tune and I was getting the *blues as fast as possible* when He changed it suddenly and scraped away on the violin as fast as it was possible for mortal to do winking his eyes at the same time in a most quizzical manner, that it started me off in an immoderate fit of laughing to the wonder of my next neighbour, who retained the most profound gravity. After a while I turned round to see wether any others were struck with the *ridiculous* on my right hand when lo! I sees our Bec nearly laughing herself off the bench, and Bill laughing first at one then at the other, to see what was going to be done next. With some degree of trouble on my part to behave myself, and to assist in restoring order, I at length succeeded, and in due time we returned to our respective homes and to bed.

Maebyl is now performing here. He had his chess playing, rope dancing, and the Carrousal, the Melodian which I take to be some kind of musical instrument.[10] I dont know what, but he has a different piece of music performed there every evening. If I should favour him with a visit, thee shall be favoured with a description. At present I am almost as ignorant of it as thyself. Last night it was opened for the first and I understand the house was filled and the audience went away highly gratified.

JGM [John Guest Merrefield] calls his son George Williams Merrifield. Maria Woodside has moved up into Third street in one of those new stores, and I believe does a pretty good business. *Debby Lupon is married to Thomas Kites son.* I believe I have spent my budget of news for the present. If I should hear anything new thee shall be favored.

OCTOBER 2ND

Lizzy I have just recieved a letter from Chandlers full of reproach for not hav-ing written to them before. Abby [Chandler] tells me to act consistent with my better feelings and scribble an account of your departure and wether I have heard from you, what I am doing myself and wether I have forgotten them. But I can solemnly assure them that is not the case. I love them all as much as ever and I think shall always feel very much interested for their well-doing—and I think I can promise for thee also. Abby writes that Rachel [Chandler] was visiting the other day, and they showed her a piece of poetry written by thy father. She said she had no doubt but thee would have loved to have seen it. She tells me if I have received the *young wolves* to be careful with regard to their education. Bring them up under good discipline and frequently make use of the rod of correction (I can tell thee one thing Liz by way of information—that I had thee here I would freely make use of one over *thy back* for not writing to me). Chandlers heard the other day that I either had been or was going to pay a visit in the neighbourhood and they seemed a good deal hurt at it. But I have not been in the country since thee left. It does not seem like any summer I have passed for several years.

Poor Betsy with the approach of winter suffers more pains.[11] The rest of the family are well and wish to be remembered. I intend writing to them and give them an account of what you are doing as far as I am able and must I tell them too that my Coz has not taken the trouble to write to me yet. Maybe Liz thee has turned into a pollywog. If so I must make every allowance for thy silence. When thee does, write Coz. I wish thee would be particular in letting me know wether you use *chop-sticks,* also, if the folks walk on their heads—their heels answering for a sign post.

Ask Tom what kind of wood would be most suitable for a crutch as I sprained my wrist yesterday. I am very glad to hear you are pleased with the prospects you have, and your expectations fully answered. I must have a full description of the farm from the house down to the chickens, but above all do have a romantic name for it. When any one asks me if I ever expect to visit you, I tell them no. I never should survive crossing Lake Erie. I am sure it would be a tremendous undertak-ing. Uncle Sammy [Samuel E. Coe] has threatened repeatedly to add a few lines by way of postscript and somehow or other he has not yet accomplished it. If he does, I will inform thee in another letter.

In my next I must give thee a description of the wedding.[12] It would not be worth while to commence it in this. Joshua Longstreth has lost his youngest daughter. She died a few days ago. I saw Sarah Dorsey a few days ago in the street, but we only exchanged nods and ventured a smile or two. I begin to fear now this news, will be rather aged before it reaches your retired habitation but if it should and the contents are at all interesting I shall be requested to write in a more connected type. At present, I have to write pretty much by snatches which must be my apology for the style.

Ann

ELIZABETH CHANDLER *to* HANNAH TOWNSEND
Michigan Territory, n.d. {ca. October–November 1830}[13]

I sat at the side of the vessel, gazing on the scenery that was passing before me, with my thoughts divided between the land I had left, and that which was in view, now reverting to the past, and now dwelling on the untried future; and often, very often, resting with the gathered band at Cherry Street, amongst whom I supposed thee then to be.

As we approached Detroit, our Governor's mansion on the bank of the river, was pointed out to us.[14] It is merely a log building white-washed; but the grounds about it have quite the appearance of a gentleman's residence. Detroit is rather a dirty-looking place; here we remained, however, only one night, and set off early the next morning for Tecumseh.[15]

After proceeding a short distance, the stage suddenly stopped, and the passengers began, very orderly, to make preparations for leaving it. For what cause this was done, I was at a loss to determine, as besides that it was much too early for breakfast, there was no appearance of a *house* anywhere in the vicinity. However, we quietly imitated the example of our fellow travellers, and descended to terra firma, when it appeared that the measure was one of prudence, required by our approach to a long series of worn, loose, and uneven logs, denominated *a bridge!* and stretching across a stream dignified by the appellation of the *river* "Rouge!"[16] A real *backwoods* bridge, this! thought I—and, as I walked over it, I perfectly acquiesced in the wisdom of dismounting, as well from a due regard to preserving the flesh uninjured, and the bones in their proper sockets, as from the danger of our weight proving too great for the frail structure for such at least it seemed, however, strong it might in reality be; at any rate, I have not heard since that it has given way, neither have any of the others, which we crossed in the same manner.

This was no very favourable augury for the roads of Michigan; but they were, in general, much better than I had expected—sometimes rough, but not dangerous; and as our carriage was sufficiently strong to bear the jolting over logs and such kind of *rail-ways,* we arrived at Tecumseh in the evening, battered, to be sure, in a most ungentle manner, but at least with undamaged bones, by whatever amount of sore flesh, reeling of heads, and excessive weariness, they might have been accompanied.[17] It was so long since I had enjoyed a night of comfortable sleep, that I was almost worn out, and could scarcely sit up long enough to drink my tea; yet when I lay down, the motion of the boat (of which I still retained the feeling as when actually on board) interfered sadly with my rest and my dreams, and caused me to pass the night with almost as much discomfort, as if actually tempest-tost.

On the next First-day, we attended Meeting. The road wound through quiet and beautiful openings, dotted occasionally with log dwellings, and small spots of improved land; but for the most part, still remaining in their own native loveliness, crowned with scattered trees, now gathered into picturesque clumps, leaving a clear space open to the sun-light, then spread out into an almost regular grove, and sometimes giving place entirely to a small stretch of bright green prairie, contrasting finely with the rich sunlight tint of the sod on the openings, which seemed coloured, as well as *covered,* by a profusion of *wild-flowers* and yellow "braken."

Yet beautiful as they are, one of the greatest charms of these "openings" is their perfect tranquility.[18] Oh, how I wish thee could breathe with me, if it were only for one short half hour, the exquisite, the *religious* stillness. There are varieties even of silence, and I dare say thou hast felt it so. Contrast the hush of a starry midnight, with that of a moon-lit evening, or of one of our religious meetings, or of an open field,—and they have each their own peculiar character. But the stillness I speak of is like none of these—and must be felt in order to be understood. It was indeed almost the only thing I did *feel,* in attempting to describe the scenery around me, for some time after leaving Philadelphia. There were many scenes that I saw were beautiful—most beautiful—grand, picturesque, or magnificent—and I gave them my admiration and my praise; but that was all, or nearly all the sensation they could awaken. There were some spots on our route that did, indeed, almost arouse a portion of my former enthusiasm; but it is of what I have witnessed since our arrival in Michigan, that I have spoken most particularly.

JANE HOWELL *to* ELIZABETH CHANDLER
Philadelphia, September 8, 1830

Thee may well suppose my dear Niece that the receipt of thy long and very interesting letter gave me, and the rest of thy friends a great deal of pleasure.

After allowing you time for your journey and the mail to return to the City, I became so impatient and uneasy about you that it almost unnerved me. It was indeed a great satisfaction to hear that you got through your journey without accidents and in good health. I watched the weather and counted the days until I had reached seven which I expected would have landed you on the shores of Michigan, after that time I felt more lighthearted supposing you were on Terra Firma, among kind friends and doing well—but on the contrary for several days you were dashing and splashing, thumping and bumping on that most tremendous Lake. It makes me shudder almost to think about it but exclusive of that, I think you must have enjoyed your journey very much. Such a variety of scenery, and the sublimity of some part of it, must have made it very pleasing.

We were very glad to hear that you have fixed upon land having so many advantages, the towns of Adrian and Tecumseh being so near, and friends meeting house and the stage road such a short distance from it, must certainly make it much more valuable: and then having such kind neighbours joining your premises will make it very agreeable. John Lovett has called several times since you left us to inquire after you, and his father was here yesterday. He was very much pleased to hear from you. He says he feels as much interrested as if you were part of his family. He thinks his land is about two miles from yours. Anna Coe is waiting for a private opportunity to send thee on a packet of letters. I hardly think she will meet with one before John Lovett goes, which will be about the middle of next month.[19]

Lemuel informed me this evening that the Widow Greenfield in company with some friend (I did not hear his name) is going to her Southern Plantations to set her Slaves at liberty. Is it not astonishing that one of her sordid disposition, who is grasping at wealth, and who is apparently dead to all the finer feelings inherent in the breast of the philanthropist, should come forth in direct opposition to her worldly interest, yes even to her poor African Slaves "to undo their heavy bands and let the oppressed go free."[20] It is a great and noble undertaking and may she have the blessing of an approving conscience for her reward, which I should suppose would be far sweeter to her, than the thanks and praises of thousands.

James Coe and Rebecca Hall are to be married the 25th day of this month if nothing prevents. Anna will give thee the particulars. I did not go to the Sea Shore as I intended. My health has been so much better that I thought home was the best place for me.[21] There is not one of your friends I believe that feels more interrested for you than Lemuel. I do not think there has one day passed since you left us, but he has talked about you. He says next Spring if nothing prevents he will certainly come and see you. George Guest has been very ill here in the City. The Physicians were apprehensive of an inflamation on the brain[22] but he is now better.

Caroline Morris is engaged to be married to a young man by the name of Dupont. He is in the Navy. They have been betrothed to each other more than a year, but none of her friends knew it until within a few days. I have not heard when the marriage is to take place. Ann Jones and Husband set sail for England the 20th of last month, to the *joy* and *sorrow* of many. A safe voyage to them. Anna Marrifield has a fine son. I hope John will have no more time for Hipo now. Last week three Houses were nearly destroyed by fire in Third Street, one belonging to Rakestrace a Printer, another to Loyd a Morrocco dresser,[23] and the other to Abram Lower Cabinet Maker. It broke out at night and made such progress that very little was saved from the flames.

Please tell me the next time thee writes whether Thomas continues to take the journal of Health.[24] Two numbers have been handed in since you left us.

Lemuel, Ann, and I went to Haddonfield [New Jersey] about three weeks since. Hannah Roberts was much disappointed in not having a visit from you. John [Roberts] has a high opinion of Michigan, and says if he was about thirty years of age he would purchase and settle there. We should like to know what prices you have to pay for horses, cows, sheep, hogs, &c, &c, for every thing is interesting to us. Do tell us if you have had any dealings with the Indians and how they comport themselves. I think I should feel prodigiously afraid of them even in their most civilised state. And as to having a house without shutters I could never agree to, for bar's and bolts I should hardly think sufficient to keep out the nightly intruder. Poor little Roy[25] for several days after you left here appeared as if he hardly felt himself at home. He would come into the house and look about and then run into the Street hardly allowing us time to feed him. He is now quite in his usual spirits.

I called to see friend Woodside this morning. She and Maria [Woodside] were much pleased to hear from you. They both desired a great deal of love. They are about removing into Third Street near Green. Maria intends writing as soon as she can meet with a private opportunity.

William Loyd Garrison delivered three lectures in this City on the subject of Slavery. He proposes to publish a weekly paper in Washington City to be called the "Liberator or Journal of the time." He says in his prospectus, "I shall exercise a strict supervision over the proceedings of Congress and the conduct of its members. The representatives of a Moral and Religious People should walk circumspectly, not as fools but as wise Men lest they be brought to public shame. This paper will be a terror to evil doers but a praise to them that do well."

Louisa left thy letter at Cousin Guests for their perusal but they were placed in a sad predicament for they could not read it; it was written so small. But fortunately Elisa Tunis came in, and she read it to them. They were very much pleased with it, and said they hoped I would let them see the next one I received.

I called on the Widow Greenfield this morning to ask her for a few grapes for a person who is sick in our neighbourhood.[26] She received me very kindly, took me into her garden, gave me several bunches of grapes, and invited me to come and get more. She is very busy preparing for her journey: she had two large packing boxes filled with whole pieces of Muslin Calicoes Canton flannels &c &c which she intends to take to her slaves.[27] I did not say anything to her about their emancipation, as she was full of business and I did not wish to detain her.

Samuel Comfort called here yesterday to inquire after you. He expresses much pleasure that you were likely to be so comfortably situated and hopes Thomas will write to him as soon as he has leisure as he shall feel very much interrested for him. He wished to be remembered to you.

We feel anxious to hear how many acres Thomas has purchased, and how it is watered and wooded, and wether there will be a good spring near the house. We have not parted with little Miss yet, nor the Stove.[28] I hope to do both soon to advantage. I must inform you "amoung the Wonders of the time" that Anna Coe Sen[r] spent an afternoon with me. I think it must have been about the time you encountered the storm on the Lake. Israel and Louisa Estlack has taken part of Joseph Gatchels house. I think a little persuasion would induce them to become inhabitants of Michigan. Aunts spent a day with me a short time since. They take great interrest in your wellfare. I hope you will have something to send them this winter as a rememberance. I think wild Turkeys will soon become scarce in Your Territory if the Population continues to increase as it has done, and we shall have to put up with tame ones.

I suppose you have heard of the revolution in France and the elopement of the King with Crown and the Jewel.[29] It was quick work but I hope it will terminate without more bloodshed. I have not seen Hannah Townsend yet but I shall I expect in a few days when I intend to gratify her with a perusal of thy letter.

On the twentieth day of last month (August) John Hare Powel and Edward Bund with their respective families chartered a vessel and set sail from this Port for England to their large estates which had been left them there but great rumours have been in circulation for several days past as to their safety as it is generally believed (from many circumstances) that the ship has been wrecked in the gale which we had a few weeks since. If so, I hope the crew has been all saved.

Aunt Amelia informed me a few days since of the decease of Titus Bennet. It will no doubt be a great loss to his family. I did not hear the particulars of his illness.

I have given thee a complete "Epitome of the times" but it really seems too bad to send one thousand miles a letter so full of blots and blundering. I intended to have copied it off but indeed it is too great a task for one who dislikes writing as I do. But away with apologies for I seldom call for their aid.

Do keep a sharp eye after they Aunt Ruth so that she does not work too hard or expose herself to the inclemency of the weather. Remember the distance that divides us.

Aunts are well and our friends generally. My own health has improved very much—and with much love to my dear sister, Thomas and thyself I remain thy

affectionate Aunt
Jane Howell

———◦—◦———

THOMAS CHANDLER *to* JANE HOWELL
Michigan Territory, September 8, 1830

My dear Aunt will excuse a half sheet as she will see my motive by looking over the other which I would thank her to seal and send to the Post office. We have all enjoyed good health since our arrival and have good reason to think it a healthy country. As I have little room I will try to give thee a description of our plans, prospects &c in as few words as possible. After spending a few days in viewing the country I was so much better pleased with the neighborhood of Adrian than Tecumseh that I concluded to select a place in that part. We therefor have taken a room in the house of friend Comstock as a temporary residence and I have chosen a lot adjoining his farm which is said by every one who has seen it to be some of the best land in the country. We are now about erecting a log house 20 by 26 feet on a gentle rise of ground which commands a fine view of our neighbor Comstocks house and farm that gives it almost the appearance of an old settled country. The prospect is really beautiful. On one side a glance of the eye may take in a view of a large tract of cultivated land perhaps 200 acres with two large frame barns and the house of our neighbor surrounded with trees which at a distance has the air of a gentleman's seat in the vicinity of Philadelphia. Indeed there are few more showy houses in Pennsylvania. It is a two story frame painted white well finished about 40 by 50 feet in size.

My farm will be but little trouble to clear as the trees are generally small on about 50 acres & so few in number as not to interfere with the plough without cutting any down. I expect to put in a few acres of wheat this fall enough for a years supply at any rate. Much more I cannot attend to on account of fencing. The situation of our place is very eligible being in a friends settlement about a mile from meeting. And within the distance of a mile and a half we shall have 8 or ten neighbors that I know of, though it is probable there are more. It is about midway between the towns of Tecumseh and Adrian 5 miles from each. A stage runs daily to and from these towns. We have taken passage several times without charge. Quite a convenience isn't it?[30]

Fruit trees thrive well though they are not yet old enough to bear as it is but four years since the first house was built in the neighborhood. Melons grow as fine as in Jersey as we have daily proof through the kindness of friend Comstock's. Potatoes are as fine as I ever saw and I have not the least doubt but sweet potatoes would grow as fine as any where but they have not been tried till this summer. Turnips are said sometimes to grow as large as a wooden bucket and very fine. Tell Uncle one of our neighbors the Widow Comstock is a connection of his. She is sister to his Aunt Hathaway's husband and is really a very fine woman— also that carpenter's are so busy that it is a difficult matter to get work done by them.[31]

In a few years I think this will be one of the most beautiful countries—it is just hilly enough to give an agreeable diversity to the prospect without being enough to render it difficult to cultivate. The oak-openings now present a different appearance from any other country I have seen. The trees are generally not very large but straight and tall and about as thick on the ground perhaps as trees in an orchard. In some places they are almost free from underbrush with the ground covered with grass and wild flowers offering a delightful place for a promenade. Aunt Ruth and Elizabeth sometimes have strolled in the woods by themselves without fear—though there is but little cause for fear. There are said to be no rattlesnakes except in the swamps and wild beasts are seldom seen. I have seen several wild turkeys since coming here when I had no gun with me, and pidgeons in abundance.[32] We find the country in most respects as we heard it described and of course are pleased with it. A bill has passed the legislative Council of the territory incorporating the Pontiac and Detroit Rail Road Company,[33] and I have no doubt but in the course of a few years a similar road or a canal will pass near this place to Monroe which will render the price of transportation to and from New York very low.

We have [been] disappointed in not hearing from thee before this time. Aunt R says she is very anxious to know how thee is. That we may speedily have our disappointment and anxiety removed is the request of aunt and sister as well as of thy affectionate nephew

Thomas Chandler

THOMAS CHANDLER *and* ELIZABETH CHANDLER *to* WILLIAM CHANDLER
Michigan Territory, October 10, 1830[34]

My dear brother

About six weeks have elapsed since we have been inhabitants of the western country and no doubt thee must feel anxious to know how we to whom the change is so very great are pleased with our location in this land of promise—and I am happy in being able to inform thee that we like it very much. In passing through the state of New York I made a practice of observing closely the land in the new settlements, in order to compare it with that of Michigan and as far as my judgement is correct, the latter is much preferable, in some respects greatly so—but I will try to give thee a description. The soil I believe is a sandy loam (very different from Jersey though) and very easy of cultivation and produces good crops. Although corn or wheat has been on the same field for several successive years no deterioration is apparent. There are large tracts of land denominated oak-openings which do not offer half the obstacles to settlers which they are compelled to encounter in clearing heavily timbered forests. On these the trees are principally white oak and none of such enormous size as some that we met with in the timbered land. They are likewise much more distant—in many places not standing thicker than apple trees in an orchard and being little disadvantage to the cultivator.

I have selected an eighty acre lot of this description which takes in a portion of meadow or river bottom. It is in a very pleasant situation about half way between the towns of Tecumseh and Adrian and about a half mile from the river Raisin and one mile from friends meeting. Our next neighbor Darius Comstock has about 200 acres cleared and fenced immediately adjoining, which almost gives it the appearance of an old country. We have placed our house on a rising piece of ground which commands a fine view of the greater part of my place and the cultivated part of our neighbor Comstocks whose buildings and house in particular form a prominent feature in the scene. Indeed it is very pleasant to stand—at the door of our house in the woods and have a view of two large frame barns and a house which would receive and deserve the appellation of first rate in any part of the country and reflect that four years ago this was a wilderness.

Our humble dwelling is composed of logs, its dimensions twenty by twenty six feet which is divided into three rooms down stairs and may be conveniently partitioned above hereafter. It is a story and half high and the logs hew'd down on both sides and has two doors & four windows down stairs and a window up stairs in each gable end and is said to be the best log house in this part of the country. I hired a man to erect the log part and undertook the carpenters part of the business myself at which I have succeeded—rather better than I expected. I had the assistance of a carpenter for three or four days in putting on the roof and gable ends and employed him to make the sash.[35] I think I have saved considerable by doing the rest myself as carpenters wages are from a dollar to a dollar and a half per day and the one I employed told me while we were shingling that by working myself I was saving a dollar a day. Carpenters have full employment— at one time I was doubtful whether I should not be entirely unable to get one.

But perhaps I have been needlessly particular in talking about the house when I have not half told thee about the country. The face of the country may be called level though it is by no means flat but partly undulating—generally more so than I had expected but there are few hills so steep as to be inconvenient for ploughing and very little indeed so level as not to admit of water passing off without standing. The openings in the early part of the season are said to resemble a wide extended flower garden and even at the time of our arrival in the latter end of August the variety of wildflowers was very considerable and in some places had a beautiful appearance. The timbered lands contained the kinds of trees which we see in Pennsylvania with several others among which are sugar maple, boxwood, cottonwood &c. Grape vines are very numerous in some places also wild plums. It does not appear to me to be half the undertaking to commence the cultivation of a tract of opening where the plough can be started at once as to enter a dense heavy forest where recourse must be had to the axe even to prepare a space large enough for a garden. Neither is it such and the land on the openings is generally thought to produce better after the first crop which is sometimes not so good owing to the sod not being sufficiently rotted. I have enquired of a number of persons the average quantity of wheat raised to the acre. Those that rate it the lowest say about twenty bushels. This quantity is thought by our neighbor Comstock to be about a fair estimate for this or any other country in which he has been but others say from twenty five to thirty bushels. Friend Comstock left a fine farm in the best part of the state of New York but he gives this country a decided preference. He tells me I can raise corn on my place which I can barely reach the top of with a walking [stick] erected at arm's length.[36]

OCT 20

I forsook my writing when I had got thus far to witness or assist in the taking of a bee tree which are very abundant in this country. The quantity of honey obtained from this tree was about thirty or forty pounds though some are said to yeild from seventy to eighty. I have endeavored in speaking of this country

· 25 ·

to be strictly candid and do not wish to [say] one word in its favor more than it deserves. The advantages it possesses over the country west of Pennsylvania for immediate settlement are considerable as we may take into consideration the better prices of produce, there being now a good market for any overplus. The facility for making canals or railways will undoubtedly open a vent for the surplus.

At the last session of the legislative council a company was incorporated to establish a railroad from Pontiac to Detroit—and I expect one will be made here after (either that or a canal) running through this section of the country to Monroe, from the St. Joseph's country in the western part of the territory. If this be the case there will certainly be more carriage on this route than any other in the territory as the St. Joseph's is thought by some to be the richest part of Michigan or even of the western country. But I prefer this part greatly for several reasons among which, to say nothing of its being so much nearer to our old home, is the difference in the society which there is said to be of a much lower order a great part composed of people who are satisfied to live *any how* or if thee does not understand this phrase such as have not enterprise sufficient to improve their farms sufficiently to give them an air of comfort, but are willing to exist year after year in a state of contented apathy exercising industry sufficient for the support of their family and spending the remainder and chief part of their time in hunting or indolence and of such as are, though industrious, devoid of any kind of ambition. Here the society is much more like that in the eastern states though it cannot be expected it should equal in refinement some neighborhoods in Pennsylvania. I do not think it would suffer by a comparison with Little Britain. Still it is different—there is more equality.

I do not think there is a person in the neighborhood addicted to drink. At least I have not seen or heard of one nor although I have been a good deal through the country have I seen a bottle out in a single instance. There is but one tavern in Tecumseh and that has no bar. So much for the temperance of the people.

The mode of farming practiced here is not so good as in Pa, but is better than I was led to suppose from what I had heard of western country agriculture. They continue one crop too long on the same ground and too often sow wheat where corn has been the same year. The soil is admirably calculated for the growth of melons. We have eaten of some very fine watermelons and cantelopes raised in a corn field quite equal to those raised in Jersey. Potatoes are as fine as I ever saw although the season has been uncommonly dry and turnips are said to thrive extraordinarily well. Comstock says he has raised them as large round as the pump. There is no doubt but this will be a fine country for the cultivation of grapes. I saw some very thriving vines at Musgrove Evans' at Tecumseh which had been set out a year or two. Some of them were French kinds and already bore some fine clusters of grapes although the greater part of the vines appeared to be the groth of the present season.

I think I shall take up another eighty acre lot adjoining mine which will make a better size farm and give me plenty of woodland. This lot contains from forty to fifty acres of heavy timbered land on a rich river bottom from 15 to twenty of open meadow without any timber except an occasional coppse and the remainder about fifteen acres is that denominated openings. The possession of this lot would give me some decided advantages especially in raising stock in the meadow. Ground would there be very valuable and would require but comparatively little trouble to make it first rate land for hay or pasture and the wood land would also be very valuable for timber. There is on this lot a large quantity of black ash said to be equally durable with chesnut for rails and to split much easier than oak. With this addition I shall have as large a farm as I want and one combining as many advantages as I could expect.

Almost every person who sees my lot congratulates me upon having made choice of a first rate piece of land and I have not yet seen an equal quantity of new land for which I would be willing to exchange it. About fifty acres are of a description called Burr oak plains which is said be the best kind of land in the territory. The timber on this part is small and scattering and will not be half as much trouble to clear as it would to free some of your Pennsylvania land from blackberry bushes. I have not "a stream of water running through my place" yet there is water on one end which by a proper arrangement of my fields at that end, can be appropriated for the use of cattle on them & at the other end the water at the house will not be inconvenient and springs appear to stand a drought well. Nearly three months elapsed this summer without rain yet I have not heard of a well having dried neither did the streams diminish much. It is said a fresh spring occurs in the river.

Perhaps it may be interesting to thee to know the price of stock, produce &c. Wheat sells for 75 cts—corn I believe about 40—oats about 30. Rye is not grown here. Potatoes are now worth about 50 cts but I do not think they will remain at that price. Hay from 4 to 6 dolls per ton. Horses are not much used here yet. They may be bought from 40 to 80 dollars. Oxen from 35 to 45 a pair. Cows with calves from 12 to 14 dolls. Of sheep, I am not informed of the price. Hogs and pigs perhaps of the same value as with you. Pork will be worth 4 or 5 dollars the hundred. The whole surplus produce is now disposed of to settlers. The price of course will fall somewhat when this demand is less than the quantity raised. About Ypsilanti which is an old settlement the storekeepers pay 50 cts for wheat which they send in waggons [ ] from whence it is conveyed to a market on the New York canal.[37] With a water communication to Lake Erie it would warrant the payment of [ ] price.

We are apt to associate with our thoughts of the western country the idea of wild beasts and rattlesnakes. At least I did when in Penn. Since we came here I have seen but one wolf and very few snakes all of which I thought were of a harmless species. There are said to be some rattlesnakes but very few now on the openings. There are some wolves and they will always run from a man. A very few bears and no panthers that I have heard of. Deer are not very plenty yet they are frequently seen. Racoons are quite numerous. There are also some muskrats. Remains of beaver dams are numerous but I believe there are no beavers left. Pigeons, partridges, pheasants, wild turkeys, geese, and ducks may be said to be as plenty here as almost any other place.

If I have omitted any thing that thee would like to be informed of please mention it when thee writes and I will endeavor to satisfy thee. I have delayed writing longer than I intended for which I must plead having a good deal of business to attend to—but do write soon and tell us what thy prospects are and when thee expects to come and see us. I often think how much it would add to my satisfaction if you were somewhere near us. I often look toward a lot adjoining mine which is not yet taken up and wish my brother was located there. One thing in particular speaks favorably of this place, there is hardly a person who is not well satisfied with the country and all seem anxious to add to the improvement of the country. But my dear brother do let us hear from thee soon. Recollect how very interesting every item of intelligence must be to backwoods people. With a great deal of love to thyself and Sarah

> I remain as ever thy affectionate brother
> Thomas Chandler

I cannot suffer brother T. to send off his letter without adding a few words if they be only those of greeting. I wish very much to hear from you—and to know your plans for the future. I seldom look round me from our log habitation without wishing you were near us. Do not pray suffer all the lots adjoining us to be occupied by strangers—it would be so delightful to see the roof of your dwelling peeping out from behind one of the flowery knolls that swell up behind us. Then brother Will might work at any of his *hundred trades* to his hearts content;—"keep *accommodation*" if his chosen; there is an excellent situation for that purpose adjoining us that is not yet taken up—and no *bar* is necessary. People are crowding very fast into the territory—and there appears to be much fewer inconveniences and hardships to sustain than might reasonably be expected in so new a settlement. So far as we have been very well satisfied—things have gone on well and smoothly and I think I like the country even better than I did at first. At any rate we, coming in all among strangers, had a more formidable prospect, and more difficulties to contend with than any of our friends who may come after us. I think I may freely and safely say I am glad we came—and that we came *here*. Brother seems so happy and satisfied that I could scarcely be otherwise even if I were disposed to be so—he is now independent of the world and master of a fine farm which requires only industry to insure him a regular competence. He feels now settled—and may look forward with as much confidence as the uncertainty of the world admits of or renders allowable, to a gradual improvement of his circumstances. And there is some comfort too in expecting the *roughest* part of the undertaking to come first. I need scarcely say with what pleasure we look forward to seeing brother Will next summer even though he may not gratify the whole of our wishes and bring his wife with him. But Thomas is waiting and I must not detain him. So adieu with much love from Aunt Ruth as well as your "far away" sister.

E.

JANE HOWELL *to* RUTH EVANS
Philadelphia, October 10, 1830

My dear Sister—

When I for a moment think of the distance which divides us I feel amazed, and when I dwell upon it my heart almost sickens at the thought; but as it must be so, I strive to conquer those feelings by thinking as seldom as I can on the subject. I received my dear Nephews letter dated September 8th which was very acceptable. I hope by this time you are comfortably fixed in your own log house; by your own fire side. There are pleasures inexpressable in it. Let it be ever so homely. I feel anxious about Thomas, I fear he will have more to do than his strength will be adequate to; I wish he had a boy to help him. It is a great satisfaction to hear you have met with such kind friends. Their attentions and kindness to you makes one feel much more resigned to our seperation.

I, and I believe all the rest of your friends are very much pleased with the location of your land. Eight farm houses within a mile and a half must make it quite a thick settled neighbourhood. I think the Oak openings must be beautiful in summer from the description I have had of them but how is it with the more heavily timbered land. I suppose the trees attain to a greater size than the others.

James Coe and Rebecca Hall were married the 27th day of last month by the Mayor at their own house. They had a snug little wedding. Anna Coe and Margaretta Hall were bridesmaids I did not hear who waited on them.[38]

Aunt [Hannah] Gamage and her daughter Sarah from Hudson are here on a visit. They have been with us about three weeks and expect to return home in the course of a few days. Aunt was much disappointed in not seeing thee in the City. Thee is a great favourite of her. She desires a great deal of love to thee—Her daughter Sarah has been ill for a long time with the liver Complaint. By my desire she applied the Tar plaister and found almost immediate-relief from it.[39] She continues to wear it. The pain in her side has entirely left her. I have prevailed on Amelia [Evans] to spend the winter with me. I shall feel much more easy to have her here in case of her being sick and her home was very disagreeable to her. She had had a bad cold but is now better. Hannah Townsend was here a few days since. She says she has several pages written in readiness to send by John Lovett. She is well and anxiously waiting for a letter from Elizabeth. Cousin Guests take very great interest in your concerns. They have seen both the letters which I received[40] and indeed they would have felt very much slighted if I had withheld them from them.

Jane Parker was here a few days since on her way to Abington. I was not at home at the time but she said she would spend a day with me on her return to the City. She informed Ann that her husband and family were going to remove in the Spring to Michigan. She seems much pleased with the prospect. I hope they may settle somewhere near you.

I am waiting an opportunity to send your letters on to William. I have not heard from him since you left us. I do not know how to direct a letter to him or I should have written by post.

If you are now occupants of your new log house your domestic duties must nearly fill up your time for where there are cows to milk butter to churn bread to bake &c &c &c there will be but little time for sedentary employment.

I must now say something of Roy. He is fatter than when you left him and his spirit is sometimes almost unbounded. He is quite a copartner with Carlo[41] in the affection of his Master. Lemuel often says if he had to part with either he should not know which to give up; but he says if he should go to Michigan he will take Roy with him.

The marriage engagement between Robert Coe Jr. and his girl is broken off. I cannot tell why it is so as I have not heard the particulars about it. Aunt Amelia [Guest] told me, but did not wish much said about it. I expect his parents are pleased with it.

There has been a Law Suit in New York between the Orthodox and Hicksites (as they are termed) about the division of the property. Richard Mott plead that the Orthodox were the real proprietors of it. He was then questioned by the Lawyers respecting the number of the members on each side but their queries he would not answer until the Judge threatened him with imprisonment. They then asked him if he thought there were two Hicksites to one Orthodox. He answered in the affirmative. It was then decided that it should be equally divided according to the number of the members on each side. There has another suit of the same nature taken place in Jersey but I have not heard the decision.

That paragraph in Thomas' letter respecting the Widow Comstock was very pleasant to us all, in a far distant land among strangers, to meet with a family connection. Let that connection be ever so distant would afford me heart felt pleasure prov'd they were kind affectionate and respectable.

The Widow Comstock Aunt Gamage says is a very fine woman. She was much pleased to hear from her, and also that you were to be such near neighbours. Please tell her that Aunt Hathways health is much better than when we were in Hudson.

Mother Howell has returned to the City in good health and desires a great deal of love to you. She was very sorry that she did not see you before you left us.

Tell my dear Elizabeth that I hope it will not be a great while before I receive a long a *very long* letter from her—I am very impatient for her Journal. It is selfish in me I allow knowing her engagements, but I cannot help it. Both letters from you have been travelling amoung our friends almost ever since I received them. They are expected home tomorrow.

> With much love
> Adieu
> J Howell

We are all well. I do not expect to write by John Lovett. There will be so many sent by him that mine will be more acceptable another time. Aunts are about in their usual health and desire their love to you.

JANE HOWELL *to* RUTH EVANS
Philadelphia, October 22, 1830

My dear Sister

I have written so recently by post that I did not think it necessary to write by J Lovett but I have become so very uneasy at not hearing from you for such a great length of time that I cannot omit sending a few lines to beg you to relieve my anxiety by letting me hear from you. Joseph Taylor was here last week. He says William & Sarah are quite well. I sent the letters which I received from you, for their perusal. Hannah Peirce is declining fast in health. The Phisician has very little hopes of her recovery. I sent her a box of tar ointment thinking that perhaps it might relieve the pain in her breast in some degree. Aunt Gamage and her daughter expect to leave the City tomorrow for New York. They have been here five weeks. Esther Chesnut has a young daughter which she calls Sarah Jane. Sarah is after Samuels first wife, Jane after myself. Aunt Gamage Sarah and I drank tea with Aunts yesterday. They were well and much pleased with their new visitors.

The pamphlet which I have sent contains a letter from a young woman (a Presbeterian) to Doctor Parrish, and his answer. I thought you would like to read it, thee need not return it. Thy stove has not been disposed of yet but I hope as soon as the weather becomes a little cooler we shall find a purchaser. I felt much disappointed in not seeing any thing of Elizabeths in the last Genius. I hope it was only for want of time not indisposition that prevented her. With the price of Elizabeths doll I have purchased the annals of Philadelphia and sent them on by this conveyance![42]

I believe I have nothing new to tell thee but the pleasure to say we are all well, and our friends generally. I have written in great haste being seventh day morning and a great deal to attend to and with much love to Thomas Elizabeth and thyself

I remain affectionately thy Sister
J Howell

In looking over the news paper yesterday; in a review of the Atlantic Souvenir for 1831 I saw the following encomium on the production of my dear Nieces pen which I have copied verbatim.[43] "Miss E. M. Chandler has frequently distinguished herself in this annual, by chaste and vigorous poetry her poem entitled Brandywine will add to her enviable fame."

I have sent thee on ten dollars in silver—on account of thy Coal Stove. As soon as it is sold I will remit thee on the rest of the money. I hope it will bring a good price.

thine &c &c
JEH

Do write more frequently. I have not heard from you since Thomas wrote, and I am so uneasy that I am almost sick. Do not pay the postage and write once a month.

—————•◆•—————

ELIZABETH CHANDLER *to* JANE HOWELL
Hazelbank, December 23, 1830

I write at last, my dear Aunt once more, from "beneath our own roof and by our own fireside." In the midst of one of the wide openings of "out of the world Michigan!" There is indeed as thee observes, something startling in the thought, and it seems at times almost impossible to realize the truth of our being so far separated. We did not leave Comstocks until the 2nd of this month having been delayed considerably longer than we expected on account of the well which had to be sunk much deeper than we expected. It is about 38 feet in depth and the water is excellent.

We received last week the packet which thee sent by John Lovett, with what pleasure I need not tell thee, for I dare say thee can fancy how triumphantly I sat in the midst of my treasures, scanning handwriting, breaking seals, and pressing first into one thing to read at a line and then into another, as if I feared they might elude my grasp unless secured by the spell of eyesight. John had some pretty rough passages in his journey, which occupied 6 or 7 weeks, being obliged to encamp out one night in the midst of a swamp, and as might be expected in so long a journey performed at the season of the year to submit to some pretty rough passages and other not very agreeable encounters. But he arrived with his family in good health and spirits, and has got settled in part of a house about 3 miles from us and very near his own place.

We continue to like the country as much as ever and are particularly well satisfied with our choice of a situation, even though thee will probably be surprised to learn that brother has already the occasion for the assistance of a lawyer in some of his business. He was not however exorbitant in his charges, and conducted the affair I believe quite to Tom's satisfaction. Brother's lot is universally spoken of as one of the best pieces of ground in the neighborhood. J Lovett heard it spoken of as such by a person who is an entire stranger to T at the distance of 6 or 8 miles from here—and I do not suppose it would have been so long unappropriated, but that Wm Jackson our next neighbor had intended adding it to his own farm. The lot contains, or consists mostly of a "burr oak basin," of which the soil is said to be of the richest quality.

95 bushels of corn have been raised off of one acre of the same kind of land immediately adjoining it; but we must not expect such crops till the ground has been a year or two under cultivation. Fruit is yet scarce here except such as is natural to the country. For vegetables the soil is excellent. I have seen monstrous

onions raised from seed planted this year, and turnips of 8 or 9 pounds weight are by no means uncommon. I saw some not long since in Comstocks cellar as big as a full grown dinner plate. Our house, which is pronounced by the neighbors to be a *"real slick one"* is nearly all, except the logging, of brother T's workmanship. He employed a carpenter to assist him about the roof and to make the window sashes, and the remainder as well as the greater part of the furniture is the work of his own hands. It is situated on a rising ground about the center of the lot, which spreads out in a plain towards friend Comstocks, and commands a fine view of this and even Jacksons farm. All else around it is the uncultured opening, sloping down on one side towards the basin, and swelling up behind in a beautiful variety of undulations, as wild and as graceful as the motions of a romping kitten—while the hills seem to enfold themselves as if to open a path to some other habitation immediately behind them. This however is not the case as we are with one exception the last family in this town (Logan) and they are about a mile behind us.

Our house is in dimensions 20 by 26 feet about 8½ ft high in the lower apartments, and four logs above the floor in the upper. It is one story and a half in height, with a door and two windows in front and four more disposed in other situations. It is divided below into 3 rooms which suffice for our present accommodation; the upper apartment is yet unpartitioned, but will make two good chambers. I often wish thee could take a look at us, and I can just fancy the mingled expression of curiosity and mirth, with which thee would eye our "home manufacture" furniture and apartments. But I can assure thee that our house is by no means despisable. It was pronounced by the *Lawyer* who did the outside *plastering* or pointing, between the logs—(*what strange uses things are put to sometimes!*) to be the *snuggest log house in Michigan!* The logs both within and without have been squared off by an expert axeman, which adds much to the neatness of its appearance. The doors are of walnut, which is in very common use here, and the partition boards as well as the chamber floors are planed and fitted together by grooving, a thing unknown in any other log house about. The windows are neatly framed and glazed, which latter operation was performed principally by Aunt R and myself; and in the spring we intend having the walls within doors also pointed, (not covered with a full dress of plastering) that having been deferred till then on account of our not wishing to incur any risk of taking cold from the dampness of the mortar.

On entering that apartment which may be best described by the comprehensive appellation of "the room"—as it is conjointly "parlour, kitchen, and hall"—the most conspicuous object is a large flour bin (situated by way of sideboard at the parlour end) over which from a wooden pin depends the looking glass. On either end of it stands Aunt Ruth's *walnut* box, and my cabinet. Against this wall, lengthwise of the room, on one side of the window stands the dough trough—on the other a long box covered by a walnut board and answering the purpose of a shelf or table; between them, and behind the stove is placed an oaken bench, which with another of somewhat better manufacture, and Aunt R's working chair, comprises our whole wealth of seats. A whisk broom, *brushes* are not in vogue—some kitchen utensils, and the red chest[44] placed on one of its ends against the partition, and covered with a green cloth, to support my desk, with Benjamin Rush and thy landscape picture hanging over it, about complete the catalogue of our furniture in the room.

Our sleeping apartment is about 10½ feet square, and brother Ts something smaller. Our bedsteads and the straw mattresses, on which I assure thee we sleep very comfortably, are both of his manufacture. In each chamber we have a dressing glass, a toilet[45] (that is a covered box) and a couple of pictures! Our books are arranged on shelves against the partitions, and with the floors covered with rug carpeting, curtains to the windows, and the chests containing our cloths to set on if needful, the rooms really look very comfortable. Feather[bed]s and chairs are not now procurable here, but we fortunately find that we can do *without them* till they are so. How very little is actually necessary to supply our wants if we can but think so!—and in our case we have so much—so very much to be thankful for, that we cannot regard at a straws value, a hundred of such trivial discomforts— if such they may properly be called which rob us of no portion of our enjoyment.

On the first night we slept here, we every one were awakened by the sound of the wind among the trees around us—poor little Emily jumped up and came to our bedside in a great fright calling upon Aunt Ruth, and as I listened to it, it reminded of nothing so much as lying close beside a large waterfall—it came on with such a steady monotonous, which Aunt thought only of the steam boat and the *lake.*

By the bye I think you have formed quite too terrible an opinion of the lake. It is seldom in the summer season that the weather is so rough as that we encountered; and, for my own part, with my experience of it I should not hesitate at all to recross it. But to proceed—we have not since been disturbed by such stormy noise, perhaps because we have become accustomed to it, and when the winds *are still,* thee can scarcely imagine a more total quietness than that which usually surrounds us—a *sound* is quite a strange thing—especially if it is near us—for we are far off the road, though the voice of cultivated life frequently comes on the clear air from the neighboring farms, to remind us that we are not quite in solitude. We have not heard the howl of a wolf since we arrived, nor have we yet had any communication with the Indians. I have seen but four I think since we arrived here in Lenawee Co.

27TH

Brother T. is busily employed whenever the weather is suitable in felling trees to clear and fence his ground;—and when it is stormy he works within doors–upstairs—at his *trade.* He intends when he has leisure to make us some tables, a settee, &c.; and also to enclose a small shed over the well, which is but a few feet distant from the house, for a summer kitchen. He does, as was remarked by one of our acquaintances the other day when looking over the house, try to frame everything as convenient as he can *for his women folks*—and as he is not near enough to look across my *shoulder,* I may as well add that he appears to be held in very good esteem, as the friends say, throughout the neighborhood. There is not a bit of danger but Thomas will do well, said neighbor Comstock the other day.

And as for Uncle Darius—for so he is universally called even by those as old or older than himself—I actually love him, for the share which he has given Tom of his good graces! And in truth he is a man whose good opinion any one may well value—he is a real *gem*—one of those characters that put you so much in a good humor with human nature! A man who "when he dies will have a tomb of grateful tears rained on him." He is a blessing to the settlement—a model of both public and private usefulness. I believe there are few around him who have not at some time or other experienced the benefit of his kindness, and all seem to turn to him as a sure "friend in need." He is about 63 years of age, possessed of a sufficient fortune about 20 or 30,000 dollars to enable him to indulge his generous and benevolent feelings, and I think there are few persons who will be able to give a better account, in that respect, of their stewardship! I do not think there is an item of covetousness about his heart and I really believe he sometimes refuses to dispose of the surplus produce of his farm to those who could pay him for it immediately, in order to reserve it for such new comers as being more destitute of means could not so readily supply their wants elsewhere. With all this then is no ostentation—it is true nobleness of nature and he does not appear to have a thought of claiming credit for the performance of any thing more than the common every day duties of life. He is highly intelligent too, and possesses much general information. And his wife is a very fine woman quite deserving of him.

Daniel Smith, our preacher, and his wife are another clever honest hearted couple—though with them, as well as our neighbors generally, we are less acquainted, except Aunt Sally Comstock. Most of the leading members of our meeting are orthodox—among the others there is some division of sentiment, but very little of feeling, is at least obvious. With us I am sure it makes no difference, nor do I think it does *towards* us. There are no meetings yet for business and those for worship are held only on first day. There is considerable difference in some of the modes and customs here from such as we have been accustomed to. For instance—we are told it is the fashion here for strangers to pay the first visits—

and on first day evening the women—aye the gallery friends even (by the way, they got *Aunt Ruth* seated in among them the other day at meeting)—get out their sewing or their knitting and work away as industriously as if it was the most privileged working day of the [week] all without so much as a vision of scruple about the matter. But do not imagine there is any thing more than an ideal gallery in our meeting house. I speak of it only as it exists in my imagination, from the place where it *should* be.

Thee requests me to mention the prices of different articles. For a cow and calf we paid six dollars—pigs 2—pork is worth 5 dolls per hundred—wheat 75 cts a bushel—corn 50—potatoes, at present 37½. T. has not yet purchased oxen as he did not wish the expense of providing food for them through the winter, without they would have been more useful. Horses are not yet much used on account of there being more troublesome for new settlers to provide for. People sometimes employ their oxen to carry them to *meeting*. The rapid ingress of population affords a ready market for all kinds of produce, and probably will do so till a canal or railroad facilitates its carriage to Monroe or Detroit. About 40 families have settled in the township during the past year.

Thee does not in thy last letter mention any thing respecting Jane Parker. If thee has seen her we should like to know more particularly respecting their prospects. I should be very glad if they would come out and settle near us. I think Israel Estlack might do very well here. There is at present but one blacksmith at Adrian, and he is a kind of "jack of all trades," who has "so many irons in the fire" that his work is seldom performed punctually. Iron work is charged for at the rate of 2 shillings—25 cts per pound.

And now after saying so much about ourselves and our country, let me ask a few questions about Phila. How are you all coming on there? We are delighted at the prospect of having a visit from uncle—and Aunt R says she can scarcely wait for the time to come. We all talk a great deal about it—and about you. How are Aunts too—dear Aunts! I often seem as if I could see them just as they used to sit last winter in their little front parlour! I am very much pleased with what thee tells me respecting the Widow Greenfield, and if thee has any further particulars respecting the number of her slaves, their destination &c—I will thank thee to let me know.

Poor little Roy! I often think how he would enjoy scampering over the openings in company with his master. Thee is right in supposing them very handsome—they are indeed so.

Give our love to Cousin Guests and tell cousin Anna Lovett that I think she would admire this scenery, her favorite forest trees show to so much advantage and are really so much more beautiful and graceful in their proportions than in a thick wood. We are very glad to hear that Aunt Amelia [Evans] is going to spend the winter with thee. I hope she has quite recovered from the cough thee spoke of. Aunt Ruth intends writing to thee soon—and she says please when thee writes say particularly how aunts are—and also mention how friend Woodside and Maria are coming on. We felt disappointed in not receiving a letter from Maria. I hoped also that Aunt A[nna] G[uest] would have written a few lines to me. Give our love to Anna and tell her that I have grown quite fat. I was looking at her "hearts" a few days since. It is safely placed in a keepsake drawer of my cabinet.

So thee thinks, Aunt, thee could not like to sleep with unshuttered windows! I can assure thee we go to rest with quite as much feeling of security here in our lovely cottage, as we did when we barricaded behind "bolts and bars," with the watchman pacing his nightly promenade beneath our windows.[46] For the first few nights we slept here, our doors—the outside ones I mean—and they were in fact the only ones we had—were not even so much as latched. They had swelled with the damp weather before we came, and we preferred having them shrunk again by the heat of the fire than to have them planed at once to fit and endure large cracks afterwards, so we merely laid a *stick* against each of them to *prevent their blowing open* and retired quite satisfied and unconcerned. We do usually now put a nail or a gimbet over the latch, but I believe it is more from the remains of old habits than any thing else. Our fears are certainly not strong enough to induce us to get up and apply the fastening when it happens to be forgotten.

I am much obliged for the papers &c which thee sent. Any thing from Philad is so interesting. Do please write soon—Aunt R says immediately—and direct to Adrian instead of Tecumseh as we have very often opportunities of sending and receiving letters from there with the T's going himself for them. I should like thee let Esther Davis know how we are coming on as she seemed much interested about us and particularly requested it. Please remember me to her, and both Aunt and myself to Eliza Lippincott. And with much love dear Aunt to thyself and the rest of our friends, and wishes for *a happy new year,* I must, as T. has just heard of an opportunity of sending this, conclude

thine affectionately
E.M.C.

When thee sees Em's mother thee can let her know that the child is very happy in good health and a very good girl.

Aunt Ruth sends her love to Aunt Amelia. The Journal of Health was taken in Aunt R's name. She will be obliged to thee to pay for the present volume when they call on thee for the subscriptions and then order it discontinued. Thee can send them out when uncle comes.

———◆———

JANE HOWELL *to* RUTH EVANS
Philadelphia, December 30, 1830

My dear Sister

I have been waiting these four months past and looking day after day for a letter from you but have not yet received one line. Have you forgotten us or do you think we care nothing about you. Three letters I have written but no answer and if it had not been that I heard from you through the letters which were written to William Chandler and Anna Coe I should have fancied the worst things had befallen you: indeed many times I have been almost sick at your silence. Do write soon and often but do not pay the Postage. Lemuel says he would rather pay a dollar for every letter than be kept in such suspense.

William has a prospect in the Spring of taking a long established Tavern Stand near London Grove Meeting house. The present Occupant who is the owner has been there about fourteen years and has become so wealthy that he is going to retire from business. He has kept a Drove Inn which is much the most profitable. There were twenty applicants for it but the Landlord gave William the preference altho an entire stranger to him—it shows how high his character stands. Anna Coe was much delighted with the letter she received from Elizabeth.[47] She had almost despaired of receiving one.

In the last Genius Lundy said he thought he could make arrangements for the future to issue it in the early part of every month but here is the 31st and none arrived yet. I hope when it does come it will have something of Elizabeths in it. Joseph Merritt was here a short time since. He says he intends writing to Elizabeth and took her address. Roberts Vaux is very anxious to get that work in the press which she has undertaken, and to use Josephs words "Roberts behaves quite foolish about it."

I was at Eunice Royers wedding a few evenings since, it is too far to send you some of the Bride Cake. Her Sister Euphemia expects to be married in a few weeks.

I hope before this time that John Lovett and family has reached Michigan in good health. I saw his father a few days since. He and his family are well, and are anxiously looking for a letter from him, and then, thro' him, I hope to hear something from you, if there is no other way of hearing, to be sure it is a beggarly way, but a hungry person will catch at crumbs. Abby Chandler was here last week. She has subscribed for the "Genius" purposely for Elizabeths apartment in it. Abby says there was a wedding at friends Meeting house. (I think it was at New Garden) a few weeks since. The bride was a widow about sixty eight years of age and the groom about twenty two leaving the trifling difference in their ages about forty six years.[48] Abby saw Cousin William Chandler a short time since. He asked very particularly after you and appears to feel very much interested for you. Aunt Mary Brinton is well. Tell my dear Elizabeth when she writes to me to let it be a letter that I can send amoung our friends generally as it will cause a great deal of jealousy if I withhold it from them—but at the same time let there be another sheet just for myself alone with everything in it. Let it be even so trifling in domestic concerns as I feel anxious and interrested to know all and every thing about you. Little Roy is as frolicksome as ever, he has grown very fat. Lemuel thinks a great deal of him and he is attached to his Master.

There are none of your friends that appear to take more interest in your concerns than Cousin Guests. They have expressed a wish several times that I would let them see my letters from you, when I received them. Aunts are well and talk a great deal about you. Aunt Amelia intends writing by the first private opportunity. She has procured a quantity of different kind of seed which will be forwarded as soon as possible.

Since writing the above Anna Coe informed me that Rachel Chandler was at Cousin William Chandlers, and when he heard that you had gone to Michigan he was very much surprised and sorry. He said he had made arrangements for Thomas and it would alter his plans; he also said that he had remembered the children (as he termed them) in his will. I hope Thomas will write to him before long. I have no doubt but it would gratify him very much, and some attention is certainly due to him. I am very much pleased with having Amelia {Evans} with me this winter. She appears very happy and contented. I should be glad to have her with me altogether but I expect in the Spring she will take the small house on Samuel Dixons place if the present tenant should leave it. Do write to her or say something to her in the letters to me. Thee knows her disposition.

Ten days ago we heard that a near neighbour of Samuel Lovetts was going to start yesterday for Michigan. Last week there were several letters written to send by him to you but we could meet with no opportunity to forward them on to him. The Atlantic Souvenir is now out. I hope they will send one on to Elizabeth. I wish I had an opportunity to send you on an Almanac[49] to let you see how the time goes for I do not wether you have such things in your *Outlandish* Country.

There is to be next month a great Eclipse of the Sun here. I suppose you will see it if you are not too far to the West. We have had a great deal of warm rainy weather since September, and but two cold days this winter. We had the most beautiful rain-bow the last day in the year I ever beheld. It seemed to attract every ones attention.

I wish I could send Thomas on the papers. They are full of foreign news, rebellion is making rapid strides, and all Europe appears as if it would shortly be involved in war.[50]

I saw friend Woodside a few days since. She always makes many enquires about you, her health is about as usual. Our friends generally are well. My health has been uncommonly good this winter and with much love to thee and my dear Nephew and Neice,

> I remain affectionately thy Sister
> Jane Howell

JAN 4TH 1831

Markwell, This is the fourth letter that I have written since I have received one from you—is it not too bad?

———————

CHAPTER 3

SETTLING IN, 1831

When Thomas and Elizabeth Chandler and Ruth Evans ushered in the new year, they had been in the Michigan Territory for six months. Despite their reassurances and positive reports throughout the year about their new homestead, Jane Howell continued her vigil of disquiet.

RUTH EVANS *to* JANE HOWELL
Hazelbank, February 5, 1831

My Dear Sister

Six months have now passed since we left Phil^a, since we bid farewell to our Dear relatives and friends—and it is most probably many more may lapse before we shall have the pleasure of visiting that city. It is true the privation is great. I feel it much, however we continue to feel firm in the belief that our removal to this place is the very best we could have done situated as we are.

Farming suits Thomas's inclination far better than any business he could have pursued in the City. He has worked very hard since he came here and has gained considerable flesh. He is this winter preparing for enclosing sufficient ground for corn oats and spring wheat. John Lovett and wife have been to see us. They are in good health and spirits.

Tell Brother L. [Lemuel Howell] we look forward with the utmost pleasure to his promised visit. I have one favour to ask of thee which I hope thee will not deny, it is to request we rather intreat thee to accompany him. Thee says thy health is much better which I am glad to hear, but still it may be entirely restored by such a journey. I am aware of the disadvantages and inconvenience of leaving the family, but all that when put in compilation with the restoration of thy health is I think of little consequence; therefore I hope thee will decide in favour of what I have proposed. The journey can with care be effected in ten days and the distance is ten Hundred and twenty miles Nine hundred and thirty of which is by water that is extremely pleasant.

We arrived here the 15th of August. The weather from that time till the last of November was remarkably fine. The first of December we moved to our log House/which is very comfortable I assure thee. The 5th we saw a snow storm and it has continued extremely cold ever since. The snow is at this moment 18 inches deep. A person in Detroit told D. Comstock there has not been such cold weather here for 20 years.

Do when thee writes say how the weather is with you. I am glad Amelia [Evans] is with you this winter. Give my love to her. I hope she is well, tell her I wish she would write to me. I quite regret William has engaged in the business he has at Grove. I think he could have done much better by comming to the West. He could have procured a good farm with some labor for a small sum. Since the cences was taken which was in june last, forty families have moved in this township, and I suppose as many in Tecumseh. It is believed this year there will be a much greater congregation. A great number came from York State. They differ greatly from Pennsylvanians in dress and manners.

We have very good neighbors in the Comstocks. Aunty Sally is spending the winter with him. Ann /Darius wife/ is a very amiable woman about fifty. She is his second wife. She has one child little girl near Emily age. They sent their slay over for us a few days since, had an excellent supper prepared and served up in handsome stile. Aunt Sally Comstock is a woman of good sense and affable manners. She and Ann are the most intimate friends we have, and we have reason to believe there is not a family in the territory they feel a greater esteem for than ourselves. They often remind me of my two Dear Aunts. There dress would be as plain if it was not for there caps being taped with ribbon the width of mine and borders set on full which is the prevailing fassion among the prominent Yorkers.[1]

Our stock at present consists of one cow and calf and two pigs, expect an addition soon of a pair of oxen and another cow. Thomas has taken up but one lot yet.[2] There is another adjoining that will suit him well, half of which is heavily timbered. He intends adding it to his farm in the spring.

Thomas has made us a dining table settee and stand all of walnut. We have a well of excellent water pure as possible, but it cost more than we expected owing to the unusual depth. We made from one hog weighing 220 weight 40 pounds of lard and as much sausage meat and scrapple; better I never ate. It was made by Elizabeth.

If thee continues to take the evening post,[3] we should be obliged if thee would occasionaly send us one by mail. The expense is but 1½ cent. Pleas [do] not enclose it in paper. After folding it narrow and tying a thread round thee will please direct on the margin to Thomas Chandler, Adrian, Michigan.

There is a great demand for grain this winter owing to so many later settlers. Wheat has advanced from six shilling to eight, corn from four to six, potatoes from two to four shillings.[4] Thirty thousand bushels of wheat was sent out of the territory in the fall. A few days since Thomas received a letter from Merrideth saying he had taken the bank stock himself, and after deducting the expenses which were five dollars it left a ballins in Thomas favour of 318 dollars. Please give our love to my Dear Aunts, also Cousin Guests. I hope they are all in there usual health. My love to friend Woodside and Maria. I presume there health is no better. When the[e] sees Emily's Mother please tell her she is in perfect health grows very tall and fat and happy as possible. Indeed she is a fine child and very useful. Thee says Lemuel intends bringing Roy out with him. I think I cannot concent to that. I could not deprive you of him, morover conveying him here would be very difficult. Our love to the Coe family. Eliz^th wants Anna to write by mail and direct to Adrian.

How often I wish thee could see how snugly we are fixed. Every one admires our location. Our house is situated in the middle of the lot, a more beautiful spot I think I never saw. However I hope thee will be here next summer and judge for thyself.

If the stove should sell for ten dollars it is quite as much as I expected—do write so. I cannot express the pleasure it gives us to hear you are all well. Write closer, stow in as much as thee possibly can. Everything is interesting. My love [to] Brother L. and his Dear Mother. Thomas intends writing to his Uncle soon, also to cousin William Chandler. Elizabeth intends as soon as she has a few moments leisure to write to my Dear Aunts. We are much obliged for the seeds Aunt A [Amelia Guest] has been so kind to procure of us. My love to Hannah Roberts. I should have been glad to have seen her before we left. I suppose thee has heard Joseph Tucker /John Lovetts Cousin/ who came out last fall, was frightened out of the territory, with hearing of a few cases [of] ague.[5] He had nearly intended to take a lot adjoining us, when they concluded they should feal most easy to go to Ohio. John Lovett regrets it much knowing he could have done much better here. I should not be surprised if he should return here in the spring for he was very much pleased with Michigan and we have good reason to be sure a more healthy country cannot be found. About five years ago friends enclosed a piece of ground for a graveyard and there has never been but one interment in all that time and that was a child. Neither have we heard of one death since we came into the Territory.

We feal a hope we shall receive a letter from thee next third day. I hope we shall not be disappointed. My love to Ann and Louisa. I must say we are all well and conclude with much love to thee I am affectionately thy sister.

Ruth Evans

My love to neighbour Herregas.

———◆——

JANE HOWELL *to* RUTH EVANS
Philadelphia, n.d. {ca. January–February 1831}

Why has thee My dear Sister let so many months pass by without writing one line to me? Does thee not think my letters worth answering, or has thee nothing interresting to communicate? The first may be the case, but the last cannot, for every thing respecting you, even that which appears the most trifling to thee, would be highly interresting to us even if it was to say you had sticks and stones in Michigan. But with me it is otherwise, for I can with truth say that often when I set down to write I feel as if I had nothing to tell you, everything here remains so much the same as when you left us.

Our landlord George Henk died about three weeks since with a pulmonary complaint. He has left his Widow the whole of his estate as long as she remains single, but if she should marry she is to have but one third. She has let the Bake house with the front brick buildings to Mr. Sherburn a former tenant for 450 dollars and the shop next to us for 150, the room over it she [has] given to us. Mrs. Herregas has a young son about six weeks old which she calls George Washington. John Merrefield calls his son George Williams. It is but a few days since they fixed on that name for him. Elisa Tunis buried her son Richard about a fortnight since. He was seized with the scarlet fever, from the effects of which he never recovered.[6] She bore her loss with more fortitude than was expected. Amelia Guest has been ill. She has undergone a course of medicine and is now much better.

On the 15th and 16th of January we had a great snow, such a one has not been known to fall for twenty and some say not for sixty years; it was very much drifted, and some of the small houses in the country were almost buried in the snow—and until the roads were broken milk was sold in Market Street from 25 to 37½ cents per quart.[7] We have had a continuation of cold weather ever since that snow fell until within a few days past. There has been much suffering amoung the poor and a great many thousand dollars has been raised for their relief, there were many that perished with the cold. We have taken the coal stove for our stove and find it to answer very well. I have sent on five dollars the remainder of the price of it, for I would not let it go for less than fifteen dollars. Poor Mary Pleasants met with a sad accident this winter. She fell on the ice and broke or dislocated her hip bone, which will entirely disable her from ever walking again.

Little Roy is a great Pet with us. He has grown much fatter, but is as playful, and as active as ever. We think more of him as we have lost Carlo. He died last fall. I expect thee will say I *am glad of it* as he was no favourit of thine. About two weeks since Lemuel went to John Roberts. Hannah was well and had a great deal to say about you.

When thee writes to me do let Thomas or Elizabeth copy it off. Thee writes such a running hand that I feal I cannot read it and that would be very mortifying to me, and another objection, thee writes the lines so far apart that I am afraid I should not get good measure.

I have stoped the Journal of Health as the half year has expired. They said if you wished to have it continued they could forward it on to Michigan at one cent and half per number postage. I have sent a few news papers and regret that I could not send more but I was afraid of imposing on the good nature of the Lawyer.[8] Elinor Lippincott desires a great deal of love to you. She had not time, or she would have written to you by this conveyance. Thee must excuse me for sending thee some blank paper for indeed the notice was so short that I did not think I could write at all, but I thought a few lines would be better than none. Lemuel promises himself a great deal of pleasure in going to see you next summer, he thinks and talks a great deal about you. We are all well. Ann desires her love to you, also Amelia {Evans} and Lemuel. I must now conclude as I am encroaching on bed hours.

Affectionately farewell
J. Howell

Tell Thomas I intend to write to him soon.

JANE HOWELL *to* ELIZABETH CHANDLER
Philadelphia, n.d. {ca. March 1831}

I am much obliged to thee my dear Neice for the last letter which I received from thee. Thee gave such a description of the house, and the arrangement of your furniture that I can almost fancy that I have been with you and can see everything as they really are, and I feel no doubt, but that after Thomas gets further on in farming and some other things necessary to your accommodation that you will feel very comfortable and happy. Wait until you have your farmyard stocked with poultry, your fields waving with grain, the trees bow'd down under the weight of their fruit, and the fleecy flocks sporting in the meadows—and as far as the eye can reach everything in the highest state of cultivation, and then say, is not our situation envyable? Who can deny it? Not the citizen. Let him rank as high as he pleases; for he is in my opinion as a captured bird in a gilded cage.

I feel the greatest anxiety for your health, and when I receive a letter from you, I am almost afraid to open it, and often read the last part first to see wether you are well. Thy aunt and thyself have never been accustomed to exposure and hard work. To be sure you have not had much to do yet to expose you to the weather but milking, and that I hope Emily will soon be able to do; but when the time for gardening comes on I hope you will be careful; and as to Thomas I think with the rest of his friends that he had done wonders. Aunt Amelia Guest predicts that he will become a very popular character and be much respected in Michigan. I feel no doubt of that. I wish I felt as fully assured that his health and strength would be adequate to the hard work he has to undergo. I wish he had a boy to assist him, if we could hear of a suitable one without parents or friends, should we send him on to you when Lemuel goes. The Asylum is crowded with children.[9]

Anna Coe was much delighted with the letter from thee. I did not see it or hear it read, but she told me some of the contents. The pieces in the Genius addressed to her pleased her much.[10] We feel thankful for every thing like a remembrance from thee in that way. Hannah Townsend was highly gratified in receiving thy letter. I called on her just after I received thy last. She said she had been looking daily for some months past for one from thee, and that she had almost began to conclude that thee had declined the promised correspondence, but when she heard that I had received but two letters from thee since thee left Philad[a] she quite excused thee for thy apparent neglect towards her, and said she had felt hurt, as she expected that thee was very frequently writing to thy friends in the City. She favoured me with the perusal of her letter. Some part of the contents was *not* very satisfactory to me.[11]

John Rutter from Westchester was at Robert Coe's a few days since. He has finished his studies and is going on to Michigan. He is advised by his friends to settle in Detroit. He has offered to take a package of letters to thee. We have sent two by him consisting of letters, 6 numbers of the Journal of health, and some papers. I have written to thy Aunt Ruth and enclosed five dollars, the remainder of the price of the stove. Aunt Amelia Guest, Hannah Townsend, Anna & Rebecca Coe, and William Hall, has written by this conveyance, and how many more I cannot tell as Anna Coe made up one of the packets. John Rutter started from here the 3rd of this Month (March). He intends a few days at Pittsburgh and a little while I suppose at Detroit so that this will I expect reach thee before thee sees him.

How far did the Eclipse of the sun last month answer thy expectations? Here it appeared at its greatest obscuration about the size of the new moon when first visible, and was about as light as a quarter of an hour before eight o clock in the evening of the longest day in summer. I must say I felt a little disappointed for I expected it would have been as dark or darker than it was at the time of the other eclipse many years ago, but it was not as much so.[12]

If the Lawyer thee alludes to in thy letter can afford to live by such clients as Thomas I hope he may find full employment for his trowel. George Weaver son to the person who owns the rope walks and who drew a prise of forty thousand dollars just before or after you left the City is now bankrupt. He has taken Johnny Gibbs in for twenty thousand dollars, and a great many others for smaller sums amoung which is Margaret Hall but I believe not for more than two hundred dollars. He purchased tickets on credit for a great amount. It is said between thirty and forty thousand dollars and is able to pay but 25 cents in the dollar. I wish the lottery trade was entirely abolished I think it is a great nuisance to the City.[13]

Yesterday I had the pleasure of receiving my dear Sisters letter. Two in so short a time makes me feel quite rich, I wish I could be oftener gratified in the like manner. It is often hearing from you that makes the seperation more supportable. I was much pleased with the proposition of sending on the Evening Post. They are useless to us after they are read and it will be pleasant to you to know what is transpiring in the City, and at present the papers are very interresting as they contain a great deal of foreign news relative to the warlike disturbances throughout Europe. I will try and forward them on every week but if I omit it sometimes do not be uneasy for it may be that they may not get to the office in time for the mail.

Jane Parker did not stop here on her return home last fall as she promised and we have not heard from them since. I was not at home at the time she was here but Ann said she spoke as if they had fully made up their minds to move to

Michigan this spring but to what part I cannot say. If I knew where her Aunt lives in the City I would enquire of her. We have not heard from the Widow Greenfield since she left here. She told Abby Warnock she was going to set free all her slaves which was one hundred and fifty in number. She took on clothing enough to last them all one year. She owns a large tract of land not a great distance from where they are, and I heard she intended giving each of them a piece of ground sufficiently large, if they are industrious to make a comfortable living on. The deeds are to be drawn in such a manner that they cannot dispose of it.

I cannot tell what has become of Emilys Mother. She has not been here but once since you left here. I am glad to hear she is a good girl and likely to be useful soon. Tell her when she can milk the cows well I will send her a present. Maria Woodside and her Mother enjoys better health since they have lived in 3rd Street. Maria is now looking about for another house that will suit better for business. She goes on just about as she did when you were here. I expected she would have made a change before this time but I think Joseph Merritt assists her a great deal. Mother Howell has spent the winter with us. She is quite well and desires her love to you. She expects to go back to Jersey this spring in the early part of the summer.

I think you must have felt quite like farmers while you were trying your lard, and chopping your sausage meat. Thy Aunt did not say wether it was one of your own fattening but I suppose not, as you would [not] have all the corn. Grain is very high in Michigan. It commands a greater price there than it does here. I wish you had several thousand bushells to dispose of—but one year more and I hope you will.

Samuel Lovett was here yesterday in good health and spirits. His wife and friends are well. If thee sees John please tell him. It is a great satisfaction to us to hear you have such a friend in Darius Comstock. Thomas is young and inexperienced in farming and he can look up to him as a father for advice and instruction. Thy aunt says Aunt Sally Comstock is spending the winter with them. I felt disappointed when I read it. I thought she was another near neighbour and no probability of losing her. I feel quite interrested to hear where her permanent residence. I love her altho I have never seen her.

Robert Coe intends moving into Market Street. He is quite the dandy now. He wears his golden gilt guard chain his clothes made in the tip of the fashion and a gold ring on his finger. Perhaps he is looking out for a wife but as to that I cannot say. The lot on which Lemuel's shop stands is sold. He has taken a lot on ground rent just back of the house you lived in in Buttenwood St. fronting on that wide St. designed for a Market house. I believe it is called Spring Garden Street. The lot has two fronts. He intends putting his shop on the back front. He is to pay two dollars per foot. It is thought by all who sees it to be very low rent.

Tell Thomas it would please his Uncle much to receive a letter from him. I hope he will write before long. I have not heard any thing from William since I mentioned him in my letter. I think it probable we shall see him soon in the City. Aunts are well and our friends generally. My own health has been uncommonly good this winter. I have escaped a cough which is a very rare thing with me in cold weather but I attribute it in great measure to wearing the tar plaister on my breast and side constantly.

Lemuel desires a great deal of love to you, also Ann, and Amelia [Evans]. Thee must excuse blunders for I have written so much that I have hardly time or patience to connect it. I must now, with much love to my dear Sister, Nephew, and thyself, with sincere wishes for your *health, prosperity,* and *happiness,* bid you an affectionate adieu

J.H.

BENJAMIN LUNDY *to* ELIZABETH CHANDLER
Philadelphia, April 2, 1831

Esteemed Friend:

Thee will, probably, be a little surprised to see this letter dated at *this place.* I came this way upon business, and being a short time detained, concluded to drop thee a line before returning home.[14]

Thy very acceptable letter (2 mo 4th) came to hand just before I left Washington. I had not leisure to answer it then; and it occurred to me that I might have it in my power to give thee some information relative to thy connexions, after my arrival here. I find, however, that you keep up so active a correspondence, my agency, in this case, will avail but little. I called at L. Howell's yesterday, and had a short conversation with thy aunt. I understood that they were all in usual health. They inform me that thy brother William expects to work his farm, the present season, instead of pursuing his mercantile business. He and his family were well at the date of the last accounts from them.

I mentioned that I came here on business; but I had an *interesting* time of visiting, on the other side of the [Delaware] river [in New Jersey], last week. My sister Lydia has just renounced the state of "single blessedness," and joined a young Pennsylvania *widower* in the "holy bands of wedlock." She was married last Fifthday, to Jack Wierman, of Adams County, in this state. I expect thee was not acquainted with him. They left the paternal mansion, *the next day,* and after visiting Baltimore and Washington, they will proceed to their intended home about

16 miles northwest of York. They had a very agreeable company at the wedding. Hannah Townsend was the bride's first attendant, and my brother Richard officiated in the same capacity for the bridegroom. Several young people went from the city. Besides Hannah Townsend and her brother, two of Jonathan Sleeper's daughters, a young lady of the name of Vessey, (I do not remember her christian name) and Frederick Turnpenny, were in attendance. The company was quite select—not more than about thirty, besides the family dined with them. For my part, I did not arrive until both the ceremony and the dinner were over!—a pretty way to attend a sister's wedding! thee will say. But I could not help it; and as I endeavored to acquit myself well, the short time I was there, they seemed willing to excuse me while, it is also to be hoped, they sincerely commiserated my hard lot for being deprived of the dinner! I did not regret it *much,* for there were so many handsome young ladies in the company, I soon forgot it! Notwithstanding the impressive gravity of some of the young as well as the aged, we had, I assure thee, quite a lively time of it. I have not latterly been much in the *rhyming mood,* but *some one* of the company composed the following, upon the occasion, for one of the young ladies from the city. Hoping it will give thee a moment's amusement, I have *obtained permission* to copy it.

THE COUNTRY EXCURSION

We dress'd for the journey—'twas not very long.—
A wedding there was on the tapis.—
We found them all cheery—the aged and young—
Their welcoming did not escape us.
At a neat Quaker Meeting, we saw the young bride,
And the bridegroom, by kind friends attended.
They vowed, before Heaven, with each to abide,
Until life's toilsome journey be ended!
We saw them again, in the joyous career,
At the pleasant paternal mansion;
And we spent a few hours—partook of their cheer—
Well pleased with their friendly attention.
And then we returned, without e'en a regret,
To mar our happy diversion.
As life passes on, may we frequently, yet,
Take a similar *country excursion.*

Edwin
Philad^a 3rd mo. 25 — 1831

I will now take leave of this "interesting" subject; and, *interesting* as it is, must beg thee to excuse me for dwelling so long upon it.

A scene, of a very different discription, presented itself in this city last Fifth-day. Richard Allen, the venerable bishop of the African Methodist Church, died the 7th day previous, and was accompanied to the tomb, on 5th day, by the largest concourse of people that I ever beheld upon such an occasion. It is said there were *eleven hundred* in the procession! This was independent of the vast multitudes irregularly assembled in the streets, extending in a seemingly dense mass from 5th street nearly down to 3d street. Nearly the whole were colored people. Perhaps not more than a dozen white went into the meeting house to attend the funeral service, and very few were seen in the crowd. A few of the members of the Abolition Society attended. It was well that the white people staid away. It gave the others an opportunity of exhibiting to the best advantage their great respect for the virtuous dead. Would not this be an excellent subject for an elegy? I should be very glad to have one, next month; but I shall hardly obtain it, unless *thee* will do me the favor.[15]

One more incident, that I have witnessed here, must be related. But as it is not my province to comment on such matters, the facts of the case, merely, will be stated. I attended *Cherry Street meeting* last First-day. Towards the close, a man (some distance from the gallery) began to preach. He had not proceeded long before he was taken out of the house, *by force,* and much against his will. He is an Englishman. The circumstance created a good deal of confusion. Many were opposed to it. *My* feelings were never so hurt in a religious meeting before.

I am glad that thee has not contracted such an affection for the "woods," yet as to be pleased with *everything* about them! I fear, however, that when the summer comes, with its train of variety and fragrance, thee will be more strongly attached thereto. Ah! What enticement—what prospect of gratification, fame, or *usefulness,* could be held out to thy view, to dispel the charm, and draw thee from a deep seclusion, that almost hides thee from the face of the world? My valued friend, if thee but knew of *half* the good thee is doing in the holy cause to which thee has so nobly devoted thy attention for a few years, I am sure thee would see the propriety of placing thyself in a situation where thee might have every advantage that the most extensive and early information of passing events would give thee. Thee knows me too well to think me capable of bestowing unmeritted praise in cases of this nature;—and thee will please consider it merely intended for *information,* when I say, that the extensive circulation of the essays, through the medium of various periodicals, is producing an exceedingly beneficial effect. I have seen many of the articles copied into more than twenty papers—some of them introduced in terms of high commendation. But if it *must* be so—if thee *cannot* see thy way clear to take up thy residence where thee could benefit by the advantages above mentioned, rest assured, that I shall use every effort to furnish thee with whatever thee may request, or that I may consider useful to thee. I shall forward a small packet soon, and something further after a while. The number of the "Album," which thee requested, is not in my possession, but I will try to obtain it, before I leave this city, and immediately forward it.[16]

I will also very soon, send thee something respecting Prince Abduhl Mahahman. I highly approve thy proposal respecting the use of his story. Our fancied *great ones* are all swayed by *great names.* Unless an object be really *dazzling,* they can see nothing of it.

Thy "description" of your section of the country (tho thee does not give it that name) is very *natural.* I think that I possess "woods-wisdom" enough to judge of it perfectly. There was so much *melody* in the statement, that I was quite gratified with it, for I am fond of music—especially on *winter-evenings.* In short, I am glad thee philosophises so wisely. Surely thee could reconcile thyself to most situations in life! Music *among the trees,* in the midst of a dreary northern winter! Very well;—the *idea* is truly "poetic," and it was poetically expressed, too. But did thee not sometimes almost imagine there was *too much* of this music for the excitement of *pleasant sensations?* Did thee not, occasionally, grow weary of listening to the *tones* of nature's magnificent Aeolian? *I* never could fancy *all* the changes of clime exhibited by the skill of an *arctic Boreas,*[17] when touching the strings of this wonderful harpsichord? The "treble" is often too sharp and *thrilling,* (is it not?) and the "bass" sometimes affords, in my estimation, little more delight than the growl of the great northern Bear himself! But when people are *determined to be pleased* with any thing, it is useless to undertake to thwart them in their purpose; and so, begging pardon for my *unwelcome* criticism, I will fault thy *fancy* no longer.

Thee seems to have a great antipathy to "stumps." I expect Thomas has broken his sleigh tongue, a few times, among them. Thee denies the necessity of driving *over* them; but thee does not say that *running against* them is at all time avoidable. Thee must not think me easily deceived by a *play upon words!* I shall expect thee to boast less of thy skill in *farming,* after this—and will not commence *before* next season! I do not much wonder at thy declining the performance of your *mason-work*—not merely because the very *lawyers* practice that *art* of industry among you! but I should be surprised that any woman, at this day (except Mrs. Royal), should even countenance *the masonic* fraternity. They tell of the comforts brought to the domicils of many, by the labors of their craft; but, latterly, a vast proportion of the *chimnies,* in some parts of our country, are proven to be incapable of drawing off *all the smoke* produced at the hearth or in the hall. Then at the *fireside,* as well the *desk,* and the *bureau,* are much annoyed by it. The *glazing* was a more appropriate business for thee. Those who strive to *enlighten* others, must be *fond of light themselves.*

Thee has not, it seems, as yet become personally acquainted with native forest lords [Native Americans]. No doubt thee correctly anticipates some disappointment in their appearance and demeanor. We *read* little about them, save accounts of the *most conspicuous* among them. Thee has, I trust, heard of the late decision of the U.S. Supreme Court, as well as the course pursued by the government, relative to the Southern Indians. The whole would afford an excellent theme for a poetic effusion, to appear in the G.U.E. on the next 4th of July.[18]

I read the statement of the *slave hunting frolic* of Adrian,[19] with delight. Would that all such excursions might be crowned with *similar success!*

It rejoices me to find thee so ardent in the good cause. And it will in turn, be pleasing to thee to learn, that my prospects are now better than ever they have been since I commenced the publication of the *Genius.* I shall be able, I trust, to make a good establishment in Washington, so soon as I complete the *great tour* that I have in view. I cannot, however, reconcile to my mind the idea of relinquishing that. I expect, indeed, to set out in two or three weeks upon it. I shall go by way of New York, and Canada; and if nothing occurs to prevent, you may all expect to see me. I shall give thee more information, then, relative to my future prospects. The place of your residence will be very little out of my way, as I wish to go a little west of Columbus, in Ohio, to view a tract of land that I have recently procured—and, if convenient, to arrange with some person to improve it. I shall have so much to do before I set out on my journey, that I fear it will be out of my power to write thee as much, at length, as I could wish, for some time. But I hope thee will never have the opportunity, again, to rebuke me so severly as thee did in thy last. Over *"six months"*!! 'Tis *not possible* (is it) that I have been so remiss! Why, surely, thee could not have remembered *dates!* But if it is so, I have nothing to do but *ask pardon,* as humbly as I can, without delay. It is true that I have, for some months past, been very busy indeed; but I have no sufficient excuse for neglecting my duty to that degree.

I was in *Baltimore* one day and two nights, lately—but heard nothing from my *persecutors.* I received a letter from my agent at Washington, yesterday, informing that he had received another letter from thee, since I left home. The last that I have seen, was the double one, containing the private communication, to which I have above averted. We shall now have matter enough for two numbers, besides the one for March, which is just out. Should thee wish, however, to communicate anything particularly, send it on, at any time. It is rather uncertain what arrangement I shall make for printing, while performing my tour. Probably I may have it done *here.* If not, I shall get it done *at different places, on my way.* Thee will, no doubt, smile at the idea of an *itinerant editor!* and, probably, laugh outright, to think of an *itinerant periodical!!* But never mind. I have often coined the *negro maxim* "Continuance half work, massa." I will "continue" many schemes, before I abandon a purpose that I have once resolved on.

Please write me, *at New York,* as soon as this comes to hand, and inform me when to send thee a box of books, pamphlets, &c. I shall pay the freight from Buffaloe to whatever place thee will choose to have them forwarded. Please also to let me know how far you reside from Detroit, and what town I should enquire for, on leaving that place, to find you the most conveniently.

Well, I have written a long letter, whether it will be entertaining or not; and having *little* more room, will conclude for the present.

Thy Sincere Friend,
B. Lundy

JANE HOWELL *to* ELIZABETH CHANDLER
Philadelphia, April 4, 1831

I received thy letter my dear Elizabeth, and also thy Aunt Ruth's.[20] For both I am much oblidged. You write to me in a very sattisfactory manner, and the picture looks pleasant to a superficial observer, but I fancy I can see sometimes a little too much shading to make it altogether what I would have it to be. The style of thy letters (altho not to me) bespeaks I think regret, or should I say unhappiness at the wide seperation between thee and thy friends. The first is natural, for who can leave the scenes of their childhood and every thing that time has rendered dear to them, without often mentally, casting a "long lingering look behind"? Very few I beleave; but the last I hope rests only in my own imagination.

Tell thy Aunt Ruth when she writes again to keep her pocket handkerchief near her, that she can apply it to her eyes when occasion may require it, for several words on the first page of her letter were rendered illegible; nay almost entirely obliterated by something that appeared to me to be tear-drops. If they were not, I think I never saw a better imitation. Now thee sees my dear Elizabeth I view every thing concerning you with a very scrutinizing eye, but I cannot help it for your health, prosperity, and happiness are the secret prayers of my heart.

Carey & Lea has forwarded on to me three copies of the Atlantic Souvenir for thee, with two letters, I cannot tell who they are from unless the Editors. Anna Coe was here when I received them. She wishes me to open one of them that she might take a peep at thy much admired piece—"the Brandywine." My desire to see it was as great as hers and so I acceded to her wishes, and to pass my opinion on it. I think it is the best written piece in the book. I think I shall very soon have an opportunity of forwarding thine on to thee, as Samuel Lovett says there is a person going to move from his neighbourhood to Tecumseh in the course of a few weeks. Thee may then look for a large number of letters, &c &c. Please tell John Lovett that his Father, Mother, and friend are all well. I hope you received the

Saturday Evening Post regularly every week. I will try to send them to the office on one particular day so that you will know what time to send for them.

When John Rutter was here he mentioned the decease of a young man by the name of Caverly. Robert Coe's family was apprehensive it was Peter, but on enquiring found it was not him, but another whose name was Charles.

Benjamin Lundy was here a few days since. He purposed setting out on a long tour in a short time. He intends visiting the Colony at Canada.[21] He told me the route he calculated taking, but I have indeed almost forgotten it, but he is to go thro' Ohio. He intends travelling in disguise as Journeyman Saddler. I hope you will recognize him when you see him for he intends paying you a visit. He says he shall put up a packing box full of Books, Pamphlets, Papers for thee and send them on to a friend of his in Buffaloe where they will be left until he can convey them on to thee, which he thinks he can do without much difficulty. Benjamins Sister Lydia was married a few weeks since to a very respectable man, every how agreeable to her friends. I have forgotten his name but I believe he is from Maryland. At any rate they are going to live there, and I expect it will suit Lydia's inclination as she will be in a slave country, and can better exercise her time, and talents in the Cause of Liberty. Hannah Townsend was bridesmaid to Lydia. They had about forty guests at the wedding, seven or eight went from Philadelphia.

Robert Coe Jr. has opened a store in Market Street above 9th South side. It is only a few days since and I have not heard how he likes it. He received Thomas' letter. I have not heard any part of the contents except that you were well. I received a letter from thy brother William about ten days ago. He and Sarah were quite well. He has abandoned all thoughts of going to London Grove, and says he thinks he will never keep Tavern again. He has taken a small place joining that on which he lived, and says he can get as much work at Carpentering and Jobbing as he can do. He has bought a second handed Lathe very low, and has been making Bedsteads tables &c &c for Joseph Taylor who was married a short time since. Poor William I expect still hankers after the Western Country. He says in his letter he intends going to see you next Fall if nothing prevents him. He writes in very good spirit and says he received several papers from Thomas but no letter.

I think thee and thy Aunt Ruth must have been up to your eyes in business when the Big Hog was killed. You must have appeared the *farmers* indeed chopping your meat and trying the lard. I am glad to know that you have been providing meat for the summer. I hope you will eat more than you did in the City to enable you to bear up under the fatigue of a Country life, particularly my dear Nephew. I have sent your letters to thy brother William. I make it a practice to do so as I know it affords him so much pleasure. I hear that the price, customs, extravagance, and dissipation of large Cities are creeping, nay making great and rapid strides into your Territory. Even poor little modest Tecumseh has fallen a victim, for I hear that a large and splendid ball has been given there, attended by one hundred Gentlemen and seventy ladies dressed in the greatest style. Good-bye rural simplicity, if that is to be the order of the day. Thy Aunt Ruth expresses a wish that I would accompany Lemuel to Michigan. I think that would be almost impraticable. What go a thousand miles from home merely on a visit. Why it would almost make me start as from a Dream, by the time I had got half way there.

There is a young woman from New York in the City by the name of Ann Johnson,[22] not in membership with friends, who embraces the principles of Frances Wright. She has made every effort to get admittance into Green and Cherry Street Meeting houses to hold forth her impious doctrines. She has been so bold and persevering in her attempts, that friends have been under the necessity of placing a constable at the door during hours of worship to keep her from entering. Lucretia Mott has advocated her cause, which has lessened her in the esteem of many of her warmest friends.

I hope Thomas has written to his cousin William Chandler. It is an attention that is due to him, and there is no doubt but he feels very anxious to hear from you. Amelia [Evans] is still with us. Her health has been better than usual I think. She desires her love to you. The weather since March came in has been mild and pleasant. Shad have made their appearances about two weeks earlier than they generally do they are fine and very plenty. Maria Woodside and her Mother are about in their usual health. Maria has made no change yet. Mrs. Herregas desires her love to you, she often speaks of you. Emily's Mother never calls to ask after her. I cannot tell what has become of her. I think she can hardly feel a natures affection for her child. Charles Williams has taken the lot on which his shop stands. In ground rent, he is to pay one hundred and twenty six dollars a year. He is about removing his shop, and is going to build a three story brick house on it, the first floor to be appropriated to his business—the back building and upper part for the accomodation of his family.

The friends are beginning to come in to yearly meeting.[23] I suppose in a day or two our streets will look quite lively with drab-coloured bonnets. I shall send this week two numbers of the Post, one of them is an old one, but I thought perhaps there might be something in it that might interrest thee. I hope they never charge you with postage either on letters, or papers, for it is always paid here. If they should, please let me know. Mother Howell desires her love to you. She was very much surprised when she heard you had removed to Michigan. She often said she would have been very glad to have seen you before you went.

I suppose before this that thee received the packages by John Rutter. Thy letter to me was at Robert Coes at the time he was there. Anna read that part, where thee speaks of the Lawyer, and the uses things are put to. He laughed most immoderately, so much so, that he raised himself off his chair. Perhaps he felt a presentiment that he would ere long be dabling in lime and sand, or fancying to himself the fine figure he should make at such an honourable occupation. The Widow Greenfield has not returned yet—but as soon as she does, I intend calling to see her and then I will write and tell thee all I hear from her. Aunts are well except slight colds. They desire a great deal of love. I was at Cousin Guests a few days since. They heard I had received a letter from thy Aunt R. They wished me very much to read it to them. By the bye I had sent it to thy Brother.

I expect the Country will soon begin to look beautiful. I shall almost envy you after a little while. The further you progress in farming the more interresting it will be. I hope after a short time you will have your place well stocked with every thing that will be useful and profitable to you. Tell thy brother I intend writing to him soon. His uncle has been looking for a letter from him for some time past, but his business excuses him. Our love to him. I hope he will take great care of himself. We are well and with much love to you

> I remain affectionately thy Aunt
> JH

Anna Coe says that both the letters which she has received from thee had the seals broken. She thinks wafers[24] would be better than sealing wax—not so liable to crack. Elisa Lippincott desires a great deal of love to you.

ELIZABETH CHANDLER *to* JANE HOWELL
Hazelbank, April 15, 1831

My dear Aunt

I have been thinking so much about Philadelphia that I seem almost bewildered in finding that I am not actually among you. I suppose the city, as is usual in this month is thronged with country friends. Some of whom probably I should like to see and hear. The meeting of the "free produce Society,"[25] too, will I suppose be held this evening, and I can only *imagine* what is transacted! As to our selves, here in *Michigan,* we are passing quietly along through the usual, but not very striking diversity of a country life. Brother T. is very busy with his spring's business. He has been through the winter engaged in chopping, and splitting rails;—and now in fencing ploughing &c. He has got an excellent yoke of oxen, well broken and gentle, and I dare say thee would scarcely know him, could thee look out yonder and see him enveloped in a large *tow frock,*[26] at work beside them, busily employed in logging. He and one or two of our nearest neighbours propose to exchange work occasionally and to unite their oxen when there is any heavy labor to be performed; so that he can have assistance when he requires it, and will be obliged to work less alone.

We have not yet begun to garden; the spot we intend for it is just before the house, and we shall have it fenced and laid out as soon as T. has time to attend to it. It is as yet too early in the season to do much at planting and the spring with us, is said to be more backward than usual. The navigation from Buffaloe is expected to open by the 15th or 20th of this month, and as soon as the canal is clear of ice, I expect there will be a great influx of strangers into the territory. There are two lines of stages to be run from Detroit to Tecumseh this summer, and there is a talk of having a steamboat to stop at Monroe. There is also an addition to be made to the Buffaloe and Detroit line of Steamboat, and the price of passage is to [be] lessened.[27] From what we can learn of the weather here, we are inclined to believe that the fall season is more open generally than in Pennsylvania. We had last fall the longest and most uninterrupted succession of fine weather that I ever remember, a short spell of damp weather before winter set in, and then cold weather, much colder than is usual, almost regularly, until about the first of March, when the snow melted and disappeared rapidly. But we have not yet had much warm weather.

Since I wrote last I have paid a little visit of a couple of days at Tecumseh. Musgrove and Abbi Evans were here and insisted upon my returning with them promising they would send me home whenever I wished it, so I concluded to return with them and remain from first day evening until third day evening and even that I thought a long time to leave Aunt Ruth.

We have not yet recieved the packet of letters which thee tells me are upon the road, but I feel quite sick in the base expectation of recieving so many. I was not a little surprised on reading the name of their bearer; but it will be very pleasant to see an old acquaintance, after being so long entirely among strangers. I wish thee had seen him, that he might have told us how thee looked, and what thee said. It would have been a little more like seeing thee. The Saturday Evening Post is always a welcome visitor, and finds eager auditors, as thee cannot doubt, for all is news. It seems almost like conversing with a Philadelphian; but do not pay the postage Aunt J., for it must be considerably more inconvenient than merely to drop it in the mail box, and we can settle quarterly. Letters &c are now usually about two weeks in reaching us, and in summer I should suppose the time would be considerably shorter. Mail day stands out from the others in a kind of bold relief, and we have no sooner heard tidings from the post office on one week, then we begin to look forward to the same important day on the next. We had been looking for two or three weeks for thy last letter, and should have been a good deal uneasy, had it not reached us as it did.

Our neighbour Comstocks seem to feel very much interested in our concerns. Ann was saying the last time she was here how glad she should be to see thee out here, and they generally enquire, when we have letters, what is said about your paying us a visit. I think you will be quite well acquainted with each other against thee and Uncle comes out. Aunty Sally C. has resided with a married daughter of hers about 2 miles from here. She is now one of Darius' family.

The walking is now good so that we can get out much oftener than during the winter, and shall probably also have more frequent visitors. John Lovetts two daughters were here the day before yesterday. His family were well. They are very much pleased with Michigan. Our neighbour Comstock a few weeks since sent us over a parcel of chickens to stock our farmyard with—so that what with the cattle, pigs &c. it really begins to look quite *farm like.* And I hope we shall before long—by the time thee gets out here—have quite a pretty garden. I should like very much when there is an opportunity to have some slips of honeysuckle if thee can conveniently procure them.

Last month was the sugar season. I wished to have seen the management of a "sugar bush," but did not compass it, as there were none very near here. The fresh maple sugar is delicious.[28] I wish you could have some of it. It comes in large cakes weighing from 30 to 40 pounds and quite solid. It has a stronger flavor than the west indian (but to my taste very pleasant/and is I think sweeter). Do you still get your supplies from Price's?

18TH

We have had beautiful weather for several days past and the vegetation is coming forward rapidly. Brother yesterday brought us some beautiful wild flowers—some of the springs earliest and I expect the openings will soon be covered with them. We have heard the wolves howling around us at night several times since I wrote last, but T. is the only one of us that has yet been favored with a sight of them. It seems strange sometimes when I am rambling to think that the ground on which I am treading has perhaps but a little while before been passed over by their feet, or those of the "good red deer." But they (the wolves) are not now numerous and every season decrease their numbers. If the season is favorable I expect we shall have plenty of wild strawberries. The openings are covered with the vines, and we intend transplanting some into the garden, where they will probably be much improved, by cultivation. I have been at work today preparing some flower beds about the house, and I suppose we shall soon be deeply immersed in all the "*mysteries*" of gardening.

The day of the "Eclipse" was quite cloudy, but not so much so as to conceal the sun entirely. It was not at any time, that I could observe, perceptibly darker for the intervention of the moon, and but a small portion of the sun was obscured by her. Towards the south I suppose it was more satisfactory, but I have not heard anything respecting it.

I feel disappointed at hearing nothing further about Jane Parker. I should have liked them very much to settle near us, and I was in hopes they intended doing so. Tell Aunt Amelia Guest that I feel very much obliged and grateful by her having written to me—for I take it for granted that it *is to me* her letter is directed, though thee does not exactly mention.[29] I intended to have written to her and Aunt Anna before now—before writing another letter to any body and am waiting now that I may answer the one from her that I am in daily expectation of recieving. How often I dream of them. How often I think what happiness it would be if we could have them with us, and hear their conversation, and wait upon them, and see them looking with affectionate interest on all our arrangements and improvements. Aunt Anna's kind smile is before me now so vividly that it seems scarcely possible that it should be only an illusion! What pleasure too it would be to accompany dear Aunt Nancy over the openings in search of wild flowers, or berries, or hazlenuts!

I suppose next time I visit Philadelphia I may have a ride on a rail-road—but really if they are no more comfortable than some short patches of *rail road* that we have in *our country,*[30] we need not envy you any continuity of them! But then our rails unfortunately run the wrong way across the road.

Neighbour Comstock has offered to teach me to spin this summer. I feel some ambition to make brother a coat of my own spinning, but we shall not I expect, keep sheep for a year or two, as they are a rather troublesome stock for a new settler on account of the wolves, though Comstocks have I believe been attacked but once since we have been here. The howl of a wolf is not near so dismal a sound as I had expected; much less so than that of a dog. It is softer and more bell-like, and in the stillness of the night sounds not very unmusical. But tis a strange contrast with the "past 12 o clock" of the watchman. There are not many wild animals of the mischievous sorts about here. Panther's, none—bears—very few if any—some foxes, but they are not very numerous, and no other that I know of except the before mentioned wolves.

There is to be new road laid out shortly between Adrian and Tecumseh, which will run through our place, and probably but a short distance from the house; and if so make it rather more lively for us, or less retired than at present.[31] Our situation is admired by almost every one who sees it, and when the trees again recover their verdure, will be exceedingly beautiful. Before they are again leafless I hope thee will have seen it. Aunt Ruth says she cannot give up the idea of thy coming out with uncle. She has fully set her mind upon it. Oh how I wish thee may!

I expect the next letter you recieve will be from Thomas to Uncle Lemuel. He has been talking of writing for some time but seemed scarcely to have leisure for it just now. Give our love to Aunt Amelia G. and tell her I intend writing to her. I thought of doing so at this time, but as I was a letter in debt to thee, I concluded I had better pay it, and not let any correspondence get too much ahead, especially as I shall have so many letters to answer when I get *my packet.* And she is too much of a housekeeper not to know that I must have a good deal to do. Tell my friends H[annah Townsend]. and A[nna Coe]. that I hope they will have less reason in future to complain of me as a correspondent, than, I acknowledge, they have both had hitherto. If I am not as prompt and regular in writing as they expect, and as I wish to be, they must not attribute it to carelessness, but to other engagements which render me not altogether mistress of my own will.

We have not yet had any Indian visitors—and have seen only two since our arrival to Hazlebank. Bro said they disposed of the greater part of their horses (of which some of them keep a large stock) last fall, in the expectation of an unusually severe winter. If so their judgment was correct. I went with brother last first day evening to look at one of their burial mounds, which is a short distance from here. It had apparently been opened for there was a square cavity at the top, and the earth about it looked fresher than below, but I do not think any curiosities have been discovered in any near here that have been examined. [The] families who have settled near their "trails" (that is the paths they usually traverse—I have given the customary term) are frequently visited by them; but there are none near us and unless we were better acquainted with their manners and customs or they at any rate bore greater pretentions to cleanliness than the Potawatomies[32] appear to possess, I am not sorry to be exempted from the intercourse. When Comstocks first came on here, the Indians were often at their house; and on one occasion, one of them, who was already half intoxicated, after soliciting Darius in vain for liquor or the means of procuring some, offered to sell his child, a little girl who was with him, to friend Comstock for a few dollars, assuring him that she was "plenty good papoose!" But I think it probable that after the fit was over he would have remanded her, or wished to purchase her back when he was able to do so.

The anti-masonic party here had it contemplation to appoint brother T. a member of their convention held at Detroit a few weeks since, to select and nominate a candidate for the office of Delegate to Congress; but as he was not present at the elective meeting, and they did not know whether he would be willing to go, another was appointed in his stead, and quite as much to his satisfaction, for he did not wish to leave home or spare the necessary time. The farm occupies more of his attention than politics and we should have felt very lonesome without him had he gone, for we miss him if he is absent only for a day.

I wish thee would write again soon, Aunt. It is such a comfort to get letters, and to hear that you are all well. I, like thee, look for that part of the letter the first thing—how many times they are perused and reperused afterwards I cannot exactly guess—but *we don't often skip much,* I can assure thee.

Tecumseh and Adrian both seem nearly to have doubled in size since we came here last summer, and I believe have done so. The country beyond Adrian is also settling very rapidly. A person from this neighbourhood bought land there about 2 years ago, where there was not a family settled within several miles; there are now eleven families within a mile and a half of them. A considerable portion of the land in that direction is heavily timbered which by some persons is preferred to the openings, but I do not think it can be near so pleasant, besides being much more laborious to clear. The lots adjoining ours will probably be taken up in the course of the summer; I hope by families that we shall find agreeable neighbours. We have so far been very fortunate in that respect, and in general we seem to like them better the more we become acquainted with them. Oh that we could reckon some of our dear old friends among them! But we cannot expect everything we wish and I believe the wisest plan is to endeavor to make the best of the blessing we do possess. Though certainly that would be the addition of a very great one to our present lot.

It is said to be quite unusual for a winter here to pass over without more or less thunder. We had some on the first or second day of last December, but have had none since till lately, nor any, that was very violent since we came into the territory.

I have written almost altogether about ourselves and our concerns because I know that is to thee the most interesting subjects. I have told thee many trifling things. It is because the routine of a farmer's life is made up mostly of such incidents, important only to the actors and to those whom affection interests for them. A retired life, even in the "backwoods" cannot furnish much matter for description, after it has once settled down into its usual round of daily avocations—especially when all the primary roughness of a backwoods life has been polished off—now if our grain had to be carried on the shoulder thirty miles to mill—if we had to live nine months in the year on pounded corn, and occasionally have [ ] to the friendliness of the Indians for a dinner—if the taste of a cup of tea was a rarity to be set down in a journal, and buffaloe meat a frequent accompaniment on our repasts—then indeed might our letters be crowded with details curious and strange to the ears of citizens but as this is not the case, the plain homespun annals of country life are all I have to offer.

Do not make thy self uneasy with the fear that we shall exert ourselves too much in our new vocation—we shall be prudent and careful. It is very great satisfaction to hear that thy health has been better this winter—do continue to be careful of it, and not expose thyself in damp weather. I think thee would find a little travelling this summer very beneficial in establishing it.

We are all well, and brother is waiting for me to finish so I must hasten over my "more last words" and with love to thyself, uncle and all our friends, bid thee fare well. Do let us hear from thee soon

> thine affectionately
> E.M.C.

If Carey & Lea leave anything with thee, for me, please keep it, whether letter or books, till you come out here.

<hr />

RUTH EVANS *to* JANE HOWELL
Hazelbank, May 30, 1831

My Dear Sister

I recd thy letter on seventh day by J. Cox and this day had a very unexpected visit from S. Lovett. As thy letter noted he did not expect to come before the 8th mo. Thee may conceive my D^r sister the peculiar pleasure it afforded me to converse with one who had so recently seen thee. He says thee looks quite healthy and I much hope this is so. However I hope thee makes a visit to Michigan which I trust thee will about mid summer accompanied by my Dr Brother L. I wish thy friends in P. would encourage thy coming. Our friends here wish much to see thee particularly Ann Comstock and Aunty Sally. I suppose Aunt Sallys permanent existence will be at Uncle Darius's. He is an excellent man of sterling virtues as my Dr Aunt Amelia says of Brother L and he merrits our good oppinion however exalted. My love to him. I look forward with pleasure to the time we shall see you at Hazelbank.

A great number of familys have come into the territory this spring and I suppose will continue coming till late in the fall. There are three very handsome lots joining ours and a friend named Charles Havalind. I admire the land much and have often secretly wished that you and our nephew William were located there. However they are no longer for sale. They were taken up a few days since by two respectable friends from York State. There are a number of familys here from jersey looking for land. I think Jacob & Ian Parker could do well here. Womens leather shoes sell for 14 shilling, morocco for 16—dry goods also sell high. I bought three skeins pattent thread[33] for which I paid 6 pence.

This probably will be the last letter thee may receive previous to your visit here, therefore I will trouble thee to procure for us the following articles, 3 yds cassmere *strong* and *cheap* for trowsers for Thomas to work in. If thee has not any,

1 think thee [can] get either of R.C. [Robert Coe] or J. M. [John Merrefield]. I mentioned Cassmere as it is exempt from slave cotton (otherwise Cassmett would do as well)[34]—also ½ yd somewhat finer for an every day waist coat for next winter. 6 yds free candon flannel. Thee can get it at Lydia White's in fifth st. Should like it thick. It is for drawers for Thomas. ½ lb ground pepper ½ lb free candle wick from Pierces. Please give our love to L. White.

Thomas went to Detroit a few weeks since to purchase a cooking stove. I wish Aunt Amelia could see the kind that are in use here. They are very superior to those made in pennsylvania.[35] The furniture belonging to them is very convenient. One large copper boiler that will hold five pails one large iron pot and several smaller copper tea kettle dripping pans &c &c. When the boilers are not in use there are covers to fit on the top which are quite orniemential. The hearth is the length of the stove, say three feet, and when the front doors are thrown open/ for it draws just as well/ it has almost the appearance of an open stove. We borrowed one for the winter of different pattent but like our own much best. With a stove of this kind a fire place is quite unnecessary. All that is required is a small chimney for the pipe to go in. There was not time last fall to put up a chimney in the ordinary way therefor was put through one of the windows by leaving out a light of glass into a wooden chimney and often it had been in use. Sometime it became very dry and foul so that it took fire whilst I was writing to thee. Fortunately Thomas was in and assended the step ladder with a pail of water to extinguish the flames from an upper window. My letter became so splashed it was hardly fit to send, however, it was that and that only thee took for tear drops.

As soon as Thomas has a little leisure he intends finishing the house but I presume he will not have time for it before the winter. He will have a great press of business till then. Thomas had not time this spring to break the land for corn and Darius having a few acres of cultivated ground let Thomas have it for that purpose. I think our garden will do well; it will be in perfection about the time you come, thee may see. I fully expect thee to bear him company. It will be a great disappointment to us if thee should not. I hope you may have good weather and good company that you may enjoy your journey. When you come on the canall boat select your births, before the best are taken. Thee will find the middle ones most desirable. Keep out of the night air on the canall and carefully avoid the bridges for there is something like 750 the captain informed us—do not forget cloaks. There is great occasion for them on the water. We found ours very useful on our journey.

The post thee wrote on Samuel expected to come we have just rec[d]. Sammy got here first. I think it would be best not to write any thing on the margin of a paper as there is a fine.

Garrison publishes a paper called the liberator. She had two duplicate numbers which she has sent to Anna Coe. He has sent her the paper regularly since the commencement. Ann Comstock intends subscribing for it, it is a very good paper! Ann Comstock, Elizabeth and myself spent a day at J. Lovetts a short time since. Betsey [Lovett] appears a kind woman. I am glad neighbour Herregas sould his house without any loss. Remember me to them.

Sally Chandlers letter to Elizabeth mentions there being in good health and William's prospect of making us a visit in the fall.[36] She says Hannah Pierce is very poorly this spring which I am sorry to hear. My love to Amelia [Evans]. I hope she is well. I am sorry Aunt Anna has had such a bad cold. I hope they are all now in there health. My love to them. It is strange Emilys mother never [ ] to enquire after her. If she should again thee can say she is well. Give my love to Aunty Howell. I suppose she has not left the city yet. My love also to Hannah Roberts, Maria Woodside & Mother. We had the pleasure of receiving a letter from my Dear Aunt Amelia [Guest]. We considered it a great favour. She said her health had been very good this winter and Cousin Guests much as when we left which I was glad to hear.

Thomas is in the field planting potatoes. He says he will send a letter to his Uncle by this conveyance but I am sure he wont have time as he has to carry this to J. Lovetts this evening [ ] time to go as he has to walk three miles so I hope Lemuel takes the will for the deed and with our united love to him and thyself

> I am thy affectionate sister
> Ruth Evans

I have enclosed $3.50 all the silver we have and Detroit notes I presume will not pass without a discount.[37] Whatever the deficiency may be I will settle when you come. My love to Ann.

RE

JANE HOWELL *to* ELIZABETH CHANDLER
Philadelphia, June 13, 1831

My dear Neice

I recieved thy letter dated the 4th Mo 15th and if it would not be too selfish I would ask for a frequent repetition of the same favours, but that I can hardly do, knowing how many things thee has to engross thy time and attention, but I am impatiently waiting the return of Samuel Lovett and hope he will be the bearer of many letters from you, if not to me, to our friends who are all buoyed up with the highest expectation. I read a letter from John Lovett to his father a week since. He says you were all over at his house to spend an afternoon, and he and Thomas the next week took a ride some distance to take a view of the Country. I am glad you live so near to each other, such a neighbour as John is very agreeable. I received a letter a short time since from thy Brother William. He and Sarah were both well. He has declined going to Michigan this Fall. He says his father-in law intends purchasing a farm for them, but he does not wish any thing said about it yet. He writes in good spirits—he continues to have full employment.

Aunt Rebecca Guest has sold her house in Sansom Street at a proffit of eleven hundred dollars, she has rented one for a year at the Upper end of Hamilton Village for which she is to pay one hundred dollars; Edward Ireland boards with her. He keeps a Dearborn[38] so that the family will not be at a loss for a conveyance to the City. Philadelphia is growing fast in size, if not in wealth. It is supposed there will be two thousand houses erected this season. Lemuel thinks a great many more. There has been a great deal of money transported to this Country from Europe for safe keeping since the Disturbance there. M Gerard has done, and is doing a great deal toward the improvement of the City; this summer he is building up a square of very elegant houses in Pine Street, which will not be surpassed in beauty by very few in Philadelphia.

I have not heard wether Robert Coe Jr has answered my dear nephews letter. If he has not, his business I suppose must plead his excuse for his Market Street store engrosses almost all his time. I was surprised to hear John Rutter had returned to West Chester and taken to himself a wife. I feel quite impatient to know wether thee has received the packets that were committed to his care. Pretty fellow indeed to play us such a trick. Anna Coe has received another letter from the same one that sent her the piece of scarlet cloth. He mentions that Abby Chandler has been extermely ill, but is fast recovering. I did not hear any more of the contents of the letter altho I was favoured with the whole of the first. Cousin Thomas Guest sent for his sister to go down. He wished to see her; accordingly she did so in company with her husband. When they arrived there he introduced them to his wife—who had been a widow about one year with six children the youngest about eighteen months old. She is about 32 years of age. What Cousin Anna's feelings must have been at the moment can better be felt than described—they made but a short visit. It is about ten days since they returned and about four weeks since the marriage took place. I have not seen Anna since I went down one evening but she was from home!

I am really astonished to hear of the great number that are emigrating to Michigan. The Post says from the 17th to the 24th of last month (May) there were nearly two thousand persons passed from Buffaloe to Detroit. Such a great influx of Inhabitants must cause almost a famine in the Territory. The next time you write do tell me particularly about the crops you have in the ground, how many acres they occupy, how they look, &c &c &c. Thee knows I am a great hand at calculating, and as you have given me the average quantity of grain to an acre in a former letter I can form some Idea of the state of your granary beforehand. Do not smile at my impatience for I feel the greatest solicitude for you. Thee gave such a description my dear Elisabeth of the maple sugar that I really felt a great curiosity to see and taste some. In going down Second Street a few days since I saw on a store window "Maple sugar for Sale." I went in determined to buy some. The seller of it brought me a piece to look at. At a short distance from the counter I took it for dryed beef or a lump of tobacco. He shaved a little of it for me to taste, but I came away well satisfied that I should never like Maple Sugar.

The good Samaritan I think is strongly delineated in the character you have given of Darius Comstock. He is exactly such a man as I admire—a true friend and christian. His wife must be a very kind and amiable woman. I feel very thankful that you have been so fortunate in having such agreeable neighbours.

I called to see the Widow Greenfield a few days since. She says she emancipated eighteen of her Slaves and sent them to Liberia.[39] She has two left but they were unable to go, I suppose thro' indisposition. There were several visitors there at the time and I did not ask her as many questions as if she had been alone. She said when she first left her Slaves she had a great many but they had died (perhaps thro' bad usage) and she had but twenty left when she returned to them. She has a great many friends calling to see her especially since she has embarked in such a great and good cause. Sixteen were there in one day. I think from the quantity of clothing which she took out for her Slaves that they will have a supply for some years. It has always been said of her that she was a very eccentric character and I suppose not without truth, but human nature will err. But I believe she has been bro't to see many of the misteps which she has made and to view her past life as in a Minor; and may she through the regenerating influence of Divine love stand ready to enter into the Vineyard and labour, even now at the eleventh hour of her day.

Cousin Guests are very desirous to see all the letters that I receive from Michigan. I sent thy last by Louisa. I intended taking it myself and reading it to them but the weather was so warm, and the distance great made me decline it. Rebecca Pemberton called to see them and read it to them. They were very much pleased to hear that Thomas had entered so much into the spirit of farming. They had no doubt they said, but, that he would do well. I was quite amused with their prognostication. "I think" said Cousin Betsey "that Elisabeth will become one of the first women in Michigan, and I have hardly a doubt but that she will settle to advantage there." Cousin Anna [Guest] replied "I do not know who it would be to then, except to an Indian Chief."

I am a friend to the Indians and commiserate their condition, but indeed I often feel very glad that you have so little to do with them for they are a people that I think I could never feel any confidence in. They have been so badly treated by the Whites in many places and the spirit of revenge seems inherent in their nature. Sometimes I fancy you taking a strole gathering wild flowers, and commenting on the beautiful scenery around you, until you have wandered a considerable distance from home, then perhaps a slight rustling noise arrests the attention; with scrutinizing eye, and palpitating heart, you discover something emerging from behind a clump of trees more dreadful than a Sea Serpent (an Indian) bending his course towards you. The screams of My dear Sister—with "come along Elisabeth" seems almost to sound in my ears—and with hurried step, and without doing as Lots wife did,[40] you reach your habitation followed closely by the Indian, who asks in the mildest tone "Will you buy some of my baskets?"

Our friend B Lundy was here yesterday. He expects to commence his journey in a few days and says he thinks he shall not reach Michigan before August or September. William Garrison is now in the City attending a Convention of the Coloured people.[41] It occupied nearly the whole of last week. I was invited by Benjamin to attend one of their meetings and I should have done so, but for the distance, and want of Company. The Orthodox friends are now raising several thousand dollars by subscription for the purpose of liberating and sending to Lyberia a number of slaves in Carolina. Our relatives have nearly all subscribed, and when they call on me, I shall do so too with the greatest pleasure.

Please tell Aunt Sally Comstock when thee sees her that we have recently received letters from Hudson [New York], and Aunt Hathway and family were all well. The first opportunity I have I will send thee some slips of Honeysuckle or a small root if I can procure one. I entirely forgot it when S. Lovett went from here. I have been calculating for some time past upon going out to see you this summer but I hardly think I can make it practicable as Ann's health for sometime past has not been very good. Her complaint I think is rheumatism in the head,[42] and when the attacks come on she has to go to bed, so now my dear thee knows exactly how I am situated, and if I do not come, you must accept the will for the deed. Amelia [Evans] is still here and enjoys pretty good health. She intends spending a few weeks in the Country soon. I hope the books I sent got safe to hand without injury. When thee writes again please let me know. Mother Howell left the City a few days since for Little Egg Harbour [New Jersey]. She desired me when I wrote the next letter to give her love to you. She heard of the death of her eldest grandson a young man about twenty one years of age, Son of John Howell. He broke a bloodvessel and died in a few days. Our dear Aunts spent a day with us a short time since and likewise Anna Coe. They were well and as is common had a great deal to say about you. Lemuel and I, I expect will have the pleasure of escorting them to North Meeting before long—perhaps next first day. It is a great while since they were there but many as old as they are attend.

Friend Woodside is not as well as she has been for some time past. Her eye sight seems to be failing fast. She continues to feel an interest in your concerns; and Maria's health is about as when you were here. Anna Coe told me to tell thee a great many things that she would do to thee if thee was within arms length of her, for not writing to her sooner, but I have really forgotten them. I hope she will excuse me. Your Profiles[43] which I thought not at all striking while you where here appear excellent likenesses now. I often look at them with a great deal of pleasure I have a very good one of thy Aunt Ruths taken several years ago.

If Lemuel goes to Michigan this summer which he expects to do, I do not suppose it will be before the latter end of July or the beginning of August as he has considerable work on hand. Our neighbourhood is very much altered since you were here. There are six dry good stores from Brown St. to Poplar Lane.[44] The famous Agnew is one of the number so thee may think we are not overdone with business. Domestic goods have taken a great rise. They are at least twenty five per cent higher than they were twelve months since which makes the sale of them very slow.

We are well, Ann [Rowe] desires a great deal of love to you, and so many of your other friends that I believe I cannot take time to name them now, and with the most hearty wishes for your *Health,* which is my greatest concern for you in the land of Strangers,

> I remain thy Affectionate Aunt
> Jane Howell

If you should want any thing please let me know (*do not be backwood*).

ELIZABETH CHANDLER *and* THOMAS CHANDLER *to* SARAH CHANDLER
Hazelbank, June 28, 1831

My dear Sister

I had little thought that so long a time would have elapsed without thy recieving a letter from me, but the necessity of much other writing, and occupations of various kinds have led me to procrastinate from time to time, in despite of my repeated resolutions to the contrary, till so many weeks have imperceptably slipped away. I am glad—exceedingly glad—that you have retired from your former business [inn keeping]; I think you will be so much more comfortable in your quiet little cottage home, independent of the cares and anxieties of a public life. You are very often in my thoughts, though my pen has not very often conveyed to you any intimation of it, since we have been here; and I have, I fancy, formed in my own mind quite a complete picture of your snug dwelling; which, from thy description, I think must be very prettily situated, and with its neat little garden, its big shadowy tree (is there not one?) standing beside it, and some honey-suckles and rose bushes growing about it, I dare say looks quite picturesque. There is less mellowness in the picture of our residence; there is more *newness* about it, though the situation is unquestionably beautiful. At the north end there is a cluster of oak-trees, and the ground slopes down to a rich basin, which with the exception of a ten acre field, lies open in all the wildness and luxuriance of its natural state. In front of the house, at a little distance, is the garden; not yet, as I suppose yours is, surrounded by a white palling, but enclosed for the present by a zigzag worm fence.[45] Our flower garden is less limited for it extends over all the wide unfenced openings, and contains moreover no contemptable variety of blossoms. I need not go far from the door to fill as many flower pots as I wish.

I long to hear from you again, that we may know whether brother William still has it in prospect to visit us this season; oh how rejoiced shall we be once more to have him among us. The very thought of it has so much of happiness, that it seems as if the reality must scarcely be anticipated, as a thing that may actually occur. We have some hopes that Aunt Jane, too, will be prevailed upon to accompany uncle out here. To see him alone would be an exceeding great pleasure; but to have them both seems almost too huge a bliss for even imagination to grasp. And the idea of seeing all three is "so famous a castle" that I almost fear to indulge in the contemplation of it, but it should indeed prove to be only *a castle in the air,* and my eyes after being dazzled by its "gold leaf and gilding," refuse to rest with satisfaction on more sober hued objects.

I am very glad that brother Will finds his trade to succeed so well; he has decidedly a talent for mechanical pursuits, and I dare say makes a very good workman. Brother has undertaken to handle the plane and saw, in the cabinet-making line, sometimes since we have been here, when the weather has been unfit for him to work out of doors and has made us some very creditable furniture as tables &c.

We have not any horses yet, as oxen are much better suited to the convenience of new settlers; so that we have not yet seen a great deal of the country out of our own neighborhood, though as yet, if we had been provided with the means we should not have had much leisure for travelling. But from what we can learn of the country, there is no part of it, I think that we should like so well as that where we are situated. A considerable quantity of land has been taken up about us this season, and the whole number of acres that have been purchased in the territory must be immense. Even before the navigation opened from Buffaloe, strangers were crowding into the territory by hundreds, or waiting at that place in like numbers, for the ice to disappear; and two of the first boats that came over, brought *seven hundred passengers.* This may serve to give some idea of the rapidity with which the country is settling, and the favorable opinion entertained of it in the other parts; and besides these are to be taken into consideration the numbers who came in from Ohio &c. So that even allowing only one tenth of those who enter the Territory to purchase and remain here, it still would leave it a very large access of population. Brother is in error in supposing the winter weather to be exceedingly severe; from what we can learn of the older inhabitants than ourselves, we should judge it to be usually not much colder than in Pennsylvania. We had it is true a long spell of very cold weather, and snow, last winter, but I believe that was the case almost every where; and was said here to be almost unprecedented in the memory of even the oldest settlers about Detroit.

I too wish most heartily, dear sis, that you could "sometimes step in and spend an evening" with us. It would be most delightful; but as long as that cannot be, I wish you would write to us more frequently, that we might sometimes spend our evenings in reading of what you are about. Every thing respecting you, even to the most trifling item of your concerns, is interesting, and you may be certain we will be gratified by the most minute particulars.

We do not visit much, though we are well pleased with our neighbourhood, and our neighbours generally seem to improve upon acquaintance. There was last week a monthly meeting established in our settlement, but under the direction of Orthodox friends; so that we of course shall be excluded, though we shall continue to attend meetings of worship as usual; but it is probable there will be another meeting established before a very great while, and a monthly meeting as soon as there is a sufficient number of *solid members.*[46]

I have a volume of the Genius of Universal Emancipation that I want to send to William when I have an opportunity. It is the last weekly volume, and the first that contains the Ladies Department. The G.U.E. is now published monthly, and reduced to the price of one dollar a year. Would you not like to take it? I should like you to do so, because it would give thee particularly a better opportunity of becoming acquainted with my sentiments; and *besides I should have an opportunity now and then, along with the rest of the folks, about the making use of slave produce.* It is possible, for we have been such strangers that I cannot certainly tell, that you may give the preference to goods of the other class; but *when* I *was acquainted with brother Will,* he was quite indifferent about it. If he is so still, tell him, dear Sarah, that it is his sisters earnest request, that both he and his wife will become better *Abolitionists* and will promote the use of *free* produce as much as it is in their power.

I am very sorry to hear that Hannah Pierce continues so ill. We were in hopes, as the last accounts spoke so favorably, that she was almost restored to her usual health. Please give our love to her when thee sees her.

I hope in future that our correspondence on both sides may be more regular. Had we not heard from you sometimes through Aunt Jane, we should have felt very uneasy; and knowing from her that she had several times sent on letters to you, rendered us better satisfied with our silence, and consequently more dilatory. But thee tells me thee will now have more time for writing, and if thee will oftener so apply it for my benefit, I think I may venture to promise that I will profit by the example. I am, dear Sarah with much love from Aunt and brother as well as myself, very affectionately

> thy friend and Sister
> Elizabeth Chandler

I am not able to give any satisfactory reply to my dear brother's enquiry respecting A[nti] S[lavery] L[eague]—no provision was made for release in any way but I am inclined to think there will be no difficulty. I should like to fill the remainder of this sheet if my time would permit but I shall endeavor to take an early opportunity of giving thee some account of my progress in the character of an emigrant—at present I can only inform thee that [I am] getting along as well as I could have reason to hope for—what does the[e] think of the sample of Michigan papers? If thee at any time has an interesting paper which thee does not wish to keep it would be very acceptable—

> affectionately thy brother
> TC

Please direct to Adrian instead of Blissfield. The latter place is ten miles distant.

ELIZABETH CHANDLER *to* JANE HOWELL
Hazelbank, July 7, 1831

My dear Aunt

We were last evening gratified by the reception of thy very welcome, but rather unexpected nor unhoped for letter. It seemed a very long time since we had heard from you, and I had been during the whole week eagerly and impatiently looking forward to the arrival of the Mail, and but a short time before we recieved it, I had been expressing to Aunt R. my hopes and wishes upon the subject, which thee may be sure were heartily responded. I suppose our packet forwarded by Samuel Lovett, must have reached you very shortly after thy letter was sent. His stay here was very short, and our opportunity for preparing letters still more limited, so that we did not send so many as we should otherwise have done. Last first day we understood that we should probably have an opportunity this week, if our letters were ready by fourth or fifth day, and consequently a packet was made ready as spedily as possible, but as the person will not go quite so soon as he then expected, I shall have time to answer thy letter by the same conveyance.

I need not tell thee my dear Aunt, with what pleasure we read the sentence expressive of thy intention of paying us a visit—the very thought of seeing thee makes my head almost dizzy with delight and though thee afterwards expresses a doubt of the practibility of thy putting thy wishes into execution, still we cannot but indulge in the hope that all obstacles to thy leaving home will be removed, and that we shall yet have the joy of seeing thee in company with uncle.

Aunt R. and I yesterday morning walked over to Satterthwaites (a family from Jersey that thee may probably recollect my having mentioned in my first letter from Michigan) to pay them a visit and take the packet of letters which we had prepared for her father to be the bearer of. Mabel Satterthwaite is a young woman, lively and agreeable, and seems quite like an old acquaintance, for she has been a good deal in Philadelphia, and has a great many acquaintance there, so that we can talk over the old gossip of the place and discuss persons and things almost as well as if she had been a citizen. We expect her father to dine with us on next first day, and perhaps some of the rest of them. Her sister and her husbands brother, also man and wife, are among the settlers who have lately come in to the Territory. She also appears a fine woman, and it is probable they may become rather nearer neighbours to us than Reuben and Rachel. As we were returning home in the evening a couple of deer bounded through the bushes at a short distance from us, and after a few leaps, turned and gazed at us for two or three moments and sprang off again. They are a very handsome animal. We passed Lovetts yesterday but had not time to stop. One of the girls was here a little while last week, when they were all well.

Our new cow (Jane) is very gentle and good tempered. She is well acquainted with her name and obeys a call by it immediately.

I do not suppose John Rutter entered the territory any farther than Detroit, as he gave a couple of letters that Abby Chandler had sent by him, to a person who was coming on here, at the falls of Niagara, to be forwarded on to me. The other packets he sent by the stage from Detroit. My [Atlantic] Souvenirs arrived safely and without the least blemish. I think the engravings are very fine.

I am sorry thee is so disappointed in the character of Maple Sugar. I do not think thee could have had a good specimen but I hope thee will like the taste of ours better. I do not think we have ever more than once seen Indians within the precincts of Hazlebank and they merely crossed the opening at a considerable distance from the house. I suppose brother has given thee the information thee wishes for respecting the quantity of land he has in cultivation. He expects shortly to put in some buckwheat, but I do not know what quantity.

In one of thy former letters, my dear Aunt, thee expresses a fear of my not being entirely happy and satisfied with my situation, as thee fancies there is a tone of melancholy feeling, pervading the pages of some of my correspondence on account of my wide seperation from so many of my friends. I cannot help feeling gratified at the interest in my feelings, which such a watchfulness of my expressions manifests, and it gives me pleasure to inform thee that I am quite contented and happy; and that I have felt much more so during the time that has past than I expected to when I left Philadelphia. I felt then, as if last winter would prove the severest trial of my strength, for I knew that it must bring many solitary hours when I should be left to the unbroken companionship of my own thoughts and remembrances, and to feel in their full force the value of what I had abandoned, and the reality of what I had ventured upon. The winter has now past, and left the memory of far fewer melancholy moments and struggles with rebellious inclination than I had anticipated. But I should be very ungrateful if I was not satisfied, when all our expectations have been so well realized; and though I suppose my situation would not be considered by many of my young acquaintances, a very enviable one, I am very sensible it has many blessings that the *inexperienced* are not perhaps aware of. I felt pleased with the country at first; but I think I like it still better now; at any rate I feel *much* more at *home* and that is not so easily transferred into a strange place, at least not by me as the person.

10TH

I intended to have written thee a longer letter in return for thine, for the closeness of its lines was not lost upon me; but I have been a good deal engaged, and yesterday, when I intended to have filled my sheet, a remarkably fine day for gardening induced me to bestow some more of my time than I intended, as it seemed very much to require some attention. But as brother T. has written and told thee I suppose most that is particularly interesting, I feel better satisfied with my imperfectly filled sheet; which however should not else have been sent so. We shall attend to thy advice respecting not exerting ourselves too much, and have heretofore avoided doing so. So I hope thee will not be uneasy on that account.

Please give a great deal of love to Aunt Amelia [Evans]. Tell Ann [Rowe] that we are sincerely sorry to hear of her being so much troubled with pain in the head; and that she must apply our good wishes and the love we send her to the part affected the next time she is attacked, and see if she does not find it beneficial. I am Dear Aunt, in great haste

> very affectionately thy neice
> E M Chandler

As thee likes long letters, I should be obliged to thee if thee thinks of it to bring or send me a quire of that large writing paper such I procured last summer also a quire of letter paper.

I got it in Front St. just below Market St. Tell Louisa not to forget us. Love to Maria [Woodside] and her Mother.

JANE HOWELL *to* RUTH EVANS
Philadelphia, July 31, 1831

My dear Sister

I received thy letter by Samuel Lovett also the money for the articles thee sent for which shall be forwarded on by the first suitable opportunity. Lemuel and I have intended paying you a visit this summer but I think we shall have to give up all thoughts of the kind for the present as Lemuel has so much building and jobbing on hand that it would be attended with great inconvenience and loss to leave it unfinished. Therefore great as the disappointment is we must submit to it. But if nothing prevents us next summer we will try and make our arrangements earlier in the season so that we can spend more time with you.

Anna Coe Jr. was delighted with her package and present from Elisabeth. She has written a great deal to send by the first conveyance. She and her sister Rebecca is now at Brandywine. Their Father took them down in a Dearborn about two weeks since. Abby Chandler has just recovered from a severe fit of illness. They expressed a great deal of pleasure at seeing the girls as they had written for them to go down in the early part of the season. I hope Anna[Coe]'s health will be bennefitted by the visit for she looks very thin and pale this summer.

About eight days since an express came up to Cousin Robert and Anna Coe informing them of the illness of Thomas Guest who was seized with the Billious

Cholic a few days before and it was apprehended a mortification had taken place.[47] They immediately closed their Home and went down but he died before they arrived there. For several weeks he had complained of feeling rather indisposed but not so as to cause much uneasiness until within about three days of his death when he was attacked with the billious cholic (a complaint which he was subject to) but as soon as the Physician came he said it was too late, he was past recovery, but for the sattisfaction of his friends he would do all he could for him. They then proposed to Cousin Thomas to send for his sister but he said he did not think it necessary. It would be a warm tiresome ride for her and the Doctor would do all he could for him. He never spoke afterwards but sunk into a leathargy from which nothing could arouse him until he died which was before daybreak on seventh day morning the 23rd Instant. Anna and Robert arrived there in the evening and he was inter'd the next morning about nine oclock. He left no Will. I suppose his Widow will recieve one third of the Estate.[48]

Near four weeks ago George Williams, Hannah, Sarah and the child left here for the Sea Shore. They write that they are enjoying themselves very much. I think they are taking time enough for it. I recieved a letter from Mother Howell a few days since. She was well and urges my going down there if I do not go to Michigan, and then they will take me to the Beach, but I would not like to go without Lemuel and he cannot go without great inconvenience. John Roberts has persuaded and at last prevailed on Lemuel to build an addition to his Tavern in Haddonfield. It will take him with his men I suppose near two months to do it. He will spend first day with me. I shall feel almost lost without him, and if it had not been that I thought the Country Air would benefit his health I would not have consented to it. I expect he will begin it the first of September. Ethan Wilson has purchased the House at the corner of Second St and Poplar Lane. Lemuel is to lower the floor and put it in order for two dry good stores, one on 2nd Street and the other on Poplar Lane now used by Charles Amolds as a parlour. Lemuel has a prospect of building several houses in our Neighbourhood. I am pleased with it as I shall have more of his company.

There has been a general Turn Out[49] with the Butchers. Both in the City and Suburbs, every Market House has been entirely vacated by them except one stall in 8th St. Market owned by a person by the name of Shaffer who stood every day with beef guarded by Police officers. Indeed one day the Mayor had to attend and it was supposed the Marines would have to be called out. The excitement of the Butchers was so great towards Shaffer that it was feared they would take his life. They carried his effigy thro' the streets tar'd and feathered and then set it on fire and burned it. Last week some of them returned very shame faced to Market having been threatened by the councils with a forfeiture of the stalls. Indeed they have been great losers by it—the loss of time, feeding their cattle, paying their journeymen and losing public patronage have amounted beyond the calculations for the public mind was very much opposed to such proceedings for many very many have said that they have done dealing with Butchers. They were absent about two weeks. The Post will give you their reasons for acting as they did.

A few days since George Guest and another young man were riding in a Gig[50] some distance from Pottsville when they were accosted by a Highway Robber who presenting a pistol to their breasts ordered them to alight and deliver. George putting on a smile to make him suppose they were not frightened told him they should do no such a thing as to get out of their Gig—he then sternly bid them deliver up their money or abide the consequence. George told him if he would give them enough to bear their expenses home they would. He agreed to it. They then handed Him forty dollars. He returned them five and they drove off. I have heard of several being rob'd in that neighbourhood.

Cousin Betsy Guest has been very ill of the dysentery for a few days. It was thought she would not recover. The Doctor wished another Physician called in but she would not consent. She is now slowly recovering. Aunts are in their usual health and desire a great deal of love to you. They spent a day with me a short time since. John Rutter told Abby Chandler that he did not go within a great many miles of your place or he should have done himself the pleasure of delivering the packages himself. We have not heard from the girls since Robert returned. Amor [Chandler] is expected in the City in a few days. I received a note from Hannah Townsend last evening wishing to know what day I was going to start for Michigan as she has a great deal written to send to Elisabeth but she did not wish to close it until I was ready to go. I sent word that we had declined going this summer but that I expected a person to go from Bucks County in a few weeks, and I would send her package with others by him. I have forgotten his name but he is intimately acquainted with Samuel Lovett. Please tell John Lovett that his Father was here a few days since in good health—the rest of his friends are well.

I hope my dear Nephew has got his crops in safe. The farmers here or a great many of them had a great deal of hay and wheat spoiled by the great quantity of rain that fell about the time they were cut. However S. Lovett was a great deal more fortunate than a great many of his neighbours for he got his crops in in good order.

Aunt Rebecca Guest has become a member of 12th St. Meeting. She has rented a house in Hamilton village for one year but I believe she intends boarding in the City this winter. Rebecca I expect will be with her sister Elisa, and Amelia [Guest] and the young woman who boarded with Aunt Rebecca has taken a House near Elisa's in Sansom Street and intend opening a boarding house, the boarders to consist altogether of Episcopalians. They are to pay 450 dollars a year rent. Does thee not call that a wild scheme? I cannot see how friends here can be so blind as to sanction such an undertaking and yet they do appear to highly approve of it particularly Cousin Guests and Elisa Tunis, and as to Aunt Rebecca her children can scarcely do wrong she appears to think but in this case I believe they will all find they have been making miscalculations. In the first place Amelia's health is very delicate. She has never been accustomed to domestic concerns and must be quite a novice in the arts of Housekeeping. In the second place, Amelia has but one hundred dollars in the saving fund and the young woman has not a great deal more. How then are they to furnish a House suitable for such boarders as they would wish to have, lay in a stock of groceries &c &c, have money always at hand to go to Market pay wages, house rent &c without going very much in debt and how are those debts to be liquidated? I hope not from Aunt Rebecca's purse; but yet I fear they will and I think she has nothing to spare.

Rebecca Teese is in very declining health. She took cold the week before the Yearly Meeting in cleaning house. The Doctor says it is the dropsy on the Heart.[51]

I received a letter from William since I wrote last. They were well. I sent your two last letters to him. He is about putting up an addition to the house which he now occupies, he is to be paid for it. I found a pair of dark cloth pantaloons in the Garrit after you left here which I think must belong to Thomas or William. I should like to know which to send them to. When thee writes please tell me. Amelia [Evans] spent a few weeks in Bucks County on a visit. She is well and desires her love to you. She thinks you ought to write to her.

Lemuel was much pleased with his letter from my dear Nephew altho it was but a very short one. When he has more leisure I hope he will exercise his pen more freely. Until then we must excuse him. I do feel very anxious to hear what you have already raised on your farm and how the corn is likely to turn out and the late potatoes for I am sure that I cannot wait with patience until they are gathered in before I hear. So only tell me what you think about them now.

An intimate acquaintance of Maria Woodside's was here a few days since to ask some questions about Michigan. He is a Shop Carpenter by trade but for the last few years has been building Canal boats. He is tired of the City and wishes to remove to the Westward. His desire is to farm but at the same time he would like to be in a situation where he could work a little at his trade. He appears to be a very respectable man. He has a wife and several children. I thought a situation near Monroe as they have talked of running a Steam Boat there. It might be an eligible place for him. To save expense he does not wish to go until he can take his family with him. He first thought of Ohio until friend Woodside spoke of Michigan. I expect he will go from here the first of September. We will write by him.

Ann is making up some little presents for you. She desires her love to you. Lemuel brot a little basket of Prune plumbs and green gages from Hannah Roberts.[52] I have saved the stones for you. Anna Coe has got a variety of flower seeds to send on to you. The Honeysuckle she intends to put up so that it can be conveyed to you without danger of being killed. I often look at the Cantelopes in our Market and wish you had some of them. You have not told us what kind of fruit you have. We want to know every thing relative to the Country.

I was sadly disappointed the other day. The Post boy came in and handed me a letter. I took it for granted it was from Michigan and was giving him the postage when he said it was only two cents. I opened it and it was your letters under a blank cover from William. Do write soon I am anxious to hear from you.

Do my dear Sister be careful to keep out of the morning dew and evening air in the Fall of the year. Great caution is necessary to keep off intermittents and billousness.[53] We are well with much love.

Adieu

J.H.

RUTH EVANS *to* JANE HOWELL

Hazelbank, September 8, 1831

My Dear Sister

I received thy letter a few days since informing us Lemuel and thee had concluded to postpone your visit to Michigan, until next year, a very distant period to look forward too, seeing every thing is so uncertain, this side the grave. Truly it was very appaling to my feelings, but thee knows few can bear disappointments much better than myself, and when I reflect how far the season is now advanced and the fall a very unhealthy time to travel and Lemuel's great press of business, all these things I have considered, and I have come to the conclusion it is better to delay it, till the first of next sixth month, but not longer, if all things suit.

I was sorry to heare of the death of Thomas Guest. I presume his departure from this state of instability was very unexpected at that time. I hope he was prepared for the final event. Thee says Aunt Howell would wish thee to make her a visit, and go to the beach. I think it would be extremely pleasant and benefit thy health if Lemuel could accompany thee, but I think not otherwise. Give my love to her when thee writes. I was sorry to hear Cousin Betsy Guest has been so ill but hope she has quite recovered. It gives me much pleasure to hear my Dear Aunts are in their usual health. Our love to them, and also to Cousin Guests. Altho one thousand miles seperates us, still we are not unmindful, of our Dear friends in P. for I believe we think of you daily.

A young man from Delaware, an acquaintance of Chandlers, spent a few days with us, a short time since he became acquainted with Elizabeth whilst on a visit to Brandiwine. He has made a tour through the Western Country with the intention of purchasing a farm. He first went to Indiana and through Ohio to Michigan. He appeared extreemly pleased with our territory, and said he should prefer it greatly to either of the states if he wished to farm only, but he wants to establish a woollen manufactury also, and he thinks this country almost too new. Therefore I believe he has decided in favour of Indiana. Elizabeth would have written by him but we concluded you were on your journey at that time. I expected you every day for about four weeks.

I hope Lemuel will not engage in two much business. I must give him the advice thee has given Thomas to keep out of the morning and evening air whilst he is at Haddonfield. Should thank him to give my love to Hannah Roberts. My love to my aged friend Sarah Woodside also Maria. I hope they are well. Dose Emily's Mother ever call to enquire after her? If she does please say she is in very good health and grows very fast.

Thee says thee would like to know how our crops are likely to turn out. I will therefore inform thee as nearly as we can judge. Thomas put in but three acres in corn and he thinks it is probable he will have about one hundred bushels. He has half an acre in late potatoes, which will likely produce one hundred bushels. He has put one acre in turnips, and expects at least one hundred and fifty bushells. Uncle Darius says it is quite common for one acre to produce four hundred bushels, but our land being new, will not do so well the first season. Thomas has raised many waggon loads of pumpkin, which are very good for cattle in the winter. He got his hay in without being injured with rain. We have abundance of watermellons and cantalopes quite as good as those raised in jersey and we think would grow much larger was the same pains taken with the culture. The Carolina seeds Dear Aunt A[nna Guest] gave us has produced very fine melons. We shall have abundance of seeds to share with our neighbours.

Thomas has broke up and fenced in ten acres for wheat, and it is not a small job. After it is broken up it has to be ploughed and harrowed again and again before it is in order for the seed. Thomas thinks it probable he will have something like twenty bushels to the acre. It is nere the house and will soon look quite green. He intends breaking up another ten acre field this winter. He has done a great deal of work since he has been here, and yet he has abundance to do. However it never appears the least toilsom for him. He has had excellent health since he left P. till a few weeks since he had a slight attack of chill feaver as it is called, but with a dose of salts and some rhubarb pills he quite recovered in a few days.[54] John Lovett and family have been out of health for some time with the same complaint. They are now getting better. Many of the late settlers in and about Tecumseh, have had the chills this summer but our neighbourhood it is said is always healthy, and we believe it is so.

Elizabeth intends completing a painting she intends for thee, also thy patchwork bedspread, against thee comes out. We want to hear from William and Sally. We regret there is no probability of there removal here. Thomas intends as soon as he can raise enough off his land, to add another lot to his farm. It is the only one nere us and we presume there is no danger of its being taken up soon, as it would not do for a farm, owing to its being all bottom land. But it would suit Thomas extremely well. It would produce excellent grass and leave a sufficient quantity of timbered land.

Two physitians from York State Orthodox friends have recently purchased land here, nere by us. I presume they will have to abandon there professional occupation, for farming and I believe they intend to do so, for while the country is as healthy as it has here been many Doctors are not requisite. There is also another man from the above State taken land nere us. His family consists of a wife and ten small children seven of them at three births.

It would give me peculiar pleasure My Dear Sister to know you would even at a distant period become inhabitants of this territory. I think it would suit my Dear Brothers disposition much better than the hurry and bustle of a City life. The longer we are here the more contented we feel, and I trust shall become perfectly satisfied, and hearing so frequently from you contributes to our comfort greatly. Tell Lemuel when he comes out next summer not to do as Thomas did, fall in the canall. He thought he would jump off and walk a spell, but by some means his foot caught in the tow rope which was the cause of his falling in. However he soon extricated himself from his unenviable situation and came on the boat dripping wet. He changed every article of his cloathing and escaped cold.

Our cow/Anne/the one we purchased last fall [is] not proving quite as good as we wished. We thought best to make beaf of her this fall. She is extreemly fat with the good pasture she has in the openings. We shall keep one quarter which will be sufficient with the pork we shall put up. Our cow/Jane/we bought last spring out of a drove suits us well. She is gentle as possible and gives a considerable quantity of milk.[55]

We have no preserves to eat with our cream, neither do we crave any. We think dried apples sliced quite a luxury, they require no sugar, and to eat them with cream I can almost fancy they are a excellent preserve. They are infinitely better than any I ever eat in pennsylvania however. I presume it is altogether owing to the manner in which they are dried. It is the common practice after they are pared and quartered to string them on thread and suspend them from the joice till they are sufficiently dried.

Give my love to Amelia. Tell her the next letter I expect will be to her. Tell my Dear Aunts we want to send them a wild turkey, but the distance makes it impossible, but if a private opportunity should offer I think we shall send them some hazelnuts.

John Lovett rec'd a letter from his father a short time since. Sammy said thee and the family were well which we were glad to hear. I wish he would always mention how you are when he writes to John. Our letters and papers we receive without any detention. We have only to send to Comstocks for them. Uncle Darius's son [Addison Comstock] keeps the post office at Adrian and sends them with his fathers papers. I suppose before this thee has rec'd the packet sent by friend Atkinson. This is mail day, we hope to receive a letter from thee.

The pantaloon thee mentioned I presume belongs to Thomas. Elizabeth is very anxiously waiting for Hannah Townsend and Anna Coe's letters. Sammy Lovett says a person from new [ ] is coming out soon. I wish thee would write by every conveyance. I can scarcely express how much I disapprove of Amelia Guests engaging in the business she has. Her delicate health I am certain cannot endure fatigue and the much exposure which she cannot avoid. I wish she may succeed even beyond her most sanguine expectations, but I am confident in the belief it will terminate in disappointment. Give my love to Ann. How is the rhumatism in her head? How is thy own health? Is the pain in thy side quite removed? I hope thee will be very careful and not expose thyself.

Aunt Sally and Ann Comstock spent yesterday afternoon with us. Sally had just heard of the death of her brother at Hudson. He died of Appoplexy. She heard nothing from Aunt Hathaways family therefore I presume they are well as usual.

We have just bean informed of the death of Mary Lovett second daughter of John Lovetts. I feal very much for the family. It must be a very [ ] trial. The inteligence will be very distressing to her grandparents no doubt. She was about sixteen and I think a very fine girl.

Our love to Cousin Coe's. I hope they are well. Having come nearly to the end of my paper, I must conclude with much love to Lemuel, thyself and Louisa. I remain

                                    thy very affectionate sister
                                    Ruth Evans

We are all in health. Mary Lovetts desease I believe was dropsey. Do write soon as always—feal anxious to hear from you.

JANE HOWELL *to* RUTH EVANS
Philadelphia, October 15, 1831

My dear Sister

One two three and almost four months had gone by since I had received the last letters which were written by my dear Nephew and Neice and handed to me by friend Atkinson from New Jersey and altho I have not answered them yet, still I have been so selfish as to be looking for others almost daily, and sadly disappointed at not receiving any. Some time ago John Lovett mentioned in a letter to his father that Thomas had had the chills but was better, and not hearing from you I began to fear the worst, and as I have a fertile imagination in forming hideous pictures, thee may be sure I had got pretty well under way with one that made me almost heart-sick when thy letter unexpectedly made its appearance. I should like to have seen my own Phis in a glass,[56] and caught the exact expression of my countenance at the Moment, for it was made up of surprise, joy, and fright. Such counteracting causes must have made me have quite a ludicrous appearance if I looked as I felt; I made my exit out of the store as quick as possible up to my chamber, and there with trembling hand broke the seal to peruse the contents of they letter; but how rejoiced I was to hear Thomas had quite recovered, and that you were all in good health. I wish I could conquer such timidity. It costs me a great deal of anxiety but it is a weakness I cannot get over.

I will ask thee one question in this letter which I hope thee will not forget to answer candidly in thy next, and that is, wether thee has entirely recovered from the fall thee had just before Samuel Lovett paid you a visit last summer. Do not keep any thing from me.

I received a few days ago a letter from our dear William informing me of the birth of his son a very fine healthy little boy. I expect they are highly pleased with it. They call him Thomas Evans Chandler. I would rather they had left out the Evans; and then he would have had a name unaltered that is very dear and precious to us all.

Soon after I received my Nephews and Nieces letters I took them up to Cousin Guest at their request and read them. They were very much pleased with them. Indeed I had to read the greatest part of them over twice. They praised Thomas very much for his industry, and both desired when I wrote to give their love to you all. I think you are quite reinstated in their favour. Cousin Betsey [Guest] slowly recovered or nearly so from the attack of dysentery which she had last summer. She has been down stairs but one day since. About two weeks ago, she took a severe cold which seems to have settled on her breast and for want of strength to throw off the phlegm. Her Physician has been apprehensive of suffocation, but within the last day [or] two past she has appeared better. I hope she may be spared a while longer to her sister and friends. I called there a few days since to enquire after her health not intending to see her as I am well aware that much company is very injurious to a sick person, but when she heard I was there, she sent for me to come into her chamber. She very soon asked me if I had a letter from Michigan lately, and if I would read it to her, but when I informed her that I had not brought it with me but would bring it and read it to her when she was better, she desired me when I wrote, to give her love to you, and tell you that she wished you a great deal of success and happiness in this world, and in that which is to come; her eyes filled with tears and I left her bedside.

Sarah Cox, Sister to John Cox, was here to day. She is very anxious to hear from her brother and family. She says he promised to write as soon as he arrived there but she has not received one letter from him. The next time either of you writes, please say something about him; she wants to know if they are well, wether he has purchased land, and where, how he is coming on in farming &c &c. Anxious as I am to hear as much from you as the sheet can contain, yet I am willing that a small corner should be filled for her.

Emily's Mother was here a few days since. She is well and the reason she has not been here, is, that she has been living in the country a considerable distance from the City. She desires her love [to] Emily and says she must be a very good girl, and when she has an opportunity she will send her a handsome present.

The Country in almost every direction round the City, has been very unhealthy this Fall. Hannah Roberts has been ill but is now much better. Polly has had a complication of diseases so that her life has been dispaired of but I have not heard for a few days past wether she is living or not. Lemuel has finished his work there and returned home in good health. I was very sorry to hear of the death of Mary Lovett. It must have been a great tryal to her family. It was to her Grandparents. Poor Samuel came in and with a faltering voice told us he had bad news from Michigan. He could say no more for a little while, and then proceeded with the particulars of her death. O my dear Sister if thee had not written to me or mentioned it, what would my feelings have been? I should have taken it for granted that something direful had befallen you.

Barny Harris' sister was here a few days since. His Fathers family were well or nearly so. His Mother had been indisposed but had nearly recovered. She gave us some account of the storm which they encountered on the Lake. She says also that they have become inmates with you for a while. I was pleased to hear it. If there is room enough to be comfortable it will make it more cheerful for you all during the winter. Jane Parker was in the City a short time ago. I did not see her, or know she was here until after she left Philadelphia. I understood they intended leaving Lancaster Co. and coming to the City in the Spring. If so they must have abandoned the idea of going to Michigan. I should like to have seen her and had some conversation on the subject.

This letter is in my own hand writing but I am using a metalic pen and it is so stiff that I can scarcely guide it. Indeed it really looks as if I had very little command of my finger joints but I have been at a great loss since you left the City to get a pen to suit me.[57]

It must have been a shock although no great surprise to you to have heard of the death of our esteemed friend Sarah Woodside. Her advanced age and delicate health prepared us for the event. I was there late in the afternoon previous to her death. I thought she appeared to be in her usual health and spirits. She talked a great deal about you, as she generally did when she saw me and selected two engravings from a great many others to send to Elisabeth as a present from her; and about half past twelve oclock that night, her spirit took flight to the regions of everlasting happiness. Maria's health is very bad, and her great loss depresses her exceedingly. She has taken Genthers store a few numbers below us where she intends carrying on business for the winter, and if she finds it answers perhaps she may continue it longer there.

Anna Coe Jr. received a letter from Abby Chandler a few days since. She mentioned the young man thee alluded to in thy letter (I have forgotten his name). He was very much pleased with his tour to the west and thinks Thomas has begun business in a way to succeed well in it. He is now in the City. Anna expects to see him and then I shall hear more from you.

Amelia [Evans] is still with me and enjoys good health. Do write before long to her. I saw Aunts yesterday afternoon. They are well and desire a great deal of love to you. Aunt Anna seemed very much pleased at receiving some hazlenuts from you in case there should be an opportunity of sending them. She wants to eat or handle something that is the production of your Soil.

Lemuel is [a] great favorite with Elisabeth Greenfield. She stop'd him a few days ago and told him she intended coming to see his wife. It quite surprised me when I heard it, for I never thought of inviting her not supposing that she would come, but I shall be quite pleased with a visit from her.

I wish Elizabeth would write a piece to the Memory of Sarah Woodside. I think it would be very gratifying to Maria. Remember me to Aunty Sally and Ann Comstock. I feel that I love them altho I have never seen them, for such disinterested kindness to you, Strangers in a distant land, has knit them close in my affections. Ann seems to be nearly recovered from the Rheumatism in her head. She desires a great deal of love to you. My health is better. I have had no severe attacks since you left us. Lemuel is very full of business but enjoys good health. He often talks about you and desires to be remembered to all.

I have several kinds of seeds to send you as soon as I have an opportunity. I hope I shall hear of one before a great while. If I do I will send a root of honeysuckle. Give my love to my dear Nephew and Niece and tell them that I intend writing to them soon. The next letter I receive from Elizabeth I hope will be on one of those Mamoth sheets I sent her. Much as I dislike writing I generally make a long letter, but how interresting I cannot say, but this much I know that yours cannot be too long for me. I must now come to a conclusion for fear I shall not have room to sign my name

Jane Howell

CHAPTER 4

A YEAR OF GROWTH, 1832

The next year of letters reflected tremendous growth and improvements both in the Michigan Territory and in Philadelphia. Nearly four months had passed since the Michigan family had last written to the waiting relatives in Philadelphia. The sunup-to-sundown labor required in a pioneer settlement left little time and energy for writing letters. However, Jane Howell did not believe that no news was good news and thus began her first letter of the year with a lengthy query and chastisement. A fear associated with the cholera epidemic descending on the nation also became a frequent subject in the letters.

JANE HOWELL *to* ELIZABETH CHANDLER
Philadelphia, January 1, 1832

My dear Elizabeth

The question is so often put to me by my friends, have you lately heard from Michigan? that I am quite tired of answering in the negative, and in fact if it had not been for one Anna Coe received, and another that John Lovett wrote to his father, both of which mentioned your being in health, I think I should have been quite sick through anxiety about you. What is the reason of your silence? It cannot be for want of paper for I sent thee a good supply. Are quills scarce with you? I should suppose not when wild geese are so plenty; and as to ink, thee might extract a liquid from roots, herbs, or berries which would answer as a substitute, no matter what colour so as it would make the writing legible. But I think I have not quite hit the nail on the head yet. Perhaps it arises partly from a disinclination and the want of time. If so, I will try and remove that difficulty also by telling thee that I will endeavour to be quite satisfied if you would write once a month and let your letters consist of but six words vis "we are well and doing well" if it is in reality so: not but what I am extremely fond of lengthy letters from you informing me of every thing which concerns you but a little bit is better than nothing.

I was sorry to hear Barny Harris had not received his goods which he sent a few days previous to his leaving here. I hope they will soon come to hand. I hear he is pleased with the Country and that his house is nearly completed. When he is under his own roof; and cultivating his own land, he will then begin to feel the independant life of the farmer. Robert Martin was at Wilmington a few days since. Barny's friends were all well. I am sorry to say Cousin Betsey Guest is no better. She is reduced to a mere skeleton. She continues much as she has been for six or eight weeks past unable to hold up her head without assistance. She sees none of her friends but those who wait on her which are principally Aunt Rebecca, Elisa Tunis and Amelia Merrefield. She suffers but little pain. Her mind is clear and she appears anxious for the change.

About four weeks since Joseph Merritt left here with his family for Cincinnati. He intends settling somewhere in the Western Country. He will spend part of the winter in travelling about to see where he can suit himself best. He says perhaps he may go to Michigan. If so, he will go to see you. His wifes father lives in Cincinnati is the reason why he took his family there. Many were surprised at his leaving here in the winter but he wished every thing in readiness to commence his printing business in the Spring. I wish him much success in his undertaking.

Jane Parkers aunt was here a few days since. She says Janes health is very delicate and that they have declined going to Michigan. She desired Jane's love, and hers to you. We have been looking for Abby Chandler in the City for some time past. I believe her health is much better than it was. The Young Man who caused thee to let the *bucket go* is to accompany her.

We heard from William and Sarah a few weeks since. Little Tom grows finely. If we should have good sleighing I shall look for them in the City.

Aunt Amelia Guest has had an attack of influenza which confined her to her bed for several days but she is now much better. Aunts Anna and Nancy are well. They all desire their love to you. Samuel Lovett spent the evening before last with us. They were about in their usual health. He and his wife intends (if nothing hinders) to go to Michigan in a Dearborn or light waggon next summer. They both say Lemuel and I must go with them, but as I was disappointed last summer I intend making no calculating on it before hand.

I hope Thomas will purchase that lot of woodland which he spoke of in one of his letters. Lemuel wished me to say that he will lend him a hundred dollars to pay for it and if we should ever go there to reside he could let us have half of it if we should want it. If Thomas approves of it please write and we will forward on the money immediately but give us instructions in what way to send it.

Robert Coe I believe has entirely declined moving his family to Salem [New Jersey]. The girls were opposed to it. Rebecca has a very attentive beau. His name is Washington Train. Report says they are going to be married but how true it is I cannot say.

I wonder what spot on the Globe Benjamin Lundy inhabits now. He comes as near Perpetual Motion as any man I know for he is forever on the move. I hope he is not in the Southern States for the excitement is so great there against those opposed to Slavery that I think his life would be in danger if he gets amongst them.

The winter set in with us much earlier this year than common. The rivers have been frozen over for several weeks past. Oak wood for a short time sold from 12 to 14 dollars per cord, Hickory 18 dollars owing to the small quantity on the wharves. Schuylkill coal raised in proportion, but within a week or two past a great quantity of wood has been brot in from the Country which has reduced the prices very much.

When you write do say how the weather is with you. I hope you will keep warm and comfortable thro' the winter. If your feet should get frosted a mixture of soot, sweet cream, wheat flour and lard will cure them if applied two successive days to them. I hope you will have something better this winter than a wooden chimney to carry your smoke off. I think they are attended with dangerous consequences. Do tell me what improvements you have made—the crops you have raised &c &c &c. You cannot tell me any thing but what will be interesting.

Gerards Will now seems to be the general topic of conversation. There are many surmises and misrepresentations about it. In a few days I expect it will be printed in pamphlet form. The Executors to the Will are each to receive for settling the Estate five thousand dollars.

We heard from our friends in Hudson about two weeks since by a person direct from there. He informed us that our friend Maxwell went on the Hudson with his Scholars to Skate, the ice being very strong. But a large place had been cut in it the day previous to fill an Ice house which he not being aware of went on it. The place being frozen over but not strong enough to bear his weight and he and his son both went under. A rope was immediately thrown which was caught by the Son which saved him but Maxwell was drowned. They however fortunately found the body. Poor fellow. We were almost daily looking for [him] the latter end of last summer. He intended placing his son apprenticed to a person in Chesnut Street. It is a very severe tryal to Uncle Gamages family. They were particularly attached to him as Aunt Gamage often expressed when she was here on a visit.

But great as the tryal has been to them poor Aunt Hathaway has had perhaps a greater. Her Son in Law Jenkins who carried on a very large manufacturing establishment a few miles from Hudson died about two months since leaving ten or eleven children. Aunt Hathway has taken her Daughter home who was in a state of mental derangement brought on by grief for the loss of her husband. I did not hear how the children were disposed of but I suppose they are with Aunt. I did not see the Messenger of the woeful news or I should have known every particular in such an Interesting Case. He stopped at John Warnacks and they sent for Lemuel. What a poor tottering foundation we have to build our mundane happiness on. We rise step by step until we have gained the very summit of earthly [ ], and then by an Over Ruling Providence, are often brought down to the very depths of Misery. "But how can finite, Measure Infinite?"

I have not seen Hannah Townsend for some time past. I have often thought of calling to see her thinking perhaps she has received late letters from thee and by that means I could hear from you. Roberts Coes family are all I believe about in their usual health now altho I think this prevailing cold has gone through their family. It is said by way of burlesque that every one who escapes the Influenza shall receive a premium; I hope our family may be amoung the number.

Anna Coe Jr. was much delighted on the receipt of her long look'd for letter from thee. Thee would have laughed heartily many times if thee could have peep'd at, or overheard the variety of punishments she had in store for thee, when the letter Courier would provokingly pass by the door with a careless look in, as much as to say, he had something in his Budget[1] for her.

Emily's Mother has called several times lately to enquire after her, she desires a great deal of love to her. Says she must be a very good little girl and do nothing naughty, but mind every thing that is said to her and then she will send her some handsome presents (so much to the child). There was a well dressed woman stop'd sometime ago at the Store and said she owed thy Aunt some money. She had had the bill, but I believe mislaid it. She appeared anxious to settle it and said she would call again and in the mean time wished us to ascertain the amount. I believe she lives a little distance from the City. When either of you write, please tell me her name and the amount, and we will collect it. Ann desires her love to you. She seems almost as much interested in your welfare as I do. Maria Woodside keeps store a few doors below us. She has been with us for two weeks past. The place where she boarded did not suit her, but next week she is going to a very suitable place near her store. Her health seems better than when you left here. She desires her love.

The City has improved very rapidly since you left it. I suppose not less than Four Thousand houses have been built in the time and there has been such a mania for attaining the fronts of the stores in Market Street, that I can scarcely tell what streets I am between when I get into it, and have frequently to stop to see where I am. (You must excuse dirty greasey news papers for so many of our neighbours borrow them that they are hardly fit to send sometimes.) Amelia [Evans] is with us and enjoys tolerable good health. When it is convenient do write to her. She rather feels herself neglected. Many of thy Aunt Ruths Jersey customers[2] have desired their love to her. I have forgotten their names.

I must now conclude but I expect I have omitted a great many things which I wished to tell thee, but however as business begins to slacken I shall have more time to write. Remember me to your friends, for your friends feel to me as my friends and perhaps in a twofold degree. I have not received the Atlantic Souvenir for 1832. I expect it will be forth coming in a few days and then I will forward them on as soon as I can to thee.For fear thee will not know who this letter is from, I will sign my name

Jane Howell

I have written in such haste that I hardly know what I have written. If I have left out words patch it together as well as thee can for I have not time to read it over and correct it.

———◆———

JANE HOWELL *to* RUTH EVANS
Philadelphia, January 15, 1832

My dear Sister

Perhaps thee will be surprised to receive a letter so soon after the one which I wrote to my dear Elizabeth but I have to announce to you the death of our Cousin Betsey Guest—an event which you no doubt have been looking forward to, being informed from time to time of her illness which has been very protracted considering her great age and infirmities of body. Her mind was strong and clear throughout her illness, except at short intervals. She often expressed a great desire to be removed and was sometimes fearful that she was too impatient for the change but she said the cloud of doubt as to her eternal welfare was removed and she felt a full assurance of a happy admission into the Kingdom. She died last third day evening at half past nine oclock and is to be Inter'd tomorrow morning (second day) at 11 oclock. I feel for Poor Cousin Anna [Guest] very much. She bemoans her desolute situation, not the loss of her sister. She says she has gone before, but she expects soon to follow her and for that reason she will strive not to grieve. I sat up with the remains of my dear Cousin the second night after her decease. There seemed very little change in her countenance from the time I had seen her last which I suppose was near two months.

I called this morning after Meeting to see Cousin Anna. He handed me a manuscript written by Roberts Vaux which had been printed in several of the Daily papers, thinking perhaps I would like to send you a copy, which I will do, and is as follows:

Note attending the Obituary—viz

Roberts Vaux offers his respectful regards to his friend Anna Guest, and encloses a small tribute to the Character of her honoured sister which appears in Poulsons paper[3] of this morning. Some slight errors of the press, are corrected in this manuscript. Mulberry Street, 1st mo 13. 1832

Obituary

It is with Sentiments of great respect for her Character and memory, that the writer would briefly record the death of *Elizabeth Guest,* which occurred on the tenth instant in the eighty third year of her age.

This truly Christian lady was descended from one of the first European Settlers of Pennsylvania, who assisted in the early legislation of the Province, as a member of the Assembly. She was born in Philadelphia and furnished a rare instance of an individual uninterruptedly resident within its limits, through so long a period of time as was allotted to her earthly existence. Her knowledge of persons and events derived from extensive observation, rendered her conversation especially interresting to those who felt any pleasure in the history of the progress of our City information, which she would impart in the most agreeable manner. It was her happiness to have been one of the pupils of *Anthony Benezet* and she entertained toward her honourable preceptor and friend, the highest esteem, often dwelling with delight upon the more prominent traits of his character. This conscientious concern for the welfare of those entrusted to his care wether it was shown for their literary improvement, their religious advancement, or by the inculcation of lessons of practical benevolence made a deep impression on her mind and uniformly gave an animation to her recitals of those proofs of his kindness, which convinced such as were favoured to listen to them how much she had profited from his instruction.

Deprived of her ability for much movement by an injury which she received many years ago, her time has since been passed in the comparative retirement of home, where her society however was sought by a large circle of sympathising friends.

She was distinguished for the refinement of her feelings, for patience, humility and true dignity of mind, and when her delicate frame was assailed by the disease which terminated her valuable life, she manifested becoming resignation of the Divine Will. A practical believer in the great doctrines of christianity, she reverently depended upon the merits and mercies of her Redeemer, and her pure spirit is no doubt gathered to that unspeakable reward, which fadeth not away.

SECOND DAY.

This morning we attended the funeral of our cousin. It was tolerably large, her remains were inter'd in the Western burial ground in a plain Walnut coffin. Cousin Anna bears up under her affliction remarkably well if it does but continue, but I fear after a while she will feel her loss more sensibly. The greatest part of her relatives who attended the funeral were invited to dine there. Lemuel and I prefered returning home which we did. Cousin Anna saw none of the company as she immediately retired to her chamber and wished to be left entirely alone.

Aunt Amelia Guest is better than when I wrote last, she and Aunt Anna desire their love to you. Maria Woodside has expressed a wish that Elizabeth in some of her leisure moments would pen down a few lines to the memory of her Mother. I expect it would be a great gratification to her. Samuel Lovett was here a few days since. They were all well. I have bought the Kaleidoscope[4] for Elizabeth and I have many more little things to send her when I have an opportunity. We are all about in our usual health. I must now conclude and with much love, I am affectionately

thy Sister
Jane Howell

Do write soon. Cousin Anna Guest allways inquires when she sees me, wether I have received letters from you. When I do, I shall take them and read them to her, as she always expresses a wish to hear them. I believe she loves you as affectionately as ever she did, and feels exceedingly interested in your welfare. (*All old things are done away with her.*)[5]

ELIZABETH CHANDLER *to* JANE HOWELL
Hazelbank, February 12, 1832

My dear Aunt

We received thy letter on last first day evening, which announced, though not unexpectedly to us, the decease of our dear cousin Betsy Guest. We had already recieved information from the "Friend"[6] through the medium of our neighbour Comstock, of an event, which cousin E's advanced age and lingering illness had taught us to anticipate. The Obituary notice we were much obliged for; I consider it a mark of respect that was quite due from the writer. I am not at all surprised that cousin Anna should appear to bear her loss with considerable fortitude. She may be emphatically termed a widow—widowed at heart—but its feelings of loneliness cannot be cast out by the out-ward exibitions of violent grief. I am not much accustomed to the sight of death, and I do not know that, for myself, I entertain more than a usual dread of it; but the idea of the grave carrying over one whom I have loved never comes to my thoughts without bringing with it a sensation that I can scarcely describe. If it were not for the certainty of a future state of existence, I think the word would never cross my thoughts without bringing with it a shudder of horror. As it is, even the desolation of the grave sometimes appears almost beautiful, from the light that radiates from beyond it; especially when, as in the present instance, the barrier between the two worlds was wasted to almost a shadow. Yet still "The fire side shows a vacant land" and it is this feeling of bereavement and loneliness that I doubt not presses most heavily on cousin Anna's heart. They have so long been every thing to each other that the absence of that one from this earth is like shrouding the sun in a life long eclipse. When thee sees cousin Anna, please give to her our affectionate remembrances.

The paper thee has sent me is of such a formidable size, my dear Aunt, that I cannot attempt to write a *letter* upon it of only one sitting, so thee must consider as after some fashion, a sort of journal. Our friend B. Lundy left here on 6th day for Ohio. He found in our neighbour Aunt Comstock a tolerably near relative of his; and in the wife of our next neighbour on the other side, a first cousin. One or two other neighbours also were friends or relatives to some of his acquaintance. He had no public meeting, but several persons subscribed for the paper, which I hope will be the means of extending the Emancipation spirit that already prevails in a very good degree through our settlement.

I felt considerably surprised to hear of the step that Joseph Marot has taken, though Mary Harris had before said that his expectation of their leaving the city as a thing of not very improbable occurrence. We have not seen any thing of him in Michigan yet. By the way, Aunt, did thee write by Samuel Marot, when he came out with Barney Harris last fall, I suppose thee heard that he had turned back without reaching here and he did not continue [ ] and a letter which Barney tells us he had in his possession for brother T. and which we concluded cannot have been written of thee, though thee has never mentioned it. If there is to be any thing like a book for me in the vest pocket thee cannot doubt that I shall be very much interested for an early opportunity presenting for its transmission. But that I always am, for the reception of a packet of letters is like six weeks summer of Greenland, amidst a year of storms. I am sure that Mohounts famous "Tuba-tree of Paradise"[7] can produce no such happiness. Besides a book from thy hand would be almost like a long letter, and I shall enjoy in reading it the double pleasure of its contents, and the thought of thy remembrance of me.

I hope dear Aunt Amelia Guest has quite recovered from the effects of the influenza. From the accounts in the papers the city must have suffered very severely from that disease; and it is one which to Aunt A's delicate constitution must have been put daily trying. Dear Aunts! How often I think of them till I almost feel as if I was again seated beside them in their little parlour. I hardly know while I was with them and with you all, wether I really knew how dearly I did love you. Oh how I sometimes long to be with you again for a few days! I could almost find it in my heart to play the baby when I think how far we are separated. But these are feelings that I do not cherish. I have chosen my lot, and *I am satisfied with it.* I believe that I am in my place, and that we did well in coming here.

I do not know whether I mentioned in my last letter, that it is proposed shortly to charter a company for the purpose of having a rail-road constructed from Port Lawrence, a town about being laid out on a fine harbour on Lake Erie, to our neighbouring village of Adrian.[8] This will probably be commenced before a great while, and will much augment the value of property in its neighborhood. A branch of it will very likely be carried on to Tecumseh immediately along the edge of this farm and within sight of the house. Owing to the natural facilities of the route, I supposed the expense attending it will not be very heavy. There is sometimes, though not in that account that I know of, already pretty close racing between two or three persons for a selected lot, especially when a stranger or new-comer into the territory is one of the parties who wishes it. The Land Office is at Detroit, and in such cases goes to the best fellow that can get there first. Even uncultivated lots are already frequently valued at double their original price.

I want to see my little nephew Tom prodigiously; I expect he has grown by this time to be a fine boy, and he is at an exceedingly interesting age too. Little

Tom Harris always reminds me of him whenever I see him. Brother Will has never told us who he looks like, or even what is the color of his eyes. Will still talks of paying us a visit, and I hope he will do so. At any rate, it is a pleasure even to think that there is some prospect of such a visit!

Tell Aunt Amelia [Evans] we have a cat which often [ ] by rattling at the latch of the door. [ ] at all of letting itself out at any time of the night it chooses, by lifting the latch and pushing open the door; without thinking it necessary even to mew for entrance. Many of the people about here are accommodating enough either to their cats or to themselves, to have a little swinging door made at the bottom of the other one purposely to afford them easy ingress and egress. But we have not thought it necessary to adopt the fashion.

Yesterday there was a slow sleet falling nearly all day, and in the evening we had considerable lightning, with some thunder, one clap of which would not have been considered very light, even in summer. During the night there was some heavy showers of rain, and this morning the trees, bushes, &c, were encrusted with the heaviest coating of ice that I ever remember to have seen. They look most beautiful even the branches of the sturdy old oaks are drooping gracefully beneath the weight of their fairy covering, which is in many instances too heavy for them to sustain, and their limbs are crashing and falling around us in all directions. Even our yard is strewed with their ruins. Such kind of weather as this brother T. makes use for doing his carpenters work. There is yet a sufficient quantity of it needed about the house, to keep him in employment, during the hours which are not fit for out doors work; though our "down stairs" rooms are pretty nearly finished. A snug staircase having taken the place of our old ladder, and walnut doors [instead] of the *check curtains* which for a time were made use of as a substitute for them.

By a new arrangement of the mails, since the first of the year they have been brought into Adrian twice a week; very much to my satisfaction as I do not have to look forward quite so long without the hope of recieving something from the post office. Communication too takes place in a much shorter time, between here and Philadelphia that it has done for some time past; the distance between Detroit and that city being traversed by the mail in seven days. Letters &c. reach us from there in about ten days.

As brother the other day was standing by the window he summoned us to his side to look at three deer who had just come in sight and were browsing on the tops of the bushes, quite fearlessly, at a short distance from the house. T had lent his gun to one of his neighbours, so he offered them no disturbance, and they kept their station for I suppose about 15 minutes, when they started off and were out of sight in an instant. They are very pretty creatures, and their near approach to the house seemed so innocent and confirming that I did not feel very sorry to see them bound off undisturbed.

We have had company every first day for this six or seven weeks until the last one; as the spell is broken now, I suppose we may look to be oftener alone for a while. The people in our settlement are sociable but I do not think it can be called a very visiting neighborhood.

14TH.

As the afternoon was very pleasant and the walking pretty good, I took a ramble over to neighbour Comstocks to see if there was any good luck from the post office. Luck excellent—a "Post," a "Liberator" and a letter from Anna Coe.[9] I had been looking for the latter a long time. Tell Anna I am much obliged and intend returning her as long a one so soon as I have time. What a comfort a bit of written or printed paper is to one, out here in the "back woods." We have not seen any of Lovetts for several weeks, but Aunt R. was talking the other day about paying them a visit before long; and we may very likely do so before I close my letter.

19TH.

First day. We have not been out to meeting today, nor has any body been here. We have never yet so far lost our reckoning of time out here in the woods as to be unable to tell what day it was, or to get entirely wrong in the arrangement. All our neighbours however have not been so fortunate. One of them, last winter went out on seventh day morning, as he thought it a pretty good day to work in the woods and his wife was busy with scouring, baking, scrubbing, and all the etcetera of seventh day's work. She had just got the house a little tidied up in the afternoon though the floor was still wet when her sister went in and in some surprise demanded what she had been doing and why she was not at meeting. She equally surprised that her sister should have been [ ] replied that she expected to go the next day, and was not a little "struck of a heap" as the folks say to find that herself and his liege lord had been so outrageously trespassing on the sabbath. Barney Harris, too told us last week that Comstock, the first day before, had been very near catching his "women folks" at the wash tub. They had kept the day before for first day, and had very innocently engaged in their second day's work on the wrong one.

29TH.

We have just my dear Aunt received thy letter to brother T.[10] with its contents safely enclosed though it has been a longer time than usual in reaching here;

and contained more blank paper than we could have wished, though we cannot I acknowledge be so unreasonable to complain a syllable; and as I have so far advanced over the second page of one of my "large sheets," I hope I shall manage to finish my letter so soon to prevent any on thy part of my tardiness.

We have had much cloudy and some few days of very cold weather during this month, but the [ ] of the season that will commence tomorrow brings with it ideas, at least, of warmth and pleasant weather, and it will start the business of farmers if it shortly introduces the reality. Brother T. has just finished cleaning a space of ten acres, ready to fence and break up as soon as the field is clear of snow and fire. There has been a great deal of good sleighing here this winter, but we have not availed ourselves of it as much as we perhaps should have done had we been provided with some better manner of conveyance than an ox. It is too slow a way of traveling for evening visits, unless for quite a short distance or for very cold weather.

I have just heard very much to my satisfaction, for a scarcity of books is one of my greatest grievances, that a Library Company is about to be organized at Adrian.[11] I expect the collection will for a time be small but I think the attempt to get up such an establishment is creditable to so new a settlement. We are beginning again to look forward to the ingress of Emigrants. It is thought by some that the number this year will double that of any preceding one, but there were so many last season that it seems scarcely possible. I hope the warm weather may at any rate bring some visitors who have never been here, and that they may be well pleased with the country. We look forward to the time of expecting you with the greatest interest, and spring is doubly wellcome because we can say in three months it will be summer. I hope you will as you intended [ ] the time of [ ] I think there may be both pleasure and profit in the employment.

When thee next writes I hope it will be thy power to say that Aunt Amelia Guest is quite restored to her usual health. We love her too well to feel satisfied while she is suffering from any remains of indisposition. It is a comfort that Aunt Anna still continues in good health, and I do hope she may escape the troublesome epidemic,[12] which has prevailed almost every where; and Aunt Nancy also.

We have visited very little, or none, I believe so far as to bring good walking; and then we shall have plenty of business on hand of different kinds to render us at no loss for employment at home. Gardening is to me a very agreeable one. But you must not expect to find that we have done much in the way of ornamental gardening.

MARCH 1ST.

Spring has entered very pleasantly, though the weather is not I believe quite so warm as yesterday. The ground is yet covered with snow, or nearly so, but not to any considerable depth; and the public roads I expect are bare. Aunt Ruth and I have just been lamenting the existing scarcity of any interesting circumstances to communicate to thee. We have neither done, seen, or heard anything scarcely lately that is worth relating. Events here seem like the stones on a gravel path; all about the same size and all little together—one large enough to stump the toes against would be worth noticing.

I am sorry to hear that Jane Parker's health is so delicate, and we feel quite disappointed that they have declined moving to Michigan. We should have liked to have Jane near us, and it is probable that Jacob could have done very well here at his trade. I suppose business has been quite brisk in the city this fall, or to speak more correctly, for I forgot the present season of the year, that it was so last fall. The Saturday Evening Post is exceedingly interesting to us. I hardly know now how we did without before we received them, for when any thing prevents their being sent from the post office at the usual time, which is now third day or evening, we feel as if there was a something wanting, till it arrives. It is very pleasant to know what is going on in this world that we came from, even if we are in such an "out of the world place" as Michigan.

When thee writes again, please say whether you still talk any thing of coming by land with Samuel Lovett. We are anxious to know all about your prospects in that respect. I suppose Samuel L. still talks of removing to Michigan when he can dispose of his farm, as he has sent word on to John to have some land broke up for him. We shall be glad to have him for a neighbor, but we should be still better pleased to have *another family that he occasionally visits,* near us. We often say how pleasant it would be if you were settled close by us. I dare say we should be quite neighbourly and intimate; and if thee will step over tomorrow morning to see if thee likes the place, and take a "bit of dinner" with us, notwithstanding my complaining above of a scarcity of intelligence, I dare say we could find *something to say* to each other to keep up conversation; and I will promise to dress a couple of dishes of "Suckatash" and "Samp"[13] in my very best manner, in addition to the boiled pork and turnips. Will not that be some temptation, Aunt, to a mornings ramble?

I almost wonder thee has heard nothing yet from Carey and Lea; I gave them thy direction, on the sheet I sent them last spring, that I should suppose they were not at any loss in that respect; but I suppose I shall hear from them after a time, when it suits their convenience, or they think of it.

Brother was a little uneasy during the unusually severe cold of the winter that the potatoes, which he had buried in the fall, should be injured by the frost; but on an examination into them he finds his care was sufficient for their security. Many potatoes were lost in that way last winter. I believe we have at different times mentioned the price of the principal articles of produce. They still continue to furnish a very fair profit to the farmer, and will most likely always do so here.

I suppose the Cholera forms a very frequent subject of conversation in

Philadelphia, and indeed all over the country, and in some persons is an object of great uneasiness, but I hope the wide space of water that separates our country from the continent may be sufficient to preserve us from its ravages. I have written my letter so much at different times that I scarcely know what it contains, and it is too formidable a task to attempt to read it; so if there are blunders and mistakes I must leave it to thee to correct them. If thy letter had reached us a day or two sooner I should have, as I intended, entirely filled the sheet. But it is too late to write much more tonight, and I suppose thee would rather excuse some blank paper on the fourth page than a detention of two or three days till the next mail; so I suppose it will be best to send it tomorrow morning as it is. I want to keep space enough for the lines I promised for Maria [Woodside], and so my dear I must bid thee good night, with the hope that my present promptitude will afford thee grounds to give me credit for a practical repentance of my neglect on the score of letter writing.

very affectionately thine
EMC

———◆◆◆———

Elizabeth Chandler *to* Jane Howell
Hazelbank, March 27, 1832

My dear Aunt

I am glad that thee intends writing thy next letter to me, for I have been bragging for some time past that I got the longest ones, and I hope a full sheet will bear me out in my boast. We received they last letter to brother last evening,[14] and with it the Mulberry seeds and newspapers mailed at the same time, just ten days from the time of their leaving Philadelphia. I am very much obliged to thee for the trouble thee has had in procuring my mulberry seed; it is quite time enough to plant them, and I hope thee will see them next summer flourishing finely; and that I may in the course of two or three years have the pleasure of presenting thee with a pair of silk stockings of my own manufacture, and raising.[15]

Spring work has now fairly set in; brother expects to commence breaking up tomorrow, in a field that he has fenced this spring, where he intends planting corn and perhaps oats. He does dearly love the business of farming, and seems very happy in his situation, which he often contrasts with his former occupation in

Philadelphia. The ground on the openings is covered by a tough sod and requires for the first ploughing, three or four yoke of cattle to break it up with two hands; one to drive the oxen, and the other to guide the plough. The voice of the driver is in almost constant requisition; so much so that it made brother when he first commenced last spring, several times quite hoarse. We were quite amused at first with watching the process. In this kind of work T. goes upon the principle of exchange with his neighbours, both for cattle and an assistant. In doors we have been pretty busy to day making candles. Aunt R. has been the Principal in the manufacture; and has dipped all of them, near two hundred in number; enough to last a long time.[16]

We have had very warm and pleasant weather generally, since this month came in, with the exception of a few days, when it seemed suddenly to revert back to January, the thermometor sinking I think one or two degrees before zero one morning, while a snow sheet again covered the ground from which it had just disappeared. Brother's grain-field already looks beautifully green, and almost every day makes a perceptible difference in its appearance.

I fear Aunt A[melia]. Guest has been much more seriously indisposed than we were at first aware of; her recovery has been much slower than we had hoped for and anticipated. To learn that she is still growing better is certainly a great satisfaction, but I hope the time is not far distant when thy letters will state that she is restored to her usual health. Please give her our most affectionate remembrances, and also Aunts Anna and Nancy. And tell Aunt Nancy that I wish she come and help me gather the wild-flowers, which in the course of a few weeks will be blooming in profusion.

Aunt R. and I were over at Harris's last seventh day afternoon. They were well, and little Tom in a high good humour. He is a very good baby, and a dear little fellow. Sally Ann Lovett has been spending several days with us. Her health is much better than it was for some time. We were about three weeks since very unexpectedly called upon to attend the funeral of our friend Abi Evans. I believe I have mentioned her in my letters, and thee will probably recollect the name as that of the person with whom we boarded at our first arrival at Tecumseh. She had been in very poor health last fall, so that very little hopes were at that time entertained of her recovery, but she had during the winter regained her usual health, and we were almost daily looking for a visit from her when we heard of her death. She was taken ill on sixth day afternoon, very suddenly, and expired on first day evening. Her funeral was an exceedingly large one, for she was the first female inhabitant of Tecumseh, was widely known, and universally respected, and beloved very generally. I think several hundred persons must have been in attendance. Her death was rendered a much more severe stroke to her family by the absence of her husband who had a short time previous gone to Washington.

I entirely forgot to tell thee when I wrote last that we had had the honour of a second visit from Uncle Darius Comstock, in company with his wife and Aunt Sally. A visit from him is no small compliment, I assure thee, for even his children consider it a great favor to receive one from him, and one of his sons when he first heard of his coming here was quite incredulous upon the subject. Uncle D. says he has already visited us oftener than he has any body else in Michigan. So that thee sees such a circumstance forms quite an *event* in our chronology.

Aunt R. often says she can fancy Uncle and thee talking about us of an evening, but though we have told you a good deal about Hazlebank, I do not expect you can tell quite as well how to place us, as we fancy we are placed as we can you. If talking about people will make their ears burn, I think yours must be hot pretty frequently.

Almost every spring, and frequently in the fall some part of the openings is burnt over, by fire communicated to them from burning brush heaps and sometimes other causes. The fire has never yet run very near us, or so near us to get upon our ground, but we did not know at one time last seventh day evening whether we should not have had a visit from it; in which case, it might perhaps have made brother some work in pulling down part of his fencing, in order to preserve it. There was a bright glow of light along the sky north of us from dusk till ten or eleven o clock, when it gradually disappeared. The blaze and red wreaths of smoke were frequently very plainly perceptible; but though the wind was high the road besides lay between as a bar to its progress.

29TH.

Brother T. has just sent to the Land Office for his lot, and before I write again, or thee receives my present letter, I suppose he will be in possession of it. Besides being very valuable to him on account of its timber, it contains some very fine and valuable bottom ground or flats, which will make excellent meadows with but little trouble, and are much better suited to grass than the openings.

If you have as pleasant weather at present at Philadelphia, as we have in Michigan, I think some of the folks there will long to escape into the country. I know I used always to wish it at this season of the year, when the weather was fine. The birds around us sing delightfully and March seems almost to have forgotten to act up to his character of creating a hurly burly among the winds.

I think the procession on the 22nd [George Washington's birthday] must have [been] a very showy spectacle and no doubt made much talk both before and afterwards. It was celebrated there with much more expense and unanimity than I believe in any other city. Here it passed off very quietly without even a ball at any of the villages.

It is sometime since we received a letter from brother Will, but we are looking for one by every mail. I want much to hear more particularly about them. Aunt R and brother have just been upstairs weighing her candles, which muster 27 lb strong. I must tell thee what we are about occasionally even if it does seem trifling, or I should be at a loss for circumstance to fill my sheet; and besides thee says that every thing concerning us is interesting. We heard from John Lovett's family a few days since; they were well, with the exception of one of the little boys who had a touch of the ague.

I suppose Louisa has by this time grown almost a woman, and become quite a good hand behind the counter. But unless I was to see her, she will still seem to me the same little Louisa that she used to be, for this long time to come yet.

I am glad that a suitable opportunity offered for brother T. sending for the patent for his lot, as it prevents the necessity of his going himself to Detroit or the risk of sending by mail. We feel very lonesome without him when he is away, and he could not besides have left home at this time without inconvenience, for he has so much business on hand.

Philadelphia has been so much altered in many of its streets since we left there that I expect we should scarcely recognize many places that we were *once* well acquainted with. I hope I am sure that the people will not alter too, so much as to pass for strangers by the time we see them again.

The sky has for several evenings past been brightly illuminated in various directions, by the fires on the openings, which I mentioned above, and on seventh day evening, and first day morning a general conflagration took place around us. We had for a week warm and dry weather, and the ground, by the aid of what the sailors call a pretty "stiff breeze" was burnt over in fine stile. On seventh thy afternoon brother went to a raising in the neighborhood; we thought it probable the openings were on fire, from the smoky appearance of the air, and the night previous it was evident they were so, though we supposed on the other side of the river. Towards the latter part of the afternoon, sooner than we expected his return, I saw him hastily cross the yard, and prepare to yoke up his cattle. We knew this was something unexpected, and on enquiring the reason, we learnt that the openings were on fire east of us, that the fire was advancing, and that all our neighbours in that direction had resolved to burn off the ground about their house, in order to prevent its coming on them in the night. Thomas said he did not know whether he should burn or not, as it was probable the fire might not cross the road, and if it did not there would be no occasion for it. He had been over to Uncle Darius Comstocks, to tell him of the fire that he might secure from it, a young grove of timber which he highly valued. Uncle D. was much obliged to him for his information and the offer of his assistance, as he was quite unaware of it, and all his own hands were absent at another raising; and T. was taking his cattle to assist him in ploughing around his trees, that he might set what they call "back fires" to meet the other that was advancing.

By the time it was dark fire after fire was seen springing up, and before a great while the openings were covered with a bright sheet of blaze. It was a beautiful sight. The fires that Uncle Darius set were just north of us, and about a quarter of a mile distant; as soon as his hands returned he had them all on the spot, to preserve brothers fence, and prevent its spreading further than they wished. The place where it was first set was covered with a thick growth of bushes, and a strong westerly breeze sent it along beautifully. At first as it ran along the edge of the farthest field and by the furrow that they had ploughed, it seemed to rush along like a rapid and turbulent stream, and gradually overleaping its banks to spread its waves of flame out into a stormy lake. The piled up volumes of red smoke that hung over it, and rolled up continually, the changing colour and aspect of the flames, the broad flashes of blaze that would every once and a while, leap up amidst the branches of the trees to feed on their withered leaves, gleam out for a moment brightly amid the red smoke, and vanish; the strange aspect of the trees themselves which the fire had not yet enveloped, but against whose bare limbs its light gleamed strongly, the dark forms of the men as they passed rapidly along against the strong light, driving back the flames, or touching their blazing torches to the dry bushes and lighting up a long line of fires, which swept forward to meet those which were more gradually approaching them from the east, all these formed a scene highly interesting, and striking in its character and entirely new to us. All the inequalities of the ground were marked out by fire, as it advanced over them, and the trees on the back ground were strongly illuminated.

Our own house looked most beautiful. The sky behind it was clear, but apparently *black* and the house with the few trees at the end of it, were painted distinctly and perfectly like a picture, against the dark sky, while a few red clouds hung over it, and the tall grey trunks of the trees wore a faint tinge of crimson.

About ten oclock brother came up again for his oxen, the fires had run across the road and they were growing, to plow round it and again set back fires. Shortly after there was an unexpected shower which lasted about three minutes, and slackened the pace of the fire. By this time it had nearly burnt out opposite to us, but the remains of it looked in the darkness almost like an illuminated city. They then concluded it would not be necessary to burn round our house that night, as the fire could not approach us very rapidly against the wind, and might perhaps go out, without threatening our fences at all. So it was concluded that as the men were tired and hungry, not having taken time to eat their suppers, they should then go home, and return again if it was necessary. Darius Jackson came back to watch with brother.

The intentions of the fires seemed uncertain, as it appeared to be alternately advancing and receding, till about one oclock, when they again went out, and as the rain had deadened it, succeeded in putting out the spots where it was burning on this side the road; and after watching a while longer they went to bed, while Aunt R and I continued to sleep and watch alternately. In the morning after breakfast they went out again to reconoitre, and returned with the intelligence that it was apparently out; and brother and myself were preparing for meeting, when the sight of smoke curling up, which soon extended into a long line, altered our intentions. Brother went to look at it, found it advancing towards us, and went over to Comstocks for assistance, for if it was suffered to run, Jackson's fences as well as our own were in danger. Uncle Darius and all his men except one had gone to meeting, but D[arius]. J[ackson]. returned with brother, and after an examination they concluded to draw a furrow and make ready to burn. They did so, and before they had finished Uncle D. and half a dozen attendants came over, and in the south and east the openings were soon covered with flame. It did not approach the fences at all, and by the latter part of the afternoon had burnt off within sight of us, but not so far distant as not to light up the sky at night. As soon as it became dark old burning trees were discovered standing, like huge torches, about us in all directions, some of which continued burning during all the next day and evening, and of whose fall were sometimes notified by the crash attending it. It is all over now, and I suppose we shall have no more very troublesome fires this season.

Brother last evening received the reciept for his lot from the land office. These reciepts or duplicates or patents as they are called, are given by the land office when the money is paid in, till the proper deed can be sent for and transmitted from Washington.

> We are all well, and with much love to all "the folks"
> I remain very affectionately thy neice
> E.M.C.

Please write soon and mention particularly how Aunt A[melia]. Guest is.

JANE HOWELL *to* ELIZABETH CHANDLER
Philadelphia, March {April} 1, 1832

My dear Neice

I received thy mammoth sheet about ten days after it was mailed, filled with a great deal of interresting matter. Thee says "Aunt Ruth and I have just been lamenting the existing scarsity of any interresting circumstances to communicate to thee." What does thee call interresting circumstances my dear? To me they are any thing and every thing from the greatest to the smallest that concerns you so that you never need to be at any loss for subjects to fill the largest sheet.

I saw Hannah Townsend a few days since. She was well, and very much pleased to hear from thee. I told her thee intended writing to her soon. She said she should be delighted to receive a letter from thee as she had been waiting a great while for one. Cousin Anna Guest expressed a wish to hear thy last letter. I took it and read it to her. She was very much affected at that part which alluded to the death of her Sister. She appears to feel her loss much more sensibly than she did at first, and indeed she says she feels the seperation more and more every thy. Her friends and neighbours are very attentive in calling to see her, but still she is a great part of her time alone. She desired me when I wrote to give her love to you.

Maria Woodside was very much pleased with the lines thee wrote on her Mother. They were truly gratifying to her. The letter which Samuel Merrit had with him, at the time he returned from Buffaloe was a letter from Maria to thee with a few engravings enclosed which he says he put into the Post office at that place. I suppose the bundles I sent by Barny [Harris] got safe to hand.

William Hall is very ill. I believe his Physicians have very little hopes of his recovery. He is at his Uncle George Williams. He was first taken with the Pleurisy from which he nearly recovered, but I suppose from improper treatment or exposure, he went into declining health and no doubt a few weeks will terminate his existance here. Charles Williams' youngest child, a little girl born a short time before Cousin Betsys death and named after her, died in fits last week. Cousin Anna about two weeks before, sent it a new silver can marked with its name. Anna Merrifield has another son which they call John, he is about four weeks old.

Aunt Rebecca has moved into Cousin Anna Guests house in Ninth near Spruce St which she is to have rent free. I suppose during Cousin Anna's life, Elisa Tunis is to have the one she occupies in Sansom Street on the same terms. So much for their attention to Cousin Betsy. Cousin Anna sent fifty dollars as a present to Betsy Smith (widow of John Smith). I expect Cousin Betsy wished her to do so as she was in low circumstances.

I hope before this time thee has received the Mulberry seeds. They would have been forwarded on sooner, but there was some mismanagement at the Post office. I have not heard a word from Carey & Lea. I wish I had reminded Joseph Merritt of it before he left the City. I have sent by this conveyance the Kaleidoscope and some engravings, the one with the house on in which Sir Isaac Newton was born is the one which Friend Woodside selected out for thee the afternoon before she died. The others are all of my own choosing, does thee not think them very pretty?

Samuel Lovett drank tea with [us] about a week since. In the evening we all went to see a very large collection of animals which are now exhibited in the City, consisting of a very large black maned African Lyon a hunting Leopard two Panthers a very large Tyger another Lyon and Lyoness a Porcupine a Zebra which is a beautiful Animal about the size of small Poney the hair on his skin over his body and head is in black and white stripes about an inch wide and look as if they were penciled. There were two Camels two Lamas and an Elephant, with a great many others the names of which I have forgotten.[17] They were fed with raw beef while we were there.

I was much pleased to hear that there was a probability of a Library being established at Adrian. If it was not for encountering wild animals and Indians I should think nothing of walking five miles for a book.

Aunt Amelia Guest is a great deal better. For many weeks we thought she would not recover. The Doctor said he thought her lungs were nearly gone, but now her cough and spiting has nearly left her, her appetite is good, she is gaining strength fast and her spirits are much better than they were. If the weather is fine this week I expect she will ride out, and I hope she will soon be able to resume her usual seat in the parlour. Aunt Anna has enjoyed excellent health this Winter. They desire a great deal of love to you.

There has been a great many failures amoung the wholesale Merchants in the City within two months past, the Freshets in the Western Country having ruined or disabled the Merchants there from making their usual remittances, and the closing of Gerards bank has been very sensibly felt by those concerned in it. I am sorry to say that Jonathan Willis of the firm of Willis & Yardly have failed, at his advanced time of life and with a family which I should suppose could do but little towards a maintenance, makes it peculiarly trying. Abby Warnock received a letter from Hudson a short time ago. Aunt Hathaway had been ill of the croup but was much better. Her daughter Sarah still continued in the same deranged state of mind. The rest of our friends there were all well.

Our City has made rapid improvement since you left it. It is supposed that a great number of houses will be built this spring and summer. Lemuel has undertaken two for Joseph Pickerings brother, in front Street not a great distance from us.

I suppose thee thought I was not epicure enough to know what Suckatash and Samp was. It is a dish I do not think I should be very fond of, tho Lemuel likes it very well. Mary Walker, Lewis' wife, is in the last stage of consumption. It is thought she will not continue many days. I was there not long since. The girls were asking particularly about thee. Their brother Joe who has been absent for thirteen years has returned but wether to stay I do not know. He was so much altered in his appearance that I did not know him. He has been a great trouble to his parents.

Thee did not tell me how Benjamin Lundy was pleased with Michigan or your part of it. It must have been an agreeable surprise to him to have met with such near relatives so far from home. I shall feel quite anxious to see him when he returns that I may hear all about you. I expect he will be quite tired of answering my questions for I have never seen anyone from there but Samuel Lovett since you left us. Ann Walton spent part of a day at Aunts about two weeks since. She says Nancy Welsh is deceased, also Esther Linton.

I hope every precaution may be used to prevent if possible an introduction of the cholera into this country, it is such an awful disease that the very idea of it is enough to make one shudder. The communication between here and the infected parts of Europe is so great that unless every part in the United States is closed against their vessels I do not see how we shall escape from it.

I am writing in great haste and with a pen that would try the patience of Job. I hope thee will be able to read it for I have not time to copy it off. We are all well and with much love.

I am affectionately thy Aunt.
Jane Howell

I mentioned sending the enclosed book before I had read it and from the title I thought it was something better but at any rate it may do for Emily and I will try and send thee something better.

The seal of the last letter to me was cracked across so that any one might have opened it. Would not a wafer do better?

ELIZABETH CHANDLER *to* JANE HOWELL *and* AMELIA EVANS
Hazelbank, April 11, 1832

My dear Aunts Jane and Amelia

Though I am limited for time, and have written quite lately, I cannot feel satisfied to let the present opportunity escape with[out] addressing you with at least a few lines. Aunt Ruth has already written, and probably communicated all the more important intelligence—if any thing important there was to communicate—so I must rest me contented with the gleanings.[18] We are waiting impatiently to know what spot uncle has fixed upon for your future residence; that we may know once more where to seek you and where to direct to you, in your great city. We shall I hope recieve a packet of letters by the return of this conveyance, but expect to hear from you by mail, perhaps before this reaches Philadelphia. The packet for Anna Coe, containing what letters I had intended sending her by Samuel Lovett, with some addition, Aunt Jane will please have forwarded to her, if they have left the city, when opportunity offers.

We have had much delightful weather this spring, and I found wild flowers in full bloom, tell Ann, I think as long as two weeks ago—perhaps more than that. Brother has been deeply engaged this morning in grafting and planting a nursery of young fruit trees. Some of my young Mulberry trees he set out a few days since in several situations in the door yard. Some of them are as tall as myself, but the larger part of them are much smaller.

Give my love very affectionally to our dear Aunts, and tell them that could we but enjoy their presence here, it would add ten-fold interest to the pleasure of endeavoring to improve the appearance of our little cottage. It is true it is but little in the way of ornamental appearance that we can yet aspire to. The severe and more necessary labours of the farm engross brother's almost exclusive attention— and it must be so I suppose for yet a while longer. In a few years perhaps we may be more able to pay attention to embellishment. Oh could you but note year after year and comment on the improvements we make, or have made on our untouched farm how delightful it would be! Aunt Jane I hope we shall see with uncle in the course of the summer and glad I should be if we had the same pleasant prospect in view with regard to the other Aunt I am addressing.

William and Sarah I hope are well. We have not heard from them lately. While brother Will is so deeply engaged in business, I suppose we need scarcely expect a visit from him. Little Tom must be quite a great boy by this time.

The bank question, we see by the papers, continues to be unsettled and strongly agitated. I think the pressure and unsettled state of the currency, must create a very great stagnation of business.[19]

Brother has come up to the house for the purpose of bearing off our packet, so I must speedily draw to a conclusion—though in a vicinity to the top of the page that I am not wholly satisfied with. Our grain grows beautifully this fine weather. The ground now looks richly green. The grass is starting also on the openings, but the trees, which are oak, and do not bud early, have not yet altered their winter appearance. I have time for no more except to subscribe myself affectionately

> Your Neice
> E.M. Chandler

Give my love to Ann and tell her to let me have a letter by the return of this opportunity. I do not know what stay John Hunt will make in the city, but I hope you may have time to prepare letters. If we knew whether you had removed or not, there would be a better chance of Aunt Jane's seeing Hunt and having more time to prepare letters, but we do not know how to direct him. This we purpose directing to the care of J. G. Merrefield and if thee he does not find you out I suppose your packet could be left there for him as we shall desire him to call a second time.

<hr>

ELIZABETH CHANDLER *to* JANE HOWELL
Hazelbank, May 5, 1832

My dear Aunt

I received thy letter last third day morning, very unexpectedly, although I had for weeks been looking forward to the reception of one about that time. Aunt R. and myself had concluded to pay a visit that day to one of our neighbours, and had stopped by the way for a few minutes at neighbour Comstocks. Almost the first thing was to enquire for letters, and papers. Of the first we were informed there was none, and respecting the last they were not quite certain, but invited me into the next room to examine for myself; Aunt R. followed, but we had not been there many minutes before Aunt Sally came in to say that there was a gentleman in the other room who had been enquiring for us. We immediately concluded it must be somebody from old Phil. or there away, though considerably surprised and not at all able to guess who; but without waiting to spend much time in *wonderment* we went to see, and I was delighted by seeing a packet inscribed with my name emerge from the gentlemans coat pocket.

The engravings are indeed most beautiful, and I am exceedingly obliged for them. I have not yet decided which I admire most, but they almost all have the power to awaken some train of thought—some by arousing old remembrances, others by leading imagination into distant lands, and scenes with which is connected some idea of reverence and romance. I am very fond of pictures, and I can sometimes read them almost like so many pages of a written volume. They are to me, to borrow an idea of a term, from Nat Willis, *unwritten reading.*

I have got all my mulberry seed planted, and I expect some of them will shortly peep above ground, though they do not come up very soon. It was not a very trifling job; I assure thee to drop them all separately in the earth at proper distances from each other, and they occupy quite a respectable portion of our garden. I hope they will grow well. I am much obliged for the Kaliedescope, and do not feel at all inclined to dispose of it in the way thee mentioned. Its contents are not I admit of the higher order of literature, but I expect I shall find amusement and probably some instruction in its pages.

Brother desires me ask thee if thee will please request John Child to procure from the Clerk of Green St. Meeting, a certificate of his membership with Friends. Such a certificate will exempt him from all trouble with Militia duties, as by the laws of the Territory Friends are exempted from such duties. Brother has not as yet had any warning to attend muster and has escaped all trouble, but he thinks it best to be provided for the future. He says the certificate of the clerk merely will be sufficient.

I have had several invitations to keep school since I have been here, and a week or two since a very pressing one, from a neighbour of ours who lives about three or four miles distant. She appeared very anxious for me to go there and take charge of her daughter and some other girls for a few months. On some accounts I should have been very willing to do so, but I could not feel satisfied to leave Aunt Ruth, and therefor declined it. Could I attend to a school with profit, at such a distance from home that I could return at night, I think I might do so, because I could then still *extend* a care over *home,* but I cannot think of leaving Aunt R. altogether.[20]

Our Cow, Jane, brought us home a very fine little calf a few days since. I am often very much amused with watching its capers; it is one of the most playful little creatures that can be, and is delighted to have any notice taken of it, which is manifest by all the antic tricks it is capable of. Tell Ann that a pair of Robbins have built their nest in the pig pen near the house, and they sing most delight-fully. The nest now contains 3 or 4 eggs, and if they do not unfortunately happen to get disturbed, I expect we shall have them about us nearly all summer. I wish thee could see brother's grain field; it is an object of daily admiration with us the colour is so exceedingly beautiful. I was proposing to Aunt R. to send thee a *sample.* The openings too are beginning to wear a less sombre hue than they did after having been burnt over. They look quite green. And the trees in the woods also are assuring "nature's livery." Wild flowers have long since made their appearance. And I have transplanted some of them to a situation nearer home.

6TH—

John Lovett took dinner with us to day in company with Samuel Marot; and after dinner they went over for Barney Harris, intending to take a walk round the country; but brother who has just returned says they got no further than John's where they staid to tea. His family are all quite well, except his Mother in law who is indisposed.

From the Saturday Post which we have received today we learn that William Hall is deceased. Poor fellow, when I last saw him he was in blooming health; and had it not been for thy having mentioned his being so ill, I should scarcely have thought of his being the person alluded to.

Our friends Darius and Ann Comstock, talk of leaving us for about a couple of months next summer, on a visit to York State. They propose setting out on their journey towards the latter part of June. We shall miss them very much, and Ann does hope they may not be away at the time you come out. She appears very anxious to see thee.

Brother has planted the principal part of his potatoes and expects to get his corn in the ground this week. It is a busy time with farmers now; but there is very little of the year when it is not so.

I believe B. Lundy liked this part of the country very much; better considerably than he expected he should. But winter does not show it off to so much advantage as the other seasons.

The stages have now commenced running every day; and the lake navigation has also opened but I do not know whether entirely so. The Monroe and Tecumseh stages pass here, or at least along the road at a short distance of us, twice each day, and I expect they will generally be well filled with passengers. We are looking forward to a large influx of population from New York State in a short time. Twelve families of *one name* [Aldrich] expect to come here during the summer, who anticipate forming a settlement not far from us across the river. Eight of them have already sold their places in York State. Forty families from their neighbourhood, it is said intend coming out here this season. I shall be glad if some clever Pennsylvanians move out here also. There was quite a gathering of Pennsylvanians at John Lovetts, as they had other visitors who were from that State as well as the three from here. John's wife remarked that it was not often they had so many together about them.

We have had very pleasant weather through nearly all of this spring and as few days of disagreeable weather as I ever remember.

Emily has been to day busily employed in writing to her mother. It was a high gratification to her. She has been for a long time anticipating writing a few lines to Mrs. Howell in one of mine or Aunt R's letters when there was a private opportunity for sending it, and perhaps at some future time thee may be *favored*. I think she will make a good writer, but being entirely unaccustomed to handling a pen has occasioned to write more awkwardly than she does on the slate.

I have been writing to Aunts, but not a very long letter. I had no idea of Samuel Marot's intending to return so soon, and I shall not have leisure to write as much or to so many of my friends as I should have done had he remained a week or two longer.

I should be much obliged if when a private opportunity again occurs, thee would send me out a Pike's Assistant.[21] I expect they can be bought there for lit-tle more than half the money probably that they could here, besides the incon-venience of procuring one from Detroit. I find that my memory would need furbishing up considerably in Arithmetic if I should undertake to play teacher, and in case of having an offer made sure that I could accept, I would not like to be obliged to decline on that account. But at any rate now while I have the oppor-tunity of doing so, I wish to fit myself to become a teacher if at any time it should be necessary or advisable for me to follow that occupation. I wish to feel that, if I am blessed with health I can always depend upon myself and my own resources for support; and besides even if no other end is attained I shall have the satisfac-tion of improving myself.[22]

Please give my best respect to little Roy, and tell him that I hear he is as lism as ever, notwithstanding he is so fat. I wonder [if] I am to expect an answer to my last letter before this reaches thee; but I suppose that is a point on which I can-not be satisfied exactly at present. I am an exceedingly punctual correspondent in *looking for letters,* I assure thee, whatever may be my misdemeanors on the score of writing them, though by the way Aunt I do not think I have *answered* thy letters to *myself* so very irregularly. Tell Aunt Amelia Evans I should like to write to her by this conveyance if I had time for it; as it is I can only enclose my love in thy letter. I should be glad if she would write to me. Thee does not mention any thing about cousin Coe's family but I suppose they are well; I happened to have some writing on hand for Anna, which I shall send, otherwise I suppose I should have had a scolding from that quarter.

It is quite bed time for back woods folks, and my eyes have been for some time very frequently reminding of that circumstance, and at length behave in such a rebellious manner that I believe I must discontinue writing for to night. Give my love to Ann and Louisa, and be assured that I am with the utmost sin-cerity

> very sleepy & thy neice
> E.M. Chandler

P.S. Aunt Ruth says if it is convenient when thee comes she would thank thee to bring a bed tick which thee gave her before we left Philadelphia, but which was forgotten to be packed among our things. If thee has made any use of it, she desires me to say it is of no consequence. She would like also to have a little white patent thread, a small bladder of scotch snuff, and a pound of pepper from James Peirce's. Aunt Ruth desires her love to thee and, with mine also, to cousin Anna Guest.

I have just been out to look at my mulberry seeds; (this is tomorrow morn-ing not last night at bed time, that I am writing now) they are I believe about

coming up but are so small that I can scarcely distinguish them. They are sometimes a month in coming up, and never I believe vegitate very quickly. Aunt
Ruth is about churning; she says she wishes thee could have some of the buttermilk; but I with an eye more to the "main point" propose to her opening nego-
tiations with thee for the sale of a pound or two of fresh butter.

I do not expect this will reach thee very speedily;[23] as S. Marot this morning
tells us he talks of going down into Ohio again to see Joseph. I had nearly forgotten to add the important sentence "We are all well" and with that intelligence
once more arrive at a conclusion. Brother says if thee does not see Samuel Comfort
his letter can be left at the Red Lion Tavern.

JANE HOWELL *to* ELIZABETH CHANDLER
Philadelphia, June 3, 1832

My dear Neice

Last second day evening while Maria Woodside and I were sitting back in the
kitchen talking over the common occurrences of the day Samuel Merrit, to my
great surprise and I may say exceeding great joy, made his appearance. His return
was a thing quite unlooked for by me as he said when he left here for Ohio that
perhaps he should not return if he found Michigan or any other place to answer
his expectations in regard to his Manufactoring concern. I felt sorry on his own
account that he did not, but he returned in good health and spirits and was so
much pleased with his tour that he says it fully compensated him for all the trouble and expense of the journey. "It is an ill wind that blows on one any good," is
an old saying, but I must confess it came forcibly across my mind when I saw
him. I hardly knew how to behave myself. I had a hundred questions to ask him
about you and I scarcely knew which to ask him first, but to my comfort his
answers were all very much to my satisfaction. I told him that I had heard a great
deal about Michigan but I had never seen any thing that was produced on the soil
and asked him why he did not bring me something that I could see and handle
if it was only a stick or a stone. He immediately took out a hazlenut from his
pocket and told me he picked it up off of Thomas' land. I set a high value on it.
It proves you *really* live on Terra Firma.

Thy packet of letters were joyfully received by all to whom they were
addressed. I immediately sent Anna Coes to her for she had for many weeks been
casting severe reflections on thee for not writing. She said she feared thee was for-

getting her and that was too provoking a thing for her to bear with, and by way of retaliation she would not send a very long letter which she had written to thee, but the breach is healed over now and she is in as good feeling with thee as ever.

Aunt Amelia Guest intends writing to you very soon. She has nearly recovered from her long indisposition. I expect she will spend a day with me this week in company with my other aunts. They desire a great deal of love to you. Samuel Comfort expressed a great deal of pleasure at the receipt of Thomas' letter and says he shall answer it very soon. Tom is a great favourite with him.

Samuel Lovett was here a few days ago. They were all well. Samuel intends sending a box of a pretty large size to John. He says he thinks there will be some room for me if I have any thing to send to you. I was glad to hear it as it will be a good opportunity to send the things thee wrote for. I was sorry to hear that John had lost two of his horses. I expect he feels himself quite unfortunate but he should not as the health of his family is so much improved.

Hugh McConkey was here last week! He says William and Sarah are well and that little Tom is a very fine healthy child. I sent some of thy last letters for Williams perusal as he was very anxious to hear from you and I had not time to write by him. Joseph Taylor expects to be in the City in a few weeks and William is to write by him. McConkey says William is full of business. He is at present building an addition to his store. He says there are several family's intend moving to Michigan next Fall from their neighbourhood. He did not say who they were. Perhaps William may accompany some of them. It would be a good opportunity for him. I saw Hannah Townsend sometime ago. She expresses a great love for thee and was very desirous that your correspondence should be kept up.

Last first day evening I went over to Pattersons Church[24] to see a couple of Indians who where to speak there. One was of the Mohawk the other of the Chickapa tribes. I was very much pleased with them. They where dressed in dark cloth made plain and were accompanied by a Methodist Missionary whose religion they have embraced. I think they were from Canada or near the lines. One of them (the Chickapa) spoke english tolerably well and his discourse which was something like giving in his experiences it is termed was very interresting. The other who could not speak english sufficient to address the meeting delivered a prayer in the Mohawk tongue, the words of which I suppose were understood by no one present but the Missionary. But the solemn and reverential manner in which he addressed the Throne of Grace was I believe felt by all who where present. They sung a Hymn together each in his own native tongue which tho not very loud was sweet and melodious keeping time and tune together. I feel quite prepossessed in favour of Indians now. I do not think I should be much afraid to live amoung them especially if they were in some degree civilized for I do not think they would injure any one who would treat them kindly.

Poor William Hall departed this life at his Uncle George Williams where he was during the greatest part of his illness. A few hours before the close he was asked by his Mother wether he would rather die or live, he answered die. He made a beautiful prayer on behalf of his Mother his Sisters and self and in the agonies of death he expressed a wish that the doctor who was standing by his bed-side would apply a mustard plaister[25] to his side, but the Physician saying it was unnecessary to do so he replied that then he knew he had not long to live. His voice soon failed him but he appeared to be in supplication until life became extinct. From the commencement of his illness until his death was about seven weeks and he was so reduced in flesh that there was scarcely a trace of his former appearance remaining. Margaret [Hall] grieves very much about him. I feel for her. I am glad to hear thee was pleased with the engravings I sent thee for if they are not of much worth in themselves yet the particular pains and the pleasure I took in selecting them for thee will I think enhance the value. I shall be pleased to see B. Lundy when he returns, I expect he will have a great many things to tell me about you. It must have been very pleasing to him to have met with so many relatives so very unexpectedly.

We have had a very wet cold spring and vegetation has been very backward. It has been very different from the weather you have had from the accounts thee has given me in thy letters. I have not seen Emily's Mother for some time past. I expect she will be delighted to receive her letter. Indeed it was exceedingly well written. Tell her she must write to me. I hope she will continue to be a very good little girl and then when I go to Michigan I will take her some very pretty things. Her Mother is married again. I do not recollect her husband's name. He is a rope maker by trade.

I think thee must have summoned a great deal of patience to thy aid whilst thee was planting singly and seperately the mulberry seeds. I hope every wish may be realized in the culture of them, and also of thy silkworms, the raising of which, when thee gets under way, I think will be a very interesting employment.

Thy friends all approve of thy keeping a school, provided thee can have one at home. It will be the means of beguiling many a tedious hour if there is no other advantage arising from it, but to attend one any distance off would be very unpleasant to my feelings. I think thee and thy Aunt Ruth in such a wilderness should not be seperated for one hour. You would feel your loneliness too much.

I feel very sorry as regards yourselves that your kind neighbours will be so long absent from you on their tour to New York. I hope when I pay you a visit they may be at home but I scarcely think it probable I shall see you this summer for Lemuel has undertaken so much work that I fear he will hardly get thro' in time for so long a journey. I will not give up the idea of going yet.

Cousin Anna Guest looks pale and dejected. She appears to feel her loss now as much if not more than she did at first. She scarcely even leaves her home for she says it seems so dismal to her to return. She weeps a great deal and some of her friends have expressed their fear that it will bring on imbecility of mind. She is a great deal of her time alone, but I believe it is her choice. She never sees me but she makes a great many enquiries about you and very frequently desires me to send her love to you. She has not heard the contents of thy last letter yet as I have not been there since. We are all in our usual health and with much love

I remain thy Affectionate Aunt

Jane HowellI hereby certify that Thomas Chandler is a member of the Religious Society of Friends—and that he belongs to "The Monthly Meeting of Friends held at Green Street, Philadelphia."

John Child Clerk of said Meeting
Philadelphia 5th Month 29th 1832[26]

JUNE 5TH—

From some accounts in this days paper we see that the Indians are assuming a hostile appearance not further than three hundred miles from you.[27] It has filled us with alarm for your safety. If there should be danger from them leave all and let Philadelphia be your place of refuge until all animosity or the spirit of revenge has subsided amongst them. John Child wrote a certificate of Thomas' membership on this sheet. He did not know wether it was necessary to sign any names to it more than his own. Please tell my dear Sister Ruth that I intend writing a very long letter to her before long. She must not think that I neglect her. Barny['s] Father was at Maria Woodsides yesterday. He and all his family where well. Ann desires a great deal of love to you. She says thee must save the Robbins nest for her until I go to see you and some of their sweet notes too.

ELIZABETH CHANDLER to JANE HOWELL
Hazelbank, June 20, 1832

My dear Aunt

I had the pleasure about two hours since, of recieving thy letter, after not a few unsuccessful walks over to Comstocks in pursuit of one. And as thee speaks of your feeling alarmed on account of the reports respecting the hostile attitude of the Indians under Black Hawk, I have almost immediately sat down to assure thee that we apprehend no kind of danger from them here, and it is not thought there is any probability of their venturing even as far eastward as Chicago. The reports respecting them have been exceedingly exaggerated; it is not supposed that they are within four or five hundred miles of this place,* or that they can get much nearer if they wished to, which I do not believe they do. The defeated militia mentioned in the papers, lost only eleven, instead of fifty two men, and the probability was that some of them were only missing. The settlers beyond Chicago, who on the first alarm had retreated to the forts, by the latest accounts were represented as returning to their farms. Here, in the Territory there has been at no time cause for terror, though the reports it is true on their first reaching here wore a formidable appearance enough, and as our men were immediately called out and marched westward, for a day or two, matters wore quite a military aspect. First came a report that our red skinned friends were ravaging the country *between* here and *Detroit*. But before people had time to be frightened came on the heels of it a flat contradiction, but accompanied by a summons to the militia to assemble at Tecumseh at two o clock, and adding the statement that the standing force, at a military post near Chicago, consisting of seven hundred men had all been cut off. Next it was said that they were in the St. Josephs country with fire and tomahawk, then that they were assembled in a force of from 15 hundred to 2000 men at White Pigeon prairie, about a hundred miles west of this, then that they had burned Chicago &c &c.**

Some few folks about Adrian and Tecumseh were rather scared, I suppose, but in our neighbourhood no serious apprehensions of danger appeard to be felt, except in one or two instances, and then not beyond the first alarm. We ourselves at no time felt afraid for we knew no reliance was to be placed on such rumours. Hazlebank throughout the whole was as peaceful and tranquil as ever, and indeed had it not been that I chanced to be over at neighbour Comstocks for several days just at that time assisting them to sew, we should scarcely have known one half of what was rumoured. The men from here went a few days march and returned again.

Emigrants are coming in fast. The land on the other side of the river, which opposite here has hitherto lain quite unoccupied is now taken up rapidly. Four families have purchased land there within a week or two past, and an old friend from Massachusetts [Aldrich], an elder of the meeting, about the same time, took up seven lots there, and four in other places, with the expectation of removing here, with all his children and grandchildren, amounting to forty persons. The land on the river is very good, and there is a fine range for settlers. Our meeting

---

*or ever have been much nearer in force

**I need scarcely to say that they were all false.

house which when we first came here, was amply sufficient to contain both men and women in its little end, now notwithstanding the addition which has been made to it, requires a fresh supply of benches to accomodate all its attendants. And I do not know of one discontented person in all the neighborhood.

I was at a "quilting" last week; there were about twenty girls besides myself, and in the evening about the same number of young men. Their dress and manners generally were such as I suppose would very little accord with the idea you city folks have formed of the people of the back *woods*. The young people in our neighborhood do not dress near as much as they do in Tecumseh, but in general well, and frequently tastefully. And there are several of our plainer and older folks that might be seated down in any of the Philadelphia meetings on first day without their being known from their dress to be strangers there.

We have paid and received several visits since I wrote last; and are engaged next first day to dine at Samuel Satterthwaite's formerly from Jersey, and of consequence almost like an old acquaintance. We were at John Lovetts not long since; they were well and in good spirits, and looking forward with a great deal of pleasure to seeing Samuel and his wife out here, either next fall or spring.

An expression which caught my eye in thy letter just now, put me upon running over in my mind the number of families just now within about a mile of us; they muster fifteen, and some of them not small ones either. But they are not all in separate houses, nor will they all remain within that distance, but none of them are going very far off. One house not far from us, consisting of either two or three rooms, contains families to the amount of twenty seven persons. We expect a couple more families within that distance shortly.

It is very good news to hear that Aunt Amelia Guest is so far recovered as again to be able to visit her friends. I should like much to have been one of the company at thy house when she and my two other Aunt A's [Anna Guest and Amelia Evans] were there, but I hope you talked a little about us.

Brother is so busy with his corn; harrowing and hoeing it; it looks so far very well. The season has as yet been very favorable.

We are very glad to hear that some people from Brother Wills neighborhood, intend coming out here. It will be delightful to have somebody that can talk about him with us. We have been some time expecting a letter from him. If, as I hope he does, he still continues to wish to pay us a visit, it would as thee says be a very good opportunity for him. As to Uncle and thyself, we can scarcely yet give up all hope of seeing you, though I confess it has been with me all along rather a *hope* than an *expectation;* for though the prospect is a delightful thing to dream about, it seem *too delightful* almost to seriously look for its becoming reality. And for my own part I am not so accustomed to out of the way enjoyments as to be surprised at not recieving them. Yet thy saying that thee is not willing yet to give up entirely the idea of the journey affords us still some encouragement, and knowing that you *wish* to come, anxious as we are to see you, we cannot urge you to do so against your interests.

The country at this time looks most beautiful; the openings are not covered so profusely as they were with flowers, two or three weeks since, but they are still almost, or quite, numberless, and I am never weary of admiring the beautiful green of the trees and openings. Brothers wheat is in head, and looks finely. Its smooth, wavy surface presents a beautiful contrast to the bushy openings.

Uncle Darius C. and his wife have not started yet for York State, and it is quite uncertain what time they will go. Aunty Sally expects to set off next first day, in company with several other persons from here, and Adrian.

I suppose our *library* will reach Adrian sometime this week. I want very much to know what books they have got, and how many. I think the selection will be a good one; novels are excluded. The character of the people here is decidedly intelligent, and that in no very trifling degree. That they are a reading people may be inferred, both from the circumstance of their taking so easily an opportunity to furnish themselves with materials for it, and from the quantity of newspapers taken and supported in the Territory. There are five weekly papers published in the Territory, all of which have a general circulation here;[28] papers from Philadelphia, New York State, Boston, &c are also taken by several. As a necessary consequence of this, and the pains taken to secure a good education, *bumpkins* are very rare, and the young people are growing up respectable and intelligent, and with a far greater degree of intellectual superiority generally than we met with in many neighborhoods in Pennsylvania, when the advantages might be supposed to be greater. I have also noticed with pleasure the general absence of all petty meanness and closeness, and in several instances that have come under my notice, of that of a disposition to take no advantage of the scarcity of an article to demand an exorbitant price for it.

Brother took about a day this spring for an *exploration* through the woods in search of ornamental trees of several sorts of a suitable size for planting round our *cottage*. He procured a number of the sugar maple, and some other very pretty trees most of which look very flourishing, and will when they grow a little larger be a great improvement to the looks of the house, and if I could get any body to send me a slip or two of honey suckle, of which I believe there is not a bit in the territory, to clamber about the door and windows, I think in process of time it would look pretty. Tell Ann her robin's nest is gone; what destroyed it I know not, but I felt quite sorry about it.

A new road has been lately laid out, which is rather nearer to us than the old one. Brother is Path-master and next week I suppose will muster the men for working on it, after which it will be more generally used.

SECOND DAY MORNING—

I have kept thy letter open and unfinished longer than I expected. With respect to the Indian affairs, I believe I have nothing more to inform thee of them, and have only to add to not be in the least uneasy about us; we consider ourselves in no danger from them at all. We yesterday dined and drank tea at Samuel Satterthwaite's in company with John Lovett and his wife. Their family was well.

My mulberry seeds were so long coming up that I began almost to despair of seeing them, and to feel a sort of growing enmity towards the whole tribe, but the plants now look very well, and though the seeds have not all come up, I think I shall have a respectable number of trees, and I think it not unlikely that some more of them may yet make their appearance above ground. Some of them I expect are an inch and a half high, some of them yet very small; but they all look healthy.

We have not yet anything better than worm fences to boast of round our house and garden but I hope by next season brother may be able to prepare a paling for the latter, as it will look much neater and be better. But the farm is of far the most consequence and must be attended to first.

In addition to the articles mentioned in my last, we should like to have a couple of shillings worth of *free sewing cotton* which I then forgot to mention; and if you should come out yourselves or an opportunity offers that thee can send them without any inconvenience I should like to have fifty or a hundred quills; they are among the rarest and dearest things in Michigan, and by cutting off the tops would not take a great deal of room. One dollar per hundred is the price here for very inferior ones. For these, as well as other items, I hope at least, we may have the opportunity of settling with thee personally before the summer is over. If not, as thee is not near enough to dun us very frequently, I do not know but we may take a little longer credit.

Aunt Sally Comstock left here for York State on a visit yesterday; I think it scarcely likely that Darius and his wife will go this season, as they think they can hardly make their arrangements so as to leave home.

We just got home last first day from meeting, so as cleverly to escape one of the heaviest showers I have almost ever seen. One minute's exposure to it would have drenched a person completely. Since April (which here this season seemed completely to have changed its character) we have had frequent showers, which with the warm sunshine, has been very favorable to the growth of vegetation.

Please give our love to our dear Aunts, and to cousin Anna Guest; also to Aunt Amelia E. and to Ann and with much love to Uncle and thyself I remain very affectionately thy niece

E.M.C.

We are all well. I hope you are the same.

It would afford brother a great deal of pleasure to escort Uncle over his farm, and I doubt not but it would be reciprocal; and I cannot say that I should have much objection to perform the same part by thyself. We have a beautiful place that is certain, but description can give you at best but a very uncertain idea of its appearance. I intended to have sent a sort of sketch of our house to you by S. Marot, if I had had time to take one, but I was then very much hurried as I had also the G.U.E. [Genius of Universal Emancipation] to attend to just at that time; and besides I was much in hopes that you would shortly see it for yourselves. But a picture would not, even if it were done well, look nearly so well as the life; because the place should be seen *whole* to show to advantage. Merely the house and its worm fences would possess little of the picturesque, but might to you notwithstanding be more interesting than a handsome view of another spot.

There is not much *romance* about our scenery—at least not the romance of rocky and water scenery. Yet even the most indefatiguable tourist who had spent season after season "a being a seeing of waterfalls" could not I think but be struck with the peculiar character of our country, and give it credit for the perfect beauty of repose. There are some parts that remind me of Pennsylvania, but much of it is quite different in its appearance. That immediately about our home is so—but though it might be more beautiful for the presence of water within sight of the house, still it is beautiful without it.

JANE HOWELL *to* RUTH EVANS
Philadelphia, July 25, 1832

My dear Sister

I have intended writing to thee for a long time past, but some how or other, I always find my letters addressed to Elizabeth. She is such a dear good girl in writing to me, that I feel myself in duty bound, as far as I can, to answer her very interresting letters. I received a letter from our dear William a few weeks since, also a present of a very nice ham, of his own raising and curing, which doubly enhanced its value with us. They were all well. Little Tom grows finely, and their neighbours say he is a very pretty boy. I wrote to Sally for the first time by the same conveyance.

Hannah Pierces health is better than it has been for a long time. Maria Woodside has closed her business, and gone with her Uncle to Washington to spend the summer, and perhaps longer if she likes it. Her health is very delicate, and Doctor Shoemaker recommended her going into the country during the warm weather. Cousin Betsy Morris departed this life the 15th day of last month. She was attacked about two weeks before with her old complaint, in which she appeared to suffer very much. She was deprived of speech, and almost of recollection until a very short time before she died. Her daughter Elizabeth was married about a week after, to Samuel Canby of Wilmington.

In my dear Elizabeths last letter, she says you apprehend no danger from the Indians. I was delighted to hear it, for I was very fearful they would invade the Territory or that there would be some skirmishing amoung them, for indeed I think they are such a revengeful people when they feel themselves wronged, that they will invent many ways for retaliation. They do not appear to discriminate between those who have injured them, and those who have not. All appear to come under their vindictive spirit. Yet I do consider them a very abused and injured people, driven about almost as a football, looked upon hardly as rational beings, their rights trampled upon, and they, who were once exclusively the proprietors of the soil, are now almost banished from their native country. Let many that pride themselves on being called Christians blush at their conduct towards them. Let them feel with full force, the grevious injuries which they have sustained by them, and let them make them a suitable remuneration, or else, they deserve no better name, than that of the Heathen they so much despise.

I have not seen Samuel Merritt since the first evening he called here. I do wish he would come again that I might ask him more, and repeat the same questions to him that I did when he was here before. Repetition is tiresome to most people, but I do not care how often I cross-question those who came from Hazlebank. Aunt Amelia Guest intends writing to you soon. She is nearly as well as when you left here. Aunt Anna enjoys excellent health, and takes a very lively interest in your welfare. They desire a great deal of love to you. I have not seen Emilys Mother yet to give her her letter.

The public mind has been a good deal excited from the apprehension that the cholera may make its appearance in this city, but every precaution is used to prevent it if possible. The board of Health and a committee of five men to every square, are very vigilent in closely examining into, and causing to be removed any filth or nuisance, which may come under their notice, and I sincerely hope, that by the adoption of those measures the city may become so well cleansed, that should it make its appearance, its progress may be arrested in a very short time. Our Physicians advise the citizens to clothe themselves warm, to sleep under a blanket, avoid the night air, exposure to the sun at noon day, and to refrain from eating many kinds of vegitables such as cucumbers, cabbage, beets &c &c which I as an individual strictly adhere to, and I hope you will do the same my dear Sister. The old adage, an ounce of prevention is worth a pound of cure, should be regarded by us at this particular time. I do not know of one case of the disease in the city at present. I do hope it may continue in the same way. I do not think much milk should be used in familys nor any thing else that will sour on the stomach.[29] All these things I know thy prudence will dictate to thee my dear Sister.

Samuel Lovett has just left here. He says he has received a letter from John and that you are well. I feel very much indebted to John for the care he takes in mentioning you in his letters. It often relieves me from a great deal of anxiety about you. Please give him my thanks and tell him, his parents and friends are well.

I was very much pleased to hear that your winter grain was likely to turn out so well. I hope all your other crops may do the same. Do tell me all about them when you write. I am glad to hear that so many of Elizabeth's mulberry seeds have come up. I hope they may grow fast, and that she may experience much pleasure and amusement in raising her silk worms, and that her trouble, or rather labour, may be amply rewarded. I had written a very long letter and mustered together a number of little articles, besides the things Elizabeth wrote for, to send them in Samuel Lovetts box, which he was going to forward on to his son John, but he has declined sending it on at present, and we shall have to wait, or look out for another opportunity.

John Merrefields youngest son about five months old, and called after himself, died on seventh day and was buried yesterday; he was ill but two days with dropsey on the brain. It is a great tryal to John and Anna. Rebecca Guest is going to be married to a young man in Baltimore [Aquila Giles]. He is I believe great grandson to Jacob Giles, cousin [to] Betsy Morris' grandfather. It is very pleasing to all parties. Rebecca was on a visit to Baltimore at the time he made proposal of marriage to her. He brot her home in style to ask her mothers consent, which thee may think was readily granted. I suppose it will take place in the Fall. Amelia Guest continues at housekeeping. Her brother Jonathan says, she looks like a little old woman; her health is very delicate. Hannah Roberts spent an afternoon and night with us last week. She desired her love to thee.

O I wish it was so that I could invite thee to put on thy bonnet and take a walk with me to the western part of the city. I should enjoy the surprise which would be expressed on thy countenance at the wonderful improvement which has been made since thee left us. The novelty of the Railroad which commences at the junction of Spring Garden Street and Ninth attracts daily many thousand of the inhabitants, some to see the elegant cars, which carries passengers to and from Germantown, and others to enjoy the ride, which indeed appears as something as sailing.[30] There is a very large three story brick house built at the corner of Green and Ninth Street, and occupied as a Hotel, which rents for one thousand dollars a year, and is generally crowded with people. Ground is rising rapidly in value, and blocks of very pretty brick houses are going up fast in that neighbourhood.

I often think that you have greatly the advantage over me, for when my imagination pays a visit to Hazlebank, she no doubt deceives me grossly by her misrepresentations, as to the general face of the country, your house, farm, out houses, cattle, improvements &c &c, but as I have never had an occular demonstration of the facts as they really are, I shall have to depend a while longer on her caprices. But you have only to turn your thoughts to No. 477 North Second Street and there you may see us, just about as you left us, except that we have our middle room papered, and painted. I wish I had paper enough left for a curtain for thee, but as I have not I will send thee a little piece when I have an opportunity that thee can fancy better how we look at home. Thee may think me very childish, but in such things I admit I am, for I delight in any thing like a remembrance, when I am parted from those I love, and I am apt to think others are like myself in that respect.

I called to see cousin Anna Guest a short time ago. She was well. I think she seems more reconciled to the loneliness of her situation. She desired me when I wrote to give her love to you. Tell my dear nephew that all his friends here give him a great deal of credit for his great industry, and good management in farming. I hope he will be careful not to expose himself too much, or work beyond his strength. When I heard your kind friends, Darius Comstock and wife, had declined going to New York state this summer, I felt very glad on your accounts, for I thought you would feel their absence from home very much, and as the cholera prevails in many parts of the state, I should have felt apprehensions for their safety. I hope Aunt Sally may return in good health to her friends.

I suppose by this time the Library at Adrian is established. I hope it may consist of books from which its readers may derive the greatest amusement and instruction. I was very much pleased to hear it was to be located so near you, and that novels are excluded, for there are very few in my opinion that pays for the loss of time in reading them.

Robert Coes family are all well. Anna is waiting impatiently for her manuscript from Elizabeth. Lemuel is very anxious to go to see his mother and friends in the country, but he says he will not go unless I accompany him, and then we are to go to the sea shore. If we go I expect it will be in the course of a week or ten days. I have not quite made up my mind about it yet. Tell Elizabeth she need not throw out any more of her enchantments (in grand descriptions of the country about Hazlebank) to draw me to Michigan this summer for to tell the plain truth I do not think I shall come. Perhaps Lemuel may accompany Samuel Lovett in the Fall if he is not too full of business, and it should be healthy thro the country. We are all in our usual health and with much love from Lemuel, Ann, and myself, I am affectionately thy sister

Jane Howell

Amelia [Evans] is in Bucks County, where she intends spending a few weeks. Neighbour Herregas desired her love to you. She gave me several little presents in glass ware to forward on to you from her, when there is a private opportunity.

———◆———

ELIZABETH CHANDLER *to* JANE HOWELL
{Hazelbank}, n.d. {August 1832}

I have just, my dear Aunt, finished off a number of the G.U.E. [Genius of Universal Emancipation] and in spite of some weariness of the pen, and a headache which has been persuading me to take a nap, I have continued at my desk to commence a reply to thy last letter. The increase of Cholera, mentioned by the papers in Philadelphia, makes us feel very anxious respecting our friends there, though the circumstance of its selecting its victims so generally from the imprudent or dissipated and worthless, renders us much easier respecting you, as we know it can have no claims on any of you on the one score, and we hope you will not suffer it to have on the other. Still it will be a great comfort if thee will write frequently. Its continuance I most earnestly hope will not be a long one in your city, and from the precautions that have been taken, and the genial cleanly character of the place, I think it surely will not. Our own neighborhood continues healthy.

Brother has harvest[ed] his crop of wheat successfully, and has reason to be well satisfied with it. It is of a most excellent quality, and I wish thee, and some of the others of our friends in P. who take an interest in our concerns, could eat some of the beautifully white bread it makes. It was quite a "brag" crop, for the first season. Our pumpkins do not flourish so well as last year. It is not so good a season for them. The corn looks considerably better that brother anticipated, for new land, and of potatoes also he expects to get a good crop. As to our domestic affairs, we have had reasonably good luck with our poultry, and have not had our churning "bewitched" more than once during the season.

Aunt Sally Comstock has not returned yet, but is almost daily expected. We learn that she has had the ague since she has been in York State, which must have deprived her of much of her expected enjoyment.[31]

I am glad to hear of R. Guest's engagement. I hope she may be settled happily. I should suppose Amelia[Evans]'s delicate health but ill-suited to the cares of her business, which must I think involve considerable anxiety in its duties.

We shall be highly gratified to recieve another letter from dear Aunt Amelia Guest. We feel very sensible of her kindness in writing and grateful for it. But her heart is all kindness. I do hope they may all keep well during the summer.

If thee paid thy talked of visit to the sea shore, I suppose thee has hardly more than returned by this time, but as the wrapper of the last "Post" was directed in thy hand writing, we concluded thee had probably declined going.

I think it probable that Maria Woodside's health will be benefitted by her visit to Washington, and that she will derive much pleasure from it. I should for my part prefer Michigan and an air of *freedom,* to the tainted breezes of our Seat of Government, though with that exception I think it likely it may be a pleasant enough plan. Folks begin to talk about having our Territory converted into a state; and the subject may perhaps be brought before Congress next winter.[32] To me as an individual it is a matter of very little consequence.

We have not recieved a letter from Brother William this long time, but I am glad to hear from thee that my dear little nephew grows finely. I do want to see him exceedingly. I dare say he is a pretty child. I suppose we shall again be disappointed this fall about seeing William, but I would not wish him to come unless the country was healthy through which he must travel.

We are quite pleased to hear that neighbor Harrigas still remembers us; please return her our thanks and transmit our love to her. If Uncle and Samuel Lovett do come out this fall I will try to have a big packet of letters to send back by them. I begrudge monstrously to be obliged to suffer a private opportunity to pass without being able to send as many letters as I wish.

When thee sees my friend Hannah Townsend, please give my love to her and ask her if she will not write to me soon. Tell her I want a letter from her very much, and when she writes I want her to tell me whether Java coffee is the production of *free* labour.

I hope aunt Amelia Evans's health may be benefitted by her excursions into the country, but I hope she will not expose herself to the night air, which the physicians say is, particularly at this time, prejudicial to health.

Brother mowed the most of his hay this season on a prairie several miles from home, so that for about a week we had the pleasure of seeing him only in the mornings and evenings. He has since then been making preparations for getting some of his own land in grass, which will be a great advantage to him. He hopes to be able to mow some of his new meadow land next summer. The strip of land which he sowed last fall with grass seed, on the openings, looks very well and I hope by another season will yeild some hay. He is now busy threshing. One of his neighbours has already engaged his seed wheat of him, and there is no doubt but that he will meet with a ready sale for all he has to spare. He expects, I believe next week to commence harrowing the ground for what is to be sown this fall.

The weather generally this summer has been cool and pleasant though we have had some warm days; and there has been as yet a sufficiency of rain. While brother was abroad at his hay, there were several showers which we apprehended would give him a ducking, but they were uniformly so slight where he was at work, though heavy with us, that he escaped, with the shelter the wagon afforded without a single wetting. There were several of the neighbours at work at the same place, which made it much pleasanter. One of them worked in partnership with T. and they rode out together in the morning, with all the appurtenances of their business, turned their cattle out to graze and returned in the evening in the same style. Carts seem quite unknown here; I have not seen one since we came into the territory.

I wrote till dusk last evening, and then laid aside my pen till the return of daylight. I take it up now only during a short intermission of my morning's employments. A most delightful morning it is! I wish thee was here, to look out with us at the landscape in its still and motionless beauty, and to ramble along one of our winding paths that lead off into the depth of the green solitude. I do not know that our country will be so interesting to me in its natural character when it becomes more cultivated, but it certainly now possesses a charm, for me, at least, which I feel that I can very inadequately describe.

I have no doubt but the rail-road mode of riding presents great attractions to our good citizens, but I think it must be too rapid for much enjoyment except only as a novelty—for a person of my gravity at any rate. I at least like to have time to think and to breathe as I am whisked through life. But business folks will no doubt find them very advantageous.

John Lovetts family were well when we last heard from them. They have dined with us since I wrote last, and we have been talking something of returning their visit tomorrow. But I do not yet know how it will be.

It is afternoon. Will thee step in and "talk a bit?" Aunt Ruth looks as if she was very much interested in a volume of "Josephus,"[33] but I dare say she would lay it by with pleasure, to welcome thee, and if thee wants to see if thee would recognize thy former nephew, we will send Emily over to Jacksons barn to summon him home. Thee says thee cannot be certain that thee is quite correct in thy notions of our homestead, I hope then it will be an additional inducement for thee to come, "when the proper time comes," as aunt Ruth sometimes tells Emily, and take a look at it. I should be mighty glad if that "proper time" would come reasonably early when you could pay a happy visit to Hazlebank. It is a comfort amidst our disappointments to hold it still in prospect for sometime.

The front part of our house looks quite pretty with the vines that creep round the door and over the windows. Every morning gives us a fresh and luxuriant show of "Morning Glory's" which contrary to the usual transient character of their beauty, sometimes (as they have the benefit of shade for half the day) remains in bloom throughout the whole day. The Tulip roots thee sent us, did not do very well this spring, but perhaps by another season they may get more naturalized. Some of my mulberry trees are nearly half a yard in height, and appear in very good health.

I believe I forgot to tell thee that brother has made us a milk house, which as we have no cellar is a very great convenience.[34] Our house inside remains pretty much as at my last description and I do not recollect that there have been any important alterations that I have not told thee of, out doors.

Aunt R. has just been reading over my letter (which is more than I expect to do myself) and she tells me it seems to contain very little information—and has thrown out a hint that it would be best to occupy my remaining paper to better purpose. My reply was a question whether she would have me to coin events, for really there are so few transpire worth mentioning, that though I am perfectly sensible of the poverty of my letters in that respect, I can think at present of no other remedy—and that is one which I expect thee would not feel very thankful to me for applying.

SECOND DAY MORNING.

We did not go to Lovetts yesterday. We had company at home. And nothing at all interesting has I believe occurred since I laid aside my letter. Brother this morning commenced harrowing this morning (or rather a boy whom he has engaged for that purpose) for winter grain. The price of wheat for this season is not yet entirely settled; but it will probably be a dollar. Brother had an offer of 75 cts for fifty bushels, but declined taking up with it. There is little doubt but that he will dispose of to much better advantage, for its quality is such that it will command the highest price in the market. A dollar was its price last year, when we first came out it was seventy five cents.

I was obliged this morning to postpone the completion of my letter by the arrival of company. They have just gone, and I am again at my station at the desk, very dutifully leaving aunt Ruth to wash up the tea-things. Brother has just returned from his work on his meadow land, and is about going over to Comstock on an errand and if I add that Em is about her evenings work of getting kindling stuff for the morning's fire, feeding chickens &c. thee will have an idea of all our employments, just at the present time.

The second anniversary of our leaving Philadelphia and coming here has past. It seems strange sometimes to think it is so long, and at other times, it seems as though half a dozen years might have passed since then. We have however to be thankful that they have left no dark traces of grief or misfortune.

If I thought I should be able to fill one of thy big sheets, in journalizing, by the time of wanting to send it, I would attempt it; if however, I do so, thee must make allowance, for the homebred incidents and trifling remarks that I foresee, will form the character of much of its contents. I hope thee will write soon after recieving this, and I will endeavor not to keep thee waiting long for an answer.

Brother was yesterday afternoon at a "raising" across the river. He has assisted at a great number this season. It is often rather inconvenient for him to leave his business to attend to them but as it usually requires as many hands as can be raised, he thinks it no more than right to make some sacrifice of his own time to assist a neighbour. The earliest settlers I think must have found it quite a tax, for living here so much longer they must have had so many more to assist at, and find no exemption by the increase of inhabitants, now. The older settlers are now building themselves barns, and some of them better houses, and the new comers, want dwellings to live in, so that it makes raisings very frequent.

I hope tomorrow to get a Post from Comstocks; we feel very anxious to hear from Philadelphia. Oh how I hope it may contain favorable accounts respecting the Cholera! I have tried several times over at Comstocks to get sight of the late "Friend" when our own papers were not there, but I believe they have not recieved any late ones, or none within two or three weeks. Sometimes they reach here a week after their date, and sometimes, as at present, are I suppose in some way detained on the road.

The Post is a very interesting paper, and contains so much, that thee can readily imagine how eagerly it is welcomed; especially when it contains assurances of the general health of the city. Besides it is something that comes from there — thee has handled it, and read it, and it is from thy hands that we recieve it, seeming still almost to retain some virtue from the touch, and it seems even to speak of you, and to give us some assurance of your welfare. It is here in "the Backwoods" a most valuable friend.

I had last week a gentle spell of the swelled face and jaw ache, but my cheek has now quite recovered its natural proportions. Thee may well smile at this as I have no more serious calamity to communicate.

Tell Ann that the little humming birds very often visit our door and windows, with the whirring music of their rapid wings—like scraps of a rainbow torn off the arch and rolled up into a narrow ball. Dear little creatures, I allways was fond of them, ever since when as a very little girl I can remember watching them flitting round the honeysuckles in our yard in Market St.

There have been some changes in Second St. since we left Philadelphia. I think the removal of Williams's must have seemed to make considerable difference for a while, as they had lived there so long; and it must have seemed strange to Coes at first to have strangers next to them. But suppose these changes are quite familiar to you now, though to us, if we were to visit Philad. they would still be new. But I expect there are many parts of the city that we could scarcely recognize. Think thee will recognize Hazlebank when thee sees it? Or must we introduce it?

We desire to be affectionately remembered to all our friends, and we feel gratified by the words of remembrance from them, which wecieve through the medium of thy letters. We are all well. And I, though I have scarcely left space so to subscribe myself, am very affectionately thy neice

E.

JANE HOWELL *to* RUTH EVANS
Philadelphia, August 22, 1832

My dear Sister

You are undoubtedly very anxious to hear from us, at this time particularly; and I have the pleasure to inform thee that we are well. We still continue in the city, and likewise all our friends, except Cousin Anna Guest who is now boarding at Chesnut Hill, with Elizabeth Paul. She has taken Patty with her. We have a place to go to in Bucks County in case there is a necessity to go, and also our dear Aunts; but as the cholera appears to be fast subsiding I feel a hope that we shall be able to stay at our respective homes, for excepting this disease I think the city now, is much more healthy than the country. I received a letter a few days since from my dear kind friend Hannah Roberts with a very pressing invitation to come with my family, and continue with them, until the city became healthy. If they would take us as boarders, and we were inclined to leave home, it would be a delightful place to go to, but as it is, I feel very much indebted to her for her kindness, and care for us.

I received a letter from our dear William. They were well. Samuel Lovett lodged one night here, last week. They were all about in their usual health. We are always very much pleased to see him. We can talk about Michigan and some of its *inhabitants* without ever tiring. It is a subject which never wears out. Our dear aunts are well, and desire their love to you. I do not feel at all in debt to thee for *letters,* and as I am always glad to have a plea for writing short ones. I shall avail myself of it, at this time, knowing that a few lines will be more acceptable than none at all, so thee must excuse the blank paper with an assurance that it is for want of time to fill it. Amelia [Evans] is in Bucks County. I received a few lines from her yesterday. She was well.

I must now ask the reason why none of you have written for such a great length of time. Is it because you think we have left the city, and you do not know where to direct your letters? If so, we are in the same old spot No. 477 North

Second Street, and I shall expect very speedily to hear from you, or rest assured I shall feel *very very* anxious about you. With much love from Lemuel, Ann and myself to you all I remain affectionately thy sister

Jane Howell

When you write, tell me wether Aunt Sally Comstock has returned from York State. I have felt anxious about her for fear she should have an attack of the cholera and wether Uncle Darius and his wife set off on their journey. I hope they did not. They were undecided about it when Elizabeth wrote last. I hope soon to have a private opportunity to send on the things you wrote for.

———— ◆-◆ ————

BENJAMIN LUNDY *to* ELIZABETH CHANDLER
Union Village, Ohio, September 6, 1832

Esteemed Friend:

Yesterday I was highly gratified by the receipt of thy well filled and interesting packet, mailed at Adrian on the 27th ultimo. Had it reached me a little sooner, I should have issued the first No. of Vol 13 at Cincinnati. But as I had nothing for thy department, I put out another *extra half sheet,* to let our patrons know the cause, in part at least, of the delay in publishing the paper. Thee will have received that Extra, no doubt, before this comes to hand. Tho I could have wished that my letter had reached thee sooner, that I could have had them at an earlier day, for the purpose aforesaid, I do not know but it will, after all, be best as it is; for I have just concluded an arrangement which will make it very agreeable to begin the new volume subsequent to it.

Thee will be pleased to learn, that I have succeeded in engaging the assistance of *another coadjutor* in the good cause, who will immediately repair to Washington, and superintend the publication of the paper whenever I may be absent. (I do not take him into *partnership,* but employ him to assist me at a stipulated salary.) And if, upon a fair trial, he shall determine to continue with me—as he now calculates on doing—he will, occasionally travel and deliver lectures, while I attend to the business at home, myself. Thee is impatient to know who it is? Probably thee is not acquainted with him, personally; tho thee certainly has some knowledge of his family. His name is *Samuel Yorke Atlee.* He is a brother of *Dr Edwin I Atlee* of Philadelphia—one of the most decided and *active* friends of our cause in that city, and, also one of the most particular and intimate friends that I have, to my knowledge. Samuel has received the benefit of a good education; and, for a few months, has done something in the way of practicing Law, in Cincinnati. But the competition being great in that place, and as many eminent lawyers were already located there when he commenced, he found that, in order to succeed, he must pursue a course of *management,* which the native honesty of his heart revolted at. To use his own language, in a letter to his brother, announcing his determination to join me in my public labors: "Such a thing as a poor, *honest* lawyer, must be a rarity, even if it be possible for one to live, in this country." This is the purport of what he said if not the precise words expressed. He is a well loved, decent, and talented young man; and I hope much from his co-cooperation—if, indeed, he do not (like all the rest—*thyself excepted*) quit me at the end of *six months,* or sooner!"[35] We may indulge the hope that, as our cause becomes more popular, the public mind will be more sensibly impressed with its high importance; and under these circumstances, some more *honest* hearts, that yet be dormant, will be roused to action.

Thee wishes to know something of my past "adventures," since we saw each other, as well as my present prospects. The limits of a reasonable sized letter will not contain the *twentieth part* of what I wish to tell thee!—and then, it would take a long time to *write* it.—But, briefly:

After leaving Cincinnati last spring, I placed all my papers in safe hands, put on a rough dress, procured a knapsack, adopted the cognomen of "*J. Iynul,*" and plunged into the "lion's den" of slavites, slave traders, and all the devils in human shape that infest those "nether regions," the slave Golgothas of the South! (Perhaps I am on too high a *key,*—but thee must not expect much *madination,* if I *must* speak at all on this subject.) I went to Louisville, Ky., and from thence to Nashville, and Columbia, Tennessee. At the two last named places I found some cordial friends, who kindly "wished me well" in a very significant way, (to a pretty smart *amount,* &c.) and bade me "God speed" with the honest aspirations of prayerful hearts. From Nashville, I went by Steam Boats, as a *deck* passenger, to New Orleans. As there were no vessels going, *soon,* to either of the Texas ports, I got a passport of the Mexican Consul for "*J. Iynul,*" to Nacogdoches, via Natchitoches, on the Red River. I was detained at N.O. [New Orleans] nearly two days, and then took a *deck* passage again on a Steam Boat. It was a *rough* kind of accommodation, and every *gunman*—and *lady* too—looked upon me with quite as much *contempt* as they did upon the negroes and even the *dogs.* I was glad of it! (Thee need not laugh, for I *certainly was,* as it saved me the unwelcome task of conversing with many of them, and avoided, perhaps some exposure.) When I reached Natchitoches, I shouldered my knapsack and *footed* it 120 miles to Nacogdoches, in Texas. The latter place is 70 miles beyond the line between this republic and that of Mexico. The first night, I found comfortable lodging; but the second I had to encamp with some creole tramsters. In the night there came up a violent thunder storm, and I crept under one of the waggons, for a shelter. I had not been there long before a surly great *Dog* came and disputed my right to *that place!* However, he was a pretty *reasonable Dog* and somewhat kind withall, and contented himself with barely room for his own accommodation. He laid down by my side, and we had no further quarrel. I *rested* poorly that night. I made several other *encampments* afterward, but I *have not room* to tell of all, here. Before I reached Nacogdoches, an alarm was spread that the insurrectionists (of whose movements thee has, doubtless, already heard) were marching towards the place, and some said that I would not be suffered to pass, even if they did not put a gun in my hand and make me assist in defending the garrison. I halted, a couple of hours at one time, to consider the matter; but then determined to *go on,* at all hazards.[36]

When I arrived, the village was thronged with Indians, who had come, *armed* to assist in defending the fort. As I went along the street, numbers of people ran to me, enquiring the news, as they supposed from my appearance, that I came from the scene of turbulence below. There were many *elongated* phiz's[37] among them. I began to think, myself, that I should see some fighting. After changing my clothes, and taking some refreshments, I went to the Commander of the garrison. He could not understand my language, neither could I *his.* But, politely inviting me to take a seat, he sent for an interpreter. While the latter was coming, he ordered a bottle of wine, and bade me partake of it with himself and brother officers. We then *conversed a little,* by signs and naming places. The interpreter soon came, and we were enabled to understand each other better. Instead of throwing any difficulty in my way, he gave me to understand that I was at perfect liberty to go where and when I pleased. He treated me with a great deal of politeness, and the next day paid me a visit, in company with another officer. In the evening of the second day after my arrival, news came, by express, that all the disturbance below was at an end. Much rejoicing was the consequence; and those who wished, or those who *did not* wish it, saw no bloodshed.

I staid at Nacogdoches six days. With what I saw and what information I procured in other ways, I felt satisfied without going further. I have petitioned the government for a grant of land, and the privilege of colonizing 400 families. The citizens, to whom I communicated my design, approve it highly, and think I will succeed. I became acquainted with a very influential man, who was lately the Secretary of State [Lorenzo de Zavala]. He proffered his assistance, in the most cordial manner, giving me important information how to proceed. He also wrote to the governor, introducing me in the most flattering terms, and urging my proposition upon his attention. A very intelligent and respectable colored man seemed *overjoyed* when he learned the object of my visit. It was the *first* proposition ever made to open the door in that country for the admission of *free* colored people, and he said I might rely on it that there was no other place in the world so suitable for them. He walked with me a long distance, when I came away, and parted with the most ardent entreaties to persevere in my undertaking.

Returning home, I came 200 miles on *foot,* through the burning sun, and a part of that distance I went through settlements where half the people were *down sick.* I had to come via N. Orleans again, where the *yellow fever* prevailed, (tho not extensively), yet my health was excellent, the whole time, until I reached Louisville. Then, I took the *ague!* However, I soon stopped it, by the use of quinine, (essense of peruvian bark,)[38] and I am now well again.

I expect soon to go on via Lockport, N.Y., and Philad to Washington, where I shall be glad to hear from thee again. If Thomas can conveniently, he will much oblige me by sending my trunk, immediately, via Detroit, to care of *Isaac S. Smith, Buffaloe, N.Y.* If he will pay the expense of sending it to Detroit, I will see that it shall be refunded. The key may be fastened some way on the outside.

Thy last packet is an excellent one. Thank thee for "*Warner Miflin.*"[39] Please continue the "Sketches." Persevere, dear Sister—there is happiness in store for us.

I am now at the "Shakers" Village near Lebanon, Ohio, waiting to get our old friend, Aquila M. Botton, to translate a new Mexican Colonization Law for me. He is now a thorough going "Shaker." Did thee ever see any of these singular people? Nothing on earth will compare with this plain, unostentatious neatness and decency. (Did thee know that I. Marot, from Philad[a] keeps a tavern in this part of the country?).

> Sincerely, Thy Friend,
> B. Lundy

ELIZABETH CHANDLER *to* JANE HOWELL
{Hazelbank, September 1832; first part of letter missing}

. . . indisposition. She was to have been here for the purpose of looking over with me some paper relating to the subject of slavery, so that it was rather a disappointment.

I believe I have not mentioned to thee that brother, on a more thorough examination of his lot, has discovered that it contains a collection of thriving young maples sufficient in number to form quite a valuable sugar-bush. There are not a great many of them, but more than he supposed when he purchased the lot, and they of course add considerably to its value. Himself and his friend J[ohn].

H[unt]. (one of our visitors) walked down to thy to look at that end of his farm, and J. pronounced it a very fine little sugar bush, adding a wish for one such upon his own farm. The trees will be fit to tap in a year or two, when we may have sugar as well as wheat off our own land, and then tell me, aunt, when we send you up a specimen cake, that thee is *convinced thee will never like maple sugar!*

13TH—

We were disturbed several times last night by a racket among some of our chickens, but though brother went out he was unable to discover what it was that was in pursuit of them. We expected to find in the morning a greater destruction among them than had really taken place, two or three only, and those of the smaller ones, being missing.

In the afternoon I went over to Uncle Darius's to return some borrowed newspapers, and on entering the house was informed that Aunt Sally had returned this morning from "York State." She seemed very glad to see me and quite pleased by thy enquiring about her, which I mentioned. Uncle D. and his wife have quite given up the idea of going this fall. Aunt Sally seems in very good spirits and good health. She has been expected for some weeks past. She says she went to the post office many times while she was about in hopes of recieving a letter from me, as she had requested me to write, before she left me, but before I had leisure to do so, I understood that she was expected back the next week, and of course thought it unnecessary.

Brother enquires if this is a newspaper, and tells me I should call it the "Journal of the Times."[40] I replied with a hint for a contribution in the shape of a paragraph, but he would not. He is hard at work in his corn field. Probably he thinks that the sphere of his penmanship lies there at present. I suppose thee has before now recieved my last letter. One reason of my not writing sooner was the supposition that thee would probably be about at the shore; or at least this supposition rendered me more easy to a delay occasioned by the occupation mentioned in my last letter.

14TH—

Half clear, half cloudy. We talk this afternoon of paying the visit which was postponed on third day on account of the weather, and may perhaps be again for the same reason. It will be as they say "killing two birds with one stone" for there are two families to both of whom we owe a visit resident in the same house. One of them is the last arrival in the neighborhood, Smith Lain and family, who[se] land joins our and who will be our next neighbours. The wife, Abigail, is a preacher, *high proof orthodox.* They have one daughter just growing up, or grown up, who has been at our house and seems to have much desire to be well acquainted, and one or two others not much younger.

Caught our friends this afternoon at the washtub. They had put off washing on fourth day, on account of expecting us, next day was preparative meeting, and today they were obliged to set about it. However they had about finished, and said they should have been extremely so, but having to wait for the men to hawl them some water. One of the ladies was mopping the floor, but as we both had practiced at home, the sight was not one of much novelty. They expressed and seemed to feel much pleasure at seeing us even though it was "all on a washing day," and on our leaving them expressed their intention of returning our visit quite shortly.

15TH—

Brother still busy in his cornfield but with the expectation getting the remains of it cut off today, and his seed-corn selected. For ourselves, baking, churning, house cleaning &c all afoot. About the middle of the morning one of the pigs came home from the woods, with five pretty little youngsters at her heels, three of them closely spotted with black; and the others almost white. The only incident, I believe that occurred to day.

16TH—

We got to meeting early enough this morning to make up for our delinquency last first day. Brother did not go with us, but came up sometime after we had been seated in Satterthwaite's dearborn, and immediately behind them uncle D. Comstocks family in their new carriage. He procured it from "York State" and as it has just reached home, to day was its first appearance. It is a close carriage, and a very handsome one—one that would be called "stylish," even in Philadelphia, and contrasted rather strongly with the more numerous ox-wagon's that comport *"wilderness country"* as thee terms it. The first time we attended meeting in Michigan, the vehicle we rode in was I believe the only one there, and there was not more than one horseman, if that. Friend Comstock has had a dearborn, but he thought it too much worn for their extended journey.

Brother heard at meeting of the arrival of a family in the neighborhood from New York city. They expect to live about three miles from us, and are I believe, friends. All their relations in this neighborhood are so. We understood at Smith

Lains last week that there were four families at Detroit from York State on their way here. They will probably fix across the river, not far from us, where there are several of their relations.

17TH—

Mary Harris came over early this morning with her children to spend the day. *Little* Tom grows finely—he is not so large as some children of his age, but fat and very healthy, and very good. I do not remember that I ever heard him cry for five minutes at a time in the course of his life. His name makes him quite a pet with us. I went over to Comstocks after they left, but got only a "Liberator." I suppose, however, there will be another opportunity of hearing from the Post Office before long. It looks quite natural to see Aunt Sally Comstock at home again.

We heard today indirectly that a person from Pennsylvania had lately arrived at John Lovetts. No letters, I suppose, or they would have forwarded them to us, so we can conclude thee did not know of his coming. They have been expecting their father out this fall, but when we saw them last did not know certainly what were his intentions. We have not been to see them very lately, but intend going before a great while. It is rather a long walk for warm weather. The thermometer stood today at eighty five in the shade, which is much higher than it has been for some time past. Brother's wheat has been up for I believe these two weeks, or near it and grows finely, forming now quite a thick carpet of verdure.

18TH—

I think today has been even warmer than yesterday. When using much exercise the weather has been, as some of the folks about here would say, "quite tedious"—interpretation, quite *uncomfortable*—the word being used in an entirely different sense from what we give it. We have been at home and alone all day minding our work, like good children.

20TH—

"Monthly meeting" day, but not for us; nor a very pleasant one for any body. There was a gust last night, and to day has been damp and chilly with intervals of rain. Brother has been hawling off his corn shocks and fencing them in, to afford his cattle the use of the stubble field for pasture-ground; 'tis better than hunting them. Our little pigs grow nicely. I think they are [ ] or quite twice as big as they were when they first came home, and very lively. Brother says in about a week he expects they will be in all the mischief they can come across. He has been to day hawling his pumpkins. It has not been as good a season for them as last year, but he expects to have from a dozen to eighteen wagon loads. The cattle are exceedingly fond of them.

The next letter thee gets will probably be from Aunt Ruth. She has not forgotten that she is in debt to thee, though she has devolved the task of *telling nothing* so much upon myself. We want much to hear again from Philadelphia. Oh, how I wish thee would, if it was for once only, write in a letter as long as this. We so soon arrive at the end of one of ordinary length, and then there is such an ungratified longing for more! Read them over and over as often as we may, it will not lengthen them or add a single line that was not there before.

2 1ST —

A beautiful day. This afternoon we walked over to neighbour Comstocks to "set a bit." They are about getting their home papered. Three rooms by the hall and staircase, were completed, and the paperer was employed at the fourth.

By a number of the Friend of later date than our last Post, I percieve that the Cholera has so far abated that the Board of health have discontinued their Reports. This is indeed welcome intelligence.

Aunt Sally mentioned that yesterday at meeting, Certificates from York State, for *sixty one persons* were read. They must have had a busy time of it; and the meeting did hold, I think she said, till about 4 o clock. She has not yet been to see us since her return, but talks of visiting us before a great while.

Brother the other day brought up one of his corn stalks to the house as a premium. From the door sill it reached nearly to the eaves of the house—and he said there were many such and probably some taller, as he had not taken any pains in selecting it. For *new* ground (that is for the first year's tillage) it was not bad.

Would thee like to see a specimen of our Michigan newspapers? The idea just struck me that thee would like to know what manner of such things they can manufacture in this "*wilderness country*" and I will endeavor to get one or two for that purpose. We do not take any ourselves.

I should like thee to see what a fine big pile of yellow pumpkins there is before our window at the bottom of the yard. In general they are not as large as last year, but then some of them were enormous, and some of them this season are very large.

22D—

A blustery, fall-like day. Brother this morning commenced ploughing on his corn ground for the remainder of his wheat. This afternoon he expects to go to a "raising"—the house of our next neighbor on the north. If it was the raising of a house for his uncle L. Howell, now, *why I wouldn't mind helping to get some supper for the men!*

23RD—

Rode the greater part of the way to meeting with Samuel Saterthwaite and family—listened to two or three sermons—shook hands with a number of folks after meeting, and with a little coaxing I accepted an invitation to go home with an acquaintance, in company with two or three others. I had thought of going to Dr. Webb's, but as the girls were in company I could as well pay my visit there another time, which I expect to do next fifth day. The three or four other families who were expected on have arrived, and will shortly I suppose give the monthly meeting folks more business at reading certificates. The meeting house now is generally *filled full.* I think they will shortly have to set about the building of another.

24—

Though yesterday was a most splendid day, with scarcely even the shadow of a cloud, we were wakened this morning by the heavy pattering of rain, accompanied by some little thunder. Several heavy showers through the day have brought brother up from his work, to the house for shelter. The weather is cool again, and the frost has left the print of its fingers on some of the trees and bushes. They are not yet much changed but wear a sufficient tinting of sunset colours to make them beautiful.

25TH—

As I knew I could not take any letter over to Comstocks yesterday, I did not finish it, though I think it is almost time it was finished. We want another letter from Philadelphia badly, and I hope before long we shall recieve one in reply to my last letter. Tis a lovely morning and I expect shortly to carry over this long string of gossip to neighbour Comstock, as its final stage to Philadelphia.

Has thee heard any thing further of the folks who expected to come out here from Lancaster county? I wish somebody would come out from that way. I should love to hear particulars about brother, wife and family and to talk to some one who was acquainted with him. I should love a good packet of letters, too, *monstrously.*

There is room enough for "quite a letter" under the seal and tho I do not know that I have any thing in particular to say, I cannot afford to send blank paper. Please give our love to our dear Aunts and all our friends. It is an exceeding great comfort to know that you breathe again in a comparatively healthful atmosphere, but do not too suddenly abandon your habits of precaution. Emily wants to know if I will send her love to Mrs. Howell. She generally enquires when a letter comes, if there is anything in it about her mother. I do not know but there is more affection on her side than on that of the parent. I suppose Aunt Amelia E. has remained in the country during the Cholera season. Please give our love to her when thee writes. We are well

and with much affection I am dear Aunt, thy
E.M.C.

—— ◆ ——

JANE HOWELL *to* ELIZABETH CHANDLER
Philadelphia, October 2, 1832

I received thy letter my dear Neice about a fortnight since, informing me that you were all well. I have felt very thankful that you have not had the cholera in your neighbourhood this summer for when I heard it was in Detroit I felt very apprehensive for your safety, as its desolating influence seemed to be felt in the country as well as the cities thro which it has passed. You may now congratulate Philadelphia as being nearly rid of her troublesome guest, whose appearance caused dread and dismay throughout her inhabitants, whilst its rapid strides thro our streets laid low in the tomb many of the most respectable of our Citizens. Yet we owe a great debt of gratitude to the Great Disposer of Events that the evil has been so speedily averted, and that health is again restored.

I saw Hannah Townsend a few days since. She was well. She says she has written to thee, and is waiting a private opportunity as she has some pamphlets which she wishes to accompany the letter. She says Java Coffee is of free production as it comes from the East Indies. Hannah is going to be married soon, so her father told Lemuel but he did not say who to. I felt provoked that Lemuel did not interrogate him on the subject, that I might have told thee all about it. Samuel Lovett was here a few days ago. They were all well. He has almost declined going on to Michigan this Fall, but he still thinks he shall send on a box, which if he does, we shall pay part of the expense and send some things on in it.

I am delighted to hear that my dear nephew has been so successful in raising his crops. Such persevering industry will be amply rewarded, and I hope he may soon find himself on the high road to independence and health his constant companion. I heard from William a short time ago. They were well. Aunt Amelia Guest has been quite ill with Influenza which has prevailed here for a few weeks past, but she is now much better. Dear Aunt Anna enjoys good health. Cousin Anna Guest has returned from the country. She had an attack of Cholera Morbus[41] after she came home but from the timely advice of her Physician she soon recovered. Rebecca Guest expects to be married the ninth day of this month. The next day she is to set off for Baltimore. She is making great preparation. Cousin Anna Guest has given her silver plate to the amount of one hundred and ten dollars, viz, sugar bowl cream jug and slop bowl. Eliza Tunis is in bad health. She has complained of a sore throat ever since Thomas died. It appears to increase and the doctor is very fearful it will affect her lungs.

The Match between Young Dupont and Caroline Morris is broken off. I have not heard the reason of it. Jacob Morris and his wife have broken up housekeeping and are at boarding, he says it will be attended with less expense. His estate is worth at least sixty thousand dollars and he has one child. Is his poverty not pitiable? Emily's Mother was here a few weeks ago. I gave her letter from Emily. She wished me to break the seal and read it to her. I did so. She seemed quite agitated at first, but was very much pleased with it and was quite surprised that she could write such a good hand. She desired her love to Emily and says when I go to Michigan she will send her a beautiful Parosol with a flowered border around it.

Roy is one of the most playful little animals I ever saw. He is very fat and I think as active as ever. I often call over your names to him, and he will stop and throw back his ears as if he understood what I said to him. Maria Woodside is still in Washington. She has been ill with billious fever, but is now on the recovery. I have written a long letter to her and as soon as she is able she says she will answer it. Robert Coe is to be married to Eliza Broom in the course of a few weeks. She has attended in his store for several months past. I believe she is a clever girl and has some property. George Guest has just returned from Buenos Ayres, I have not heard wether he has made a prosperous voyage or not but I suppose he feels himself very fortunate, that he has got here in time for his sisters Wedding. Eliza Bind expects to be married shortly to Stephen Phipps. He is a Man that is highly respected and is supposed to be worth about one hundred thousand dollars. She has resigned the Yard-stick to her sister Anna.[42] I do not hear that either Amelia or Anna Coe has any particular suitors. They must take care or they will get on the Old Maids list. They are all in looks and health about the same as when you left them.

I should be very glad to receive a letter from thee written on one of those large sheets if thee has courage enough to undertake it, for be assured that if it is written ever so small, and the lines crowded it will appear but short at last for I am so desirous to hear all, and every thing about you, that a volume would hardly satisfy me. Amelia [Evans] is still in Bucks County. I received a letter from her a few days ago. She was well but did not say when she should return.

Thee has not said any thing about your Library at Adrian since its establishment there. I feel quite interrested in it, for if the books are well selected it will be a great acquisition to the neighbourhood and with you "twould tend to drive dull care away." I am very desirious to send thee a root or two of Honeysuckle if I should have a private conveyance. Some say they think they could not be carried so far to live but I think by putting the roots in a bladder and wetting the earth well and tying it closely up that they would go safe, be it as it will I think I shall try it, and at the same time I will send thee on some seeds. Cousin Anna Guest says she thinks they will bear flowers three years after planting. She desired to be affectionately remembered to you; whenever she sees me she inquires very particularly after you and if she hears that I have received a letter from you, she always asks me to bring it and read it to her, which I sometimes do. She seems very much altered since Cousin Betsy's death, so low spirited. I do not think I have seen a smile on her countenance since.

Sarah Lukins, Daughter of Sarah Pennock, died about two weeks since. She left three children the oldest a girl about seven years old, an Idiot who has never walked, another a fine little boy two years of age and the youngest about three months olds. I believe Sarah thought her disease was of the heart, something like assification,[43] but her Physicians could hardly make up their minds what it was, but they rather thought it was consumption, but I believe they were not allowed after death to ascertain the fact by opening her.

Robert Coe and Anna his wife set off yesterday to their place in Salem Co[unty, New Jersey]. I suppose they will stay a week or ten days. I hope the jaunt will benefit their health, for Cousin Robert has been weak and delicate ever since his attack of cholera this summer, altho it was but slight. Mary Guest, Acquilla Giles' sister, and Caroline Morris are to be brides Maids to Rebecca Guest. John Merrifield and Anna, and Amelia Merrifield are the only ones of the family that are to be at the wedding. I believe Anna Coe is a little hurt that James and Rebecca were not invited, as Rebecca Guest was brides maid at their wedding, and so nearly connected. Acquilla will bring two of his groomsmen from Baltimore, and George Guest will make the third. The Groom elect is about twenty three years of age quite small (Aunt Nancy says not bigger than Rebecca). He received a Salary of 7 or 8 hundred dollars a year in the bank. He is a young man of domestic habits and through economy has laid by sufficient to build himself a snug house on a lot which his father has given him. They are going to board with an Aunt in Baltimore until the house is completed.

When you write tell me what quantity of Potatoes and corn Thomas has raised this year. Do you raise sweet potatoes in Michigan? I should suppose the soil well adapted to their growth, and they are an excellent vegetable. If you have none, I could send on some small ones for planting.

Doctor Noble who has been attending Aunt Amelia Guest in her last indisposition says the common black walnuts are excellent for the consumption.[44] He says some years ago he fractured a blood vessel which threw him into very bad health, and by eating very frequently of the nuts, which he would have by his bedside at night, the fracture healed and he was restored to health. He mentioned several patients who came under his care with consumption who were entirely cured by the use of them.

We are all well. I do not think I shall talk any more about going to see you, until I really put it in execution for it appears to me exactly like grasping at a shadow. I feel quite provoked at Lemuel sometimes. He will come and sit down by me and talk about going to Michigan exactly as tho there were no ifs and buts in the way, and thee knows that I never bear disappointments gracefully.

{Jane Howell}

A little while ago I received thy last letter for which I was much obliged.

———◆———

RUTH EVANS *to* JANE HOWELL
Hazelbank, October 22, 1832

My Dear Sister

Thy last letter came to hand at a time when my mind felt much disquieted on account of my Dear friends in Philad[a], learning through the papers the Cholera had reached your city, and thinking it most probable it would spread, although much care was taken to prevent it. Yet I was fearful you would be in danger, and we so very remote from you, caused me many an anxious hour. Thee says our relatives are all in the city, except cousin Anna Guest. I think she can now return to her home with safety. I hope she is in good health. I have deeply sympathized with her, in her very severe affliction, and I doubt not, but she has had the consoling assurance, that her sister's pious life, has secured her an admission into that city, "whose maker, and builder, is God." And I hope, and humbly trust, Cousin Anna will feel reconciled to the loss of her Dear departed Sister, for He who calmed the waves of the sea, can also calm, and comfort, the troubled mind. I have had myself to pass through seasons of heart rending trials, but when favoured to look to the right source for support, and guided by the unerring light within, we may be able to surmount the most poignant grief, that the all Wise Creator may be pleased to Afflict us with.

Through Elizabeth's influence we have established an Anti-Slavery Society here.[45] Our first meeting was held at the meeting house two weeks ago. They are to be monthly. We suppose there will be about twelve new members at our next meeting. They heartily unite with it although perhaps may have seldom heretofore thought much on the subject. However, I trust they will endeavour to abstain from slave raised articles as much as practicable.

John Lovett and his wife five or six weeks since were taken extremely ill with billious fever, for about ten days.[46] There was little or no hopes of Johns recovery. The Physician was very attentive day and night, and I am now happy to say they have quite recovered. We expect them to spend a day with us shortly. Our country has been very healthy. I believe I have not heard of more than [ ] sick persons in this settlement, for six months past. There has been one case of cholera at Adrian owing to the woman eating a quantity of grapes, but did not prove fatal.[47] I believe a great number have fallen to that distressing disease by there own imprudence. The Cholera and Indian War, has been a great disadvantage to imigration this season. However a considerable number came and I believe every lot nearby is taken up.

Aunt Sally Comstock made a very pleasant visit to York State, this summer. She says if ever she should go there again, she will visit her friends in Hudson. Her niece Sarah Jenkins continues in the same ill state of health. Aunt Sally has a daughter in York State, who intends coming here next spring. She is very anxious to see Elizabeth. The Society is rapidly improving. Elizabeth has a very intimate friend in Julia Webb. She is about three years younger, and has a well informed mind. She is a very interresting girl, extremely fond of reading and has free access to Elizabeth's library. The books in the Adrian library, we believe have been selected with judgment, the price of a share is three dollars. Thomas procured one share by giving books to that amount. Since I commenced my letter we have had the pleasure of hearing again from our friends in P. Thy letter informs us of the health of all, except our dear Aunt Amelia [Guest]. Her feeble constitution seems unable to bear such repeted attacks of such a weakening complaint, but I hope when thee writes again which I trust will be soon, it will be in thy power to say she is quite restored to health. It is a great comfort to me dear Aunt Anna continues so well; at her advanced age it is unusual. I imagine they all look much as when I left, dear Aunt Nancy industrious as ever. Give my love to them, and also to Cousin Anna Guest.

I little thought my dear sister, when we parted from you, so much time would have elapsed without seeing thee, and Dear Lemuel at Hazlebank. However I trust it has been altogether for the best you did not undertake the journey this summer, as the country through has been very unhealthy. However, we must still anticipate a visit from you next year. We have had but one letter from William since the birth of his precious little boy. When thee writes to him, I want thee to tell him, Thomas and Elizabeth had written. We are fearful he has not received them, otherwise I think he would certainly have replyed to them. Thee says Amelia [Evans] is at Bucks County. I hope she will return before cold weather. I think she would be much more comfortable with you. Give my love to her. I hope she enjoys good health. In a former letter of thine thee wished me to inform thee, if I had quite recovered from a fall I had just before Sammy Lovett came out. I trust I can answer thy request in the affirmative.

Thee wishes to know how Thomas's corn, potatoes, &c. &c. have turned out this season. His corn far exceeded his expectations as it was planted in new ground. He put in but about half an acre of potatoes, which produced one hundred and fifty bushells. He has the best wheat that has been raised in the neighbourhood, all he has sold has been at one dollar per bushell, which is the current price for first rate wheat. Thomas has been very much hurried with business this fall. He is breaking up five acres for an orchard, which he will sow with oats in the spring. His neighbours are surprised he can effect so much with out any assistance. I have heard several say he would make a first rate farmer. He has put to fattan three large hogs. I suppose they will weigh eight hundred. He has one hog and six pigs to keep over.

Please tell Emily's Mother she is well. She is very anxious to write to thee, as soon as there is a private opportunity. She is a fine child and very useful. She desired her love to thee and Louisa. Thee dose not say how Ann's health is. I hope she has got [the] end of the rhumatism in her head. Tell her I think she would like Michigan much. She and I formed quite an erronious oppinion of the society here. They are realy quite refined, and pollished, for back woods. My love to her. How is Dear Aunt. Give my love to her, and also to Hannah Roberts.

11TH MO.

As thee may see from the last date of this letter it has been aside for some time. My reason for retaining it, was to say something more about Lovetts, as I have daily expected John and his wife here for some time. Still they have not arrived, however I presume I can say they are all well. They were when last I heard. I want thee to give our united love to Cousin Coe's. Elizabeth thinks it really singular Anna has not written to her. Elizabeth is also looking every hour for thy reply to her very long letter. I wish thee would write on those large sheets. If thee knew how often we go and send to Comstocks for letters, I think thee would not be willing we should so often be disappointed. However I believe we are too selfish. I think we cannot accuse thee of negligence in writing. The evening post, which I seldom took in my hand whilst living in the city, I now read with the greatest interest.

A few days ago we spent the afternoon and evening at Comstocks. Ann is a great favourite of mine, Aunt Sally is also a very fine woman. They want very much to see thee and Lemuel. They often remind me of my two dear aged Aunts. I hope before many days we shall have a letter from thee, that will inform us, my dear Aunt is in her usual health. I have realy felt very uneasy since I heard of her indisposition.

With much love to thy Dear L. and thyself, I remain thy affectionate Sister

Ruth Evans

The next letter I write must be to Amelia.
We are all well.
Remember me to neighbour Herregas.
Thomas has done all his breaking up for this fall. He intends in a few days to point our house inside. It has not been done yet. It is the prevailing custom here, not to finish there houses for two or three years, that more important business may be attended to such as breaking up, ploughing, draging, as it is called, fencing, &c. &c. I hope in one more year Thomas will be able to build a barn, which he will really need. We have however got along admirably. May I again enjoin thee to write frequently. I would we could hear from you every month. It would in measure console us for not seeing you this summer, when I think we shall not probably see you before midsummer next, the thought is really quite appalling.

ELIZABETH CHANDLER *to* JANE HOWELL
Hazelbank, December 13, 1832[48]

My dear Aunt

By the desire of Aunt R. I am once more seated at my desk for the purpose of commencing the manufacture of another scrap letter. And in the first place, for my own satisfaction, I must say, that we have been looking in vain for a letter so long that I feel right down impatient, and nearly downspirited, and Aunt R does not comfort me at all, for she says she is sure something must be the matter, as it is now more than two months since thy last letter was mailed. We were quite disappointed, too, on last fifth day afternoon when on paying a visit at John Lovett's, we found there a woman who had arrived only a couple of days before immediately from his father's house, and no packet for us. And such a delightful surprise, as it would have been, too, to have received one. Well I suppose there is no remedy but patience. But really my vial has very little remaining in at present, but some dregs that are not good for much and I do not think they will last much longer. Every body seems of the same mind, too, as I tell Aunt Ruth—Anna Coe—Brother Will—Hannah Townsend—nobody writes—and yet all of them, and thyself too, Aunt J. owes me a letter. I do not suppose that all this complaining will be very interesting to thee, but as I said before, it is for my *own* satisfaction. And having thus far relieved my mind I shall endeavor to make the rest of my letter satisfactory to thee. Oh if I was in Philadelphia and you in Michigan, what letters I would write!

We have had very fine weather this fall in Michigan, and it still continues so. The farmers are still ploughing, and may perhaps do so for some time longer. Brother went up to Tecumseh on fifth day to see about getting us some chairs, which thee may think we by this time need; he is to give wheat in return for them.[49]

17TH.

Yesterday we had a visit from a couple of friends who have recently removed into this neighborhood from Mount Pleasant, Ohio. Joseph Gibbons and his wife, and a young man from the same neighborhood, whose parents expect to remove here in the spring. They were accompanied by two of our old neighbours (I don't mean old people though) at whose house they at present reside. J. Gibbons is a Philadelphian, and has parents now residing there. He left Phil[a] about ten years since, but in the interim has paid several visits there, with his wife, the last of which was something more than a year ago. Since we have been there ourselves, I think we shall find them very agreeable neighbours. He has purchased land about two miles distant from us. Joseph {has plans} of delivering occasional lectures this winter at the schoolhouse, on Chemistry, Astronomy, and some branches of Natural Philosophy. The first one is to be delivered next fifth day evening. He has invited us to attend.

21ST.

No letter yet!—and we have been anxiously looking for one this six weeks I believe. What can be the reason—have we not cause to be uneasy? Brother expects to go to Adrian tomorrow, but I have almost given over looking for a letter. It seems as if we were to learn to do without.

1 MO. 1ST, 1833.

A happy New Year, Aunt! and the same to all the rest of you!

2ND.

Brother returned from Adrian last evening with the same old story—no letter. I feel very little in spirits to go on with mine, without there was some hope of hearing from you. We got papers however, which was some satisfaction, as our "Post" of last week tarried by the way till its brother came up, and left us more completely in the dark than usual. The mail does not come now as frequently as it did during the summer.

27TH.

Well, my dear Aunt, after expecting a multitude of wishes, wonders, sights, fears, and all the etcetera's of such matters, our anxiety is at last relieved by the reciept of a letter with the welcome intelligence that you are all well.[50] I have just finished taking my turn at reading it for the second time, and as thee sees have recommenced on my old sheet, for though the beginning is dated so far back, as it was on my large paper I did not like to throw it aside. Brother went up to Adrian this morning, and though we have been so often disappointed, that I scarcely dared to expect a letter, yet if he had not brought one this evening on his return, I believe we should have been downright *scared.* We really do like to get a letter now and then, for there are some folks in Philadelphia that I suppose we think about *at least as often as once a month,* and it [is] quite pleasant to learn occasionally how they are coming on.

Thee speaks of sending us weekly something like a substitute for a letter in the Post, and I am delighted to be able to tell thee that I expect we shall next summer be able to gratify thee in the same manner. We expect to have a newspaper published at Adrian. About a thousand dollars have been subscribed for setting up the establishment, and a printing press is to be procured as early as the navigation opens. An editor has not yet been procured or selected, but I hope we shall have a good paper, and be able to prove to thee that we can find something to talk about even in Michigan. The pleasure of sending it to thee was one of my first thoughts when I heard of it; and I know by the interest with which we recieve and read the Post, that let it contain almost what it will, it will be interesting to thee.[50]

Thy mention of our dear Aunts brings them so freshly to my mind that it seems almost as if I could see them before me at the moment or see aunts Anna and Nancy entering the door of 477 for the purpose of passing the day with thee, as they did on Christmas. How glad I am that aunt Amelia has so far recovered as to resume her seat in the parlour. Still through the season of influenza's and colds we cannot but feel very anxious about her. Our thoughts are very often with them.

Cousin R Coe should be involved in the pecuniary misfortunes of his sons. I am sorry on their own accounts, especially for James who has a family depending on him for support, but far more so that it should be the means of disturbing the comfort of the rest of the family, which I hoped was at last pretty firmly established. I am glad to hear that Anna is writing to me. I have been looking a long time for a letter from her, and I can assure thee she has no cause to be jealous of J[ulia]. W[ebb]. or any one else.[51] I have been expecting, for a long time, too, a letter from my friend Hannah [Longstreth]—(I have no affinity for her new name yet)—and I almost begin to fear that her change of circumstances has occasioned a change also in her friendship. However, I must not judge too hastily.

Aunt R. says thee has given her credit for only half the number of letters she has actually written. She and I some weeks ago, had a grand numeration of all we have recieved from thee. As we could get no new one, we concluded we would at least have the satisfaction of going over the old, and by assuring ourselves that we had actually recieved letters aforetime, kept up our hopes that the like event might befall us in the future. Had thy letter not reached us as it did, I suppose we should have had another reading match shortly and gone over the same ground again.

Thee need not feel under any anxiety respecting the ice causing us to caplon the bottom of the well, for the curb round it is so high that it forms a secure barrier against intrusions of that sort.

FEB.

We paid a visit some days since to our friend J and C Howard. They informed us that a number of friends from Jersey talk of removing into Michigan during the course of next season and farming on their settlement, some dozen or twenty miles distant from this place. The evening was very pleasant and our *horned horses* gave us quite a pleasant [ride] as we returned.[52]

9TH.

Took tea and spent the evening at our nearest neighbours—Smith Laings. A while before tea brother, who had been up to Adrian, came in and gave me a letter from my dear brother Will. We were very glad to hear from him, but his letter disappointed a hope that we have indulged of seeing him in Michigan during the course of next summer. He tells us, what thee, I suppose, by this time also knows, that he has taken a farm &e. for three years.

10TH.

A day of snow. We had as yet very little this winter in Michigan; and not much cold weather. John Lovett took tea with us this afternoon; his family were all well.

15TH.

We had another very heavy fall of snow yesterday. Brother thought in the evening it was 15 or 16 inches in depth. Went this evening over to Uncle Darius. My letter comes on slowly. I have not been in the mood for writing for several days.

16TH.

We expected John Lovett and part of his family here this evening in time to go with us to lecture. They did not come, however. We had quite given them out and were preparing to go to tea, when himself wife and daughter came in. There has been so little sledding that farmers are obliged to make the most of the present snow, and have not much time for sleighing in the day-time.

17TH.

Towards evening three or four young friends called to see if we would take a short sleigh ride. Brother and I were soon ready, and after a pleasant drive of a few miles, we returned home and they took tea and spent the remainder of the evening with us. Thy engravings contributed as they have often done before, to our entertainment. They are very much admired.

21ST.

Brother to day went up to Adrian, but as we had previously recieved our newspapers, and there were no letters he brought nothing from the post office. He has been busy for the two last days at threshing. He will have about 150 bushels of wheat; near half of which is yet in the sheaf, but will I suppose be out before long. He has been much engaged this winter with chopping, and splitting rails, as he wishes to fence about twenty additional acres in the spring.

We are delighted to hear that there is a prospect of any one coming out here from Philadelphia. I hope we shall recieve a large packet of letters and I really want one for they have come in a very stinted stream lately. I shall be very much obliged for some slips of honeysuckle if thee thinks they will grow, for I am very impatient to see some growing about our house. They will give it such a home look, and I should like if thee can get them without trouble some of the seeds also, of either the coral or scented monthly, or still better of both, and any other seeds which may happen to come in thy way. I have a number of rose bushes of different sorts, set out round the yard and we intend getting grape vines as soon as we can—but the honeysuckle is not known here, and was always a great favorite of mine since early childhood.

FIRST DAY.

Last night was a fall of snow, and this morning we had a sled ride to meeting. Two young friends returned with us dined and spent the afternoon.

26TH THIRD DAY.

Brother was going up to Adrian with some grain, and we rode the greater part of the way with him to pay a visit to one of our friends, and had the pleasure of returning in a snow storm. The last time we visited them Aunt R. and myself were both obliged to stay all night on account of a heavy rain, (as we then walked) and let brother come home by himself and get his own breakfast next morning. The sleighing had been going very fast during the day, but this snow quite rein-forced it for a while. The Temperance Societies both of Tecumseh and Adrian had meetings today, but we were at neither.[53] We reached home tolerably well powdered but took no cold, as we were well sheltered by cloaks.

28TH.

This afternoon we had a visit from Johnathan Harned and his wife and a neice of hers who came out last fall from Jersey. Land lookers and emigrants are beginning to come in already, the former in considerable numbers, and it is thought that emigration will probably be greater than during any previous season. We have heard of a number of families who expect to come in as soon as the navigation opens.

My paper here holds out amazingly—or else my stock of intelligence has run to a very low ebb, for the sheet fills very slowly. We are looking for a letter from thee, for thee said in thy last thee should write again shortly, and Aunt R. has not forgotten that thee owes her a letter. Oh dear how I wish it might be a big one. It seems to me that a great many things must have transpired during the winter that we should love to be acquainted with—while our situation in that respect with regard to you is very different.

I expect master Roy would by this time have no recollection of his Michigan friends. However tell [him] they are glad to here of his well doing. I am beginning to think again about gardening and warm weather and such things—and not least the opening of the navigation on the lake. I do hope when there is an opportunity my friends will be kind enough to send me a good parcel of letters after the starving time I have had of it lately. I have recieved no letter either from Hannah [Longstreth] or Anna as yet, though as thee told me they both intended writing, I have been in daily expectation—until I am almost tired of looking. Brother is still threshing away at his grain or at least has been during the present week.

Aunt R. says she would be obliged to thee to get from Lydia White enough free coloured muslin to cover an umbrella and parasol, and send them by the next conveyance; also something to make a couple of sun-bonnets—coloured muslin if she has not any lower priced that is suitable for the purpose. And for that as well as other things we hope to have thee a *personal* settlement next summer.

I believe I have fairly come to a full stop; so surely adding the important intelligence that we are all well, I shall endeavor to put my laggard letter in a way of reaching Philadelphia as soon as possible.

I am very affectionately thy niece
EMC

Aunt R. desires me to send a message from her to you all.

CHAPTER 5

A YEAR OF WAITING, 1833

The letters of 1833 reflect the sense of sameness and routine that settled on the Chandler/Evans household. Both those in Michigan and those in Philadelphia had become reconciled to the distance between them, and the excitement had worn off, though the anticipation of a visit from Lemuel and Jane Howell never dissipated. The Michigan family continued to wait for visits and for letters. Worry is less apparent in Jane's correspondence, and Ruth's and Elizabeth's letters manifest resignation to their situation and occasional homesickness.

JANE HOWELL *to* ELIZABETH CHANDLER *and* EMILY JOHNSTON
Philadelphia, January 9, 1833[1]

I thank thee my dear Elizabeth for thy large sheet or sheets so well filled for I believe there are several of thy letters yet unanswered by me but thee must not care for that but continue to write. The Evening Post which I send every week serves in some degree as an apology for letters. I often think how I should like to receive something from your hands weekly even if it was but a piece of blank brown paper. But by the by thee asked me some time ago if I would not like thee to send me on one of your Michigan papers as a specimen. I must say I should like to have one very much to see what is looks like for I cannot contrive what you can find to put in them so far in the back woods unless it is to inform the different parts of the Territory that the frogs croak louder in one ditch than they do in another, for springs I suppose are rare in your country.

Benjamin Lundy called to see us some weeks since. I was glad to see him return in such good health and spirits and it was a great sattisfaction to be able to question and cross question him so closely about you. He gave a pretty good account of you, and seemed very much pleased that he had met with relatives so very unexpected in your neighbourhood.

I suppose before this thee has received a letter from thy friend Hannah Longstreth. I understood she intended writing to thee soon after her marriage. Maria Woodside has returned to the city. Her health is better than it was before she left here. She has not got a situation in a store yet—but is looking out for one. She desires her love to you.

I had been anxiously looking for a letter from you for some time past when to my great pleasure I received one from my dear sister about three weeks since. I think it is but the second one that I have received from her since you left us but her many domestic occupations excuses her.[2] I intend taking an early opportunity in answering it.

Our dear Aunt Amelia Guest is much better than she was. She is able to ride out and take her usual seat in the Parlour, but she continues very weak and I fear another attack of the same kind in her present state of health would be too much for her to get through with.

Aunts Anna and Nancy spent Christmas with me. They, with Aunt Amelia were spending a week at John Merrefields and while there I had the pleasure of frequent but short visits from my dear Aunt Anna. She was much pleased at hearing thy Aunt Ruths letter read. She said it was so very sattisfactory. The production of thy brothers Potatoe Patch seemed almost to astonish her. She continues to take great interrest in your welfare. John Merrefield cannot articulate one word yet, altho he appears to understand all that is said to him. The little boy they lost was a very fine child. They called him John.[3]

I am very much pleased at thy writing in the form of a journal. Thee mentions a great more little incidents that are very interresting to me and brings you in fancy nearer to me. I am very much pleased that the Country around you is becoming so speedily populated with such respectable inhabitants who will all contribute to its rapid improvement. The Praire lands will soon become fruitful fields, trees which can boast of no fruit, planted by natures hand, will no doubt give room to those of the Apple peach Pear and plumb of which I suppose you have seen none since you have been in Michigan.

I hope by this time you have exchanged your wooden chimney for one of a less combustible nature for if it was more fire proof it might prevent people from falling down ladders, hurting their sides and spattering water on letters nearly finished to the great discomfort of the one who receives them. I do think you Michigan foot travellers have greatly the advantage over us Pennsylvanians for you have no stones to stump your toes against or bubbling streams to impede your journey for a moment. I do wish your well had a pump in it. I hope the ice nor any other accident will compel you to explore the bottom of it this winter.

I am very glad that John Lovett and his wife have recovered from their illness.

Samuel was here a few days since. He wished me to say they were all well. I was sadly mortified that I did not know in time of the woman going on to John's. I had been waiting a long while very impatiently for a private opportunity to send some things on to you, and then when such a good one offered, to think I could not avail myself of it, was rather trying I assure thee. James Gamble, a Journeyman of Lemuels, a very sober industrious and good principled young man will go with his family early in the spring to settle in Michigan. He wishes to take a letter of introduction to Thomas as he thinks he should feel very forlorn without something of the kind. I have not heard from thy brother William for some time past. I intend writing to him soon. The last time I heard from him they were well.

I hope in the spring to send thee on a few roots of honeysuckle. Cousin Anna Guest says she has raised them from the seed without any difficulty. I have not seen her but once since she returned from the Country but I believe she is well. She seems to take quite an interest in thy silkworm Concern.

A few weeks ago Hannah Woodside returned from Wilmington. Barney Harris friends were all well. Robert and James Coe have been unfortunate in business; they have made an assignment and will pay about forty cents in the dollar. Their fathers name is on their paper, which will be a great disadvantage to him and I have no doubt but it will be the means of breaking him up. If it should be so I think it probable they will remove to Salem Co[unty, New Jersey]. Young Anna has heretofore been very averse to going. I do not know how it is with her now. James Coe has opened a lottery office opposite to us. He and his wife are boarding with Margaret Hall. Robert will try to get into business soon and then I suppose he will be married. His intended spouse has several hundred dollars which I suppose will serve as a capital for him. Rebeccas intended has also failed, which I suppose will postpone their marriage a while longer. Aunt Rebecca is boarding with Elisa Tunis. Jonathans wifes sister has taken Aunts house and Jonathan and his family are boarding with him. Amelia Guest is so much pleased with house keeping that I believe she has no intention of declining it. George has gone again as Super Cargo to the same place he went before (Buenos Aryes). He is not fond of sea voyages, but nothing better seems to offer.[4]

I think great credit is due to my dear nephew for his great industry and perseverance in farming. I fear sometimes he will injure his health by his great exertions, but you must do with him as is Commonly done with too free going horses, hold in the reins.

We have had very warm pleasant weather so far this winter. Until within a day or two past I do not think we have had ice thicker than the eighth of an inch and that only for a few days. Last week it was almost like May.

I did not tell Anna Coe that thee had a very intimate friend in Julia Webb, for fear she might think that she would supercede her in thy affections. That I am sure would be a great tryal to her. Her friendship for thee is so great, that it seems her greatest pleasure is talk about thee. I expect she has a very long letter waiting for thee to send by private conveyance, as I heard several weeks ago that she was writing to thee. She is pale and thin. I have no doubt but she very keenly feels her family misfortunes.

Lemuel says perhaps he will reach Michigan in time to help Thomas build a barn. If he was to, I think it would afford him a great deal of pleasure. He desires me to give his love to you. Thy Aunt says Thomas' wheat was of an exceptional quality and that his corn exceeded his expectations, but did not say how many bushells he raised. I feel anxious to hear all and every thing about you.

John A Williams had the Rheumatism to such a degree that he had to use crutches, but he has now nearly recovered so that he can walk out. Cornelia Knox is going to be married. She is about selling out her stock of dry goods. It is said her intended husband is a wealthy man. I do not recollect his name.

I hope the winter will not injure thy young mulberry trees after all the trouble thee has had with them. I suppose by this time they have attained a considerable heighth.

I expect Lemuel will in a few days get down in the country to see his Mother. She has been indisposed, but is now much better. If I had known that there had been a case of cholera as near you as Adrian I should have felt very much distressed about you at the time. I heard it was at Detroit and I thought that distance very near. How envyable is the lot of those who can have all their friends near them. It is a blessing which we can hardly be too thankful for.

When I heard your kind neighbour Comstocks were going to visit York State I secretly wished that they would extend their journey as far as Philadelphia that I might in some degree express my thanks to them for their kindness to you. I love them altho I have never seen them.

> We are all Well and with much
> love to you all I remain thy
> Affectionate Aunt
> Jane Howell

Roy is quite well and in his usual high spirits. Lemuel says he sets a much higher value on him as he belonged to you.

EMILY JOHNSONS LETTER

Well my little Emily I saw thy Mother and Sister Sarah a few days ago. They were well. Sarah says she would like very much to live in Michigan. I hope thee is a very good little girl and always tells the truth, for it is very wicked to tell a fib. And I hope thee will try and do every thing thee can to help Miss Evans and Miss Elizabeth and mind every word they say to thee for they are the kindest and best friends thee has in this world. And then when I go to Michigan I will give thee a great many pretty things for I like to reward good children, but if they are naughty I cannot love them or make them any presents. When Miss Evans (or Aunt) thinks is proper thee must write to me and tell me how many chickens you have and wether you have any geese and goslings and Turkeys and little lambs. I should like to hear all about it. I expect thee will be very happy as all good children will, when they have such kind friends to take care of them as thee has. I must now conclude from thy friend.

Jane Howell

THOMAS CHANDLER *and* ELIZABETH CHANDLER *to* WILLIAM CHANDLER
Hazelbank, February 3, 1833

My dear brother

The whole of the year 1832 has passed and in its course no letter has been received at Hazlebank from thee. The constant expectation of hearing from thee has been one cause of my deferring writing till now although two letters have been sent to thee since thy last. I can assure thee the receipt of a letter from our friends now we are so far removed from them is a circumstance that is not lightly appreciated but I do not wish to chide. I am willing to acknowlege my own remissness but only to remind thee that sixteen months have gone by without our receiving any direct intelligence from my dear brothers family. *verbim sat.*[5] When does thee expect to visit Michigan? The anticipation of seeing thee coming the last season was the source of many bright moments of pleasure which I hope will be realized in the course of the ensuing season. We hardly know whether to expect we will ever have you for neighbors but still continue to hope that this may yet be the case.

Our country is filling up fast but the Indian war and the Cholera have been great drawbacks on emmigration during the last season. Although the hostile Indians were two or three hundred miles from us many fabulous and exaggerated accounts respecting them were spread abroad sufficient to deter numbers already prepared from removing at that time, and immediately after the appearance of the

Cholera in various places was a sufficient cause to arrest the tide of emmigration. Notwithstanding this we have had a considerable accession of settlers and a number of new neighbors near us. There are three times the number of friends in this settlement now than were here at the time of our arrival, a greater part of whom are orthodox. But there is now a prospect of a settlement of *Friends* being formed some miles south of Adrian when I hope we shall have a sufficient number to form a monthly meeting.[6] It is intended to establish a press at Adrian in the course of the ensuing spring for the purpose of issuing a newspaper. A meeting was held there a few weeks since at which sufficient funds were immediately subscribed I expect the county seat will be removed there during the present session of the council.

FEB. 10.

Having received thy letter yesterday I have told Elizabeth I would leave her room to reply to it and therefore conclude this abruptly assuring thee that I am as ever

> thy affectionate brother
> Thomas Chandler

2ND MO 11TH

Dear Brother

I am really glad to recieve some demonstration, at last, that thee has not utterly forgotten the existence of thy sister, and other Michigan friends. We have been for a very long time anxiously expecting a letter from either Sarah or thyself, and had it not been that we have heard from Aunt Jane occasionally of your health, your very long silence would have occasioned us no little alarm and uneasiness. Of my sister S. I have no complaint to make. However gratifying it would be to recieve a letter from her frequently, I know her time now must be much occupied and will not urge her writing. But surely, brother, thee might spare a few moments occasionally of an evening, to devote to those near relatives, who have no other means of communicating with those they love, than this, at best imperfect one of the goose quill. I know thee does not love letter writing, but surely it can be no more trouble to write to Michigan than to Philadelphia, and let the task be as disagreeable as it may, it cannot be so much so as the pain which thy silence causes us. But as we have at last recieved our dear letter, I will give over scolding for the present; though had I commenced on the other page instead of brother T. I should not have been so good humoured as he has been. Thee speaks in thy letter of having written twice, without having recieved answers. We have recieved none since the fall of 1831, and to the one which then reached us, brother replied long before I wrote my last letter.[7]

I cannot say that I read thy letter with unmingled sensations of pleasure. It has dashed a hope, which though disappointed from time to time, has been fondly and ardently indulged—that of seeing my beloved brother in Michigan, before a very long time, as a visitor at best, and perhaps at a rather more distant period as a resident. This then it seems we must no longer look forward to, for these long years. The anticipation was too sweet to permit of our not feeling the disappoint-ment sensibly. Still delightful as it would be, I should be far from urging, either a visit or a removal. You are the best judges of the expediency of both. Do not suppose though that I intend to give up the idea of kissing my dear little nephew some time or other. I am mighty proud of him, and I have no doubt that he is just as pretty and roguish as need be. When thee goes to Philadelphia, do not for-get to take a lock of his hair to Aunt Jane for me. Let me at least see a part of him.

But to return to a graver and less pleasant subject. Thee mentions thy inten-tion of trying tavern keeping again. It will most probably be greatly more prof-itable if thee has good success, than the business thee is now engaged in and I have but one objection to it—and that is a very strong one—but can if thee chooses, be obviated. I allude as thee will I suppose guess, to the selling of liquors. Do not my dear brother accuse us of an unwarrentable interference in thy concerns. I do not wish to assume the grave aspect of a counseller—I ask of thee only before commencing thy new business to think for thyself upon the subject, and talk upon it with Sarah, with a mind unbiased by the lure of interest, and a determination to act according thy conviction of its propriety. That it is a very profitable branch of the business, I do not doubt, but if thee might recieve for every drop an equal portion of gold, I would still say, renounce it. A clean hand and a clean conscience are of greater value and I cannot but consider the traffic in question exceedingly wrong—so much so that the idea of thy being engaged in it is very painful to me. Thee must not feel offended with me brother, for having spoken so plainly. It is a sister's privilege—perhaps her duty; and I love my brother too dearly to regard any thing that concerns him with feelings of indif-ference. It is not on the score of the irrespectability of tavern-keeping that I object to it in the least. It is only for the cause I have mentioned, and that I am sure if thee sees proper to remove that objection thee will never regret having done so. Not for my sake, but as a sacrifice to doing right.

We have had during the present winter, but little cold weather and very lit-tle snow. I think thee has formed rather an erronious opinion of the coldness of the winter weather. We consider it very little if any [ ] the spring season is perhaps rather more backward, but scarcely perceptably so. Sufficient snow fell yesterday to make tolerable sleighing, but I do not suppose it will last long. Brother T's main business this winter has been chopping, and splitting rails. He expects to fence twenty five acres more in the spring, five of which he broke up last fall, and the remainder he expects to get done next summer. He does not complain at all of being obliged to work too hard, and often contrasts his present situation with that behind the counter. I feel satisfied that his present enterprise was the best he could have engaged in. He is obliged to work, it is true, but his labour yeilds him a fair profit, and any capital pays well whether invested in land, labour, cattle or buildings. He has not yet been able to build a barn, but expects to prepare timber for the next winter.

Uncle L. still talks of visiting us, and [ ] we hope to see Aunt Jane, though she says she will not talk of coming for fear of being again disappointed. I do not think the "York State" people mind journeys as much as the Pennsylvanians. Every summer some of our neighbours take a trip across the lake to see their relations.

The Adrian Library contains a very good collection of books. Brother has a share in it, and it affords us quite a material addition to the pleasures of a winter evening. T. has threshed out seventy five bushels of wheat from his last year's crop, and has about the same quantity yet in the sheaf. The current price is one dollar a bushel which he has obtained for all he has yet sold, and it probably will not be lower. Some farmers have sold for less, but brother's was very fine, and has commanded the highest price.

Tell my sister that I shall probably continue to trouble her with a letter occasionally, and that if she cannot find time to answer them, I hope we shall both some time or other be able to pay off all old scores of that sort, by actual "word of mouth" over a sociable cup of tea, and that in the mean time I wish to impose upon her the task of occasionally reminding my negligent brother that perhaps his poor faraway sister is getting quite out of spirits, because he has not written to her for such an unreasonable length of time.

We have this winter had a couple of gratuitous lectures on different scientific subjects, delivered at the school house by a friend from Mt. Pleasant, Ohio who last fall came to the Territory [probably John Hunt].

Kiss little Tom for his two Michigan Aunts though they had much rather do it for themselves, if it is possible. Thee is not mistaken in supposing that he would be a great pet, if he was but near enough. We talk very often about him and his parents. We are all well. With much love to Sarah and thyself, in which Aunt R. unites, I remain very affectionately

thy sister
E. M. Chandler

Please inform us where thee intends moving and when. What is the nearest Post Office &c? Some description would likewise be interesting.

T.C.

———•••———

JANE HOWELL *to* RUTH EVANS
Philadelphia, March 23, 1833

My dear Sister

I have just been counting up the time since I have received a line from you, and according to my calculation it is six months. Is it possible? Yes six tardy months have elapsed since I have received a letter from Michigan, and I suppose it is at least two months or more since I have heard from you thro the medium of John Lovetts letters to his father. Your silence has caused me many anxious hours; my fancy paints many unpleasant pictures, both asleep and awake, but thee knows the timidity of my disposition, but I cannot help it.

Why not then relieve the anxiety of my mind by writing a few lines. Dearly as I love to receive long letters from you, yet I would much rather receive a short monthly, with only one line written on it, informing me how you are, if you cannot spare time to write more than to receive one six feet square, well filled, and but once in six months. The letter carrier too, has been very tantalizing for some-time past; he frequently makes a halt on our pavement as he passes by with his hands full of letters, as if purposely to raise my expectations on tiptoe, and then disappoint me. You hear as it were every week from us, by receiving the Post directed by me, and I think you ought to write six letters, where you receive one from here.

Aunt Amelia Guest is much better, but still continues weak, but we think when the weather is suitable for her to ride out, that the air, and exercise, will strengthen her. Dear Aunt Anna is well. She often talks about you.

I received a letter last month from our dear William. They were all well. He said he intended paying us a visit some time in the month if the weather and roads were good, but we had not the pleasure of seeing him. He has had the offer of an excellent Tavern stand and a farm attached to it, at a low rent. He thinks he shall take it. It is a great stopping place for Drovers, and a great deal of money has been made there. He also had the offer of a Clerkship at an Iron Furnace in Hartford County, Maryland, which he conceived to be very flattering until he went to learn particulars. The house which he was to occupy had but two rooms, and he would have to board six of the workmen who were of the lowest grade, which quite discouraged him from undertaking it. Otherwise it would have done very well. He says they have had a lady boarding with them this winter from Baltimore. Her husband is in bad health and has taken a Sea Voyage. To use Williams words he says Tom has become a great fat wild and troublesome fellow busy from day light until ten oclock at night in mischief and play. Dear little boy how I should like to see him.

John McClellan, a Journeyman of Lemuels, started from here about two months since for Ohio. He thought it probable he should reach Michigan before he returned and I gave him a letter of introduction to Thomas; but he has returned without going there. James Gamble, another of Lemuels men, expects to go this spring or the early part of summer immediately with his family to Michigan to settle. By him I hope to be able to send the things you wrote for. Anna Coe is writing I believe a great many pages to send by him; She feels almost offended that Elizabeth has not written to her for such a great length of time.

Maria Woodside has got a situation in Woods silk store. She receives five dollars a week, which I think is a great recompence for her services. Her health is better and she wishes to be remembered to you. Joseph Merrit is at Tavern-keeping near Cincinnatti Ohio. He sent for his brother Samuel to go on there, as he thinks it will suit his business. He approved of it, and has gone. Last Spring Clifford Smith and Charles Poultney made an assignment to their creditors. Charles called here a few weeks ago to make inquiry about Michigan. He wished to know if it was healthy, and wether a pretty good business could be done there. He said he thought he should write on to Thomas for information. Daniel Temple has been on the point of writing on the same subject for some time past. I hope they may both decline it, as I think it would be quite an interruption to Thomas' business to answer their letters.

About a month since I dined, and spent part of a day with Cousin Anna Guest. She asked very kindly after you, and told me when I wrote to give her love to you. She enjoys pretty good health. She expressed a wish to see some of Elizabeths last pieces in the Genius. I sent her a few of the numbers by Amelia Merrefield who said Cousin shed tears on hearing them read. Amelia was proposing to Aunts to discontinue the use of slave raised produce.

Emilys Mother was here a short time ago. She was well, and says she has purchased a beautiful brown silk parasol with a white border around it, to send on to Emily as soon as there is a good opportunity. I hope she is a very good little girl.

How does your sugar maple trees come and I feel quite interrested in your sugar making concern, but I suppose my dear nephew has employments of more consequence to attend to at present. I paid you a visit a few weeks ago, in my sleep, but I must confess that I met with a very cold reception, to be sure. I caught thee at the wash tub in the yard, in the act of wringing out some clothes, and altho I went in, very unexpectedly, thee neither expressed surprise, or pleasure at seeing me, which thee may suppose, could not be very agreeable, after having travelled such a distance, and alone, to see you.

24TH—

I very unexpectedly this morning received a letter from my dear Elizabeth. What a burthen did it take off of my mind; the weight of which, might almost be compared to a Mill Stone. O how delightful it is to hear you are all well, and next to that doing so well, and that you are surrounded by such kind agreeable neighbours. My heart ought to expand with gratitude, to the Great Dispenser of such blessings.

Benjamin Lundy was here a few days since. He expects soon to commence his Journey to Mexico. He was in good health and spirits. His oldest daughter is married to a man about 35 years of age, a near relative of her Aunt Lydias husband. He is a man that is much respected, and wealthy. The only objection Benjamin had to the match, was the disparity, in their ages she being about seventeen. Benjamin wished me to tell Elizabeth to direct her letters or packages now, to Philadelphia, as the Genius is to be published here during his absence.

I hope Elizabeth will write soon to Anna Coe, she feels hurt that she has delayed it so long, but I would rather she would not say any thing about their misfortunes as I should not wish her to suppose that I informed you of it. I expect she will tell you all about it, when she writes.

To day there has been a great parade of the hose and Engine companies. There were about forty Hose Carriages, and Engines, the greater part of which were drawn by four horses, and very profusely orniminted with wreaths of artificial flowers. Some of the men who drove the horses, were attired in a very grotesque manner. Some with red jackets or spencers, with full, large white muslin sleeves, petticoat trowsers of same drawn close round the ancle with a broad ruffle, white cotton stockings and red morrocco slippers, white muslin Turbans with white plumes on their heads, concealing all their hair, and if it had not been for their mustaches, they would have had more the appearance of women than men. The Washington was drawn by four elegant white horses. In front of the carriage on an elevated seat, sat a little boy, of about four or five years of age, equiped in the same uniform as the company; over which was thrown an Arch of evergreens, and Artificials, with a large Portrait of General Washington. But the last, and most imposing of all, was the William Penn. It was preceded by a grave looking portly man, with a wig, three cornered hat, and his other clothes, representing the Founder of Pennsylvania; he carried a large scale in his hand, on his right and left was a sham Indian Chief. Behind him several men in the plainest Quaker garb, with ten or twelve Indians, to appearance, painted, with long black hair, their cars ornimented with a variety of trimming and with their blankets drawn close around them. They had a very natural appearance.

I do not recall wether I mentioned in a former letter that Smith and Burnet had behaved unfairly to A & J Coe. They had agreed with the rest of their creditors to take 40 cents in the dollar, and let them go on in business, provided they would give their notes at four months, for that amount, endorsed by their Father. When Robert presented them with their notes, with his fathers signature, Burnet put them in his pocket book, and then they told him, they should only give him a receipt for that amount, and afterward, look for an equal dividend with the rest of their creditors. Robert was very angry, and exposed them publicly in the papers; and by that means, they had to give up business. Their Father has made over every thing to Amelia Coe, even to his life time in his wifes Estate. He is going on in business under Amelias name I suppose.

Samuel Lovett stopped in to say, that he had received a letter from John. They are all well. Tell my dear Elizabeth that it was seventy seven days from the commencement of her letter, until the completion of it, and then the sheet was not filled, but I excuse her, if she will write more frequently, but I need not say one word on that score, for know how far I stand back, on the ground of correspondance. I think from the great increase of Friends in your neighbourhood, that you will very soon have to build a new Meeting house, for I cannot think how you can all stow in such a little bit of a place as Elizabeth described in one of her first letters. I suppose before a great while your Territory will be converted in to a State, and when you are within the limits of the United States, it will seem as if you were nearer to us, for the word Territory has such an Out of the World sound, as if it might be the abode of Satyn and such like beings. We understand that land in Michigan has fallen in price to fifty cents an acre. That will hold out great inducements to emigration. A man with a large family and very small capital may settle very comfortably there, and raise his children to respectability, and independance.

Ann desires her love to you, and she intends writing a long letter to thee. She feels a warm interrest in your concerns. We have had a very mild open Winter and very little snow until the beginning of this month when we had excellent sleighing which lasted eight or ten days and made the City very lively, as it brought great numbers in from the Country. Lemuel enjoys good health. He desires a great deal of love to you. I believe there is no thing that would give him more pleasure than to pay you a visit, but from present appearances I think there is but little probability of his being able to put it in execution as he is likely to have a great deal of work to attend to this summer, but I am determined not to fix my mind on it for fear of disappointment. Perhaps Lemuel may be able to arrange his business so as to leave it. If he can he will, for I can assure thee he requires no coaxing.

Give my love to Aunt Sally and Ann Comstock. I expected before this to have been personally acquainted with them. Your friends feel to be my friends and I love them that have treated you kindly. Elizabeth did not say how much Thomas was to pay for his chairs. I expect they demand a much higher price than they do here. I wish you had some good feather beds, I think straw ones must be very uncomfortable in cold weather.

A little while ago I discovered that I had made a wrong calculation as to the time of the last letter which I received. I fully believed that it was in the early part of the 10th month, having mislaid the letter, but from some circumstance I recollected to day, that it was about Christmas, which takes off nearly one half the time. Well thee must excuse me for the mistake, for thee knows I am a great blunderer.

We are all well, and I believe our friends generally. And with much love I am affectionately

thy sister
Jane Howell.

———•◆•———

BENJAMIN LUNDY *to* ELIZABETH CHANDLER
Ancocas, New Jersey, March 30, 1833

Esteemed Friend:

Again I have neglected writing *too long!* But thee knows something of my engagements, and *I am sure* will save me the trouble of apologizing for it. Indeed I *have not room for that* now, as I have so much else to write about.

I am preparing to pay a second visit to the Mexican Republic; and it is possible that I shall, this time, go as far as the city of Mexico and Vera Cruz. I *hope* to get my business transacted, without proceeding further than *Leona Vicario,* (formerly Saltillo) the seat of government for the State of Coahuila & Texas. But if the law excluding the citizens of this country, shall be still in force, when I reach that place, I shall be under the necessity of visiting the capital of the Republic. I have procured excellent credentials, and expect to set out in a few days for Pittsburg. From thence, I shall proceed down the Ohio and Mississippi, and probably up the Arkansas, to "Little Rock"; then across the country, to "*Pecan Point,*" on the Red River; then through the Indian country to Nacogdoches, on the crossing of the Trinity river, in Texas. After exploring the country a little on this last mentioned river, I shall probably pursue the San Antonio road, to the fort now called Texar, and thence south about an hundred miles towards the Gulph of Mexico. Here I shall wish to examine the country a little. Then I shall go as direct as I can to the seat of the State government, unless I may think proper to visit Matamoras, on the "Rio Bravo del Norte."

If nothing unusual occurs to detain me, I hope to perform this journey in four or five months. In the mean time, I have made arrangements to have my paper issued in *Philadelphia.* The editorial management will be confided to *Evan Lewis,* an old, and faithful abolitionist; (though I wish this kept a *profound secret,* as he is, thee is no doubt aware, something of a *religious controversialist;*) he is the author of the *prize essay,* published some months since, in the Genius of Universal Emancipation. Thee is, therefore, requested to forward thy communications, until further notice to *Philadelphia,* instead of Washington. But I wish them directed *to me,* or in *my name,* as usual.

We have, at length got the publication going on, *I hope* pretty well. The number for this month is out, and I expect by this time mailed. But, unfortunately, in removing the copy to Philadelphia, some of thine was left at Washington, and I had to do the best I could with thy department. Several original pieces were admitted, as well as some selections, that should have passed under thy inspection. I hope, however, thee will excuse me; yet if I have done wrong, do not be backward in telling me so. Thee will be gratified to perceive the movement of our friends in Ohio. The article, signed "Sophanisba," is the production of a young colored woman, the writer of the enclosed letter.[8] She had, by some means, found out thy name, before I knew of it. The drawing is her own work. She presented me with a very appropriate one, at the same time. She is considered a highly respectable young woman, and is on terms of intimacy with Lydia White, and some of the rest of our friends. The article, signed "Edna," is from the pen of *Alice E. Bettz,* of Philadelphia. I presume thee is acquainted with her. I have ventured to copy a little from the pamphlets, sent us by our English friends; but I wish thee to attend to them, as well as everything else that thee conveniently can, for thy department. I did not dare to put the extracts from the little work, entitled "Reuben Maddison,"[9] in that part of the work, as I feared thee would object to the language of a portion of it.

Among the papers, &c. forwarded by the Secretary of the Ladies' Anti Slavery Society, I received a letter, of which the following is an exact copy.

"West Bromwich
May 16, 1832
Dear Sir,

I have intended to write you a long letter in return for your very interesting and valuable one; but our 7th Report, which is just come from the press, and which I waited to insert in the parcel, is only ready as I am about to leave this place, and all I have to do is obliged to be done in a hurry, without the possibility of replying to your excellent letter as it deserves. Above all, I am vexed to tell you that Miss Chandler's "King Fisher," or rather, I should write it "The Kingfisher," has never reached me.* I hope it will, if you favor me, as I entreat you, with more of your publication. In "Reuben Maddison," and our 7th Report, you will see we have availed ourselves of your kind help. I have been much encouraged by Miss Chandler's exertions; and I hope if life and health are vouchsafed, to thank her with my own hand, as Secretary, for her aid, when I have read the poems you speak of. I will trust to you to present her with the Humming Bird, and one each of the publications enclosed.

I the less regret that I cannot write more, because the "Questions on Slavery" speak much (and in the words of Scripture) that I could write. I beg I am soon to hear of your having returned safe from your tour, and the like to hear of your success. I entreat that "Reuben Maddison" may be well circulated in America.

I shall be too late to finish this parcel if I add more than that. I remain, with much gratitude,

> Yours most truly
> Lucy Townsend Sec.

Surely this is encouraging language. Thee is *beginning* to see the fruits of thy labors. *Hold* on, my dear sister—the time is at hand when the happiest results will be realized. Already the effusions of thy muse have attracted the attention of *thousands*.

> O suffer not that harp to rust,
> Nor hand it on the willow bough.

Thee will perceive that I have *republished* the "Tears of Woman"; and if I cannot send our correspondent the *King Fisher,* I will re-insert that also.

For a few days, I have been at the house of my father, near Burlington, N.J. The state of things here is much changed of late. My step-mother departed this life a few months since. Another sister was married while I was to the westward; and this very day my brother has brought home a charming young bride. The girls in Philadelphia, too, are marrying off as fast as they can! One of Jonathan Sleeper's daughters was married to Hannah Townsend's brother, some time ago, (thee surely heard that she had wedded a young widower!) and within a week

---

*Nor 'Tears of Woman'"

past, Martha Sleeper—Jonathan's second daughter—also "perpetrated matrimony." While upon this subject I wish thee to *disbelieve* the curious report that *my* oldest daughter has chosen a companion, as well as the rest. It *will not do* to let a story pass *unrefuted!*

Before leaving Philadelphia, a few days since, I called at thy Aunt Howell's, and was pleased to learn that they were in usual health. They had just received a letter from thee. They tell me that William and his family are also doing well. I likewise called on thy friend, Anna Coe. She appears in excellent health, I spent a few moments very agreeable in her company. She wants to see thee very much. And, by the way, there are *some others,* there, who *would* like to see thee. I think not a few in number.

Does thee remember *Ruth Logue?* She formerly resided near Centreville, in Maryland; and says she knows your family well. She is now married to a very clever man, named Nathan Galbreath, and resides at a place called Newgarden, in Columbiana County, Ohio. As I was travelling through that part of the country, last summer, I called at their house. They had heard a great deal about me, and knew that thee assisted in conducting the paper. But Ruth was quite disappointed in my *appearance.* She observed, in very pleasant way, that she "should have expected to see me dressed in a *white hat* and a *drab coat*"! She gave me clearly to understand, however, that she did not *fault me,* for my "dress." I found she was not one of those who insist on the necessity of wearing *any*one's "*living*"; and was much pleased with her company. Her husband now takes the paper.

What does thee think of our friend Garrison's *ostentatious parade,* in *begging money* to go to England? For my part, it pains me to see it. I have no objection to the object of his mission; but I am sorry to see such a *public "alms"*-gathering, for the purpose expressed. They require $500. to fit him out; altho they expect him to collect money, as soon as he gets there! I fear they will *spoil him.* He is naturally vain and egotistical; and to add to this *public begging,* is too much to be endured. I like *modesty* in such matters.

My friends have also insisted on my receiving some *donations,* to defray my expenses to Mexico, &c. and several have contributed handsomely towards it. The Free Produce Society has also made an appropriation of $50; and the American Convention &c has given some assistance. But this is not to be publicly trumpeted throughout the country. If I *must* procure means through such a medium, I would say to the generous donor: "When thou doest thine 'alms,' let it be done *in secret.*"

Has thee seen Brother [Charles W.] Denison's paper recently established at New York?[10] I will have it forwarded to thee. I had, the other day, interviews with both the editors of the Album and the Lady's Book.[11] By some singular fatality, they were *both discontinued,* soon after the first few numbers were forwarded! They promise me that they will see to sending them on, hereafter. They were paid for at first.

I have engaged a very good *printer* to do our work. He will want the copy early in the month, as the paper hereafter will be printed about the middle, instead of the latter part, as formerly. Thee will see by this month's number, what part of thine has been inserted. If thee has written since the letter that contained some of the matter in the last No. we shall have enough for next month—if not I will see that matter is furnished for it, before I leave home. I do hope that the business will go on regularly hereafter. Please drop me a line at *Cincinnati,* Ohio, upon the reception of this letting me know how you all are, and whether thee is satisfied with my arrangements.

Perhaps I shall write thee again before I leave Cincinnati—at any rate, I shall before I go out of the United States. Yet, in view of a long journey, and several month's absence, I would, most respectfully, bid thee, *Farewell.*

> Dear Sister adieu, I must hasten away
> To the land of the Sun, where the wild men play,
> To purpose an asylum for Slaves, in duress,
> Whose prayers ascend unto God, for redress.

I wish my best respects presented to thy aunt and brother; and please inform Ann Comstock of the particulars which I have stated relative to my father's family. She is a little related, and will feel somewhat interested in the matter. We are all in reasonable health at present. My sister Mary sends thee her respects.

> Sincerely, Thy Friend
> B Lundy

ELIZABETH CHANDLER *to* JANE HOWELL
Hazelbank, April 24, 1833

My dear Aunt

Though thee speaks in aunt R's letter of writing to me shortly, I believe the best way to endure it, will be to sit down and write myself, that thee may not expect another till thee does write. More especially it wise to commence in season if my letter is to be "seven and seventy" days in its completion. But remember my dear Aunt, that my former one, came to a *full stop,* of I know not how long, in its centre, out of sheer uneasiness; for I could not bear to go on any longer with my rigmarole of trifles, while my fears were raising phantasms of evil [ ] our distant friends. Besides, Aunt, is it any fault of mine that so little occurs in Michigan? So little at least that will bear narration in a letter. There is plenty to do but not much to write about.

Spring is a very busy season in the country, and this spring to us more so than any we have yet had in Michigan. There is sowing oats, fence making, ploughing, harrowing, planting corn, and I know not what all. Part of it is done and part is yet to do. Brother put in this spring between four and five acres of oats. He is now about putting up the rails which he split last winter round about twenty acres of ground, which he wishes to break up, or some part of it, during the summer. He has also a *big gate* to make, part of his oats ground yet to enclose &c in the way of fence making. Corn planting time has not arrived yet.

Gardening now occupies several hours of my time almost daily, and will I suppose keep me pretty busy for some time longer, even more so than at present. It is a business I am not very skilful in, but one which I think I shall grow very fond of as I improve in it. So please do not forget me when thee has a chance of getting seeds, whether flowers or vegetables, if the latter are not very common ones. I have now a basket of roots to plant, which were sent me by one of our neighbours, and must go and attend to them, having been only writing while waiting for the frost, of which there was a little last night, to get off the ground. When I am tired enough to quit work, I shall probably come in and resume my pen.

And I am here again.

"Raisings" have been going on quite briskly in our neighborhood this spring. Brother was invited last week to four, two of which he attended and one the week before. There is also to be a sawmill raised tomorrow, and after that I hope they will be nearly done with for this season in our immediate neighborhood. These raisings are quite a tax upon the time in a new settlement, but they are things that cannot very well be done without.

The lake navigation has I believe commenced, and I suppose the influx of emigrants will soon render the country quite lively. Uncle Darius expects a brother of his to remove here next month, a man who is said very much to resemble him in character. And there are a great number of friends from York State expected besides. There are, I have understood, about thirty families who calculate on coming out at nearly the same time this summer. Our little meeting house a long time ago recieved an addition of more than its original size, but it will either be further enlarged, I suppose, or, what is more probable, a new building erected before a great while. It is however in contemplation to build another meeting house across the river, this summer, when some more of the folks who are expected, come over.[12]

The report of land selling, here at fifty cts. an acre is not correct. At least we have heard nothing of it in Michigan. Emigration is rapid enough at 125. But half lots (40 acres) are now sold, to actual settlers, but not less than 80 acres to those who purchase merely for speculation. Breaking up and fencing land is allowed to raise its value to ten dollars an acre, though it most frequently I believe in selling a farm bears a higher rate than that. But farms are not sold here as yet, by the acre, actually, but in the lump. This makes the selling a partially improved farm quite a profitable affair, very often; and improved land is frequently a considerable object to persons just coming in, who have large families to provide for, because they can so much more derive their support from the land, while to those who have a supply of all things about them, a second removal into the woods is not near so formidable, while the additional capital they acquire, can be invested to excellent profit. This occasions frequent changes and removals in a new settlement, especially among those who are not very well off, or who have any thing speculative in their dispositions!

Brother has not yet tapped his maple trees. It has not been a very favorable spring for making sugar, and he has so much business on hand that it would have been more expensive for him to attempt to make for himself than to buy, especially as the greater part of his trees are yet almost too young to tap. The openings have not yet been on fire, very near us this season, though they have been in different directions at some miles off, several times. Last evening the sky in every direction, north, south, east and west, was lit up with distant fires, but I think it not likely that they will come near us, now this season. The country does not yet look green, except the grain fields, but grass and wild flowers are starting up over the ground, and in a little time will look beautiful.

Brother gave a half dozen bushels of wheat for his chairs—6 dolls for the half dozen. They are windsor, not very handsom, but answer very well for our dwelling. They are Tecumseh manufacture.

I received a letter a few weeks since from Hannah Townsend—or Longstreth, I suppose I should write it—and very much surprised I was to find that she was the wife of a farmer, and settled down in the country.[13] She says she has some pamphlets which she should like to send me, when private opportunity offers, the notice of which can be left at her brother's southwest corner of Green St. and Old York road; but I suppose it would be necessary to give the information some time before hand.

I hope this fine weather will quite restore dear Aunt Amelia's G's usual strength. It is a favor indeed that Aunt Anna so retains her health. Give our love most affectionately to all of them, and tell them that they are very often in our thoughts.

A couple of our neighbours [came] to tea with us yesterday afternoon, so that of course I was prevented from continuing my letter, and as Aunt R. and myself are just now bound for a walk down to the river bank, I shall be under the necessity of deferring further conversation until our return. I should not have commenced writing now but she has summoned me to attend her something sooner than I expected.

We brought back our hands full of wild flowers to plant,—a neat pretty little blossom, with which the bank is studded in hundreds of bunches—fragrant, star shaped, and colored of different tints, from white to a deep blue; with many of them a lilac. We got about a dozen fine large currant bushes, a few days ago, from uncle Daniel Smith, and a number of cuttings; so that in another season I hope we shall have some fruit of that sort. I hardly expect they will bear this summer after being transplanted.

Aunt R. says she will be very much pleased to recieve a letter from Ann, and desires her love to her. Will thee ask her if she would like me to send her the seeds of some of our Michigan wild flowers? If she would I will try to gather some for her when they are ripe.

My good Anna is rather unreasonable to complain of my not writing to her. I have not recieved an answer to my two last letters yet, the last of which was forwarded by mail the latter part of last summer, or, commencement of the fall, and I have been looking for one almost ever since; so that I think she ought to leave all complaining for me to do. Will thee tell her so next time she grumbles? adding however at the same time that I am desperly pleased to hear she is writing me, and that I am doing the same good turn for her, to send when a private conveyance offers.

Aunt R. says please when thee writes again, mention particularly Aunt A. E. and when thee sees or writes to her give our love. I should like very much to see her. We have had for a week past another house in sight—Joseph Gibbons's who purchased some land of Uncle Darius. It seems rather singular to see houses springing up around one in this manner—a vacant space one day, and a house the next. Aunts Sally and Ann Comstock drank tea with us a short time since. Uncle D. still talks of going to York State this summer, if nothing occurs to prevent.

Brother this afternoon has gone up to Adrian. It is now the time for laying up our supply of maple sugar, and it necessary to see to getting it, in season as there is a demand equal or more than equal to the quantity made. I always feel in hopes of something from the Post Office when brother goes up there, but I do not today expect any letters; or even newspapers, unless they come earlier than usual.

I am sorry that William has again rented a tavern stand, for it is a business to which I have a very great aversion, on account [of] the bar. If it were not for that I should make no objection to it. But I felt quite disappointed in being obliged to give up the idea of having a visit from him as I suppose we need not expect it if such is the business he engages in.

Brother this morning brought home a purchase which he made the other day,—a sow and eight pigs, for which he paid twelve dollars; as they are of a superior kind, the price is not considered unreasonable. Yesterday morning he brought home the cow from the woods, with a fine little calf by her side. The live stock of Hazlebank, in case thee should have any curiousity about the matter, now consists of five head of cattle, (calf inclusive) fourteen pigs—big and little—some twenty chickens, and a couple of *cats*—one of them a minor. We expect to get another cow before long. Some of our hens have [not] as yet brought off any broods this spring, but will I suppose before a great while. I quite want to see the pretty little creatures. I am very fond of watching them when they are quite young.

Brother saw John Lovett a few days ago. His family were all well, and himself also. A Friends family from Indiana removed into this neighborhood, (near Tecumseh, at least) last week; and yesterday we understood that a very respectable Friend from Ohio had come in with the intention of purchasing. The wife of the Friend first mentioned, is a daughter to friend Atkinson of New Jersey, and has two sisters residing near Tecumseh, by the name of Satterthwaite, of whom I think I have spoken before.

The price of a cabin passage across the lake has been still further reduced. It was formerly ten dollars—then eight—and now is six and Aunt R says that when you come out she desires you in particular to take a cabin passage. The expense at the present rates, is but little more than the steerage, and in case of a long passage may be less; while the latter is infinitely disagreeable, and exceedingly exposing to the health. We had intended taking a deck passage when we came here, but brother had not sooner seen the accommodations and the company, than he said it would not do. However by getting Em. and all our goods brought over free, the expense was reduced to probably nearly what it would otherwise have cost us; and we were comfortable and escaped colds, which I think we should not have done, or perhaps more serious illness, had we undergone the exposure of a deck passage. The Steerage cabin was crowded with the lowest order of swiss emigrants—going I know not where—we saw nothing of them—as dirty as need be, so that even if we had had beds, which we had not, we could not have gone there—and had we remained on deck we should have been thoroughly drenched by rain, and the spray of the waves, which both nights that we were on board washed every part of the deck. We all of us begrudged the rhino,[14] at first, no little, but we have never regretted that we paid it.

Please give our love to cousin Anna Guest when thee sees her, and to cousin R Coe's family. And *let me know* as soon as thee wants a letter. Thee says we ought to write more frequently than thyself, not taking into consideration how much more thee has to tell, and that some of my letters are equal to two or three common sized ones—and I assure thee *we dont mind the trouble of reading letters here at all.* We shall be quite ready to receive one as soon as it can get here. I believe I have told thee every thing I can think of at present that would be likely to interest thee and now I suppose the next best thing will be to send it off, lest it should miss a conveyance to the Post Office. We are all well—and I am

very affectionately thy niece
E.

JANE HOWELL *to* RUTH EVANS
Philadelphia, May 5, 1833

My dear Sister

I have the Melancholy task of informing you, that our dear Aunt Amelia Guest, departed this life, on fifth day morning, the 25th Ultimo—She suffered by very little pain during her last illness, but seemed to waste away, until nature became quite exhausted, and in a state of lethargy, which continued about three hours, her pure spirit, quitted its tenement of clay, "for that House, not made with hands, eternal in the Heavens."[15] Indeed, who could better be compared to one of the wise virgins, than She? Ready, at a Moments warning, "to enter the Bridegrooms chamber." And altho it is indeed very trying to our Natural feelings, that the grave should conceal forever from our view, that form, and those features, which we were always delighted to gaze upon, Yet it would have been selfish in us, to have wished her retained here much longer, under her bodily sufferings, and at her advanced age. And, altho another link is broken in the chain which binds our affections to this world, Yet we must bow in submission to Him, who is all Love, and in the secret of our hearts say, "Not My will, but Thine be done."[16] The remains of our dear Aunt was inter'd the following first day afternoon at 3 oclock in Cherry Street Burying ground attended by a large number of relatives and friends.[17]

Dear Aunts Anna and Nancy did not attend it. Anna Merrefield, and I, staid with them. They have borne up under their tryal surprisingly well. Poor dear Aunt Nancy, I expected it would have gone hard with her, but she has exerted herself to support Aunt Anna. They have broken up housekeeping and are boarding with John Merrefield. Little Mary [Merrefield] is to go to Westown boarding school,[18] and Amelia [Merrefield] intends qualifying herself for Teacher and then open a School. The best of Aunts furniture is reserved, and the rest will be sold I expect this week. The house which they occupied is to be Aunt Anna's and Nancy's during their lives. I think it probable they will get 275 dollars a year for it, which with their other income, will be more than sufficient for their expences.

Dear Aunt Anna enjoys excellent health. I am very much pleased to have her so near me. Sister Amelia [Evans] has been several weeks with Aunts, which was a great comfort to them, and sattisfaction to her self. She is well and desires her love to you.

I wrote a letter to my dear Nephew during the Yearly Meeting, to send by friend Satterthwaite who expects to start for Michigan in a few weeks. Anna Coe has also sent four letters by the same conveyance. Joseph Taylor was in the City a few days since, he says William and his family are well, and that William is doing a very good business. We are all well, and with much love I remain affectionately

> thy Sister
> Jane Howell

Lemuel saw Cousin Anna Guest, who inquired after you, and on hearing that I was writing to thee, she desired him to tell me, if I had not closed my letters, to give her love to you.

———— ·•·•· ————

ELIZABETH CHANDLER *to* JANE HOWELL
Hazelbank, May 25, 1833

Dear Aunt

We received on the 22nd thy last letter containing the very painful intelligence of the decease of our dear Aunt, Amelia Guest. It is a stroke which, sooner or later, we knew we must submit to, yet one which we still, from the last favorable accounts recieved of our dear aunts health, fondly hoped might have been averted yet a while longer. She I believe has long been *always ready;* but when ever can the hearts of those who are to be forsaken, make themselves ready to part with those whom they love? Bright as is that life to which we have yielded her, with us there must still be sorrow that we "shall see her face no more"—no more when have seen her, amidst those who loved her, with her kind eye beaming affection on all around. Oh what a privelege we should have felt it, to have seen her once more! But it is in such moments a consolation to reflect that this world is not all. I think thee may indeed feel happy to have dear Aunt Anna so near thee—not that thee may seek to comfort her for she has in her own bosom a better and true consolation than any that can be offered her—but that thee may be frequently with her— with both of them—and cheering them with thy presence and attentions. It was very satisfactory, both to Aunt R. and myself that Aunt Amelia Evans was with Aunt A. during her illness. She is such an excellent nurse, and so very attentive, that I am sure Aunt A. could not have been better provided for; and I think it must be very satisfactory to her own feelings.

I think Aunts will be much better off than if they had continued at house-keeping. It would have been quite to fatiguing for Aunt Anna to have had any of the charge of household affairs, and they will besides be less lonesome, and more in the center of their friends. I dare say dear Aunt Nancy feels the stroke very severely, for she is of such a tender affectionate disposition, and was so strongly attached to her sister. Please give our most affectionate love to both of them.

I suppose A[melia]. G. Merrefield will still remain there. I hope she may find success in her prospects, and that her intended occupation will prove agreeable to her. When she engages in it, I should like to hear further particulars respecting her. But I should not suppose any inducement could prevail on her to be separated from Aunts, except during school hours. Give her my love and good wishes.

Brother at present is about from home, and has been for about a couple of days, on a little excursion, the first he has taken, except when he went, on necessary business to Detroit, since we have been in the country. His primary business at present was to attend a convention assembled about 20 miles from here, to which he was appointed a delegate; though not present at the meeting at which he was nominated.[19] And, as he has got through the press of his present business, he talked of continuing his journey, after the business of the convention was concluded, something farther, to see a portion of the country, which he feels desirous of becoming acquainted with; and at the present opportunity, the company of one or two young men of his acquaintance who wished him much to go, will render his little journey more pleasant. He has been working hard and close this spring, and we are glad for him to have a little relaxation. We expect him back either this evening or tomorrow.

I am very glad thee happened to hear of friend Satterthwaite's coming out here. We had calculated on sending letters by him on his return, but to recieve some from him, is better fortune than we had hoped for. I suppose he will reach here in the course of a week or two. Emigrants are coming in very fast. We seldom see any of our neighbours, without hearing of some one or another who either has just arrived or is expected shortly. The last time I saw our neighbour Comstock's, they mentioned that on the day previous they had counted, at different times, ten wagons loaded with household goods and all moving towards Adrian. And a few nights before, twenty strangers had lodged with them. There are at present two lines of stages running between Adrian and Detroit. Now settlements, further back in the country, are forming very rapidly. And we begin to find [it] quite difficult to keep up our recognition of all the faces at meeting—even on the women's side.

Brother finished his planting the early part of this week. He has made considerable fence this spring and on the road exhibits a fine large six barred gate—an appendage to a farm that is not yet very frequently met with in our new country.

We are glad to hear that Brother Will and family are well. It is always a satisfaction to hear from them, and know they are so. If Will was not so very dilatory about writing I should begin to expect a letter from him. He did not mention when he last wrote whether he expected to leave his old neighborhood, or merely the situation he then occupied.

I recieved a letter from Anna Coe, at the same time thy last reached us.[20] Tell her I am exceedingly obliged, and that I hope to send her a tolerably clever sized packet by friend Satterthwaite, and intend moreover [to] write as soon as I can by mail; but if I should not do so previously to sending her packet, she must not feel disappointed or impatient, as it may be that fd Satterthwaite may return almost as soon as I should have time to prepare a letter, and if he should not stay long, I shall probably be somewhat hurried with writing. Aunt R. intends writing to thee by that opportunity. We had had quite a warm dry spring this far. Rain at one time began to be quite badly wanted, but within the last two or three weeks we have had tolerably frequent showers. The "Post" tells us that business is quite brisk in Philadelphia; and the spirit of improvement and building, it appears is not yet laid to rest. Old Phil. must be amazingly altered since we last saw her.

27TH—

As we were going to meeting yesterday a couple of wagons passed us completely loaded with people. We afterwards learned they had just come into the country from one of the eastern states, and were part of the family of a friend Aldrich, who purchased land here last season, and expected to bring in altogether 40 persons—25 of them I believe arrived yesterday—his children, grandchildren &c. The great influx of strangers renders our country very lively.

Brother returned yesterday afternoon, after a very pleasant excursion. After the business of the convention was over on sixth day afternoon, they set off for Vistula, on lake Erie, at the Mouth of the Maumee river, reached there about ten oclock and as the place was much crowded, for it is but a new one, found some little difficulty in procuring lodgings, which however they succeeded in doing. The next day, they took a steamboat excursion of about 9 miles up the Maumee river to Maumee and Perrysburg, in Ohio. Towards evening they left Vistula and rode as far as Whites Settlement, near Ottawa Lake. This is quite a new settlement, and they were obliged to find accommodations for their horses at one place and themselves at another half a mile off. Brother says there is some fine land down that way, but he does not like it any better than our own situation. The public houses between Adrian and Vistula, he says were all crowded with business. But we do not yet see any body from Pennsylvania.

We had a delightful rain last night, and vegetation this morning looks as if it might be advancing rapidly. Brother's corn is nearly all up, and looks nicely; and the rain will be a benefit to it. Uncle Darius expects to start for York State about the middle of next month. We shall miss them very much.

Brother says I have been talking of the emigration into our country, why do I not tell Aunt Jane that in the course of twenty four hours from last seventh day noon, to first day noon, about one *hundred fifty persons* came into this our town of Logan. What number of these may be actual settlers I do not know. Many of them were the families of those who had already taken up land. Some probably only visitors, to see the country, and others intent on making selections of land. T. has just returned from an errand over to Comstock's—he says he met two loaded wagons on their way into the interior. All this does not accord very well with the idea of the scarcity of strange faces, which I dare say you had formed as a concomitant of the "back woods," previous to our coming here.

Brother is about to take a load of grain to mill, and will afterwards go to Adrian, so I must conclude my letter, in order to give it the chance of the conveyance to the post office. Please give our love to cousin [Anna Guest, and to cousin Anna, John, Rebecca, Robert, and Amelia] Coe's family; also to Uncle Aunt Amelia E., Ann, and I may add our friends in general. Our dear Aunt Guests I have already mentioned. I hope when thee writes to hear of their continued health, and that they are restored to comparative cheerfulness.

We are all well. And hope to hear from thee again before a great while. With much affection I am thy niece

E.M. Chandler

Aunt Ruth says, when a suitable opportunity offers, she would thank thee to send out a pound of Lydia White's knitting cotton. It is for stockings for brother, and thee can judge of the quality suitable—please get unbleached, if she has it.

———·—·———

Ruth Evans *to* Jane Howell *and* Amelia Evans
Hazelbank, June 10, 1833

My Dear Sisters Jane & Amelia

The afflicting intelligence of thy last letter was very trying to our feelings, although I was in measure prepared for the event. The feebleness of our Beloved Aunt's delicate frame, and a protracted disease of a very weakening nature, combined with lengthened years, seemed scarcely possible she could continue here much longer. All who knew her, knew her intrinsick excellence, and all will lament her death. In her strong and cultivated mind was centred virtue, and her heart was fraught with love to all her fellow creatures, her hand was ever ready to releive the wants of the indigent, and she could deeply feel, and sympathize with the afflicted. Lovely indeed she was, from youth, to the latest period of her life. She strictly adheared to her Blessed Saviours precepts, and her pure soul was stayed upon the immovable rock of Ages. She has now joined the Church triumphant in Heaven.

It gave me much satisfaction Dear Amelia to hear thee was with her during her illness—a great comfort no doubt to thyself. I feel much for my Dear Aunts but I trust they will become reconciled, knowing she has only gone before. But they will feel their loss severely through life. I can say from experience. I believe I feel the loss of our preacious Mother [Elizabeth Guest Evans] as much at this moment as at any other period, and trust I shall through coming life. I have written a few lines to the memory of her. I will transcribe them for you. No eye has seen them save my own.

THOUGHTS ON THE DEATH OF A BELOVED MOTHER WHO
DEPARTED THIS LIFE THE 26TH OF THE 2ND MONTH 1826

> Methinks it seems as yesterday,
> Thou pressed me to thy breast,
> And with affections fond embrace,
> Soothed my sorrowing mind to rest.
> Ah yes!—it seems as yesternight,
> Thou couldst converse with me,
> But before the coming morn,
> Deaths hand was laid on thee.
> Upon thy couch insensable,

I watched thy parting breath,
And Christ, I trust was near thee,
In the closing hour of death.
Although thy time was lengthened out,
To more than four score years,
And thou wast fit at any hour,
To quit this vale of tears.
But still the blow is keenly felt,
Though many a year's roll'd by,
And many a poignant heartfelt pang,
Relieved by Him on high.
Ne'er O ne'er shall I forget,
Thy kind maternal love,
Thy ever great solicitude:—
Now rests thy soul above.
Oft I think upon thy virtues rare,
And think how thou was blest,
So calm, such sweet serenity,
In seasons of distress.
But now thou art forever gone,
To Heaven, beyond the sky,
Thy joy is now transendant,
With God, and Christ thy Saviour, nigh.

Emigration to our country this season is really surprising. A great many of the new comers are obliged to [go] further west, as it is difficult to procure land in our settlement. Darius Comstock and wife are again preparing to make a visit to York State. They intend setting out on their journey next second day. They will travel in their own carriage. They were disappointed last year on account of the Indian war and Cholera.

There has been quite a demand for wheat this spring. Thomas has sold all he had to spare at eight shillings. There was ninety five bushels—corn four and six pence, potatoes two and six pence. Thomas has a great deal to do. In addition to his ordinary business, he purposes breaking up about twenty acres of land this summer, and if nothing should prevent he will prepare in the winter for building a barn.

Please tell Emily's Mother she is in good health, and perfectly happy. Julia Webb spent yesterday afternoon with us. Elizabeth went home with her in the evening and I expect she will return this afternoon. Give our affectionate love to Dear Aunts, and Cousin Anna Guest. They all have my Deepest Sympathy.

I was pleased to hear Aunts were at J. Merrefield's. I think they will be very comfortable there. Anna is extreemly kind, and I trust will be very attentive to them. Give my love to her.

Elizabeth is daily looking for a letter from thee Dear Jane, in reply to some of her's. Do not disappoint her. I would we could receive letters more frequently. Tell Ann I have not forgotten the one she has promised me. I hope it will arrive soon. My love to her.

A few days ago Thomas purchased a first rate Cow and Calf. He gave twenty five Dollars, from fifteen to twenty are the ordinary prices—of middling Cows. Friend Saterthwaite made us a visit a few days since. The letters sent by him we have not yet received, they were put in a box, with other things, that was sent by another conveyance. It is expected in a few days. We regret much they were not put in his trunk, but conclude there was not room. He expects to leave here on second day next.

13TH.

Yesterday we walked to J. Harned's. They live three miles from us. We dined and drank tea with them. They have a neice living with them from New York City. She is very much attached to Elizabeth. In the evening we received a letter from William.[21] He says they are well, and seems to be encouraged in business. I often wish they were here, feeling confident in the belief he could do altogether better. However I am aware, it would be extreemly trying for Sally and her near relatives to be so far seperated, and I seldom indulge a hope of the kind.

I saw in the evening Post the death of two of Joseph Mathor's children, a great afflication, certainly—but they have been taken from the evil to come. I have not heard from J. Lovetts for some time, but presume they are all well. Emily wishes me to give her love to you, and also to her Mother. She is much delighted with the parrosoll her mother has promised to send her.

Our friends here, Dear Jane, often enquire of us if thee and Dear Lemuel intend making us a visit this summer. What may I tell them? May I answer in the affermative? My affectionate love to Dear Brother L. Thomas intends writing soon. He could by this conveyance but is much engaged. Remember me to Cousin Coe's. Elizabeth has written to Anna. I must now conclude, and believe me to be

youre very affectionate Sister—
Ruth Evans

JANE HOWELL *to* ELIZABETH CHANDLER
Philadelphia, June 23, 1833

My dear Niece

I do not know how many letters I am in debt to thee for, but thee is a dear good girl, and gives me a long credit on them. I know I impose on thy good nature, but as soon as I become fonder of letter writing I will make amends for all deficiences, that thee may rest assured of. I received thy two last letters one dated 4th M° 24, the other 5th M° 25. I was much pleased to hear my dear Nephew had spent a few days in travelling, a little relaxation from his laborious business is really necessary to his health, and then, it was gratifying that he should be put forward in public business, it makes him more known, and wherever known, his merit will make him respected.

I had the pleasure a few days since of seeing a person from Tecumseh by the name of McNeer; thee may depend I questioned, and cross questioned him about you all, and his answers were very satisfactory. He was going on to New York, to purchase his goods, or I certainly should have troubled him with a box or bundle. I suppose you feel quite *stiff* since you have got your new Windsor chairs, they can hardly look consistent for "Back Woods" people. Do tell me what else you are going to buy that will make you look in the land of stumps, more like Civilized folks; 'tis strange what a spirit there is for imitation. I suppose soon, glass tumblers will take the place of calabashes, as an article to drink out of, and where looking glasses are not to be had, they will answer in some measure as a substitute.

If out of the world people were not so accustomed to discordent sounds, I should think your ears would be greatly annoyed with the mooing, mauwing, and grunting of your livestock of oxen, cows, calf, hogs and pigs, nineteen in number "but use is second nature." Old Phil, as thee calls her, is not like the generality of aged dames, who, as they increase in years decrease in beauty. It is the reverse with her. She is growing so rapidly in size, that she makes quite a jigantic appearance alongside of her sister states, and then, her face is altogether so very much improved, that many of her former features can hardly be traced.

George Guest returned from his last voyage a few weeks since: He brot Cousin Anna Guest an air plant. It is a great curiousity. She has it hung up on a nail in the yard over the Piazza door, during the summer, and in the winter, it will be hung up in her back parlour. It vegetates without the aid of earth or water, but I do not know how they are propogated, unless from a slip. They increase considerably in the course of a year, and bear a kind of blossom. I have not seen it yet.

Amelia Merrefield gave me a description of it. I hope the next time I write, I can tell thee more about it.

He also brot with him an Orang Otang, or wild man of the woods. He is more than six feet in length or higth. He was secured on board the vessel in a large case but by breaking some of the bars, he extricated himself from his confinement, and walked himself about the deck most majestically, to the great consternation of those on board. The captain in some way offended his lordship, and he took up a washing tub nearly full of water, and threw at the captain. They then thought it most advisable to remain quiet and not irritate him until some means could be devised to entrap him, which George succeeded in doing by mixing in a pint of wine, of which he was very fond of, a tablespoon full of Laudanum, and placing it near a strong ring and staple fastened in the floor of the deck. He soon scented it, and in a few minutes drank the whole of it, which in a short time so stupified him that he fell into a sound sleep. They then chained him down to the floor and afterwards sawed off his tusks. The Captain and George brot him to this country in Partnership, expecting to get a great price for him. I have not heard how much they sold him for. George is about setting sail again, I believe he is going first to France, and then to Spain, on a trading voyage.

Aunt Rebecca Guest intends going in a few clays to Baltimore to spend six months with her daughter and friends. My dear Aunts, Anna and Nancy, spent yesterday after noon with me, they were in their usual health. Thee can judge better than I can tell thee, the great pleasure it affords me in having my dear aged Aunt, so near me. Her mental faculties remain I think just about as when you left her, her sight and hearing about the same, but her bodily strength seems declining a little. They seem quite comfortably situated at John Merrefields. Aunt Anna feels the separation from her dear departed sister very keenly, but she strives as much as possible, to hide it in her own bosom. She desired me to give her love to you all. Amelia Merrefield is now qualifying herself for a Teacher, under the tuition of Martha Tyson in the School room formerly occupied by Ann Bedford. She seemed quite pleased at being remembered by thee. Indeed I think Amelia has mended her manners considerably for the last twelve months past. She seems to feel the loss of her dear Aunt sensibly, perhaps a retrospect of her treatment to her, makes her feel it more keenly.

I suppose thee has heard that Robert Coe Jr. has been married eight months ago, but on account of his business it was kept a secret until within a few weeks past. They are at boarding and will continue so until next spring, when I suppose they will take his Father's establishment when he removes into the Country. James and his wife are boarding with Margaret Hall. They have a young daughter which I believe they call Angelina. M Woodside is in Baltimore attending a store for a person there. She is pleased with her situation, but her health continues bad. I believe her complaint is Rhumatism.

I went home with Samuel Lovett last week and returned in the Doylestown Stage[22] the next day. I had a very pleasant little visit. Aunt Sally wished me to stay a week, but I could not with convenience leave home any longer. Jonathan Roberts was buried about two weeks since, the particulars of his death you have no doubt heard. His daughter Ann [Roberts] is in very bad health. Her recovery is rather doubtful. The rest of the family are well.

I received a letter from thy brother William a few weeks since. They were all well. He said he was going to write to his brother Thomas. Little Tom grows finely. He runs alone and is full of mischief. Their new residence is about a half a mile from the old one. McConkey says he is doing a great deal of business, and is very much respected by all who know him. I should like very much to go and see them this summer but Lemuel is so very much engaged in business that he could not leave it to go with me, and I do not like to travel alone.

There was a great storm of wind and rain passed over Montgomery County the 2nd day of this month, which caused great destruction to houses, trees, barns, fences, &c &c, our paper gave an account of it and I have been informed that Joseph Mather was one of the greatest sufferers. It is said his loss was between two and three thousand dollars. I suppose you saw some time ago in the Post the death of two of his daughters with the scarlet fever. I have not seen any of the family since you left us.

I had not the pleasure of seeing Black Hawk and his companions whilst they were in the City. There are many of their tribe I dare say, who would be willing to be taken prisoners if they could be treated precisely as these where.[23]

Anna Coe and Rebecca and their beaus, took a ride in the steam boat up to Borden town. They stoped at the Widow Longstreths the same house which you went to on your way to Michigan. The tragical scene which took place there this spring in the murder of Mary Hamilton, has touched the hearts of so many, with sympathy for the relatives of the deceased, that their house at times has been crowded to excess, and altho it has brot a great deal of custom to the establishment, yet it must cause the heart deeply [ ] with woe, from the late direful event, a pang, to be thus exposed to the public eye. Emily's Mother was here a few days since. She is very anxious for an opportunity to send her parasol. She is well. I feel sorry for your sakes that your neighbour Comstocks are going to York State. I suppose they will be absent several Months, but selfish as I am, I hope they may have a very pleasant journey, and excellent good health. I suppose Aunt Sally will not accompany them as she went last summer. Give my love to her. I feel almost as if I was acquainted with them.

I shall soon be looking for friend Saterthwaites return, and then I suppose I may expect a letter from my dear Sister. I am really astonished to hear of the great ingress of Strangers into Michigan. A paper mentioned last week that there were twelve hundred landed from the Steam boats at Detroit in the space of one week.

I should suppose government land would all be disposed of in a little time if emigration continues long as it has been. To be sure the Territory is very large, and will admit of a very vast number of inhabitants. Lemuels journeyman still intends moving his family to Michigan this summer or Fall. I feel particularly anxious for it, as I have many things which I want to send under his care. Ann desires her love and would be much oblidged to thee for some of the seed of your wild flowers. Indeed we should take great delight in raising flowers from your neighborhood. I hope soon to be able to forward on to thee new roots of Honeysuckles. They are in a pot and can be packed in a box. I have not heard wether you raise sweet potatoes in Michigan. I should [think] your soil would suit them. If I have an opportunity at a suitable time, I will send some seed on to you.

Has your news paper establishment got into operation or not? If it has, I should like to have one of the papers very much just to see with what kind of matter it is filled. Have you had any marriages in your settlement since you have been there, or is matrimony quite out of vogue? That is a subject which thee has never touched upon, altho it is so universally interresting. I should think young men would be a mere drug there. It must make the girls very saucy in selecting Husbands.

I do not recollect wether the Post mentioned that Westown School house had been on fire and very materially injured it. J. Merrefield is there. He wrote home a very ludicrous account of the behaviour of the Scholars on the occasion. Mary is to go there on fifth thy next.

Our Germantown rail road attracts a great many spectators and makes that part of the town very lively. There are about fifteen Elegant Cars. They attach two and three together to the locomotive Engine, each one holding about thirty passengers, certain hours in the day, they have them drawn by horses. Spring Garden Street is opened as low as Sixth and as high as Twelfth Street. There is to be Market houses erected this summer from 6 to 8th Street, between 11 & 12th St. They are preparing to build up the square with handsome 3 story brick houses. This will give you a little Idea of the improvement of the City and Suberbs. Charles Williams has moved his family in fourth near Willow Street and his currying shop, to the corner of Second and Margaretta Street. John A. Williams has been very ill with inflamatory Rhumatism. He has been in a very critical situation, but is now much better. We are all well, and with much love I must conclude, and very affectionately

thy Aunt J. Howell

I have just heard of the decease of Benjamin Tucker!

JANE HOWELL *to* RUTH EVANS
Philadelphia, September 1, 1833

My dear Sister

I received thy very acceptable letter by friend Saterthwaite and was very much pleased with those lines on our dear Mother. They were written with a great deal of feeling and were very beautiful. I was from home at the time the young man brought the packet. I had been spending the day with Cousin Anna Guest it being the fourth of July and did not return home until about ten oclock in the evening. Ann held something behind her and wished me to make a bid for it. She said it was very valuable but I believe the highest offer I made was two cents, when to my great pleasure she produced the packet. Poor Anna Coes patience was put to the test that evening. She accidently stop'd in just after the young man had left here. She used every persuasive argument to induce Ann to open the packet but all without avail. She went home and returned but with no more success Ann thinking it improper to open it in my absence. On my return I immediately sent hers to her which she joyfully received. I went to Lydia Whites to procure the things thee wrote for, coloured muslin for umbrellas and ginghum for bonnets I got there, but she had neither knitting or sewing cotton and could not say when she would have it. I bought from her a remnant of table diaper and some coarse domestic muslin.[24] Her assortment is not very good so thee must excuse me for not sending thee better.

Emily's Mother is a very strange woman. She has several times told me that she had purchased a parasol for her and seemed very desirous for an opportunity to forward it on to her. About a month ago I saw her in the Market house and went over to her and told her that I expected to have an opportunity to send it in a few days as James Gamble then thought of going. She said she would bring it, to me in a day or two and I have not seen her since. I have sent an old frock or two of Louisa's which I thought might do for her, also a cloak and woolen shawl. They are hardly worth sending such a distance.

I called a few days after the interment of Benjamin Tucker to see the family. They all seemed to feel their loss keenly but poor Theodocia, her memory and mind is so much weakened that I expect she is hardly sensible of her loss. She asked very particularly after you all. Sarah Williams has purchased the house in Second Street at the corner of Margaretta Street occupied a few years ago by Jonathan Guest. Charles has moved his currying shop to it and has sold his new house a few doors below us to his Brother John A. Lemuel is about fitting it up for a dwelling and dry good store which will cost John I suppose from ten to fifteen hundred dollars.

Maria Woodside did not like Baltimore and left there and has been spending the summer with her friend in Wilmington and the Country. I expect she will return shortly to the City, and try to get into some business. She gave me some time ago a piece of linen lawn[25] to send to thee and desired her love to you. Amelia Merrifield intends at the close of her present quarter to commence schoolkeeping. She has copied several pieces for Elizabeth which she thought very beautiful and I have sent them by this opportunity. I do think there is a great change in Amelia for the better, and I am glad to see it if it is only on her own account. Coe's and she are quite intimate. Neighbour Harrigas has a young daughter which she calls Catharine Louisa. If it had been a boy it would have been William Thomas, after our dear Nephews. The other she called George Washington, he is about two and half years old and a very fine little fellow. She desires her love to you. I have sent her little presents of glassware which she gave me some time ago for you. Ann has written a long letter to thee but I do not know wether I shall be able to persuade her to send it or not.

I am very much pleased that my dear Elizabeth has such an intimate friend in Julia Webb. I think she must be very amiable and if there is a congeniality of mind they must indeed be happy in each others society. The Honeysuckles which I have nursed with so much care are all dead but one, and that is very dwindling so that I thought it best not to send it, but I feel in hopes that later in the season I may have an opportunity to foreward on some that are more healthy and they will bear the removal better.

After reading dear Thomas' letter to his brother which was unsealed, I forwarded on by mail immediately. I was surprised to see that he had fenced in as much as forty acres. I have no doubt but that he could get a very handsome price for his farm if he was disposed to sell it, but I should feel very sorry if he was to after so much hard labour on it, and every year will make it much more valuable.

My dear Aunts spend an afternoon with me every week and sometimes a day, it is delightful to have my dear aged Aunt Anna so near me. She retires early to bed in the evening and I frequently go in and set at her bedside and talk to her until she falls asleep.

One of the pieces copied by A. Merrefield entitled a Dream of Heaven was written by a young minister who boarded a long time with Amelia Guest. When Aunt Rebecca returns from Baltimore Rebecca Giles and her young son Acquilla are to accompany her. I expected they would have called him John Guest after her own dear father. I forgot to say that Lydia White informed me of the death of Wilburforce in England. I suppose it must have been a great disappointment to Garrison that he did not get to see him as he was so very anxious for it.

The last time Lydia heard from B Lundy he was at Texas and in good health.

Lydia in company with another young woman went on to New England a few weeks since to see the young woman (I do not recollect her name) who has suffered so much persecution on account of opening a school for coloured children.[26] She was very much pleased with her, her number of Scholars is about seventeen and under good regulation. The excitement against her by the inhabitants of the town seems to be very much subsidiary. Some have become quite friendly, whilst others are quite hostile. Lydia mentioned a few instances of their unkindness to her. She was sick, her Sister went to the Stores to purchase a cup to make gruel in, but they would not sell her one. A Young Man some distance off went to see her, but as soon as he got to the town he engaged lodging for the night at the Tavern. In the evening after he left her, he went to the Inn but was spurned from the door by the Tavernkeeper because he had been to see her. Now the best constructions I can put up on their behaviour is, that they are a parcel of blockheads.

Close confinement to business has somewhat impaired Anns health. I persuaded her to spend a few days at John Roberts, which she did, and enjoyed herself very much. Hannah desired her love to you. I have sent a drawing of Aunt Nancys which she drew purposely for thee. I know thee will value it, Not for its merits but for her sake. She talks a great deal about you. Charles Williams has removed his family to a very pretty house in fourth Street near Callow Hill. He has a young son which they intend calling John or Charles. Cousin Anna [Williams Merrefield] made Grace [Williams] a present of her two ingrain carpets[27] which she had on her parlours. Ought I not to be jealous? Aunt Nancy has partly made and draped a pasteboard doll for Emily. She was spending the afternoon here yesterday, and for her amusement I got her to do it. I was sorry she didnt complete it, as I have had no time to day for doing it, and the box must be closed this evening. Perhaps Elizabeth will undertake the important task herself. Tell her the one she finished off in such style before she left the city lies safely and snugly in my trunk.

Amelia [Evans] has spent the summer in the country; she was here a few weeks since and was quite well. I think it probable she will spend the winter with me. She was very much pleased with the letter she received. Cousin Anna Guest desired her love to you. I wonder the interest she appears to take in your welfare, does not slacken her purse strings a little. James Coe is now at his fathers. Margaret Hall will not allow him to live with his wife. She is at her Mothers and James pays for her board. I should suppose such conduct from her would deter young men from marrying either of her other daughters.[28]

We are all well. I have taken seven bottles of Wilsons Panacea[29] which has improved my health very much. I must now conclude a with much love to you I remain

Affectionately thy Sister
Jane Howell

Tell Elizabeth that as she would receive so many letters by this conveyance, that I thought I would postpone writing until another time, as it would be then more acceptable to her.

Anna Coe has sent a plant, but has not said what it was.

ELIZABETH CHANDLER *to* JANE HOWELL
Hazelbank, September 2, 1833

My dear Aunt

We have been for several weeks almost daily looking for a letter from thee. I think it must be almost three months since we recieved thy last one, and we begin to feel very anxious about you. Aunt Ruth's letter by friend Satterthwaite and brothers and mine by mail, I suppose have long since reached thee—though we should be glad to hear certainly. Thee has also I suppose heard of us from Anna Coe. I have begun to write at present, not with the intentions of sending it now, but because I happen to have a little leisure and thought perhaps I might not be so well off, when the time came that it was necessary for me to do so.

Things move on at Hazlebank very much as usual; brother has finished his grain and hay harvest, and is now preparing again for his wheat crop. His corn promises very favorably, and it will soon I suppose be time to cut it up. The season here has been a very favorable one for vegetation—warm suns and frequent showers—but the weather today and yesterday has felt rather autumn like.

Uncle Darius and his wife reached home again rather more than two weeks since, after a pleasant journey, performed without any accidents and during which they both remained in good health. They went through Canada and returned by way of Ohio, travelling in all about a thousand miles; and uncle Darius says in all his journey he has seen no land that he likes so well as his own neighborhood in Michigan Territory. John Lovett and his wife and daughter, yesterday week dined with us. They have enjoyed very good health this season.

We yesterday received a "Post." They are a great satisfaction to us—and it is a satisfaction that the accounts of the health of the city so far still continues favorable. I hope I am sure that they may still do so.

Brother got a horse and dearborn a couple of weeks ago and took me up to Adrian, where we had an invitation to spend the afternoon and take tea. The village has grown considerably since I was there before, which was not for a long while; it is quite a bustling little place. There are four or five stores there now—

and some of them keep large assortments of goods—one of the merchants there is just getting on a new supply of thirty or forty tons of goods.

We have seen nobody from Philadelphia or any where near there the whole season—which has not been the case before since we have been here. The journeyman of uncles that thee has spoken of has not yet reached here—whether he still intends coming we cannot tell till we hear from thee again—unless he should chance himself to be the bearer of the letter containing the information. I felt almost certain we should get a letter yesterday, but was mistaken and disappointed.

Our plumb orchard, a collection of wild fruit trees down in the woods, has this season been very productive, and the fruit is excellent both for eating and preserving. I think your market can shew few of any species finer flavored and richer than some of them. Brother intends transplanting some of the trees that are young enough to bear it, into the vicinity of the house. When eating of them we have wished that you could partake—we have dried some of them for winter use.

Building, it seems by the "Post," has been going on so rapidly in Philadelphia this season as at any previous period. There must have been an immense quantity of houses built there since we came away.

John Lovett still expects his father to move out here next season. He has not yet sold his place I suppose, but calculates on doing so. His daughter and family also wish to come to Michigan. We have not yet had a visit from our friends Comstock since their return but they talk of coming shortly.

Aunts I hope still continue well—remember us to them when thee sees them most affectionately. I suppose it looks down at cousin Coe's pretty much as it did when we came away, except some alteration in the appearance of their store which Anna tells me they have made. Will thee tell Anna that I am looking very anxiously and impatiently for a letter—and that she must not let her pen and fingers get the rheumatism for want of exercise. Tell her that I shall feel much disappointed if she does not write to me soon—or rather if I do not soon get a letter—for I think one should be at least, *almost ready* by this time for a journey to Michigan. I felt almost certain of recieving a letter from thee sometime last week, but must I suppose hope on for the present one—perhaps it will be more accommodating in the matter.

The country here still looks fresh and flourishing, but I suppose a change will be perceptable in the appearance of the foliage. I admire autumn scenery—but it reminds one, in its very beauty, that it is on the verge of [ ] withering and decay.

First day afternoon, Sept. 8th.

No letter yet from my dear Aunt. When are we to hear from you? Brother says 'tis not quite so long since we got our last letter as Aunt Ruth and I thought it was. Election day, on which we recieved it, he says was in the seventh month—we thought in the sixth—but we were not quite so far wrong in our calculations as thee was in thy late letters—and at any rate it seems a monstrous while since we heard from you. Tis now more than three years since we left Philadelphia—rather more than three years since we reached Michigan—and we have not had a visit from you yet.

A new bank has recently been established in Michigan, at Monroe, called The Bank of the River Raisin—the notes are very showy, and handsome—one of the figures is an Indian.[30] Aunt R. and I have been this afternoon over to Harris's a little while. The weather to day has been delightful, but quite warm for the season. Brother this fall expects to put in about fifteen acres of wheat. He had this season about nine of the same crop. The grain is beautiful and makes excellent flour. We have been for some time using of it for the demand for wheat before harvest that he parted with all he could spare. He cut this summer quite a clever sized stack of hay off of the ground he sowed with grass seed, with his first wheat. He was not obliged to get near so much hay from a distance this season as last, though he has a greater number of cattle. He has provided this greater portion from his own land, and will have a good supply of corn fodder. He wants this winter to make preparations for building his barn, which will be a great convenience to him when finished. How I wish you could take a peep at him in the midst of his labours and improvements—I think I shall always love Hazlebank because he has made it what it is.

TENTH—

'Tis almost time my letter was finished, from the date of its commencement—but I have no letter yet to reply to. Must I finish, and dispatch it as a messenger for one? I scarcely know whether we shall get one without—perhaps the interval seems more than usually long from our impatience.

Brother is still busy with his grain. The present is a very busy season of the year perhaps as much so as any time in it, except the few weeks of harvest and scarcely less so than those. As soon as his grain is in the ground the corn, must be cut up—pumpkins gathered in—potatoes dug, and stored away—there will be more fencing—rails to split—more breaking up to do, if he can—and probably some ploughing to prepare the ground for next spring—so thee may suppose he is not at a loss for business—hiring, too, so little as he does. The land here differs very much from the ground in Pennsylvania, with respect to wearing out—that is best when new, and becomes poorer, if not sustained by manure, with each successive crop which it produces—but this will bear crops year after year without exhaustion, and is much better after having been worked a few years than it is at first. It will even bear being sewed or planted with the same crop for several years in succession—yet to judge from looks only, when it is first turned up, a person might suppose it was but *poor* stuff. On the Burr Oak land particularly, which is of the first quality, the little ugly straggling trees, are calculated to produce, on one unacquainted with them, anything but a favorable impression. It is one proof among many of the impropriety of judging solely from appearance.

I suppose the fall business has by this time fairly set in, and gives you plenty of occupation—tis a stirring season but its cool fresh arms are bracing, and enable the system better to sustain an increase of exertion. Has thee been travelling this season? I hope thee has taken some relaxation, and enjoyed at least a little release from the cares and confinement of the city. The Omnibuses are a new invention started since we left Philadelphia.[31] They must, I think be quite a convenience to men of business residing at a distance from the places of their employment. How much change has taken place, in various ways, in that city, since we left there.

Thee generally expresses an interest to know the amount of brothers crops. His wheat he perhaps mentioned when he wrote—I do not know what numbers of bushels he expects to have—some of his corn he thinks will yield fifty bushels to the acre—his potatoes we can tell nothing about yet. Of oats he did not expect a large crop—they turned out I believe as well as he expected.

Other employments, for several days past, have prevented the completion of my letter, which I now once more resume.

I was at a quilting party last sixth day afternoon; and ate peaches. We had a very pleasant party—and there were only thirteen persons in the wagon I rode home in, which was driven by the help of a lantern. There were two girls there who are out on a visit from York State. We had a prodigious variety of cakes at tea—and there were two tables full sat down—first the girls and then the young men—though the party was not so large as the first one I attended after we came here. I was at another a few weeks ago, but twas not so large nor so pleasant a one as this.

There was a wedding at Adrian on first day. The bride was an acquaintance of mine, and lived some two or three miles off. With her chosen I was not acquainted. He has not been in the country very long. She was a friend by birth right—but as he was a baptist she humored him by having the ceremony performed in Baptist meeting. It is quite common here to have marriages performed on first day at the place of worship—or rather it is not uncommon. I was not invited to the wedding, nor any one else I believe from here. If she had any company it must have been only some of his friends—but I rather think there was to be no company. In case of thy feeling any curiosity as to the dress of a *back-woods bride* I will tell thee that she was to wear *white shoes,* watered silk dress &c.

It is to day very cloudy and rainy, with some thunder and lightning—I suppose it is the equinoxial storm. There was frost two or three nights last week—quite heavy—which obliged brother to go immediately to cutting up his corn that he might save the fodder, which the frost injures very much, if it is left standing after being touched. His wheat is not all in the ground yet, but will be finished as soon as possible. He was greatly in hopes the frost would have kept off till his wheat was in, as it would have suited him much better—but such things must be taken as they come.

It is said that several families of Mount Pleasant, Ohio, are turning their attention to Michigan—and that some may probably be expected here this fall or winter. I shall be very well pleased to have some more families from that neighborhood near us. A friend from England is now in the neighborhood, with the expectation of settling here with his family.

I do not know whether Brother mentioned in his letter that uncle Darius contemplates building a Grist Mill on his farm, which will be quite a convenience to T. by saving a considerable portion of time which the greater distance of the present one necessarily occupies. We will perhaps also have a fulling mill[32] and woolen factory—perhaps a saw mill—but I do not recollect whether I have heard the last one spoken of or not. I think it not improbable that there may sometime be a village in the Valley, as it is called, near Comstocks.[33]

If thee has not written my dear aunt, when thee recieves this, do please do so as soon as thee can. I expect to take this over to Comstocks some time to day if the weather is fit, and may possibly be so fortunate as to recieve a letter—as they expected to hear from the Post Office last evening. We got a "Post" on seventh day last, by which it appears that the city is still healthy. Our neighborhood is also so.

Give my love to Ann. I think she has never yet sent me word how she likes Hazlebank, from description, nor how she likes the name itself. I should like to know just what idea you have formed of it; and of our country altogether.

Thee has not I suppose, seen Hannah Longstreth since her marriage, or thee would have mentioned it—unless indeed it had been since thee last wrote to us. Has thee paid a visit to Jersey this summer? I think when thee wrote last thee scarcely expected to go, but if the weather in Philadelphia has been as warm as it was for a while in Michigan, I think it must have been uncomfortable remaining in the city.

Please give our love to Cousin Anna Guest and to Cousin Coe's family—and the rest of our friends—and recieving a large portion for uncle Aunt Amelia [Evans] and thyself, believe me to be

> affectionately thy niece
> EMC

We are well—and I am sure *we hope that you are the same.*

JANE HOWELL *to* ELIZABETH CHANDLER
Philadelphia, September 29, 1833

Well my dear Elizabeth what does thee think of thy Aunt Jane by this time? Is thee not almost ready to cast her by as an unworthy correspondent letting thy letters lie from time to time unanswered. Well I do allow that I am a great delinquent and I believe that is all the apology I shall now make hoping thee will pass it over to the account of proffit and loss and perhaps I will do better in future. I was much pleased to hear Samuel Lovet intends paying you a visit this Fall. Do send a plenty of letters. I say plenty, but plenty signifys enough, and if you write enough you would have to write them by the score and that I am sure would be a great imposition on your time and patience so I will try to be sattisfied with one or two, but do send me something which nature has produced on your soil, or climate, if it is only a *chickens feather,* you surely cannot withhold such a humble request.

I heard a few days ago from thy brother William by Mary Decline who lives in Front near Green Street. Her sister whom she went to see lives a short distance from William. She was there and he desired her to call and let us know they were all well. She says William is doing an excellent business, and is very much respected in the neighbourhood where he lives. She was very much delighted with little Tom, says he is one of the finest looking children she ever saw. She said he might be compared to a young Apollo his form was so beautiful.

Hannah Roberts spent part of two days with us last week. She was well and desired to be remembered to you. I saw Samuel Comfort yesterday. He asked particularly after Thomas and his farming and was much pleased that he was progressing so well. Maria Woodside returned to Philadelphia from Wilmington last week. Barny Harris' friends are all well. I think Maria looks better, but she is still very much afflicted with Rheumatism. She intends going into a store if she can meet with a good situation. She wishes to be remembered to you.

We were alarmed last night with the cry of fire, and on inquiry found it to be in John Merrifields houses in Poplar Lane. One of his tenants having heated her stove for baking and it being placed in contact with the partition which divided the two kitchens and it being made of plank, and lathed and plastered and the heat being so great it took fire inside and burned considerably before it was extinguished but I believe the houses were insured so that John will not sustain any loss by it.

Aunts continue to pay me a weekly visit and sometimes two. I like dearly to have them with me, and they express great pleasure at coming. Dear Aunt Anna enjoys good health. Aunt Nancy has had a bad cold and something like rheumatism in her back and shoulders, but she has nearly recovered. Amelia Merrifield has not commenced schoolkeeping yet. She is still improving herself but as soon as a suitable opening should offer for a school I expect she will embrace it. I have not seen anything of Emilys Mother yet. I think she has behaved very strangely.

Sarah Pennocks son Casper is to be married about Christmas to Caroline Morris. They have been travelling together this summer in company with some others. They went to the Falls of Niagara and whilst there one of the young men remarked that there was a great view of the country from the top of a very high eminence composed of rocks but which very few dared to ascend on account of the danger attending it. However some of the young men thought they would venture and Caroline seemed determined upon it altho they tried to dissuade her from it. They all reached the summit in safety and were very much delighted with the prospect from it but in descending which each one had to do separately as there was no assisting each other and they were about half way down Caroline heard something crack above her head and steping aside made way for a rock which came tumbling down and grazed by her as it fell. All expected to see her killed, but fortunately she was only bruised altho at first it was thought her leg would have to be amputated. She has now quite recovered, I have not seen her lately but I expect she is the same rough uncouth Caroline as ever and I am astonished that such an accomplished young man as Doctor Casper Pennock should think of uniting himself to one of her mind and manners, but I expect her purse was the loadstone.

Charles Williams' Currying Shop which he sold to John A. Lemuel is fitting up as a handsome Dry good Store and dwelling house and which will take him until Christmas or after to finish. If he had known in time that Samuel Lovett had been going to Michigan he would not have undertaken it, and would have gone with him. He wants to see you very much and I think the journey would have been of service to him after such close application to business. He desires his love to you.

Last fourth day Anna and Rebecca Coe went to "Village Green" [Pennsylvania] to spend a few days. They expected to spend a day at Brandywine before they returned. Cousin Robert and Anna are about in their usual health. Robert says if he was a young man in less than a month he would be alongside of Thomas. Robert Jr. has a young daughter. They have named her Rachel Broom Coe after his wifes brothers wife. They have no children and are quite wealthy. He was so much pleased to hear the child was called after his wife that he put a thousand dollars out at interest for the child, and probably he may do a great deal more for it should it live. So much for a *name.*

I suppose before this time Darius Comstock and his wife have returned from York State. It must seem delightfull to have them back again. I hope they have returned in good health. If they heard from our friends in Hudson, I should thank thee to let us know how they were. It is a great while since we have received letters from there and Lemuels friends are quite anxious to hear from them. Aunt Rebecca returned from Baltimore last week. Rebecca Giles and her young son Acquilla came with her to spend about two weeks. They came up to see Aunts but I had not the honour of a visit from them, but I assure thee I did not *grieve* myself sick about it.

Aunt Rebecca has received letters from her son John lately. He says he has had two attacks of the Cholera one last summer and the other this; he intends coming on to see his friends about Christmas if nothing should prevent. Persons from the place where he resides say he is a young man of the first respectability there. He is better than six feet high and well proportioned. He must be astonishingly altered since he left here. I hope I shall get a peep at him when he comes if it is only thro' a key hole.

The sketch the[e] took of your cottage[34] and sent to Anna Coe answered very near the idea I had formed of it, but not the grounds about it, but that I made allowance for, as I supposed thee had not time to finish the picture, but I did not think to take notice whilst I was looking at it wether you were standing at the windows. If you had been, and were well portrayed I think I should have looked at you with a great deal of interrest.

I expect soon to spend a day, or part of a day with Cousin Anna Guest, and then she will want to hear all about you. She appears to feel great interest in your wellfare, and while she is feeling, I wish she would in her *purse.* After Lemuel sold his lot on Spring Garden, he put his shop on another lot on Coates Street near 11th St. He seems desirious that we should move up nearer to him, I think it probable after he has completed Johns building we shall and then I shall be at more liberty to visit my friends.

I hope James Gamble and family has arrived safely to Michigan. I feel quite interrested for them. When thee writes say what thee knows about them. Ann Roe has sent thee as a small remembrance a white woolen tippit[35] (very much worn here) a black silk apron, a little fancy box some pieces from the Diary of a Physician which she cut out from news papers and a piece of white sattin ribband for thy bonnet. She wished me to apologize for the color of the ribband it being the best which we had in the store and she did not wish to go elsewhere to buy. She has sent Tom a little silk Hdkf. To my dear sister Ruth she has made up and sent a white flannel petticoat a white tippit and blk silk apron also some white soap to wash flannels with,[36] and to Emily a pair of mitts and a pincushion which she has had ever since she was eight years old, and desires to be remembered to you. I have sent thy Aunt Ruth a couple of canton flannel jackets which I hope she will wear when the weather becomes cold, also a remnant of gauze flannel for thy use. The canton flannel I bought of Lydia White, sewing cotton she has not, but knitting cotton she will have in a few days. She desired her love to you.

Thy Aunt Amelia [Evans] came to the city yesterday. I expect she will spend the winter with us. She is well and desires her love to you. Roy is frisking about the floor in great spirits. He is very little changed since you left him.

9TH MO END—

Cousin Anna Coe was here last evening. The girls have returned. They were at Brandywine, and thy friends there made great inquiry about thee. They were well except Hays who has been very ill, but was much better when they left there. Anna Jr since her return has had a pain in face, but Cousin Anna said if it was better to day she would finish a letter which she has been writing to thee and send it by this conveyance. I must now conclude as Saml Lovett will be waiting to take it. We are all well. I must just say that I am pleased thee puts the above words which are of the highest interrest to me in large letters so that immediately on opening thy letter which is generally done with a trembling hand and a palpitating heart I am at once relieved from anxiety and can then begin to read the letters with almost unbounded pleasure. With much love to my dear sister, Nephew, and thyself, I remain in affection as ever

> thy Aunt
> Jane Howell

I am afraid sometimes there is a repetition in my letters as I write without copying them off. I have nothing to refer to and by that means may take up the paper with subjects which I have already told you. If I do, excuse me. I have sent Emily a pair Germantown stockings,[37] but I do not know wether they will fit her.

JANE HOWELL *to* RUTH EVANS
Philadelphia, October 2, 1833

My dear Sister

Yesterday I received a letter from my dear Elizabeth expressing a great deal of anxiety at not receiving a letter for such a length of time. I wrote by James Gamble who I expected would have arrived then some time before Elizabeths letter was mailed.[38] I hope no accident has happened to him, or his family. His baggage did not go on until after he left here and perhaps he has been waiting their arrival at Detroit. There is a friend going from here to Michigan by land, it is not *Lemuel.* He expects to arrive there about the 22nd of this month if nothing prevents. I have written a long letter to Elizabeth, so that you can see I have not been as negligent as you supposed. Ann by this opportunity has sent some little remembrances to you. She has written several letters at different times but I never could prevail on her to send them, she thinking them too worthless to send one thousand miles. When this *friend* returns we shall expect letters, so you may as well prepare them in time for I do not suppose he will stay with you more than two weeks. I am not going to write much now, for I have written so many letters to you lately that perhaps they will be like Dry goods, when they are a [ ] in the Market they depreciate in value.

My pen is bad, my time is very limited this morning, and I have no information to impart except what I have said in my other letters which are going and gone so I would have you remain satisfied.

We are all well and with much love to you all I am affectionately thy Sister

Jane Howell

William and Sarah and little Tom were well a few days ago, and our friends in general enjoy good health. I will try and answer Elizabeths very acceptable letter soon.

———◆———

RUTH EVANS *to* JANE HOWELL
Hazelbank, September {October} 11, 1833

My Dear Sister

I received thy letter by J. Gamble. We expected and wished him to come with his family immediately to our house, but he stoped at Lovetts to leave a letter, and John engaged him to build a Kitchen &c &c for him. After staying about half an hour there, he came on to Hazlebank, and I was really rejoiced to see some one who had so recently been with you. I questioned him about thy health previous to opening thy letter. He said thee had been very unwell but was then much better. Thee has not mentioned in any former letter thy having occasion for so much pattent medicine. Thee says it has improved thy health very much. I am glad to hear it, and hope thee will have no need for any more of it. Thee did not say what complaint thee took it for, I am fearful thee is not careful enough of thyself. I will therefore commission Ann to keep a watchful care, for I am too far off now to advise thee as I was wont to do. I am induced to believe from the healthiness of our country, if thee could spend a few months with us, it would be far more beneficial to thee than medicine. If nothing should intervene I hope thee will arrange for making a visit next season to Hazlebank. I am sure Dear Lemuel will urge it, and accompany thee at any time.

I am now seated at my favourite window, and the prospect before me is really splendid, the foliage of the trees are very richly variegated and the winter grain of such a beautiful green makes a very handsom contrast. Do not imagine Dear Jane that I am so delighted with country life, and the beautiful scenery it presents, that I do not devote a proper portion of my thoughts to my Philadelphia relatives. I assure it is otherwise. I think of you daily, and I believe I may say hourly, particularly my beloved Aunt Anna. Kiss her and Aunt Nancy for me and give our love to them.

Emily bore the loss of the parasol well, but still it was a great disappointment, and she was willing to make every excuse for her mothers apparent neglect. She is very much attached to her mother and sisters, and desires her love to them, and also to thee. I think she is a fine sensible little girl. She is very forward in her learning under Elizabeth's tuition. I think I never knew a child of her age to read better. She wished me to inform thee she done all the milking which consists of two cows each giving a considerable quantity of milk.

My Dear Elizabeth went yesterday to Doctor Webb to make a visit to Julia. I expect she will return this evening. I fear their intimacy will not be of very long continuance as I suppose Julia will be married before long to a Lawyer in Adrian. I should think it a more suitable connexion if he had belonged to the society of friends. However I hope he may prove deserving of her.

James Gamble was not here more than two days before he was engaged in business at Tecumseh. He recieves ten shillings per day also his board, and tools he is supplyed with gratis his not having yet arrived. His wife is boarding at John Lovets till there goods come on, then they will occupy a small house John built for a man in his employ whose time is now out. There is no doubt but James will have abundance of business. There are at this moment a number of persons waiting for him to work for them. Mechanicks are much wanted here.[39]

Barney Harris has offered his farm for sale. His price is Eight Hundred Dollars. He has improved twenty acres, has a good house, and well of good water, excellent neighbours all around him, but he belongs to the Methodist society and is anxious to be amongst them, and there is a settlement of them some ten or twelve [miles] off where he intends going as soon as he can effect a sale which I think will be soon, as improved farms are in demand and his is very cheap certainly. His little Tom C. is a fine little boy and very healthy.

16th.

Last first day a little before sunset, Jacob Hoag, a neighbour of ours and a very worthy friend was so unfortunate as to have their house burned to the ground, whilst he and his wife were from home. They were very careful previous to there leaving the house to secure the fire and fasten the doors, and leaving there little children at Smith Laign's, his brother in law. They proceeded to meeting. After meeting accompanied by Smith Laign and his wife they visited a friend of theres and stayed till after dark. On there way home they were informed of the distressing intelligence. We went over to Smiths and spent the evening and could deeply sympathize with them. They estimated there loss to be about five hundred dollars. The wind was extreemly high on that day, and it is believed it blew down the chimney so violently as to scatter the coals over the fire from the house, save one bed. They remained at Smiths about one week during which time the neighbours sent them cloathing, and furniture sufficiently to keep house with and they removed to a school house near by that is not at present in use. There they will stay till Jacob can rebuild, and I presume his friends will all assist him.

Fanny Webb and her daughter Julia was here one day last week. Julia persuaded Elizabeth to spend two days with her which she did, the second visit she has made there since I commenced my letter.

We are extreemly anxious for the arrival of our box. Dear Elizabeth is quite impatient to read her letters, and I do hope I shall find one in it from Aunt [Anna].

22nd—

Yesterday Aunt Sally and Ann Comstock and three young women by the name of Bixby were here. Ann handed me thy letter dated 10th Mo 2nd informing us a friend was about starting for Michigan to make a visit to us, but who this friend is we cannot imagine. Thee says it is not my dear brother, therefore we finally concluded it must be William G. Chandler, and hope he will arrive safely. Thee says Ann has sent some little remembrances for which we feel very much obliged to her, but I am really sorry she destroyed her letter as I fully expected one from her. Give my love to her, and tell her I often think of her. Remember me to my friend Betsy Herregas. We have not yet seen the present she sent us. Please give her our thanks.

Darius Comstock when in York State purchased a side board and a number of other articles of furniture amounting to a considerable sum. He has heard nothing of them since. He is fearful some accident has happened on the Lake. He has had his house very handsomely papered and new carpets on several rooms, also the hall and stairs. Aunty Sally Comstock received a letter from her daughter in York State who made a visit to Hudson. She says Aunt Hathaway enjoys very good health much better than for many years. When thee sees Aunt Howell remember me affectionately to her, and also to our kind friend Hannah Roberts. I was pleased to hear Ann was there a little while this summer.

Thomas is very busy digging his potatoes. He thinks he will have between one hundred & fifty and two hundred bushells. He has just sold a man fifty bushells of Corn. He supposes he will have about two hundred bushells. He sold it for three shillings, but it is believed it will bring four or perhaps five shillings per bushell towards spring. His wheat is all in Smith Laigns barn. What quantity he may have, I cannot say, but it turned out extreemly well. His oats he stacked at home. He will have six fat hogs this winter—three we shall keep and three he will sell in pork. One looks now as if it weighs three hundred. He will have eight fine hogs of a very good kind to keep over winter.

26TH—

The friend has not yet arrived. Elizabeth says she feels certain it is her dear Brother William. I would she may not be disappointed. I have told her if it was him thee would have said so. Certainly, thy letter has been read by her again and again. Still she is confident in the belief the friend is her Brother William. It will also be a great disappointment to Thomas, however, when the friend comes. I suppose we shall recognize him, if it should not be William.

Elizabeths friend Julia Webb is now Julia Chittenden. She was married two days ago, to the above mention person. She is very desirous the intimacy may continue, but as she will reside in Adrian there cannot be the same intercourse. She says she hopes she shall see thee when thee comes to Hazlebank. Give my love to Maria Woodside also my thanks for the piece of lawn. I have not seen it yet, but hope it will not be long first. Thee says Amelia has been in the country this summer. I think she would be altogether more comfortable with you—this winter.

Yesterday afternoon we had the pleasure of seeing the much talked of friend, and conversing with him about thee and all the inmates of your house, and reading thy long and interesting letter, and examining with feelings of gratitude the remembrances sent by Ann and thyself, and their being so neetly made up, still tends to enhance their value. *Samuel* [Lovett] said he thought Lemuel would have come on with them if he could have left his business. I believe I can say I am really glad he did not come, cause why? Because the season is now so very unpleasant and his time would be so very short, that the pleasure of seeing him however great would scarcely compensate for the reluctance we should feel at parting with him so soon. I wish such an opportunity may offer in the spring and you could leave home to stay at least two months with us with out Lemuel's making to great a sacrafice.

It is my intention to write to Amelia and Ann by this conveyance, if I can possibly find sufficient time, but really domestic concerns seems to occupy almost all my time. Therefore if I should not write give my love to them, and say I will endeavour to write to them by the next private opportunity. I feel disappointed in not receiving a letter from Ann. I am very sorry she destroyed it. If she knew how gratifying it would have been I am certain she would not have done so. Elizabeth has written to Amelia, Ann, and thyself, and also to Anna Coe. I suppose R. Coe will remove in the spring to there farm. I should think they would find it a pleasant change. When thee sees Cousin Anna Guest give our love to her. I often think of her, she must be very lonely. I hope she enjoys good health.

It is strange R. Giles did not call her boy after her beloved father. I think that Aunt R. made quite a visit with her at Baltimore. Thee says you have a prospect of leaving second street this winter and I am very glad to hear it. I think the city must be much improved since we left. I should be glad once more to see it if but for a very short time, and once more to see my beloved and aged Aunt, but as it is impracticable I do not indulge a hope of the kind. I often think how happy thee must feel to have her so neer to thee and that she is able to visit thee so often. Remember us to John, Anna, and Amelia Merrifield. I wish Amelia may be successful in school teaching. The things thee sent for Emily are very acceptable, and I am much obliged for them. Thee says thee wishes to see something from our country however truing in value, I have proposed making a pound cake as the ingredients will be all of our raising except the maple sugar, and being made by us would make it acceptable. We have sent you some hazlenuts. We gathered a great quantity last fall and laid aside half a bushell for you but had no opportunity to send them and those gathered this fall I presume are rather better and have sent them in preference.

I am very glad James Gambles goods have come. I began to feel anxious concerning them as there has been several accidents on the Lake this fall. The winds have been unusually high, but property is nothing when compared with the loss of lives. James we think will do extreemly well here. He will have as much business as he can possibly do. They like the country much. We expect a visit from them soon.

Thomas is preparing for a barn this winter, and has engaged James to build it in the spring. B. Harris offers his farm low. Thomas would not be willing to sell his for double that sum, but ours is very superior in point of situation and improvements certainly. I wish we had our sausage made that we could send some to you; it is common here to put it in bags made like pudding bags, and hang up. It will keep a long time good, and when wanted for use it is cut in slices about an inch thick. I think it is altogether better than putting them up in skins.

> With much love to dear Lemuel
> and thyself we are all well—
> I remain thy affectionate sister
> Ruth Evans

We feel extreemly sorry not to be able to send on the things we had prepared for you. Elizabeth had written six sheets of paper full for A Coe, a letter to Aunt Anna, Aunt Nancy, Amelia, Ann, and thyself. I broke the seal of mine to make this addition. Thee may look for a long letter from Elizabeth soon. I hope we shall hear from you soon.

We both had a hand in making the little cake, and it has got burned so it only confirms the old adage that too many cooks spoil the broth. We have sent you a little sample of our flour. We frequently have it whiter. It is owing to the grinding. The onions we have sent as a specimen have grown from the seed sown in the spring. When Sammy Lovett left here the other day he engaged to dine with us today, but he started yesterday without letting us know. We felt fearful he was to do so and Thomas went to J Lovets this morning and to his surprise found he was gone.

Ruth probably sent the following poem with the preceding letter.

IMAGINATION

From early morn till eventide,
My thoughts will wander far and wide
Oer mountain, hill, and fertile vale,
And murmuring hill and verdant dale.
And through the lone and gloomy wood
Where many an oak for ages stood,
And nought is heard save the rustling leaves
Fanned by the pure and gentle breeze.
Here pensively I wander through
For nature's works I love to view
And oft I feel at such an hour
Dependant on Almighty power.
Amidst the forrest's peaceful gloom,
I pluck the wild flowers in full bloom.
Sweet is their fragrance neath the lofty trees
And sweet to me indeed are hours like these.
But I must now no longer linger here
I leave this scean where all is hushed and drear.
I must bid adieu to the distant west

To the land of my Father's I go in quest.
Before the autumnal leafs will fall
I'll away, away, to my native soil
There the rose and the myrtle blooms
There I can visit my Kindred's tombs.

R. Evans
10th month 1st 1833

———◦•◦———

ELIZABETH CHANDLER *to* JANE HOWELL
Hazelbank, October 28, 1833

My Dear Aunt

I wish sincerely thee could just at this moment take a peep in a[t] Hazlebank, or could have done so any time within the last three or four hours. It has been, as I have just remarked to Aunt R, quite an eventful day with us. In the first place though, to make thee understand all things correctly, I must go back to last fourth day afternoon, Oct 23rd, and tell thee to look in the glass at our little log dwelling, about two oclock in the afternoon. Aunt R, myself, and three of my young acquaintances were sitting quietly conversing, when one of the girls, looking out at the window, observed that a couple of friends were approaching—who proved to be Aunt Sally and Ann Comstock. Pretty soon Aunt Sally remarked that she had brought us a letter which she produced to our delighted eyes. Our first emotion on the discovery of so much blank paper was alarm, and I watched Aunt Rs countenance very anxiously till I discovered by the expression that all was well. Then, as soon as our friends had left us, commenced a *guessing match* brother and I soon arrived at the conclusion that the friend must be brother Will, which opinion we very dutifully persisted in, in opposition to Aunt Rs better judgment, and as is usually the case with wise acres, were doomed to gather a disappointment. Seldom has [a] letter been oftener read or the contents more carefully scanned than that of thine—from lamenting the non appearance of the box, we took to watching for "the friend," or at least introduced the former only as a varying paragraph in our impatience—or perhaps I should say *mine,* as I generally have the greater share of the talking to do on such occasions, as thee may readily suppose. Well one day past after another and neither box nor friend yet made their appearance. Aunt R assured us we need not expect to see Will this fall, but our faith still remained *almost* unshaken—but it went to the winds this morning.

Brother went over to Comstocks, where he found a letter from *William,* bearing an *Ohio post mark*—for a moment his hopes ran high—the next moment the words "favored by John Webster" caught his eye, and they fell again *below*—The letter stated that the bearer was from Wills neighborhood, who had proposed when he left them coming to Michigan, but by his sending the letter on by mail had we knew of course turned back. Could he be "the friend?" I must confess my dear Aunt, to having to hold up the "Post" pretty closely before my face for a few minutes, to conceal some symptoms of disappointment. As I contemplate the scattered and broken fragments of my bright visions, and fancied my *long letter,* that I had anticipated with so much pleasure, reaching an unwelcome destination in Philadelphia. Soon however brother and Aunt cheered me by arriving at the conclusion that John Webster was certainly not "the friend" and though he was not William, it was somebody that we should see yet—when the time came— and we gave up guessing and concluded to wait patiently.

About the middle of the afternoon, as I was sitting by the window, I saw a couple of men on horseback coming down the hill on the road about a quarter of a mile distant from the house. I would not concern myself much about them— though my work did not gain much while they were passing over the space which intervened between them and our big gate. They reached it—halted—I began to open my eyes a littler wider—but didnt think best to feel too much elated—they came in—came to the inner gate—brother passed the door with the corners of his mouth all puckered up, and presently ushered in Samuel Lovett! And he tells us my dear Aunt, that he left you all well—that he saw you but a short time before his departure. And I have read my long and very interesting letter—and we have opened our package, and looked over all the evidences of thine and Ann's kindness—and does thee wonder that I wished thee could take a peep into the cottage at Hazlebank and see how happy we look? Besides I forgot to tell thee, the box has come—not here yet but to John Lovetts—so that we have that to look forward to, and the letters which it contains. James Gamble's goods reached him this morning, so that Samuel Lovett was the bearer of that intelligence also.

Samuel and his friend took tea with us, and left about dusk since when thee may suppose I have been pretty busy to assist in all the talking that has had to be done, stand foreman in examinations, and all that sort of thing, and write a tolerably well sized letter to boot. It does not it is true contain much—it is not such an answer as thine deserves and I do not consider it an answer to *that*—but Aunt Ruth is writing thee a long letter and will I expect tell thee all the news and all the events of the day in Michigan. After however that has been perused, my scribbling may perhaps find acceptance, with all its imperfections on its head—for though I am aware, that I might send thee a better sample of penmanship, had I been more deliberate in writing, or by copying it off. I am not certain by any means that the latter operation would not render me unwilling to send so long a talk about nothing, as I am conscious that it is only as giving thee the prevailing feelings of the moment, that it is not altogether worthless.

Aunt R. has raked the fire, and as we are at the present season of the year, tolerably early risers, I suppose I must conclude for this evening at least, though it is not yet very late in the evening, or if it is, it has passed so rapidly that I am not aware of it. And with many thanks my dear Aunt for thy kind remembrances, I remain most affectionately

thy niece
Elizabeth

P.S. 11 mo. 3rd—We wish forwarded by this conveyance, a trunk belonging to Benjamin Lundy, which he was unable to carry with him when he left here. Enclosed in it are the few articles we have sent to you as a specimen of Hazlebank products—some hazelnuts—a little packet of flour—a cake—and a packet of letters—the other things belong to Benjamin, and we would be obliged to thee to take charge of the trunk till his return.[40] The picture—I had forgotten to mention—it is the one I have been painting for thee—it is not so well done as I could wish, by much, but I was obliged to paint by guess, and consequently could not do so with the same correctness. I should like to have sent thy patchwork by this opportunity, but have not yet got it finished, as sewing cotton run[s] low with us, and I felt unwilling unless compelled by actual necessity to purchase any of the slave manufacture. I shall not be able to make it the full size as I shall not have pieces enough. It will I expect require a border, perhaps of the width or a breadth of furniture calico.

— ◦ —

ELIZABETH CHANDLER *to* ANNA ROWE
Hazelbank, October 29, 1833

Dear Ann

The arrival of Samuel Lovett here is an event which will occasion quite a brisk motion of quills in this region, and fortunately it occurred at a time when we are not necessarily encumbered with much other business, and not which I believe has been the case before when there has been any private opportunity of sending letters from here to Philadelphia. The kind remembrances which thee sent to us reached Hazlebank in perfect safety, and thy beautiful little box bore its journey without the least diminution of its brilliancy. We are much obliged for all of them, and when worn or looked upon, will not fail to remind us of the giver. Aunt Jane's letter was quite a feast, and I have boasted myself not a little over Aunt and brother, who each, last week and yesterday, received a letter when I had none; but which were written on one page only, while mine was so well filled.

When James Gamble first came here, I was, as the folks say, "quite in a taking," letters for Aunt Ruth and brother, and none for me. And what made matters worse, I could not ascertain whether any were coming, for Aunt R. who was busy talking to James insisted on reading hers first, and she moreover actually got brother Tom's letter into her pocket also, so that I was left with nothing to satisfy my impatience but the letter of introduction, till brother compassionately give me permission to open his letter when he was talking with James, and I consoled myself with hoping that more might come, and Aunt Jane said nothing about it, and I thought she perhaps would have mentioned if any had not written. I can assure thee that it is not a little of an event to receive letters at Hazlebank from our distant friends—and when I find they are all well, it is such happiness.

I passed two days in the early part of last week with my friend Julia Webb, who was on the twenty fourth married to Esq. Chittenden of Adrian, a lawyer and a young man very highly thought of his acquaintances. He attends also to the business of the post office. We expect them to dine with us next first day. I shall miss Julia very much when she goes to Adrian. We understand that John Lovetts daughter Sally Ann is also going to be married to a young man residing not very far distant from them—but have not learned when it will probably take place nor are either of us acquainted with the young man who is spoken of as her intended. As to myself I still keep true in allegiance to the single sisterhood. The Society here has much improved since we first came on; there is a much larger circle, particularly of females, who seem to maintain the majority with us, though I believe it is not very customary for them to do so in new countries.

I think from the description of brother William's little Tom he must be a very pretty child, and I should love most dearly to see and to kiss him. While we were looking for William out here, we concluded he had paid you a visit in Philadelphia—but I suppose you have not seen him since ourselves.

We are a quill-driving set here just now; Aunt Ruth, Emily and myself have all been diligently occupied this afternoon with writing, and I hope we shall among us muster together no inconsiderable packet of letters. Brother alas of our household has made no alliance with pen and ink to day. He is employed in the [ ] task of assisting to raise a log house, for the neighbor who a short time ago [ ].

The country now looks what you citizens would call, I suppose, dreary. We do not feel it so, although it is now the time "of wailing winds and naked woods and meadows brown and serene." They are however at present whitened by quite a respectable coating of snow, which, much to the surprise of the Michiganians, has made us such an unseasonable visit. We have had yesterday and to-day, quite wintry weather, but I do not suppose it will last very long at present, though it is possible it may return, and establish its quarters with us sooner than usual. But we shall expect Indian summer and pleasant weather we still expect that

"Warm still days will come,
To lure the squirrel and the bee from out there winter home
When the sound of dropping nuts is heard through all the wood still
And twinkle in the smoky light the waters of the mill."

The autumn season is generally delightful here but the present one has been rather [ ]. High winds have prevailed considerably. By some, an early and cold winter is foreboded and indeed from present appearances it seems quite probably that it will be so.

I suppose a boarding school will this winter be opened in our neighborhood. Whether we shall have evening lectures again, I do not yet know, but I think it quite probable that there will be, as I have heard the subject several times spoken of, and a desire expressed for the delivery of another course which I think the lecturer will be willing to gratify. I expect if nothing occurs to prevent in the course of a week or two, to pay a visit of two or three days in the neighborhood of Tecumseh—principally at Samuel Saterthwaites. Emmeline Bixby, a daughter of one of our neighbor's is to accompany me. I went home a few first days ago with Eliza Clark, a young woman who came from Jersey about a year ago, and remained till the next afternoon when we paid a visit together and I returned in the evening. She had a short time before paid a visit of about the same length, and we had one of the longest rambles together that we have had [ ] for ramblings sake since we have been in Michigan, venturing fairly across the river and to the woods opposite, a thing I have by no means sufficient courage for when alone. I am talking some of these days when brother can escort me over the fallen tree that bridges the stream at another point, and convoy me through the woods beyond it, of paying a visit, of [ ] across the river.

I inquired of Samuel Lovett if you all look just as you did, and whether Ann is as lively as ever—he tells me, yes,—and while I am looking back I seem almost as if I could fancy myself among you again. But before I visit Philadelphia, many more changes then those which have already occurred, will probably have taken place there. There has already been not a little change and removal among my friends & acquaintances there. Hannah Townsend I should miss much, if I should visit there. I suppose you have not seen or heard any thing of her since her marriage. Brother returns his thanks for his hand some black handkerchief—and Emily is delighted with her presents—she talks of writing to thee herself and is highly pleased with having permission to do so. I am much obliged for the newspaper pieces thee sent me, they appear to be very interesting, but I have not yet indulged myself with the perusal of them. The ribband for my bonnet is very handsome, and I think those tippets will be most comfortable things for the neck besides being very pretty. I should love dearly to be able to send thee something of my own manufacture in the spinning line—but as we have as yet had nothing to spin, I have not made any proficiency in that branch of country economy. Perhaps in a few years I may be better able to astonish you with some specimens of my industry. I have left myself scarcely room enough to subscribe myself,

affectionately thy friend
EMC

13TH—

Thee may suppose my dear Aunt from the quantity I have written that by them I have been kept pretty busy for a couple of days past. I am now not a little sleepy and scarcely know whether I can muster resolution to carry me to the bottom of the sheet; but as I suppose this will go to the office tomorrow I must conclude tonight. We spent this afternoon at our friend Comstocks. They were all well. I had prepared thy cow picture to send thee by S. Lovett, but it still remains (as I cannot transcribe it to send by mail) in my own possession. In the box I found, very unexpectedly, a packet and letter from Hannah Longstreth which was very acceptable, as I had not heard from her for a long while, and knew not that she had written. I think from her descriptions she must have a very pretty situation for a residence, and I should like much to visit it. The box, brother brought with him on his return from Lovetts, in a wagon passing them on its way to meeting—and how much we regreted as we opened it that one was not on its way to Philadelphia! John Lovett expects to go up their sometime towards spring, or sometime during the winter. And thee may depend we shall keep a sharp watch that he does not get off without taking charge of letters at any rate. I hope dear Aunt we shall again have the pleasure of hearing from thee again before long. The articles in the box were very acceptable and we are much obliged for them.

I could not get quite to the end last night, and now I have only time to add a few words just to save my credit from the charge of sending blank paper. We are on the verge of setting out to pay a visit—riding with brother on his way to mill; and as we must not keep him waiting I am of course in hurried—not a little—for I have been otherwise engaged the former part of the morning and have not been able to attend to the finishing of my letter before. I wish thee or some of you could go with us this morning and try how riding goes with us. The weather now looks as if we might be going to have a spell in Indian summer, but

I do not know how long it will last. So dear Aunt please write very soon. We are all well—

and I am affectionately thy niece.
E.

ELIZABETH CHANDLER *to* AMELIA EVANS
Hazelbank, October 30, 1833

To Aunt Amelia

A private opportunity of forwarding letters from Michigan, having again occurred, I avail myself of it, to give thee what intelligence I can respecting thy friends in this place. Nothing however out of the usual order of events, has I believe occurred since I last wrote to thee. Day and night, summer and winter, seed-time and harvest, have passed quietly away, and returned again, since we came here, and left the record of no unusual events. We may look back with thankfulness to peaceful years, unstained by the traces of any overpowering source; not brightened by the remembrance of any unusual joy, but, which is perhaps the safest track of life, passed calmly amid seclusion and necessary labours. We learn from Aunt Jane's letter that thee has recently returned to the city, intending, I believe, to pass the winter there. During the summer the country is much more pleasant and I expect agrees better with thy health, but in winter I think the city offers thee decidedly superior advantages for a residence. I feel very thankful that the city, and surrounding parts of the country, have been so healthy this season and have escaped a second visit from the dreaded cholera. We felt during the summer much anxiety respecting it and I almost for a time feared to open the newspapers, lest they should contain a statement of its re-appearance.

Our own neighborhood has also been healthy; and I think may be allowed to claim a very fair character for salubrity of climate. Emigration has poured into our country this fall in a full and rapid stream. But there is ample room from the accommodation of settlers,—not in our immediate neighborhood for that is already full, except where a farm is sometimes portioned off, or [ ] to accommodate a wishful purchaser—but on the north, south, and west there is range and variety of land, enough to suit all sorts of people. And to some, the more unsettled parts present for the greater attraction, while others prefer and are willing to pay an advanced price for farms which have been already brought under some cultivation.

There have no few changes taken place in the appearance of the country around us since we came here. And I have now become so familiar with the sight of fences and houses, that it looks almost strange when I happen to get into a spot where there are none visible, I have not yet paid a visit to the new settlements across the river Raisin, though I think I shall sometime have the curiosity to do so. They have a Preparitive meeting over there, but it is yet held in the house of one of the members. When I look at the alterations and improvements that have been made here since we first came, and think of those that have occurred in Philadelphia, I am sometimes almost at a loss to determine imediately what length of time has really elapsed since we left there; and more than once when I have been asked the question, I have been obliged to pause in my reply in order to consider. In the whole and thickly settled parts of the country years pass away and make little alteration either in the appearance of the country or the neighborhood; but here not only the appearance of things but the people themselves are less stationary, both as to numbers and sameness. The population not only increases in denseness, but the farms are more frequently transferred to different owners. Several of those about us have passed into different hands from those by which they were held when we came here; and several others will probably change owners in the course of another season. I learned this morning that a very respectable family of Friends from Mount Pleasant, Ohio, have this week come into our neighborhood and expect to settle somewhere not very far distant.

There has been a considerable quantity of peaches raised this season around the neighborhood of Tecumseh, and some in this settlement. They are not a very certain product here, for the finer weather in the fall is apt to start the buds, which the frost of the winter afterwards kills. This season I believe all kinds of fruit have been abundant, if we may judge from the produce of the wild fruits in this neighborhood, and the few cultivated ones that are brought into bearing. It seems of so much more importance to procure the staple articles of life, that farmers are apt to postpone for awhile the planting of orchards; but some of the earliest settlers have trees which have commenced bearing tolerably well.

Samuel Lovett's visit to Michigan seems to have afforded an opportunity of coming out here almost good enough to have tempted some of you to avail yourselves of it; but he stays so short a time that it would hardly pay for the fatigue of the journey, if there was a necessity of going back with him.

I do not know whether thee is aware that we have not such a thing as an open fireplace in our whole house. We have a stove, which for cooking by I like much better than an open fireplace, and I think they warm a room also better. But it would seem queer in Pennsylvania to have a house built in that manner. The cooking stoves that are in use here are, however, I think, much superior to any I ever saw in Philadelphia.

I should be much gratified if thee would write to me some of these times, when opportunity offers. Aunt Ruth intended writing to thee by the present conveyance, but she thinks she will scarcely have leisure for doing so. She and brother Thomas both desire their love to thee. Brother has so much business on hand that he has scarcely time to write to any body. He still continues to like farming as well as ever, and is allowed by his friends here to succeed extremely well. I think he has increased in size considerably since he has been here—but he is not so much altered that you would find any difficulty in recognizing him.

Our neighborhood has become so civilized that we have not heard the cry of the wolf for a long time; but there are still some lingering about not very far distant, though their number is still decreasing; every season more or less of them are shot and trapped by the hunters; but they are yet sufficiently numerous to render the keeping of sheep troublesome and far less profitable than it would otherwise be, as they must be penned every night to defend their safety, in a place inaccessible to the prowlers, or defended in some way from their oppressors. This has deterred brother as yet from purchasing sheep, as he could not afford the time necessary to hunt them and bring them from the woods each evening. I have never yet seen any wild animals since we have been here except deer. They are very pretty creatures, especially when running. There are some bears, but they are not numerous, as thee may judge from the circumstance of four dollars having been paid last summer for a young one, captured somewhere towards Tecumseh, by a young man who wished to carry it to the state of New York. Several have been shot this fall, I understand, across the river. I have not yet had the pleasure of tasting the meat, but it is said to be very good. I cannot say that I feel very desirous to become acquainted with its flavor. The fire has grown low, and Aunt Ruth has more than once proposed my deferring the conclusion of my letter till tomorrow; but I have so nearly reached the [ ] boundary of my paper that I shall have no more than sufficient space to subscribe myself, dear Aunt,

very affectionately thy niece,
E.M. Chandler.

———•◆•———

ELIZABETH CHANDLER *to* JANE HOWELL
Hazelbank, November 11, 1833

My dear Aunt

I doubt not thee will feel much disappointed at Samuel Lovett having returned and brought nothing from thy friends at Hazlebank, but thee will not be more disappointed and worried than we ourselves have been about it. Probably Aunt Ruth's letter will reach thee before he returns, as it was sent off immediately when we found he had gone, but as it was already so full as to admit of only a very brief explanation, I will mention the circumstances more fully.

On second day afternoon the day after they reached John's, Samuel Lovett and his friend came over to see us. They took tea with us and on taking leave, engaged to dine with us the next first day, and we pressed them to visit us in the interval if they could, to which they assented. We then set to work most industrious to write letters for Philadelphia; being desirous to send so many as we could by so good an opportunity. Our box, Samuel informed us, had that morning reached John Lovett's. As thee may suppose, we were impatient enough to receive it, and have an opportunity of examining its contents, and I was doubly eagerly waiting for [it]. Third and fourth days, brother was busy working at Jacob Hoag's, so there was no chance of getting it thus far; and as we expected we could have it brought up by one of our neighbors on fifth or sixth day, and brother was exceedingly busy; we thought it as well to be patient that long—especially as there seemed to be no real necessity for our getting it just then and we concluded that I should have time to answer the letters it contained the next week, or if I did not, as I had so much written it would be of less consequence. And we supposed if we did not get it before we certainly should on first day, as we knew it would be no trouble for Lovetts to put it in the wagon and bring it up with them. We were looking for them almost every day through the week, and should have liked to go over there ourselves to have talked as much as we could with Samuel about you. We were so engaged, brother without and ourselves within, that we were not able to do so. Brother's wagon too was away at the blacksmith's shop for the purpose of being repaired, which was another reason for his not going there.

On sixth day he went over to the shop, with the intention, if he could get it, of going to Lovetts, and Aunt R. had intended to ride over with him. It was not however finished. On seventh day afternoon he went over there again and then learned that Samuel talked of going sooner than he had at first calculated. That day morning he walked over directly after breakfast, but twas too late. Samuel had started the day before. He was very much worried. He said that hurried as he was and important as his business was, he had rather have lost three whole days in going over there than it should have happened so. And though he would have gone fifth or sixth day if his wagon had been mended, yet if we had in the least urged it he would have borrowed one—but we both told him he had better leave it, as under such circumstances he would have lost a whole day, and the weather was very uncertain to continue fit for his business, till it was completed.

He was, and still is busy husking corn—fifty bushels of which he engaged week before last—and it is work, which if not done in season in the fall, is sometimes obliged to be left till the next spring, which he could not do without much disadvantage—and week before last winter seemed to be coming upon us almost immediately. The weather has been much more unpleasant and unsettled this fall than usual, and it is thought probable by some that the winter will set in early.

Uncle Darius yesterday received safely the goods which he imported from Lockport, as which he was apprehensive had been lost in the passage. David Steer and family, very respectable Friends from Mount Pleasant Ohio, moved into our neighborhood about two weeks ago, and have purchased a farm a few miles distant from us. His wife, and the first wife of Isaac Bonsale late of Philadelphia were sisters. He had some idea of purchasing Harris's farm, in which case we should have had them for near neighbors, but they could not agree upon terms. Harris has not yet sold.

Brother has engaged all the pork he will have to spare to five dollars a hundred [pounds]. The digging of his potatoes is completed and he has secured them for the winter—or for sale if demanded; but the larger portion of this crop is usually disposed of in the spring. He wished much to get some ploughing done this fall if possible.

Tell Anna that I am exceedingly obliged for her packet and intend writing to her very soon—my [ ] work of writing to her will have to be delayed till another opportunity, but I will endeavor to finish a letter next week to go by mail or etc. for my other letters. Those intended for thyself Aunt Amelia and Ann, I believe I will do with as I threatened when I first heard Samuel had gone—copy them all off on to a *big sheet,* and send them to their place of destination together—though copying a letter is what I much dislike, even to read it over being a task that I very often do not burden myself with. Yet if you will in the present instance accept of them in this form, I will undergo the penalty of discovering all their imperfections and re-writing them, with pleasure.

CHAPTER 6

MAJOR CHANGES, 1834

*The year 1834 brought major changes in the lives of the Chandler/Evans house-
hold in Michigan and the Howell household in Philadelphia. Thomas built his
barn. The Howells moved to another section of the city, and Jane gave up her dry
goods business. The anticipation of Lemuel and Jane Howell's oft-discussed trip
to Michigan resurfaced and then again dissolved. But the single most significant
and difficult development was Elizabeth's protracted illness and finally her
death on November 2.*

JANE HOWELL *to* RUTH EVANS
Philadelphia, January 20, 1834

Whilst I was reading thy letter my dear Sister which I received by Post, after
Samuel Lovett had left you, and my spirits highly elated in hearing from you and
my imagination actively employed in dividing the cake, distributing the nuts,
and in shewing the specimans of flour, onions &c &c amoung my friends interested in your welfare; how greviously was I disappointed when thee informed me
that Samuel had taken his departure without seeing you. I was ready to say with
Soloman, "all is vanity and vexation of Spirit"[1] and indeed I do not know wether
Job's patience would not have wavered on a similar tryal; but be that as it may, it
produced the spirit of grumbling in me which extended down as far as Robert
Coe's. It was so sadly provoking that I felt as if I could hardly see him when he
returned. To think he was so near you, with such a ready mode of conveyance, the
friendly footing which we have been on for so many years, the great distance
which seperates you from me, the pleasure I have allways expressed to him, when
thro' Johns letters I have heard from you, admits of no excuse that can be any how

satisfactory to me. And I will strive to annihilate any thing like resentment, altho thee knows my dear Sister with what an ill grace I bear disappointment. I am not like thyself, think every thing is for the best. I do not look behind the curtain, but view things in their present form, which perhaps causes me moments of discontent. To see, taste, and handle, are real realities and which I thought I had realized until I came to the cross lines in thy letter—and then how shockingly provoking it was, to find it all vanish just like waking from a pleasant dream, and leave nothing but disappointed.

Samuel Comfort was here a few days since. He was making many inquiries after Thomas, and his farming. He appeared much pleased to hear he was progressing so well. He has intended writing. He says it is a task he seldom undertakes unless he has urgent business. He desired to be affectionately remembered to my dear Nephew.

Margaret Hall is about opening a Tavern, in Second below Coates Street, to be called the Fifth Ward Hotel. It is no doubt a great tryal to her friends that she should follow such an occupation. Her daughter Rebecca and her two children board with her. James Coe is at his fathers. She will not allow them to live together.

We have been reducing our Stock of dry goods for more than a year past with an intention of moving into the Western part of the City. Lemuel allows me to choose a house in any direction within six or seven squares from his shop, which is in Coates Street above Eleventh St but I do not suppose we shall leave here before the second or third month as Lemuel does not wish to make a change until he has finished J. A. Williams house which I suppose will be done by that time. We have found the cloak business quite brisk this winter. We have made a proffit of between 3 and 4 hundred dollars on them.

Since the removal of the public funds from the United States Bank, the mercantile business has declined to a very low ebb in the City, oweing to the great scarcity of money, caused by the Banks refusing to discount. Mark Richards and many of our *big* men have stop'd payment, or broken, and a vast many of our greatest Merchants will be placed in the same predicament if they do not speedily obtain relief from their pecuniary embarrassments. I should suppose Jacksons friends would have their eyes pretty well unbandaged now, to see how they have been duped and drawn by his mismanagement in public affairs, into a labyrinth of perplexity and trouble, from which, no doubt, they will find it hard to extricate themselves.[2]

I am not going to fill my sheet with politics so I will turn to something of a more interresting nature. Were you eye witnesses to the great Phenomena, which appeared on the morning of the 13th of November last? I think no national being could have viewed it, without being filled with awe. To see thousands of flying stars (as they are so called) shooting at the same moment in every direction from different centres, leaving behind them long trails of light, was truely grand, and to those who could divest the minds of fear, a very interresting sight. One of those centres or starting places (if they may so be called) appeared immediately over our Yard, so that we had a very fine view of them, and the light emitted from them when clashing against each other, appeared almost like lightning. It commenced I believe about two oclock in the morning and continued until day light. I suppose they were seen in every state in the Union.[3]

John and Anna Merrefield were thrown into great consternation a few weeks since by their black woman being taken ill with the variloyd.[4] They immediately sent her to the hospital and the whole family, excepting my dear Aunts, underwent vacination.

Tell my dear Elizabeth I received her long and very interresting letter and I intend as soon as I have leisure to answer it. Anna Coe received hers a few days since. She thinks she will not write by Post, but wait until John Lovett returns. She spent an evening with us a short time since. She regrets leaving the City for a country life. I should think situated as they are, that she would greatly prefer it, and I should suppose that her health would be benefitted by the change. I do not hear when, or wether Rebecca is going to be married. Washington [Train] still goes there, but I rather think he is not in a business sufficient to support the expenses of house keeping. Cousin Robert Coe's health is better than it was some time ago, but Cousin Anna has been unwell for several weeks with a pain in her breast. Indeed I feel apprehensive sometimes that the drudgery and exposure attendant on a country life will be more than their constitutions can bear. If that should not be the case I think it probable they will enjoy better health. Cousin Robert went down to their place a few weeks ago and took his english walnut tree and a variety of shrubs plants with him as he thought it would be a better time than the spring for transplanting them.

The day after Christmas I had the pleasure of having my dear aged Aunt Anna and Aunt Nancy to dine and spend the remainder of the day with us. The reading of your letters to her affords her much pleasure as she takes the greatest interrest in your proceedings. She seems as if she could hardly praise Thomas enough for his industry and good management in farming, and looks forward to his becoming a rich man, and rising high in public esteem. Our dear Aunt appears just about the same as when you left here. She participated with me in the disappointment in not receiving the things you intended sending by S. Lovett.

How has the winter been with you so far? With us it has been uncommonly wet, every few days rain. I do not think we have had more than two weeks real cold weather this season. The Captain of the vessel in which George Guest sailed for South America has returned and says George is engaged to be married to a girl there. I did not hear any particulars about her as to her riches, beauty &c which I suppose she must possess or she would not suit Georges high notions. Mary

Guest (Jonathans wife) is in very ill health. It is very doubtful wether she will survive Jonathan's return—which is expected in the spring. I believe I mentioned in a former letter that he had gone to South America.

Next month I expect Louisa Hull will commence in the Mantua-making trade, as I expect she will leave me to go to her Mother after she is of age, which will be about the middle of August next, as her brother Washington is very desirous that they should all get together and make one family, their Mother being in delicate health, and out at service a few miles from New York.

I expect soon to spend a day with Cousin Anna Guest, and then as usual I shall be closely questioned about you. She speaks with admiration at Thomas' industry and progress in farming, and soon after you left here a great change in Cousins sentiments towards you, from a cold indifference to a warm affectionate regard for you, and an interest in all your undertakings. The first time you sent your love to them was in a letter to dear Aunts. Cousins seemed much gratified by it, and for the first time desired me when I wrote to give their love to you. And I do expect it was a great sattisfaction to dear Cousin Betsy [Guest] in her last illness to feel that the breach was repaired, for I do believe as she expressed herself, that she died with love to all. Cousin Anna has become more reconciled to the loneliness of her situation than she was, altho she says sometimes she feels as if she had not a friend in this world, and her house is a dismal home. Her home to be sure is a very altered one, but still she enjoys good health and the society of her friends which ought to be appreciated as a blessing. I wish sometime you would write to her or put a paragraph in one of my letters for her. I think it would be so very gratifying to her. I think it is quite time all hard thought should be laid aside.

As soon as we move I shall write and let you know where to direct your letters. We have all been hurried in our business so much that we have had but little time to look out for a house. I was looking at two in Seventh near Green Street both very pretty houses and pleasantly situated but they were too near a brick pond.[5] Ann is well and desires her love both to thee and Elizabeth and intends writing to you before a great while. Samuel Lovett was here yesterday. He and his family are well. We had the pleasure of hearing from you in a letter from John to his father. Tell John that I am much oblidged to him for so often mentioning you in his letters. Please give my love to the family.

I have not seen Emilys Mother since I wrote last. Her behaviour is very unnatural. I am very glad to hear that Emily can milk the cows and do so many things to help the best friends she has in this world. Give my love to her and tell her if she continues to be a good girl when I go to Michigan I will take her some nice presents. She must write to me when there is a private opportunity. I should like very much to receive a letter from her. Lemuel thinks and talks a great deal about you. He says it would be such a tryal to leave you after having paid you a visit that he thinks it would almost overballance the pleasure let it be ever so great, but I cannot adopt his sentiments there, for altho a great deal of bitter would be mixed with the sweet, yet the sweet would greatly preponderate. At any rate I shall be willing to try it next summer if no thing prevents. Lemuel desires a great deal of love to you.

Amelia is still in the Country. She was to see us a few weeks since and I heard from her last week. She was well. I have not heard from William since I wrote last. I intend writing to him soon, and then I hope I shall have a letter from him. We are all well and with much love to you all

> I remain affectionately thy sister
> Jane Howell

Please remember [me] to Aunt Sarah and Ann Comstock.

ELIZABETH CHANDLER *to* JANE HOWELL
Hazelbank, January 27, 1834

My dear Aunt

What can be the reason of our having received no letter for such a very long time? Are any of you ill? Or have thee written and the letter never reached us? It is more then three months since we received thy last one, and we have heard indirectly but once since, which was from a letter written by Samuel Lovett shortly after his return. Samuel then said you were well—but that was a long while ago, and we have looked and looked for a letter till it seems almost as if we were not [to] hear again from you. J. Lovett was here a few week ago. He had then received two letters from Pennsylvania since the return of his father, and we have not all this time received one. The "Post" still reaches us and the covers are directed by thyself, which seems some assurance that Philadelphia has not vanished altogether, and as we cannot suppose that thee has become quite indifferent to us, what can we imagine but that thee is not well enough to write, or that some other of our friends is sick? Or if we would try to console ourselves by supposing that possibly some unknown reason may have prevented, still we cannot help feeling much anxiety and fearing the worst. Aunt Ruth, particularly, has long been very uneasy; and I, though not very prone to anticipate evil, can think of no satisfactory reason by which to plausibly account for thy silence.

So my dear Aunt, as we cannot get a letter to reply to, in order to spare thee the anxiety which we feel, we have concluded that it is best to write again, though it is for the third time, without an answer. I think it scarcely needful now to say, "do write to us," for if thee has not done so before sufficient time will elapse for the receipt of this, there must undoubtedly be some painful cause for thy silence, and thee can easily conjecture that if we should not receive a prompt reply imagination would not be idle in picturing the worst. But I can not think that so much time will pass before we hear from you. Thee surely must have written before this time.

Well, thee wants, I suppose, by this time to know how Hazlebank and its inhabitants are coming on. As to the former, it has been covered two or three times this winter several inches deep with snow, but it at present wears only a coating of about an inch in depth. At a short distance from the house are lying some long pieces of hewed timber, which are next summer to favor a position of a barn. It is to be 30 by 40 feet in size, and the carpenters work to be done for 55 dollars, part paid in wheat, and the hands boarded. Brother had expected that James Gamble would do it for him, but he had engaged in another job, which he could not leave and brother could not wait its completion on account of drawing his timber during the winter season, which must be done, or he would be obliged to defer it another year. James is delighted with Michigan. He says he could not like it better, and shall always feel grateful to uncle for advising him to come out here. He has bought a house and piece of ground of John Lovett, and has had plenty of work with good wages ever since he came here—much better wages brother says than he could have made at building his barn, at the price (which is the usual one) that he is to pay for it—which made brother more indifferent about his undertaking it. His wife too is much pleased with the country and well contented.

Sally Ann Lovett was married some weeks ago. She and her husband have since paid us a visit. He appears like a clever young man and quite suitable for her. There has not been very much sleighing here this winter. We have had some cold weather, but only a few days severly so. The third and fourth of this month were the coldest there has been this winter. The thermometer in the evening of the fourth was several degrees below zero.

I see by the last number of the Genius that the paper is to publish in Philadelphia. We have not yet learned whether B. L. has yet returned from Mexico, as the January no. has not yet reached us—if it has been published.[6]

David Steer and his wife, from Ohio, paid us a visit some weeks since. He says Hazlebank is the prettiest place on the openings that he has seen in Michigan. He enquired of several persons when he first moved in, if brother would not sell, but received no encouragement to apply to him. His wife and daughter also were delighted with our situation.

Application has lately been made to the Legislative Council, to set off a part of the town of Logan, and give it the name of Raisin—which town we shall be in.[7] Brother was strongly solicited to accept the office of Magistrate, but he would not consent, not being persuaded even by the temptation of being dubbed Squire Chandler, or writing his name Thomas Chandler Esq.

Brother is as busy as a bee this winter. He has his hands full with preparing for building. A little more snow would be an assistance to him in drawing his logs to the mill—and probably in the course of a few days we shall have more. The hewed timber for the frame he to day completed drawing up to its station. He wishes also to make preparation for building a kitchen sometime during the course of next summer—which will be a great convenience to us.[8]

As for Philadelphia we know not what is taking place there, except as the newspapers inform us; and as they do not usually contain much intelligence respecting our particular friends and their concerns, we are quite as much in the dark on that point as is desirable. I suppose Cousin Coe's are by this time quite busily making preparations for moving. Anna has I expect long since received my letter. Tell her I am impatient for a reply. I hope they will be pleased with a residence in Jersey.

You too, have you put in operation the contemplated change in your residence? We have endeavored to hope that the occupation and care attendant upon a removal may perhaps be the cause of thy long silence. But if so how are we to know to direct our letters unless thee thinks proper to enlighten us? This poor thing itself may perhaps be a homeless wanderer—but I hope I am sure that it may eventually reach its right destination, for I have no inclination to have the Clerks at Washington peering into the recesses of any of my letters.

Does thee know, Aunt, that it is *four months,* except a very few days (either two or three) since the date of thy last written letter? Aunt Ruth says thee is not setting us a good example. Does thee think it is? We have been looking for a letter by every mail for these six weeks or more and thee knows a disappointment lasting six weeks is rather a formidable attack on one's patience. If we only knew that you were well, we might be more contented; though every thing passing among you is very interesting to us, and I think during so long a time many things must have occurred. We go on just about as usual—soberly and quietly—brother making gradual improvements, as he can manage them.

The scarcity of money, occasioned by the removal of the bank deposits, which the papers complain of, I suppose must have considerable effect in making business dull—though I do not recollect that the papers say it is so. There has been much talk here lately about constructing a railroad through the territory. Meetings have been held on the subject, and I believe it is intended to apply to Congress about it. It would be a great advantage to the inland farmers, and the face of the country generally, favours the undertaking very much, as it will not be so expensive by much as over a broken and irregular surface. If constructed, it will pass through Adrian, I suppose.

2D MO 1ST—

February has come in most pleasantly. The sun is shining clearly and the air quite mild—but I do not pretend to prophesy how long it will last. Brother has been for a couple of days past working on the roads. They are building another bridge across the river. Our new country requires the formation and laying out of many roads, but luckily they are not generally very difficult or tedious in the making—but through the timbered and bottom lands they require more work than on the openings.

We have several times in our letters, thee will probably remember, mentioned Samuel Satterthwaite's family. His wife, a very fine woman, died very suddenly a few weeks since. It is an exceeding great loss to him and to their children and the information will doubtless be very distressing to their Jersey friends.

EVENING—

Brother has just gone over to Comstocks. They expected this evening to hear from the Post Office, and he has gone to see if there is any thing for us. Will he bring a letter? Or is this state of suspense to continue yet longer?

I believe I have said all concerning ourselves and our affairs that would be of much interest to thee. I can however think of nothing more at present. Brother has brought no letter. We must again look forward to the arrival of the mail—perhaps again to be disappointed. But I do not wish to worry thee with complaints. We will still endeavor to hope for the best. Give our love to our dear Aunts, Cousin Anna G. and our other friends. Tell Ann Aunt Ruth says she must not give up the idea of writing to her, but put it in practice. Our love to her and Louisa—with much to uncle, Aunt Amelia and thyself. I should have been glad to acknowledge the receipt of a letter before closing, and have delayed closing my letter for several days; since its commencement in the hope it might be so—but it seems scarcely worthwhile to detain it longer. Thee must be anxious to hear from us by this time—and I have the satisfaction to annex the important words We are all well—I remain with much affection

thy neice
EM Chandler

JANE HOWELL *to* ELIZABETH CHANDLER
Philadelphia, February 18, 1834

My dear Niece

I have just received thy letter expressing a great deal of anxiety at not receiving a letter from me for nearly four months but I assure thee that I wrote a very long one to my dear Sister Ruth and dispatched it from here three or four weeks since in company with an Almanack and two numbers of the Post. I hope my letter will yet come to hand for like thyself I should be averse to having the contents scan'd by the eyes of strangers. I am very sorry that you have suffered so much from my long silence, for indeed it was a long one, even at the time I last wrote, for I know from sad experience the tortures of protracted suspence. I feel strongly convicted, plead to be excused and will try to do better for the future.

Samuel Lovett was here a few days since. He and the family are well. He says John intends coming on to see them in March. Anna Coe says she has been filling several sheets with her pen to send on to thee by him. She received thy letter by mail. I am sorry she feels so much reluctance at going into Jersey to live, and what adds to it, Rebecca will be married before they go, if Washington [Train] can get a house to suit him. I pity Cousin Robert and Anna Coe very much. They are so much devoted to their children and have their interrest and happiness so very much at heart, and then to have to leave the greatest part of them, situated as they are, almost pennyless, and the times so adverse to making a livelihood, and James's health so very delicate, must make them feel quite uncomfortable and may I not add very unhappy. I am glad to hear James Gamble and his wife are so well pleased with Michigan. John McClellan another of Lemuels journeymen thinks he shall go on there before long. Please remember us to them.

Lemuel has just finished Cousin John Williams house, and has commenced a pretty large job for Joshua Lippincott in Market St. but I suppose he will finish it in time for us to go to Michigan, but if you are going to build this summer you will have no room nor time for visitors, but if we go we will promise to lend a hand. Our dear Aunty Anna and Nancy spent last seventh day with me. They were well.

I think my dear Nephew was nearly right in rejecting the office of Majistrate and all its attendant honors for I should not think it a very lucrative calling in your *back woods* but might suit some more aspiring character. I cannot give you a correct idea from words how much I want to see you but you must ask your own hearts and I think they will tell you. I hope you will retain your former looks so that I shall recognize you when I see you or half the pleasure of my visit will be lost.

Ann desires her love to you and intends writing soon. Indeed she proposed writing today in answer to thy letter, but I thought I could scratch a few lines in less time as I wished them put into the Post office to day, so as to relieve your anxiety as speedily as possible. We have not moved from Second Street yet not having found a house to suit us. There are a great many unoccupied in the Western part of the City but they are too near brick ponds but as soon as we move I shall write and let you know.

When I began this I expected to have written but a few lines, not as an answer to thy letters. I would pay them a greater compliment but merely to allay your feelings, but if I keep on I shall make it out quite a long letter which will do to go against one of thine. I hope thee will be able to read it for I am in such a prodigious hurry that I hardly know what I am writing. Amelia Merrefield gave me a copy of some lines written on the death of George Dillwin. I thought my dear Sister Ruth would like to read them and I have copied them on this sheet. Thy Aunt Amelia is at present in the country. She frequently comes down to see me. She desired her love to you. I intend writing to thy brother William soon, for I do not believe I shall get a letter from him until I do, altho I wrote to him last. Lemuel was delighted as well as myself to hear from you to day. I must now conclude with much love and remain affectionately

> thy Aunt
> Jane Howell
> We are all Well.
> We are all quite well.

ON THE DEATH OF GEORGE DILLWIN OF BURLINGTON
> Fully ripe like the ear of the reaper
> He met the pale Messengers word
> O! Sweet is the sleep of the Sleeper
> That rests in the name of the Lord
> For the Storm that on earth often gathers
> To unknown in the Heavenly clime
> They have placed the cold earth on his ashes
> They have given him up to the tomb
> But the light of his virtues still flashes
> The pathway of Truth to illume
> He is dead—but his memory still liveth
> He is gone—his example is here

And the lustre and fragrance it giveth
Shall linger for many a year
He stood in the might of his weakness
With the snows of long years on his head
And sublime with a patriarchs meeting
The Gospel of Jesus he spread
The path of the faithful he noted
In the way of the faithful he trod
And his life was with and our devoted
In the cause of religion and god
Like the stream that in the Cataracts pouring
Frets and chases and turmoils in its foam
And for many a mile in its roaring
Till it finds in some calm lake its home
So he long in this lifes rugged station
Through the world and its vanities prest
And now having closed his probation
He enters the Haven of rest
He has wandered away like the setting
Of stars in the dead of the night
But we are not in the darkness forgetting
The Fountain that rendered it bright
Let his name be a beacon to light us
And guard us from slumbering snares
O! that we may die as the righteous
And our Journeys end be like to theirs.
For theres joy in the grief of the weeper
Whose loss may above be restored
And sweet is the sleep of the sleeper
That rests in the name of the Lord.

ELIZABETH CHANDLER *to* JANE HOWELL,
Hazelbank, March 9, 1834

Thanks, my dear Aunt, for thy prompt reply to my last letter. It reached us last sixth day evening (day before yesterday) and I have sat down to give it an early answer, while we may know where to direct, but in much better spirits for writing than when I commenced my last letter. Thine, to Aunt Ruth reached us a day or two after mine was sent off, and what a relief it was to our anxiety, I need not tell thee. The Almanack, I suspect made a little call somewhere on the road, as it did not reach here till near a week afterwards. The fun, however, was not "all read out of it," nor is yet for it was but the other day it excited the visible faculties of some visitors of ours in no small degree.

It is a great satisfaction that our dear Aunts continue so well, and is it pleasant to hear of their visiting thee frequently. It seems to approach the nearest to a participation in their society, that we now may, unless in memory or imagination, and then we at least have the satisfaction of thinking that you frequently talk of us. Give our love to them most affectionately, I should think Aunt Anna and cousin Anna Guest would take great pleasure in each other's society, though the distance between them I suppose must prevent their enjoying it very frequently. How lonesome cousin Anna must be. She has many relatives and friends it is true, but there are none who can supply the place of her she has lost. How much of the hearts happiness can depend upon one tie.

I was quite surprised to learn that there was a prospect of Rebecca Coe's being married so soon as this spring. Anna must indeed anticipate the parting from her with much pain, for no doubt it will be a great trial to her. She would miss her very much if they both remained in the city, but much more in the retirement of a country life, the pleasures of which are so enhanced by the company of those we love.

And are we really my dear Aunt to permit ourselves to anticipate a visit from uncle and thyself next summer? How much delight the idea affords us, and how much we talk about it, I need not attempt to say, for thee can readily imagine. Thee speaks of it more confidently than thee has hitherto done, and our hopes rise in proportion. We being to feel as if we may let our hearts jump about at the thought of seeing you, without bidding them be quiet with their tantalizing. As to our being engaged with building and work people, do not give thyself a moments concern about that, for we expect to get through quite early in the season, and moreover shall not have more than one or perhaps two hands employed about the remainder of it, except the raising. These framed barns and buildings do not require so much work and so many labourers as the substantial stone ones of Pennsylvania, and that part of the work which requires most hands is now done. The kitchen brother will not I expect, do anything at all till his barn is completed, and the hurry of his summer business over—and it will not occupy more than one hand, when it is engaged in—which may not be till late in the fall.

We have had a very mild winter this season, and very little sleighing. Last month, particularly, the weather was warm and spring like. March came in cold and snowy, but soon changed—but whether the spring will eventually be as forward as the weather has seemed to indicate is yet to be known. Emily brought me in some Johnny Jump up's, in bloom, from the garden several weeks ago; and I expect some gardening work could have been very well attended to had we been prepared for it.

Last third day afternoon, the books were opened at Adrian, for subscriptions to the stock in Erie and Kalamazoo Railroad. It is to pass through Adrian, and that part running from Port Lawrence to Adrian will be commenced shortly and first completed. Fifty thousand dollars was the amount to be subscribed at present, at fifty dollars a share, and it was all taken up in less than three days. Upwards of twenty five thousand dollars were subscribed the first afternoon—and the greater portion of the stock is divided in small portions round the neighborhood from two to five, and ten shares being the amount most usually taken. Brother when he went up to the village had not intended taking any, but he concluded that he would be quite safe in venturing on a couple of shares as the money is to be paid in by small investments during the course of several years. There is no doubt but it will be a safe, and probably a very profitable investment for money, when the road gets under operation. There must be in time an immense amount of produce sent out to the lake, and the rail-road will be the most ready mode of conveyance from this section of the country; and by the stock being mostly held in the neighborhood, it will not even carry from the country the money received for toll, the rates of which can also be measurably regulated by the farmers themselves.

We were over spending an afternoon at Comstocks last week—and in answer to their enquires had the pleasure of telling them that we expected a visit from you next summer. Aunt Sally took tea with us last fifth day. Brother has engaged her youngest son, a lad of fifteen, to work for him this summer, and he is now with him. We are glad for brother to have some assistance about his work, and such a lad, in some kinds of business can be as useful as a man. He is to allow him six, or six dollars and a half a month—the wages of a man is twelve dollars—most frequently that much when engaged for the year round—when but for a few months during the long days, more than that. Labourers are scarce and much in demand and consequently the rates of payment are high.

We have not seen John Lovett very lately but he has promised very faithfully to let us know before he goes to Pennsylvania. However, brother intends going in the course of a few days to see him about it. We have been expecting a visit from them for some time past, and probably they will pay it before he goes.

We have not received a letter from brother Will for several months past, but he is so irregular a correspondent that we do not feel much surprised at it. Did we not occasionally hear of him from thee, in addition to his infrequent letters, we should often have cause for uneasiness. He owes us a letter now, but when it will come I know not—perhaps when like thyself we write to him again. Please when thee writes give my love to them, and tell them to make haste and learn little Tom to write letters to his Michigan aunts.

Brother has already commenced with his ploughing, on the ground which he intends for oats. He had great deal of business on hand this spring but thinks he shall be able to get through with it in good season. While I am writing I am thinking almost continually of your expected visit—so if I blunder and blot a little thee need not be surprised—Heigh ho—that visit! We talk of it, and re-talk—and we shall appreciate it too, for we know what an exertion it will require to leave home, and that it will be attended with some sacrifice. However I hope you will find your journey a very pleasant one, and feel your health benefited by it.

Thee did not mention in thy letter whether Cousin Robert Coe's family expect to remove. The third month was talked of some time ago, but if this wedding takes place I suppose it will be delayed by it for a while.

We see by one of the last papers that Joseph Mather has met with another severe affliction in the loss of some of their sons—and the suddeness of his death and the manner of it, must add to their grief of his parents. They seem to have had many trials lately, in the loss of children.

There has been a travelling Professor of Elocution [R. W. Ingalls] lately delivering a course of lectures at Adrian. His terms were fifty dollars for a course of thirty lessons to be "administered" during the course of ten days. He taught on a system peculiar to himself. He was engaged at Tecumseh for two courses—at Detroit for several and expects yet to teach in several other places in our Territory. He purchased a village lot at Adrian, on which he talks of erecting a printing office and establishing a newspaper.[9] It was rather a compliment to our village as it seemed to show that he considered it a more enterprising and thriving place than Tecumseh.

Brother has engaged some young apple trees and grafts, wherewith to set us out a small orchard this spring—which, though anxious for it, he has not been able to do before. So you must not expect us to treat you with apple dumplings and cider, when you come to see us—though as to the latter, we are such temperance folks here, that I do not know that there will be any presses erected, even when fruit is plenty. Anti-slavery principles too are gaining ground. Daniel Smith last first day mentioned the subject in his sermon, and spoke upon it for some time. Thee may suppose that I listened to him with much pleasure. Uncle Darius is very much interested in the subject as is his wife also.

Barney Harris has not yet sold his place but probably will when emigrants come in, without any difficulty. He thinks he may improve his circumstances by selling his and buying new land again, at government price. Give our love to Maria Woodside when thee sees her. I suppose she is still in the city.

The navigation, if the weather continues this open, will commence I expect, on the lake earlier than usual—the canal also will be much sooner free from ice if the weather in the state of New York matches ours. Another census of the population of Michigan will probably be taken next summer, as it [is] thought that the Southern Members of Congress will object to our territory being received into the Union, unless a slave state could be admitted the same time—so it must be able to demand admission with a population of sixty thousand inhabitants. That number it probably contains now, or not far short of it—and perhaps more, for it contained forty thousand when we came out here, and has increased no little since then. The new town Raisin has been set off by the Council so we are no longer inhabitants of Logan. Hazlebank, however, still continues in its old place—and its inhabitants are still "at home." We are still in the same town with Uncle Darius, but the limits of his place form the boundary as far as they extend, between Raisin and Logan. A surveyed Town contains six miles square, but they are set off in larger divisions till they become settled.

Give our love to Ann, and tell her she must be sure and write by John Lovett. I hope we shall receive a large package by him. Tell Anna that I [am] very glad to hear that she is writing, and that I hope she will continue. I did intend to have written to her by mail again before they moved, but did not get any letter finished in time—so she will get it in a packet with the others. I shall look for John's return with a great deal of interest, and I hope the other girls will also then write to me.

Thee does not mention what time in the summer you will be most likely to undertake your journey, but I suppose you can scarcely tell yourselves yet. I dare say you feel curious to see what sort of a country. Description will not fix the picture on the mind like eyesight. But you must not anticipate too much. Remember where we are. Our country is very different in its appearance from what you have been accustomed to and may at first appear rude, and less pleasant than to us who have been longer familiar with it. I do not however fear that you will be disappointed. I do not think my descriptions have done it more than justice, though they may have failed to give a correct idea of it. But you must not look for neatly railed fences, grass plots and flourishing shrubbery studding them at graceful distances. No—we are new yet. Make up your minds for worm fences, girdled trees, and stumps. Do not expect to set at the window and inhale the scent of clover fields and newly mown hay, nor to see a picture cottage, with all its softened tints and its low mossy roof peeping up among the umbrage of beautiful trees. But before very many months pass, perhaps you will yourselves tell us what you think of it—and that will be better than all this letter writing—good as that is in the want of a better mode of conversation.

Please give our love to cousin Anna Guest—to cousin Coes family and with much to Aunt Amelia and yourselves I am, on behalf of Aunt Ruth and brother, as well as myself,

affectionately, thine
E.M.C.

We are all well. Thee has not, my dear Aunt, mentioned, whether you intend quitting the dry good business, or only to retrench it. Will thee please say when thee next writes? for we are, as thee is aware, very much interested in all that concerns you. I suppose you will remove before [ ] and we shall feel very desirous to know where you have fixed [ ]. No doubt thee will inform us, but do not defer writing too long, for [ ] or be able to tell us. We are always impatient to hear.

— · —

RUTH EVANS *to* JANE HOWELL
Hazelbank, March 16, 1834

My Dear Sister

I received thy very acceptable letter about eighteen days after it was mailed, and should have replyed to it before now, if I had known certain you had not removed from Second Street. We think it probable J Lovett will go to Pennsylvania before long, and we will endeavor to send letters by him, if he dose not serve as like his father did. I can assure thee we were sadly [disappointed] in not forwarding on to thee by Sammy the things we had prepared. Elizabeth wished to send the painting she has finished for thee, and wrote divers letters, and the pound cake was a very handsom one for we had taken peculiar care in manufacturing it. The bag of hazlenuts will remain unopened ready for the next conveyance. It was really extremely trying when such a good opportunity offered to be deprived of it through carelessness on there part. Thee says my dear Jane I think every thing is for the best. I grant I do in some instances but in the one attended to I must confess I thought it otherwise.

We now look forward my dear sister with the greatest pleasure at the prospect of seeing Dear Lemuel and thyself this summer. I sincerely hope nothing may occur to prevent it, and that you may so arrange your business as to have your minds quite at ease whilst here with regard to home that you "can make us quite a visit," as the phrase is here. I trust your journey thither will be very pleasant, if the weather is fine, and I hope it may be so. The sail over the Lake I think will be very delightful (if the wind is not too high) and I trust will benefit your health. In journeying on the Canall beware of the bridges for they are very numerous. (Thee will perhaps smile at my caution, but thee well knows I am apt to anticipate evil, and I believe my anxious disposition increases with my years.) I will not attempt to tell thee how much we want to see you, neither can I tell thee how rejoiced we shall be to welcome you to Hazlebank. Suffice it to say you will be uppermost in my mind till the wished for period arrives.

Spring has come in very mild and pleasant. The season is fast approaching when strangers will be coming here to view our Territorial land, and those who purchased last year I presume will come to settle this summer. Thee says our dear aged Aunt [Anna Guest] enjoys good health, which is a great comfort to me to hear, I believe I think of her every day, and I would I could once more see her. Indeed I indulge a hope that I shall though the period may be distant. Remember us affectionately to her and dear Aunt Nancy, and also to Cousin Anna Guest. Her home must and probably will continue to feel very altered indeed, her fireside no longer shared with the presence and pleasing converse of the beloved object now mourned. Some there are when overwhelmed with affliction of the most trying nature, restrain not there grief, and feel it with the utmost poignancy, for a season. By and by the departed is no longer remembered. Not so with our Cousin. She will more and more feel her loss, but will I trust become more and more resigned thereto, having substantial reason to believe she is now at rest with God her Father. When I took leave of her, I felt it was for the last time, I felt I was bidding her a final farewell, and it is the desire of my soul when we are called from hence, to be in her lamblike state, to have nothing to do but to die, then every tie however strong can easily be broken this side Eternity.

There is a committee consisting of twelve men and women friends appointed by Farmington Monthly Meeting in the state of New York to visit friends in Michigan with a desire to establish a meeting here, this summer; but we think it will not be desireable at present. There are but few of us in number, and those not of the most weighty and solid character, and as there is a meeting here that we can and do attend, makes it less important that we should have another, and I think it would not be adviseable under present circumstances.[10]

The Genius makes no mention of B. Lundy. I am really fearful some ill has befallen him. It is now about a year since he left Philad^a. His journey has been a very hazerdous one. Still I hope and desire he may return in safety. The Liberator published by Wm L. Garrison some three years ago is an excellent Anti-Slavery paper. W^m has sent it to Elizabeth from the commencement gratuitously. She also received a paper equally good, from New York City, called the Emancipator, free from expence save the postage. Our papers with the addition of some eight or ten taken by D. Comstock furnishes us with a considerable stock of information.

It is really strange Emily's Mother so seldom calls on thee to enquire about her child. If thee should see her please inform her she is in good health. She talks a great deal about thy coming here this summer and the extra pleasure it will give her to see thee.

We have not seen J. Gamble for some time but expect a visit from him and his wife shortly. Thomas wishes James to have had the job of building his barn, but he had previously engaged to build a large house for a person who was in a great hurry to commence; to get a great deal of business, and it cannot be otherwise, when there is so much building going on, and he is I presume by far the best workman that there is in the settlement. We expect our barn will be raised in about two weeks. Only think how many apple pye's, and nut cakes, we shall have to make for something like forty men. However, we shall prepare them most cheerfully. It is quite a frugal supper, but it is not common here, to provide anything more on such occasions.

4 Mo 9th—

We have been informed J. Lovett has declined going to your country this spring. We learn however, J. Hunt from Bucks County intends going on in a few days. By him we purpose sending a packet, and hope on his return to receive letters. Thee says Amelia is still in the country. I hope her health is good. Give my love to her, and tell her she owes us several letters. If Aunt Howell is in the city, remember me to her, and also to Hannah Roberts when thee sees her—and also to M. Woodside, and Betsy Harrigas. I feal much interrested for all my friends in the City.

Give my love to Ann. Tell her I want she should write to me by the bearer of this. If she does, I so hope she will not destroy it as heretofore or probably I may feal some degree of wrath. I have written a few lines for her but scarcely think them worthy her acceptance. I will however reserve a small portion of my sheet for them. Thee says thee expects to part with Louisa some time in the course of the coming summer, a tryal I am sure it will be to thee. Give my love to her, for I feal much love for her, and I hope she will strive to keep in the narrow path, that will lead to life Eternal.

I suppose R. Coe^{Sr} has gone to his farm before now. I wish they may all enjoy good healths, and I hope the change they have made may prove for the best. Thee has not informed us wether Amelia Merrifield has commenced school teaching. Every thing respecting our relatives is interresting. Give our love to her. I wish she would write to Elizabeth.

Our friends here, anticipate a great deal of pleasure in seeing you. Remember me to dear Lemuel, and believe me to be thine as ever—

Ruth Evans

AN ACROSTIC ADDRESSED TO A.R.

And now I am absent from thee, and many a mile between,
Nor canst thou my friend, conceive how beautious is the scene,
Nature is most glorious here and the earth with flowers she strews,
And the lone wood, neath the noontide rays, tis lovely there to muse.
Receive these lines my friend from one, who often thinks of thee,
Our bygone days doth often recur, and dost thou think of me?
Secure may we beyond, the tomb, a home amongst the blest,—
Eternal life with God, and Christ, in endless joyous rest.

R.E.

JANE HOWELL *to* RUTH EVANS
Philadelphia, May 15, 1834

My dear Sister,

How gratifying it is to receive letters from our absent friends especially from those we most dearly love and to hear that they are well and happy. To me it is one of the very greatest pleasures and the most exhilarating to my spirits for I must assure thee that they get a great deal below par sometimes when I reflect on the distance which divides us. And yet I am almost ready to charge myself with ingratitude to the Great Disposer of Events when I think how many blessings have been dispensed unto you and what a protecting care has been over you and you have been sheltered from the Storm of Pecuniary embarrassments which have pervaded our United States through a wrong administration of Public Affairs which have shook to the very foundation a vast number of our most opulent Merchants. Every class of People feel the times from the Richest to the poorest but our wise President said he would bring all on a level. The times in Baltimore I believe are much worse than they are in our City. So many of the Banks there are broken. The old bank of Maryland owned by Evan Poultney which stopped sometime ago has caused great distress there as a great number of widows and orphans and the labouring classes of people had deposited their money and hard earnings there, as that bank allowed interrest on deposits and consequently it was a strange inducement considering the high standing of the bank for thousands to entrust their all there for safe keeping. Evan Poultney married Jane, Sister to Tom Tunis. They lived in Baltimore in the greatest splendor their house almost like a

Palace, and parties from one to two hundred persons were given by them very frequently thro' the winter. The day after the Bank stop'd Evan's house was mob'd and it was not until he promised to give up all his property Real and personal that the people dispersed. Jane has about fifteen thousand dollars left to her by her brother John which the creditors cannot touch, and also a small house a few miles from Baltimore. They sent their children with their nurse during the summer. That small house now has become their place of residence. What a change & what a reverse of fortune. When I heard it I thought of the words of Isaiah, How are the Mighty fallen.[11]

Samuel Lovett came here about two weeks since to inform me that his wife intended starting for Michigan in about eight days from the time he was here and she was very desirous that I should accompany her. If every thing had suited I should have liked it very much, but I could not think of going without Lemuel, and he still hopes to be able to go this summer. He has had so much business on hand for the last two years that he has had scarcely one days relaxation except first days, and such close application to business has made him look quite thin and pale. But his health is as good I believe as when you were here.

A. G. Merrefield seemed pleased at being remembered by thee. I mentioned her writing to Elizabeth. She said she has felt very much hurt that Elizabeth had not asked her to write before she left home and that she did not doubt but that she had asked Anna Coe.

I must now inform thee that we have moved to No. 400 Coates Street six doors above Tenth Street South side into a very neat new three story brick house two handsome parlours folding doors and marble mantels a very commodious kitchen and four handsome chambers close shutters in the 2nd story and green venitian to the 3rd. We have a beautiful yard about 66 feet clear of the buildings a white painted fence with a border of flowers and shrubbery around it a paved walk and in the middle a long grass plot with an english walnut tree which I raised from the nut about the time you left here and which had nuts on last year. I have a coral honeysuckle in the yard in reserve for dear niece when a suitable opportunity afford to forward it on to her.

Coates Street is curbed and paved out as far as the Ridge Road and nearly built out to it with near 2 and 3 story brick houses. Do not think we are in a retired situation. Far from it. It is astonishing at the great number of Persons who pass and repass in a day both on horseback in carriages and on foot. The Gerard College which is going up on the Ridge road attract vast numbers to see it and that perhaps is the cause of so many passing by.[12]

I expect in the course of a week or two Lemuel and I will go down to see his Mother. After we return I should like to go and see William. am quite a Woman of leisure—now having no store to attend to. We have packed up our goods and deposited them in our back 3rd story chamber. Occasionally we can part with some of them to the Journeyman and perhaps trade some of them away. Lemuels carpenters shop is about a square above us. The most of our nearest neighbours on the South Side are respectable friends. Our house we pay 150 dollars a year, a very low rent it is. Abby Warnock says not as good houses in their neighbour-hood rent for 400 dollars. She lives in 10th near Arch Street.

An Omnibus run starts from a tavern just below us out to the Gerard College and from there to Mansyunk a distance of 5 miles for 12 cents so that we can have a very cheap ride when we want one. The rail road is on Ninth Street better than a square below us but we can stand at the front door or back chamber window and see the Locomotive with 3 and 4 elegant cars which will carry thirty persons each attached to it going as if by magic along the road. It is a great distance to our Meeting, but friends belonging to North Meeting are looking out for a suit-able lot which will be more central for a Meeting house. The committee saw one at the corner of 6th and Willow Street which they thought would do, but the owner asked too great a price for it. Spring Garden Market is about 4 squares from us. Many of the Jersey friends who attend Market have taken stalls there. Spring Garden Street will in time be a very handsome street. It is as wide as Market Street and they are putting up very good houses. It runs out to Schuykill.

Cousin Anna Guest was delighted with Elizabeth's piece entitled Christ-mas.[13] She wished me to lend it to her that she might get Elisa Tunis to coppy it for her, which I did with pleasure. She always asks me when I call to see her wether I have received late letters from you, wether I have them with me, and if I will read them to her. She quite approved of Thomas' not accepting of the office of Majestrate. She said she thought it would interfere verry much with his other business and without yielding him much proffits. She passes many encomiums on Thomas for his industry and perseverance in farming, and she says she has no doubt but that he will make a very rising character and stand high in Society. For my part I think he stands a fine chance, if he does not work too hard, of becom-ing a rich man. I have been wanting for some time to write a long letter to him. I quite excuse him for not writing as his time is more proffitably employed. Give my love to him and tell him that I often see him in imagination just as he was when he left us only a little fatter and a good deal sun burnt.

The Spring came in very pleasant. We had some very warm weather in March and the early part of April, but ever since we moved here, which is four weeks tomorrow, until within a day or two it has been cold and windy, which has put back my garden considerably. There was a very brilliant Auroraborealis a few weeks since, and I have remarked for some time past that cold wind then follows their appearance.

It is now about one year since I have seen Emilys Mother. It is a pity that her promised present should have been the means of keeping her from calling to enquire after her child which I do expect has been the case. Give my love to Emily and tell her I am very much pleased that she is learning to be such a good scholar, and as soon as there is an opportunity she must write me a long letter.

I saw Elmira Atherton some time ago. She asked particularly after Elizabeth. She has taken a very serious turn, and dresses as plain as Hannah (Townsend) Longstreth.

Ann was very much pleased with her acrostic. I told her I was quite jealous for no one had ever wrote one on me. I am quite impatient to see my picture, and to have the pleasure of hanging it up in one of my best rooms. I have had the frame and glass for it more than a year past. Perhaps I may be the bearer of it myself. I hope Lemuels business may be so that he can go for I believe he is as anxious as myself for it. My health has been uncommonly good this spring, and indeed thro' the winter. I think the Panacea was of great benefit to me.

I suppose if we go to Michigan we shall get there before Aunt Sally Lovett returns. If we go, we shall calculate upon being from home about two months and I think they will be two of the happiest months I ever spent or at least that part of the time spent with you.

Ann has written her letter but because she has blotted it a little she is not willing to send it unless I will coppy it off for her so I must set about it,[14] but I must first say we are well, and with much much love, bid thee farewell.

J Howell

Amelia is still in the country. She came in about three weeks ago to see me but got wrong directions from some of the girls in John Merrefields store and had to go out of town without seeing me. I have written to her and sent the number of this house.

———◆———

JANE HOWELL *to* ELIZABETH CHANDLER
Philadelphia, May 15, 1834

My dear Niece

We received your letters by John Hunt and were highly delighted in having an opportunity of conversing with a person who had so recently left you. At first I felt at a loss to understand him owing to the defect in his speech, but Ann was my interpreter as she had been in his company about half an hour before I came home, having gone to market. But I very soon could understand him without much difficulty. He came here in the afternoon lodged and took breakfast with us next morning. We should have been better pleased if he could have spent more time with us. He gives a very favorable account of you and several times in a jesting way I would hint at your makeshifts and the inconveniences you had to encounter, but he would away with them all and say how very comfortable you lived and thee may depend it afforded me heartfelt pleasure.

Cousin Robert Coe moved his family to N Jersey about the 15th of last month. I have not sent thy packet yet. I expect Robert will be up in a few days when I expect he will bring Annas packet for thee. I hope it will arrive in time to forward it on by John Hunt. If not, Samuel Merritt expects to go on to Michigan in a very short time and then I will send it by him. Anna intended leaving it with me before she went but she thought she would have so much to tell thee after she got to her new home, that it would be best to send it up by her Father. I went down to Cousin Roberts the evening before they moved to invite the family to breakfast with us as they were to start about seven in the morning, but they declined it as their son Roberts furniture was there and everything convenient for them. I declare my heart ach'd for them for their spirits were down to a very low ebb. Their being unfortunate in business was nothing when compared to their other troubles. James' misconduct in taking with another young woman who was employed in their store has almost broken his Mothers heart and caused a seperation between him and his wife. Rebecca and Hellen the youngest child are with George Williams at present, and perhaps may continue there. Rebecca has been dangerously ill but has recovered so far as to be able to ride out. The Doctors were very apprehensive that she would go into a consumption. Wounded pride and stifled troubles is thought to have been the cause of her illness. Poor James drinks to excess and I fear his brother Robert is not a great way behind him. Robert occupies his fathers old stand and James tends in the store.

After the Lottery business was broken up Margaret Hall went to considerable expense in fitting up her house for a Tavern but not being able to procure a license she was under the necessity of breaking up house keeping. Margaretta and Sabina were offered a home at their Uncle George Williams, since which George has placed Sabina at a boarding school in Abington. Margaret Hall has a few weeks since taken a small house in Camden N Jersey for the purpose of selling lottery tickets. She says she can supply her old customers here in the city with them without any danger of coming under the penalty of the law of Pennsylvania for so doing.

Joseph Taylor was to see us perhaps five or six [days] since. He said that William Sarah and little Tom were all in excellent health, and that William was doing a very good business but I have one thing to say against him, and that is that he is very remiss in writing to his friends. It is a very great while since I received a letter from him, but I think I shall jog his memory soon by writing a letter to him.

Aunt Rebecca Guest set off from here the 3rd of March for St. Louis having heard from William Warder from that place that her son John had had several severe attacks of illness which had reduced him very low. But having reached Baltimore her friends insisted on her continuing there until she could receive further information from him by an interchange of letters and it was very prudent she did for she would have travelled unaccompanied by any one she knew, the roads extremely rough, and weather unsettled. She has since received a very satisfactory letter from him informing her that he has recovered and expects to pay a short visit here about next Christmas.

Lemuel some time ago received a letter from James Gamble. He was very much pleased to hear that he was doing so well and that Michigan more than answered his expectations. His wife appears like a very industrious, but backward unassuming woman. James speaks in very high terms of the kindness of John Lovett to him since he has been there. I hope he may still meet with encouragement in his trade for he is undoubtedly a very good workman. Another of Lemuels Journeyman who has worked for him about six years intends seeking his fortune amoung you before long.

When I wrote to thee last I expected Rebecca Coe would have been married in a short time as they were looking out for a house, but it is put off until next fall and Cousin Anna told me the evening before they moved that perhaps it would never take place for he [Washington Train] was not in suitable circumstances to many. And to judge from appearances I should think it a very unsuitable connection, but I believe Rebecca is very much attached to him and perhaps he is to her. But he is so very inactive in business that I should take him to be a real lazy young man. I may perhaps do him injustice, but I only judge from what I have seen. His mother too is strongly opposed to it, not that she has anything against Rebecca but she looks upon him as her stay and support being her only son now and her daughter in such delicate health. Indeed I have often been surprised that Rebecca's parents sanctioned it as long as they did.

I expect our dear aged Aunt Anna and Aunt Nancy will spend next week with us or the greatest part of it. Does thee not almost envy me? I assure thee it will be a great gratification to me to have them with me that long. I shall have a great deal to tell them about you which they will hear with the greatest interrest.

Amelia Merrefield is so delighted with our new residence that she is going to bring cousin Anna Guest to see me if she can get her consent to foot it which Amelia thinks she could do with ease. I have not seen Cousin Anna for a great while. I am very soon to go and see her. She seems desirous for me to pay you a visit.

I called a few days ago to see Lydia White, but she was on a visit to New York. She was so much discouraged in her free-good business that she has given up her store (which was in fourth street a few doors below Arch) and deposited the remainder of her goods at Joseph Sharpley's. I met Joseph in the street this morning. He says they heard from Benjamin Lundy about six weeks since. He was then in the upper part of Ohio but expected to return back to Mexico. I believe Joseph got his information from Evan Lewis who has since deceased, and in his Death the Cause of Emancipation has sustained a great loss for indeed he was a great advocate for the slave. There is a young man who has opened a free grocery store on a small scale in the front of Joseph Sharpley's china store, which is I believe the only one in the city of the kind.[15]

I intended calling on friend Townsend to enquire after Hannah Longstreth but I believe I shall not have time before I close thy letter. Anna Coe I expect will be in the city I think in about six weeks. She is to be bridesmaid to her cousin Julia Ann Randolph. I suppose it will be a very stylish wedding. I think she is to pass meeting next month and it is probably Anna will stay with her until she is married. But when thee receives her packet thee will hear all about it.

There has lately been enacted in Camden opposite the city a Lighthouse which it is said will throw a strong light on the eastward part of our [ ]. The design is for the benefit of vessels coming in at Night.[16]

Our New Exchange surpasses in beauty any other brick building I ever saw.[17] It attracts vast numbers to see it, and the rooms are all open for the admission of visitors. How I should like to see thee rambling our streets this summer. I can almost fancy I see the pleasure and surprise that would be expressed on thy countenance at the wonderful improvements which have been made since you left us.

17TH—

I am afraid Anna Coes packet will not arrive here in time to forward it on by this conveyance. I expected Cousin Robert would have been in the city before this time. Ann is writing to thy Aunt Ruth but she is so unaccustomed to letter writing that she is afraid your comments on it will not be much to her liking and she has half a notion not to send it.

Maria Woodside is still out of employment. The Dry good business is so very dull that it is a difficult matter to get a situation in a store. She has been thinking of opening a school for small children or an Infants school something on the Lancasterian plan,[18] but she finds it difficult to get a room in a suitable situation for one. She still continues in delicate health. As I wish to leave my letters at Vances Tavern early tomorrow morning for fear John Hunt should go and leave them as he told Lemuel that he should [be] gone on the 18th if nothing prevented, I must now conclude after saying what thee already knows, that I am

> thy affectionate Aunt
> Jane Howell

Give my love to my dear Nephew and tell him that I am very glad to hear that he has a boy to assist him this summer. I think it will be a great advantage to him as it will enable him to get thro more work which will count up more than his wages, and at the same time lighten his labour.

———◆———

Elizabeth Chandler *to* Jane Howell
Hazelbank, May 28, 1834

My dear Aunt

I must write for I should feel willing so far to violate the golden rule, as to suffer so good an opportunity for forwarding letters to pass unimproved—but I set myself to my task almost idealess. It is so long since we have received a letter—so long a time passed without a syllable of intelligence respecting you having reached us that there is a feeling of vagueness and uncertainty over my mind, very unfavorable to the business of letter-writing. We *expect* letters, it is true, by John Hunt, but I do not like to answer a letter upon expectation and we have seen Samuel Lovetts wife and been told that you were well when Samuel last saw you and have removed somewhere. I wish they had called at your house passing through the city, for if your letters were ready at that time they would have reached us sooner, and we might have had a chance of hearing again by Hunt. Of cousin Coe's family we have heard nothing since thy last letter of last winter, but I suppose that they too like yourselves are *somewhere,* and perhaps Anna may sometime think proper to edify you with the knowledge whereabouts it is. Aunts we hope are well. They have always our love. Yet, if it is only for the sake of bringing ourselves a moment before them, we must desire thee to offer it to them particularly. Please remember us affectionately also to Cousin Anna Guest and to our other friends. And now my dear Aunt, after adding that we are all well, shall I conclude? Or can thee really have patience to peruse the *fourth* unanswered sheet? (one from Aunt Ruth inclusive)

Well then, if thee wishes me to go on, I will do so. We had our barn raised several weeks ago. It went up snugly and safely. There was a large number of hands, between forty and fifty altogether, and if thee had happened to step in on the afternoon or morning before the raising, thee would have found Aunt R and I quite deeply immersed in preparations of pies, puddings, and cakes—such being the articles provided for refreshment. We had intended setting our tables out of doors, but the afternoon was rather cool and dusty so that we were obliged to spread them within—not for the men to sit down to, for that would have been out of the question—but to cluster round as well as they were able, or obtaining their supplies retreat to another part of the room and give place to others. A clearance was soon made and our room was left again to its proper occupants. So much for a "raising" in the "back woods."

The spring this season has been much more than usually backward with us. Quite early in the season the weather was quite warm, and vegetation appeared to be coming forward rapidly; but one or two cold spells of weather since checked it very much. The weather has not however been more unfavorable here than in many other places—nor as much so—and less injury to farmers has been sustained by it. I do not know that it has seriously injured any of the crops—though some of the oats looked rather frost bitten for a while. Brother [said] it will not be any disadvantage to his. Fruit, we have not yet—and there is not a great deal in the neighborhood. What there is, except apples, I expect has been destroyed. In Ohio and Indiana we understand that some of the crops, rye especially, have been much injured by the frost. Will you not engage your supply of pork for next winter of us? We have nineteen fine young porkers, about two months old which will make nice pork in the fall.

Lovetts have just sent word that their mother is going to leave tomorrow. We expected another visit from her but she leaves sooner than she expected. So I must immediately conclude and send off any letters. I believe I have said all that is of much interest about ourselves. We are very anxious for our packet by Hunt in the hope it may say something of the time of your visiting here. Friend Lovett could tell us nothing about it.

We are all well and with much love I must hastily conclude. I intended writing to Aunt Anna but cannot now. Affectionately and with much love from all

> thy niece
> E M Chandler

———— ◆ ————

JANE HOWELL *to* ELIZABETH CHANDLER
Philadelphia, July 1, 1834

My dear Niece

I received thy letters and purse with the eagles feather by Sally Lovett but thee did not say who thee intended the purse for and so Ann claimed it until we should hear further about it. It is very pretty and quite a curiosity but what greatly enhanced its value with me was that it was made by thee. Aunt Sally spent almost a day with us which was indeed very gratifying to me for I had so many questions to ask her about you and yet after she was gone I found there was a great deal more which I wanted to know. I am very doubtful of our reaching Michigan this summer for it will be so late in the season before Lemuel will get thro his work which he has engaged to do that it would allow us too short a time to stay with you.

Tell my dear sister that I think I bear disappointment better than I used to do. Perhaps I equal her now in that respect. Our dear Aunt Anna, and Nancy spent near two weeks with us since we moved into Coates St. I expect next month to have another visit from them. Aunt Anna looks remarkably well, but her hearing is not as good as when you left here. Otherwise she is much the same. She desired me when I wrote to give her love to you. Anna Coe was here about ten days ago. I gave her thy last letter. She said thee was a dear good girl for writing and she must make thee suitable returns. She intends writing soon and will I suppose give thee a detail of the wedding affairs. I think the girls will enjoy themselves a great deal more now they are released from business. Anna looks better already. I enquired after Hannah Longstreth this morning. Her mother returned from there yesterday. She enjoys good health. She has a son I believe about a year old.

George Guest has returned from sea. He has made an unproffitable voyage, scarcely enough to cover his expenses owing to bad markets at all the ports where he stopped, but he intends going again in a few weeks as there is nothing that he can do to any advantage in the city. Jonathan [Guest] is expected in soon but I expect it will be pretty much the same case with him. Aunt Rebecca has gone to Baltimore to spend the summer with her daughter Rebecca. Her son John has recovered his health and expects to visit his friends in the city next winter.

We like our new residence very much. It is so very lively. We have a full view of the cars on the rail road passing and repassing. There are often 8 or 10 of them attached to the locomotive, crowded with passengers the fare being but 12½ cents to Germantown. One of the cars is called Tecumseh and it is quite unlike the rest perhaps as much so as that town is like our city. I am getting ready to go down with Lemuel to see his Mother and from there I expect we shall go to the sea shore, but I do not know wether I shall venture into the surf. I was delighted with the account Aunt Sally gave of my dear nephew's farming and of Hazlebank altogether. The pig pens which was near the house were so clean and so much taste displayed in the arrangement of the ornimental trees that she thought it was the handsomest looking place that she saw in Michigan. She also said how comfortable you lived every thing so neat and nice. But hers was like a story twice told for John Hunts exactly corresponded with it, and thee knows that out of the mouth of two or three witnesses the truth is established.

The Mercantile business is almost at a stand in the city. Thomas Tell told Lemuel a few days since that he thought half the stores in Market Street would have to shut up very soon unless there was a change.

8TH MO 3RD—

When I first commenced my letter I expected to have sent it on immediately by William Dunlap the bearer of this who was ready to commence his journey at that time, but Lemuel having undertaken a very heavy job he concluded to stay and help him a few weeks. He is a real clever man and I hope may meet with friends and encouragement at this trade in Michigan! His correct habits entitles him to it. I hope James Gamble is doing well. He is a man that requires advising with. When thee sees him and his wife please remember us to them.

This being first day Lemuel has just left me to spend the day at John Roberts in Haddonfield. I should have been glad to have accompanied him as he nor I have spent one hour in the country this summer oweing to his close confinement to business and on first day being too tired to leave home. But I hope in a few weeks he will be able to go and pay a visit to his Mother and friends and take a trip to the sea shore. If he does I expect to go with him.

Ann and I have had very little leisure time since we have lived in Coates Street. We have had so much sewing to do in making Lemuels summer cloathes and a set of linen for him. Also setting out Louisas who will be of age in about nine days and who can do nothing for herself as she is learning her trade.[19] And in addition we have had a great deal of company since we have been here, so that in the aggregate thee may suppose that we have not spent much idle time. I have stop'd the Post and commenced taking the Saturday Courier,[20] but if you would prefer the Post I will take it again. My reason for changing was the Courier was a larger paper and contained more interresting matter. The last number of the Genius I received had nothing of thine in it and that was nearly three months since. I intend calling on Doctor Atlee to know what is the reason it is not issued more regularly, or if it is, why not sent to me.

I saw Cousin Anna Guest about two weeks since. She according to her usual custom had a great deal to say about you and when I told her how clean Sarah Lovett said Thomas kept his pig pens, that she said was a sure mark of a good Farmer. And in leaving her she said "when thee writes give my love affectionately to thy Sister and to Elizabeth and Thomas." Now Tom must not be jealous because she placed thee before him. I suppose she forgot his seniority. I saw Cousin Robert Coe a short time since. He looked exceeding well and seemed in good spirits. He said his family were all well and there seemed nothing wanting but a little more society. I saw dear Aunt Anna a few days ago. She was well. She says they are going to postpone their visit to me until the beginning of October and then they are to stay about a month with us if nothing prevents. She desires her love to you.

I think if president Jackson was to visit our city at this time and look at some of the shop windows he would see in what estimation he stands in the opinion of the people. He is so ludicrously caricatured often assuming in body the form of a full grown pig but there is always an excellent likeness of his head and face. I think the coming Elections will be carried on with great spirit.[21] The Freedom and prosperity of the country is at stake and the most latent fealing of the public mind will be aroused in defence of its rights and interrests. I always detested female politicians and of course will bridle my tongue altho I cannot my fealings, for who can remain in a State of Apathy when the Country's rights are trodden down.

I have not seen anything of Emily's Mother for more than one year. The parasol affair has I suppose kept her away. I hope when Emily has a good opportunity she will write to me. I am very much pleased to hear she is such a good girl. Lemuel is sadly disappointed that he has not been able to pay you a visit to you. Thy Aunt Amelia went from here a few days ago. She was well and wished me when I wrote to give her love to you. We are all well and with much love I remain affectionately

Jane Howell

I hope soon to have more leisure and then I want to write a long letter to thy Aunt Ruth.

———◆———

JANE HOWELL *to* RUTH EVANS
Philadelphia, September 22, 1834

My dear Sister

I have just received thy letter[22] with the distressing intelligence of my dear Elizabeths illness but I hope before this she will be restored to health again. I shall be extremely unhappy until I hear from her. Do write immediately on the receipt of this and tell me exactly how she is. Never mind filling the sheet. If there is but a line or two it will do.

I wrote a very long letter to either thee or Elizabeth I forget which and sent it by William Dunlap a journey man of Lemuels who went from here in the early part of August but who I understand from thy letter has stopped at Detroit until his goods arrive. He is also the bearer of Anna Coes packet to my dear Niece. I am very sorry he did not forward them on by his cousin who was at John Lovetts. William Dunlap expected to have left here in the seventh month for Michigan. I wrote a letter to send by him then, but Lemuel having undertaken a heavy job of work he concluded to stay about a month longer to help him. So thee sees my dear sister that I was not so remiss in writing if my letters had come to hand. I have been extremely uneasy for some time past at not hearing from you. I have been on the point of writing several times but expecting a letter every day, I defer'd it on account of answering it as soon as I received it. I felt a presentiment that something was the matter and told Ann I should be afraid to open the letter when I received one which was the case to day. But on opening it how relieved I was for a moment as I cast my eyes first at the bottom of the page and seeing the Initials of my dear Elizabeth's name and venturing a line or two higher I saw the delightful words "Aunt and brother are both well." I exclaimed with joy to Ann, "they are all well."

I then began with a very light heart to read the letter but how soon were my feelings changed when I read of my dear Niece's indisposition. Had I have known that she had been ill, I should it is very probable, have ventured alone to have been [with] her. Kiss her for me, and tell her I hope soon to receive a letter from her.

It was a great disappointment both to Lemuel and myself, that we could not get to see you this summer but he had so much work on hand that he could not possibly leave it without giving offense to his employers. I have since wished that I had accompanied Sally Lovett. Lemuel seemed rather desirious I should fearing that his business would be so that he could not leave it.

Amelia Coe has been in the city for the last few weeks. Cousin Anna thinks of paying us a visit this fall. Anna Jr. also. They like their new residence much better than they expected. I expect my dear Aunt Anna and Nancy to spend about a month with me. They will come next week. They are both well. I have not heard from my Nephew William since we moved into Coates St. A short time before that, he was well and doing well. I have intended writing to him and giving him our address, but thinking I should pay him a visit soon has detered me.

Our Sister Amelia was here a few days since. She was well. She lives in Smithfield [Pennsylvania] and keeps a small shop of trimmings &c. She thinks she will do very well at it and is in good spirits. The country suits her health and inclination much better than the city, or else we would rather she would be with us. Amelia Merrefield is at schoolkeeping. She has about eleven scholars at three dollars per quarter. She began about two weeks since, but I think she will soon get tired of the confinement unless she should meet with more encouragement. She is to pay sixty dollars a year for her school room which is in Fourth Street, in an alley between Market and Arch Street. Lemuel has taken a prentice boy about

17 years old. He is to be at no expense with him except his board and Lemuel has made a bargain with his Father that if he goes to Michigan next summer he is to send him home until he returns. He is from Bucks County and of very respectable connections. He is so handy with tools that Lemuel thinks he will soon acquire a sufficient knowledge of the trade as to be very useful.

We are very much pleased with our residence in Coates Street. The air is so pure and the house so convenient and pleasant that I think we could not be better suited. Next seventh day I expect to go with Lemuel down to see his Mother. She has been ill but is now better. Hannah Gamage from Hudson spent seventh day afternoon with me. She is on her way to Ohio to spend the winter with her Uncle there. Aunt Hathaway and family were all well except Sally Jenkins who continues in the same distressed situation.

I hope William Dunlap may soon arrive and he can tell you all about us, and I hope Anna's packet which is a very large one may afford my dear Elizabeth much amusement.

Give my love to my industrious Nephew and tell him that great praises are bestowed upon him by his Philadelphia relatives for his perseverance and good management in farming. They all think he is on the high road to independance. Ann was quite distressed when she heard Elizabeth had been sick. She desires her love to her, and thyself. I must now conclude, and with a great deal of love from Lemuel and myself I remain with much

> Affection thy Sister
> Jane Howell
> We are all Well.

Ruth Evans *to* Jane Howell *and* Amelia Evans
Hazelbank, September 29, 1834

My dear Sisters Jane & Amelia,

This day we received the packet of letters sent by Wm Dunlap, but not one for myself. It matters however little to me, who they are addressed to provided they, could be more frequently received by either of the inmates at Hazlebank, which I must confess has not been the case of late. My last letter informed you of the illness of Dearest Elizabeth.[23] At the time I wrote we indulged the hope she was much better, but a few days convinced us it was only temperaerry. She is still confined to her bed, but we hope and believe she will soon be able to set up, being now evidently much better, for several days past.

The Doctors united in believing mercury must be used in order to effect a permanent cure, and the blue pill was seemed the safest and most shure course. She has taken them for some time and will continue to until she becomes slightly salavated. She has taken one in six hours for two week past, and probably may have to continue them two weeks longer, unless meanwhile her mouth should become sore. She has taken several ametic. Blister upon blister has been applyed, and most powerful cathartic which have reduced her exhumly. Six weeks she has been confined to her bed, and amidst all her bodily distress she has been perfectly calm and reconciled.[24]

10TH MO 7TH—

This evening I received my Dear Sister Jane's letter. We were truly glad to hear you were in health. You doubtless must feel very anxious about our beloved Elizabeth. She does not set up yet, but I hope and believe it will not be long first. She has for several days past felt some stronger, and more inclination to eat. We still watch with her through the night, as she must take nourishment very frequently. She has taken about one hundred blue pills, which will be discontinued now as salavation is going on well. Today her mouth is sore and salava runs freely. She is in good spirits and I believe is very happy.

Her friend, Julia Chittenden, is now a widow. Her husband was buried this afternoon. He was ill about five weeks. Julia will deeply feel and mourn his loss. Indeed his death is much lamented by all his friends which are very numerous. I hope you will not feel to anxious about Elizabeth. Rest asured if she is more poorly I will inform you. At present she is certainly doing well.

Thomas has purchased a span of horses and waggon on very good terms. He gave his oxen and waggon and sixty dollars in cash, or grain.

Our united love to our dear Aunts, and Cousin Anna Guest. I often think what a privilege you enjoy in having in your power to see them so frequently. Give our love [to] Dear Lemuel. Tell him a year seems a long time to look forward for a visit from you. I am however very glad you declined it as the season was so unhealthy, the cholera prevailing in many places, particularly in Detroit. Give my love to Ann. Tell her I should have been glad if she would have written me by some of the late conveyances. I am watching with Elizabeth therefore believe I cannot spare more time to write at present and will conclude with much love to you.

I remain your affectionate Sister,
Ruth Evans

8TH

This morning Elizabeth's much as usual. She passed rather a tedious night. She desires her love to you, and wishes you would write soon. I hope before long to be able to tell you she is much better. The desease however seems to be removed, but she is extreemly weak which the salavation tends to increase. She takes many things to strengthen her, which I hope may have the desired effect. We cannot expect her to be otherwise than weak after a confinement of almost eight weeks to her bed. She is however one of the most patient ones I even knew.

R.E.

Thomas and myself are well, and Emily also, if her mother should enquire for her.

I believe I have given you a correct statement of Elizabeths situation, knowing it would be most satisfactory to you.

———◆◆◆———

JANE HOWELL *to* RUTH EVANS
Philadelphia, October 28, 1834

My dear Sister

I received thy second letter informing me of the continued illness of our beloved Elizabeth. I had flattered myself from the contents of thy first that she had nearly recovered, and it was with feelings of sorrow that I perused thy last; but not without a strong hope that in a little while she would be restored to health again. Hers is a disease which causes great prostration of strength, and the remedies which has been used has been of a very weakening nature. The blue pill is very much used here in that complaint, but I think it took a great many to salivate my dear niece, but I hope it will entirely eradicate from her system every vestage of the disease so that she will never have another attack of the kind. Do write again my dear Sister soon. I do not care how short thy letters are now. I am so very anxious and I may say unhappy until I shall hear from you.

I received a long letter from our dear Nephew William, a few days ago. They were all well. He says he has written one if not two letters to me since I wrote to him, which have never come to hand and I think it probable it has been the same case with his letters to you. From his letter it appears that he has a prospect of removing to Michigan. I will coppy a paragraph from his letter, "I think I men- tioned in my last that our thoughts still wandered to Michigan and the prospect continues to grow as Sarahs mind inclines more and more to remove there. In fact we think it highly probable that we shall go next year. The owner of the property (Dr. Sappington) has advertised it for Sale (see Evening Post) and if he sells it we shall probably have to remove in which case I should like to go immediately to Michigan."—"We do not sell any Spirituous liquors and altho it curtails our prof- its considerably yet it is a source of much greater satisfaction to us." He says Sarah has accompanied a family of their friends as far as Baltimore who are removing to the Western Country. She expected to be about a week from home. He did not say a word about little Tom, but I suppose he is well.

Anna Merrefield has a young son about a week old. They have now two chil- dren. She would much rather this last one had been a daughter. Anna Coe Jr. has come to the City, I expect to spend the winter. I have not seen her yet. She is at her cousin Julia Ann [Randolph]s. It will throw quite a shade over her pleasure when she hears of dear Elizabeths illness. Amelia Coe has been spending a few weeks in the City but has now returned home. Her father has lost a very fine cow a few weeks since. They made from her six pounds of butter a week, besides a free use of milk and cream. I believe James is with his Father, Rebecca and her youngest child is still at George Williams. She attends in their store. Cousin Anna Guest was here a few days ago. She was very sorry to hear of Elizabeths indisposition and desired me when I wrote to give her love to you and said if she was thirty years younger she would like to go and see you.

Our dear aged Aunt Anna and Aunt Nancy has been with me about three weeks. I expect they will stay a week longer. They desire a great deal of love to you and particularly to our dear Elizabeth. Aunt Rebecca has gone to Balti- more to see her second little grandson. I think Rebecca promises to have a large family.

George Guest set sail a few days ago for South America. He thinks it proba- ble he shall not return for five years. He has a great dislike to the sea, and as there appears nothing for him to do here, he thinks he will establish himself in some kind of business at the Spanish Islands. Jonathan [Guest] also intends doing the same. They have both been very unsuccessful in their voyages as supercargoes. I believe I mentioned in a former letter that Jonathan had been shipwrecked, on his way home and all the cargo lost, but fortunately no one perished. Jonathan suf- fered very much from great exposures, and short allowance of food so that he lost about thirty pounds of flesh, and his nervous system had become so relaxed that his friends were fearful of a derangement of mind, but he has now quite recov- ered, and intends soon to set off again. If he does his wife and two little sons will accompany him. He has had some offer in South America which he seems will- ing to accept of and I suppose that place will be his residence for several years.

John Guest is expected on a visit from the Western Country about Christmas. From accounts received of him he is conducting himself very well, and is upwards of six feet high. Hannah T. Longstreth is mother of two children. The last time I heard from her she was well.

If my nieces stomach should be irritable so that it will not retain food a little wheat flour put before the fire and slowly scorched until [it] is a fine brown colour, and then made into a thin gruel is the best thing to stay on the stomach and at the same time very nourishing. It seemed to be that, that saved John Childs life at the time he had the cholera, the Phisicians had removed the disease but his stomach would retain nothing, and they thought he must die for want of food, but a friend stepped in and mentioned this gruel to them and how to make it, and it was prepared and given to him as speedily as possible and from the time he took it he began to recover. (There is a little salt put in it, and sweetened to the taste.) (Some take it without salt or sugar.) Do make it for Elizabeth. It will be so good for her.

I feel very anxious about thee my dear Sister. I fear thy great solicitude on account of my beloved niece, the exposure attendant on nursing, watching at night, and the drudgery thro the day, will be too much for thy strength to bear. I do hope you will act with great caution to thy self. I wish I was with thee that I might help thee bear they burthen.

Kiss my dear Elizabeth for me and with it a great deal of love, and tell her I hope it will not be a great while before she will be able to write me a long letter. Also with much love to thee and my dear nephew I remain

thy affectionate Sister
Jane Howell

I omitted to say we are all well and that Ann desires a great deal of love to thee and Elizabeth. Lemuel desires his love to you all.

JANE HOWELL *to* RUTH EVANS
Philadelphia, November 16, 1834

My dear Sister

It is now more than five weeks since thy last letter was dated and it seems a very long period to look back to for one that feels so much anxiety on your account. Has thee been sick thyself, my dear sister? Or has thee written and thy letter miscarried? I wrote very soon after I received thy last, and have daily been looking for a letter for some time past. I received a paper from my dear Nephew about ten or twelve days ago, but there was very little satisfaction in that. It did not tell me that my dear Niece was better, or that the remainder of the family was in health. If it was a suitable season for travelling, I think I should be tempted to undertake the journey alone.

I must now inform thee that Cousin Anna Guest was taken suddenly ill on the 7th Instant and died the third after, which was last first day evening. The morning she was taken ill she came down stairs to breakfast apparently well. After a short time she complained of pain and dizziness in the head and said she would go and lay down, which she did, and gave some directions for dinner but in a few minutes after she was without sense or motion except that caused by respiration which indeed was very difficult and continued so until she expired. She was intered last third day afternoon in Cherry St ground. Her will was not read after funeral as is generally done, but it is to be recorded, and afterwards read to the legatees. Charles & George J. Williams, and Jasper Cope, are the Executors. Charles says that William G. Chandler, Thomas, and Elizabeth, are to receive one thousand dollars each, and thyself, Amelia and myself each one thousand. Cousin Anna Coe is to have two thousand dollars, but I believe that none of her children is remembered. We have not heard the particulars of the will yet, or very little more than what concerns ourselves, but I suppose in a few days we shall hear all about it. Cousin Anna Coe came up to the City last evening to make arrangements for making over, or securing her two thousand dollars, from the creditors of her husband and sons. And thee and our Nephew William will have to do the same as speedily as possible. I have written to William telling him how to act, for if it is delayed in all probability you may lose it.

Our dear Aunt Anna and Nancy spent four weeks with me. They returned home about ten days ago. They are well. Aunt Anna desired a great deal of love to you and is very anxious to hear from Elizabeth. Anna Merrefield has a young son about three weeks old. They think of calling him John but they are not quite determined upon it.

Our Sister Amelia is here. She is well and desires her love to you. She is very much pleased with her legacy. We are all well and with much love to you all but particularly to my dear Niece, I am

> thy affectionate sister
> Jane Howell
> Excuse blank paper

Cousin Robert Coe is going to give me a coppy of his bill of sale drawn by his lawyer which I will send on in a day or two. You had better employ a lawyer and have the thing properly executed as perhaps it may make a difference between our city and your Territory. If thee chooses thee can sell it to Thomas or to Lemuel Howell as Roberts lawyer says there is no way of securing it but by bona fide sale.

JANE HOWELL *to* RUTH EVANS
Philadelphia, late November 1834[25]

My dear Sister

It was with the most heart-rending feelings that I heard the contents of my dear Nephews letter, altho my mind was in a great measure prepared for the event. It is a bereavement which will be ever felt by us. The hand of time may soothe, may soften and mittigate our sorrow, but it never can efface it. No, such worth, such loveliness as hers, is not to be forgotten, but will live, as an Evergreen in our Memories, until the end of time. She was a plant too pure, too ripe for bliss, to be long an inhabitant here, and into a Clime more congenial to the purity of her nature, she has been removed, there to flourish forever, and ever. And, now my dear Sister, knowing that our loss on earth, is her gain in Heaven, that she has only gone before us; should we not humbly strive, and pray for strength, to mould our wills, to the Will of Him, who is the Great Judge of the earth, so that we may not murmer at any of his decrees, for it is His right to Rule, and Reign, in Heaven, and in the Earth, and why should we call in question any thing that He doeth. He gave, and it is His right to take away. He lendeth to us for a season, precious pearls, jewels of inestimable value, but, when He calleth for them, should we wish to hold them back? And altho the seperation from our dear Elizabeth, may be indeed, like the dividing between the bone, and the marrow, yet, the consoling hope, of meeting her after we have done with time, is like a balsom to our lacerated hearts. Yes my dear Sister, if she could but tell us, how she passed the valley, and shadow of death,[26] when the veil of mortality was drawn from her view, to feel herself as in the immediate presence of her dear, crucified Redeemer, with his arms extended to receive her, and this gracious invitation, "Come thou blessed of my Father, inherit the Kingdom prepared for thee." Would she not say, He, to whom I looked, hid not his face from me, nor, He in whom I trusted, did not forsake me. His presence was as a light to my feet, and as a lamp to my path, to guide me to the Portals of everlasting Peace.

What greater attainment could we wish to arrive at, than that our latter end may be like unto hers. And altho thy bereavement, may make thee feel, like a lone sparrow [on] the house top.[27] Yet, the reflection, that her transition from this frail tenement of clay, has reunited her to kindred spirits, in that Glorious City, where she, with them, are singing praises to their God, and King, will I think, to thee, be like Oil poured upon the troubled waters.

I believe we are allowed to weep, when the heart is overcharged with sorrow,—Jesus wept at the grave of Lazarus—but to grieve immoderately at the dispensations of providence, let the cup we have to drink of be ever so bitter. It is certainly wrong, it seems to betray an unwillingness to bow to the will of Heaven. It destroys health, brings on disease, which often ends in death.

Therefore my dear Sister, let me plead with thee to summon up all thy fortitude against the present trying dispensation, and look unto Him, who can say to the most turbulent waves of the mind, "Be Still" and there will be an immediate calm. Willingly resign the precious lamb that the Great Shepherd of Israel has been pleased with the crook of his divine love to draw within His Heavenly enclosures. And may His will, be our will, is the sincere wish of

> thy truly affectionate Sister
> Jane Howell

I have had Obituary notices put in the papers.[28]

> Her spotless soul freed from its cumbrous clay.—
> On Angels wings to Heaven it sped its way.

RUTH EVANS *to* JANE HOWELL
November 1834, {excerpt}[29]

Thou canst, my dear sister, sympathise and deeply feel with me, in my sore affliction; but thou canst not know the full extent of my loss. She was my heart's delight—she was my earthly treasure. She was all goodness—all excellence—too sweet and too lovely to consign to the cold and silent grave. Oh! how I have wished that thou couldst have been with her through her protracted illness, and seen what a perfect pattern of patience she was. Never shall I forget her sweet engaging countenance, nor her affectionate language. I nursed her faithfully more than three months, before she was entirely confined to her bed, but saw with heart-felt sorrow that she was evidently declining.

A few weeks before her departure, she asked me if I supposed she would recover. I told her I thought she would be spared, if no new complaint should set in. She replied that she hoped she should; and if favoured to recover, she would endeavour to be more thoughtful, and more devoted to her Maker, than heretofore. I remarked that I did not think she could have a great deal to do. She answered, "I know that I have a merciful Saviour, and all-wise Father, but I feel as if there was something more for me to do. Yet if I should be removed, it will be for the best, and I hope I may feel reconciled."

I believe she cherished the hope that she would recover, until within a week of her decease; but about that time a new symptom appeared, which still increased her debility, and afterwards she failed very fast. One of the physicians having paid her a visit, she asked him what he thought of her case. He observed there would be a change before many days, which she seemed rather surprised to hear. I left the room for a moment, but returned immediately after the doctor had gone out. She then addressed me in the most affectionate manner, saying, "My dear aunt, do not be too much troubled at what the physician has said; it will no doubt be for the best." I seldom left her bed, except for a few moments at a time. She frequently addressed me affectionately, saying, "Aunt, let me go."

Two or three days before her death, we expected it momentarily. On First-day morning, the 2d inst., she quietly departed, and was received into the mansions of perfect peace and rest. Solitary, indeed, do I feel, for in her was centred my earthly happiness. She approached nearer perfection than human nature generally attains to. She was all I could desire—and is much lamented here by all who knew her.

RUTH EVANS *to* JANE HOWELL
Hazelbank, December 21, 1834

My Dear Sister

I have transcribed from the Liberator my precious one's death notised by Garrison, knowing anything relative to her will be interresting to her friends and relatives. We purpose supplying Garrison with sufficient materials for writing her biography, and publishing the selection we shall make which I am certain thou wilt approve of!

DEATH OF A MERITORIOUS FEMALE ABOLITIONIST
Our heart is sad—our breast is filled with melancholy emotions, on perusing the following letter, which contains tidings the most painful. Elizabeth M.

Chandler is a name not familiar either to the eye or the ear even of abolition-ists;[30] and yet there is not a female in the United States who has labored so assid-uously, or written so piously, in the cause of the oppressed, or who has such claims upon the gratitude and admiration of the colored people of this country and their advocates, as this departed friend. The effusions of her pen are chiefly to be found in the pages of the Genius of Universal Emancipation, to which publication she has been a constant contributor for eight or ten years, and for the five years she has conducted the Female Department in that paper. She has also contributed many articles to the columns of the Liberator, which have obtained a wide circulation. She was a prodigy in literature and philanthropy. Her genius was singularly original and fertile, and her taste exquisitely pure and discrimi-nating. Her prose articles are very beautiful, but she excelled in poetry. One of her pieces is the popular and pathetic hymn, commencing—

> Think of our country's glory,
> All dimmed with Afric's tears—
> Her broad flag stained and gory
> With th' hoarded guilt of years.

She was a member of the Society of Friends, and ardently beloved by all those who were intimately acquainted with her. It was owing to a modesty, as rare as it is admirable, that her name was not given to the public—for she cared not for her own celebrity, but only for the triumph of mercy and justice. Now that she has gone, however, it is meet that her worth should be known and praised, and that her name should stand first upon the catalogue of female phi-lanthropists in the cause of injured humanity in the United States. We shall ask permission of her relatives to write her biography, and to gather up the best of her productions in a small volume, so that she "being read, may yet speak" warn-ingly to the oppressor, and soothingly to the slave.

The following letter, communicating the intelligence of her death is from her afflicted brother. We trust he will excuse us for publishing it entire.

Near Adrian Mich. Ter. 11th Mo 4th 1834
To WᵐLloyd Garrison:
Respected Friend,

Although thou art personally a stranger to me, yet I feel as if I can commune with thee as a friend, for thou wert the friend of one who was to me the dearest object of a brother's love. It has pleased the Almighty, in his infinite wisdom, to take unto himself my beloved sister Elizabeth Margaret Chandler, in the prime of her life, and when her mental pow-ers were just fully developed. After an illness of eleven weeks, during which time she was wholly confined to her bed, and which she bore with the greatest patience, not a murmur or complaint having passed her lips through the whole period, on the morning of first day the 2°~' instant she breathed her last. Her character through life has been almost perfectly virtuous and guileless, and her sympathy for suffering humanity has rarely of latter times suffered an opportunity to escape, even in the social circle, of urging the claims of the oppressed, or of awakening an interest in their behalf. Of the efforts of her pen in the same holy cause, thou art already, to some extent, aware—but they are now cut short. I would thank thee to notice her death in the Liberator:

Died at the residence of her brother, near Adrian Michigan Territory, on the morning of the 2nd inst, of a protracted remittent fever, Elizabeth Margaret Chandler, in the 27th year of her age.

Mayst thou, my dear friend, be spared to grapple with, and assist to overcome, the savage monster with which thou art now engaged.

> I am thy friend,
> Thomas Chandler

I have so recently written thee my Dear Sister I believe I shall now send thee a little blank paper, as I do not wish to afflict thee by writing on the same melancholy subject, and I cannot write on any other for she is scarcely ever absent from my mind. Neither do I wish she should be, for she was dearer to me than I have language to express.

> with much love I remain thy
> affectionate sister
> Ruth Evans

I so fully expected my Dear brother and thyself to make us a visit last summer, that I must now abandon all hope of it in future, and shall endeavour to visit you next spring. The pleasure of seeing our dear relatives will amply compensate for the sacrifice Thomas would have to make. I do not however build upon it certainly, but Thomas thinks he can so arrange his business to make a short visit without being much disadvantaged. I want much to see my Dear aged Aunt. I want to see you all.

CHAPTER 7

MATTERS OF LIFE AND DEATH, 1835–1837

The family was devastated by Elizabeth Chandler's death. Ruth Evans took the loss especially hard—she was now without her household companion and the young woman she had raised as a daughter from infancy. Jane Howell responded to Ruth's uncharacteristic despondency, assuming the role of consoler. Despite their sadness, the family's efforts to publish Elizabeth Chandler's poems and essays energized them. However, also during this period, Thomas Chandler and Jane Howell faced more life-altering events when both Ruth Evans and Lemuel Howell died in 1836.

———◆———

JANE HOWELL *to* RUTH EVANS *and* THOMAS CHANDLER
Philadelphia, January 7, 1835

My dear Sister

I received thy letter yesterday, after passing thro a great deal of anxiety on account of not receiving one before, and deeply, very deeply do I sympathize with thee, in thy heavy, and indiscribable affliction. Yes my dear sister, the billows of Affliction has passed over thee, almost to overwhelming, but I trust that He, to whom thou lookest for help, has, and will stretch forth his hand and prevent thee from sinking—for to Him alone can we look for support under such deep baptisms. Thee says thee wished I could have been with our dear Elizabeth thro her protracted illness, and seen what a perfect pattern of patience she was. I wish I had. I think I could have resigned her with more willingness to have watched by her, to have waited on her, to have heard her sweet voice, and to have taken a last,

last look at her, would to me have been a great consolation. But that comfort was not for me, and I must submit. Oh! at such seasons as these, how trying to be so widely seperated. Year after year have I looked forward with the sweet pleasing expectation of meeting, and joyfully embracing, my dear distant relatives whom I so tenderly loved. I thought no joy on earth could be more extatic, more unmixed with alloy. But how is the scene altered—let me draw the curtain.

Rarely, very rarely is there to be found such a combination of all that is good, and lovely, as that which was possessed by our dear Elizabeth. Who could know her and not love her? Yes, she twined the cords of love strongly around the hearts of those with whom she was acquainted, and those who were nearly allied to her by affinity, must feel keenly, very keenly, the pangs which such a seperation must create. And altho it is very hard for our natural feelings to bear up against it, yet it is our indispensable duty so to do, seeing that it was the will of her Heavenly Father to take her to his bosom, where, she is secure from all the storms, and tribulations with which, this world abounds. Let me persuade thee my dear Sister, to strive to dry up thy tears. Every thing was done for her that could be done. Thy health calls for a remission of grief; for the strongest constitution is soon undermined by it, and disease of an incurable nature is often times the result of deep seated grief.

Therefore my dear Sister beware of the ill consequences, before it is too late. Remember, how many there are, whose happiness depends on thy good health, and if thee cares not for thyself, care for them. Grief, and mourning, will not bring the departed back, even if we were selfish enough to wish it. She is happy, superlatively so, and with such an assurance, should not sorrow subside, and cheerfulness resume her former seat in thy bosom. I do not ask impossibilities of thee, but I know it is in our power to do a great deal for ourselves, not forgetting, that the "hand that dealt the blow, is all sufficient to heal the wound." It is said, "Those He loveth he chasteneth."[1] "Let us therefore kiss the rod." In deep humility say "not my will, but Thine be done."[2] And with much love as ever, I remain

thy truly Affectionate Sister
Jane Howell

1ST MONTH 7TH 1835

My dear Nephew

What changes my dear Thomas does a few months produce, and how little can we calculate upon the future. I can hardly realize the departure of our beloved Elizabeth. At times, it seems to me it cannot be, to think that I am never more to see her in this world, is to me, a very great tryal; but to thee, and thy dear Aunt Ruth, her loss is incalculable. I feel the greatest sympathy for you, but I hope your minds will be brought into a perfect state of resignation, believing, that in the best of Wisdom she was taken. Thy brother William spent a few days with us nearly two months since. He had not heard until he arrived here of the painful event. Poor fellow it was a close tryal to him. He was well, also Sarah and the child.

According to thy wish Doctor Atlee was informed of the decease of thy beloved sister. He mentioned directly having obituary notices put in the public prints, but that I had already done, having put them in eight papers which were the most circulated. If there should be any thing of the kind in the New York or Eastern papers, it would be gratifying to me to see them. The piece that appeared in the Courier about two weeks since, was it sent by thee for publication? Or did some other kind hand put it in. It is the belief of Doctor Atlee that Benjamin Lundy is no longer an inhabitant of this world, not having heard from him since last summer.[3] The Genius has not been published for many months. Poor man, how much his death is to be regretted, away from home, and friends, if it is so but I feel a hope, that it is not the case, and that he may yet return.

Lemuel feels anxious to hear how William Dunlap is coming on. He is quite interrested in his wellfare, and would be glad if William would write either to him, or his friends here. Charles Williams has not yet I believe paid any of the legatees the money which was left them, but suppose it will not be long before he will do it. Thee must give me instructions how to transfer yours on to you. I suppose Charles will keep it in his hands until he hears from you, if I act for you, I suppose it must be a power of Attorney. Thy brother William read the Will. There was one thousand dollars left to each of you "but if either one died, that thousand was to be equally divided between the surviving two." I have not seen it myself. Charles brought it to read it to me but I was from home.

Our dear Aunts are to receive the interrest of seven thousand dollars during their life time. Jonathan Guest had the house Aunts lived in in Callowhill Street, but has since sold it to John G. Merrefield. I will try [ ] to send thee on the particulars of the will, when I am better informed myself. Lemuel went to see Aunts last evening. They were well. Dear Aunt Anna desires a great deal of love to you.

We have had very severe cold weather since the 3rd of this month, but I hope it may soon moderate on account of the poor, who I think must suffer exceedingly by it. My dear Lemuel has deeply sympathized with you in your trouble. His tears have attested to it. He desires his love to you. Ann also has felt very much for thy dear Aunt Ruth, and wishes me to remember her affectionately to her. Thy Aunt Amelia is in the country. She was well a short time since. She wishes in the spring to move to Camden [New Jersey] opposite the city. She thinks she can do a snug little business in the confectionary line. I am quite of her opinion, and approve of it. There are so many going there, every day thro the warm weather and taking their children for a little recreation, that I think she might sell a great deal.[4] And as she will live alone, I would rather she would be nearer to me.

I must now conclude my dear Nephew with a heart overflowing with love for thee and thy dear Aunt, and may health, and every thing that can tend to your happiness be with you is the fervent wish of thy Aunt

Jane Howell

We are well. Do let me hear very soon from you. Do not take the time to write long letters. Leave that for me to do, and only let me know how you are, as often as you can with convenience.

JANE HOWELL *to* RUTH EVANS
Philadelphia, January 21, 1835

I received thy letter my dear Sister with a copy of the obituary notice, from the pen of Wm Lloyd Garrison. It was expressed in words which pleased me much. It spoke loudly in praise of the deceased to those unacquainted with her, but to all who knew her real worth, words are not adequate to convey a just estimate of it. I felt very much oblidged to him, and was desirious to have it published in a few of our city papers. I applied to three of the Editors, but they all made one objection, and that was, to the name of Wm Lloyd Garrison. They said that he had sunk so low in the estimation of the citizens since he has espoused the cause of the coloured people in the way that he has, by approving of their intermarrying with the Whites &c. &c. that they thought it would be a great disadvantage to the memory of the departed, to have his name any how connected with it. Would it then be proper my dear Sister for him to publish her biography? Seeing how unpopular he is here, and what part of the Union would it be more eagerly sought after, than in this our City, where she was so well known, and so very dearly beloved. Let nothing be done that can in the smallest degree tarnish the luster of her unspotted character.

Can it be possible my dear Sister that I am to have the supreme felicity of seeing thee and my dear Nephew next spring, if nothing prevents? My heart bounds with joy at the very thought. If Thomas will not make too great a sacrafice by it, I think the journey will be of benefit to your health, but be sure not to come until travelling on the Lake is quite safe. I hope we shall not be disappointed, but I will try and not build too much upon it.

I have not heard from my Nephew William since he left here. I intend writing to him soon. I was very much pleased when he told me what a comfortable living he had made, and had been enabled to purchase a good deal of stock, and household furniture. He looked very well. I expect he will be delighted when he hears you intend paying us a visit. I have not mentioned it to any of my friends yet. I want to hear more about it first. How will our dear aged Aunt look when I tell her? She takes such great interest in every thing concerning you. I do not see any change in her since you left, either bodily or mentally. During the four weeks she spent with me a few months since, we frequently walked out after dinner, and several times she walked six, or eight squares, without appearing to be much fatigued. I want soon to write thee a long letter for at present I have not time as I wish to send this in tomorrow mornings mail, so thee must excuse a great deal of blank paper now. Ann desires a great deal of love to thee, and with no small share from Lemuel and myself to thee and our dear Nephew I am as ever

> thy affectionate sister
> Jane Howell
> We are all well.

I forgot to say that our Sister Amelia was here a few days since. She was well and wished me when I wrote to give a great deal of love to thee and Thomas. *Do write Soon.*

I have sent an Almanac for the present year.

———— ·◆· ————

JANE HOWELL *to* RUTH EVANS
Philadelphia, February 15, 1835

My dear Sister

Yesterday I received thy letter mailed the 1st Instant,[5] and I am grieved to find that thy fortitude has so far forsaken thee. Thee must not dwell so much upon thy loss, and cherish sorrow as thee now does. It will not do my dear Sister. Thy own good sense and religious feeling must tell thee so. Then why act against both? It is greatly in our power to stem the tide of sorrow, and it is our duty as far as we can to do it. If we indulge our natural feelings, we may esteem it almost a luxury, to weep and mourn after that which we held most dear, but why should we do so, when it places health and life at stake? And if we set no value on our lives, it is our duty to do nothing to shorten them. Thy heart, I know, is pierced to the very core, but there is a balm for every wound, prepared by the Great Physician of Souls, and as there is a right looking unto Him. He will have pity, and heal, and bind up the broken heart. Therefore my dear sister let me persuade thee, to use all thy endeavours to bring thy mind into a perfect state of resignation, believing that in the best of wisdom, she was taken from the evil to come.

How I long my dear Sister to embrace thee again, to see, and converse with thee and my beloved nephew. It affords me too much pleasure to dwell long at a time upon it, for fear I should be disappointed. I feel as if I could hardly wait until the time arrives. I hope it will be in my power to arrange domestic affairs so as to return with you. Lemuel says he shall be very glad if he can do the same, but he thinks his business will hardly admit of it. I think dear Aunt Annas eyes will fairly glisten with delight when I tell her you are coming. She has so often expressed a wish for it.

Thee mentions some pieces in an Adrian paper sent to me about eleven weeks ago. I have never received but one, and that was the first number dated October 22nd. I should be glad to receive the one thee alluded to.

The piece entitled "The Forrest Vine" is indeed very beautiful,[6] and highly valued by me. It is strange that it was not published before, but it is probable it was mislaid.

Cousin Robert Coe and his wife were in the City a few weeks ago. Smith & Burnet I beleave had made an attachment on Cousin Annas legacy, which is still in the hands of the Executors. They had previously made an assignment of it to Richard Coe, but I believe it was not quite properly executed which made it necessary for them to come up and secure it in some other way, which I understand cost them fifty dollars. I did not see them whilst they were here as their stay was very short.

I do not know when the Executors intend paying the legatees their money, but I suppose it will be before long. It takes some time to draw in the mortgages &c but I think to avoid all risk, they ought to have paid Robert Coe, as Smith & Burnet, are so exasperated against Robert and his sons, that they are determined to levy on any thing that they can lay hold on, but they have I believe secured every thing in such a way that I suppose they will get nothing. They may blame themselves for their improper conduct towards Robert and his Sons in the first place. Robert has been advised to act as he has done by the other creditors.

I took off my dear Nephews note from my letter and gave it to Lemuel to hand to John Child. I believe John takes no active part in any kind of business now. He has been quite low in his mind for some months past, but at times is much better. He has never been in good bodily health since he had the cholera, two years since. It is supposed that dwelling so much on the loss of his two Sons who died at that time and combined with other predisposing causes, has brot his mind into its present state. His family entertain very little hope of his ever being much better. His Son Samuel takes his place in meetings of business and is very active.

I expect Amelia will be here before long and then I will give her thy opinion about her living in Camden &c. I quite coincide with thee, and hope she will change her mind.

Ann met with a sad accident a few weeks ago, which caused us great anxiety, as we were apprehensive it might terminate in the locked jaw. She ran a pin in her arm just below the elbow, which swelled exceedingly, and became very much enflamed, and around the wound about the size of a cent, it was almost black. She complained of great pain shooting from her arm to different parts of her body, and a chilliness which was very alarming; but with the application of warm lye and milk poultice, and Jamaca Spirits taken internally she became more easy.[7] It has discharged a great deal since, and seems now in a fair way of healing. The sore is about the size of half a dollar. She desires a great deal of love to thee, and is delighted at the prospect of seeing thee in the spring.

I cannot think our dear Nephew William has abandoned the idea of moving to Michigan. It seemed to be his wish when he was here, but he thought it would be unpleasant to Sarah's Mother to part with her, and he did not like to say much to her about it. I think my self it is the very best thing he could do. I intend writing to him soon, to inform him of your expected visit, so that he may arrange his business that he can spend some time with you while you are with us.

John Merrefields youngest sister has lately come on from the State of Ohio. She is about seven years old. John has now four of them to provide for. Anna has full employment, with a young infant, the care of the Store and a family of seventeen to look after, but she seems to get along admirably.

I have no doubt dear little Roy will recognize you, and be delighted to see you. His memory is very retentive. He is as active and playful as when you left here, and has a great many pretty little tricks.

Lemuel is delighted at your proposed visit. He talks a great deal about it. He told me I must send a bushell of love to you, so I have mentioned the measure. When my dear Thomas sends News papers on to me I wish he would do them up something in the way that I do, by making them larger at one end than the other. It prevents them from being drawn out to be read on the way, and there is a better chance of their getting here safe. Thee did not say in whose care Thomas was going to leave his farm and his cattle during his absence from home. I must now conclude, and with a great deal of love to thee and my dear Nephew

I am affectionately thy Sister
Jane Howell
We are all well.

RUTH EVANS *to* JANE HOWELL
Hazelbank, March 5, 1835

My Dear Sister

I received thy letter last evening, and I am sorry to hear Ann has suffered so much from the wound caused by a pin. Indeed the symtoms were very alarming, and I hope there is now no danger to be apprehended. I learn from thy letter I received last month that Wm L. Garretson is not much respected by the Citizens of Philada. I hope however they do not generally feel so much hardness towards him. I presume he has many enemys that would rejoice at his downfall, but I do not give credence to all that is said against him. He is we believe highly esteemed throughout the State of New York, and all the Eastern States and we trust he merits the good character he bears, and with regard to his wishing the Whites and blacks to amalgamate, I presume it would be as repugnant to his feelings as to any other one whomsoever—but with respect to the publication we shall do nothing precipitately. We shall consult with thee previously, as I presume we shall be in the city before we decide on a publisher.

Yes truely, my dear Sister, it is our determination if favoured with health, to make you a visit as early in the fifth month as we can leave consistently. Yes already I have begun to count the weeks that must elapse, before we can arrange for leaving. Oh the comfort I anticipate in again seeing my dearest relatives. Yet the thought of visiting you unaccompanied by my ever loved, and precious one, that bore me company thither, is poignant indeed. Yes I say the bare thought seems to rend my verry soul, but alas, I must submit. It cannot be otherwise.

I wrote to Wm G. Chandler a short time ago, and I hope we shall hear from them before long, but he is extremely neglectful in writing. I wrote him a few months since, and I told him more than a year had elapsed, and not one line from him, had reached Hazlebank.

I presume our Territory will become a State, before long, as there are now more than eighty thousand inhabitants, and sixty is a sufficient number. It is believed there will be a great many newcomers this year, but they will have to go further west. I do not know of one lot of government land for sail, within many a mile of us. There will soon be a great settlement at bear Crick about fifteen miles [west] from us, the land is of the first rate quality.

If the Executors can have the money ready for us against we go to the City (and I hope they may) I intend to invest it in land there, as the probability is in a little time it would be worth double what it would cost. Darius Comstocks nephew has three lots of land near to us, which he offers for sail at six hundred dollars, and I presume they are worth it, altho there is not a cents worth of improvement thereon. He lives about thirty miles from here. Thomas has written to him and offered him five hundred dollars for them. He has not heard from him yet, but I presume he will take up with his offer. They would make a very valuable farm if any of our friends should ever think proper to move to Michigan!

There is certainly cause for alarm on account of B. Lundys long absence, but I think not more than there has been heretofore. I hope, and trust, he will before long return to his friends, and again publish his useful paper, but it will not be read by his subscribers with the same interest, it has been for some years past.[8]

A person in New York City lately deceased, and left a estate amounting to half a million of dollars, chiefly among coloured people formerly slaves. He has made them all independant, and some of them verry wealthy. [To] B. Lundy, he left fifteen hundred dollars, and to Wm L. Garretson five hundred dollars.

I will copy on this sheet, the pieces I alluded to in my last letter, fearing if I should send the paper, it might not reach thee. The few lines of prose writin by Joseph Patterson, I like well. The poetry by Elija Brownel is very common place, but any thing relative to that dearest one, will ever be interresting to us.

> Died,
>
> In the Township of Raisin, Lenawee County, on the morning of the 2nd Inst of a protracted remittent fever Elizabeth Margaret Chandler in the 27th year of her age.
>
> Modest and retiring in her manners, this amiable young woman had cultivated a mind of no ordinary cost, with a course of select and well digested readings. Some of our best periodicals have been adorned by her contributions.
>
> To her expanded and contemplative soul, the curse of slavery appeared in all its horrors, and called forth, at times, some of the most beautiful productions of her classic pen. It were indeed painful to witness the extinction of so much worth and talent, were we not assured of the more perfect views of her Creator.
>
> Lines suggested on hearing of the death of Elizabeth Margaret Chandler, which took place at her residence in Raisin, Lenawee County, M.T. on the 2nd of 11th Month, 1834, in the 27th year of her age.

> Alas! For a sound that awakens a feeling,
>   Innate in the bosom alive to the call;
> For anthems impressive, by language revealing,
>   What mortals inherit, and mortals befall.
> When Friendship is severed, and friends are departing

No more to be greeted on this side the grave;
Their virtues, their merits, shall mem'ry imparting
Their loveliest relics be faithful to save.
When talent, when genius, and muses are fading,
And leave a vain world to the pilgrim behind;
What heart that keen sorrow shall fail of pervading,
And fill with regret at the loss of the mind,
A gem is now taken from earth in full bloom,
And Africa's sons, and daughters may mourn,
The early, untimely, and sudden entombing,
Of her, who converted their cause to her own.
Much were her thoughts and her pen in conversing,
With scenes of distress, and of sorrow and woe,
Strong was her pleading their lot for reversing,
Undoing their burdens and letting them go.
Tho' sons of oppression may cease from deriving,
In future that aid they were wonted to share.
Her labours, like incense, before them arising
To freedom's fair prospect their way shall prepare,
The circle is broken, no more to be mended
And the scenes that are past, shall never return,
To the dead, another in glory's appended,
To tenant the lonely and mouldering urn.
United on earth in the bonds of affection
The grief of dissolving that mutual tie,
To a source of the greatest and keenest affliction,
Which draws the spontaneous tear from the eye.
In Fancy we drew the long line of enjoyment
Thro' a series of future and far coming years,
But alas the stern hand of cold disappointment
Can blast all the prospect our imagery wears.
Where then is the hope, or the strong consolation
The staff and the stay in sorrow's dark hour,
But in Him, through whom is eternal salvation,
Of infinite goodness, and boundless in power.
In vain are the jarrings of time in commotion,
In vain are the frowns that fortune may wear,
To a mind rightly in real devotion,
The anchor of souls will surely be there.
Then welcome to all the scenery changing,
And thankful alike for the smile or the frown,

'Tis but a Providence wisely arranging,
 The best to promote His glorious renown.
    · Logan 2nd of 11th Mo 1834
    E.B.

If thee should see Emily's mother, I think thee had better not tell her I expect to visit you. She perhaps would think I should bring Emily, but there would be no advantage whatever, her studies meantime would be neglected, she would suffer much from sea sickness, and it would be an expense, without the least profit to her, and she has not the least desire to go. I made a visit to Lydia Gibbons last first day, and told her our prospect of visiting Philad[a]. She was much surprised and also pleased, she thought it would be very benefitial to me. She asked me if we intended taking Emily. I told no, if she would board her during our absence which she agreed to without the least hesitation. They have a prospect of moving to bear Crick in the fall which I much regret. They are as well fixed where they are as they could wish to be, but some near relations of theirs have gone there, and they are very anxious Joseph and Lydia should be near them. Lydia wants to see thee very much. She says she knows she shall love thee from what she knows of thee.

Give our love to Lemuel and tell him I hope he will be at liberty to visit Michigan this summer. When thee sees Amelia remember me affectionately to her. I hope she will be in the city whilst we are there. Give my love to Ann. Oh the happiness I anticipate in the society of my dear distant friends. Remember me to my dear aged Aunt. What a privilege I shall esteem it if we are permitted to meet again—which I hope will be in ten weeks at farthest. There is however a great deal of work to be done in that time, corn, oats, potato's, &c, &c all must be in the ground. Thomas intends letting Darius Comstock have his horses, another neighbour the cows. The young cattle and hogs will run at large, on our own unimproved land as usual. Our house we shall make secure, and I trust nothing will suffer in our absence. Do write soon. We are well, and with much love I am

        With much love to dear Thomas
        and thyself I remain
        thy affectionate sister.
        Ruth Evans

JANE HOWELL *to* RUTH EVANS
March 23, 1835

My dear Sister

I have been anxiously waiting for an answer to my last letter dated the 15th of the 2nd Month. It seems a very long time since I heard from you. I should have written before now, but I have had a larger share of domestic concerns to attend to, than usual, as Ann has gone into Cousin John A. Williams' Store as an attendant; her health being hardly adequate to the work she necessarily has to do, and another consideration was, that her wages would be double, as she is to receive two dollars a week, and to board in the family. I encouraged her going, and I believe she would not have left me. I miss her very much as thee may suppose; being with me nearly eight years. Her arm has got quite well. I have a very smart half grown girl now, but I am looking out for a suitable young woman, which I hope I shall be able to meet with before a great while. Any how by the time thee gets here, so that I can devote all my time to thee, and my dear nephew.

I was quite alarmed in reading the last numbers of the Courier, at the threatening aspect of political affairs between your Territory and the State of Ohio. I cannot understand why they should wish to hold the reins of government over Michigan, on which claim they have upon it, I sincerely hope all things may soon be amicably settled, without recourse to arms.

Lemuel is building a very large store house for Wetherals & brothers, on Schuylkill Front and Walnut Streets, the roof of which takes 26 thousand 3 hundred shingles. It is let for two thousand dollars a year.

Aunt Anna a few weeks ago was a good deal in disposed with a cold, but has quite recovered. She desires a great deal of love to thee, and my dear Nephew.

Aunt Rebecca was here a few weeks ago. She is sadly disappointed that Cousin Anna Guest left so little to her sons. Cousin some time before her decease gave Eliza Tunis her choice of the house she lived in, in Sansom Street, or the one Cousin occupied in Arch Street. She of course chose the one in Arch Street as it was the most valueable. The wood and coal in the cellar, a new brussel carpet in the front parlour, and the silver tumblers were also left to Eliza.

The house at Eliza's death is to go to her daughter Rebecca. To Amelia Guest, Rebecca Giles and Mary Guest each Fifteen hundred dollars. To Aunt Rebecca, the house in Ninth Street near Spruce, to go at her death to her Son George. George is also to receive ten shares of Schuylkill Stock, and that is all. The house which Aunts occupied in Callowhill I believe I mentioned before, was left to

Jonathan, which he has sold to J. G. Merrefield and has gone to Washington, and most probable in one year he will spend his last dollar. I am surprised Cousin did not entail it to his children. John Guest was left one thousand dollars. He wrote since he heard it to his Mother, and says, it seems very little, but little as it is, it will be of great help to him. Aunt was pleased that he bore his disappointment so well. Cousin has left both of those houses in Walnut Street to Charles Williams and considerable stock beside amounting it is said to Thirty Thousand dollars, and a great part of her plate to Grace, his wife. George G. Williams has one of the Sansom Street houses, and I believe some money beside. His brother John A. has the house in Race Street and five hundred dollars, also the book case, and part of the books. Mary Ann Williams received nothing but each of her two children one thousand dollars. Margaret Hall and her children nothing. One of the houses in Sansom Street is to be divided between John G. and Amelia Merrefield. Aunts are to receive the interest of seven thousand dollars in bank stock as long as they live. Afterwards it is to be divided between Sarah Williams and Anna Merrefield. Judge Smith in Salem a first cousin is to receive four Thousand dollars, his son and daughter each one thousand dollars, Rebecca Pemberton three Thousand dollars, Patty and Elisa who lived with cousins each five hundred dollars. To Westown School six thousand, to the black Shelter six hundred dollars. I do not know wether there was anything left to any other institutions. The collateral law it is said will take from twenty to twenty five thousand dollars. Cousins left me some of their old plate vis. 7 table spoons 3 dessert or pap spoons 10 tea do—a small silver slop or sugar bowl a pepper box and four new salt spoons with the initials of Cousin Betsy's name, and on the inside Howell, two of the table spoons I have given to our sister Amelia.

She spent a few days with me about a fortnight ago. She was well, and has declined moving to Camden. She wished me to give her love to you. I intend writing in a few days to William. I expect he will be delighted to hear of your intended visit.

We are all well and as I wish to send this to the post office this evening thee must excuse a little blank paper and a very badly written letter. I hope thee will be able to read it. With much love from my dear Lemuel and a great share from myself to thee, and my dear Nephew, I remain

thy affectionate Sister
Jane Howell

I hope soon to have time to fill another sheet for thee for I have many things to tell thee, but do write in the mean time. I am very desirious for those papers which Thomas sent, and never came to hand.

JANE HOWELL *to* RUTH EVANS
Philadelphia, April 9, 1835

My dear Sister

I received thy letter dated 3rd M° 5th containing those pieces which thee copied from the Adrian papers. The prose does credit to the writer, although it is very short, it is expressive and beautiful. The poetry, if not the first rate, yet I feel grateful to the author for it, or to any one else who has written on the same subject. That from Wm Lloyd Garrison has been published entire, except Williams name has been left out. John Merrefield cut it out of Poulson's paper some time ago and gave it to Lemuel for me.[9]

Our dear Nephew Wm G. Chandler paid us a visit a few days since. He has a young daughter about three weeks old which he calls Elizabeth Margaret. I have made the little darling a present of a silver pap spoon marked E. G. which had belonged to Cousin Betsey Guest. William was quite surprised to hear that thee had not received his letter in reply to thine. He thinks he has written several letters to Michigan which has never come to hand. He wished me when I wrote, to give his love to thee, and his brother. He was very much pleased to hear that you were coming so soon to Philadelphia. He intends bringing Sarah and the two children to see you. He hopes nothing may prevent you from coming! He went to Charles Williams to know if he could let him have the amount of his legacy, but Charles told him he could not until the year was up. William then told him that you intended paying us a visit in the 5th month as he supposed it was the only time in the year that Thomas could leave home without subjecting himself to great inconvenience, and wether he could not let you have the money when you came, but he replied in the negative, stating, that if he paid one, he must pay all, and then if there should come in any debts against the Estate of Cousin Anna, he should be liable for the payment of them. A very frivolous excuse indeed. He must be well aware that there is nothing of the kind against it, and indeed I think there is a great deal of injustice in it, as those who were to receive the real estate are put in full possession of it. I hope it may not prevent you from coming. Perhaps Charles may alter his mind or you can make arrangements with him to forward it on to you when he is ready for it.

I have not seen Emily's Mother I believe for more than two years. Perhaps she is not living. If she was, I should think she would certainly make some enquiry after her child. Samuel Lovett came up to see us a few days since. He and his family were well. Our dear aged Aunt Anna is well. She is very much pleased at the prospect of seeing you.

I am so full of business now, having at present but a half grown girl, that I have not much time to write, but I hope soon to have more help, and then I will make amends in writing long letters to thee, until then excuse blank paper. I have many things I want to tell thee but shall have to wait until I write again.

John Child is nearly recovered his usual health. He will have your certificates ready next month.

I must conclude with a great deal of love to thee and my dear Nephew I remain

> thy affectionate Sister
> Jane Howell
> We are all Well.

———— ◆◆ ————

No letters were written between mid May and early July, the period Thomas Chandler and Ruth Evans spent in Philadelphia with their loved ones. When they returned to their log home in Michigan, the letters resumed.

———— ◆◆ ————

JANE HOWELL *to* RUTH EVANS
Philadelphia, July 29, 1835

My dear Sister

Yesterday I received my dear Nephew's letter informing me of your health and safe arrival at Hazlebank.[10] It relieved my mind of a great weight of anxiety for I had been looking for a letter nearly two weeks allowing you about eight days for your journey and a tarry of two days at New Brunswick. I am very glad you found all things safe at home and that Thomas' grain looked so well. By this time I suppose your harvest is over.

Poor Thomas Orr met with many misshaps on his journeying to the West. Before he reached Pittsburgh the place where his goods were which he took with him caught fire from the locomotive and consumed a box containing about twenty dollars worth of new clothing and at the same time had another stolen containing wearing apparel. One large box which he sent several days previous to his leaving here has returned back to Philadelphia. After they had embarked in a Steam Boat I believe it was on the Mississipi it sprung a leak which alarmed the passengers very much and about the same time two persons were seized with the Cholera. They left the boat and took shelter in a log hut which was so infested with rats that they could not lie down at night. The next day they took another steam boat but they had not proceeded far before the boiler burst but not in such a way as to injure the passengers and they had to paddle to shore. When they had got within 22 miles of Jacksonville they put up for the night at a tavern but the accomodations being so bad they started without breakfast for their kind friends in Jacksonville whose house they had kindly offered them for a home until they were suited in one of their own, but when they arrived there altho they informed them of their long ride without breakfasting, they did not offer them a morsel to eat and it was then after ten oclock and in the evening they had to provide themselves with lodging. Every thing is so different there from what was represented to them that they are very much disgusted with it, and are now I suppose on their way back to Philadelphia.

Benjamin Lundy was here a few evenings ago, and again this afternoon he was very desirous to hear particulars of our dear Elizabeth. I handed him two or three letters and the obituary notice by Garrison. He shed many tears in perusing them and paced the room for some time. He wished me to say that he intends writing a letter to thee and my dear Nephew very soon and desired his very best respects to you. He is very desirous to take upon himself the publication of the book you have in contemplation and would wish to have it done as speedily as possible. He was very sorry that the sheets had not been left here that no time would have been lost in going on with the work as he will have to leave the United States after the course of some weeks and will not be able to return before next spring. The thought of giving it to Carey & Lea or some other eminent book seller and to sell them the copyright for the first edition receiving as many numbers as you would wish, he thinks as much or more might be made in that way than in any other and with much less trouble to yourselves, but he wishes to leave it to your judgement. He says if there will be no immediate private opportunity to convey them on, he thinks they had better be sent by mail either rolled up closely and well sealed or done up flat and very legibly directed. He says he would wish to have her Biography, but if Thomas has not drawn anything up in that form, if he would send on facts relative to her parents the place of her nativity her age &c &c he will do it himself. He appears very unwilling that Garrisson should undertake it. He says if there are any pieces on other subjects than Slavery he should like them sent so as to make the work miscellaneous, but if not no matter.

Elizabeth Merrefield was very much pleased with her present from thee. She

wished me to send her sincere thanks to thee for it. I heard from our dear Aunt
Anna a few days ago. She was well. Ann has left John Williams.' She says the
business was too heavy for her. She is now with George Coleman and boards at
Richard Bailes in Second Street.

Thee may judge from my writing that I have an intolerable bad pen, which
makes it almost labour to write so I believe I must conclude.

> With much love to dear Thomas
> and thyself I remain
> thy Affectionate Sister
> Jane Howell
> We are well.

I hope soon to receive a long letter from thee giving me the particulars of all
that occured on your journey. I was glad to hear that your goods arrived safe and
particularly those that I had a hand in packing. How comes on your flowers? I feel
great interest in every thing that is yours. Eliza Tunis and Mary Guest has accompanied Jerre Warder and his wife home to Cincinnatti and expects to go still further west. Eliza went on account of her health. Charles Williams has I believe
quite recovered. He has a young son about five weeks old. Richer and Richer.

BENJAMIN LUNDY *to* THOMAS CHANDLER
Philadelphia, August 6, 1835

Highly Esteemed Friend,

Most sincerely, do I console with thee and thy dear aunt, on account of the
great loss which *we all* have sustained, in the demise of thy dearly beloved, philanthropic, and amiable sister. Altho the circumstance has unquestionably been to
her an *eternal* gain, to us the loss is truly *irreparable*. And alas! how fully do we realize the truth of the saying, (as applied to all created things,) the tenderest, most
beautiful, and most fragrant flowers are the earliest to fade, and the swiftest to
decay. Permit me, my dear friend, to mingle my sorrows with thine, upon the
mournful occasion. While thee has lost thine *only* one, I *too,* am thus deprived of
the dearest *sister* I had upon earth. Never, indeed, will the vacuum thus opened in
our afflictions be filled—for *"never* shall we look upon her like again!"[11] Yet while
we deeply lament the awful and sorrowful dispensation, let us bow in humble res-

ignation to the unerring will of Divine Providence; and when bedewing with our tears the silent tomb of our dearly beloved, O may we prepare to join her spiritual and immortal form in the everlasting mansion of peace and never-ending felicity.

I have conversed with thy aunt Howell, since my arrival here, and learn from her that you have selected some of Elizabeth's writings with the view of publication in book form. She also tells me that you are willing to allow me to assist in publishing the work. Most gladly will I attend to it, and aid you therein as far as I can. I wish you, therefore, to forward the manuscript to me, with such facts, &c. as you may think proper to furnish, relative to Elizabeth's biography, if you have not yet got that prepared. Thy aunt, here, can assist me in procuring information on this point; but I wish you to send me everything, at hand, that you may consider proper to be used in the publication. The best plan that we can probably adopt, will be to sell the copyright, for the *first edition,* to some popular and influential bookseller. My engagements will not permit me to superintend both the printing and sale of the books. You can reserve a certain number of copies. Thee will inform me what you may wish to have done, in this respect, when the manuscript is forwarded. It will be the best to send it *by mail* to Philadelphia, or, else, by some safe conveyance to me, care of my friend Lyman A. Spalding, of Lockport, in Western New York. I shall visit him, on business, in the course of a few weeks. I repeat, it will afford me the greatest pleasure to assist you in this matter. I shall never be able fully to discharge the obligation which I am under to the family, for the inestimably valuable labors of our dear departed sister, in conducting my periodical work.

> My best respects to thy aunt; and
> believe me—
> Thy Sincere Friend
> B Lundy

Nashville, 5th Mo. (May) 14th, 1835

ESTEEMED FRIEND:

Again, I take this method of communicating some private information to my personal friends, relative to my proceedings in Mexico. My last visit to that country (like the one preceding) having been prolonged far beyond the period which I had anticipated, I feel it incumbent on me to explain the causes thereof, especially to such as take an interest in the enterprize in which I have engaged, and those who have kindly assisted me with means to defray the expenses of my journey, &c.

Soon after the date of my last printed letter, which was issued from this place, I went to New Orleans, with the intention of taking a passage, by sea, to some port in Mexico; but after waiting in that city about two weeks, and finding no opportunity to obtain one, I proceeded up the Red River, and journeyed through Texas again, by land. My health continued very good for some length of time; but when I reached the middle part of the Texas country, it was my misfortune to come again in contact with the direful *"Cholera,"* and again I was the subject of its virulent assaults. My detention was great, and my affliction pretty severe; though I finally expelled the disorder as I had done before. My sufferings were somewhat aggravated in several instances, by the fearful prejudices of the people among whom I travelled. I was very anxious to get through my journey, and often essayed to travel, before I was, in fact, well enough. The consequence was, that I frequently took relapses, and sometimes had to lie out, under trees, even in time of rain, within sight of houses,—the people being unwilling to give me shelter therein, fearing that my disorder was contagious. At length I reached the Mexican town of *"San Antonia Deflexar,"* and there I tarried, until I had got pretty well rid of the Cholera. I then pursued my journey to Monclova, the seat of government for the State of Coahuila & Texas, in company with several Mexican gentlemen and foreigners. Previous to this time, I had travelled several hundred miles, entirely alone, and generally encamped in the woods or plans, at night.

On my arrival at Monclova, I was doomed to encounter "misfortune" of a very different character. Here I found that the Englishman, (mentioned in my other letter,) with whom I had contracted to petition for two grants of land,[12] *had totally failed in his application.* The petition had been laid before the Governor, and he was about issuing the grants, when he received a decree from the legislature, which was then in session, forbidding him to grant any more land, under any pretext. This measure was taken to prevent the great land speculators from carrying on their swindling operations in Texas. An act was soon after passed by that body, repealing all their colonization laws; and thus every hope that I had so fondly entertained, and each fair prospect, seemingly so near its realization, *was instantly blasted and utterly destroyed!!* If ever the fortitude of man was tried, mine was then. If ever stoic philosophy might be successfully called to the aid of human courage, I felt the necessity of invoking it upon that occasion. Nearly two years of toil, privation and peril had been wasted. My sufferings had been great, though my spirit had soared on the buoyancy of hope. Now, the fair superstructure of an important enterprise, whose ideal magnitude had employed my mind, to the exclusion of many hardships endured, suddenly vanished from my sight, and left before me a hideous and gloomy void, with no other encouragement than total disappointment, conscious poverty, and remediless despair!

What *should* I then have done? My health was restored, but my detention and consequent expenses had been so great that my funds were nearly exhausted. I came to the country for an important purpose, and I reasoned with myself thus: Although my way is closed, in this State, cannot something be done *elsewhere?* I will not boast of the stoutest heart among me, but mine *must not quail.* Something further *must* be done, if possible; and—I WILL TRY.

In the course of my travels, I had seen a part of the adjoining State of Tamaulipas, and had been informed that the colonization laws thereof were liberal. I was even aware that some parts of it are more suitable for the culture of the sugar-cane, than any tract I could have obtained in Coahuila & Texas. And, upon a little reflection, I determined to make further investigations in Tamaulipas.

As soon as my horse was a little rested, I set out, alone, on a journey of between four and five hundred miles, part of the way through an awfully mountainous region, and much of it an uninhabited wilderness. I encamped out almost every night, during the whole journey, very seldom near any human habitation. I had no fire-arms, nor anything to defend myself against the ferocious beasts of the forest, which I had evidence to convince me were frequently numerous, and not far distant. In about two weeks, I reached the city of Matamoras, in the State of Tamaulipas, quite destitute of funds, after parting with almost every disposable article belonging to my wardrobe, &c. The people of this place being all perfect strangers to me, I did not for a while unfold to them the real object of my visit; but instead thereof, I opened a shop, and commenced working at my old trade, the *saddling business.* I soon got as much work as I could do—supported myself—replenished my pocket—made some acquaintance with a number of people, and obtained more information respecting the colonization laws of that State.

A few weeks elapsed, while I was employed in this way. I then mounted my horse again, and proceeded to the capital of the State; and, after negotiating for some time, with the Governor and Council of State, I succeeded in obtaining a grant of land, upon advantageous terms. I then performed another journey of almost 250 miles, *"alone,"* to Matamoras again; and soon thereafter embarked for the United States.

My friends will thus perceive that I have not been *idle;* though much time has been occupied in my last expedition. I shall not attempt to excite their sympathy, by exhibiting the *twentieth part of what I have suffered.* I do not even like to *look back* upon some of the scenes through which I have passed. But thanks to a kind and all-sustaining Providence,—complete success has, at last, crowned my exertions. I strove hard to command it; and I leave it to others to say whether I have *deserved* it or not.

The terms upon which I have obtained my grant of land, will be noticed in a *public* address, which I shall forward with this letter.

Since my arrival in this place, I have been confined by sickness; but I am now convalescent, and shall visit my friends to the eastward, as soon as circumstances will permit.

I cannot close this communication, without an expression of my sincere thanks, to those kind friends who rendered me assistance in defraying the expenses of my last Mexican tour. Their favors will be most gratefully remembered, and I shall feel myself under additional obligations to labor for the melioration of the condition of the poor and suffering *slave*. In the next number of the "Genius of Universal Emancipation," I shall insert the names of those who have contributed to aid me in the prosecution of my enterprise, and correct information, relative to all proceedings therein, will be given in the pages of that work, as the business connected with it progresses.

> Most respectfully
> Thy Friend
> B. Lundy

Thos Chandler—

N. B. The foregoing will give thee *some* of what difficulties I have recently had to encounter. I believe that I sent thee a copy of the same before; but lest it may have miscarried, I send thee another with the letter annexed.

I likewise forwarded an "extra" of the G.U.E. which thee has, no doubt received. My business has kept me continually engaged, or I should have written much sooner. (My particular respects to all our friends in your neighborhood.)

> In haste, Sincerely, Thine, &c.
> B.L

P.S. My trunk was safely delivered to me by Dr. Atlee. Accept my thanks for thy kind attention to it. Please write me *soon,* as my stay in this part of the country cannot be prolonged many weeks.

> Respectfully,
> B.L.

———— ◆ ————

JANE HOWELL *to* RUTH EVANS
Philadelphia, September 7, 1835

My dear Sister

I received thy letter giving me an account of your journey home.[13] I felt anxious to hear, as my dear Nephew said you were nearly two weeks in performing it, and I was fearful that you had encountered some difficulties on the way. But how thankful I was to the Great Disposer of Events that you were permitted to reach home in safety.

The route to the Far West by way of Pittsburgh &c has in many instances this summer proved fatal to travellers; the cholera having prevailed very much along the rivers and canals. One of the persons who died on board the boat in which was Thomas Orr and family, was taken ill about day light and before 8 oclock the same morning was intered on the banks of the river.

John Warnock a few days ago received a letter informing him of the death of his brother who a few years since came to this country with his family and purchased a considerable quantity of land near Cincinnatti on which he settled, about a month since as he was on his way to Pittsburgh I believe on publick business. He was seized with the cholera and died in a very short time. He was a man that was much respected.

I was very sorry indeed my dear sister when I read in thy letter that thee was not in good health. I am very much disposed to think it proceeds in a great measure to thy using so little exercise. A sedentary life will not do for thy constitution nor mine, that I know from real experience. We have both from early years been accustomed to a very active life, and if we wish to preserve health we must use as much exercise as our strength will admit of. At the time I was making Louisas freedom clothes I sat hours together at my work for several days but I found it would not do for the pain in my side increased very much.

I was very sorry to learn that Emily attends to almost all thy domestic concerns. If thee is able to be on thy feet it would be much better for thy health to take an active part in them, so as not to over fatigue thyself. It would be good for thy mind and body. Remember whilst thee was with us in the city how much better thee was after thee began to walk about and such long walks as thee would take at a time. Do take my advice on this one subject. It is the wish of thy sister who loves thee dearly. Embrace every opportunity in riding or walking out, but avoid the evening air. If I studied my inclination instead of my health, I should love to set whole days together at my book or work. I was very much surprised when thee told me how many books thee had read and how much knitting and sewing thee had done in so short a time, altho' it was a very long time for thee to be using the exercise. I should not wonder that thy health suffered by it. I feel as if I could hardly drop the subject.

I wrote to William a few days before I received thy letter. I sent a copy of Thomas' letter to him thinking it would be more satisfactory than if I had merely made an extract.[14] I expect I shall soon hear from him and then I think it probable he will say what he thinks about moving to Michigan. I wrote to Amelia about a week ago desiring her to come and spend a few weeks with me. I have heard from her since. She was well. Lemuel has been so full of business since you left here that we have not been able to leave the City one day, and he has still a great deal of work on hand. He said a few weeks ago that he thought he had fully made up his mind if I was willing to move to Michigan in the spring without first going to see it. He is very tired of his trade, and of the City and longs to be at farming, and there is no place that he would prefer to Michigan, and I have no doubt but he would make arrangements this winter for leaving here in the Spring if it was not for his Mother. He says he would like to settle near you when he goes.

I heard from Aunts a few days since. They were well but Amelia Merrefield has been very ill for several weeks past. I suppose it must be about six weeks ago, she and another young woman were riding in a Gig together, when the traces or something broke, they both got out and Amelia endeavored to raise the Gig whilst the young woman repaired the place which had given way, in doing which she strained herself in such a manner as to cause her much pain, still she kept about for several weeks and refused to have medical advice until she became confined to her bed. She was then attended by Doctor Smith of Germantown who bled her and put her on very low diet. The Doctor called her disease the Pleurisy on the lungs. I think it hardly probable that she will recover. Her friends are very anxious to have her brought to the City but the only way they could bring her would be on a bed which she is not willing for altho' very desirous to come.

I think it is quite time our dear aged Aunt had left the country. I am very much afraid some accident will happen to her before she reaches home, for she gets up several times in the night and goes into Amelia's room which thee knows is at the head of the stairs. Eliza Williams' health is much better since her jaunt to the Sea Shore. Cousin John [Williams] has purchased another house in New Street adjoining the other which they bought some years ago. Ann has left there and is now in George Colemans Store next door to where we lived in Second Street. Hannah Roberts spent several days in the City last week. She made her home with us. She was very much gratified with thy visit to her. She desired her love to thee when I wrote. I stopped in Third Street this morning to see Margaret Hall to make some inquiry after Cousin Coes family, but she had removed into

Front near Duke Street. I got no information as Margaret was from home. Young Robert [Coe] was seen here in the City a few days ago but what he is doing I cannot say.

I am daily expecting to see Benjamin Lundy. He has not been here since I wrote last. He expected to be absent from the City for some time on business but would come to see me on his return. I forget wether I mentioned in my last letter that he wished to be remembered to you and that he intended writing to you as soon as he has a little leisure. The retaining [of] the Manuscript after the publication shall be carefully attended to.

I was much pleased to hear that Thomas got along so well with his harvest. I hope his wheat yielded him a good crop. How comes on his corn and potatoes? Cousin Lizzy and Samuel Dixon spent an afternoon with me a few days ago. She made many enquiries about you and seemed quite willing to excuse thee for not going to see her, as thee had so much to attend to.

Thomas Orr's wife, her father, and child have returned to Philadelphia. They met with much trouble on their journey home. Her father was taken ill on board the steam boat, which was supposed to be the cholera. The passengers said he should be put on shore or they would leave the boat without paying for their passage. The captain accordingly put them on Shore. They took lodgings at a Tavern until he was able to travel. Her child also was taken extremely ill and for three days she dispaired of his life. When they resumed their journey it was in the land stages which cost them twenty dollars more than it otherwise would have been if they had not left the boat. Thomas had to remain at Jacksonville to await the arrival of his goods, since which he has received a letter from the Mayor of Cincinnatti, saying, that boxes of goods had been siezed upon as stolen, marked Thomas Orr Jacksonville and he must come there and prove them to be his, which he could not do until he had sent to Philadelphia for the hand writing of the one who had marked the boxes. This will cause great detention and much expense before he gets through with it. In one of his letters he says he has been very unwell with chills and night sweats. The Doctor wishes him to leave there as soon as he can. He has regretted very much that he did not take Lemuels advise and go to Michigan.

Betsy Harrigas and her husband spent an afternoon with us a short time since. He is very anxious to sell his property and then he says he would go to Michigan and settle in Detroit. He thinks he could do a good business there. Maria Woodside is still out of business. She has been at Wilmington for some time past. Emily's mother has not called to make any inquiries after her. She could know where I lived by asking in Second Street. Emily must write to me as soon as she has an opportunity. Give my love to her. Thee did not say how many acres there was on the place thee mentioned was for sale but Lemuel thinks if the man puts in 30 acres of wheat without an extra charge it must be cheap. Abby Warnock wished me to tell thee that she was very sorry that thee did not get the patterns before thee left here. Hannah gave them to one of the little boys but he forgot to bring them.

Thee may recollect when we were at Eunice Hassingers that she said her Dutch girls sister a child about ten years of age was on her way to this country from Germany and wished me to take her. I did so, and I think she is one of the most industrious children I ever saw, and altho she cannot speak any english except yes, and no, she seems to understand almost any thing I say to her. She has been with me about six weeks. Her name is Henrietta. She is very strong and active. I think we shall have her bound before long, as there are several that are wanting her and she might be persuaded away. She is all the help I have at present, but I expect soon to have more!

Lemuel has given that note of Thomas' to me and I should like to lay it out in unimproved land if Thomas should see any that he thinks will do, and perhaps I will buy an improved farm in Michigan with my legacy, unless I should conclude to take the house we live in. It seems to afford Lemuel a great deal of pleasure to set and talk about you. He takes the greatest interest in your concerns as much so as he possibly could, were you his own brother and sister. I am glad thy purchases for thy friends suited them. They certainly were selected with much judgment.

Hannah Woodside dined with us to day. She says there is a young man by the name of Goodman who expects to start from here next seventh day for Michigan. He wishes to see the place and how he likes it before he moves his family on there. She wanted me to send this letter by him, but I thought it would reach thee sooner by mail.

I think Isaac Comstock is very fortunate in shooting deer. I expect they must be very fine eating. The shoulders and hams are very nice when cured and dryed as beef. Do have some by the time we come to see you. Hannah Woodside says Maria has had an offer to go to Virginia to assist in an infants school but wether she would accept of it she could not tell. Friend Wooley told Hannah Roberts that she was very sorry that she did not know that thee was in the City. She said if she had she would certainly have come to see thee. Do my dear Sister when thee writes drop a little ink on the paper—cross off a few words, write with a bad pen, so that they will not put my letters so to the Blush with their neatness.

Let me impress it on thee to use exercise. It will be the Hygean Medicine thee can tolerate best.[15]

Late letters from Hudson informs us that Phebe Beckman has lost her husband. It seems as if all Aunt Sallys daughters would become widows. Potatoes have been selling in our market as low as twenty five cents per bushel. It has been a very favourable year for thier growth. I expect Thomas will have an abundant crop, to judge from former years.

Thee says thee is taking the Hygean Pills, they are the same kind that I had been taking before you came to the City. They are highly recommended by many who have taken them and I think I was benefitted by them. Lemuel prefers them to any other medicine for himself. I reduced the number from 5 to 2 or 3 as I thought it was rather weakening to take so many, and so often. We call them the Morrison pills.

The spoon matched them that were [ ], and as Charles did not want it, I took possession of it. Lemuel is lowering a floor and repairing a house for Charles Witherall. We are all well and with much love to thee and my dear Nephew, I remain

thine affectionately
J. Howell.

I mix the pills in a little jelly or molasses and take them all at once. Do write soon or I shall feel very uneasy.

———◆—◆—◆———

RUTH EVANS *to* JANE HOWELL
Hazelbank, September 24, 1835

My Dear Sister:

I have been looking for a letter from thee for several days past, and I have just heard there is one at the Post Office, which I conclude must have come by this days mail, as there was none there the day before yesterday, and I assure thee it will not remain there longer than it will be practicable to convey it to Hazlebank. When last I wrote to thee, I was in a very feeble state of health, my health began to decline soon after my return home. The day after I wrote thee, I was confined to my bed for several days. I was fearful billious fever would set in. Thomas wanted I should have medicle advice, but I could not concent to it. I put no confidence in the arm of flesh. It is to the Lord I look for help. He can raise from a sick bed whom He will. I made considerable use of the Oil of Tar, and I also took the hygean pill, anti billious pill, salts, and what not, without any apparent relief for some time. Still I was not discouraged, altho the words that were spoken to King Hezekiah very often came into my mind, "Set thine house in order for thou shalt die and not live."[16] This preparation of heart is what my soul craves. It is ten thousand times more desireable than all mundane enjoyment however glorious, and O that our time this side Eternity, may be protracted for the purpose of becoming prepared to meet the messenger of death.

Thomas has just returned from Adrian with thy long letter which is very acceptable. I am sorry to hear Amelia Merrefield is so much out of health. I fear her recovery will be very tedious. I think she and dear Aunts would be much more comfortable in the city now, if Amelia could be removed. Remember me affectionately to them.

Thee has my dear sister no doubt felt uneasy on account of my sick state of health, but I have now the satisfaction to inform thee, I am as well as I was during my visit to you in Philadᵃ but when last I wrote I thought it possible it might be the last letter I should ever write, but I have admirably recovered, for which I strive to feel thankful for. I quite unite with thee in sentiment respecting exercise. I think and have thought for many months past, it is of more benefit to me than medicine. Thomas had often urged me riding, and as we have a good light waggon and a span of horses which we believe to be perfectly faultless, I can enjoy it without the least fear of danger. How I wish thee was here that we could ride on horseback. Such exercise I am sure would be of great advantage to thee and myself, and I hope and trust the time is not very far distant when I can visit with thee, without my going all the way to Philadelphia.

Tell dear Lemuel I rejoice to hear he entertains so favourable an opinion of Michigan, but I presume it is no better than it merrits, for I believe it is as fine section of country as America can boast of. I do not want you should purchase any more property in the city. I want you should have nothing of that kind to tie you there. The farm I mentioned in my last letter contains one hundred & forty acres. It is three quarters of a mile from us, and I presume there is more than fifty acres under cultivation. It is on the Adrian Road and will be very valuable. There is no government land to be bought now any where near us, but as soon as Thomas has leisure we purpose making a visit to some of our friends at Bear Creek, and there it is probable a good selection of land may be made. We wish to invest our money in unimproved land there, as it more than doubles in value every year.

I have written to Sarah Chandler, and have somewhat relieved my mind by pointing out the advantage that would arise by their coming to the West. Heretofore I have written little or nothing to them on the subject altho it is the desire of my heart he should be near his brother. I am really sorry Williams letters do not come to hand. It must be owing to misdirection certainly.

We received a letter from B. Lundy some weeks ago. Thomas wrote him without delay and sent the manuscript by mail, the postage he paid was eight dollars and twenty five cents. I regret I did not leave it with thee. It would have forwarded the business as Benjamin is limited for time.

I think I never heard of any travellers to have encountered such a series of perplexities in so short a time as the Orr family. I really do not know how I should have got along in a similar situation, but conclude it would have caused great depression of spirits particularly when detained on the road with sickness. Give my love to Uphemia and tell her if they should conclude to come to Michigan now or at any distant period, we should [like] to see them at Hazlebank. I presume they would meet with a very different reception from what they did at Jacksonville, and I trust by coming here they would do well.

When thee sees Amelia give my love to her. I should think she might often spend a little time with thee. It would be a very pleasant change for her. I should like to know how Cousin Coes get along amidst their trouble. I really feel much for them.

Thomas is very busy ploughing for winter grain. I wish we could send you a barrel of our beautiful flour. His crops have all turned out well. He will have considerable for sail, and there is a great demand for all kind of produce. He will also [have] a very fine beef, and I cannot say how many hundred weight of pork to sell this fall. As soon as thee receives this letter please reply to it without delay. I cannot however impute any neglect to thee on that score. I want thee should write compact, and tell me every event, every thing is interresting to me relative to my far distant friends. Remember me to thy dear Lemuel and with love to thyself I remain

thine as ever.
Ruth Evans

— ◆ —

THOMAS CHANDLER *to* LEMUEL HOWELL
Hazelbank, September 24, 1835

My dear Uncle,

Aunt Ruth has left a portion of her paper for my use to write a few lines to thee which I shall appropriate in telling thee something about Michigan which is making rapid strides towards a high state of improvement. Property has sold higher this season by far than heretofore and the price of produce is full as good as in any former year. A. J. Comstock sold a lot in the village of Adrian about ? an acre for 1500 dollars and an individual who purchased two village lots a few years since for one hundred dollars sold them this summer for one thousand. Uncle Darius sold two build lots about a mile from us for six hundred dollars, the back of which is rather inferior—he likewise sold 120 acres of which ten were improved for 800 dollars. The last he purchased two years since for 450 which was then thought a good price.

The railroad from Adrian to Toledo is progressing finely. It is thought it will be completed next summer. The Toledo War I expect has entirely blown over us. It is probable Ohio will be content to wait now to have the question decided by Congress as it eventually must be. It was the intention of Ohio that a court should have held in the village of Toledo, thereby formally organizing the disputed territory as a county belonging to that state. Governor Lucas of Ohio was to be present with an armed force to protect it from the civil authorities of Michigan but he failed to make his appearance. The reason is thought to be the inability to procure men as a large majority of the reflecting inhabitants of Ohio are utterly apposed to his violent measures. Our territory sent a force of 1500 or 2000 men to assist the sherrif of Monroe county (in which Toledo is situated) in arresting them but after waiting a few days and finding no intruders they returned.

William Dunlop worked two or three days for me a couple of weeks since. He has broken up some land which he expects to move on after he makes some more money to improve it. I believe he is doing very well. John Lovett was here lately. They were all well. I have not yet made a selection of any kind but expect to go on an expedition in company with some friends for that purpose shortly. I remain very affectionately

> thy nephew
> Thomas Chandler

———————◆———————

JANE HOWELL *to* RUTH EVANS
Philadelphia, October 1, 1835

My dear Sister

I have not received an answer to my last letter yet, but I hope there is one on its journey here and will arrive in a few days bringing agreeable intelligence with it. Benjamin Lundy called here last week to inform me that the Manuscript came safe to hand after being on the way nearly one month. He is at present engaged in getting a pamphlet relative to Mexico ready for publication. He will then go on immediately with the other.

Aunts returned from the country about three weeks since. Dear aunt Anna is about as she was when thee saw her last. Amelia Merrefields disease took a favourable turn and she has nearly recovered but looks very thin and pale. She has made a very great change in her dress since her illness. Her caps and bonnet is quite as plain as Grace Williams. I hope her heart is changed also.

Last week I received intelligence of the decease of Cousin Robert Coe. Poor Cousin Anna how much sympathy I feel for her in her overwhelming troubles and this last one I fear will be more than her delicate health can bear. Cousin Robert came to the City some time in the 8th month to meet friends with whom he was under dealings on account of securing Cousin Annas property from his creditors. He was then disowned, which was a very great tryal to him. He went up Second Street to go to his Son Roberts, not knowing what had happened, but just as he was entering the door he was observed by John Merrefield who called to him and told him that his son had left there and strangers had taken the house and store. And where has the fellow gone? exclaimed he in astonishment, and being informed that he was boarding in the Tavern nearby opposite, he went to John Merrefields and cried (Anna says) like a child. He went home and was taken unwell and continued to get worse until a day to two before he died when I believe he was siezed with Apoplexy which terminated his existance. I have not heard from the family since, but I understand Richard Coe was going down to persuade Cousin Anna to move back to the City. I do think it would be best for them to come, I believe there is none of them except Amelia that likes living there, and it is certainly unhealthy.

Sister Amelia was to see me a few days ago. She was well. I believe I mentioned in a former letter that Hannah Gamage had gone on to see her friends at Hudson. She called to see me yesterday, she started this morn on her journey to the West. She left her Mother and family well and Aunt Hathaway is about in her usuall health but her daughter Eliza has been quite ill. Her physician has been apprehensive that it would terminate in the black jaundice[17] and thinks her ill health has been brought on by grieving at the death of a little daughter of Meritts about eleven years old to whom she was very much attached. Phebe Beckmans husband died about two months since, which was a very great tryal to her. Sarah Jenkins remains in the same distressed situation.

Thomas Orr still remains at Jacksonville. He has got some of his boxes of goods but they have been opened and many things stolen from them. I expect he will return before a great while wether he receives the remainder or not. Aunt Betsey Vinsant (Attys Mother) died very suddenly about two weeks since. She was getting ready to go and see her daughter went into the garden and fell down and expired.

I am very much pleased with my little Dutch girl. We have not had her bound yet but I expect we shall soon. She never seems so happy as when she is at work. She begins to say many things in english and she understands almost any thing I say to her.

I do hope the people of Ohio and Michigan will settle their dispute without bloodshed. I thought the affair was to lie still until Congress met to decide on it but it seems they had been spitting and snarling at each other like two angry Dogs and what the result will be I am unable to foresee, but I hope it may not bring on a Civil War.

Charles Williams has purchased a very handsome large three story house in Fourth near Taminy Street. I suppose he will move his family into it.

I am glad Thomas has Isaac Comstock to help him. I think he must find him very useful. Ambitious boys of his age can nearly do a mans work. I am so much engaged now with preserving &c &c &c that I shall be under the necessity of sending thee a good deal of blank paper but I will try to fill the next sheet. By that time perhaps I shall have a little more blank time than I have at present. Abby Warnock William Brown and Lemuel desire their love to you and with mine included I remain thy

> Affectionate Sister
> Jane Howell
> We are all Well.

— • —

RUTH EVANS to JANE HOWELL,
Hazelbank, October 25, 1835

My Much loved Sister

Thou hast been so kind as to write me again, without waiting the arrival of mine, which I sent some two or three weeks ago, and I conclude it has reached thee before now. I am really glad my dear Aunts have returned to the City, and are well. Amelia Merrefield has great cause for thankfulness in being restored to health. I presume the desease that assailed her, was of a very dangerous nature, which should cause her to feel the highest degree of gratitude to her merciful Creator, for her restoration. And I trust she has in measure.

And I am induced to believe that during seasons of bodily suffering, there is oftentimes much solid happiness experienced when the mind becomes disincumbered, and weaned from the gewgaws, and fascinating allinements of this fleeting and fading world, and thereby becomes in a more fit situation to hold communion with Him who knoweth the inmost recess of the heart, and in His unlimited goodness and mercy will guide us in the way we should go. If we are faithful to his divine will, we shall then clearly discern, that this world, with all its glory is nothing, nothing I say when compared with joys unutterable beyond the grave, and which will endure forever. Remember me affectionately to her, and also to my beloved Aunts.

I very much regret I could not have more of there society, whilst I was in your City, but as it was otherwise, I must be content. I can scarcely express how very deeply I sympathize with Cousin Anna Coe, her trouble previous to her recent affliction seemed almost insupportable, and now the loss of her truly affectionate companion is distressing in the extreame. We who were not present at the scene of sorrow cannot realize the misery of that afflicted family. I would write to her, and offer the cup of consolation, but I conclude it would not in the least, mitigate her grief, nor sooth her almost broken heart.

I wrote to Sarah Chandler about two weeks ago. I hope we shall hear from them soon. I wish they would tell us they had concluded to remove to the "far distant West." We have now a Post Office established half a mile from Hazlebank. Darius Comstock Jackson is Post Master. It will be a great accomodation to us. Thou wilt please direct, Raisin Lenawee Co Michigan Tr.

One of my friends here, has a little girl about three weeks old, she has named Ruth Amy, after her deceased sister, and myself. It is a very pretty Child.

My health is very much improved. I am much better than I have been for some eight or ten months past. I believe Morrisons pills have been very benefitial to me, and would be good for thee also.

There has been gennerally great crops of wheat, corn, and oats, for which there will be considerable demand. Wheat sells for nine shillings pr bushell, and probably will be higher shortly.

On the third page of this sheet, I will transcribe a few lines I have unexpectedly written on *her* who was dearer to me than language can express, and who lives fresh indeed in my mind, and I hesitate not in saying, will continue to until my heart shall cease to beat. It is now almost twelve months, yes twelve long, long months since her departure, and yet it seems as but yesterday. Many there are, who feel deep affliction with the utmost poignancy for a season. It is otherwise with me. It strengthens with time. Let us therefore my dear whilst opportunity offers improve it. Let us prepare to meet *her* and all those loved ones gone before! in that blessed world, where all sorrow and sighing is at an end, and where we shall meet *her angel spirit* to part no more.

> With much love to Amelia,
> Lemuel, and thyself,
> I am sincerely thine
> Ruth Evans

[Thomas Evans to Lemuel Howell] I would thank my dear uncle after having received and deposited in bank the money for those legacies to obtain from R Pitfield the cashier a certificate stating that so much specifying the amount has been deposited on my account, or subject to my order, in the bank of the Northern Liberties. It would be better to place "of Adrian Michigan Ter." after my name. This certificate I should like forwarded on by mail. This is thought to be a perfectly safe way of making a remittance and some delay might take place in receiving the cash for a check of my own at a bank where I am not known. T. Chandler

TO THE MEMORY OF A BELOVED NIECE

Dearest—the precious form now lies,
    Beneath your tranquil mound,
There thou slumberest, undisturbed,
    By those who weep around.
And o'er thy tomb with watchful care
    I'll rear the choisest flowers
And when that sacred spot I view
    How solemn seems the hours.
The sunny vines with odour sweet,
    Will flourish round thy grave,
But dearest—how unconscious those,
    While they doth softly wave.
The myrtle too, and rose shall bloom
    And spread their fragrance round
But dearest—thou canst know it not,
    Nor who frequents the mound.
'Tis vain to grieve or wish thee here,
    Amidst life's changeful scene
There's many a thorny path to trace
    And many a cheerless gleam.
No grief of mine, can ne'er molest,
    Thy mould'ring form so dear,
I linger in this joyless work
    Which now, to me is drear.
'Tis vain I say, to sorrow thus,
    And there to sadness given,
It was the Great Jehovah's will,
    that Thou shouldst live in heaven.
Then hush'd be all my sorrows now
    Let peace pervade my mind,

With thy Redeemer now thou art,
  And I should feel resigned.
Then whilst I sojourn in this vale
  Of sorrow and of tears,
Be pleased O Lord, my soul protect,
  Be near through coming years.
And when my God shall seem it fit,
  In death my eyes to close,
Then dearest—by thy side I'll lie,
  And gently there repose.

WILLIAM *and* SARAH CHANDLER *to* RUTH EVANS
Little Britain, Pennsylvania, November 8, 1835

Dear Aunt Ruth

We gratefully acknowledge the favour of a letter from thee received a few days ago and are much concerned at the intelligence of thy ill health—but very glad to learn that it is becoming better. We have since heard from Aunt Jane that thee is still better and I hope that thee may soon find it reestablished. I still indulge the hope of seeing you before very long though you must not be disappointed if it should not be in the ensuing spring, as was my design when I saw you last. But as soon as I can feel at liberty to leave home and my business I will certainly see you. We are much obliged for thy again repeated wishes in our behalf on the subject of our removal to Michigan—and I trust that time will see us settled there—but obstacles still present themselves as yet—so that I some times wish you had not gone as we cannot follow. I should however be much better able to come to a conclusion myself, as will satisfy my friends by seeing for myself. Thee does not mention whether Thomas has made any purchases of land since your return. I should have been glad to know; and also the amt of his crops when he has ascertained. You have in all probability heard of the death of Cousin R Coe so I need only mention the circumstance—but as Sarah is waiting for the paper to write a little I can only again express my wishes for the restoration, of thy health, and my remembrance to brother Tom—and assure thee that I am as ever

thy affectionate nephew
W. G. Chandler

11TH Mº 8TH 1835

My Dear Aunt

I have very often intended writing since I had the pleasure of seeing thee, but have postponed from time to time thinking every day that we should receive a letter from you at Hazlebank. We are now happy to acknowledge the receipt of thine but I need only repeat what William has said that we are extreemly anxious for thy health which I hope is now restored to its natural state. Autumn and winter is to me by far the pleasanter half of the year and I hope the coming season may have a salutary effect with thee. We are sorry, very sorry that thy visit to us should be productive of so much distress to thyself.

I returned two weeks since from a visit to Grove. Sister Hannah was here and spent two weeks while she staid the election for little brittain was held here and she lent a hand to assist me. I then went home with her and spent a week. I had not seen little Thomas for nine weeks. He was up to pay a visit in the summer and was so well contented going to school that we let him stay and he can now spell in three letters. It seemed almost an age since I had seen the little fellow, he was telling us to-day how many uncles he had, and among other things said that uncle Thomas throwed him up on his knee. He is very fond of his little sister who by the bye is now a fine fat playful babe nearly 8 months old and just beginning to creep but as she is too fat and heavy to get forward she imitates the crab and moves backward but makes the desired place after a while. She weighed when in Grove 25 lb and is a charming good girl. My sincere desire is that she may inherit the virtues of that dear one whose name she bears. Oh how much I do regret never having seen her that I might still have a sketch of her features in our little E. M. but what is our loss compared with her eternal gain.

We feel very anxious to hear what you have done, or are going to do with the manuscript prepared for publication. There is a great stir among the abolitionists and Garrison stands conspicuous and it seems by the papers has not altogether escaped persecution, but it is to be hoped that this spirit of revenge may soon die away, and that the chastisement may fall where it is most deserving.

Brother Franklin has again started to seek his fortune. He left home while I was there in a great hurry, to join the engineers on the Chesapeak and Ohio Canal. This was a great trial to mother, but his mind has been wholy absorbed with it since he was out in Ohio, and I think it better that he should follow the bent of his inclination as farming to him is mere drudgery.

Mother is still afflicted with sore eyes and I think her health in general is goodeal impared. She spent a week with us in the summer and thought her eyes were benefited by the change of air. She procured the eye water thee recommended, but it did not have the desired effect.

I have now to inform thee of the decease of Susan Taylor, also of Jonathan Peirce, and his youngest son is in a deep consumption not likely to survive his father many months. They are indeed an afflicted family. Joseph Taylor too is much to be pittied as he is left entirely alone in the world.

I do hope my dear Aunt that thee may be careful of thy health untill it is perfectly restored. I am fearful that thy little Emily however useful she may be, is hardly sufficient, and I suppose it is difficult to procure help in your neighbourhood. What a consolation would it be if thee could only have the attention of *her* who was everything! I often think of this and have to wonder at the ways of providence, not doubting but that Thomas is everything that it is in the power of man to be, but his business necessarily calls him away, and it is not in his power to attend so closely as a female could. But as it is his will we must submit not doubting but that all was done in wisdom; I hope thee will not neglect us so long again for we shall feel very anxious untill we get an other from you.

Please excuse the hurry in which this is written as it is growing late, and believe me thy affectionate niece

Sarah Chandler

JANE HOWELL *to* THOMAS CHANDLER
Philadelphia, January 3, 1836

My dear Nephew

I have been waiting, anxiously waiting to hear again from thy dear Aunt Ruth. Thee said in thy last letter that she was mending slowly, I hope by this time she is much better.

I had a letter written several weeks ago to send to her, but Lemuel wished me to delay forwarding it on until he could learn when your legacy would be paid in. They have within a few days paid off several. Amoung the number was thy Aunt Ruth's. They deduct 2½ percent from every legacy which is twenty five dollars on a thousand. It is certainly a very unjust thing if the collateral law comes upon the legacies, when there is such a great overplus after every one is paid. Lemuel says he shall make inquiry wether such proceedings are lawful. The executors have made it quite a matter of favour that they have paid as many as they have. They say that they have done it on their own responsibility that they had no right to do it until after the 13th day of this month when the will and every thing relative to the Estate is to be laid before the Auditor appointed by the Orphans Court for proper adjustment.

For every legacy which they have paid they have required a refunding bond that in case any heavy debts should be brought in against the estate which should overbalance the overplus (which is thought to be about twenty thousand dollars) that the Executors should not be losers by it, every heir or legatee refunding a certain proportion according to what they have received. Charles Williams knowing the state of Cousin's affairs to be entirely unincombered by debt considered it a very unnecessary thing, but the lawyer and Cope wished to have it so, and it was done.

Lemuel gave his bond for thee and thy Aunt Ruth. I do not think I shall apply for mine until after the 13th of this month and then perhaps a bond will not be necessary, and the Executors wishes thine left until that time, and also the other. Lemuel says as he has seperate power of Attorney from thee and thy Aunt Ruth. It is necessary to have an order from thy Aunt Ruth wether he shall send it on seperately, or with thine. Thee mentioned in a letter some time ago how thine should be forwarded on which will be done in the way thee proposed.

The next letter thee, or my dear sister writes please write the order from her at the bottom of the sheet so that it can be taken off. Lemuel thinks it would be safer perhaps to send them seperately in case of the certificates being lost, say two or three days between the time of sending them.

Please write as soon as possible that they may be forwarded on to you. Have you any thing in prospect to purchase with the money for it is thought it will be a very critical time with the Country banks whilst the United States Bank is calling in her notes. It is said that many of them will be broken up. I thought if you did not wish to make use of the money now wether you would not like to have it put in the Northern Liberties Bank in thy name and entered in thy bank book which thee left with me and when you want to make use of it send an order to the Cashier for it. Indeed I would not trust it in any of the Michigan Banks. I should think it much safer in your own house provided it was in Philadelphia money. I thought I would merely suggest the thing to you, and leave it to your own discretion how to act.

We are well and with much love to my dear Sister and thyself I remain

Affectionately thy Aunt
Jane Howell

Lemuel desires his love to you.
I feel extremely anxious to hear from thy dear Aunt Ruth.

JANE HOWELL *to* RUTH EVANS
Philadelphia, January 14, 1836

My dear Sister

In a letter from my dear Nephew I received the painful intelligence of thy indisposition which thee must be well aware caused me the most intense anxiety. I kept it to myself. I told no one until I received another saying that thee was much better, then I vented my feelings with a flood of tears which I could no longer suppress. I hope thy health may continue to improve and that thee may feel no more of the pain in thy side; the blue pill is given now generally by the Physicians for affections of the liver, and then a gentle cathartic to carry it out of the system. If thee would frequently rub thy side with the oil of tar before going to bed Id think thee would find great benefit from it. It would strengthen the part. I do not suppose thee would experience much benefit in two or three rubbings but by persevering in it a little longer thee would feel amply repaid for all the trouble of using it. I have often taken from five to ten drops on Sugar or in water sweetened. It is very seldom now that I feel any pain in my side and shoulder. I have had but one severe attack since we have lived in Coates' Street. My remidy is when the attack comes on to rub with the oil where the pain is and bathe my feet in as warm water as I can bear, with mustard, ground pepper and salt about two table spoons full of each thrown into the water. Mustard plaisters to the side and soles of the feet is active in removing the pain. I wish thee to remember these things in a similar case, but I hope at the same time that thee may never have occasion to use them.

Last evening George Hank brought me a letter from my dear Thomas and a note from Ann Rowe saying that Samuel and John Lovett had called to see her, and that they had intended coming up and lodging at our house the night previous, but their friends in the City would not let them, and the next morning the roads were getting so bad on account of the melting of a deep snow that they had to hurry home without seeing me. It tryed me exceedingly when I heard it. I thought it was so unkind in them. Ann says John expects to return in the early part of next week. I am writing but I do not know wether I shall be able to send it or anything else on by him.

About seven weeks ago William, Sarah, and her sister Lydia, with their darling infant spent a week with us. They were all well and in good spirits. It was a very cold day when they came and continued so until they returned. They appeared to enjoy their visit very much. They were out every day either in shopping (as

Lydia had many things to buy for her friends) or looking at the handsome public and private buildings through the City. We went to the Navy Yard but had not a very good view of the ship, for our heads became giddy before we had ascended half way up. Every thing was new and pleasing to Lydia it being the first time that she had been in the City. We laughed heartily at her one day, a short time before they left the City. She had a few things to buy, and thought she could go alone, as all her purchases had been made in Second, between Coates' and Chesnut Streets. She started with full confidence of knowing the way, and went down until she came to Third Street which she mistook for Second and down Third Street she went until she came to Market Street. The Shope where she was going was in Second a few doors from Market She stood a little while to make up her mind wether to venture down the street, or retrace her steps back to Coates and then down to Second Street. She preferred the latter in preference to the risk of getting lost altho it was a severe cold day.

It was a delightful task to me to be Childs nurse in Sarahs absence. I think a more lovely babe could not be found. She is very fat, her face is almost round, her eyes black or very dark her nose is short and I think will be something like her father, and a more intelligent countenance I never saw in so young an infant. She could [ ] almost alone and laughed and crowed almost the whole day. She was not the least afraid of strangers, but would put out her little arms to go to any one that would take her. She cut her first tooth whilst she was here, and I think I may say I did not hear her cry more than two or three minutes at a time, and that was when she was either hungry or sleepy, during their stay with us. Dear little Tom fancies himself quite a man. He wants his father to get him a long tailed coat with mettle buttons and a pair of long square toed boots. He is very fond of his sister and often asks if she will not be a boy when she grows a little bigger.

Thomas Orr has returned safe and in good health to his native City he feels satisfied to settle down for a while and be satisfied with making a bare living for his family. He regrets very much that he did not go to Michigan instead of the place he went to, but he is now out of funds, having lost and spent about eight hundred dollars.

William will I expect be up in a few days to receive his money from the Executors. I am to write to him as soon as I hear from them which I expect will be in a day or two. He intends paying you a visit in the spring and wishes to go in company with us. I think we shall not go before the middle or latter end of the 5th month. Sarah's mother seems still opposed to her leaving her. She is fearful the Country is not healthy, her father I believe has nothing to say against it. Franklin Taylor left home I think for some part of the West—a little while before Sarah came to the City. She said her mother shed a great many tears at parting with him altho she expected him to return in a few months. When Sarah was here, she went to John Merrefields to see Aunts. Anna Coe was there. She said they were all very much pleased with her easy manners, and admired her very much. I was sorry they did not see the babe but it was too cold to take her out.

Margaret Hall has declined going to New Orleans. She had bespoke her passage, had some of her things on board and she was to have started in the vessel the next morning at seven oclock. She took leave of George and Charles and then went to bid John farewell late in the evening. He was so much agitated when he heard her errand that after having conducted her into the parlour he retired to his chamber to give vent to his feelings. Whilst he was there Sarah [Williams] and Hannah [Williams] came over. When he returned to the parlour he asked them if it was possible that their sister had to seek for a subsistance in New Orleans and a woman that was so well calculated to make a living here if means was given her to do it. He then proposed raising a sum sufficient to put her in business here. He said he would give two hundred dollars, he then went to his brothers and interceded for her and from each of them and Sarah he got two hundred more when made eight hundred dollars. Afterwards they went to Anna Merrefield and wished her to put the same sum to her name which they had on the paper, but she positively refused giving any thing. Margaret intends boarding this winter. Margaretta and little Helen are at George Williams. In the spring Marge yet intends taking a house and Store in Second Street not far from her brothers, and going into the dry good business. I hope she will be more prudent and successful than she has been heretofore.

John Willits bricklayer has purchased this Fall twelve hundred and fifty acres of land about fourteen miles from Michigan City. He expects to go there in the Spring to build and make improvements on it, and then move his family there. It is not far from where his daughter Rebecca lives.

Lemuel has got thy legacy from the Executors a week since and was going to forward it on as soon as possible, but he was informed that as he had a power of Attorney seperately from Thomas' that he must have a seperate order from thee, to forward it on to thee, as in case it should get lost, thee could come upon him for damages, for remitting it on without thy order. It was quite a disappointment to Lemuel, but as he is quite a novice in this kind of business, and they have advised him to transact it in the regular way, he thinks perhaps he had better do so. He says he is very sorry that it was not thought of whilst thee was here or in time afterwards to have sent it on before this, but as soon as he receives it, a certificate for the amount will be forwarded on immediately.

Amelia has got hers and put it in bank. She has taken a small house and intends taking one hundred dollars to stock a small shop something in the grocery line, and to buy some things to make her comfortable in housekeeping, and with the rest she wants to purchase some property that will advance in value. She expects to have two little girls to board with her who have lost their Mother, their father is an able man and I expect she will be well paid for their board and tuition.

Rachel Chandler dined and spent part of a day with me last week. She left Mary well, but Amor had met with an accident that had lamed him very much. He was taking in a load of corn fodder when he fell and the horse which had been lately shod trod on the calf of his leg which cut and bruised it very much, but with the use of a crutch and cane he made out to get along. She says Abram Sharpless is deceased. He died in the ninth month. He left a very large fortune to his two sons. The youngest one is going to be married to Bishop somebody's daughter. I have forgotten the name. She did not say that he left Hannah any thing. Roberts Vaux who had lately been appointed one of the associate judges of the Court died on fifth day evening last from a very short illness. I think it was the scarlet fever.

John Guest arrived here from the Western Country about five or six weeks since. When he went to his Sister Eliza's he inquired of the girl who went to the door if Ms Tunis was at home. He was invited into the parlour whilst she went to inform Eliza that a gentleman wished to see her. She came in they bowed and the usual complements passed between them. After a little time he asked her if she did not know her brother John and not until then did she recognize him. He was represented two years ago as being upwards of six feet high and a fine figure, but it is not so, he is not near as tall as John Merrefield and not as well proportioned. He went to see Aunts and deaf Polly caught him around his neck and kissed him. He seemed quite gratified with her mark of affection. He expects to spend the winter here.

George [Guest] has also arrived. He embarked in a vessel for the United States with a great number of passengers and when about half way home the Ship was wrecked near some coast, the passengers were I believe all saved, but the Ship and cargo all lost. Fortunately for George he had not much on board, as he had freighted another vessel with his goods. He was detained for some time at the place where they landed at very heavy expenses. I believe it is Aunt Rebeccas wish that he should not undertake another voyage as he has been unsuccessful but strive to get into some business in his native country as his high expectations of independance is cut down. Perhaps it will [ ] his aspiring mind more on a level with his situation in life.

Jonathan [Guest] since he turned over to [Andrew] Jackson has got an office under him which brings him eight hundred dollars yearly. What a convenient thing it is when we can make our principles subservient to our interests. It has placed Jonathan with many a good deal below par.

I heard from Aunts a few days since. They were well. Amelia Merrefield some few weeks ago had been spitting blood. Her Physician did not think it proceeded from her lungs as she has no cough with it. He advised her to clothe herself warm and walk out every day when the weather was suitable, that she must not take medicine unless there was real necessity for it nor confine herself too closely to her room when in the house. He said he thought the air and proper exercise would do more for her than anything else he could prescribe. She has followed his directions and her health seems very much improved.

Maria Woodside is still in Garret Newkirks Store in Jersey. I have not seen her since she went there but from what I have heard she likes it very well; I hope the country air will improve her health.

We have become dear lovers of batter cakes made with an equal quantity of Indian meal and wheat flour mixed up with warm water or milk with salt and yeast and made about as thin as buckwheat batter and when light baked and pretty well buttered I think they are excellent.[18] My girl which has been living with me from Chester County recommended them. They are as strengthening as palatable. Do try them. I feel quite uneasy at your using so much Saltaratus in your bread.[19] Some constitutions may withstand its baneful effects, whilst others fall a prey to it. Lemuels brother Johns been in the habit for two or three years past of using Saltaratus in rising their bread, and wether it is that, or from some other cause I cannot say but there is not one healthy one amoung them.

I have sent by this conveyance some genuine Madeira wine without any adulation.[20] I think it wilt be very strengthening to thee to take a little every day. The ginger nuts and candies are made of free materials. They were bought at Sleepers. I would have sent more oranges and lemons but I thought they might get touched with the frost and then they would be spoiled. The figs and raisons if they are not too heavy for thy stomach I should think would be good for thee.

SIXTH DAY EVENING.

I have been down at the different Taverns this afternoon to try to find an opportunity to send the things you wrote for,[21] and this letter to Samuel Lovetts, but I was unsuccessful. Lemuel has gone down this evening on the same errand. I hope he will succeed better than I did, if not I will try it again in the morning. If it should be so that we cannot send them by John, I will keep the memorandom and we can take them on when we go in the Spring, or if an earlier opportunity offers we will send them.

Thee will have to take the greatest care my dear Sister that thee does not take cold after taking so much Mercury.[22] I wish the Physician could have given thee other medicine that would have done as well. We had a letter a few weeks ago from Hanna Gamage. Since her return to the Western Country she had a very severe attack of billious fever, but when she wrote she had nearly recovered.

If I thought cousin Anna Coe had received no information from her son Robert I would write to her and tell her what my dear nephew mentioned in his letter respecting him, for bad as he is she must feel an anxiety for his welfare. Poor dear Cousin how she has to exert herself to keep from sinking under her heavy afflictions. She told me (to use her own expressions) "that she would work until there was hardly any breath left in her, to try to draw her mind off from her trouble." She said his disownment from friends preyed very much on his spirits and on First day evening he read to his family in the bible as was his practice, and he explained several passages in Scripture, after which he said he would take a walk in the piazza which he did but soon returned and told Cousin Anna that he thought a chill was coming on. She got him to bed and nursed him faithfully until the following sixth day when he expired. He had in the 8th Month an attack of chills and fever, but had recovered from them.

[Jane Howell]

We were yesterday invited to the funeral of Charles Williams' two sons, George the oldest one and Charles the youngest aged about six months.

I have opened my letter to say that I could get no way to send this by John Lovett. He has used me so bad that I hope you will not send any thing by him or for him to take any thing to us. He is so very disoblidging. I expect to write again in a few days as soon as Lemuel gets Thomas' money he will send it on to him.

We are well. In haste and with a good deal of love I bid thee adieu

from thy affectionate Sister
J Howell

Sometime during the month of January, Ruth Evans, for whom life had become a burden, died and was buried beside Elizabeth Chandler at Hazelbank. Thomas Chandler wrote to Jane Howell, informing her of Ruth's death, but the letter is no longer extant. He was now alone at Hazelbank, except for the help of Emily Johnston.

———◆◆◆———

Benjamin Lundy *to* Thomas Chandler
Philadelphia, February 16, 1836

Dear Friend:

With much surprise, and with the deepest sympathy with thee in thy bereavements, I have just learned of the death of thy aunt Ruth. I had understood that she was somewhat afflicted, but had not the most distant idea of her being in a dangerous condition. I have no doubt that the change will be consistent with her own eternal welfare, and perhaps we should not murmur. But with thee, in thy lonesome situation, we can truly sympathize. I hope, however, thee may be endowed with fortitude, sufficient to meet the emergency, and not suffer anything in the nature of despondency to overwhelm thee. These dispensations of Providence, if rightly understood, may turn to our advantage, by directing our minds to something more substantial than the happiness which this world affords.

I have just left thy Aunt Jane, and am sorry to say that she is somewhat indisposed, in consequence of a fall, yesterday, on the icy pavement. Her right arm was so much injured, (it is badly sprained,) that she cannot use the pen. She requested me to inform thee that, on this account, she has not been able to answer thy letter—which she had received a little while previous to the accident above mentioned. As might be expected, she was greatly affected at the sorrowful news which thy letter contained. With the exception of what I have mentioned, her health, as well [as] Lemuel's, is as good as usual.

I have, after preparing the biography of our dear lamented Elizabeth, endeavored to dispose of the copyright of her works, before proposed. But I have not been able to find a bookseller, willing to take it in that way. Many of our friends are very anxious for its publication, and we have concluded to issue a prospectus, to try it by subscription. I have no doubt that it will meet with a large patronage. I expect, very soon, to leave here for Mexico, but shall send out the prospectus before I go, and direct them to be returned to Lemuel Howell. One or more will be forwarded to thee, in a few days.

This is the best I can possibly do with the work. The Booksellers all say that the market is overstocked with poetry; and I may add, they are afraid to *touch* the "unpopular" subject of "slavery." We must have the aid of our *friends* in patronizing it. The biography makes upwards of 40 pages of manuscript, the size of this letter. I have done the best I could with it; but shall have to ask, in advance, great allowance for imperfections. Hannah T. Longstreth gave me a good deal of assistance in procuring materials for it. Thy aunt and Lucretia Mott have both seen it, and expressed their satisfaction with it. None else, except thy uncle Lemuel, have yet heard it read or been consulted.

I write in great haste, and must conclude, for the present.

> Most Sincerely and Respectfully,
> Thy Friend
> B Lundy

JANE HOWELL *to* THOMAS CHANDLER
Philadelphia, March 12, 1836

My dear Nephew

With my left hand[23] I take up my pen to inform thee that I received thy letter of the 11Th Ult. I quite approve of thy letting out they farm to the shares but my dear cannot thee board some where else for I think it is sufficiently proved that Hazlebank is a very unhealthy place, probably from laying so near the river. I hope thee will take a proper view of it before it is too late. And at any time if thee should be taken sick so as to have need of a phisician (which I fervently hope may not be the case) exact a promise from him that he will not give thee a particle of Mercury or use it in any way. Let him say what he will to urge it, let the past suffice.

Lemuel will in a few days send thee on 700 dollars with a deduction of 95 dollars for collateral tax the other 300 dollars will be forwarded on to William. He has not received any of his money from the Executors yet but I expect after the 18th the court will confirm their accounts and all will be settled with and then the remainder of thine will be sent on. As soon as thee receives the money write and let us know for Lemuel will feel anxious for its safe arrival. Something in the form of a receipt is necessary.

Every thing is now ready for the publication of the manuscript. B Lundy has sent about one hundred and fifty prospectus's to the Eastern states and elsewhere and it will be soon known wether there will be a sufficient number of subscribors to defray the expenses which will be about 200 dollars. The printing, the proposals 200 in number, cost two dollars and fifty cents, which is all the expense yet incured. If there should not be quite subscribers enough would thee wish the publication to go on but from present appearances I think there will be. Thee must let me know by the early part of next month. Benjamin would like to have in the collection if thee has them, "the Duelist's Soliloquy" and "the conscripts farewell" if thee can get hold of them without much troubles.[24] If so thee could copy them in a letter to me.

I must now stop writing as it pains my right arm in useing my left hand. I fell on the ice near 4 weeks since and dislocated my wrist. The Doctor thought I could not bear the pain of having it drawn in place as it was so very much swelled and he bandaged it to a shingle until wither a few days past. It is better but such hurts mend very slowly so thee sees my dear Nephew one trouble does not always come alone but it is our duty to strive to bear up under them. Thy aunt Amelia is with me. Lemuel desires his love to thee and with a great share from myself I remain more than ever

thy affectionate
Aunt J Howell

Since I wrote the foregoing Lemuel went to R[obert] Pittfield to know which would be the best way to send the money on and he told him it would be necessary as there was no will to have an instrument of writing drawn up and signed by the heirs at law making over Amelia and my lawful interest in it to William and thyself. Thee can have it done in a proper manner with thy signature to it and on the same sheet a draft on Lemuel for 675 dollars which Robert says will be thy receipt for the same. I am glad the legacy was disposed of in the way it was but I dislike the formal way of your receiving it. It makes it so troublesome. Please send word how the money shall be sent on. I think from what Robert says their banker has no dealings with the Michigan banks. I think he said they could send a draft to one of the New York banks and thee could get it from there. I have not been able to go and see Robert myself. Do try my dear and have the writings properly done for we are very anxious to have the money sent on without further delay. Make every thing safe and secure at home which are not wanted for use so that strangers shall not meddle with them. I cannot say any more now but fare well and take a great deal of care of thyself. My anxiety for thy health is greatly hightened now.

Did thee receive a Newspaper that I sent to thee?

There are no letters for the last nine months of 1836. During that time Lemuel Howell published Elizabeth's biography and writings, with financial assistance from Thomas Chandler. In August, Lemuel died, though the first mention of his death in an extant letter occurs in Jane Howell's October 22, 1837, letter to Thomas.

Five 1837 letters specifically pertain to the family's affairs.

———•◆•———

ISAAC TRESCOTT *to* THOMAS CHANDLER
Salem, Ohio, February 5, 1837

Dʳ Friend Thomas Chandler

    I have a wish to publish the life & writings of Elizabeth Margaret Chandler, if on examination into the circumstances it shall be thought advisable and I thought it proper to address thee in relation thereto, to know on what terms thy consent can be obtained &c.[25]

> Please answer at thy earliest
> convenience,
> Thine truly,
> Isaac Trescott

Thou canst know who I am by referring to David Steer.

———•◆•———

JANE HOWELL *to* THOMAS CHANDLER
Philadelphia, April 25, 1837

My dear Nephew

    I received thy letter to day and quite approve of sending the books on the way proposed as I should have felt reluctance at asking Samuel Lovett to have any care over them as he has wounded my feelings several times in that way I do not wish to put it in his power to do it again.

I have put up one hundred in a box with a little bundle of pamphlets &c &c which was sent from the AntiSlavery Society* more than a year ago to thy dear Sister. I have also sent a few ingraved likeness's, the same as in the books.[26]

Thee says thee hopes the use of my hand is restored. It is partially so. I can use my thumb and forefinger tolerably well, but my hand remains very stiff yet and at times there is considerable pain in the wrist, the ligaments still being swelled. But from the way it was hurt, it has mended as fast as I could have expected. My general health is about as it has been for several years past.

I am sorry Darius Comstock mends so slowly, but I am pleased to hear that he can go on crutches. If there is no dislocation of the joint or fractured bones, I should think he would get well.

Aunt Rebecca Guest, Eliza Tunis and family, Amelia and George Guest are all going to embark for Europe in the course of this summer. They do not expect to return before four or five years and perhaps longer. A warm climate has been recommended to Eliza on account of her health which not very good. Their residence they think will be in Italy or some part of the South of France. George Guest last fall went to Michigan and purchased Government land to the amount of seven thousand dollars at 125 per acre, since which he says he has been offered six dollars an acre for it. He is going on soon to sell about two thousand dollars worth, and that money he intends travelling on. The remainder of the land is to remain until he returns back to America.

I still hope thee may succeed in purchasing government land such as thee approves of, for it appears money cannot be more profitably invested than in land. I hope thee will not work too hard, or expose thyself too early in the morning, or late in the evening, especially later in the season, when the dews are heavy.

5TH M° 7TH

The box of books &c I sent about a week since, and a receipt for the same from the Transportation Company, which I directed to thee, and sent by mail. I hope the box may arrive safe and in good order. I have nearly fifty books in hand which I think I can soon dispose of, as thy brother, and Joseph Taylor, each want some, as soon as there is a conveyance for them.

A sad accident happened yesterday on the railroad near Coates Street. A boy about 16 years of age was run over by the cars and his head severed from his body.

May the protecting hand of Providence be ever over thee, my dear nephew, to guard thee from harm is the sincere desire and prayer of thy ever affectionate

---

*In England

Aunt
Jane Howell

I forgot to tell thee that I sent a book in thy name to thy aged cousin William Chandler. I thought it was a mark of respect due to him, and I have no doubt but he will value it very highly. I hope thee will approve of it.

JANE HOWELL *to* THOMAS CHANDLER
Hillside, New Jersey, August 22, 1837

My dear Nephew

I received thy letter dated 17th of last month.[27] I felt very anxious about thee as an interval of several months had elapsed without hearing from thee. I was pleased to hear that the books had arrived safely, and in good order. I have thirty or forty on hand yet which I expected thy Brother, and Joseph Taylor, would have sent for, but perhaps it has been for want of a suitable opportunity. I expect to spend a few weeks with William before long. He has written for me several times. I am now on a visit to Cousin Anna Coe. She expects to move her family to the City this Fall, if she can rent her place to satisfaction. She and her family are well. She wishes James to go on to his brother at Adrian. My dear aged Aunt Anna and Aunt Nancy spent a day with me a short time ago. They are well.

Thy Aunt Amelia has been building an addition to her house this summer. The first one was a new three story house 16 feet square, single pitched roof, the addition is the same size which makes a double house, large, and commodious, with a lot 70 feet deep, fronting on 13th and Olive Street. The whole expense of her house, stands at between 11 and 12 hundred dollars; and I expect she could now get two thousand dollars for it, if she wished to sell it. Barney Harris' father is very anxious to hear where he has moved to since he has sold his farm, Barney has not written to him, I think, since he left them. Emily Johnsons mother is not in good health. She wishes very much for a letter from her.

Anna Coe Jr. says there is a broken finger ring, which belonged to our precious E which she is very anxious to have that she can have it mended, and wear it. If thee can part with it, she says she will set the highest value on it for the sake of the one it belonged to. If there are any pieces of writing, which thee thinks was designed for her, she would be oblidged to thee to forward on to her, when there is a suitable opportunity. From some mention made in a letter to her, she thinks there must be a considerable number.

Benjamin Lundy says he expects soon to receive money from several subscribers who have not paid yet. I am very anxious to settle thy account, and as soon as I have it all collected in, which I hope will be soon, I will send thee on a statement, and then I should wish thee to let me know how I shall forward the money on to thee.

Aunt Rebecca a few weeks ago received the sad intelligence of the decease of her son John. I have not heard any particulars yet. They have declined going to Europe this Fall, on account of the Times, but next month they intend setting off for the South.

I am treated with the greatest kindness and attention by my friends here, but I expect to return home in the course of a day or two; as the unhealthy season is coming on. I say home, but no place seems like home to me now. Home, which I once so dearly prized, has lost all its charms. I feel so desolate, so lost to everything like enjoyment or happiness in this world, that I feel sometimes as if there not a tie left. I know that it is wrong to grieve as I do, but nature overpowers reason at times, and I have to yield to its sway. Twelve long sad months have passed, since my great, and last bereavement, and yet everything relative to it, is so fresh on my mind, that it seems but as many days. I can dwell no longer on the subject now, it is too painful.

But do not my dear Nephew believe, that I murmur at the divine dispensation, hard as it is, for any natural feelings to bear the seperation, yet I strive to bow in submission to the will of Him, who in his infinite wisdom, has been pleased to call my dear husband from "works to rewards."

I will send thee a copy of a few lines I wrote a short time since. Thee must cast a veil over their imperfections.

UNTO THEE, THOU GREAT JEHOVAH,

Unto Thee, my thoughts I'll raise
Altho, my heart is deeply wounded
I will strive to sing thy praise.

From Thy hand, how many blessings,
The unworthy I receive
Give me grace, to thank Thee for them,
And, thy promises believe.

Thou, hast in thy wisdom taken
From this world my husband dear

Be pleased, my broken heart to heal
And, be Thou to me, ever near.

And, when e'er Thou seeist fit
To lay thy chastening rod on me,
May murmuring ne'er escape my lips,
But, may my heart bow down to Thee.

For all that made life dear to me,
Is raised from Earth to Heaven on high,
And in Thy presence there he lives
With his Redeemer ever nigh.

Thou know'st our hearts were knit together
By affections strongest cord,
Be pleased to look with pity on me,
And some comfort me afford.

Misterious are thy ways, O Lord!
How wonderful, how right,
Thy omnicient eyes can all things see,
Nothing is hidden from thy sight.

The lofty man Thou bringeth low,
The low Thou high doth raise,
Thy judgements all will feel who swerve
From thy just and righteous ways.

My Husband, if I loved too well,
That it weaned my heart from Thee,
Be pleased to heal the stripes and wounds
Which Thy rod hath made on me.

For, when I think of gone by days,
And the happy years I've spent
When with the one I dearly loved
My heart is sorely rent.

My isolated state sometimes
Seems more than I can bear
For, hand in hand, we went thro life,
Our sorrows each did share.

And, when my troubles rise, indeed
Like billows on the sea,

May I in faith hold out my hand
And humbly trust in Thee.

Thy pitying eye my heart can see,
Thy ear my groans can hear,
Thy hand can soothe and give relief
When no one else is near.

My once sweet home, how altered now,
Now, all is sad and drear,
No greet or smile from him I loved
From him I held most dear.

But 'tis most selfish thus to grieve
As the prize of Heaven he's won,
He now can see Thee face to face
With thy dear and only Son.

In robes of purest white arrayed,
Before Thy Throne he sings,
Praises ever unto Thee,
Thou, Mighty King of kings.

Hartman Sweet, the Natural Bone Setter, was in the City a short time since. He travels from one state to another and stays but a few days at a time in each place. I had him to examine my arm. He said immediately that my elbow and shoulder were out of place, but he set them with much less pain than I expected, and they now look and feel as well as before they were hurt. The ligaments in the wrist and hand had become so rigid and contracted that he thought it would not be safe to do much with them then, but he left several bottles with me, one containing a black oil, and the others liquid of some kind, to rub my wrist and hand with, which he said would relax the leaders, and the first of the 10th month he would be in the City again and then he would be able to set the wrist bones properly. I am in my usual health, and with much love I must bid thee adieu,

from thy Aunt
Jane Howell

ISAAC TRESCOTT *to* THOMAS CHANDLER
Salem, Ohio, September 8, 1837

Dear Friend Thomas Chandler

We send thee one doz of E. M. Chandlers works, the edition is nearly out. We bought all there was for sale in Philadelphia at $4.00 per dozen. We retail them at 62 cents per copy.

In relation to future editions, the Friend having charge of the plates in Philadelphia requires an authentic order from the heirs of Lundy provided they should be wanted to publish an Edition [ ]. Perhaps we may try to make an arrangement for a small edition with him but if thee has any advice on the subject please write to us soon. I may write thee again when time permits in relation to future editions.

In haste Thine truly
I. Trescott

JANE HOWELL *to* THOMAS CHANDLER
Philadelphia, October 12, 1837

My dear Nephew

Thy letter with the ring enclosed was handed me a few days since by T. Atkinson! Thee mentioned that thy health was good, which thee may be well assured afforded me great satisfaction, and seeing a person who had so recently left thee, and to whom I could make so many enquiries, was a source of much pleasure to me, and also, at having such a good opportunity of sending on the ballance of thy account, as the greatest part of the money has been laying useless in the Bank for a long while. But my Lawyer within a few days has entered into a suit about the Coal Land, and as it will be necessary to keep sufficient money in my hands to defray the charges as they may occur, I thought if thee did not want to make immediate use of the money, I would settle thy account by giving thee a note at 4 months bearing interest from the date. If thee should want the money please let me know, as perhaps I shall not want it, but I thought I would like to hold it in reserve. I have settled B. Lundy's bill for books, pamphlet, papers &c amounting to 18.50. He has now collected in and paid me in full for all the books he sold, and I have now left on hand 35 copies which I have no doubt but that I can dispose of during the winter.

Soon after I fell on the ice and injured my arm, and whilst in the greatest distress with it and unable to attend to any business whatever, Benjamins funds got so low that he found himself under the necessity of leaving the City and going to his Father's, not having where with to pay his board. It happened at a time when his attention was the most required in the Publication of the work and in getting subscribers. I made him a present of fifteen dollars, which enabled him to stay in the City and attend to our business. In a few weeks something offered to his advantage which put him in funds again. I never intended mentioning it to thee, had I not met with so many losses, and if thee is not quite willing to allow it in the account, thee must let me know, and I will add it when I settle with thee for the books on hand.

I have not been to thy brothers yet. I thought if I went at the time I first fixed on, I should not be at home in time to see Doctor Sweet who expected to be here about the first of this month but he has not come yet, and I think I will not wait much longer for him, or I fear all the pleasant weather will be over. William calls his youngest son William Edward. Sarah Chandlers mother has been in the City about ten week with a daughter about 15 years of age, who has been under the Doctors hands with the Egyptian sore eyes.[28] They returned home a few days since.

George Guest has taken the Benefit, his name appeared amoung the Insolvents in the paper a few days ago, very much to the surprise of his friends, as he has been in no business for a long time past, to involve him in difficulties. So much for price and extravagance.

Do not my dear Nephew work too hard. I often fear thee will, when I hear how much goes through thy hands. Thy Industry, and good management, I hope will soon make thee independent. I often wish that thee could meet with a mind every how congenial with thy own, in a person every way worthy and suitable for thee as a companion for life. Marriage when properly entered into, contributes greatly to Earthly happiness and, in thy now lonely situation, stripped of those thy heart held most dear, makes a change very advisable.

The ring thee enclosed (altho I think not the one Anna alluded to, as that had clasped hands, and was broken) will no doubt be held, and treasured up by her, as an article of inestimable value. It shall be given to her as soon as a suitable opportunity offers.

Barney Harris' father will no doubt feel glad to hear of the place his Son has removed to. Maria Woodside wrote to him informing him of the nearest Post Office so that he could write to him. I am sorry he manages business so badly.

I think it is unsafe to use sealing wax where letters are sent to a distance. It is apt to break which was the case with the letter I received from thee. A few years since I received one by Post with the Seal broken, a wafer I think much more safe.

14TH—

After I had settled with Benjamin, he told me he had forgot to charge one dollar for Elijah Brownels subscription to the 14th volume of the Genius of Universal Emancipation, and as I have my accounts made out I will turn the dollar to our last settlement.

Benjamin has laboured so hard in the Anti Slavery cause devoting his time and attention so closely to it that his health became quite impaired. His friends were very apprehensive that his lungs were affected, and I believe he was of the same opinion. He put a suitable person in his place and left the City with an intention of staying several weeks. In a short time feeling himself better, he became uneasy at being absent from his post, and returned. He now begins to look more like himself, and I hope his health will soon be reestablished. I feel under great obligations to Benjamin for his unremitted attention to the publication and disposal of the books. He has not lost one dollar by any of the subscribers. Although, when I saw how many were circulated through almost every State, I felt fearful that not one half of the money would be collected, to be sure. Some of them were very tardy in making their remittances, but he would every now, and then, jog their memories, by writing to them.

Aunts are well. Thy Aunt Amelia desires her love to thee. My health is better than it was some time ago. I must now conclude, as my arm aches considerably from using my pen, and believe me my dear Nephew thy,

> ever affectionate Aunt
> Jane Howell

I would have sent the bond thee gave to the Executors by this conveyance, but I did not know but that it might be wanted at the close of my administration, but it can be of no value to any one as thy signature is canceled.

LIFE GOES ON, 1838–1842

Jane Howell and Thomas Chandler continued to correspond during the next five years, though they did so less frequently. The letters from Thomas to Jane are no longer extant, but hers have survived. Jane was lonely and sad and forced to resume storekeeping, but her spirits were finally buoyed when she learned that Thomas was getting married.

———•◆•———

JANE HOWELL *to* THOMAS CHANDLER
Philadelphia, May 21, 1838

My dear Nephew

I received thy letter on the 9th Inst. and sat down the same day to answer it but before I had got my sheet half filled I was informed by George Williams that dear Aunt Anna Guest was much indisposed. I put by my writing and went to see her. She was in bed but complained of very little pain except in her back, and from her hips to her feet she was unable to move. Doctor Noble bled her, but he was not able to decide at first wether it was Palsey or Rheumatism.[1] She seemed much pleased when I told her that I had received a letter from thee, and that thee desired thy love to her. She appeared to be getting better for several days but on sixth day last she was attacked with the Ericipalous[2] which continued to increase until it reached her brain which terminated her existance about quarter after one oclock on 3rd day morning 16th Inst. and was buried about half past 4 oclock in the afternoon on Sixth day following. She retained her mental faculties until her last illness, and then no great change was observable, except a little wandering at times. She was in her 88th year. Poor dear Aunt Nancy bears it better than we expected. At the commencement of Aunts illness she seemed to feel it so keenly that we felt afraid of the consequence. I intend writing thee a long letter soon in answer to the two last I have received, and now with much love I bid thee farewell from thy

Affectionate Aunt
Jane Howell

P.S. I called upon Benjamin the same day that I received thy letter to settle thy account with him. He thought there was nothing due to him. He was just on the point of leaving the city to visit some of his friends in N. Jersey and he said when he returned he would call and see me on that business. I have not seen him since, but I will attend to it.

JANE HOWELL *to* THOMAS CHANDLER
Philadelphia, May 29, 1838

My dear Nephew

According to promise I have taken up my pen to answer thy two last letters. Thee must excuse me for not answering the first sooner, for I intended it from the time I received it, but one trifling thing or other has prevented me, for I am apt to let very little things excuse me from my duty in answering letters even from those who hold the warmest place in my affections. A copy of an address before a meeting of the Anti Slavery Society came safe to hand for which I thank thee. I was much pleased with it and if it was delivered as well as it is written, I think he must have made many converts.

Our fine spacious building, the Pennsylvania Hall, was destroyed last week by a mob of about three thousand who fired the house, and has left nothing standing but its naked walls. The next night they set fire to the black Shelter for coloured orphans, a new handsome building lately erected in Thirteenth Street, but the fire companies beat them off, and extinguished the flames, before a great deal of damage was done. On Seventh day night the mob proceeded down sixth street to the African church, which was I understood filled with coloured people at worship but when they arrived there, they were soon dispersed by the interference of the Sheriff, Mayor, Police, Marines, Citizens &c. It is to be regreted that they did not present themselves and use the authority that the law allowed them, in dispersing the mob, at the Pennsylvania Hall. The city seems now pretty quiet again which I hope may be of long continuance.[3]

Benjamin Lundy is going to Illinois, about two hundred miles from thee. Several of his nearest connections have gone there to settle amoungst which are his two eldest daughters (both married). He intends farming and will continue publishing the Genius of Universal Emancipation. He did expect to leave here in the early part of next month but I hardly think it probable that he will get off as soon as he expected. His health has not been good for some time past and within a few weeks he has had something like Paralytick in his face which affected one side of it very much but when I saw him last he was better. He has applied himself a great deal too closely to business. He has been visiting many of his friends in the country, and he promised to call on me as soon as he returned, but I have not seen him yet.

I am sorry that thee should have hesitated one moment at getting me to settle thy bills here. It is perfectly convenient, and it will at any time be a pleasure to me to do it.

I am glad thee has got through with thy fencing. It was a mamoth job and must have been attended with a great deal of hard labour. I am glad thy health keeps so good. Do take a great deal of care of thyself.

When thee sees Lydia Gibbons give my love to her. I have often felt sorry that I had not more of her company when she was in the City but I was in too much trouble to enjoy the company of any one. I hope she will excuse my inattention to her. Should she ever be plunged into Affliction like mine she could overlook all such apparent neglect. I wish thee had mentioned particularly how her health was.

The latter end of the 3rd month Robert and James Coe arrived here from Michigan. James said they walked nearly all the way for want of money to pay their passage in the stage or car. We did not see Robert but James looked very shabby and weatherbeaten. He said they could find nothing to do. The school Robert was employed in was closed and they thought they could do nothing better than to return home to their Mother. I believe Robert has not disposed of his land in Michigan. I think he has about 8 acres cleared.

I forgot to tell thee that Benjamin has had reprinted at different times about 1500 copies (on his own account) of the works of our dear Elizabeth. He sells them to B. Jones at about first cost, and the proffits goes to aid the abolition cause. I think he has 500 more in the Press. He intends after he removes to the West to print a second Edition. He has been striving to collect together all that he can get, so as to make a considerable addition to the work. He says they are now becoming very popular, a great many are sent to New York, and the Eastern States. The addition he intends having Stereotyped[4] at Cincinnati, as he can have them done there, as low as he can here. The price of the book will be advanced in price, accordingly to the additional cost. He says if thee should want one or five hundred copies of them, thee shall have them at what they cost him. He would be glad if thee has any pieces in thy possession that thee would like published to forward them on to him after he gets settled in his new home. He will then send his address to thee. He has often requested me when I wrote to thee, to give his love to thee, but I have always forgotten it.

Amelia Guest was married the 7th day of March to Meadows T. Nicholson of New York, an Irishman by birth and an adopted son of James Clibborns an old friend of Uncle John Guests. He belonged to the Orthodox friends, but they were married in the Episcopal church.

Mary Guest was married about three weeks since to a Doctor Smith. He was also a friend. They are going to reside about 300 miles from the City. I do not know in which direction. They are waiting Eliza Tunis' return before they go. She is expected daily.

Poor Jonathan G{uest}. has had the Sheriff on him for two thousand dollars which he owed the Union State Lottery for tickets bought some years ago. His furniture and all was sold, his wife and daughter is now boarding in Philad[a] at his wifes sisters. He has an office in Washington. Little did Cousin Anna think that a portion of her money was to go to pay lottery tickets with. She had better have left it to the widow and her orphans.

I am sorry thy brother does not write more frequently to thee but thee knows how he dislikes writing and thee must excuse him. He was here the latter end of last winter and expressed a great wish to go to Michigan, but he could not see how he could leave home to go. He is full of business. He carries on the cabinet making business pretty smartly, having journeymen and an apprentice. He attends to the farming himself. Whilst he was in the City I had very little of his company as his time was taken up in purchasing mahogany and other articles necessary in carrying on his trade. He thought he should be down again this spring.

I suppose before this thee has received my letter informing thee of the decease of our dear aged Aunt Anna Guest. Poor Aunt Nancy feels it keenly. She still bears it better than was expected. There have been four deaths in John Merrefields family within six months, averaging one every six weeks. There was first his sister Elizabeth, then Sarah Anna, next his little daughter, called after Aunt Anna, and aged about 18 months old, and lastly our dear Aunt. So that poor John has had a great deal of care anxiety and trouble.

The ring which thee forwarded on some time ago was the right one. At the time I wrote to thee about it Anna expressed a great wish to have it. She said it was broken, but she would have it mended and clasped hands put on it. I misunderstood her and thought she said it had clasped hands. She knew the ring to be the same one she wished for, but that it was mended.

6TH MO 8TH

I left my letter open until I could see Benjamin so that I could pay him and get his receipt. His account and thine did not quite agree but he would not take any more than thee mentioned in thy letter. He expected to have left here for the West the first of this month but he thinks now that he will hardly be able to go before the latter end of it. He has entered damages for the loss he has sustained at the burning of the Hall at two thousand dollars. He says he would not have taken that sum for what he lost, but he does not expect that the Grand Jury will allow him more than 5 or 6 hundred dollars. He had a few days previously deposited almost every thing he had at the Hall. He desired to be remembered to thee, and says he shall write to thee soon.

I am well, but thy Aunt Amelia is quite indisposed with a bad cold. I must now close with a great deal of love to thee I remain

thy affectionate Aunt
Jane Howell

Do take a great deal of care of thy health, and take thy work fair and easy.

Thee wished to know my dear Nephew wether I will have enough to live comfortably on. That is more than I can tell thee, until the Real Estate is disposed of which I hope will be before long, but as the Estate will be divided I think I shall not have sufficient to keep house comfortably on without taking in a couple of Boarders or some other trifling business—but I will inform thee more on the subject after a little while.[5]

———•◆•———

JANE HOWELL *to* THOMAS CHANDLER
Philadelphia, July 22, 1838

My dear Nephew

I received thy letter with the delightful intelligence that thee intended paying us a visit this Fall. I cannot express the pleasure I feel at the thoughts of thy coming although it is generally accompanied with a train of very painful reflections and recollections of the events which has transpired since I saw thee last. I wrote immediately on the receipt of thy letter to inform thy Brother of thy intended visit, that he might participate with me in the pleasure. I hope nothing may intervene to prevent thy coming.

I saw Benjamin Lundy a few days since. I suppose by this time he is on his way to the West. He wished me to inform thee that the Stereotype plates are all safe. He says he intends writing to thee soon after he reaches Illinois. He desired to be remembered to thee.

John Merrefields youngest child about 4 years of age has been very ill with symtoms of consumption. Doctor Noble said that unless they took him into the country he would not live through the summer. They have done so, and he appears better. I have been filling Anna's place as housekeeper during her absence, as she thought she could not leave home unless I did. I suppose in a few weeks she will be able to return.

Aunt Rebecca and her daughter Eliza is going to set sail from New York for Europe the first of next month. Eliza's health is no better. I hardly think she will ever return. I am surprised at her going, but she feels in hopes that the climate will suit her disease better than this, as the winters here affect her very much. George will not accompany them on account of some commercial difficulties. I should like to fill my sheet but as my ink is nearly exhausted I must think of concluding with much love from thy Aunt Amelia, and myself, I remain

thy affectionate Aunt
Jane Howell

⸻ ◆ ⸻

Thomas visited Philadelphia during the fall of 1838, and sometime in December, Jane received a letter (no longer extant), announcing his safe return to Michigan. Emily Johnston accompanied Thomas on his trip east and remained there after he departed.

⸻ ◆ ⸻

JANE HOWELL *to* THOMAS CHANDLER
Philadelphia, May 7, 1839

What is the reason my dear Nephew that thee has written but one—one single letter to me for nearly six months? Is it because thee received no answer to the one thee wrote to me? If so, I am sorry that I did not write immediately, for it would have saved me a great deal of anxiety on thy account, but I still thought my dear Nephew could not stand upon such ceremony with an Aunt who so dearly loves him, and who feels all the interest and solicitude for his health, and well doing, that a Mother could possibly feel. I do not wish thee to take up much time in writing long letters to me, for I know thee has a great deal to attend to, and can have but little leisure, but out of that little, spare a few minutes to inform me of thy health, if nothing more.

I was very much pleased when I received thy letter informing me of thy safe arrival home. The week after thee left here, I saw an account in the papers of great destruction of vessels on the Lakes, occasioned by the storm the week previous, which was the week thee left here. Thee may suppose I felt very much alarmed, but my fears subsided very much in reading in another paper, to find, that the Storm occured the day thee left here. How thankful I felt that thee did not go a few days sooner.

It makes me feel gloomy when I look forward and think what a length of time it will probably be before we shall see thee here again. Thy last visit was very unlooked for, until thee informed us thee was coming, and it has almost spoiled me, for now I feel as if I could hardly wait three years for another visit.

Soon after I received thy letter I forwarded it on to thy brother, knowing it would be more satisfactory than any thing I could write from it. I have not had a line from them until a few days ago. I received a long letter from Sarah, with two lines from William. Sarah says, William has had a great press of business in the shop this spring, and it still continues; he was also very busy through the winter. She says they have not received one line from thee since thy return. Little Elizabeth is at her Grandfathers, going to School to her Aunt Lydia {Taylor}. They were all well.

I have not gone to Housekeeping yet. I could not get a house that suited, until the winter set in, and then it seemed too cold to undertake it, so I concluded to leave it until Spring. I have been engaged this winter in assisting Amelia with her school. She has had a bad cough, and hardly able to attend to her scholars. The chief of my time has been devoted to the school, except when attending to family concerns, which left me very little time, or thy letter would not have remained so long unanswered.

The lots on Green and Coates Streets, were sold by order of the Orphans Court. I bought them, but intend selling them at private Sale after a little while. The Coal land is to be sold in the sixth month.

John Merrefield has taken a very pretty place for the Country for the Summer about two miles from town on the Frankford Road, abounding with almost every kind of fruit. There is a great abundance of Strawberries, and Rasberries. The tenant who was there last year, says he gathered as many as one hundred quarts in a day. He attended market with them. They are very desirious for me to take Anna's place in town. I have made every excuse, but it seems they will not take any denial, and as I am not suited in a house believe I shall accede to their wishes, as I shall not be so much confined, and shall have less care through the summer than if I was at housekeeping.

Aunt Rebecca expects to return to this Country next month. Eliza's health is so much better that she will leave her with her children in Italy, where I suppose they will continue for several years, as the climate suits her health.

Robert Coe intends going in a short time to Michigan. I believe to sell his land, and then he purposes coming to the City, and going into some kind of business here. If he does, I hope he may succeed better than he has done heretofore. James is some where in his Mothers neighbourhood keeping School.

I beleave I have nothing to communicate to thee that would be any how interresting, for there has nothing transpired since thee left us in our circle of friends, and relatives, of any importance. I forgot to mention to thee before of the Death of dear Mother Howell. I accidentally heard it some time after she was buried. It hurt my feelings very much, for I felt great affection for her. She had frequently within three years past, sent word for me to come and see her, that I felt as near and dear to her as any daughter she had, and that she wished to see me once more—but the way things were, it was unpleasant to go.

When thee writes do tell me how thee has succeeded with thy chesnuts, and how thy crops are likely to turn out.

I have spent an unpleasant winter, with close confinement, and the noise of the children, but Amelia is now able to attend to her school herself, and the change which I am about to make, will be much more pleasant. We are nearly in our usual health, and I believe I must conclude and with much love to thee my dear Nephew, believe me as ever

> thy very Affectionate Aunt
> Jane Howell

⬥

JANE HOWELL *to* THOMAS CHANDLER
Philadelphia, May 31, 1840

My dear Nephew

I do not wish to charge thee with neglect but merely to give thee a little hint that it is about seven months since I received thy last letter, which was answered a very short time after I received it, since which my time has been very much occupied in assisting Amelia in her school through the winter, and at storekeeping this Spring. On the 10th day of the 3rd month I rented the House No 489 North 2nd Street 3rd house from Poplar Lane (east side) at 250 dollars a year. The house is one of those built by Seltzer.

I did not wish to buy goods on my own account, not knowing how long I might continue in the business, and being aware of the loss attending the selling off a stock, so my kind friend and Cousin, John A. Williams, proposed and agreed to furnish me with as many goods as I should want at precisely what they cost him; and to take them back without any deduction in price whenever I might think proper to discontinue business. I pay him my sales every seventh day, which always amounts to between one and two hundred dollars weekly, and were the times better it would be a great deal more. I feel more happy now that I did when I had nothing to do (but I have misapplied that word, I should have said contented) as it draws my mind from my bereavements which no time can efface. I have Emily with me in the Store and with her assistance and Henrietta (my little Dutch girl) I make out very well, not having to go out for goods, as Cousin John supplies me from lists which I sent to him.

Eliza Williams took it into her wise head to back out from her husband last Fall and go into business by herself. She accordingly without his knowledge or consent took Wood's Store in 2nd near Market Street for which she pays 1500 dollars a year. She purchased a house in Arch Street and went to housekeeping, taking with her all the best of their furniture; since which not finding housekeeping seperate from the store a convenient concern, she has thought fit to return back to her husbands residence without any invitation from him; and I think it probable it will not be long before their business will be conducted jointly as heretofore.

Thy Aunt Amelia has given up her School and rented her house with the exception of two rooms which she has reserved for her own accommodation. She gets 88 dollars a year for the part she lets out, and I think she will have permanent tenants.

John Merrefield has been so unfortunate as to lose his son George. He was taken ill a short time before Christmas, and died after an illness of about two weeks. John and Anna both feel their loss most keenly. They had a cast taken of him in plaster after his decease, and a portrait painted from that, which all who see it say that it bears very little resemblance to him. It was taken by Street, for which they paid one hundred and seventy dollars.

Robert Coe's wife [Eliza Broom Coe], or her friends for her, have sued for a divorce. It is to come before the Court next month and there is hardly a doubt but it will he granted. Robert is keeping school about five miles from his Mothers residence. James has got into some employment which yields him about three hundred dollars a year including his board. He has joined the Baptist meeting, and Amelia the Presbyterian Church.

Mary (Guest) Smith is now on a visit to her Philadelphia friends. She makes her home at John Merrefields. She is subject to a singular disease, resembling Animal Magnetism.[6] After much excitement of mind, or fatigue of body, she will appear to faint, or swoon away, stretch herself out—her countenance wearing a death like appearance, and in this way she continues for half an hour or longer, answer any questions that may be put to her by those standing by. No restoratives are used during the Paroxysms and when she recovers from them, she is immediately in her usual health and spirits. She had one of her spells at George Williams, and another a few evenings ago at John Merrefields.

I received a letter from Sarah Chandler about ten days ago. They were all well. William's business at the Cabinet making is very brisk and that with farming keeps him constantly employed.

George Smith first teller in the Pennsylvania Bank, left that Institution very abruptly about three weeks since, and not returning, great fears and suspicious were felt, and search immediately made for him by his friends who traced him to Harrisburg and found him a few days ago in a state of insanity. I believe they have brought him to the city, and probably they will put him into Friends Asylum where his brother Joseph is, and has been for more than twenty years.

John Merrefield and George Williams have made a purchase at Sheriffs sale of a lot of ground fronting on Sixth, Green and Marshall Street for which they paid sixteen thousand five hundred dollars. It has a front of more than one hundred feet on Sixth and Marshall Streets and I believe about one hundred and fifty feet on Green Street. There is a handsome house on Sixth Street which they have let for four hundred dollars. They intend selling the ground off in building lots, for which they expect to get seven dollars a foot on Sixth Street and six on Marshall Street. They think they will realize a profit of about ten thousand dollars, but I rather think they will have to wait until the times get better, for very few attempt to build now.

I have had several offers for my lots on Green Street, but they were not willing to give me more than three dollars and half for them and I do not wish to part with them for less than four. That large tract of land near Pottsville of two thousand six hundred acres belonging to James Elliott on which the Estate held a Mortgage, was advertised and sold, and as it would not bring a thousand dollars on account of the scarcity of money there it was bought in for me, the mortgage and interest amounting to about that sum. So I hope when the times get better I shall be able to part with it to advantage. The former Owner Elliott has been dead for several years. My lawyer had to take out letters of Administration before he could sell the land.

A few of the chesnuts which I planted last Fall have sprouted. I wish when they get a little larger that a good opportunity would offer to forward them on to thee.

Emily thought a few days ago that she saw a man pass by that looked very much like one of the storekeepers at Adrian, I forget his name, but I hardly think it was or thee would have requested him to call. Emily seems very happy with me and is very much pleased with the business. Before I went into storekeeping I got Mary Wilson to take her to learn her trade (the millenary) which she seemed to prefer before any other, but in about two weeks she left there. I do not exactly know the cause for I have not seen Mary since and Emily says Mary did not tell her why she parted with her, more than that she could not board her any longer. Emily suits me very well in some respects, and I hope I shall be able to keep her for I feel much interrested for her, but I am afraid her family will be a disadvantage to her and make her too forward. She is well and desires to be remembered to thee.

When my dear Nephew shall I have the pleasure of seeing thee again in Philadelphia? It will now soon be two years since thee was here and that seems a long time. Turn thy attention to it next Fall, or when it suits thy business best— and let me know when thee writes to me that I may anticipate the pleasure it will afford me.

When thee writes tell me all about thyself, thy interests, and concerns and that is all I want to hear. Thee has no excuse left now for not writing once in seven months, and leaving me to answer my own letters. Thee has now always a subject to write upon, no matter if it does not quarter fill thy sheet. Remember thee has an Aunt that loves thee, and does not wish to be forgotten by thee. I must now conclude and with the sincerest wishes for thy health and welfare I remain as ever

thy affectionate Aunt
Jane Howell

I called at Douglass's in Arch Street a few days ago to see if their son had painted, amoung other Abolitionists, the Portrait of our dear Elizabeth. He had, but I thought it bore very little resemblance to her. It was painted from a minature which Benjamin Lundy had taken by Street and which I thought was a very striking likeness of her, both in features and expression of countenance. I have often, very often wished that I was the owner of it, by paying what it cost, but I do not suppose the family would be willing to part with it.

JANE HOWELL *to* THOMAS CHANDLER
Philadelphia, February 21, 1840 {1841}

I have been setting thee a bad example my dear Nephew by letting thy letter which I received last summer lay so long unanswered. I thought then that as I had so recently written, a letter after a little while would be more acceptable to thee, but the little while has turned out a great while, which I hope thee will excuse as I have very little time for writing except on First day, and then, I often meet with interruptions.

My business in the Store[7] is quite as good as I could expect in such a deranged State of the Currency, which has thrown a great many of the working class of people out of employment, and has made money very scarce amoung them; and as my customers are chiefly made up of that class, I cannot expect my sales to be a great deal until there is a change. A short time ago, every one was looking forward to the resumption of Specie payments with the greatest pleasure for there has been such an inundation of small notes, ragged, and defaced the majority of them, that their amounts were scarcely legible and it really seemed delightful to have their places filled by Specie; but the vast run upon the Banks after they resumed, especially by the Antibankites, compelled them to stop, which caused such a great excitement in the City for a few days, that many were fearful of the result; but I hope the Legislature will soon place the Banks in such a situation that they can go on again in Safety.[8]

I have not received a letter from thy brother or Sarah for several months—but Hannah Taylor was to see me in the 12th month. She left Sarah at her father's on a visit. William and his family were quite well. She said thy Brother thought of letting out his farm and taking a House in Lancaster that has long been established as a Tavern and stopping place for Country Merchants. They can also have a large number of permanent boarders. The proprietor of the establishment is very desirious that William shall take it, as he thinks he can do so well there. I felt sorry when I heard it, but perhaps he has declined it or I think he or Sarah would have written to me about it, as they always have done when they have undertaken anything of the kind, for they know how much I feel interrested for them. William has given up his trade for the purpose of collecting in his money which Sarah said was all in good hands. Sarah appeared in good spirits about moving, and if they do, I hope it will turn out well.

Anna Coe has spent a great part of the winter in the City. It is said she is to be married in the spring to Providence Ludlam from Cumberland New Jersey. He has been very attentive to her for several years, quite a wealthy young man, and of steady habits, but he is about ten years younger than herself. He came up to the City with his Carriage and fine pair of horses, and took her home.

Emily is still with me. She can sell goods very well and takes great interest in the business. I think in time she will make a first rate hand, if she will strive to have more patience. She is by no means an amiable disposition. I have thought many times I should have to part with her, and had I not studied her welfare I certainly should, but she has done much better for some time past. When thee writes say nothing about her, but what thee would be willing for her to see, or hear, as she is desirious to know all that thy letters contain.

Thy Aunt Amelia's health is much better since she has given up her school. It kept her temper constantly irritated, which I think was in a great measure the cause of her ill health. The rent of her house supports her comfortably. She has spent several weeks with me at different times this winter. She is now on a visit to a friend in the Country, who has sent several times for her to spend a few weeks with her. It would gratify her very much if there is any thing in the clothing way, which had belonged to her Mother, in thy possession, and thee has no particular wish to keep them, if thee would forward them on to her when a suitable opportunity offers, she would be very much oblidged to thee, and would pay any expense attending the conveyance.

In thy letter thee mentioned thy wheat having been much injured by the Hessian fly.[9] I hope it turned out better than thee had anticipated. I hope thee has suffered no loss on the Failure of the Banks in Michigan, or the Railroad stock. Stocks have fallen prodigiously in the City. Jonathan Knight my Landlord has lost fifteen thousand dollars on the United States Bank Stock. It is now down to about 25 dollars.

I should not suppose that Benjamin Lundy's relatives would object to parting with the portrait by sending them ten dollars, which was the price paid for it. They might value it highly, but they could not appreciate it as we should do. Benjamin, and myself thought it an excellent likeness, after many alterations, and he said that fifty dollars would be no inducement to him to part with it. If thee should send for it, be particular to send for the one taken by Street as I believe Douglass made an attempt to paint one from it much larger but wether Benjamin took it with him or not, I cannot tell.

George Williams and Joseph Fox have purchased a large lot of ground in Front Street above Poplar Lane, for which they gave twenty thousand dollars. They are laying it off in building lots, and expect to make a handsome proffit from their purchase.

How has the weather been with you this winter? With us, it has been very variable. We have not had much snow nor many days severely cold, but a great deal of cloudy, rainy disagreeable weather, exactly calculated to try the most robust constitution, but with all I believe the City has been as healthy as usual. The freshet we had this winter, done a great deal of damage on the Delaware and Schuylkill rivers. Thy papers I expect gave an account of the destruction of property occasioned by it. I suppose New York suffered as much as any other State!

John Merrefield has intended going to Washington to be present at the Inauguration of our new President, but he is such a stay at home, that it is a chance if he goes. It is said that strangers from almost every part of the Union are going to that place to witness the ceremonies of the 4th of month.[10]

22ND

I had not time to finish my letter last evening, and this morning I had the unexpected pleasure of receiving one from thee, by Joseph Gibbons, and hearing that thee was well.

Thee says thee has received but one letter from me in the course of a year. I think then we keep even pace with each other in writing, as I have received but one from thee in that time.

I am glad to hear that times are improving in Michigan. I wish I could say so of Philadelphia. As soon as they take a turn for the better, I will let thee know.

Emily will write to thee by Joseph, and if I have time I will also. If not, please excuse me.

I went this afternoon to the AntiSlavery Office. They informed me that there had not been any Executors or Administrators to the Estate of Benjamin Lundy,[11] but they could give me no information who Benjamins daughters married. I then went to Sidney Ann Lewis, but she was from home. I lastly went to Douglass in Arch Street. Met with much better success. They had forgotten their names but I was invited up stairs to look at the paintings. Their Son Albert has returned from Europe, where he went to improve himself in the art of painting. His Mother says he has made great proficiency in the time he was there. He brought a great many home with him, which he painted in Europe amount which were Benjamin West, Queen Victoria and Prince Albert. The Queen is by no means handsome, and to judge from her countenance, I should think she was a woman of very little intellect. Prince Albert is a handsome man if he would leave off his mustaches.

I will have the books in readiness for Joseph [Gibbons] when he calls. He did not say any thing about them whilst he was here, which was but a short time. I had several customers in the Store which prevented me from saying a great deal to him.

When thee writes tell me which of the Philad[a] papers thee takes. I could often send thee on one if I knew which to send. In the course of a day or two I intend writing to thy brother. I feal very anxious to hear from him. I was in hopes I should have seen him here this winter, but I suppose he has not had time, as he is collecting on his outstanding debts.

When my dear Nephew will thee pay us a visit? Thee must tell me a good while before hand that I may have the pleasure of anticipating it.

My health has been unusually good this winter. My mind, during business hours, is diverted in a great measure from my sad bereavements. I must now conclude, and with the most sincere love to thee, my dear Nephew, I remain as ever

> thy Affectionate Aunt
> Jane Howell

EMILY JOHNSTON *to* THOMAS CHANDLER
Philadelphia, February 22, 1841

Dear Thomas

I am now going to acceed to thy request to write to thee and not wait for answers from thee. I was heartly pleased to hear from thee for I had just settled myself into a dumb forgetfullness with regard to hearing from thee and just made up my mind to wait thy honour feelings. Thee may judge of my surprise when I saw Joseph [Gibbons] coming in not being aware of his intentions to pay our city a visit. I could almost have loved him just for bringing the letter. I realy think there is no one who prises a letter more than I do and yet who is there that has more cause than I for it is such a rare thing for me, and coming from such a sourse that makes them doubly valuable.

I have received a letter from C. Styles a short time ago. She told me so much news. I do think it is to bad that thee will not be in the fashon. Every one is getting married around thee and why not step forwards and gain companion and house-keepers. But I tell thee what, I do pity the girls that have been getting married there. I think if they had seen a few more years of pleasure they would not have so many of pain [and] trouble. I think it is a great peice of folly for a young girl and also a man to undertake to get married before they get anything. Is it not a pity that I came away. Perhaps had I have staid that might have chosen one for myself. However I do not feel very sorry. Perhaps should I return there will be some good grains left in waiting.

Oh how I would love to go back for a short time and just go into each house and say how do you do and Farewell like I did the day before I came away.

Caroline mentioned Jane Webb and Jane Steer's both being married but did not mention who to and even if she had I do not know that I would have remembered them for I am sure when I read her letter there were so many with whom I was so well acquainted that I had to stop and think where to place them.

I have enjoyed myself very much since I have been here for if I can make myself contented it is enough. Yet sometime when I think of my poor Brother I feel as if could grasp at every straw if it would advance any towards getting a home for him. He is now in the Hospital and I believe every attention is paid him. Sarah goes out to see him whenever she can get an opportunity and I go when at any time I can be spared. We always make it a point to take him any little thing that we think will be relished by him but I have such a distance to go and very seldom go before 2 in the afternoon that I do not get to spend much time with him. He is very small of his age. Thee knows how small I am for my age and he is not near as tall and he is now about 20.

How does thy farm improve much scince I came away. I expect thy apple trees begin to bear by this time. I wish they would hurry and bear so that thee could barrell them up like flour and then we should have the pleasure of eating them for, if they were ever so poor they would none exceed them. I often when I am eating bread think perhaps I am eating some of thy produce. How one imagination may form reality out of nothing.

I have been in the practice of going to the church where Sarah is a member nearby ever since I came to thy Aunt and almost every[one] tells me that the plain Quaker girl had turned into a Baptist and I suppose that they think will get me for a member there but that point is very undecided indeed as yet and will remain so to all appearance. Sarah is alone in her proffession for all of our relatives are Presbyterians excepting Mother.

I have not heard from Mary Titus for a great length of time and I think that thee and she may well agree in point of writing for she has never written but once to me. I was very sorry to hear that Stephen had lost his little son for I expect that they almost worshipped him. Oh how strange it would seem if I could have peeped in at them. Only think what a change from what it was a short time ago. Stephen must be getting quite old and Samuel the youngest Titus that was.

Dear me I do not know whether I shall be able to get enough to fill up my sheet but if I do not it will not be much matter for if thee has so little time to devote to writing how much less must thee have to look at this poor miserable scrawl.

23RD—

I commence again my evening occupation which if not for certain reasons would be highly gratifying to me but when I recur to the person whom I address

I think that all unseen imperfections will be passed over unregarded although not unseen by thee. Last evening I went to see a cousin after a party a night or two previous. I was invited but declined the invitation. She is to be married now shortly to a Jersy farmer and a step-cousin and I think it seems rather a blow to her vanity as she had prided herself on something higher and yet I am surprised that she should marry a man with whom she is not satisfied. I do not think that a girl that can do such a thing as that has never taken a cool and impartial view of the important step she is about to take. However I leave her to her own fortune and procceed to something more entertaining—to thee.

Oh I must tell thee about poor Roy. I was so glad to see him when I came that I hardly could beleive that it was the same pet I used to have but he has got so old that he lays about the stove and cant bear to leave it, but I think in the spring that he will get lively again. I was reading to day in the papers about the Maple Sugar and it just put me in mind of it. I wish I could come and get there in a sample and get a fair surfeit of it and then I should not think so much about it. Please when thee writes tell me all concerning the sugar and any thing else of the kind for any kind of news is received with the greatest pleasure by me.

Thee mentioned that times seemed changing for the better. I wish they would do the same here for really the dull state of times here is truly distressing. People get a little money they cling to it as if they never were to get another cent and if the times should get too prosperous just please to send a part of your good luck on to us and it shall be received with the greatest pleasure.

Phil seems to agree with me very well indeed and I still creep up by deggrees. Our folks all think thee would hardly know me but I guess there is some of the Emily yet that would betray me. I am going to be one of the small dimenutive specks in world eye but never mind (as I often tell my Uncle when he is runing me about my size) the best goods are in the smallest bundle for I get any thing to get off from his jokes.

Well I have set by the counter till every one is shutting up and my neck tells me it is time for me to do the same and my paper will storm bitterly if I do not cease. I must finish this trash by begging of thee to write if it is not to say more than 6 lines. Give my love to all my acquaintances that is left if thee please and I remain

Gratefully
Emily R. Johnston

P.S. I was so sorry that J. Gibbons' wife was not in company for I could have asked so many hundred questions that I did not feel free to ask Joseph.

E. R. Johnston

JANE HOWELL *to* THOMAS CHANDLER
Philadelphia, March 9, 1841

My dear Nephew

I promised thee in my last letter that if I had time I would write to thee by Joseph Gibbons. I am now about putting my promise in execution altho I have not much to tell thee. Joseph was here this morning and said he should go tomorrow or next day so I thought I must write this evening or perhaps I should not be able to send it by him.

John Merrefield and his brother Joseph went to Washington and were highly pleased with the proceedings of the day. The City was crowded with visitors. It was said there were fifty thousand strangers there. I suppose thee has read the Presidents address, I was very much pleased with it, and I believe it gave general satisfaction to both Parties. He received several handsome presents on the day of his Inauguration.

John and Joseph Merrefield made their home at Jonathan Guests. He lives in the first rate style. I do not know what salary he receives but I think it must be large to enable him to live in the expensive manner which John says he does.

I have sent by Joseph Gibbons 20 books which is all I have left except one which I have kept for myself and which I will account to thee for when we come to a settlement.

I have not seen Sidney Ann Lewis since I wrote last, but intend to before long. I find it difficult to leave the store during the day, and in the evening I am almost afraid to expose myself to the night air.

A few days ago I wrote a long letter to Sarah Chandler, and I have been in daily expectation of receiving an answer to it. I was in hopes I should have heard from them in time to have informed thee how they were coming on in this letter.

I have sent by this conveyance a vest pattern and handkerchief if thee will think them worth accepting. The vest was one of the most fashionable kind worn here last summer.

Emily has sent thee a mammoth sized paper, called the New World.[12] I think thee will find it quite interresting, and its immense size in your part of the world I think will make it quite a novelty.

It was rumoured some days ago that the United States Bank had made an assignment, and that the Directors had chosen Assignees to settle her affairs, but I believe it is not the case. The Daily Chronicle that mentioned it, I sent immediately on to thee thinking it might perhaps deter thee from taking her notes which thee might lose on. Her stock has been as low as fifteen, but is now about 17 or 18 dollars. Some think it will continue to rise and are speculating on it.

I hope soon to receive a letter from thee. Thee must not leave it six or seven months, and if thee has not time to write a long letter, write a short one, but never think that any subject that thee may write upon, let it be what it may, can in the last degree be uninterresting to me. Every word traced by thy pen is read with interrest over and over again.

Thy Aunt Amelia has not returned yet from the Country. I expect her home in a few days. I must now with much love to thee conclude my letter and remain as ever

thy Affectionate Aunt
Jane Howell

I love long letters but short ones are better than none.

JANE HOWELL *to* THOMAS CHANDLER
Philadelphia, June 20, 1841

My dear Nephew

I feel very uneasy at thy long silence and fear that thee is sick, or that some accident has happened to thee. I allowed sufficient time for Joseph Gibbons to reach home, and a letter to be conveyed to me by post from thee, since which I have been counting the days, weeks, and months which have elapsed, and have almost come to the conclusion that thee cares nothing about me. Be that as it may, it does not in the least lessen the love I feel for thee. I almost wish sometimes that I could think less about thee. It would relieve my mind of a great deal of anxiety, but that is a thing impossible.

I hope the box of books got safe to hand. I should think that the New York transportation line was more direct to Michigan than the Pittsburgh but Joseph seemed to prefer the latter.

I received a letter from Sarah Chandler. They had got settled into their new establishment in Lancaster, and seemed to like it very much. The house is large and convenient. The rent 250 dollars [per year]. Sarah gave me no directions as to the Street, number, or name of their House, so that I cannot answer her letter until I receive them. They were all well. William expected to come to this city some time this summer to make some purchases. I hope he will. I want to see him very much.

Anna Coe was married about the middle of last month to Providence Ludlum. They are boarding with Cousin Anna and will continue there until next spring. They then expect to go to their farm in Cumberland N.J.

Aunt Rebecca Guest has appeared in the ministry for some months past in Baltimore. I was very much surprised when I heard it, but I believe she had been under a religious exercise for some time previous.

I think I shall feel easy to close my letter now without saying much more, as this is my third letter to thee, without an answer to either.

> I am well, and with much love to
> thee I remain as ever
> thy Affectionate Aunt
> Jane Howell

Emily complains heavily because thee has not answered her letter. Do write to her. She is well and wishes to be remembered to thee.

JANE HOWELL *to* THOMAS CHANDLER
Philadelphia, September 25, 1841

I thank thee my dear Nephew for thy letter by Samuel Leeds, and also for the one I received some weeks previous. I should have answered the first without delay, but being assured in thy letter of thy good health I thought I would postpone writing until I began to feel anxious about thee, and then I would write, with the hope of receiving an answer immediately. The spectacles came safe to hand for which thy Aunt Amelia and I am much obliged, and I hope thee will not take any further trouble about forwarding any thing else. Amelia thought that there might be some articles belonging to her Mother which thee would perhaps have no particular wish to retain, and if so, they would be very highly valued by her, but she does not want thee to put thyself to any inconvenience in forwarding them on, as any future time will do.

Thee says you have had a very warm and dry summer which I suppose must have injured your later crops of corn oats and potatoes and I suppose rain now would answer no very good purpose, except for buckwheat. I am very sorry to hear your crops will come in so light, but I hope next year abundant crops may make up for the present short ones, the great demand and higher price given for grain in Europe has raised the price of flour several dollars in the barrel here.

I think I have not heard from thy brother since I wrote to thee last. I want to write to him or Sarah but I do not know how to direct the letter. I have been looking for William here this summer as I heard he intended coming, but I suppose his business prevents him.

I have felt anxious to know wether thee held stock in any of the Michigan banks, or wether thee has sustained loss from them in any way. I hope thee has not. I think stock of any kind is a very uncertain and unsafe thing to invest money in. My Landlord Jonathan Knight has lost about thirty thousand dollars on United States Bank Stock and a vast many in this City who a few years ago considered themselves quite independant are now reduced to Poverty by the fall of that Bank.

I have just been called from my writing to look at a funeral procession of a little boy of fourteen years of age son of a new neighbour who was killed the night before last by a fire Engine passing over his neck when he fell in running to a fire, and nearly severed his head from his body which I should think would serve as a warning to parents to prohibit their children from going to fires.

Emily is not with me now. Her brother died about the middle of the 8th month. She wished to go into deep mourning for him, and as I was not willing to advance money sufficient to purchase it with, she with the advice of her Sister Sarah left me without any notice. I still looked for her to return until the third day after the funeral, when she borrowed some money and came and settled the little balance between us. I did not regret her leaving me, only on her own account, for her place is better filled by another. She is at her Uncle Robert Johnstons, and I suppose will continue there until she can find some situation to suit her, but I fear she will not stay anywhere a great while, for I think very few would bear with as much as I have from her, but the interest I felt for her induced me to overlook her faults. I sincerely wish her well.

Eliza Tunis has returned from the South of France and intends residing in this City. She is nearly as large a woman as her mother. She is making her home at John Merrefields until she is suited in a house. John her oldest son is nearly as tall as John Merrefield and her daughter Rebecca is quite a woman in size. They were mere children when they left here.

George Guest and his companion still keep Bachelors hall. They have an old black woman for Cook, and a boy to wait on them. I do not know what time they breakfast, but they dine between five and six oclock in the afternoon.[13] I should like to hear what George has done with all the land he bought in Michigan. Part of it I believe he sold, and the rest was to remain until it increased in value, but I think it most probable that it has been sold and the money spent.

Eliza Kirkbride sister to Mary Ann Williams is going to be married this Fall to John Joseph Gurney the English friend that was here on a religious visit. Eliza is now in England on a visit to her friend Ann Backhouse.

Early in the spring there was an appearance of a great deal of fruit of every kind. The trees were loaded with blossoms and young fruit but the late frosts that followed destroyed nearly the whole of it. John Roberts in Haddonfield has a peach orchard with about five hundred young bearing trees and from the whole of them they did not expect to get one bushell, and from two very large apple orchards they do not think they will have apples enough for their own family use, and as to plumbs, although I am so near the Market I do not recollect that I have seen one this summer. Mellons, and vegetables of all kinds we have had in abundance. We had a very warm dry spell of weather early in the summer which lasted a few weeks and made the farmers very apprehensive that if it continued much longer it would ruin their crops of corn and potatoes but fortunately in time we had some fine and frequent showers which put them out of danger and I believe there will be very good crops of both.

Charles Elliott a dry good merchant between Brown and Coats Street has failed it is said for ninety five thousand dollars. He has compromised with his creditors to pay them forty cents in the dollar and continues on in his business. George Coleman and his father have gone to Ohio to see if they can find anything there that will do better for them than storekeeping for they think that selling dry goods the way times are is hardly worth attending to. Indeed the proffits are very light and I do not know how those who have large expensive families can support them.

Samuel Lovett was here a few evenings since. He said he had intended going on to Michigan this Fall but he thought he should decline it. I think he gave his reasons for not going but I forget what they were.

John Merrefield I expect will decline business before long. He pays very little attention to it now except in purchasing such goods as are wanted. Joseph will be of age in a few months and he rather wishes him to go into the wholesale business down in the City. He divided all that Amelia Merrefield left which I suppose must have been six or seven thousand dollars between Joseph and Mary and has had it out at interrest.

Samuel Leeds informed me that thee did not intend coming on to Philadel[a] before next year. It does seem too long a time to look forward to but thee knows when it will suit thee best and I must patiently submit.

I intended when I began, to have filled this sheet, but I have met with so many interruptions that it is now near bed time and I have not got to the bottom of the second page so I shall have to conclude as I have no other day but First day to write on, every other day is occupied in attending to business.

With much love I remain my
dear Nephew
thy Affectionate Aunt
Jane Howell

JANE HOWELL *to* THOMAS CHANDLER
Philadelphia, February 13, 1842

My dear Nephew

Thy letter which reached me a few days since afforded me much sattisfaction, as it relieved my mind of a great deal of anxiety on thy account. A few days ago Samuel Lovett called here and told me that he had received a letter from his son John saying there was some decease prevailing in his neighbourhood but Samuel had forgotten what it was, and as my fears are always alive to every thing of that kind, when those I love are within its limits, I felt fearful that it had reached thee, but thy kind letter (tho short, was long enough, if it only said thee was well) relieved me from my anxiety.

Margaret Hall had met with a severe tryal in the death of her daughter Margaretta. Her health had been rather delicate for several years past, but so that she could attend to the business in which she was engaged in with her Sister Rebecca, until about six weeks before her decease, when she took cold, which terminated in consumption. She had been engaged to be married to Robert Taylor, a first cousin to R & I Coe, for nearly eight years, but the marriage was disapproved of by her Mother, as he was in no business, and of rather dissipated habits: but still he visited her until the close of her life, which was about the middle of 12th Month last.

Last evening about half past six oclock Cousin John A Williams' son Samuel, departed this life, after an illness of five months, of Consumption; which is a very severe stroke to his parents, he being their only child, and although he had led an idle and dissipated life, they having little or no control over him, yet their earthly happiness seemed centred in him, even tho his heart seemed as impenitrable to conviction, as a rock of Adamant, and all their entreaties, admonitions, and threats, were of no avail. Yet when he was brought on the bed of sickness, the prayers of the ministers who attended him, and the mental anguish which his Mother evinced for him as regarded his future State, seemed to make an impression on him, and he was brought to see, how wide he had wandered from the paths of rectitude, and to feel that abasement, which attends true contrition, and through the mercies of his dear Redeemer on whom he seemed to rely, I trust, he has gone to rest.

Sarah Williams passed meeting last month with Samuel Fox, a widower with eight children some of them small. They will be married next month. He formerly kept school in the country and married a relation of Patty Yarnalls, by the name of Hilbert. Sarah will be his fourth wife. He is now a Scrivener and City Surveyor. Her friends all disapprove of the connection.

George Guest is engaged to be married to a young woman in Baltimore. She is about his own age, not handsome, but very rich. Their marriage is to take place next month.

I felt disappointed at thy putting off thy visit until Fall. I thought it a great while to wait until summer. I wish thee would make arrangements before thee leaves home, to stay with us all winter. The thoughts of thy crossing the Lake at a late season in the year, destroys a great deal of the pleasure of thy visit.

When thy Brother came to the City he brought little Tom with him. He is a very smart intelligent boy for one of his age, and his father says a very good one, which was a great deal for William to say, as he seldom praises any thing belonging to him. John Merrefield was much pleased with him and made him a present of a Magic Lantern, which delighted Tom highly.

I expect Sarah will pay a visit to the City before long. She intends bringing Elizabeth with her, and leaving her awhile with me. I hope she will, for since my dear Sisters removal, I feel so lonesome, so isolated, as if I stood in the world alone. No one to care for, nor none to care for me, but I find it will not do to cherish such feelings. They would prove inimical to my health if indulged in.

I have written a longer letter than I expected I should when I began, and after informing thee that I am well I must conclude and with as much love as ever I remain

thy Affectionate Aunt
Jane Howell

Thee directed my last letter N° 497 north 2nd Street instead of N° 489. It is the 3rd house above Poplar Lane.

Excuse the manner in which this letter is written for it is too great a task to copy it. Write soon or I shall fret and [worry] about thee.

JANE HOWELL *to* THOMAS CHANDLER
Philadelphia, May 22, 1842

My dear Nephew

I received thy letter a few days since, and was, as thee may suppose, very glad to hear that thee was well, as I always feel very solicitous about thee, seperated as we are so widely apart from each other. Thee said nothing in thy letter about thy intended visit this Summer, or coming Fall, to Philadel.ª I hope thee will not decline it without thee can offer a very good substantial reason for not doing so, and then we will strive to bear the disappointment without murmering, anticipating the pleasure as only a little while defered.

I feel very desirous to see Charles C. Burleigh letter which has a reference to his visit to thee. I hope I shall get the paper this week from the Anti Slavery office, and after I have perused it well, I will send it on to thy brother.

I received a letter from Sarah Chandler about two weeks since. They were all well. She says thy Brother intends paying me a visit this summer but she cannot say exactly when. They have been doing a very good business this spring, and have at present a number of Boarders. Sarah's Mother staid with me one night during the Yearly Meeting. I received a very pretty letter from little Tom. It was written in quite a Juvenile style, and he apologized by saying it was the first letter he had ever written, but he hoped the next would be better. He said he intended writing a letter to his Uncle Thomas before long. He is an uncommon smart, intelligent boy for one of his age, and by no means spoiled. I was very much pleased with him whilst he was with me.

Anna Coe, now Ludlum, left the City a few days ago. She came up with her Mother to purchase Carpets &c towards housekeeping. They have been boarding with cousin Anna since they were married. John Merrefield says he is a very nice young man, and he thinks he resembles thy brother William very much. I did not see him. Anna was in very poor health before she married, and it seems to be declining since. She has a disease of the heart, which is very dangerous, and she has to observe the greatest care in not using much exercise.

A few weeks ago I was invited to attend the funeral of John Roberts of Haddonfield. He died from the effects of Palsy. Hannah his widow is in very poor health and I think cannot continue much longer in the state she now is.

When I wrote to thee last I said George Guest expected to be married the early part of the 3rd month. The marriage was postponed on account of the badness of the times. I suppose when he marries, he would wish to set out in high style, but the way things are now forbid it.

Sarah Williams, or I should have said Fox, appears very happy since her marriage. She has a house in Spring Garden Street large and commodious, and very handsomely furnished which is the place of their residence. John Merrefield and Anna disapproved so much of the connection, that there is no intercourse between them.

In thy letter thee says nothing about the state of the times in Michigan. I hope they are better than they are here for here they are really deplorable. The Merchants, and Manufacturers I believe suffer most, goods are monstrously sacrificed at Auction, selling often at one third and fourth of their real value, to raise money to meet their payments. A great number of the first Merchants have failed, and a large number of others are very tottering; for the discounts at the bank are quite trifling, even for the very best paper.

I am glad to hear that there is such an appearance of good crops of wheat. I hope all thy other grains may turn out well.

The tract of land at Pine Grove [Pennsylvania], on which I held a claim of about a thousand dollars, and which I purchased two years since, I have had surveyed, and laid out in four hundred acre lots. It measures two thousand three hundred and sixty acres. Part of it has Iron Ore on it, and it is well timbered. There are four handsome Mill seats on it. A good part of it lies in a valley and is excellent farming land. It is about four miles from Pine Grove a town about the size of Wilmington. There are several other smaller towns within a mile of the land inhabited chiefly by Germans, many of which are farmers. I bought it at Sheriffs Sale for my claim. I have had the title examined into the Office at Orwigsburg and Reading, the towns for recording of deeds for the County Schuylkill, as far back as fifty years, and the title is indisputable, and I believe there is nothing now against it but the tax for last year, which I expect to send by private conveyance in a few weeks.

I have sent the paper thee mentioned in thy letter (United States) by this conveyance.[14] I hope it may get safe to hand.

I am much oblidged to thee for thy last letter. I hope thee will write again before long. I feel when I get a letter as if there was one left, who had not forgotten me. Short letters are as acceptable as long ones, to me, so that they only convey the intelligence that thee is in good health.

I am not in the way of apologizing, let the writing be as bad as it may, but I must say excuse this, for the pen has been so trying that it would scarcely perform its office in letting down the ink on the paper without the most coercive means being used, which does not do very well with steel pens.

> I must now conclude, and with
> the warmest wishes for thy
> health and prosperity I remain
> thy affectionate Aunt Jane Howell

I have had a bad cold this winter but am now about in my usual health.

━━━◆◆◆━━━

JANE HOWELL *to* THOMAS CHANDLER
Philadelphia, August 28, 1842

My dear Nephew

The pleasure I received from the perusal of thy last letter was not a little I assure thee.[15] It embraced too much to allow me to read it with indifference, or with a moderate share of attention. No my dear Nephew, every thing connected with thy welfare, lies too deeply embedded in my heart, to allow me to feel less, than a maternal care, and interest for thee, in all thy proceedings through life.

I have felt very solicitous for some years past, that thee might meet with some one, who would make a suitable companion for thee for life, one to share thy weal, or woe. Thee has now made choice of one whom thee thinks altogether worthy of thee, and from the character thee has drawn of her, I think she must be *far above Par* (and none but such, I should think good enough *for thee*) and I am very much pleased to hear thee has made such a choice. I feel that I love her already. May nothing intervene to prevent the union. Take her, and *may Heaven bless you.*

If it is not convenient for thee my dear Nephew, to leave home before the 10th or 11th month, I would a great deal rather thee would defer it another year, much as I want to see thee. The dread I should feel at thy travelling so late in the season, would destroy in a great measure the pleasure of seeing thee. It made me feel very unpleasant when I saw the time thee had fixed on for coming, in thy letter. My mind seemed to forebode some evil if thee came. Abandon every thought of coming this Fall, and come earlier next Year. I shall only have the pleasure of anticipating it a while longer, with the pleasure of being introduced to my *new Niece.*

I have not seen, or heard from Barney C. Harris. I went yesterday to see Maria Woodside thinking perhaps he had left the money with her, but she had left here for Wilmington. I think it probable when she returns he will send it on by her.

Cousin John A Williams has stop'd payment, but he expects to go on again, in a short time. I see very little improvement in the times here. The manufacturers are almost without employment, and if the Tariff bill should not pass, which will be known in a few days, I think there will be a great deal of distress this winter.

I believe I have not heard from William since I wrote to thee last. I have intended writing to Sarah for some time, but had not done it. I shall now have something to communicate to them. I suppose thee will have no objection. At any rate, I cannot wait until I hear from thee.

Ann Rowe is married to James Morris. He is a tailor. He is a very industrious young man and I hope they may do well together.

I am well, and as I have not much more time to write this afternoon, I think I must conclude, and believe me as ever

thy affectionate Aunt
Jane Howell

EPILOGUE

Members of the Chandler family continued to contribute to the growth of Michigan, to the cause of abolitionism, and even to feminism. The following information comes from material Minnie Fay assembled about her ancestors, much of it from a reminiscence by her uncle, Henry Clay Chandler. The material she collected is now part of the Minnie Fay Papers, Michigan Historical Collections, Bentley Library, University of Michigan, Ann Arbor.

Jane Howell outlived her sisters Margaret and Ruth and her husband Lemuel. She had no children, and nothing is known about her life or death after the letters ceased.

In 1843, Thomas Chandler married Jane Merritt, the daughter of Quakers Joseph and Phebe Hart Merritt, prominent Battle Creek, Michigan, pioneers and abolitionists. Thomas and Jane are thought to have met at a Friends' Yearly Meeting. They raised two sons, Merritt and William, at Hazelbank, and they continued to contribute to the growth of Lenawee County and to carry on the abolitionist efforts Elizabeth Chandler had begun. Hazelbank hosted many antislavery meetings, and family legend states that Sojourner Truth, whom Jane had known through her parents, visited there. Thomas Chandler was badly injured in an accident in Adrian on September 19, 1881, and died three weeks later. He was buried at Hazlebank, as was his wife, Jane.

William Guest Chandler and Sarah Taylor Chandler remained in Lancaster County, Pennsylvania, where they raised four children. (Their first son, John Conley, died in infancy.) Thomas Evans was born on September 26, 1831; Elizabeth Margaret was born on March 20, 1835; William Edward was born on February 24, 1837; and Henry (Harry) Clay, was born on December 7, 1842.

William Guest Chandler was a skilled carpenter but changed professions frequently. Sarah went along with William's many career changes, always providing a stable home for their children. In approximately 1853, William and Sarah sold their Lancaster farm and equipment and moved to Philadelphia, where William and two of Sarah's brothers ran a real estate business. After that business failed, William and Sarah took in boarders. In 1858, William, Sarah, and their youngest child, Harry, moved to Indianapolis, where their oldest son, Thomas, had established a real estate business. Sarah's brother, Franklin Taylor, later joined Thomas in business, and the firm prospered. William worked as a pattern maker for his son's firm and built a small home on West Vermont Street, where he died in 1873. Until her death in 1901 Sarah lived in Battle Creek, Michigan, with her daughter, Elizabeth Margaret Chandler Merritt.

William and Sarah's daughter, Elizabeth Margaret, taught in a country school in Chester County, Pennsylvania, and later in Philadelphia. In 1856, she traveled to Michigan to visit her Uncle Thomas and Aunt Jane Chandler at Hazelbank. Jane's brother, Charles Merritt, was there at the time, and Elizabeth and Charles fell in love, marrying on June 9, 1858. They established their home in Battle Creek, Michigan, and raised four children: Minnie, born on November 14, 1859; Charles Wendell, born on March 6, 1861; and William Guest and Maud Elizabeth, birthdates unknown. Like the aunt for whom she was named, Elizabeth Margaret Chandler Merritt was an active abolitionist: her home served as an abolitionist headquarters, and runaway slaves were occasionally hidden on the Merritts' farm. She subsequently became active in the women's suffrage movement, witnessing its success before her death in 1923 at the age of eighty-eight.

William Edward Chandler, the third surviving child of William and Sarah, was born in Little Brittain, Pennsylvania, on February 24, 1837. He married Margaret Statt in Philadelphia on August 19, 1858, and they raised seven children. He was a machinist by trade but also spent time working on a nursery farm in Lancaster, Pennsylvania. He moved his family to Indianapolis where he worked for a time at his brother's and uncle's real estate business. He served in the Civil War, and a letter he wrote on May 16, 1864, while in the service, is in the Minnie Fay Collection. He died in Rivera, California, on October 2, 1923.

DIRECTORY OF NAMES

The letters in this collection mention hundreds of people. Some, such as close friends and family members of Thomas and Elizabeth Chandler and Ruth Evans, appear frequently and were fairly easy to identify. Other names appear infrequently and could not be easily located within the sources listed in the bibliography. Because early Quaker families tended to name children after friends and relatives, it was often difficult to determine which one of several people with the same name was being referenced. Women were listed in Philadelphia city directories when they were widowed, owned businesses, or had the distinction of being "gentlewomen"; otherwise, they were not listed and, therefore, were almost impossible to find. Alternate spellings of names have been included and are cross-referenced when they do not appear immediately before or after the correct spelling.

COMMONLY USED NAMES

Ann	Anna Rowe
Anna	Anna Coe Jr.
Aunt A. E., Aunt Amelia E.	Amelia Evans
Aunt Amelia G.	Amelia Guest
Aunt Anna	Anna Guest
Aunt Nancy	Nancy Guest
Aunt Rebecca	Rebecca Guest
Aunt Sally	Sarah Comstock
Aunts	Amelia, Anna, and Nancy Guest
Benjamin	Benjamin Lundy
Carlo	Lemuel Howell's dog

Cousins Coe	Anna, John, Rebecca, Robert, and Amelia Coe
Cousins Guest	Eliza, John Jr., George, and Rebecca Guest
Darius, Uncle Darius	Darius Comstock
Em, Emily	Emily Johnston
Lemuel	Lemuel Howell
Little Tom	Thomas Evans Chandler
Louisa	Louisa Hull
Roy	Thomas Chandler's dog
Sarah	Sarah Taylor Chandler
William	William Guest Chandler

AGNEW, William. Owned dry goods store at 24 S. Second Street, Philadelphia.

ALDRICH, Friend. Probably Sarah Aldrich (b. November 8, 1789). Married to Savil Aldrich.

ALLEN, Richard. Bishop of African Methodist Church in Philadelphia.

ARNOLDS, Charles. *No information located.*

ATHERTON, Elmira. *No information located.*

ATKINSON, T. ("Friend"). *No information located.*

ATLEE, Dr. Edwin I. Brother of Samuel Yorke Atlee.

ATLEE, Samuel Yorke. Cincinnati lawyer and abolitionist; brother of Edwin I. Atlee.

BACKHOUSE, Ann. *No information located.*

BACKS, Dr. *No information located.*

BAILES, Richard. *No information located.*

BECKMAN, Phebe. *See* BEECKMAN, Phebe

BEDFORD, Ann. Resided at 81 S. Third Street, Philadelphia.

BEECKMAN (Beekman, Beckman), Phebe. Daughter of Sarah Comstock; widowed in 1835.

BENEZET, Anthony (1713–84). French-born Quaker abolitionist.

BENNET, Titus. Bookseller and stationer at 37 High Street, Philadelphia.

BETTZ, Alice. *No information located.*

BIND, Anna. *No information located.*

BIND, Eliza. *No information located.*

BIXBY, Emmeline. *No information located.*

BLACK HAWK (1767–1838). Leader of the Sauk and Fox Native American tribes; led 1832 rebellion against white settlers.

BONSALE, Isaac. *No information located.*

BOTTON, Aquila M. *No information located.*

BRINTON, Mary. *No information located.*

BROOM, Eliza. *See* COE, Eliza Broom

BROOM, Elizabeth. Mother of Eliza Broom; married to John Broom.

BROOM, John. Grocer at 379 High Street, Philadelphia; married to Elizabeth Broom; father of Eliza Broom.

BROOM, Rachel. Married to Eliza Broom Coe's brother.

BROWN, Abi. *See* EVANS, Abi Brown

BROWN, Joseph W. (1793–1880). Prominent Michigan general and politician; brother of Abi Brown Evans; migrated from Bucks County, Pennsylvania, to Lenawee County, Michigan Territory, in 1824.

BROWN, William. *No information located.*

BROWNELL, Elijah. (b. 1806). Early resident of Lenawee County (1828); first Society of Friends minister in county.

BUND, Edward. *No information located.*

BURLEIGH, Charles C. *No information located.*

CANBY, Elizabeth Morris. *See* MORRIS, Elizabeth

CANBY, Samuel. Married to Elizabeth Morris, July 1832.

CAVERLY, Charles. Resided at 8½ S. Seventh Street, Philadelphia.

CAVERLY, Peter. *No information located.*

CHANDLER, Abby. Married to Amor Chandler; mother of Amor Chandler Jr.

CHANDLER, Amor. Storekeeper in Beaver Valley in the Brandywine Hundred; married to Abby Chandler; father of Amor Chandler Jr.; great-uncle of William, Thomas, and Elizabeth Chandler.

CHANDLER, Amor, Jr. Son of Amor and Abby Chandler; second cousin of William, Thomas, and Elizabeth Chandler.

CHANDLER, Elizabeth Margaret (1807–1834). Daughter of Thomas and Margaret Evans Chandler; sister of William and Thomas; author of essays and poems; main correspondent in this volume.

CHANDLER, Elizabeth Margaret (1835–1923). Daughter of William Guest Chandler and Sarah Taylor Chandler.

CHANDLER, Hayes. Brandywine relative of William, Thomas, and Elizabeth Chandler.

CHANDLER, Dr. Joseph P. Brandywine relative of William, Thomas, and Elizabeth Chandler.

CHANDLER, Margaret Evans (1778–1807). Oldest of four daughters of Daniel Evans and Elizabeth Guest Evans; married to Thomas Chandler, May 12, 1803; mother of William, Thomas, and Elizabeth Chandler.

CHANDLER, Mary. Oldest sister of Thomas Chandler Sr.; aunt of William, Thomas, and Elizabeth Chandler.

CHANDLER, Rachel. Married to Hayes Chandler.

CHANDLER, Sarah Taylor (Sally) (d. 1901). Married to William Guest Chandler, March 18, 1829; mother of Thomas Evans Chandler, Elizabeth Margaret Chandler, William Edward Chandler, and Henry Clay Chandler.

CHANDLER, Thomas, Sr. (1773–1815). Married to Margaret Evans Chandler, May 12, 1803; father of Elizabeth Chandler.

CHANDLER, Thomas [Jr.] (1806–1881). Son of Thomas and Margaret Evans Chandler; brother of William and Elizabeth Margaret Chandler; married to Jane Merritt, 1843; father of Merritt and William Chandler.

CHANDLER, Thomas Evans (b. 1831). Son of William Guest Chandler and Sarah Taylor Chandler.

CHANDLER, William. Cousin of Thomas Chandler Sr.

CHANDLER, William Edward (1837–1923). Son of William Guest Chandler and Sarah Taylor Chandler.

CHANDLER, William Guest (1804–73). Carpenter, tavern keeper, farmer, among other occupations; son of Thomas and Margaret Evans Chandler; brother of Thomas and Elizabeth Margaret Chandler; married to Sarah Taylor, March 18, 1829; father of Thomas Evans Chandler, Elizabeth Margaret Chandler, William Edward Chandler, and Henry Clay Chandler.

CHESNUT, Esther (Hetty). Second wife of Samuel Chesnut; mother of Sarah Jane Chesnut; possibly related to Jane Howell.

CHESNUT, Samuel. Resided at 73 N. Sixth Street, Philadelphia; married to Esther Chesnut; father of Sarah Jane Chesnut.

CHESNUT, Sarah Jane. Daughter of Samuel and Esther Chesnut.

CHILD, John. Clock and watchmaker at 452 N. Second Street, Philadelphia; father of Samuel Child.

CHILD, Samuel. Son of John Child.

CHITTENDEN, Joseph, Jr. (d. 1834). Migrated to Adrian in 1833; lawyer; married to Julia Webb, October 24, 1833.

CHITTENDEN, Julia Webb. *See* WEBB, Julia

CLARK, Eliza. Grocer at 138 Lombard Street, Philadelphia.

CLIBBORNS, James. *No information located.*

COE, Amelia. Daughter of Anna Guest Coe and Robert Coe.

COE, Angelina, Sr. *No information located.*

COE, Anna Guest. Married to Robert Coe Sr.; sister of Thomas Coe; cousin of Margaret Evans Chandler, Ruth Evans, Jane Howell, and Amelia Evans.

COE, Anna, Jr. Daughter of Robert Coe Sr. and Anna Guest Coe; married Providence Ludlam, May 1841; third cousin and close friend of Elizabeth Margaret Chandler.

COE, Eliza Broom. Daughter of John and Elizabeth Broom; married to Robert Coe Jr.; mother of Rachel Broom Coe.

COE, Helen. Daughter of James Coe and Rebecca Hall Coe.

COE, James. Storekeeper at 202 N. Waters Street, Philadelphia; married to Rebecca Hall; first cousin of Margaret Evans Chandler, Ruth Evans, Jane Howell, and Amelia Evans.

COE, James G. Owned dry goods store at 361 N. Second Street, Philadelphia.

COE, Rachel Broom. Daughter of Robert Coe Jr. and Elizabeth Broom Coe; third cousin of William, Thomas, and Elizabeth Chandler.

COE, Rebecca (Bec, Becca). Daughter of Anna and Robert Coe Sr.; married to Washington Train, 1832; third cousin of William, Thomas, and Elizabeth Chandler.

COE, Rebecca Hall. *See* HALL, Rebecca

COE, Richard. Merchant at 175 Callowhill Street, Philadelphia.

COE, Robert, Jr. Owned dry goods store at 453 N. Second Street, resided at 427 N. Second Street, Philadelphia; son of Anna and Robert Coe Sr.; married to Eliza Broom Coe; third cousin of William, Thomas, and Elizabeth Chandler.

COE, Robert, Sr. (d. 1835). Owned dry goods store at 427 N. Second Street, Philadelphia; married to Anna Guest Coe.

COE, Samuel E. ("Uncle"). *No information located.*

COLEMAN, George. Owned dry goods store in Philadelphia.

COMFORT, Samuel. Owned the Red Lion Tavern (listed as Red Lion Hotel and State Office in Philadelphia directory).

COMSTOCK, Addison. Son of Darius Comstock; established Adrian post office in 1818; married to Sarah S. Dean, February 14, 1826; founded village of Adrian in 1828.

COMSTOCK, Ann (Anna) (b. 1782). Married to Darius Comstock.

COMSTOCK, Darius (b. 1768). Married to Ann Comstock; brother of Sarah Comstock.

COMSTOCK, Isaac. *No information located.*

COMSTOCK, Sarah. (b. 1781). Sister of Darius Comstock.

COMSTOCK, Sarah (Aunt Sally, "Widow"). Mother of Darius Comstock; sister of the husband of Lemuel Howell's Aunt Hathaway.

COPE, Jasper. No information found.

COX, John. Brother of Sarah Cox.

COX, Sarah ("Widow"). Shopkeeper at 120 Filbert Street, Philadelphia; sister of John Cox.

CROSSLEY, Mary. *No information located.*

DAVIS, Esther. *No information located.*

DECLINE, Mary. Resided on Front Street near Green Street, Philadelphia.

DENISON, Charles W. Editor of the *Emancipator,* New York's first antislavery journal.

DILLWIN, George. *No information located.*

DIXON, Lizzy. *No information located.*

DIXON, Samuel. *No information located.*

DORSEY, J. *No information located.*

DORSEY, Sarah ("Widow"). Resided at 309 Mulberry Street, Philadelphia.

DOUGLASS, ———. Philadelphia artist who painted Elizabeth Chandler's portrait.

DOUGLASS, Albert. Son of artist who painted Elizabeth Chandler's portrait.

DUNLAP, William. *No information located.*

DUPONT, "Young." *No information located.*

ELLIOTT, Charles. Dry goods merchant between Brown and Coats Streets, Philadelphia.

ELLIOTT, James. *No information located.*

ESTLACK, Israel. Blacksmith in Lenawee County; married to Louisa Estlack.

ESTLACK, Louisa. Married to Israel Estlack.

EVANS, Abi Brown (d. 1832). Sister of General Joseph Brown; married to Musgrove Evans; mother of George Evans, first child born in Lenawee County.

EVANS, Amelia (b. 1782). Youngest of four daughters born to Daniel and Elizabeth Guest Evans; aunt of William, Thomas, and Elizabeth Chandler.

EVANS, Elizabeth Guest (1744–1826). Shopkeeper at 14 S. Second Street, Philadelphia; married to Daniel Evans, April 1766; mother of Margaret Evans Chandler, Ruth Evans, Jane Howell, and Amelia Evans; grandmother of William, Thomas, and Elizabeth Margaret Chandler.

EVANS, Jane. *See* HOWELL, Jane Evans

EVANS, Margaret. *See* CHANDLER, Margaret Evans

EVANS, Musgrove. First settler and prominent citizen in Lenawee County; married to Abi Brown Evans; father of George Evans, first baby born in Lenawee County.

EVANS, Ruth (1779–1836). Second-oldest daughter of Daniel Evans and Elizabeth Guest Evans; sister of Margaret Evans Chandler, Jane Howell, and Amelia Evans; raised Thomas, William, and Elizabeth Chandler after Margaret's death.

FETHER, Barry. *No information located.*

FIELD, Elizabeth. *No information located.*

FOX, Joseph. *No information located.*

FOX, Samuel. Married to Sarah Williams, 1842.

FOX, Sarah Williams. *See* WILLIAMS, Sarah

GALBREATH, Nathan. *No information located.*

GAMAGE, Hannah ("Aunt"). Relative of Lemuel Howell whose family resided in Hudson, New York; mother of Hannah Gamage.

GAMAGE, Sarah. Daughter of Hannah Gamage.

GAMBLE, James. Mechanic and brick manufacturer on Walnut N Eighth Street, Philadelphia.

GARRISON, William Lloyd (1805–79). Prominent and controversial abolitionist and temperance advocate; editor of the *National Philanthropist,* the *Journal of the Times* (Bennington, Vermont), the *Genius of Universal Emancipation,* and the *Liberator.*

GATCHELL, Joseph. Blacksmith at 13 Decatur Street, resided at 57 N. Ninth Street, Philadelphia.

GERARD. *See* GIRARD, Stephen

GIBBONS, Joseph. Migrated to Michigan from Mt. Pleasant, Ohio; married to Lydia Gibbons.

GIBBONS, Lydia. Married to Joseph Gibbons.

GIBBS, Johnny. Resided at 227 S. Second Street, Philadelphia.

GILES, Acquilla. Resided in Baltimore; great-grandson of Jacob Giles; married to Rebecca Guest.

GILES, Jacob. Grandfather of Betsy Morris.

GILES, Rebecca Guest. Daughter of Rebecca Guest; married to Acquilla Giles.

GIRARD, Stephen (1750–1831). Philadelphia merchant, banker, and philanthropist; founder of Girard College.

GOODMAN, ———. *No information found.*

GREENFIELD, Elizabeth ("Widow"). Resided at 371 Mulberry Street, Philadelphia; freed slaves and sent them to Liberia.

GUEST, Amelia. Daughter of (Aunt) Rebecca Guest; sister of Eliza Guest Tunis, George Guest, Johnathan Guest, and Rebecca Guest; married to Meadows T. Nicholson.

GUEST, Amelia (d. 1833). Resided on Mulberry Street, Philadelphia; sister of Anna and Nancy Guest; aunt of Margaret Evans Chandler, Ruth Evans, Jane Howell, and Amelia Evans; great-aunt of William, Thomas, and Elizabeth Margaret Chandler.

GUEST, Anna (d. 1837). Resided on Mulberry Street, Philadelphia; sister of Amelia and Nancy Guest; aunt of Margaret Evans Chandler, Ruth Evans, Jane Howell, and Amelia Evans; great-aunt of William, Thomas, and Elizabeth Margaret Chandler.

GUEST, Anna. *See* COE, Anna Guest

GUEST, (Cousin) Anna. Sister of Elizabeth Guest; cousin of Margaret Evans Chandler, Ruth Evans, Jane Howell, and Amelia Evans.

GUEST, Betsy. *See* GUEST, Elizabeth.

GUEST, Eliza. *See* TUNIS, Eliza Guest.

GUEST, Elizabeth (Betsy) (d. 1832). Sister of Anna Guest Coe; cousin of Margaret Evans Chandler, Ruth Evans, Jane Howell, and Amelia Evans.

GUEST, George. Brother of Eliza Guest Tunis, Johnathan Guest, and Rebecca Guest; cousin of Margaret Evans Chandler, Ruth Evans, Jane Howell, and Amelia Evans.

GUEST, John. Philadelphia merchant; married to Rebecca Guest; father of Johnathan Guest, Rebecca Guest Giles, George Guest, and Eliza Guest Tunis; brother of Elizabeth Guest Evans; uncle of Margaret Evans Chandler, Ruth Evans, Jane Howell, and Amelia Evans.

GUEST, Johnathan (d. 1837). Son of John and Rebecca Guest.

GUEST, Mary. Sister of Elizabeth Guest Evans; married to Joseph Merrefield; aunt of Margaret Evans Chandler, Ruth Evans, Jane Howell, and Amelia Evans.

GUEST, Mary. *See* SMITH, Mary Guest

GUEST, Nancy. Sister of Amelia and Ana Guest; aunt of Margaret Evans Chandler, Ruth Evans, Jane Howell, and Amelia Evans; great-aunt of William, Thomas, and Elizabeth Chandler.

GUEST, Rebecca ("Aunt"). Married to John Guest; mother of Johnathan Guest, Rebecca Guest Giles, George Guest, and Eliza Guest Tunis.

GUEST, Rebecca. See GILES, Rebecca Guest

GUEST, Thomas ("Cousin"). Brother of Anna Guest Coe.

GURNEY, Eliza Kirkbride. *See* KIRKBRIDE, Eliza

GURNEY, John Joseph. Married to Eliza Kirkbride Gurney, fall 1841.

HALL, Margaret Williams. Storekeeper at 307 Callowhill Street, Philadelphia; widow of John A. Hall; sister of George Williams, Charles Williams, and Anna Williams Merrefield; mother of Margaretta Hall, Rebecca Hall, Sabina Hall, and William Hall.

HALL, Margaretta (d. 1841). Daughter of Margaret Williams Hall and John A. Hall; sister of Rebecca Hall, Sabina Hall, and William Hall; engaged to Robert Taylor.

HALL, Rebecca. Daughter of Margaret Williams Hall and John A. Hall; sister of Margaretta Hall, Sabina Hall, and William Hall; married to James Coe.

HALL, Sabina. Daughter of Margaret Williams Hall and John A. Hall; sister of Rebecca Hall Coe, Margaretta Hall, and William Hall.

HALL, William. Owned lottery office in Philadelphia; son of Margaret Williams Hall and John A. Hall; brother of Rebecca Hall Coe, Margaretta Hall, and Sabina Hall.

HAMILTON, Mary. Murdered in 1833.

HANK, George. *No information located.*

HARKEN, Charlotte. *No information located.*

HARNED, Jonathan. Migrated to Lenawee County from New Jersey.

HARRIGAS. *See* HERIGAS

HARRIS, Barney. Purchased land in Michigan, migrated to Lenawee County, and later returned to the east.

HARRIS, Mary. Married to Barney Harris.

HASSINGER, Eunice.

HATHAWAY, Eliza ("Aunt"). Aunt of Lemuel Howell from Hudson, New York; mother of Sarah Hathaway Jenkins.

HATHAWAY, Sarah. *See* JENKINS, Sarah Hathaway

HAVILAND (Havalind), Charles (b. 1800). Migrated to Lenawee County; married to Laura Smith Haviland.

HAVILAND, Laura Smith (b. 1808). Married to Charles Haviland; cofounder of Logan Female Anti-Slavery Society with Elizabeth Chandler in 1832.

HAYS, ————. *No information located.*

HENK, George. *See* HANK, George

HENRIETTA. Jane and Lemuel Howell's bond servant.

HERIGAS (Harrigas, Herregas), Betsy. Married to John Herigas; neighbor of the Howells; friend of Ruth Evans.

HERIGAS (Harrigas, Herregas), John. Tobacconist at 471 N. Second Street, Philadelphia; married to Betsy Herigas.

HICKLIN, Lydia Logue. Friend of Ruth Evans.

HILBERT, ————. Married to Samuel Fox.

HOAG, Jacob (b. 1799). Married to Sarah Laing Hoag; brother-in-law of Smith Laing.

HOWARD, J. and C. *No information located.*

HOWELL, Jane Evans (b. 1780). Second-youngest daughter of Daniel Evans and Elizabeth Guest Evans; sister of Margaret Evans Chandler, Ruth Evans, and Amelia Evans; married Lemuel Howell; aunt of William, Thomas, and Elizabeth Chandler.

HOWELL, Lemuel (d. 1836). Owned dry goods store at 477 N. Second Street, Philadelphia; also built houses; married to Jane Evans Howell.

HOWELL, "Mother." Lemuel Howell's mother; resided in Hudson, New York.

HULL, Louisa. Bond servant who worked for Jane and Lemuel Howell; sister of Washington Hull.

HULL, Washington. Brother of Louisa Hull.

HUNT, John. *No information located.*

INGALLS, Rensselaer W. Newspaper editor and publisher of the *Adrian Gazette and Lenawee County Republican,* later called the *Adrian Watchtower.*

IRELAND, Edward. *No information located.*

JACKSON, Darius Comstock. Probably grandson of Darius Comstock.

JACKSON, William. *No information located.*

JENKINS, ————. Resided in Hudson, New York; married to Sarah Hathaway.

JENKINS, Sarah (Sally) Hathaway. Daughter of Eliza Hathaway; married to ———— Jenkins.

JOHNSON, Ann. *No information located.*

JOHNSTON (Johnson), Emily. Bond servant who emigrated to Michigan with Thomas and Elizabeth Chandler and Ruth Evans; sister of Sarah Johnston; niece of Robert Johnston.

JOHNSTON, Robert. Uncle of Emily Johnston.

JOHNSTON, Sarah. Sister of Emily Johnston.

JONES, Ann. Resided at 3 Perry Street, Philadelphia.

JONES, B. *No information located.*

KIRKBRIDE, Eliza. Sister of Mary Ann Kirkbride Williams; married to John Joseph Gurney, fall 1841.

KIRKBRIDE, Mary Ann. *See* WILLIAMS, Mary Ann Kirkbride

KITES, Thomas. Bookseller, printer, and bookbinder at 64 Walnut Street, resided at 6 S. Fifth Street, Philadelphia; son betrothed to Debby Lupon.

KNIGHT, Jonathan. Jane Howell's landlord.

KNOX, Cornelia. *No information located.*

LAING, Smith (b. 1793). Emigrated to Michigan, June 1832; married to Abby Hoag; father of eight children; Jacob Hoag's brother-in-law.

LEEDS, Samuel. *No information located.*

LEWIS, Evan (d. 1834). *No information located.*

LEWIS, Nathaniel. *No information located.*

LEWIS, Sidney Ann. *No information located.*

LINTON, Esther. *No information located.*

LIPPINCOTT, Aaron. *No information located.*

LIPPINCOTT, Elinor. *No information located.*

LIPPINCOTT, Eliza. Friend of Elizabeth Chandler and Ruth Evans; member Philadelphia Female Anti-Slavery Society.

LIPPINCOTT, Joshua. *No information located.*

LOGUE, Lydia. *See* HICKLIN, Lydia Logue.

LOGUE, Ruth. *No information located.*

LONGSTRETH, Hannah. *See* TOWNSEND, Hannah

LONGSTRETH, Joshua. Merchant at 21 Church Street, resided at 185 Mulberry Street, Philadelphia; son of Widow Longstreth; married to Hannah Townsend, 1832.

LONGSTRETH, "Widow." Mother of Joshua Longstreth.

LOVETT, Betsy. Daughter of Samuel and Anna Lovett; sister of John Lovett.

LOVETT, Anna. Married to John Lovett; cousin of Margaret Evans Chandler, Ruth Evans, Jane Howell, and Amelia Evans.

LOVETT, John. Philadelphia native who migrated to the Michigan Territory and also traveled frequently to and from Philadelphia.

LOVETT, Mary. Daughter of John and Anna Lovett.

LOVETT, Sally Ann. Married to Samuel Lovett.

LOVETT, Samuel. Father of John Lovett; married to Sally Ann Lovett.

LOWER, Abraham (Abram). Cabinetmaker at 246 N. Third Street, resided at 98 St. John's Street, Philadelphia.

LOYD, Joshua. Owned leather and shoe store in Philadelphia.

LUCAS, Robert. Elected governor of Ohio 1832; involved in Michigan/Ohio boundary dispute know as the Toledo War; established Lucas County, which included disputed area and located county seat at Toledo.

LUDLAM, Providence. Married Anna Coe Jr., May 1841.

LUKENS (LUKINS), Sarah Pennock (d. 1832). Daughter of Sarah Pennock; sister of Casper Pennock.

LUNDY, Benjamin (1789–1839). Famed abolitionist who founded the paper *Genius of Universal Emancipation,* for which Elizabeth Chandler wrote; wrote biography of Elizabeth Chandler after her death.

LUNDY, Lydia. Sister of Benjamin Lundy; married to Jack Wierman, March 1831.

LUNDY, Richard. Brother of Benjamin Lundy.

LUPON, Debby. Married to Thomas Kites's son.

MAROT (MERRITT), I. *No information located.*

MAROT (MERRITT), Joseph. Bookseller at 87 High Street, resided at 69 Crown Street, Philadelphia; son of Samuel Marot; possibly a friend and/or suitor of Elizabeth Chandler.

MAROT (MERRITT), Samuel. Bookbinder at 69 Crown Street, Philadelphia; father of Joseph Marot.

MARTIN, Robert. *No information located.*

MATHER (MATHOR), Joseph. Merchant at 120 High Street, Philadelphia.

MAXWELL, ———. *No information located.*

McCLELLAN, John. Owned dry goods store at 48 N. Seventh Street, Philadelphia.

McCONKEY, Hugh. *No information located.*

McNEER, ———. *No information located.*

MERREDITH, ———. *No information located.*

MERREFIELD, Amelia Guest. Daughter of John and Mary Merrefield; sister of John, Joseph, Mary, and Sarah Merrefield.

MERREFIELD, Anna Guest.

MERREFIELD, Anna Williams. Married to John Guest Merrefield; mother of George Williams Merrefield; sister of Margaret Williams Hall, George Williams, and Charles Williams.

MERREFIELD, Anna (1836 or 1837–1838). Daughter of John Merrefield and Anna Williams Merrefield.

MERREFIELD, Elizabeth. (d. 1837 or 1838). Sister of John Merrefield.

MERREFIELD, George Williams (1830–39). Son of John Merrefield and Anna Williams Merrefield.

MERREFIELD, John. Owned dry goods store at 425 N. Second Street, Philadelphia; married to Mary Guest Merrefield; father of John Guest Merrefield, Joseph Merrefield, and Mary Merrefield.

MERREFIELD, John Guest. Son of John Merrefield and Mary Guest Merrefield; brother of Amelia, Joseph, Mary, and Sarah Merrefield; married to Anna Williams Merrefield; cousin of William, Thomas, and Elizabeth Chandler.

MERREFIELD, Joseph. Son of John Merrefield and Mary Guest Merrefield; brother of John Guest Merrefield and Mary Merrefield; cousin of William, Thomas, and Elizabeth Chandler.

MERREFIELD, Mary. Daughter of John Merrefield and Mary Guest Merrefield; sister of Amelia, John, Joseph, and Sarah Merrefield.

MERREFIELD, Mary Guest. See GUEST, Mary

MERREFIELD, Sarah Anna (d. 1837 or 1838). Sister of John, Amelia, Joseph, and Mary Merrefield.

MERRITT, Joseph. See MAROT, Joseph

MERRITT, Samuel. See MAROT, Samuel

MORRIS, Anna Rowe. See Rowe, Anna

MORRIS, Caroline. Daughter of Elizabeth Morris; relative of Margaret Evans Chandler, Ruth Evans, Jane Howell, and Amelia Evans; married to Casper Pennock.

MORRIS, Elizabeth (Betsy) (d. 1832). Widow residing at 2 Hyde's Court, Philadelphia; mother of Elizabeth Morris.

MORRIS, Elizabeth. Seamstress at 42 German Street, Philadelphia; daughter of Elizabeth Morris; married to Samuel Canby, July 1832.

MORRIS, Jacob. Merchant at Arch above Sixth Street, Philadelphia.

MORRIS, James. Married to Anna Rowe.

MOTT, Lucretia (1793–1880). Owned free produce store in Philadelphia; Quaker; women's rights advocate and abolitionist.

MOTT, Richard. *No information located.*

NEWKIRK, Garret. New Jersey shopkeeper.

NICHOLSON, Meadows T. Adopted son of James Clibborn; married Amelia Guest Merrefield on March 7, 1838.

NOBLE, Charles. Medical doctor at 258 N. Third Street, Philadelphia.

ORR, Thomas and Euphemia. *No information located.*

PARKER, Ian. *No information located.*

PARKER, Jacob. Shoemaker at 284 Race Street, Philadelphia; married to Jane Parker.

PARKER, Jane. Married to Jacob Parker.

PARRISH, Joseph. Medical doctor in Philadelphia; distant relative of the Chandlers.

PAUL, Elizabeth. *No information located.*

PEIRCE (PIERCE), Hannah. Resided at 54 Arch Street, Philadelphia; friend of Ruth Evans.

PEIRCE, Jonathan (d. 1835). *No information located.*

PEMBERTON, Rebecca. *No information located.*

PENNOCK, Caroline Morris. *See* MORRIS, Caroline

PENNOCK, Dr. Casper. Son of Sarah Pennock; brother of Sarah Pennock Lukens; married Caroline Morris.

PENNOCK, Sarah. Resided at 336 Mulberry Street, Philadelphia; mother of Sarah Pennock Lukens and Casper Pennock.

PHIPPS, Stephen. *No information located.*

PICKERING, Joseph. *No information located.*

PIERCE, Hannah. *See* PEIRCE, Hannah

PITTFIELD, Robert. *No information located.*

PLEASANTS, Mary T. Resided at 14 N. Eleventh Street, Philadelphia.

POULSON, Zachariah. Editor and proprietor of *American Daily Advertiser,* 106 Chesnut Street, Philadelphia.

POULTNEY, Charles. *No information located.*

POULTNEY, Evan. *No information located.*

POWELL (POWEL), John Hare. Resided on Walnut Street, Philadelphia.

RAKESTRAW, Joseph. Printer at Willow above Third Street, resided at 256 N. Third Street, Philadelphia.

RANDOLPH, Julia Ann. Cousin of Anna Coe.

ROBERTS, Ann. Daughter of Jonathan Roberts.

ROBERTS, Hannah. Married to John Roberts.

ROBERTS, John (d. 1842). Married to Hannah Roberts.

ROBERTS, Jonathan (d. 1833). Resided at 150 Coates Street, Philadelphia; father of Ann Roberts.

ROE, Ann. Possibly married to James Roe.

ROE, James. Part owner of Roe and Kay, storekeepers, 186 N. Second Street, Philadelphia; possibly married to Ann Roe.

ROWE (ROSE), Anna (Ann). Bond servant of Lemuel and Jane Howell; married to James Morris.

ROYAL, Mrs. *No information located.*

ROYERS, Eunice. *No information located.*

ROYERS, Euphemia. *No information located.*

RUSH, Benjamin (1746–1813). Prominent early-nineteenth-century Philadelphia physician; signer of the Declaration of Independence; member of Congress.

RUTTER, John. *No information located.*

SAPPINGTON, Dr. *No information located.*

SATTERTHWAITE, Mabel. Daughter of Samuel Satterthwaite and Hannah Atkinson Satterthwaite.

SATTERTHWAITE, Samuel (1790–1862). Married to Hannah Atkinson Satterthwaite; father of seven children; emigrated from New Jersey to Michigan Territory, 1831.

SELTZER, ———. Philadelphia builder.

SHAFFER, ———. Philadelphia butcher.

SHARPLESS, Abraham (Abram) (d. 1835). Co-owner of Sharpless and Drinkers, mantua makers, 56 Mulberry Street, Philadelphia.

SHARPLEY, Joseph. *No information located.*

SHERBURN, ———. *No information located.*

SHOEMAKER, Dr. Nathan. Physician at 210 Chesnut Street, Philadelphia.

SLEEPER, Jonathan. Owned china store at 66 N. Second Street, Philadelphia; father of Martha Sleeper.

SLEEPER, Martha. Second daughter of Jonathan Sleeper.

SMITH, Elizabeth (Betsy). Shopkeeper at 202 Chesnut, Philadelphia; widow of John Smith.

SMITH, Clifford. Merchant at 19 N. Front Street, resided at 205 Spruce Street, Philadelphia.

SMITH, Daniel ("Uncle"). (b. 1785). Married to Sene Smith; father of Laura Smith Haviland; minister in Society of Friends; charter member of the first Society of Friends meeting established in Adrian.

SMITH, Dr. Married to Mary Guest, May 1838.

SMITH, George. At Friends' Asylum for the Insane.

SMITH, Isaac S. *No information located.*

SMITH, John. *No information located.*

SMITH, Joseph. At Friends' Asylum for the Insane.

SMITH, Laura. *See* HAVILAND, Laura Smith

SMITH, Mary Guest. Married to Dr. Smith, May 1838.

SPALDING, Lyman A. *No information located.*

STEER, David. *No information located.*

STEER, Jane. *No information located.*

STOCKDEN, Tom. *No information located.*

STREET, ———. Artist who painted Elizabeth Chandler's portrait.

STYLES, Caroline (1819–1889). Married Jesse E. Barker in 1842; move to a farm in Manchester, Michigan.

SWEET, Hartman. Itinerant bone setter.

TAUNTAIN, A. Owned merchant mill on Brandywine River.

TAYLOR, Ann. Mother of Sarah Taylor Chandler.

TAYLOR, Franklin. Brother of Sarah Taylor Chandler.

TAYLOR, Hannah. Sister of Sarah Taylor Chandler.

TAYLOR, Joseph. Uncle or brother of Sarah Taylor Chandler.

TAYLOR, Lydia. Sister of Sarah Taylor Chandler.

TAYLOR, Maris. Father of Sarah Taylor Chandler.

TAYLOR, Robert. Engaged to Margaretta Hall; first cousin of Robert Coe and James Coe.

TAYLOR, Sarah. *See* CHANDLER, Sarah Taylor

TAYLOR, Susan (d. 1835). Sister of Sarah Taylor Chandler.

TEESE, Rebecca. *No information located.*

TELL, Thomas. *No information located.*

TEMPLE, David. Merchant at 65 N. Second Street, Philadelphia.

TERRY, Eliza. Friend of Anna Coe Jr. and Elizabeth Chandler.

TITUS, Mary. *No information located.*

TITUS, Samuel. *No information located.*

TITUS, Stephen. *No information located.*

TOWNSEND, Hannah. Daughter of John and Hannah Townsend; married Joshua Longstreth, 1832; friend of Elizabeth Chandler.

TOWNSEND, Lucy. Secretary of Ladies' Anti-Slavery Society, West Bromwich, Pennsylvania.

TRAIN, Washington. Married to Rebecca Coe, 1832.

TRESCOTT, Isaac. Sought to publish biography and collected works of Elizabeth Chandler.

TUCKER, Benjamin (d. 1833). Head of Philadelphia Select Academy; resided at 44 N. Fifth Street, Philadelphia; married to Theodocia Tucker.

TUCKER, Joseph. Cousin of John Lovett.

TUCKER, Theodocia. Married to Benjamin Tucker.

TUNIS, Eliza (Elisa) Guest. Sister of Rebecca Guest; widow of Thomas R. Tunis; mother of Richard Tunis, John Tunis, and Rebecca Tunis.

TUNIS, Jane. *No information located.*

TUNIS, John. Son of Eliza Guest Tunis and Thomas Tunis; brother of Richard Tunis and Rebecca Tunis.

TUNIS, Rebecca. Daughter of Eliza Guest Tunis and Thomas Tunis; sister of John Tunis and Richard Tunis.

TUNIS, Richard. Son of Eliza Guest Tunis and Thomas Tunis; brother of John Tunis and Rebecca Tunis.

TUNIS, Thomas (d. before 1831). Married to Eliza Guest; father of John Tunis, Richard Tunis, and Rebecca Tunis.

TUNIS, Tom. *No information located.*

TURNPENNY, Frederick. *No information located.*

TYSON, Martha. Widow with a dry goods store at 92 N. Fourth Street, Philadelphia.

VAUX, Roberts (d. 1836). Resided at 346 Mulberry, Philadelphia; prominent Philadelphia businessman and philanthropist.

VESSEY, ———. *No information located.*

VEZEY, Hezekiah. Tailor at 2 Shield's Court, Philadelphia.

VINSANT, Atty. *No information located.*

VINSANT, Aunt Betsey (d. 1835). *No information located.*

WALKER, Joe. Brother of Lewis Walker.

WALKER, Lewis. Hatter on Market Street, Philadelphia; brother of Joe Walker; married to Mary Walker.

WALKER, Mary. Married to Lewis Walker.

WALTON, Ann. *No information located.*

WARDEN (WARDER?), Jeremiah. *No information located.*

WARDER, Jerre. *No information located.*

WARDER, William. *No information located.*

WARNOCK, Abby. Widow and grocer at 19 N. Eighth Street, Philadelphia.

WARNOCK, John. *No information located.*

WEAVER, George. *No information located.*

WEBB, Dr. Married to Fanny Webb; father of Julia Webb.

WEBB, Fanny. Married to Dr. Webb; mother of Julia Webb.

WEBB, Jane. *No information located.*

WEBB, Julia (b. 1810). Friend of Elizabeth Chandler; married to Joseph Chittenden Jr., September 1832.

WEBSTER, John. Merchant, resided at Wade's Hotel, N. Third Street, Philadelphia.

WELSH, Nancy. Widow residing on S. Twelfth Street, Philadelphia.

WEST, Benjamin (1738–1820). American painter who resided in England.

WHITE, Lydia. Hicksite Quaker; founding member of Philadelphia's Female Anti-Slavery Society; ran a free-produce grocery in Philadelphia

WIERMAN, Jack. Married to Lydia Lundy, March 1831.

WIERMAN, Lydia. *See* LUNDY, Lydia

WILBERFORCE, William (1759–1833). British statesman, abolitionist, philanthropist, and religious writer.

WILLIAMS, ANNA. *See* MERREFIELD, Anna Williams

WILLIAMS, Charles. Owned currying shop at 463 N. Second Street, resided at 457 N. Second Street, Philadelphia; son of Sarah Williams; brother of George Williams, Margaret Williams Hall, and Anna Williams Merrefield.

WILLIAMS, Eliza. *No information located.*

WILLIAMS, George. Owned dry goods store at 459 N. Second Street, Philadelphia; son of Sarah Williams; brother of Charles Williams, Margaret Williams Hall, and Anna Williams Merrefield.

WILLIAMS, Grace. *No information located.*

WILLIAMS, Hannah. *No information located.*

WILLIAMS, John A. Owned dry goods store at 286 N. Second Street, Philadelphia; cousin of Margaret Evans Chandler, Ruth Evans, Jane Evans Howell, and Amelia Evans.

WILLIAMS, Margaret. *See* HALL, Margaret Williams

WILLIAMS, Mary Ann Kirkbride. Sister of Eliza Kirkbride.

WILLIAMS, Samuel (d. 1842). Son of John A. Williams.

WILLIAMS, Sarah. Shopkeeper at 35 S. Second Street, Philadelphia; mother of George Williams, Charles Williams, Margaret Williams Hall, and Anna Williams Merrefield; married to Samuel Fox, 1842.

WILLIS, Jonathan. *No information located.*

WILLIS, N. P. (Nathan, Nat). Literary competitor of Elizabeth Chandler; potential suitor for Anna Coe and Elizabeth Chandler.

WILLITS, John. Bricklayer; father of Rebecca Willits.

WILLITS, Rebecca. Daughter of John Willits.

WILSON, Mary. *No information located.*

WITHERAL (WETHERAL), ————. *No information located.*

WOOD, Charles. *No information located.*

WOODSIDE, Sarah ("Friend"). Mother of Maria Woodside.

WOODSIDE, Maria. Storekeeper at 377 Race Street, Philadelphia; daughter of Sarah Woodside; friend of Elizabeth Chandler.

WOOLEY, Friend. *No information located.*

WOOLMAN, John (1720–72). Traveling Quaker minister and abolitionist.

WRIGHT, Frances. British abolitionist and radical activist.

YARNALL, Patty. *No information located.*

POEMS BY
ELIZABETH CHANDLER

———————

ANTHONY BENEZET

Friend of the Afric! Friend of the oppress'd!
    Thou who wert cradled in a far-off clime,
Where bigotry and tyranny unbless'd,
    With gory hand defaced the page of time;
Wert thou forth driven by their stern control,
    An infant fugitive across the deep,
To teach, in after years, thy pitying soul
    O'er all the Afric's causeless wrongs to weep,
Where slavery's bitter tears the flag of freedom steep?

And thou didst nobly plead for them; thy heart,
    Thrilling to all the holy sympathies,
Of natural brotherhood, wept, to see the mart
    Of commerce, with its human merchandize,
So crowded and polluted, and thy voice,
    With the clear trumpet tones of God's own word,
Rang through the guilty crowd, until no choice
    Was left them but to tremble as they heard,
Or bind with treble seal the feelings thou hadst stirr'd.

The ears of princes heard thee; and the wise,
    Touch'd by the mastery of thy earnestness,
Bade their train'd spirits for a while to rise
    From their profound research, and learn to bless

Thy generous efforts, and with kindred zeal,
    Led on by thee in duty's path to move;
And kindled by thy sacred ardour, feel,
    Like thee, that overflowing gush of love,
That lifts man's selfish heart all narrow thoughts above.

The fetters of the slave are still unbroken;
    But there will come, perchance, ere long, a day,
When by their lips who wrong'd him, shall be spoken
    The fiat of his freedom;—and the ray
Of intellectual light shall radiance pour
    On minds o'er which the gloom of darkness hung
In treble folds impervious before,
    By tyrants' hands around them rudely flung,
To bind the chains that to both limb and spirit clung.

Then shall their children learn to speak thy name,
    With the full heart of gratitude, and know
What thou hast done for them; and while they frame
That history for their infants' ears, may grow
    Perchance, in their own hearts, the likeness strong
Of thy bright virtues; so thou still shalt be,
Even in thy sepulchre, their friend;—and long
    Shall those who love mankind, remember thee,
Thou noble friend of those who pined in slavery.

THE BRANDYWINE*

My foot has climb'd the rocky summit's height,
And in mute rapture, from its lofty brow,
Mine eye is gazing round me with delight,
On all of beautiful, above, below:
The fleecy smoke-wreath upward curling slow,
The silvery waves half hid with bowering green,
That far beneath in gentle murmurs flow,
Or onward dash in foam and sparkling sheen,—
While rocks and forest-boughs hide half the distant scene.

* A beautiful stream, flowing near the author's place of nativity

In sooth, from this bright wilderness 't is sweet
To look through loop-holes form'd by forest boughs,
And view the landscape far beneath the feet,
Where cultivation all its aid bestows,
And o'er the scene an added beauty throws;
The busy harvest group, the distant mill,
The quiet cattle stretch'd in calm repose
The cot, half seen behind the sloping hill,—
All mingled in one scene with most enchanting skill.

The very air that breathes around my cheek,
The summer fragrance of my native hills,
Seems with the voice of other times to speak,
And, while it each unquiet feeling stills,
My pensive soul with hallow'd memories fills:
My fathers' hall is there; their feet have press'd
The flower-gemm'd margin of these gushing rills,
When lightly on the water's dimpled breast,
Their own light bark beside the frail canoe would rest.

The rock was once your dwelling-place, my sires!
Or cavern scoop'd within the green hill's side;
The prowling wolf fled far your beacon fires,
And the kind Indian half your wants supplied;
While round your necks the wampum belt he tied,
He bade you on his lands in peace abide,
Nor dread the wakening of the midnight brand,
Or aught of broken faith to loose the peace-belt's band.

Oh! If there is in beautiful and fair,
A potency to charm, a power to bless;
If bright blue skies and music-breathing air,
And nature in her every varied dress
Of peaceful beauty and wild loveliness,
Can shed across the heart one sunshine ray,
Then others, too, sweet stream, with only less
Than mine own joy, shall gaze, and bear away
Some cherish'd thought of thee for many a coming day.

But yet not utterly obscure thy banks,
Nor all unknown to history's page thy name;

For there wild war hath pour'd his battle ranks,
And stamp'd in characters of blood and flame,
Thine annals in the chronicles of fame.
The wave that ripples on, so calm and still,
Hath trembled at the war-cry's loud acclaim,
The cannon's voice hath roll'd from hill to hill,
And 'midst thy echoing vales the trump hath sounded shrill.

My country's standard waved on yonder height,
Her red cross banner England there display'd
And there the German, who, for foreign fight,
Had left his own domestic hearth, and made
War, with its horrors and its blood, a trade,
Amidst the battle stood; and all the day,
The bursting bomb, the furious cannonade,
The bugle's martial notes, the musket's play,
In mingled uproar wild, resounded far away.

Thick clouds of smoke obscured the clear bright sky,
And hung above them like a funeral pall,
Shrouding both friend and foe, so soon to lie
Like brethren slumbering in one father's hall.
The work of death went on, and when the fall
Of night came onward silently, and shed
A dreary hush, where late was uproar all,
How many a brother's heart in anguish bled
O'er cherish'd ones, who there lay resting with the dead.

Unshrouded and uncoffin'd they were laid
Within the soldier's grave, e'en where they fell;
At noon they proudly trod the field—the spade
At night dug out their resting-place—and well
And calmly did they slumber, though no bell
Peal'd over them its solemn music slow;
The night-winds sung their only dirge, their knell
Was but the owlet's boding cry of woe,
The flap of night-hawk's wing, and murmuring waters' flow.

But it is over now,—the plow hath rased
All trace of where war's wasting hand hath been:
No vestige of the battle may be traced,

Save where the share, in passing o'er the scene,
Turns up some rusted ball; the maize is green
On what was once the death-bed of the brave;
The waters have resumed their wonted sheen,
The wild bird sings in cadence with the wave,
And naught remains to show the sleeping soldier's grave.

A pebble stone that on the war-field lay,
And a wild-rose that blossom'd brightly there,
Were all the relics that I bore away,
To tell that I had trod the scene of war,
When I had turn'd my footsteps homeward far—
These may seem childish things to some; to me
They shall be treasured ones; and, like the star
That guides the sailor o'er the pathless sea,
They shall lead back my thoughts, loved Brandywine, to thee.

CHRISTMAS

Mother, when christmas comes once more,
        I do not wish that you
Should buy sweet things for me again,
        As you were used to do:

The taste of cakes and sugar-plums
        Is pleasant to me yet,
And temptingly the gay shops look,
        With their fresh stores outset.

But I have learn'd, dear mother,
        That the poor and wretched slave
Must toil to win their sweetness,
        From the cradle to the grave.

And when he faints with weariness
        Beneath the torrid sun,
The keen lash urges on his toil,
        Until the day is done.

But when the holy angels' hymn,
    On Judea's plains afar,
Peal'd sweetly on the shepherds' ear,
    'Neath Bethlehem's wondrous star,

They sung of glory to our God,—
    "Peace and good will to men,"—
For Christ, the Saviour of the world,
    Was born amidst them then.

And is it for His glory, men
    Are made to toil,
With weary limbs and breaking hearts,
    Upon another's soil?

That they are taught not of his law,
    To know his holy will,
And that He hates the deed of sin,
    And loves the righteous still?

And is it peace and love to men,
    To bind them with the chain,
And sell them like the beasts that feed
    Upon the grassy plain?

To tear their flesh with scourgings rude,
    And from the aching heart,
The ties to which it fondliest clings,
    For evermore to part?

And 't is because of all this sin, my mother,
    That I shun
To taste the tempting sweets for which
    Such wickedness is done.

If men to men will be unjust, if slavery must be,
Mother, the chain must not be worn; the scourge
    be plied for me.

THE CONSCRIPT'S FAREWELL

Farewell, father;—
I had hoped that I should be
In thine age a staff for thee;
But when years have mark'd thy brow,
When thy step is weak and slow,
When thy hair is thin and white,
And thine eye hath lost its light,
I shall never seek thy side,
And thy faltering footsteps guide.
Where my country's banners fly
Proudly 'neath a distant sky,
To the battle forth I speed,
There to fight and there to bleed;
Not because the foeman's lance
Glitters in the vales of France;
Not because a stranger's mirth
Rises round my father's hearth;
Not at glory's trumpet call,
Nor in freedom's cause to fall;
But because ambitious power
Tears me from my peaceful bower.
Yet amidst the battle strife,
In the closing hours of life,
Think not that my heart shall quail,
Spirit droop, or courage fail.
Where the boldest deed is done,
Where the laurel-wreath is won,
Where the standard eagles fly,
There thy son shall proudly die;
Though, perhaps, no voice may tell
How the nameless conscript fell!
　　　Thy blessing, father.

　　　Farewell, mother;—
It is hard to part from thee,
And my tears are flowing free.
While around thee gloom and night
Quench'd religion's blessed light,
Still thou bad'st my lisping voice

In the evening hymn rejoice;
And my childhood's prayer was said,
Ere thou bless'd my pillow'd head.
Oh, before I leave thee now,
Place thy hand upon my brow,
And with every treasured word,
That my infant ears have heard,
  Bless me, mother.

Farewell, brother;—
Many an hour of boyish glee,
I have pass'd in joy with thee;
If with careless act or tongue
I have ever done thee wrong,
Think upon thy brother's lot,
And be all his faults forgot;
Thou may'st dry our mother's tears,
Soothe our sisters' anxious fear,
Be their shield, their guide, their stay
Throughout many a coming day;
Freely with thy father share
All his secret weight of care;
Be what it were mine to be,
Had I still remain'd with thee,
  And love me, brother.

  Farewell, sisters;—
Yonder is our favourite vine,
You must now its tendrils twine,
And when 'neath its leafy bower,
You are met at evening hour,
Think how oft in by-past days,
There we waked the song of praise,
Till your beaming eyes are wet
With the tears of fond regret;
Then together fondly bend,
And your gentle voices blend.
  Pray for me, sisters.

The Forest Vine

It grew in the old wilderness—The vine
Is linked with thoughts of sunny Italy,
Or the fair hills of France, or the sweet vales
Where flows the Guadalquivir. But this grew
Where, as the sunlight look'd through lacing boughs,
The shadows of the stern, tall, primal wood
Fell round us, and across the silent flood,
That wash'd the deep ravine. The pauseless lapse
Of ages had beheld no change in all
The aspect of that scene; or but such change,
As Time himself had made; the slow decay
Of the old patriarch oaks, and as they fell
And moulder'd on the earth, the silent growth
Of the young sturdy stem, that rear'd itself
To stretch its branches in their former place.
The wild flower stretch'd its tender petals out,
Leading strange brightness to the forest gloom;
The fleet deer toss'd his antlers to the breeze,
Graceful and shy; and when the sun went down,
The tangled thicket rustled to the tread
Of the gaunt wolf—just as in former years.
But the red hunter was no longer there;
And the bright flowers were no more twined to deck
The brow of Indian maid.

   We stood beside
A fallen oak; its aged limbs were spread
Prone to the earth, uptorn by the rude wind,
And perishing on the soil that once had fed
Their giant strength: clinging around its roots
And its decaying trunk, a grape-vine wreathed
Its fresh green foliage, draping the still grave
With its luxuriance—meet garniture
For such a sepulchre! A sepulchre most meet
To wrap the bones of the old forest race!
For we had checked our idle wanderings
To gaze upon the relics of the dead—
The dead of other ages! they who trod
When that fallen tree was fresh in its green prime,—

The earth that it now cumber'd; they who once
In savage freedom bounded through the wild,
And quaff'd the limpid spring, or shot along
The swift canoe upon yon rushing wave,
Or yell'd the fierce and horrid war whoop round,
Or gather'd to the council fire, or sprang
With proud firm step to mingle in the dance,
And vaunt of their own triumphs;—there they lie,
Brittle and time-blanch'd fragments! bones—dry bones!
Prison'd for lingering years beneath the sod,
And now that the strong wind hath torn away
The bars of their dark cell, restored again
To the clear sunshine. It seems strange to think
That those wan relics once were clothed with life—
Breathing and living flesh—and sprang away
O'er the green hills at morning, and at eve,
Return'd again to the low cabin home,
And found its shadows happiness.

    That dust—
Gather some to thee—the keen eye can mark
No difference from that spread widely round—
The common earth we tread upon; yet this
Once help'd to form the garment of a mind
Once wrapp'd a human heart, and thrill'd with all
The emotions of man's nature; love and hate,
Sweet hope and stern revenge—ay, even faith
In an undying world.

    So let them rest!
That faith, erring and dark as it might be,
Was yet not wholly vain. We may not know
Of what the dark grave hideth; but the soul,
Immortal as eternity itself,
Is in the hands of One most merciful.

JOHN WOOLMAN

Meek, humble, sinless as a very child,
     Such wert thou,—and, though unbeheld, I seem
Oft-times to gaze upon thy features mild,
     Thy grave, yet gentle lip, and the soft beam
Of that kind eye, that knew not how to shed
A glance of aught save love, on any human head.

Servant of Jesus! Christian! Not alone
     In name and creed, with practice differing wide,
Thou didst not in thy conduct fear to own
     His self-denying precepts for thy guide,
Stern only to thyself, all others felt
Thy strong rebuke was love, not meant to crush, but melt.

Thou, who didst pour o'er all the human kind
     The gushing fervour of thy sympathy!
E'en the unreasoning brute, fail'd not to find
     A pleader for his happiness in thee.
Thy heart was moved for every breathing thing,
By careless man exposed to needless suffering.

But most the wrongs and sufferings of the slave,
     Stirr'd the deep fountain of thy pitying heart;
And still thy hand was stretch'd to aid and save,
     Until it seem'd that thou hadst taken a part
In their existence, and couldst hold no more
A separate life from them, as thou hadst done before.

How the sweet pathos of thy eloquence,
     Beautiful in its simplicity, went forth
Entreating for them! That this vile offence,
     So unbeseeming of our country's worth,
Might be removed before the threatening cloud,
Thou saw'st o'erhanging it, should burst in storm and blood.

So may thy name be reverenced,—thou wert one
     Of those whose virtues link us to our kind,
By our best sympathies; thy day is done,
     But its twilight lingers still behind,

In thy pure memory; and we bless thee yet,
For the example fair thou hast before us set.

THE KNEELING SLAVE

Pity the negro, lady! her's is not,
Like thine, a blessed and most happy lot!
Thou, shelter'd 'neath a parent's tireless care,
The fondly loved, the theme of many a prayer,
Blessing, and blest, amidst thy circling friends,
Whose love repays the joys thy presence lends,
Tread'st gaily onward, o'er thy path of flowers,
With ceaseless summer lingering round thy bowers.
But her—the outcast of a frowning fate,
Long weary years of servile bondage wait.
Her lot uncheer'd by hope's reviving gale,
The lowest in life's graduated scale—
The few poor hours of bliss that cheer her still,
Uncertain pensioners on a master's will—
'Midst ceaseless toils renew'd from day to day,
She wears in bitter tears her life away.
She is thy sister, woman! shall her cry,
Uncared for, and unheeded, pass thee by?
Wilt thou not weep to see her rank so low,
And seek to raise her from her place of woe?
Or has thy heart grown selfish in its bliss,
That thou shouldst view unmoved a fate like this?

REFLECTIONS ON A THUNDER GUST*

When light'nings flash, and thunders roll,
To God, I will direct my Soul
When sorrows assails my troubled mind,
In God, I can a refuge find.
Preserved by Him, from every snare,
I'll join Him, in Heaven with Angels there;
And after death—in worlds above,

*Written on June 23, 1817, when she was nine years and six months old

If good, I'll live with Him in love.
I [can] depart this life without a sigh,
And after death, I'll soar to regions high
So now, I'll try to keep in Virtues path,
Tho heathens rage; and all the wicked laugh.

SOURCE: Elizabeth Margaret Chandler Collection,
Bentley Library, University of Michigan

SOLILOQUY OF A DUELLIST

They all at length have left me—long I wish'd
While round me with officious care they stood,
To dress this paltry wound, to be alone;
And now I find that solitude is dreadful—
Dreadful to one, upon whose burning soul,
The weight of murder rests! Oh, would to heaven
This day were blotted from the scroll of time:
Or, as indeed it seems, that some wild dream
Had wrapp'd me in its horrid tangled maze.
It is a dream,—it must be,—o'er my brain
Such strange bewildering scenes in memory crowd,
As are not, cannot be reality;
And yet this agony is too intense,
'T would rive the chains of sleep. This stiffen'd arm,
These bandages, and the sharp pain which shoots
Across my burning temples—these are real—
Oh, no—'t is not the phantasy of sleep—
He does lie bleeding, younder, pale and dead;
I, too, am slightly wounded.—Would to heaven
The erring ball, that pierced this guilty arm,
Had found a goal within my guiltier breast,
Ere I had lived to be a murderer—
A hateful murderer, still living on
Beneath the weight, the torment of a curse,
Heavy as that of Cain, the stain of blood
Forever on my conscience, crying out
To heaven for vengeance. Yet my wounded honour
Claim'd, sure, some reparation for the blot
His language on it cast. Could I have lived
Beneath the brand of cowardice, and borne

The sneer and the expression of contempt,
That would have follow'd me from every lip?
He gave the challenge, and could I refuse?
I could not—yet I might—I could—I could—
The offence was mine, and mine is all the guilt.
Why o'er my heated passions could I not
One instant hold the reins of self-control?
One single moment of deliberate thought
And cloudless reason, would have spared me all
This guilt, this agony. The approving smiles
Of peaceful conscience, and mine own respect,
Had balanced well the idle laugh of fools—
And now, what am I now? I dare not think!
The stain of life-blood is upon my soul—
The life-blood of my friend—he was my friend,
And I have kill'd him! Oh, that this dark hour
Of deep remorseful anguish might recall
The moments that have pass'd. My Wife!—my wife!
I cannot meet thee thus. I hate myself—
All whom I have loved, and e'en thou wilt hate me.
Oh! would that I were dead—I will not live
To meet thy tearful eye in sorrow bent
O'er one who once could wake its proudest smile.
I cannot pray—I dare not call on Heaven,
To pardon my offence—before the throne,
Even at the mercy-seat, his bleeding form
Would mock my agony, and drive me thence.
How can I look on those whose hearts my hand
Has made so desolate? His mother's eye
Has often smiled in kindness on my boyhood,
And such has been my gratitude, to wring
The last bright drops of comfort from her heart,
And cloud the evening of her life with woe.
His sisters, in their tears, demand of me
Their loved, their murder'd one—and there he lies,
There lies the fatal instrument, and there
Its fellow lies to tempt me—loaded still;
I dare not think—the future and the past
Are fraught alike with images of horror.
Blood calls for blood, and mine own hand shall pay
The debt of justice. Crime shall wash out crime—

I dare not look into eternity—
Oh, God! Oh, God! Forgive me for this deed!

To Prudence Crandall

Heaven bless thee, noble lady, in thy purpose good and high!
Give knowledge to the thirsting mind, light to the asking eye;
Unseal the intellectual page, for those from whom dark pride,
With tyrant and unholy hands, would fain its treasures hide.

Still bear thou up unyielding 'gainst persecution's shock,
Gentle as woman's self, yet firm, and moveless as a rock;
A thousand spirits yield to thee their gushing sympathies,
The blessing of a thousand hearts around thy pathway lies.

Slave Produce

Eat! they are cakes for a lady's lip,
Rich as the sweets that the wild bees sip;
Mingled viands that nature hath pour'd,
From the plenteous stores of her flowing board,
Bearing no trace of man's cruelty—save
The red life-drops of his human slave.

List thee, lady! And turn aside,
With a loathing heart, from the feast of pride;
For, mix'd with the pleasant sweets it bears,
Is the hidden curse of scalding tears,
Wrung out from woman's bloodshot eye,
By the depth of her deadly agony.

Look! They are robes from a foreign loom,
Delicate, light, as the rose leaf's bloom;
Stainless and pure in their snowy tint,
As the drift unmarked by a footstep's print.
Surely such garment should fitting be,
For woman's softness and purity.

Yet fling them off from thy shrinking limb,
For sighs have render'd their brightness dim;
And many a mother's shriek and groan,
And many a daughter's burning moan,
And many a sob of wild despair,
From woman's heart, is lingering there.

To a Particular Friend

We took sweet counsel together, we went to the
house of the Lord in company. —*Psalms*

We've sat beside the forest stream,
    And watch'd the bright wave rippling by,
Now flashing back the summer beam,
    Then dark'ning like a half-shut eye,
As whispering to the joyous breeze,
Down closer bent the shadowing trees.

Thy hand was clasp'd in mine, my friend,
    And heart to heart was answering then;
Although, perchance, our tones might send
    No echo down the rocky glen—
Or if we spoke, 't was language fraught
With all the others' voiceless thought.

Oh! it was sweet to linger there,
    Beneath a sky so purely blue,
And breathe the gather'd sweets, the air
    Had stolen from flowers it wander'd through—
How could there come a thought of ill
Amidst a scene so calm and still!

But yet, a holier chord than this,
    Around our breasts its power hath twined;
And though, perchance, those hours of bliss
    May fade, like moonlight, from the mind,
Can love aside be careless cast,
O'er which the breath of prayer hath past?

Oh, no! and though not oft we meet,
      Within the house of worship now,—
The hours may come, less calm and sweet
      Than those beneath the greewood bough;
Those hearts may ne'er be wholly riven,
Which side by side have bow'd to Heaven.

POEMS TO
ELIZABETH CHANDLER

———◆———

The following two poems were dated October 29, 1826, and were written by "D. M.," a former teacher of Elizabeth Margaret Chandler. Elizabeth was almost nineteen years old and, based on the words in the poems, it is easy to presume that he had more than platonic admiration for her. The letters in this collection, however, reveal nothing about their relationship.

To my Pupil E. M. Chandler

Oh, had I Shakespeare's soul of fire,
Or pensive Hammond's soothing lyre,
Could I but weave the magic lay
And hearts with pleasing rapture sway;
I'd form a Chaplet for thy brow,
As bright and pure as Dian's snow;—
Within the beauteous wreath I'd bind
The fairest Emblems of the mind:
For brilliant eyes, I would not seek,
Lips breathing balm or pallid cheek;
For tho' these transient charms are thine,
They all in *borrow'd* beauty shine,
And from thy *mind* derive their power
To brighten Friendship's social hour.—
But I would cull, with hermit care,
Each Emblem, elegant and rare,
Which marks the chaste & humble mind,

By *Taste,* and *heav'n*-born *worth, refin'd.*—
A *Heart,* with mild affections fraught.
A *Mind,* with purest morals bought.
A *Judgment* clear, a *Temper* ev'n,
And *Hopes serenely fix'd* on *Heav'n.*

Not *affectation's* pious mood
Which leaves "no leisure to be good";
But pure religion's heav'n felt pow'r,
Smiling on pleasure's harmless hour.—

Yes, *could* I choose from Beauty's bowers,
Love breathing sweets, & fragrant flowers,
I well could form the beauteous prize,
As fair as morning's cloudless skies:
But not to *Flora's* matchless art,
Is giv'n the pow'r to paint *thy Heart:*
Her flowers, in Infant glory drest,
May blush on beauty's throbbing breast,
Mingle their sweets with many a sigh
Bloom thro' their little hour & die;
For Nature's self full soon destroys
These Emblems of our transient joys;
But can these trifles of an hour,
Portray Expressions *magic* pow'r?
Or true to Nature's artless ease,
Describe the modest wish to please?
Or warm with soft compassion glow,
To avert misfortune's falling blow?

The flowers that paint the gay pasture,
Promise like Hope—and disappear;
'Tis Kindred minds alone impart,
The *tribute worthy* of the *Heart.*

To E. M. Chandler

O thou young worshipper at Nature's throne
    Whom she hath blest with that electric spirit
That *genius,* which hath stamped thee for her own

And which her votaries may alone inherit!
Grieve not while gazing on the mountain brow,
     The rocky precipice, or torrent's roar,—
That strange emotions bid thine eye o'erflow,
     And that thy heart in silence doth adore
The glory that is around thee; these are few
     Formed to partake a joy so pure & holy
As is that high and tender Melancholy
     To every *finer* feeling ever true,—
Then Oh! *Repine* not that thy throbbing vein
     Is keenly strung alike to pleasure & to pain.

My *dear, lov'd* girl, May joy thy steps attend,
And may'st thou find in every form a friend;
With care unsullied be thy every thought—
And in thy dreams of bliss *Forget Me Not.*—

SOURCE: Elizabeth Margaret Chandler Collection,
Bentley Library, University of Michigan

ELIZABETH MARGARET CHANDLER'S RECIPE FOR HONEY TEA CAKE

———•◦•———

The following recipe was adapted by William Woys Weaver for modern cooks and equipment. He preceded the recipe with the following paragraph: "This is the old and once well known recipe of Elizabeth Margaret Chandler (1807–34), an abolitionist poet who settled in Tecumseh, Michigan, in 1830. Her fiery poems were published by another well-known abolitionist, Benjamin Lundy. Her honey cake was the toast of abolitionist teas because it did not use molasses, a product of slave labor."

HONEY TEA CAKE

8 tablespoons unsalted butter, at room temperature
1 cup honey
½ cup sour cream
2 eggs
2 cups pastry flour
½ teaspoon baking soda
1 tablespoon cream of tartar

Preheat the oven to 350°F.

Cream the butter and honey together until smooth. Add the sour cream and beat well. Beat the eggs to a froth and combine with the batter. Sift the flour, baking soda, and cream of tartar together three times (to ensure a light cake), then sift this into the batter. Stir well, but do not beat too hard, or the soda will be overactivated before baking. Pour into a well-greased 10-inch square pan and bake for 30 minutes.

NOTE: A 10-inch round cake pan may be used for this recipe. The term *tea cake* meant that it was baked round and cut into eighths. This cake also takes well to elaborately shaped molds.

SOURCES: Dr. C. C. Millers, *Food Value of Honey: Honey Cooking Recipes* (Medina, Ohio: Root, [1910]), 12; William Woys Weaver, *America Eats: Forms of Edible Folk Art* (New York: Harper and Row, 1989), 151.

INVENTORY OF MINNIE C. M. FAY'S HOUSEHOLD EFFECTS, OCTOBER 29, 1935

The following inventory provides an excellent glimpse into life in the Chandler/Evans household based on their material possessions.

Mahogany dresser, wedding gift to Sarah T. Chandler by her father, Elizabeth Merritt
Sewing box on the mahogany dresser, Chandler Family
Small toilet drawer on the mahogany dresser, Chandler Family
Silver cream pitcher, monogram D.E.E. (Daniel and Elizabeth Evans)
Silver butter knife, marked E.M.C.
Pewter: large round "charger" platter, Taylor Family, 1722
Porringer, marked D. F. T., Taylor Family
Dinner plate, Taylor Family
Dishes:
> Large dinner tray (platter), Guest Family
> Fruit dish, green and white, Chandler Family
> Blue and white cake plate, Chandler Family
> Blue and white tea canister, Chandler Family
> Blue and white plate, Chandler Family
> Blue and white bowl, Chandler Family
> Chinese bowl, large, Chandler Family
> Tea cup and saucer, Ann Taylor, married 1804.
> Cream pitcher, white and blue edge, Chandler Family

Two glass bottles, Dr. Thomas Chandler
Three china plates and two saucers, Sarah Chandler's first set
Brass warming pan, Daniel Evans or Dr. Thomas Chandler
Salt cellar, willow ware, Chandler Family
Knife and fork, Sarah T. Chandler's first set
Reddish brown pottery jar, Ann Taylor
Dark brown pottery jar, Ann Taylor
Blue and white Canton platter, Guest Family
Blue and white gravy boat, Ann Taylor
Blue and white willow ware plate, Ann Taylor
Glass candle shade, Chandler Family
Glass oil bottle, Chandler Family
Black wedgewood pitcher, Ann Taylor Family
Framed portrait of Elizabeth Margaret Chandler
Silhouette, Dr. Thomas Chandler
Wine glass, Lois croft, Chandler Family
Six tea matts, Guest Family
Snuf box, Dr. Thomas Chandler
Mortar and pestle, Dr. Thomas Chandler
Two glass bottles, Dr. Thomas Chandler
Pr. knitted stockings, Ann Taylor
Piece of linen sheet marked Ann Taylor
Two towels, Dr. Thomas Chandler
Towel, marked E. E. (Elizabeth Evans)
Pr. linen pillow slips, marked M.E. (Margaret Evans)
Three towels, marked M.E.
Sheet and pr. pillow slips, marked Hannah Taylor
Pr. sheets, marked S.T. (Sarah Taylor)
Table cloth, belonged to Ann Taylor
Table cloth, linen was prepared and spun by Sarah Taylor
Two lunch cloths, made by Sarah T. Chandler
Hexagon pieced and quilted bed spread, Ruth Evans
Striped chintz and quilted bed spread, Ruth Evans
Chintz appliquéd on white, large, marked R. Guest (Rebecca Guest)
Marseilles counterpane, marked Margaret E. Chandler
Afghan, log cabin, made by Sarah Chandler
White wool blanket, marked S. T., made by Phebe M. Taylor
Two white wool blankets, marked P.T., made by Phebe M. Taylor
Brown and white coverlet (pine tree pattern) made by Sarah T. Chandler

SOURCE: Minnie Fay Collection, Bentley Library, University of Michigan, Ann Arbor

NOTES

Introduction

1. Thomas Chandler to Ruth Evans, June 31, September 28, October 23, 1806, May 18, October, November 4, 15, 26, December 1807, Elizabeth Margaret Chandler Collection, Michigan Historical Collections, Bentley Library, University of Michigan, Ann Arbor (hereafter cited as EMC Collection). The first mention of Margaret's death appears in Joseph Parrish's January 4, 1808, condolence letter to Thomas Chandler. Neither the EMC Collection nor the Minnie Fay Collection, Michigan Historical Collections, Bentley Library, University of Michigan, Ann Arbor (hereafter cited as MF Collection), includes a formal notice of Elizabeth Margaret Chandler's birth or Margaret Evans Chandler's death.
2. Typed reminiscence, MF Collection. A survey conducted in November 1810 provides these details. Margaret Evans's letters are not included in this book but can be found in the EMC Collection.
3. Thomas Chandler to Ruth Evans, October 23, 1808, EMC Collection.
4. According to the typed reminiscence, MF Collection, Thomas Chandler "attended the ladies at the Marine Hospital." A silver doorplate engraved "Dr. Thomas Chandler, No. 341 Market Street" was given to Dr. Chandler's great-grandson, Dr. Thomas Evans Chandler, who practiced medicine in Boston almost one hundred years later.
5. Typed reminiscence, MF Collection.
6. *Philadelphia City Directory,* 1806, Clements Library, University of Michigan, Ann Arbor.
7. Ibid. The early letters in the EMC collection, which are not included in this book, refer to the yellow fever plague in Philadelphia.
8. Several events caused this upheaval. The Thirty Years' War in Europe, the Civil War in England, the Plague of 1651–52 (which decimated one-fifth of the

English population), the founding of the republic in 1649, and a demographic shift from rural to urban settings all helped to "create a climate conducive to the spread of political and religious radicalism" (Richard Bailey, *New Light on George Fox and Early Quakerism: The Making and Unmaking of a God* [San Francisco: Mellen Research University Press, 1992], 2).

9. Historian Margaret Bacon points out, however, that at the heart of Quakerism lay a "delicate balance between individual freedom and group authority" (*Mothers of Feminism: The Story of Quaker Women in America* [San Francisco: Harper and Row, 1986], 20).

10. Ibid., 10.

11. Elisabeth Potts Brown and Susan Mosher Stuard, eds., *Witnesses for Change: Quaker Women over Three Centuries* (New Brunswick, N.J.: Rutgers University Press, 1989), 3. Geoffrey Nuttall observed, "There had been certainly nothing previously like equality on this scale" (Bacon, *Mothers,* 7).

12. Christopher Durston, *The Family in the English Revolution* (Oxford: Basil Blackwell, 1989), 25, 26. Phyllis Mack found in her study of Quakers in early modern England that "women were understood at two levels: in a social context, as humble, meek, and subordinate, and at a spiritual level, as immensely powerful" ("Gender and Spirituality in Early English Quakerism, 1650–1665," in *Witnesses,* ed. Brown and Stuard, 38). See also Nancy A. Hewitt, "The Fragmentation of Friends: The Consequences for Quaker Women in Antebellum America," in *Witnesses,* ed. Brown and Stuard, 93.

13. By the 1660s Fox urged all Friends to "establish women's business meetings parallel to the men's meetings on each level." He later used the women's meetings as organizational models when setting up preparative, monthly, quarterly, and yearly meetings. Friends prided themselves on their careful record keeping and, according to Bacon, the women were particularly conscientious (*Mothers,* 21). This record keeping has resulted in vast amounts of material available to historians.

14. Hewitt, "Fragmentation," 93, 94.

15. For more on the Hicksite movement, see Hugh Barbour and J. William Frost, *The Quakers* (New York: Greenwood, 1988); Bacon, *Mothers,* 93, 94.

16. Jane Howell to Elizabeth Chandler, June 13, 1831, EMC Collection.

17. Thomas Chandler to William Chandler, October 10, 1830, Elizabeth Chandler to Jane Howell, December 23, 1830, June 28, 1831, EMC Collection. The Adrian monthly meeting was established on June 20, 1831, when it received its first certificate of removal from the New York monthly meeting. The Adrian meeting opened with two preparative meetings, one in Adrian, the other in Farmington, New York. The first women's minutes were recorded on this date, and the first men's minutes appeared nearly a week earlier, on June 14, 1831. The early Michigan Quaker settlement did not have a yearly meeting of its own. Hicksite meetings, once they were established, fell under the Genesee, New York, yearly

meeting (Ann Burton, *Michigan Quakers: Abstracts of Fifteen Meetings of the Society of Friends, 1831–1960* [Decatur, Mich.: Glyndwr Resources, 1989]).

18. Elizabeth Chandler to Jane Howell, June 20, August 30, 1832, May 25, 1833, EMC Collection. The first Friends church was the Raisin Valley Church, organized in Lenawee County on June 20, 1831. It originally met at the home of Darius Comstock. By 1834 a building had been erected. The proposed meetinghouse was to be forty feet by fifty-six feet, one story high. It was oriented north-south. On the east side, a platform ran the full length of the building, allowing family wagons to discharge their passengers. Two doors opened into the building from the east: the north door provided entrance into the men's meeting, while the south door opened onto the women's portion of the house. In the center of the meetinghouse, running from east to west, was a partition that could be raised and lowered, thus making it possible for men and women Friends to worship together but to conduct their business meetings separately. In its original state, the building served the needs of the area's Friends for forty years. On June 6, 1834, the Adrian monthly meeting approved the establishment of the Raisin Preparative Meeting of Friends, and on September 18, 1834, the Society was established (Merle L. Kerr, *A History of Raisin Township from the Beginning to the Present* [Adrian, Mich.: Lenawee County Historical Society, 1976], 6, 7).

19. Ruth Evans to Jane Howell, October 11, 1833, Elizabeth Chandler to Jane Howell, September 26, 1833, EMC Collection. Quakers used the term *first day* to refer to Sunday and numbered the following days accordingly—*second day* was Monday, *third day* was Tuesday, and so on.

20. Lydia Logue to Ruth Evans, June 31, 1806, EMC Collection. This letter is not included in this book. For a discussion of Quaker women's attitudes toward marriage, see Hewitt, "Feminist Friends," 32.

21. Jane Howell to Elizabeth Chandler, June 13, 1831, June 23, 1833, EMC Collection.

22. Elizabeth Chandler to Anna Rowe, October 29, 1833, EMC Collection.

23. See Robert V. Wells, "Quaker Marriage Patterns in a Colonial Perspective," *William and Mary Quarterly,* 3d. ser., 29 (1972): 421, 434.

24. Hewitt, "Fragmentation," 104; Joan M. Jensen, "Not Only Ours but Others: The Quaker Teaching Daughters of the Mid-Atlantic, 1790–1850," *History of Education Quarterly* 24 (spring 1984): 4, 5.

25. Elizabeth Margaret Chandler, *Essays, Philanthropic and Moral: Principally Relating to the Abolition of Slavery in America* (Philadelphia: Howell, 1836), 8, 9; Chandler, *Poetical Works,* 178.

26. Elizabeth Chandler to Jane Howell, May 5, 1832, EMC Collection.

27. Jensen, "Not Only Ours," 7.

28. Jane Howell to Elizabeth Chandler, June 3, 1832, Elizabeth Chandler to Jane Howell, August 30, 1832, EMC Collection.

29. Jensen, "Not Only Ours," 3, 9, 17, 18.

30. Chandler, *Essays,* 9.

31. Bacon, *Mothers,* 22.

32. Jones, "Elizabeth Margaret Chandler," 14; Lundy, "Memoir," 13.

33. Alma Lutz, *Crusade for Freedom: Women of the Antislavery Movement* (Boston: Beacon, 1968), 4; Thomas E. Drake, *Quakers and Slavery in America* (New Haven: Yale University Press, 1950), 5, 6.

34. Drake, *Quakers and Slavery,* 13, 14; James Brewer Stewart, *Holy Warriors: The Abolitionists and American Slavery* (New York: Hill and Wang, 1976), 23.

35. For discussions of Woolman and Benezet, see Drake, *Quakers and Slavery,* 51, 59; Herbert Aptheker, "The Quakers and Negro Slavery," in *Toward Negro Freedom* (New York: New Century, 1956), 51; Lutz, *Crusade,* 4; Chandler, *Poetical Works,* 51. For Chandler's poems, see appendix 2.

36. Drake, *Quakers and Slavery,* 7, 78.

37. Stewart, *Holy Warriors,* 23.

38. Benjamin Lundy, *The Life, Travels and Opinions of Benjamin Lundy,* comp. Thomas Earle (New York: Kelley, 1971), 16.

39. Walter M. Merrill, *Against the Wind and Tide: A Biography of William Lloyd Garrison* (Cambridge: Harvard University Press, 1963), 30, 31, 37, 38; Drake, *Quakers and Slavery,* 131, 132.

40. *Genius of Universal Emancipation,* February 12, 1830.

41. Merrill, *Against the Wind,* 38, 60–64.

42. Charles S. Sydnor, "Prologue to the End of Slavery," in *The Abolitionists: Means, Ends, and Motivations,* edited by Hugh Hawkins (Lexington, Mass.: D. C. Heath, 1972), 5.

43. Stewart, *Holy Warriors,* 51.

44. Jane Howell to Elizabeth Chandler, September 8, 1830, EMC Collection. Howell apparently had confused Garrison's earlier association as editor of the *Journal of Our Times* with his intention to publish his own new paper, the *Liberator.*

45. Ruth Evans to Jane Howell, May 30, 1831, Jane Howell to Elizabeth Chandler, June 13, 1831, EMC Collection.

46. Jane Howell to Ruth Evans, January 21, 1835, EMC Collection.

47. Nancy Wolloch, *Women and the American Experience* (New York: Knopf, 1984), 4.

48. Benjamin Lundy to Elizabeth Chandler, April 2, 1831, EMC Collection; Chandler, *Poetical Works,* 175, 176.

49. Laura S. Haviland, *A Woman's Life-Work, Labors, and Experiences* (Chicago: Waite, 1881), 32; Maurice Dickson Ndukwu, "Antislavery in Michigan: A Study of Its Origin, Development, and Expression from Territorial Period to 1860" (Ph.D. diss., Michigan State University, 1979), ii, 17; Louis Filler, *The Crusade against Slavery, 1830–1860: The Quaker Dissent from Puritanism* (New York: Harper and Row, 1960), 233; Merton L. Dillon, "Elizabeth Chandler and the Spread of

Antislavery Sentiment to Michigan," *Michigan History* 39 (December 1955); Ruth Evans to Jane Howell, October 22, 1832, EMC Collection. Ndukwu gives both women equal credit (ii); Dillon credits Chandler; and Filler refers to her as a "pioneer feminist" (233).

50. Haviland, *Woman's Life-Work,* 32. The Friends to which Haviland referred were Orthodox. They still constituted the "ruling portion" of the territory and had, as mentioned earlier, all but abandoned the slavery issue to concentrate on the schisms of the period.

51. Drake, *Quakers and Slavery,* 115; Margaret Hope Bacon, "By Moral Force Alone: The Antislavery Women and Nonresistance," in *The Abolitionist Sisterhood: Women's Political Culture in Antebellum America,* ed. Jean Fagan Yellin and John C. Van Horne (Ithaca: Cornell University Press, 1994), 276–81.

52. Drake, *Quakers and Slavery,* 117.

53. Merrill, *Against the Wind,* 56. Between 1817 and 1862 fifty-three free-produce stores existed, mostly in Philadelphia, and at least five of them were run by women. In 1829 Lucretia Mott convinced her husband, James, to switch from selling cotton to selling wool to avoid slave products. Lydia White and Sydney Ann Lewis both opened free-produce stores in Philadelphia, and White's store remained open for sixteen years (Bacon, "By Moral Force," 178).

54. Chandler, *Poetical Works,* 111; Chandler, *Essays,* 28, 50.

55. Elizabeth Chandler to Sarah Chandler, June 28, 1831, EMC Collection.

56. Elizabeth Chandler to Jane Howell, August 1832, October 28, 1833, Jane Howell to Elizabeth Chandler, October 2, 1832, EMC Collection. Chandler's advocacy for free produce included providing recipes that did not use slave-produced sugar. See appendix 4 for a sample recipe.

57. Ndukwu, "Antislavery," 20.

58. Aptheker, "Quakers," 31; Bacon, "By Moral Force," 276–81.

59. Jones, "Elizabeth Margaret Chandler," 121, 122.

60. Chandler, *Poetical Works,* 57, 70, 71.

61. Ibid., 110, 111.

62. Jones, "Elizabeth Margaret Chandler," 111, 126.

63. Sarah Mapps Douglass to Elizabeth Chandler, March 1, 1833, EMC Collection; Chandler, *Poetical Works,* 59; Philip Lapsansky, "Graphic Discord: Abolitionist and Antiabolitionist Images," in *Abolitionist Sisterhood,* ed. Yellin and Van Horne, 205, 206.

64. Jean Fagan Yellin, *Women and Sisters: The Antislavery Feminists in American Culture* (New Haven: Yale University Press, 1989), 14, 31, 32, 41, xviii.

65. Lutz, *Crusade,* 9. A distinction is made here between journalism and fictional writing. Many women were publishing fiction at this time.

66. Chandler, *Essays,* 116.

67. Evidence has shown that women of seventeenth-century England wrote a greater

proportion of published work than ever before, and proportionally more Quaker women used this avenue than did women from any other sect. Hugh Barbour and J. William Frost have calculated that Quakers published more material per head than any other group. There were 650 early Quaker authors, including 82 women, "though only eight percent of the women's tracts were doctrinal" (*The Quakers,* 61). Conversely, Phyllis Mack estimates that between 1650 and 1775, the Quakers included more than 240 female preachers and writers (*Visionary Women: Ecstatic Prophecy in Seventeenth-Century England* [Berkeley: University of California Press, 1992], 38). Because these women's writings were directly related to the religious teachings of early Quakerism, they had an inherent reason for their actions, which could be justified as "following the light" available to each individual. Patricia Crawford observes that "religion sometimes served a woman as her best alibi for incursions into the male domain" (*Women and Religion in England, 1500–1720* [New York: Routledge, 1993], 10).

68. Wolloch, *Women,* 182, 186, 187, 192.

69. Nancy Cott, *The Bonds of Womanhood: "Women's Sphere" in New England, 1780–1835* (New Haven: Yale University Press, 1977), 7, 8; Gerda Lerner, *The Grimké Sisters from South Carolina: Pioneers for Woman's Rights and Abolition* (New York: Schocken, 1971), 1.

70. John Mack Faragher, *Sugar Creek: Life on the Illinois Prairie* (New Haven: Yale University Press, 1986), 53, 54. Faragher has labeled the 1820 Land Act "the single most important piece of land legislation since the original 1785 ordinance." The earlier Land Act of 1796 had "set the minimum purchase price of public lands at two dollars an acre for 640 acres, an initial investment far beyond the financial resources of most pioneers" (Fannie Anderson, *Doctors under Three Flags* [Detroit: Wayne State University Press, 1951], 124).

71. Elizabeth Chandler to William and Sarah Chandler, June 14, 1830, EMC Collection.

72. F. Clever Bald, *Michigan in Four Centuries* (New York: Harper, 1954), 155.

73. Thomas Chandler to William Chandler, February 12, 1830, EMC Collection.

74. Ibid. Elizabeth Chandler's "little work" was undoubtedly submission of an essay or poem to an abolitionist weekly or general annual journal such as the *Atlantic Souvenir,* for which she was being paid. Mary Patrick Jones found that, according to the cost book of Carey and Lea, the Philadelphia publishing house responsible for the *Atlantic Souvenir,* five and a half pages of Chandler's poetry were printed in 1820, for which she received twelve dollars. At other times, the journal paid Chandler in copies of the book—two books for three pages of poetry in 1830, three books for five pages in 1831, and two copies for two pages in 1832. The *Atlantic Souvenir* was a very reputable publication that featured well-known authors such as Washington Irving, Nathaniel Hawthorne, William Cullen Bryant, and later Ralph Waldo Emerson, Edgar Allan Poe, and Henry Wadsworth

Longfellow. The journal adhered to "the highest standards of literary and artistic excellence possible in America" (Jones, "Elizabeth Margaret Chandler—Poet, Essayist, Abolitionist" [Ph.D. diss., University of Toledo, 1981], 17).

75. Thomas Chandler to William Chandler, February 12, 1830, EMC Collection. The coal region was located west of the Allegheny Mountains in northwestern Pennsylvania and northeastern Ohio. See Kenneth E. Lewis's recent study entitled *West to Far Michigan: Settling the Lower Peninsula, 1815–1860* (East Lansing: Michigan State University Press, 2002).

76. Thomas Chandler to William Chandler, February 12, 1830, EMC Collection.

77. Elizabeth Chandler to Sarah Chandler, February 12, 1830, Elizabeth Chandler to William Chandler, June 14, 1830, EMC Collection. The first letter from Elizabeth to Jane Howell in Philadelphia has been lost. The exact date of their departure is unknown, but the collection contains an August 6, 1930, letter from Anna Coe to Elizabeth that mentions that the group was expecting to leave "tomorrow."

78. *Michigan Pioneer Collections* [hereafter cited as *MPC*], 1:222. Elizabeth's letter to Hannah Townsend is not in the collection, but excerpts appeared in Benjamin Lundy, "A Memoir of the Life of Elizabeth Margaret Chandler," in Chandler, *Poetical Works of Elizabeth Margaret Chandler: With a Memoir of Her Life and Character by Benjamin Lundy* (Philadelphia: Howell, 1836), 29–39. Wayne County was first established in 1796 and then reestablished in 1813; Monroe County was established in 1817; Mackinac and Macomb in 1818; Oakland in 1819; and St. Clair in 1820 (*MPC*, 22:483). The name *Lenawee* was derived from the Delaware Indian word *lenno* or perhaps from the Shawnee *lenawai,* meaning "man," and the equivalent of the Chippewa *inimi* (*MPC,* 17:483, 1:221). The River Raisin was named by the French for the abundance of grapes growing along its banks. Indians called it Sturgeon River because of its abundant fish (*MPC,* 17:219).

79. *MPC,* 1:223, 1:229, 2:369, 3:554.

80. Thomas Chandler to Jane Howell, September 8, 1830; Thomas and Elizabeth Chandler to William Chandler, October 10, 1830, Ruth Evans to Jane Howell, April 5, 1831, EMC Collection.

81. Elizabeth Chandler to Jane Howell, December 23, 1830, EMC Collection. A drawer in this red chest held the collection of Chandler letters until 1941.

82. See inventory in appendix 5; Caroline Kirkland, *A New Home—Who'll Follow?,* ed. William S. Osborne (New Haven: College and University Press, 1965), 73, 75, 76, 88–89.

83. This is not unlike today's women's magazines, many of which present ideals that few women ever realize in their homes. Nancy Hewitt found that "religious precepts promoting social duties and condemning finery and display limited the elaboration of domesticity within Quaker households. Even in urban Philadelphia, Lucretia Mott ordered her domestic life so that 'no excess duties,'

including unnecessary stitching or 'ornamental work' on clothes, would take time away from reading, meditation, and community work. Quaker farm women, further removed from the accoutrements of the new domesticity, would have had less time or use for the fancy dress, abundant furnishings, or lavish social entertainments that characterized affluent urbanites and those who sought to emulate them" ("Feminist Friends: Agrarian Quakers and the Emergence of Women's Rights in America," *Feminist Studies* 12 [spring 1986]: 30).

84. Emily Johnston appears incidentally in the correspondence. For example, in her August 1832 letter, Elizabeth wrote, "Emily is about her evening work of getting kindling stuff for the morning fire, feeding chickens, etc." On October 11, 1833, Ruth Evans wrote, "I think [Emily] is a fine sensible little girl. She is very forward in her learning under Elizabeth's tuition. I think I never knew a child of her age to read better." Johnston's exact age is unknown, but she was not an orphan: Ruth, Elizabeth, and Jane Howell mentioned Emily's mother and sister in subsequent letters. Emily remained with Thomas in Michigan after both Elizabeth and Ruth died but returned to Philadelphia in 1838 and never went back to Michigan.

85. Benjamin Lundy to Elizabeth Chandler, April 2, 1831, EMC Collection.

86. Nancy Grey Osterud, *Bonds of Community: The Lives of Farm Women in Nineteenth-Century New York* (Ithaca: Cornell University Press, 1991), 9, 11.

87. John Mack Faragher, *Women and Men on the Overland Trail* (New Haven: Yale University Press, 1979), 66; Sandra Myres, *Westering Women and the Frontier Experience, 1800–1915* (Albuquerque: University New Mexico Press, 1982), 7, 11; Elizabeth Chandler to Jane Howell, December 23, 1830, EMC Collection.

88. Hewitt, "Feminist Friends," 32.

89. Jane Howell to Ruth Evans, October 10, 1830, EMC Collection.

90. Ruth Evans to Jane Howell, February 5, 1831, EMC Collection. Myres observed that "domestic manufacture continued on the Western frontiers for many years after it had ceased in the East" (*Westering Women,* 240).

91. Jane Howell to Elizabeth Chandler, April 4, 1831, EMC Collection.

92. Elizabeth Chandler to Jane Howell, April 15, 1831, March 27, 1832, EMC Collection.

93. Elizabeth Chandler to Ruth Evans, May 5, 1832, Elizabeth Chandler to Jane Howell, August 1832, EMC Collection.

94. Ruth Evans to Jane Howell, October 11, 1833, EMC Collection.

95. Osterud, *Bonds,* 283, 284.

96. Elizabeth Hampsten, *Read This Only to Yourself: The Private Writings of Midwestern Women, 1880–1910* (Bloomington: Indiana University Press, 1982); Annette Kolodny, *The Land before Her: Fantasy and Experience of the American Frontiers, 1630–1860* (Chapel Hill: University of North Carolina Press, 1984), 13, 147; C. Kirkland, *A New Home,* 92.

97. Elizabeth Chandler to Jane Howell, April 15, 1831, May 5, August 30, December 22, 1832, August 24, 1833, March 9, 1834; Ruth Evans to Jane Howell, May 30, 1831; Elizabeth Chandler to Sarah Chandler, June 28, 1831, EMC Collection.

98. Elizabeth Chandler to Jane Howell, March 27, May 5, June 20, 1832, EMC Collection. Quakers frequently used silk in their clothing and bedding because it was not a product of slave labor.

99. Elizabeth Chandler to Jane Howell, April 15, 1831, February 12, March 27, August, December 22, 1832, May 25, December 22, 1833; Ruth Evans to Jane Howell, May 30, 1831; Elizabeth Chandler to Sarah Chandler, June 28, 1831, EMC Collection.

100. Elizabeth Chandler to Jane Howell, April 24, 1833, EMC Collection.

101. Elizabeth Chandler to Jane Howell, March 9, 1834, EMC Collection.

102. Elizabeth Chandler to Jane Howell, August 1832, April 24, May 28, 1834, EMC Collection.

103. C. Kirkland, *A New Home,* 104; Faragher on Turner, *Sugar Creek,* 130.

104. C. Kirkland, *A New Home,* 154; Hampsten, *Read This,* 40; Myres, *Westering Women,* 168; Karen V. Hansen, *A Very Social Time: Crafting Community in Antebellum New England* (Berkeley: University of California Press, 1994), 173.

105. Elizabeth Chandler to Jane Howell, December 23, 1830, EMC Collection.

106. Jane Howell to Ruth Evans, October 10, 22, December 30, 1830, EMC Collection.

107. Elizabeth Chandler to Jane Howell, February 12, 1832, EMC Collection.

108. Elizabeth Chandler to Jane Howell, May 5, 1832; June 20, 1832; September 26, 1833, EMC Collection.

109. Elizabeth Chandler to Jane Howell, March 27, 1832, EMC Collection. Hansen states that "the sheer volume of visitors filtering in and out of everyday routines astounds the twentieth-century reader" (*Very Social Time,* 79).

110. Elizabeth Chandler to Jane Howell, April 15, 1831, May 25, 1833, January 27, 1834, EMC Collection.

111. James H. Cassedy, *Medicine in America: A Short History* (Baltimore: Johns Hopkins University Press, 1991), 29; Faragher, 91.

112. Jack Larkin, *The Reshaping of Everyday Life: 1790–1840* (New York: Harper and Row, 1988), 84; C. B. Burr, ed., *Medical History of Michigan* (Minneapolis: Bruce, 1930), 1:198.

113. Burr, *Medical History,* 1:696.

114. Ibid.

115. Jane Howell to Ruth Evans, October 28, 1834, EMC Collection; Lundy, "Memoir," 4.

116. Robley Dunglison, *A Dictionary of Medical Science* (Philadelphia: Lea Brothers and Co., 1903).

117. Burr, *Medical History,* 1:123, 681.
118. Ruth Evans to Jane Howell, September 29, 1834; Jane Howell to Ruth Evans, January 14, 1836, EMC Collection; Dunglison, *A Dictionary of Medical Science.*
119. Chandler, *Poetical Works,* 116.
120. Transcript of speech by Minnie Fay, MF Collection.

Chapter 1. Preparing to Remove, 1830

1. The letters mentioned in this paragraph are not in the collection.
2. It is not clear what Elizabeth was working on or what she expected to get paid, but she contributed to many publications and received remuneration for her work.
3. Western Pennsylvania is rich in both anthracite and bituminous coal. The coal region lies west of the Allegheny Mountains.
4. William's current occupation was tavern keeping.
5. The Society of Friends Meeting at which Thomas was a member would "release" his membership to a Michigan meeting.
6. Penn Hill was the area where William and Sarah lived, so named because it was part of William Penn's original holdings.
7. Sarah and Elizabeth never met.
8. The *Buffaloe Gazette* provided migration and shipping information for many people considering the move to the West.
9. The Welland Canal opened in November 1829 and connected Lake Ontario at Port Dalhousie to Lake Erie at Port Calborne. The Chesapeake and Ohio Canal was never completed. Many canals were projected across Michigan, but none was completed.
10. Elizabeth was probably referring to Lenawee County but had apparently misheard its name and had not yet seen it in writing.
11. Possibly a reference to Sand Lake.
12. Exodus 22: "I have been a stranger in a strange land."
13. William's trade was carpentry.
14. The Chandler relatives lived in Centreville, Delaware, along the Brandywine River, and the area was called the Brandywine Valley or Brandywine.

Chapter 2. Arrival and Adjustment, 1830

1. Old Hundredth refers to the hymn "Praise God from Whom All Blessings Flow."
2. Sugar that was not cultivated or harvested by slaves. The alternatives to sugarcane, which used slave labor, were molasses and maple sugar.

3. Cherry Street Meeting was the Quaker meetinghouse where the Philadelphia Ladies' Anti-Slavery Society met.

4. Elizabeth's letter is not in the collection.

5. In 1829, the *Genius of Universal Emancipation,* published by Benjamin Lundy, was a weekly eight-page paper. It later changed to a monthly. Elizabeth Margaret Chandler was the editor of the publication's Ladies' Repository and wrote almost all the entries in that section.

6. A mantua maker manufactured plain-weave heavy silk fabric that was generally used for dresses but also utilized as a furnishing material.

7. Fire was a common sight in the city. Philadelphia's fire-fighting practices and precautions date back to the late 1600s. Households were required under penalty of law to keep ready a swab twelve to fourteen feet long and a bucket or a pail. In 1803 the Philadelphia Hose Company was organized, and it built the first hose carriage in the United States. The hose company worked with the Philadelphia Engine Company to erect a building to house the hose carriage. The Fire Association of Philadelphia was established in 1813, with a number of hose and engine companies and a governing board. In 1818 the association entered the insurance business.

8. Named for the Reverend Gregory T. Bedell, Bedell's lecture room was located in St. Andrew's Church at 152 South Ninth Street. A magic lantern was a lantern slide projector.

9. The Lyceum movement, named for the place where Aristotle lectured to the youth of ancient Greece, was an early form of organized adult education that had widespread popular appeal in the northeastern and midwestern United States. These voluntary local associations gave people an opportunity to hear debates and lectures on topics of current interest, especially the natural sciences. American lyceums multiplied rapidly after the establishment of the first such institution in 1826, and by 1834 the United States boasted three thousand of these societies. By 1840, lyceums had become professionalized, paying a fee for well-known speakers. The Franklin Institute was organized in 1824 to form a "library of books relating to science and the useful arts" and to open a reading room. The institute contained complete sets of patent office publications from around the world, promoted the study of scientific and technical subjects, and offered lectures. The institute expanded into the areas of mechanical and architectural drawing and finally into "all the useful branches of English literature and the ancient and modern languages" (Joseph Jackson, *Encyclopedia of Philadelphia* [Harrisburg, [Pa.?]: National Historical Association, 1931–33], 689, 690).

10. The carousel was a merry-go-round at South Street above Seventh. The melodeon is a small reed organ or type of accordion.

11. Probably the same Betsy who worked for Elizabeth's father in Brandywine at the time Elizabeth was born. Betsy attended Elizabeth's mother during her illness and

remained in the household after her death. She did not move to Philadelphia in 1810 when Thomas left Brandywine but remained with the other Chandlers and lived to an old age.

12. Rebecca Hall and James Coe married on September 27, 1830 (see Jane Howell to Elizabeth Chandler, September 8, 1830).

13. The first letter from Elizabeth to her aunt, Jane Howell, which described the trip in great detail, is not in the collection. Elizabeth also wrote several letters to her friend, Hannah Townsend, that are not in the collection. However, Hannah shared her letters with Benjamin Lundy, who included excerpts in "Memoir." This letter is presented here out of strict chronological order because the events it describes took place before the next two letters were written.

14. The governor of Michigan at this time was Lewis Cass. The house Governor Cass occupied was located near the banks of the Detroit River on the north side of Larned, between First and Second Streets. It is believed by some to have been built in 1703, and it was demolished in 1882. It was forty feet long and twenty-four feet wide and built of oak (Silas Farmer, *The History of Detroit and Michigan* [Detroit: Farmer, 1884], 367, 368).

15. Named after the famous Native American chief, Tecumseh was located approximately fifty miles southwest of Detroit and ten miles northeast of Adrian. On March 4, 1824, the village of Tecumseh became the first private land purchased in Lenawee County. During the summer of 1824, 6,320 acres of land were entered in the township. In the 1830 census, Tecumseh, including several townships west to Lake Michigan, numbered 771 sections. Tecumseh served as the Lenawee County seat until 1836, when it was moved to Adrian, which was more centrally located. Harriet Martineau traveled in Michigan in the 1830s and reported, "We reached Tecumseh by half-past nine, and perceived that its characteristic was chair making. Every other house seemed to be a chair manufactory. . . . At Tecumseh, I saw the first strawberries of the season. All that I tasted in Michigan, of prairie growth, were superior to those of the west, grown in Gardens" ("Travels in Michigan," *Michigan History* 7 [January–April 1923]: 54).

16. The stage followed the route alternately known as the Michigan Road and the Chicago Road (now U.S. Route 12), and it would have crossed the Rouge River at what is now Michigan Avenue in Dearborn, approximately ten miles southwest of the port at Detroit.

17. The process of building a road required that trees and underbrush be cut. However, it was not always possible to remove the roots of larger trees, which meant that travelers risked broken legs for horses and broken carriage wheels. Furthermore, low places held rainwater, becoming permanent swamps and marshes. Road builders (usually private individuals who built roads on their land without government help) solved these problems by cutting down trees with fairly straight trunks six to eight inches in diameter, trimming off the branches,

and laying the trunks crosswise in the road. The ribbed surface suggested the name *corduroy road.*

18. Thomas also described these oak openings in his October 10, 1830, letter to William Chandler. Martineau concurred with the Chandlers' reactions: "We fairly entered the 'rolling country' today: and nothing could be brighter and more flourishing than it looked. . . . The copses, called 'oak-openings,' looked fresh after the passing thunder showers; and so did the rising grounds, strewed with wild flowers and strawberries. . . . The ponds gleaming between the hills and copses, gave a park-like air to the scenery. The settlers leave trees in their clearings; and from these come the song of wood-thrush; and from the dells the cry of the quail. There seemed to be a gay wood-pecker to every tree" ("Travels," 55).

19. The Chandlers and Howells used both the U.S. Postal service and Lovett to carry mail between Philadelphia and Michigan, although it is unclear whether they paid him for his services.

20. Isaiah 58:6: "Is not this the fast that I have chosen? to loose the bands of wickedness, to undo the heavy burdens, and to let the oppressed go free, and that ye break every yoke?"

21. Philadelphians visited the New Jersey shore because sea breezes were thought to improve health.

22. Inflammation of the brain, or phrenitis, is a sudden attack of pains in the back of the neck shooting into the head; violent throbbing in the arteries of the neck and temples; redness about the face and eyes; incapability of bearing light or noise; confusion; and nausea. The suffering is so bad that "with any thing he can lay hold of, [the patient] attempts to destroy his life" (Daniel H. Whitney, *The Family Physician and Guide to Health* [Pen-Yan, N.Y.: Gilbert, 1833], 48). This seems to describe a migraine headache.

23. A morocco dresser prepared leather that would be used to cover furniture and line carriages as well as for shoes. It was often embossed with designs.

24. The *Journal of Health* was one of many nineteenth-century health-related publications available to general readers.

25. Thomas Chandler's dog, left behind with Lemuel and Jane Howell.

26. It is not clear why grapes would have been considered useful in this case since they were often thought to be the cause of a gastrointestinal illness.

27. Muslin is a fine cotton textile first made in India in the 1600s and later in England and Scotland. It could be plain, woven in stripes, or printed with flowers and designs. Calico cloth of many grades and varieties was first made in India and later in the West. It is made of cotton but resembles linen. The name comes from Calicut, the first place the Portuguese landed when they discovered the Indian trade. Calicoes can be plain, printed, stained, dyed, chintz, or muslins. Nineteenth-century canton was available in three different ways. Canton crape was highly finished fabric made with fine silk or cotton warp and heavier filling,

forming light cross ribs. It was heaver than crepe de chine, came in plain colors, and was used as dress material. Canton flannel was a twilled soft cotton fabric with a long nap that could be bleached, unbleached, or piece dyed in plain colors. It was used for sleeping garments, linings, overcoat pockets, household purposes, and diapers. Canton linen, commonly called grass cloth, was a fine, translucent plain-weave fabric made of ramie (china grass), which looks like linen. It was either bleached or dyed blue and was sold in oriental shops for lunch cloths, doilies, and blouses (Florence M. Montgomery, *Textiles in America, 1650–1870* [New York: Norton, 1984], 184, 189).

28. Little Miss was Elizabeth's doll, for which Elizabeth had made clothes. It may have been porcelain or pasteboard. Ruth's stove was probably a wood-burning cookstove that she could not take with her to Michigan. The cast-iron cookstove appeared in the kitchens of prosperous urban homes by the 1820s but did not become a regular item in middling city families until approximately two decades later. When such stoves first came into use, people suspected that they might cause sickness, and women had to learn completely new ways of gauging temperature and cooking times. The cookstove's even heat and waist height (which meant that women did not have to stoop over the fire) eventually convinced women of its value. Jane probably sold both items in her store.

29. The Revolution of 1830 in France involved a Liberal and republican protest against King Charles X's July Ordinances, which had established a rigid government control of the press, dissolved the legislature, and changed the electoral system in an attempt to insure an Ultra party majority. The protesters erected barricades and took over Paris's Hotel de Ville on July 29. The Marquis de Lafayette headed the radical movement, which aimed to make him president of a French republic. The Liberal deputies then turned to Louis Philippe, duke of Orléans, as the savior of the cause of constitutional monarchy. On August 7, he was offered the lieutenant-generalship of the realm, was accepted by Lafayette on behalf of radical Paris, and was proclaimed king of France by the Liberals sitting as a rump legislature. Louis Philippe reigned as the July monarch through 1848.

30. The ten-mile trip from Adrian to Tecumseh probably followed what is now Michigan Route 52 north to U.S. Highway 12, then east.

31. Lemuel Howell was a carpenter and a builder.

32. Before passenger pigeons were hunted to extinction during the nineteenth century, huge flocks flying overhead would darken the sky.

33. The Pontiac and Detroit Rail Road Company was chartered in 1830 but never progressed.

34. Thomas originally addressed the letter to his brother, William, but crossed that out and instead sent the letter to Lemuel Howell.

35. The hewn-log house differed from the round-log cabin, which was intended for use as a temporary shelter. The hewn-log house required many specialized tools

and was not simple to build. It is unlikely that Thomas had all the tools required to construct his house. Although he undoubtedly owned the axes, hatchets, saws, hammers, wedges, and so forth that he would have needed for regular farming activities, the more specialized tools would have likely been owned by the carpenter he hired to help him. In early-nineteenth-century rural areas, a variety of craftsmen also had farms. The practice of work and skill exchange was prevalent, and people often lent each other tools and implements. The Chandler log house was probably built of white oak. Any boards that were required were probably sawed at Darius Comstock's mill. For a thorough description of the tools pioneers used in building their log house, see Warren E. Roberts, "The Tools Used in Building Log Houses in Indiana," *Pioneer America* 9 (July 1977): 32–61. Martineau commented on the log houses she saw on her Michigan travels: "The log houses,—always comfortable when well made, being easily kept clean, cool in summer, and warm in winter,—have here an air of beauty about them. The hue always harmonizes well with the soil and vegetation. Those in Michigan have the bark left on, and the corners sawn off close; and are thus both picturesque and neat" ("Travels," 53).

36. A common variety of corn grown on Midwestern farms in the nineteenth century was yellow dent, which grew to ten to twelve feet tall. It would have been used primarily as feed for livestock, but when cooked in lye and water until soft, it could be made into hominy for human consumption.

37. Ypsilanti, in Washtenaw County, Michigan, was settled a few years before Tecumseh and Adrian. *Old* was a relative term. Ypsilanti lies approximately twenty-five miles northeast of Adrian. Thomas referred to the Erie Canal as the New York Canal because two other major canals were in the process of being built, the Pennsylvania Canal and the Chesapeake and Ohio Canal, although neither was ever completed.

38. The phrase "who waited on them" refers to the practice at Quaker weddings in which the meeting appointed a custodian responsible for reading the certificate at the time of the wedding and seeing that it was properly signed by the witnesses, sometimes in great numbers, as well as the groom and bride. The custodian then recorded this information in books designed for that purpose.

39. Tar was thought to prevent or cure several ailments and diseases. Many Philadelphians carried tarred ropes on their persons to ward off disease. A tar plaster or ointment would have been applied to a specific area of the body.

40. Elizabeth's letter, which is not in the collection, and Thomas's September 8, 1830, letter.

41. Lemuel Howell's dog.

42. John F. Watson, *The Annals of Philadelphia and Pennsylvania in the Olden Time: or, Memoirs, Anecdotes, and Incidents of Philadelphia and Its Inhabitants from the Days of the Founders,* ed. Willis P. Hazard (1830; Philadelphia: Stuart, 1884). Many revi-

sions and updates of this book were published throughout the nineteenth century.

43. Elizabeth Chandler's poem "Brandywine" (see appendix 2) appeared in an annual gift book, *The Atlantic Souvenir* (Philadelphia: Carey and Lea, 1830). First published in 1825, the *Atlantic Souvenir* contained short stories, essays, and poems by various writers. The books were printed on high-quality paper with specially designed bindings, sometimes of stamped or embossed leather, then encased in decorated cardboard slipcases. The first edition sold well, and other publishers created dozens of different versions of these books, which became annual publications that sold for an average of $3.50 (compared to 37.5 cents for a paper-covered novel and $1.25 for a hardback book) and generated huge profits. The contributing writers and artists were sometimes highly paid. Elizabeth's writings appeared frequently in these gift books, and she shared notoriety with such distinguished authors as Nathaniel Hawthorne and John Greenleaf Whittier.

44. The red chest over which Rush's portrait hung contained the letters in this collection, and the chest and its contents were handed down through the family.

45. A dressing table on which items for personal grooming were placed.

46. In Philadelphia, a night watchman carrying a lantern, a rattle, and a club would walk through each district of the city, calling out the hour and a brief report, such as "Ten o'clock and all's well." If something alarming occurred or he needed assistance, he would spring his rattle; the other watchmen would then spring their rattles and come to his aid. The result could be quite a racket.

47. Elizabeth's letter is not in the collection.

48. Studies on marriage during this period have indicated that, especially among Quakers, the number of available men declined. A sharp rise in male migration to the frontier could have been one of the causes, thus reducing women's marriage opportunities.

49. A proliferation of advice manuals such as farmer's almanacs were available in the late eighteenth and early nineteenth centuries.

50. In late 1830, protests and agitation among workers arose throughout Europe. Revolutions in Italy and Poland followed the French protests in July, and a rapid spread of secret societies and workers' insurrections created fear of a large-scale war, which never materialized.

CHAPTER 3. SETTLING IN, 1831

1. Almost two hundred years later, it would probably be difficult to notice the difference between the dress of the "Yorkers" and the dress of the Philadelphia Quakers. According to Elisabeth McClellen, *History of American Costume, 1607–1870* [New York: Tudor, 1937], "Only one to the persuasion born could master the subtle differences in the garb of the two factions, the Orthodox and

Hicksite Friends" (530). For a definitive study of Quaker dress, see Amelia Gummere, *The Quaker: A Study in Costume* (Philadelphia: Ferris and Leach, 1901).

2. Each lot was eighty acres. The federal Land Act of 1820 provided that minimum parcels of eighty acres could be purchased from the government for cash at $1.25 per acre.

3. The *Saturday Evening Post,* a weekly periodical published in Philadelphia.

4. The United States had established a decimal currency in 1793, but many rural Americans through the 1820s and early 1830s continued to figure prices and wages in terms of English pounds, shillings, and pence, translating amounts into American dollars and cents when the time came to pay for something.

5. Ague was a malarial disease accompanied by fever and chills that lowered the body's resistance, leaving the victim at risk of contracting more life-threatening maladies such as typhoid, consumption (tuberculosis), and pneumonia. Ague was transmitted by anopheles mosquitoes, which were especially prevalent in the swampy areas of Michigan during this period, although medical authorities did not recognize mosquitoes as carriers until the end of the century.

6. Scarlet fever was an acute and dreaded contagious disease characterized by inflammation of the nose, throat, and mouth; generalized toxemia; and a red rash. There was no known cure or preventative in 1831.

7. Watson wrote, "The old fashioned snow storm . . . of the 20th and 21st of February, 1829, [was] far eclipsed by 'the deep snow' of the 14th and 15th of January, 1831. It was really cheering and delightful, to rise in the snow-stillness of the Sunday morning of the 16th January when 'Earth robed in white, a peaceful Sabbath held—' in a double sense,—to witness such towering pyramids and deeply piled banks of glistening snow, all resting after the subsidence of the storm, in calm repose. It cheered the men of olden days, to be thus able to show to the young of the rising generation, the unexpected, and welcome living picture of scenes oft told, but difficult to be conceived, or credited by those youngsters who had never seen them. Hardly expecting to see such another storm, in *my* future life, I determined, at the time, to preserve sundry notices of its effect, &c. throughout the country, not *now* needful to relate. It laid upon the country, and was used upon the roads till the middle of February, actually exhausting all the pleasures of sleighing by its long continuance" (*Annals* [Philadelphia: Stuart, 1884], 2:368).

8. The person who carried Jane's mail to Michigan, possibly John Rutter of Westchester, who is mentioned in Jane's next letter.

9. Asylum was used to refer to any institution that cared for the blind, the insane, orphans, etc. The Society of Friends maintained several such institutions that were open to members and non-members alike.

10. "To a Particular Friend," which appeared in the *Genius of Universal Emancipation* in the February 1831 issue and is reprinted in appendix 2.

11. Because Elizabeth's letter to Hannah has not survived, it is not known exactly what Jane found unsatisfactory. However, Benjamin Lundy included an excerpt in his posthumous tribute to Elizabeth that reflects Elizabeth's self-effacing attitude toward her antislavery activities, which Jane, who regarded her niece so highly, might not have liked. Elizabeth wrote to Hannah about the Female Anti-Slavery Society in Philadelphia, "Oh how often I wish I might be with you in your gatherings! Not because I think I could be of much service, for there are many and far more useful members than myself to attend to the business, but it is natural to wish to participate in what we feel interested about. . . . I will not be discouraged, if you will hold on to your principles, and persevere in your efforts. . . . I feel exceedingly interested for this society, and cannot ever *think* without pain, of its sinking into inertness. But do not think that I *fear* for it, . . . though . . . there is enough, it must be confessed, to make the heart of any one falter sometimes, when looking at all the various difficulties that are to be overcome before our object can be attained. . . . There are times when I feel as if I could go unflinching to the stake or the rack, if I might by that means advance it. I never expected to do 'great things' in this cause—I have never indulged in speculations as to the effect of what I attempted to do, yet I sometimes feel as if I had been a mere idle dreamer, as if I had wasted my time in nothingness—so disproportioned does the magnitude of the cause appear to all that I have done; so like a drop in the ocean are my puny efforts. I am not discouraged by these feelings, because I hope that I have been, and still maybe, in some degree, useful; but I much often feel disposed to censure myself for want of sufficient exertion and interest, than to indulge in self-complacency" (Lundy, "Memoir," 39).

12. A total eclipse of the sun occurred on February 12, 1831, and was visible as far north as New England and as far south as Georgia.

13. According to the *Annals of Philadelphia,* lotteries in early Philadelphia constituted "the frequently adopted measures of raising ways and means . . . they were then fairly conducted, had public benefit in design, and tickets were generally vended by disinterested citizens without reward. . . . The earliest mention of a lottery in Philadelphia occurs in 1720 when Charles Reed advertised 'to sell his brick house in Third Street by lottery.'" The legislature eventually attempted to regulate lotteries; however, according to the *Annals,* "The history of lotteries, since our independence and self-government, and its lately pervading evil in all our cities, is too notorious and too generally lamented by the prudent and considerate, to need any further notice in this connexion. In the hands of the wily *traffickers* in these unstable wares, legal enactments have been but 'ropes of sand,' without power to fetter them." Furthermore, "By an act of the Legislature lotteries were entirely prohibited in this State. Still, tickets for lotteries in other states are clandestinely sold, and they are only still maintained by churches and religious associations!" (Watson, *Annals,* 2:444–45, 3:483). The city council made the lottery trade pub-

lic in 1748. In 1776 the Continental Congress voted to establish a national lottery to raise funds for the American Revolution, though the scheme was abandoned. Over the years the practice of holding smaller public lotteries was seen as a mechanism for obtaining "voluntary taxes" and helped build several American institutions of higher education, including Harvard, Dartmouth, Yale, King's College (now Columbia University), William and Mary, Union College, and Brown. Privately organized lotteries were also common as means to sell products or properties for more money than could be obtained from a regular sale. By 1831, 420 lotteries had been held in eight states. However, while this method of fundraising became very popular with city departments and with churches and schools, it was never without its detractors or opponents, especially the Society of Friends (Watson, *Annals,* 3:485).

14. Lundy was born in Sussex County, New Jersey, and considered it his home, although he was constantly on the move. His wife and two daughters lived in Tennessee, where his wife died in 1826 while he was on a trip to Haiti. Upon his return, he scattered his children among friends and renewed his vow to devote his energies abolishing slavery (Lundy, *Benjamin Lundy*).

15. The elegy for Richard Allen could not be located in the *Genius.*

16. The 1830 issue of the *Album,* an annual literary anthology first issued in New York in 1824.

17. The Arctic Boreas was the North Wind personified. Boreas was the Greek god of the North wind.

18. In December 1829, President Andrew Jackson requested that Congress appropriate federal funds to move southeastern Native Americans west of the Mississippi River. The president offered two rationales for the removal: (1) to have an independent Native American nation residing within the borders of any state was intolerable; and (2) for their own survival, southeastern Indians had to move away from white encroachment. Under the guise of concern for the natives' welfare, Jackson argued that if they remained east of the Mississippi, they would soon become extinct as whites invaded the land and destroyed the Native American life and culture. Intense public opposition to this proposal sprung up immediately. Massive petition drives were organized, calling on Congress to defeat removal and uphold native property rights. The measure was passed by a much narrower margin than Jackson had anticipated. Though the forces of opposition did not succeed, they did make an impact. In March 1831, in *Cherokee Nation v. Georgia,* the Supreme Court ruled that the laws of the state could have no force over the Cherokee because they were protected by federal treaties that gave them full rights to their lands. Opponents of removal were encouraged, though the Court also acknowledged that the Cherokee's legal status remained outside the Court's jurisdiction. For a comprehensive discussion of this subject, see Mary Hershberger, "Mobilizing Women, Anticipating Abolition: The Struggle against

Indian Removal in the 1830s," *Journal of American History* 86 (June 1999): 15–40.

19. As part of the Underground Railroad, antislavery activists developed several routes across southern Michigan to aid runaway slaves in escaping to Canada, but slave hunters and their subsidized sympathizers began to monitor the main lines of travel to intercept these runaways. The "slave-hunting frolic in Adrian" to which Lundy referred was probably one of these efforts to locate unregistered blacks (George B. Catlin, *The Story of Detroit* [Detroit: *Detroit News,* 1926], 321–28).

20. Elizabeth's letter written between December 23, 1830, and January 3, 1831, and Ruth's letter dated October 22, 1830.

21. Lundy described the Canadian colony as follows: "During the latter part of 1829 and the first part of 1830, a colony of several thousand coloured people, mostly from Ohio, was established in Upper Canada, the immediate occasion being the enforcement, in Ohio, of an old law, which was intended to restrain the settlement of emancipated slaves in that State. It appears from the Genius, that this even excited a strong feeling in Canada, at that time, and the House of Assembly of that Province passed resolutions expressive of its aversion to the settlement, and requested the Governor to apply to the British Parliament, for the future prohibition of such emigration. The application proved unsuccessful, and Canada remained open to coloured settlers. Lundy, who had paid a visit to Canada, encouraged the emigration of free coloured people thither, in case they had previously resided north of 34 degrees latitude, so as to be fitted to endure the climate: and the coloured people of Boston and Philadelphia, formed societies to encourage such emigration" (Lundy, *Benjamin Lundy,* 240). In January 1832 Lundy visited to the Wilberforce Settlement, on the Ausable River, about twelve miles from London, in Upper Canada: "It had been established for about twenty months, and consisted of thirty-two families, comprising in all about one hundred and sixty persons. Near two thousand coloured refugees had visited the place, but for want of means of employment, they had left and gone to other parts of Canada. The settlers were sober, industrious and thrifty. They had two schools, two churches, one being of the Methodist, and the other of the Baptist sect; and a temperance society" (Lundy, *Benjamin Lundy,* 252).

22. Possibly Mary A. W. Johnson, an active abolitionist.

23. The annual business meeting of the Hicksites, which convened in Philadelphia.

24. A thin disk of dried paste, gelatin, or adhesive paper used to seal letters.

25. Pennsylvania's Hicksite Quakers had organized the Free Produce Society of Pennsylvania in 1827. The free-produce movement fit with the Quakers' belief that passive resistance effectively rectified an unacceptable situation. Based on the theory that people who used the products of slave labor were partially responsible for the perpetuation of slavery, the members of the society supported total abstinence from the use of such slave-grown products as cotton and sugar.

26. A loose-fitting shirt made from tow, the flax fiber used to make linen fabric. Linen came in many grades and weaves. Tow garments were intended for work and were generally made from coarse thread.

27. The establishment of a line of lake steamers between Buffalo and Detroit in the early 1830s, in addition to the already much-used Erie Canal, provided travelers with safe and fairly comfortable passage from the Atlantic to Michigan for less than ten dollars.

28. Maple sugar was a free product and the alternative to slave-produced cane sugar. See appendix 4 for a recipe of Elizabeth Chandler's that uses maple sugar.

29. Amelia's letter is not in the collection.

30. Corduroy roads.

31. What is now a county road leading south out of Tecumseh and meeting Michigan Route 52 just northeast of Adrian. This road goes past what was Hazelbank. Congress had also appropriated money for a road from Monroe to the Chicago Road (U.S. 12) at Cambridge Junction, Michigan, via Tecumseh, which is now Michigan Route 50. Musgrove Evans was contracted to survey the route, which was completed in 1835.

32. The Potawatomies were the native tribe living in the Lenawee County area when settlers began arriving. After the War of 1812, the natives' power was broken and they had little recourse but to accept treaties that forced them to relinquish their land to white settlers. Several Native American villages had been located in what would in 1815 become Lenawee County, and other tribes used the area for hunting. A number of burial mounds were located throughout the county, including an important council ground near Tecumseh that is thought possibly to belong to the Hopewell tribe, which lived between fifteen hundred and two thousand years ago. Settlers at first avoided the swamps and wetlands, giving the Native Americans a false sense of security regarding their land rights. However, innovative methods of agriculture soon enabled the settlers to tame these wet areas, which were eventually plowed over, erasing most evidence of the natives' existence in the area.

33. Leather cording used to sew or repair patent leather shoes.

34. Cassimere was a medium-weight twilled woolen cloth of soft texture. It could be plain and used for clothing and furnishings or patterned and sometimes mixed with silk, cotton, or mohair for coats and waistcoats. Casinet was a light mixed cloth, a modification of cassimere, woven in a twill weave with the warp of cotton and the weft of a very fine wool or wool and silk. In American manufacture, it was usually coarse and was frequently called Negro cloth.

35. Detroit had its beginnings as the center of the American stove industry during the 1830s, when settlers in the territory grew weary of sending broken parts to Albany or Troy, New York, for repair and then waiting long periods for the repaired or replacement parts. The first stove manufacturer in Detroit was the

Hydraulic Iron Works, which made stove castings and repaired stoves (Catlin, *Story,* 472–78).

36. Sarah Chandler's letter is not in the collection.

37. Although the Bank of Monroe had been established in 1827 and was closer to Hazelbank, Ruth sent bank notes from the Bank of Michigan in Detroit, which had been chartered in 1817. Because these were territorial banks, their notes' value did not equal that of notes of the Bank of the United States in Philadelphia, and Ruth's suspicion that the notes would be discounted was valid.

38. A light square wagon that had two seat boards and a standing top and was usually drawn by one horse. In the early nineteenth century, this type of carriage was also referred to as a Jersey wagon or a carryall.

39. The July 1831 issue of Lundy's *Genius of Universal Emancipation* explained in detail Elizabeth Greenfield's actions. She had resided a long time in Mississippi and owned several plantations there and in Louisiana. Prior to her removal to Philadelphia she had sold all her slaves but those on a plantation near Natchez. As she was advanced in years, she provided in her will for the emancipation of those remaining slaves upon her death. Land was to be purchased for them in Ohio, and all necessary articles were to be furnished for them to set up businesses. However, when Ohio legislated against allowing former slaves to settle there, she traveled to Mississippi to induce her former slaves to consider emigrating to Liberia.

40. In the Bible, Lot's wife looked back as she was escaping the destruction of Sodom and Gomorrah and was turned into a pillar of salt.

41. The American Society of Free Persons of Colour had been founded on November 30, 1830, and convened its first annual convention in Philadelphia on June 6, 1831.

42. According to Whitney, "rheumatism is an affection of the extremities and external coverings of the body, having its seat in the muscles and tendons, and is characterized by pain, stiffness and swelling of the joint, attended with fever when the disorder is violent. . . . The brain is seldom or never affected." He states the cause as "cold with moisture, particularly where long applied, . . . hence it is generally attributed to sleeping in damp beds or on the ground, putting on of damp clothes, and working in damp situations." Treatment involved "large and repeated bleedings" followed by "a smart dose of salts; and to abate the fever and thirst let the patient drink freely of flaxseed tea, balm tea, barley or rice water, with a little nitre dissolved in them; and small doses antimony (tartar emetic) or Dover's powders to promote diaphoresis. And blisters applied so as to cover the whole of the affected joint. . . . These means must be repeated until the inflammation subsides. The pain must then be allayed by opium or laudanum. The system may now be supported by bark and wine and a generous diet" (*Guide to Health,* 68).

43. Before the advent of photography, it was common practice to have a profile (silhou-

ette) cut from black paper. It was less costly than having a portrait painted.

44. The western and eastern boundaries of Philadelphia's shops.

45. A common method of making fences was to stack rough hand-hewn rails in a zigzag pattern. Because no nails were used, the fences could be easily moved or added to when necessary.

46. The monthly meeting was a business meeting in which the Hicksites would not be allowed to participate. They could, however, worship with the Orthodox Friends.

47. Mortification is gangrene; biliousness described an illness marked by suffering from disordered liver function and especially excessive secretion of bile.

48. According to Virginia K. Bartlett, "Pennsylvania was unique in that the state denied a widow any part of her husband's estate—even that to which she was legally entitled—until the man's creditors had been paid off. Other states . . . allowed her to receive her share first, before the creditors made their claims. The Pennsylvania interpretation created many indigent widows dependent on children, other family members, or public relief" (*Keeping House: Women's Lives in Western Pennsylvania, 1790–1850* [Pittsburgh: Historical Society of Western Pennsylvania and University of Pittsburgh Press, 1994], 147). Thomas Guest's widow would receive a third of his estate after creditors were paid.

49. A British term for a labor strike.

50. A light two-wheeled carriage pulled by a single horse.

51. According to Whitney, dropsy arose from "excessive drinking, poor diet, protracted intermittents, schirrous tumors of the abdominal viscera, violent inflammations, and whatever may occasion too free a secretion of the action of the absorbent vessels." Dropsy of the heart, or "hydropericardium," involved "water in the purse, or membrane, which encloses the heart" (*Guide to Health,* 120).

52. Prune plums could be dried without fermenting. Green gages were small greenish or greenish-yellow cultivated plums.

53. *Intermittents* were illnesses that came and went at intervals.

54. The root of rhubarb, also called pie plant, was used in small doses (six to ten grains) as an astringent, thought to be strengthening to the stomach. In larger doses (from a scruple to half a dram) it was first a purgative, then an astringent. It was, therefore, considered "excellent medicine for diarrhea and dysentery" (Whitney, *Guide to Health,* 189).

55. At certain times of the year, drovers collected and moved cattle to market, stopping to buy and sell animals along the way. They used herding dogs to keep the livestock together and could usually cover approximately ten miles a day. Many taverns and inns had fenced pastures that drovers could rent at night. The Chandler household probably would have bought a shorthorn or a devon, all-around varieties used for milk and meat.

56. Face in a mirror.

57. Goose quills were still the common writing utensil. Jane's handwriting in this letter clearly reveals her lack of skill with a metal pen.

CHAPTER 4. A YEAR OF GROWTH, 1832

1. A leather pouch, wallet, or pack.

2. The proximity of Pennsylvania and New Jersey enabled residents to shop for their dry goods in the larger city of Philadelphia by crossing the Delaware River on a steamer or ferry. The attraction to Ruth's store also may have resulted from the fact the she had sold cotton raised without the use of slave labor.

3. The *American Daily Advertiser* edited by Zachariah Poulson. The newspaper was founded by John Dunlap in November 1771 as a weekly called the *Pennsylvania Packet* or the *General Advertiser,* and in September 1784 it became the first daily paper on the American continent, changing its name soon thereafter.

4. Several publications at this time had *Kaleidoscope* in their titles: *Kaleidoscope and Literary Rambler,* a Boston weekly; *Baltimore Kaleidoscope and Weekly Express;* and *Kaleidoscope,* published in Liverpool, England.

5. Jane mentions this breach between Elizabeth or Ruth and Anna Guest several times in the letters, but no details are known.

6. *The Friend* was a Philadelphia religious and literary journal, edited by Robert Smith and printed by Adam Waldie.

7. Muhammad, the Arab prophet and founder of Islam, spoke of a the tuba tree as greeting all those who entered Paradise.

8. Talk of building a railroad in the new settlement began with Darius Comstock; his son, Addison; Calvin Bradish; and a few others in the late 1820s and early 1830s. The planned Erie and Kalamazoo Railroad would have crossed the swamps between Adrian and Toledo and then opened up the central and western parts of Lenawee County, eventually stretching west to the Kalamazoo River. Ludicrous as the idea seemed to the settlers, who could not imagine a railroad crossing swampland, the Comstocks put up the money, secured backing from others in Toledo and as far away as New York state, and hired engineer George Crane to lay out the route. The first train ran in November 1826 between Port Lawrence (Toledo) and Adrian, making it the first railroad west of Schenectady, New York. Horses pulled the train until June 1837, when they were replaced by a Baldwin steam locomotive.

9. Anna Coe to Elizabeth Chandler, August 9, 1831, EMC Collection.

10. Jane's letter is not in the collection.

11. On March 10, 1817, the Detroit residents held a meeting to organize a "social" proprietary or subscription library. Shares were offered at five dollars each, and one book could be withdrawn for each share. Some of the more prosperous subscribers

purchased more than one share. The library in Adrian followed this method, and Thomas subscribed for the Evans/Chandler household (Floyd R. Dain, *Education in the Wilderness* [Lansing: Michigan Historical Commission, 1968], 39).

12. The troublesome epidemic was probably cholera. In 1832 a national epidemic of Asiatic cholera occurred, recalling for Philadelphians the terror of the yellow fever of 1793. Asiatic cholera had originated in the Indian subcontinent and was making its way west. The speed of cholera's spread was greatly increased by one of the early nineteenth century's most exulted achievements, the rapid pace of ocean and overland transport in the United States and Western Europe. A virulent bacterial disease of the intestinal tract, cholera caused intense diarrhea and dehydration. Cholera was not quite the wholesale killer that smallpox or yellow fever had been, but it was deadly and frightening enough. Philadelphia was hard hit. Following the main transportation routes and thriving in dense populations, cholera spared most of rural America.

13. Succotash is a Native American (Narragansett) dish consisting of kernels of corn and kidney beans cooked in bear grease. Samp is a porridge made of coarsely ground corn.

14. Jane's letter is not in the collection.

15. Silkworms spin their cocoons while living in mulberry trees. Silk had been cultivated in Pennsylvania on and off since 1725. By 1771 mulberry trees were planted in New Jersey and the counties around Philadelphia. When the Revolutionary War started, foreign silk fabrics became unavailable, so the women of the area, including Elizabeth Chandler's ancestors, began manufacturing silk.

16. Bartlett states that, according to Harriet Beecher Stowe, candle-making day was "seven-fold worse in its way than even washday." Women worked from dawn to night dipping candles. Long strings had to be prepared, the tallow had to be melted, and a rack had to be readied for hanging the candles. Often done in the fall and the spring, the tedious chore involved dipping each string and laying it across the rack, repeating it until the candle was thick enough to burn sufficiently. All the while the fire under the kettle of melted wax had to be tended and kept burning. In the spring, alum water was added to assist the tallow in hardening (*Keeping House*, 33).

17. Circus exhibitions first came to Philadelphia in the early 1800s. The exhibitions originally featured horsemanship and equestrian performances, but in 1810, Thomas Swann, a riding master, exhibited at his amphitheatre at Fifteenth and Market Streets "the largest lion that ever was seen in this city" as well as a dancing horse. Many more circuses followed in later years, and the Zoological Institute, or menagerie, was built in the 1840s (Jackson, *Encyclopedia*, 2:459, 460).

18. Ruth's letter is not in the collection.

19. This is a reference to President Andrew Jackson's elimination of the Bank of the

United States, which was replaced by state and private banks, causing great suspicion and fear.

20. Even in rugged frontier settlements, settlers sought almost immediately to establish schools. Although the school buildings were often makeshift, the pioneers' determination to provide educational opportunities for their children and maintain the cultural level from which they migrated exemplified their attitude of optimism about their new surroundings.

21. Nicolas Pike, *A New and Complete System of Arithmetic, Composed for the Use of the Citizens of the United States* (Newburyport: Mycall, 1788), commonly known as *Pike's Assistant* and endorsed by George Washington, was a famous arithmetic textbook used widely in early schools. Each page provided a rule to be memorized.

22. In her essay "Female Education," Elizabeth advocated female "school-keeping because there are so many pursuits, more lucrative and agreeable to active and ambitious young men," resulting in a lack of good instructors. She also characterized women as "by temper and habit admirably qualified for the task" of teaching school because they inherently had "patience, fondness for children, are accustomed to seclusion, and inured to self-government" (Chandler, *Poetical Works,* 9). Catharine Beecher also saw teaching as an alternative to marriage, a "profession offering influence, respectability and independence" (Jensen, "Not Only Ours," 3).

23. Carried by Samuel Marot, Elizabeth's letter took approximately three weeks to arrive in Philadelphia. Had she mailed the letter, it would probably have arrived in just under two weeks.

24. A liberal Presbyterian church housed in an imposing brick building at the intersection of Second and Coats Streets in Philadelphia.

25. Mustard seeds were used both externally and internally. The pulverized seeds could be made into a topical application and used as a "diffusible stimulus." When the seeds were taken whole they "produced a gentle evacuation" without weakening the stomach and bowels (Whitney, *Guide to Health,* 187).

26. This postscript was written in a different hand: it was the certification Thomas had requested so that he would be exempt from military muster.

27. The Black Hawk Rebellion was an Indian uprising in northern Illinois and the Michigan Territory west of Lake Michigan (what is now Wisconsin) in the spring and summer of 1832. Black Hawk, leader of the Sauk and Foxes, had earlier been forced with his people to move west beyond the Mississippi River, leaving the villages and farms of his people to white settlers. His "rebellion" involved recrossing the Mississippi into Illinois with five hundred warriors and an equal number of women and children, planning to plant the fields his people had once farmed, which was prohibited by treaty. The settlers demanded protection, and four thousand troops were sent up the Rock River in Illinois in pursuit of Black Hawk. Before Black Hawk and his people turned back, a number of settlers had been

killed. News and exaggerated rumors spread east rapidly, and Michigan began to muster its militia in anticipation of Black Hawk's advances, which never occurred.

28. Seven papers had been established in the territory by this time, though two had already been discontinued. Four were published in Detroit: the *Detroit Gazette* (1817–30), the *Michigan Herald* (1825–29), the *Detroit Courier* (1831–35), and the *Democratic Free Press* (which began as a weekly under the name *Democratic Free Press and Michigan Intelligencer* on May 5, 1831, and became the *Democratic Free Press* on November 22, 1832; in 1848, it became the *Detroit Free Press*). In addition, there were the *Monroe Michigan Sentinel* (started in 1825), the *Ann Arbor Emigrant* (1829), and the *Pontiac Oakland County Chronicle* (1830).

29. The fear of harmful effects from vegetables and milk had been a long-standing concept. Awareness of the importance of cleanliness to prevent cholera was a relatively new theory, although Benjamin Rush had been a proponent of cleanliness long before this time.

30. According to the *Annals of Philadelphia,* Oliver Evans is credited with running the "first carriage ever propelled by steam in the world in this city—from his foundry to the river Schuylkill, a mile and a half, in 1804." The first American locomotive was built by Colonel Stephen H. Long in Philadelphia in 1830 and was placed on the New Castle and Frenchtown Railroad, making its first trial run on July 4, 1831. Pennsylvania's first railway for general commerce was built by the state and was the Philadelphia and Columbia Railroad, which ran 84? miles between those two cities. Trains traveled between Philadelphia and West Chester beginning on December 25, 1833, and between Philadelphia and Columbia beginning in June 1834 (Watson, *Annals,* 3:152, 485).

31. Because ague occurred most commonly in swampy areas, Sarah Comstock may have had the disease before she left Michigan, although she did not have symptoms until she reached New York.

32. Discussions about Michigan statehood began in 1832, when the Legislative Council asked the territory's inhabitants to vote on the question. Though the number of voters was small, the majority supported statehood. The council then petitioned for statehood based on a southern boundary that stretched from the southern tip of Lake Michigan due east to Lake Erie, but the southern part of that territory, including Toledo, was also claimed by Ohio, whose northern boundary had not been clearly delineated when that state entered the Union in 1802. In July 1834, Michigan Governor Stevens T. Mason stepped up the campaign for statehood, and when the Legislative Council met in September, he asked that a census be taken as a first step. The census found a total of 85,826 people in the territory east of Lake Michigan, far exceeding the Ordinance of 1787's requirement that a territory have 60,000 free inhabitants to make a constitution and organize a state government, but the Toledo War with Ohio and the U.S. Senate's

desire to keep an equal number of slave and free states continued to hold up the effort. A constitutional convention was held in May 1835, with Mason chosen as leader. President Andrew Jackson mediated a compromise between Ohio and Michigan in which Michigan received the area north of what is now Wisconsin (the Upper Peninsula) in exchange for relinquishing all claims to the Toledo strip. Over the objections of many Michigan residents, territorial leaders accepted the compromise on December 14, 1836, and Michigan's statehood followed shortly thereafter, on January 26, 1837, when Arkansas also joined the Union. By this time, Michigan's population had reached 175,000.

33. Flavius Josephus (A.D. 37?-95) was a Jewish historian.

34. A milk house held containers of milk while the fat was separating from the liquid, after which the fat was used to churn butter. During the process, the milk had to be kept covered and cool. Depending on how much milk was being separated, the separators took up considerable space, and a milk house freed up space in the main house.

35. Lundy is referring to William Lloyd Garrison, who left the *Genius* after discovering his irreconcilable differences with Lundy on the subject of emancipation. In addition to the Atlees, Lundy also enlisted the aid of Abraham L. Pennock, Dr. Jonas Preston, Thomas Shipley, Thomas Earle, Isaac Barton, and others.

36. The Republic of Mexico, which included Texas at this time, had abolished slavery in 1829. On September 15, 1829, Mexican President Vincente Guerrero issued an order, countersigned by Secretary of State Lorenzo de Zavala, decreeing (1) that "slavery is forever abolished in the republic"; (2) that "all those individuals who until this day looked upon themselves as slaves, are free"; and (3) that "when the financial situation of the republic admits, the proprietors of slaves shall be indemnified, and the indemnification regulated by law." As a result of this decree, slaveholding U.S. colonists living in Texas revolted during the summer of 1832, and a full-blown war developed. Lundy wrote extensively about the war in Texas in *The Life, Travels, and Opinions of Benjamin Lundy*.

37. Faces.

38. Cinchona bark (a.k.a. Jesuits or Peruvian bark) contains quinine and was used as a tonic for bilious or remittent fever and ague. It was administered as a steeped tea in boiling water or in port wine (Whitney, *Guide to Health,* 18).

39. Lundy did not include "Warner Miflin" in Chandler's posthumously published *Works.*

40. A reference to Garrison's original Burlington paper.

41. *Cholera morbus* was a nontechnical term for a gastrointestinal disturbance characterized by diarrhea and sometimes vomiting.

42. The sisters owned a dry goods shop.

43. She was probably referring to ossification, a disease of the heart that doctors called angina pectoris. The most common cause was thought to be "an ossified (bony)

state of the coronary vessels of the heart (the vessels that supply the substance of the heart)" (Whitney, *Guide to Health,* 93).

44. Whitney makes no mention of black walnuts in his *Guide to Health,* although he does list the root of the white walnut tree as a curative for diarrhea or dysentery.

45. Elizabeth Chandler and Laura Haviland had formed the Logan Female Anti-Slavery Society, the first women's antislavery society in the Old Northwest, in 1832.

46. According to Whitney, *Guide to Health,* 16, "bilious or remittent fevers are produced from the same causes that intermittents are, and differ from intermittents only in being more violent. Intemperance, especially in the use of ardent spirits . . . produces fevers of the most malignant form."

47. Because eating grapes might exacerbate cholera, some people mistakenly believed that grapes could cause the disease.

48. Although Elizabeth began this letter in mid-December 1832, she did not send it until the end of February 1833, after she had received Jane's January 9 letter.

49. See Jane Howell to Elizabeth Chandler, January 9, 1833.

50. The first newspaper, established October 1834 and published by R. W. Ingalls, was called *Republican and Adrian Gazette* and was later renamed *Watch Tower.* "It was a good paper for the day, and . . . it made faithful chronicle of all marriages and deaths reported to it; . . . it published an editorial every week, and . . . immediately above the editorial it published the Democratic nominations in full, and . . . it never named them but to praise them" (*MPC,* 7:530).

51. See Jane Howell to Elizabeth Chandler, January 9, 1833.

52. Oxen.

53. The first temperance society in the Michigan Territory was formed in Detroit in 1830, and many more followed throughout the territory.

CHAPTER 5. A YEAR OF WAITING, 1833

1. This letter arrived in Michigan before Elizabeth mailed the one she started on December 13, 1832 (see chapter 4).

2. The collection contains four of Ruth's letters to Jane up to this date (February 5, May 30, September 8, 1831, and October 22, 1832).

3. John and Anna Merrefield's second son, John, was born in March 1832 but died less than five months later (Jane Howell to Elizabeth Chandler, April 1, 1832; Jane Howell to Ruth Evans, July 25, 1832). The baby's father apparently was so overcome by grief that he became unable to speak.

4. A supercargo is the officer on a merchant ship who is responsible for commercial matters.

5. *Verbim sat* is rudimentary Latin for "enough words."

6. The Friends on the east side of the River Raisin established the Logan Preparative Meeting at Sylvanus Westgate's house. Michigan never established a yearly meeting of its own during this period. The Orthodox meetings fell under the New York yearly meeting and later the Ohio meeting. The Hicksite meeting fell under the Genesee, New York, yearly meeting, which was originally called the Hicksite yearly meeting.

7. These letters are not in the collection.

8. Sophanisba was the pseudonym for African-American Sarah Mapps Douglass (1806–82), the daughter of an affluent barber, Robert Douglass Sr., and his wife, Grace Bustill Douglass. Sarah Douglass was active in Philadelphia's abolitionist movement and a dedicated teacher who wished to see more educational opportunities made available to African-American women.

9. *Reuben Maddison* was a British publication. It is unclear whether it ever appeared in print in America.

10. Denison was editor of the *Emancipator,* New York's first antislavery journal.

11. Possibly *Godey's Lady's Book,* a popular nineteenth-century journal edited by Sarah Hale.

12. Official records are scarce, but reminiscences provide some idea of where the Friends met. Richard Illenden Bonner, ed., *The Memoirs of Lenawee County* (Madison, Wisc.: Western Historical Association, 1909), states that "the Friends Church was first established at Raisin Valley by a colony of Quakers, including Darius Comstock, Jared Comstock, Abram West, Elijah Brownell, Daniel Smith; . . . there is no record of their having held meetings until June 20, 1831, when . . . the organization of the society was effected. . . . Though the record of their early activities is incomplete, it is believed that the first meetings were held in the winter of 1831–32 in a log shanty situated about one mile west of the present edifice in the village" (57). According to Kerr, *History,* 7, this original meeting place was "a log shanty 12 by 16 feet. The pews were slabs from the woods and placed on legs. The worshippers seemed happy with the seats." When this log structure became too small, a request was made to the Adrian Monthly Meeting to hold a meeting for worship and a preparative meeting at the house of Sylvanus Westgate, which was approved. Westgate's house also became too small, and the group built a "long, low, upright building facing the south with a long platform with two doors. The west door was for the women's entrance to their part of the church and the east door to the men's section. Benches were high backed separated by a low partition keeping the men and women separate." This meetinghouse was completed in 1835. The Raisin Valley Friends Church, on Michigan Route 52 just north of Adrian, still resides in this location.

13. Hannah's letter is not in the collection.

14. Money or cash.

15. 2 Corinthians 5:1: "We know that if our earthly tabernacle of this house were dissolved, we have a building of God, an house not made with hands, eternal in the heavens."

16. St. Luke 22:42: "Nevertheless, not my will, but thine, be done."

17. Quakers had very specific burial and funeral practices that fit with their efforts to remain plain and unostentatious. The discipline of the 1797 Philadelphia Yearly Meeting states that "it is wrong, and of evil tendency to have any grave or tomb stones or monuments placed at or over any grave in any of our burying grounds; and . . . those monuments . . . already set . . . should be removed, and no new ones erected." The Philadelphia and New York Quakers shared this discipline until 1810. By 1848, New York Hicksites allowed stones, and Philadelphia Hicksites followed in 1856.

18. Westtown School had opened in May 1799 with twenty students of each sex and in the following three months had admitted approximately ten boys and ten girls each month. Subsequently, each child who departed would be replaced by another of that sex so that enrollment could be limited to an equal number of both sexes.

19. It is not clear what convention Thomas attended, though it could have pertained either to Michigan's statehood or to the Treaty of Chicago, finalized on September 27, 1833, which provided money, goods, and horses for those members of the "United Nations of Indians" (Chippewa, Ottawa, and Potawatamie) who were residing on land situated in the territory of Michigan with the understanding that they would move from that land within three years and would not be disturbed before that time. They were to move west of the Mississippi River, though some of those involved requested removal to the northern part of the peninsula of Michigan (Charles J. Kappler, *Indian Affairs: Laws and Treaties* [Washington, D.C.: U.S. Government Printing Office, 1904], 2: 410–15).

20. Anna Coe's letter is not in the collection.

21. William's letter is not in the collection.

22. The Doylestown Stage, the "Sign of the Camel," was located at Second Street above Rose.

23. After Black Hawk was captured, he made peace with the U.S. government. According to F. Clever Bald, in 1833 Black Hawk was taken on a tour of the East to impress him with the foolishness of defying the power of the United States. He appeared dignified in public, wearing a long blue coat, a white high hat, and spectacles and carrying a cane (*Michigan,* 192).

24. Table diaper was a linen fabric (sometimes cotton) in a twill weave and was used to cover tables. Domestic muslin was a fine cotton woven in America. Lydia White's selection was limited because she dealt only in free goods.

25. Linen lawn is fine delicate linen used for shirts, handkerchiefs, ruffles, and aprons.

26. Prudence Crandall, a Quaker schoolteacher in Connecticut who opened a school

for black girls. Unhappy townspeople persuaded the Connecticut legislature to pass a law prohibiting the education of out-of-state blacks. Crandall fought the law with the help of leading abolitionists, was jailed three times, and eventually had her conviction reversed. However, local merchants organized a boycott, preventing Crandall from buying supplies; filled the school's well with manure; and set the school on fire, forcing Crandall to abandon her efforts. Garrison reported the story in the *Liberator,* and Crandall became a hero to Quaker women abolitionists (Bacon, *Mothers,* 102, 103).

27. Ingrain carpets, also called Kidderminster or two-ply Scotch carpets, were composed of two cloths of different colors woven together to form a type of positive-negative pattern. They were made of strips thirty-six inches wide sewn together. The carpets were first made in Scotland in 1822; in 1833 the Hartford Manufacturing Company of Thompsonville, Connecticut, began manufacturing them.

28. The Coe family's financial disgrace and unsavory reputation apparently caused Margaret Hall to forbid her daughter, Rebecca, from living with her husband, James Coe.

29. A patent medicine.

30. The Bank of River Raisin in Monroe was chartered on June 29, 1832, and was located in a two-story brick building erected on Washington Street near the public square. The bill to which Elizabeth referred was either the three dollar note, which pictured an "Indian in canoe," or, more likely, the five dollar note, which pictured an "Indian chief," a portrait of William Penn, and an "Indian in canoe." The bank closed in 1846 (Harold L. Bowen, *State Bank Notes of Michigan* [Detroit: Havelt Advertising Services, 1956], 139, 140).

31. Omnibuses were passenger conveyances that preceded Philadelphia's railroads.

32. A fulling mill cleansed and thickened wool by a special manufacturing process, also called felting.

33. A reference to Raisin.

34. Elizabeth's sketch of their log house is not in the collection.

35. A scarf for covering the neck and shoulders, usually having ends hanging down in front.

36. Probably a very gentle soap, because flannel was made from wool.

37. Germantown, Pennsylvania, was noted for manufacturing three- and four-ply worsted and woolen spun yarns.

38. Jane is referring to Elizabeth's September 2 letter. Ruth mentioned in her October 11 letter that Jane's September 1 letter had arrived.

39. A mechanic's skills involved anything having to do with the building trade.

40. Benjamin Lundy had requested in his September 6, 1832, letter that it be sent "immediately."

Chapter 6. Major Changes, 1834

1. Ecclesiastes 1:14: "All is vanity and vexation of spirit."

2. Andrew Jackson became president in 1828 with a long-standing distrust of banks and paper money and announced that he would veto the recharter of the Second Bank of the United States. This resulted in a growing number of state bank charters, creating fertile ground for state monopolies as well as corruption. A "free banking" movement followed, in which individuals or associations of individuals could establish banks by conforming to certain general regulations. The situation led eventually to the Panic of 1837. For a discussion of the bank issues during this period, see William Gerald Shade, *Banks or No Banks: The Money Issue in Western Politics, 1832–1865* (Detroit: Wayne State University Press, 1972).

3. According to the *Annals of Philadelphia,* the meteors "of the 13th November, 1833, were the most remarkable ever witnessed. A beholder says, he was sitting alone in a well-lighted apartment, at 4 A.M., when he suddenly saw through the window a shower of sparks falling past it on the outside. He supposed the house was on the fire, and rushing to the door, to his extreme amazement, he found the entire atmosphere filled with flakes of fire, (for they fully resembled flakes of snow of a stellated or radiated form,) of a pale rose red, seemingly of an inch diameter, falling in a vertical direction, as thick as he ever saw snow! Intermingled with the smaller stars, were a larger kind, equal to one in a hundred of the others, of an intense sapphire blue, seemingly of three to four inches in diameter. This shower continued up to broad day light. They were seen all over the United States, and have been variously described, but all agreeing that they surpassed all other known cases" (Watson, *Annals,* 3:369).

4. Possibly *variola,* any of several viral diseases (such as smallpox or cowpox) marked by a pustule eruption. Early vaccinations consisted of inoculations of the virus to produce immunity.

5. A place where bricks were made.

6. Benjamin Lundy's March 30, 1833, letter apparently had not yet arrived.

7. The town of Raisin was directly east of Adrian and directly south of Tecumseh.

8. The kitchen could be attached to the rear of the house, or it could be a separate building, thereby keeping the house cooler in the summer. Prior to kitchens, cooking took place in the "keeping room" or, as in the case of the Chandlers' log home, in the large main living area.

9. Ingalls established Lenawee County's first newspaper, the *Lenawee Republican and Adrian Gazette* (later the *Watch Tower*), on October 22, 1834.

10. The Farmington Monthly Meeting was the first Hicksite meeting in Michigan.

11. 2 Samuel 1:19: "The beauty of Israel is slain upon thy high places: how are the mighty fallen!"

12. Upon his death in 1831, Stephen Girard founded Girard College to educate

orphaned white boys. His will provided two million dollars in trust to the city of Philadelphia to erect the institution and one million dollars to maintain it. The cornerstone of the main building was laid on July 4, 1833, and the buildings were completed in 1847. The college opened on January 1, 1848.

13. See appendix 2.

14. Ann's letter is not in the collection.

15. The other free-produce stores specialized in dry goods rather than groceries.

16. In June 1834, Congress appropriated six thousand dollars for construction of a lighthouse at the north end of Long Beach Island, New Jersey. Work soon began on a forty-foot masonry tower, and the lighthouse was put into commission in 1835. Mariners, however, deemed its nonflashing, fifth-class light ineffective. The original structure stood until 1856, when encroaching seas toppled it. A replacement tower was built between 1857 and 1858 and dedicated as the Barnegat Lighthouse.

17. According to the *Annals of Philadelphia,* the new Merchants' Exchange, located at Walnut and Dock Streets on Dock Creek, was an "edifice of grandeur." It was estimated to have cost $160,000 to build on land that stockholders purchased for $75,000. The new brick building, with its marble facade, was the largest building in the city and elicited a great deal of interest among residents (Watson, *Annals,* 1:348).

18. Joseph Lancaster (1778–1838), a Quaker, developed a system of mass education whereby brighter or more proficient students under the direction of an adult taught other students. This "Lancasterian plan" called for between two hundred and one thousand pupils to be gathered in one room and seated in rows of ten. The adult schoolmaster taught the monitors, or prefects, each of whom relayed the lesson to his or her row of pupils. Lancaster's school, lectures, and 1803 pamphlet, *Improvements in Education as It Respects the Industrious Classes of the Community,* attracted philanthropists' attention by making education and its techniques subjects of widespread interest, and his approach provided at least a rudimentary education for large numbers of poor children.

19. Upon reaching maturity, Louisa Hull would no longer be the Howells' bond servant and would be released with enough goods to live independently.

20. The *Saturday Courier,* a weekly newspaper published in Philadelphia.

21. Probably the upcoming Pennsylvania gubernatorial election, in which Joseph Witner, a Whig, defeated Democratic incumbent George Wolf.

22. Ruth's letter and one that Elizabeth sent at the same time are not in the collection.

23. Ruth's letter is not in the collection.

24. According to Dunglison, *Dictionary, ,* the blue pill was a mercurial pill containing 33 percent metallic mercury with glycerin and honey. It was a sialagogue (a drug or other agent that increases the flow of saliva) as well as an alterative (a

medication that restores health) and a purgative (a "medicine which operates more powerfully on the bowels than a laxative, stimulating the muscular coat and exciting increased secretion from the mucous membrane"). According to Cassedy, *Medicine,* "For the ordinary antebellum regular physician, improvement increasingly meant carrying on a more-or-less ongoing process of trial and error on his patients with respect to the various therapeutic modes or options of the day" (69). In addition, home remedies were still used to supplement doctors' care. Thus, Jane's letters frequently included recipes for home remedies.

25. Elizabeth Chandler died on November 2, 1834, fourteen days before the preceding letter was written. Thomas informed Jane and Lemuel Howell of the sad news in a letter that is not in the collection. Jane struggled with the tone of this letter, composing a complete draft and then copying it over neatly; both versions are extant.

26. Psalms 23:4: "Yea, though I walk through the valley of the shadow of death, I will fear no evil: for thou art with me; thy rod and thy staff comfort me."

27. Psalms 102:6: "I have watched, and am even as it were a sparrow: that sitteth alone upon the house-top."

28. The following postscript appears only on the draft copy of this letter.

29. This letter is not in the collection, probably because Jane Howell gave it to Benjamin Lundy to include in his memoir of Elizabeth. This excerpt is taken from Chandler, *Poetical Works,* 42.

30. Her name was not familiar because she did not sign her work.

CHAPTER 7. MATTERS OF LIFE AND DEATH, 1835–1837

1. Hebrews 12:6: "Whom the Lord loveth he chasteneth."

2. St. Luke 22:42: "Nevertheless, not my will, but thine, be done."

3. Benjamin Lundy was alive. His August 6, 1835, letter to Thomas Chandler included a detailed account of Lundy's trip to Mexico and explained why no one had heard from him.

4. Camden was a vacation destination across the Delaware River from Philadelphia, and a confectionery business would be sustained by tourists.

5. Ruth's letter is not in the collection.

6. See appendix 2.

7. Pins were made of steel, but it was not stainless, and they therefore rusted. Tetanus shots to prevent reactions to such injuries had not yet been developed. The remedy they used, a warm lye and milk poultice, would have served two purposes: the lye would act as a constringent for the infection; the milk poultice, most likely made with bread and milk softened with sweet oil or fresh butter, would soothe the wound. Jamaica spirits was probably rum.

8. She is referring to the absence of Elizabeth's contributions.

9. Poulson's *American Daily Advertiser* reprinted the tribute to Elizabeth that appeared in the *Liberator* on November 29, 1834.

10. Thomas's letter is not in the collection.

11. William Shakespeare, *Hamlet,* act 1, scene 1: "He was a man, take him for all in all, / I shall not look upon his like again."

12. Lundy was looking for land on which to place freed or runaway slaves.

13. Ruth's letter is not in the collection.

14. Thomas's letter is not in the collection.

15. Hygiene medicine dealt with the preservation of health through cleanliness and improved sanitary conditions.

16. Isaiah 38:1: "Set thine house in order: for thou shalt die, and not live."

17. Blackjaundice, or Wiel's Disease, is caused by a micro-organism and is a bacterial infection of the liver. The condition turns the skin dark yellow, dirty dark brown, even green-black.

18. Indian meal was cornmeal. These cakes were johnnycakes.

19. Salteratus was a substitute for baking soda and was made from corn cobs burned to ashes.

20. Wine that fermented naturally, unlike distilled spirits, which were aided by an unnatural process and thus were unacceptable to proponents of temperance.

21. The letter from Ruth is not in the collection.

22. Mercury was used as a sialagogue. According to Whitney, "Various preparations of mercury produce salivation; calomel is most commonly used. Salivation effected by mercury is attended with pain, heat in the mouth, with swelling and ulceration of the gums, the swelling frequently extending over the throat and face. These are checked, by gentle purgatives, opium, blisters to the throat, free exposure to cool air and frequently washing the mouth with a solution of borax, alum, or sage tea sweetened with honey. Because ingesting mercury caused the mouth to become sore, Whitney also suggested taking "the inner bark of the root of sumach or shoemake, make a tea and wash or gargle the mouth with it—and take sulphur and cream of tartar, a teaspoonful of each mixed with cream or molasses, two or three times a week" (*Guide to Health,* 227).

23. Jane wrote with her left hand because of the fall Lundy mentioned in his February 16, 1836, letter.

24. See appendix 2. The pieces appeared in Chandler, *Poetical Works,* 133, 127, respectively.

25. Trescott's motives in making this offer are unclear, and it is not known how Thomas Chandler responded.

26. This portrait, painted by Sartain and engraved by Street, appeared in Chandler, *Poetical Works,* and has been reproduced as a frontispiece in this volume.

27. Thomas's letter is not in the collection.

28. Because Egyptian doctors had extensive knowledge about the eye and discovered a treatment for trachoma, trachoma became known as Egyptian eye disease or Egyptian sore eyes. It is a contagious bacterial disease that forms blisters on the conjunctiva and causes fifty percent of all blindness. Whitney, *Guide to Health,* offers the following remedy for sore eyes: "Make a decoction of fresh wild turnip or of lobelia, strain through a fine cloth, and use it for a wash. Or dissolve twelve grains of white vitriol, and sixteen of sugar of lead in half a pint of water; or instead of the water, in 3 gills of milk, and use the whey" (178).

CHAPTER 8. LIFE GOES ON, 1838–1842

1. Palsy is a loss or diminution of sense or motion, or of both, in one or more parts of the body.

2. Erysipelas is an acute infectious disease characterized by diffusely spreading, deep-red inflammation of the skin or mucous membranes. According to D. Whitney, it was "apt to follow in bad habits of the body" (*Guide to Health,* 122).

3. A mob destroyed Pennsylvania Hall on May 17, 1838, during a meeting of the Female Anti-Slavery Society. In response, the Pennsylvania Hall Association publicly stated that it was founded on "no narrow, sectarian, or party views but that it was what it purported to be, a hall for free discussion," and that it was rented out for "frequent opportunities for the discussion of the subject of Slavery" (Samuel Webb, *History of Pennsylvania Hall* [Philadelphia: Merrihew and Gunn, 1838]), 1–5).

4. Stereotyping involves making metal printing plates by taking a mold of composed type and then taking from this mold a cast (plate) in type metal.

5. Enclosed with this letter was a June 7, 1838, note from Benjamin Lundy to Thomas Chandler regarding some subscription accounts for the *Genius of Universal Emancipation.*

6. Hypnotism.

7. Nearly sixty years old, Jane Howell had returned to storekeeping, possibly for financial reasons.

8. A suspension of specie payments occurred in 1839, and a shift in the Democratic Party toward opposition to all banks of issue resulted in strong antibank forces. Bank corruption and bribery was the impetus for these political reverses. For a discussion of the "antibankites" in Michigan, see Shade, *Banks.*

9. A small fly, native to Asia, that was transported to Europe and later to North America, supposedly in the straw bedding of Hessian troops during the American Revolution.

10. William Henry Harrison was inaugurated as president of the United States on March 4, 1841.

11. Benjamin Lundy died on August 21, 1839.
12. *The New World* was an American periodical of the Universalist Unitarian church.
13. Dinner was typically a midday meal.
14. The *United States Gazette* was a daily newspaper published in Philadelphia.
15. Thomas had announced his forthcoming marriage to Jane Merritt.

BIBLIOGRAPHY

MANUSCRIPT COLLECTIONS

Chandler, Elizabeth Margaret, Papers. Michigan Historical Collections, Bentley Historical Library, University of Michigan, Ann Arbor.

Fay, Minnie C., Papers. Michigan Historical Collections, Bentley Historical Library, University of Michigan, Ann Arbor.

PERIODICALS

The Friend: A Religious and Literary Journal (Philadelphia)
Genius of Universal Emancipation (Baltimore and Washington, D.C.)
The Liberator (Boston)

OTHER SOURCES

Adam, John. "Early History of Lenawee County." *Michigan Pioneer Collections* 1 (1878) 221–24.

"Address on Laying the Corner Stone of the New Court House for Lenawee County at Adrian, June 28, 1884." *Michigan Pioneer Collections* 7 (1885): 521–34.

Alden, Bernice. "The Quakers in Michigan, 1829–1837." 1935. Michigan Historical Collections, Bentley Historical Library, University of Michigan, Ann Arbor.

Anderson, Fannie. *Doctors under Three Flags.* Detroit: Wayne State University Press, 1951.

Andrews, Clarence A. *Michigan Literature.* Detroit: Wayne State University Press, 1992.

Aptheker, Herbert. "The Quakers and Negro Slavery." In *Toward Negro Freedom,* 10–34. New York: New Century, 1956.

Bacon, Margaret Hope. *Mothers of Feminism: The Story of Quaker Women in America.* San Francisco: Harper and Row, 1986.

Bailey, Richard. *New Light on George Fox and Early Quakerism: The Making and Unmaking of a God.* San Francisco: Mellen Research University Press, 1992.

Bald, F. Clever. *Michigan in Four Centuries.* New York: Harper, 1954.

Barbour, Hugh, and J. William Frost. *The Quakers.* New York: Greenwood, 1988.

Bartlett, Virginia K. *Keeping House: Women's Lives in Western Pennsylvania, 1790–1850.* Pittsburgh: Historical Society of Western Pennsylvania and University of Pittsburgh Press, 1994.

Bonner, Richard Illenden, ed. *The Memoirs of Lenawee County, Michigan.* Vol. 1. Madison, Wis.: Western Historical Association, 1909.

Bowen, Harold L. *State Bank Notes of Michigan.* Detroit: Havelt Advertising Services, 1956.

Bowerman, Sarah G. "Chandler, Elizabeth Margaret." *Dictionary of American Biography,* 613. New York: Scribner's, 1957.

Brown, Elisabeth Potts, and Susan Mosher Stuard, eds. *Witnesses for Change: Quaker Women over Three Centuries.* New Brunswick, N.J.: Rutgers University Press, 1989.

Brown, Ira V. "Cradle of Feminism: The Female Anti-Slavery Society, 1833–1840." *Pennsylvania Magazine of History and Biography* 102 (1978): 143–66.

Burkland, Carl E. "An Early Michigan Poet: Elizabeth Margaret Chandler." *Michigan History* 30 (1946): 2:277–88.

Burr, C. B., ed. *Medical History of Michigan.* Vol. 1. Minneapolis: Bruce, 1930.

Burton, Ann. *Michigan Quakers: Abstracts of Fifteen Meetings of the Society of Friends.* Decatur, Mich.: Glyndwr Resources, 1989.

Cassedy, James H. *Medicine in America: A Short History.* Baltimore: Johns Hopkins University Press, 1991.

Catlin, George B. *The Story of Detroit.* Detroit: *Detroit News,* 1926.

Chandler, Elizabeth Margaret. *Essays, Philanthropic and Moral: Principally Relating to the Abolition of Slavery in America.* Philadelphia: Howell, 1836.

———. *Poetical Works of Elizabeth Margaret Chandler: With a Memoir of Her Life and Character by Benjamin Lundy.* Philadelphia: Howell, 1836.

Cott, Nancy. *The Bonds of Womanhood: "Women's Sphere" in New England, 1780–1835.* New Haven: Yale University Press, 1977.

Crawford, Patricia. *Women and Religion in England, 1500–1720.* New York: Routledge, 1993.

Cutcheon, Byron M. "Fifty Years of Growth in Michigan." *Michigan Pioneer Collections* 22 (1893): 479–502.

Dain, Floyd R. *Education in the Wilderness.* Lansing: Michigan Historical Commission, 1968.

Decker, John. "A Study of the Motivation of a More Common Abolitionist." 1977. Michigan Historical Collections, Bentley Historical Library, University of Michigan, Ann Arbor.

Dewey, Francis A. "Early Settlers in Lenawee County." *Michigan Pioneer Collections* 3 (1881): 553–57.

———. "Lenawee County: A Sketch of Its Early Settlement." *Michigan Pioneer Collections* 1 (1874–76): 221–24.

Dillon, Merton L. *The Abolitionists: The Growth of a Dissenting Minority.* DeKalb: Northern Illinois University Press, 1974.

———. "Elizabeth Margaret Chandler." In *Notable American Women, 1607–1950,* ed. Edward T. James, 1:319. Cambridge: Belknap Press of Harvard University Press, 1971.

———. "Elizabeth Chandler and the Spread of Antislavery Sentiment to Michigan." *Michigan History* 39 (December 1955): 4:481–94.

Drake, Thomas E. *Patterns of Influence in Anglo-American Quakerism.* London: Friends' Historical Society, 1958.

———. *Quakers and Slavery in America.* New Haven: Yale University Press, 1950.

Dumond, Dwight Lowell. *Antislavery: The Crusade for Freedom in America.* Ann Arbor: University of Michigan Press, 1961.

Dunglison, Robley. *A Dictionary of Medical Science.* Philadelphia and New York: Lea Brothers, 1903.

Durston, Christopher. *The Family in the English Revolution.* Oxford: Basil Blackwell, 1989.

Earle, Thomas. *the Life, Travels, and Opinions of Benjamin Lundy.* New York: Kelly, 1971.

Eckert, Jack, comp. *Guide to the Records of Philadelphia Yearly Meeting.* Philadelphia: n.p., 1989.

Faragher, John Mack. *Sugar Creek: Life on the Illinois Prairie.* New Haven: Yale University Press, 1986.

———. *Women and Men on the Overland Trail.* New Haven: Yale University Press, 1979.

Farmer, Silas. *The History of Detroit and Michigan.* Detroit: Farmer, 1884.

Filler, Louis. *The Crusade against Slavery, 1830–1860: The Quaker Dissent from Puritanism.* New York: Harper and Row, 1960.

Friedman, Lawrence J. *Gregarious Saints: Self and Community in American Abolitionism, 1830–1870.* New York: Cambridge University Press, 1982.

Gillard, Kathleen Isabel. *Our Michigan Heritage.* New York: Pageant, 1955.

Gilpin, Alec R. *The Territory of Michigan, 1805–1837.* East Lansing: Michigan State University Press, 1970.

Ginzberg, Lori D. *Women and the Work of Benevolence: Morality, Politics, and Class in the Nineteenth-Century United States.* New Haven: Yale University Press, 1990.

"Gravesite of Poet, Anti-Slavery Leader Is Restored Near Adrian." *Toledo (Ohio) Blade,* November 26, 1928.

Gummere, Amelia. *The Quaker: A Study in Costume.* Philadelphia: Ferris and Leach, 1901.

Hagaman, Ardath. "Women of the Old Northwest in the Antislavery Movement." 1941. Michigan Historical Collections, Bentley Historical Library, University of Michigan.

Hampsten, Elizabeth. *Read This Only to Yourself: The Private Writings of Midwestern Women,*

1880–1910. Bloomington: Indiana University Press, 1982.

Hansen, Karen. *A Very Social Time: Crafting Community in Antebellum New England.* Berkeley: University of California Press, 1994.

Hartzog, W. B. "General Joseph Brown." *Michigan History* 5 (July–October 1921): 21–25.

Hatcher, Harlan. *Lake Erie.* New York: Bobbs-Merrill, 1945.

Haviland, Laura S. *A Woman's Life-Work, Labors, and Experiences.* Chicago: Waite, 1881.

Hawkins, Hugh, ed. *The Abolitionists: Means, Ends, and Motivations.* Lexington, Mass.: D. C. Heath, 1972.

Hersh, Blanche Glassman. *The Slavery of Sex: Feminist-Abolitionists in America.* Urbana: University of Illinois Press, 1978.

Hershberger, Mary. "Mobilizing Women, Anticipating Abolition: The Struggle against Indian Removal in the 1830s." *Journal of American History* 86 (June 1999): 15–40.

Hewitt, Nancy A. "Feminist Friends: Agrarian Quakers and the Emergence of Woman's Rights in America." *Feminist Studies* 12 (spring 1986): 27–50.

Humphrey, Caroline B. "Laura Smith Haviland." *Michigan History* 5 (January-April 1921): 173–85.

Jackson, Joseph. *Encyclopedia of Philadelphia.* 4 vols. Harrisburg, [Pa.?]: National Historical Association, 1931–33.

Jeffrey, Julie Roy. *The Great Silent Army of Abolitionism: Ordinary Women in the Antislavery Movement.* Chapel Hill: University of North Carolina Press, 1998.

Jensen, Joan M. *Loosening the Bonds: Mid-Atlantic Farm Women, 1750–1850.* New Haven: Yale University Press, 1986.

———. "Not Only Ours but Others: The Quaker Teaching Daughters of the Mid-Atlantic, 1790–1850." *History of Education Quarterly* 24 (spring 1984): 3–19.

Jones, Mary Patrick. "Elizabeth Margaret Chandler—Poet, Essayist, Abolitionist." Ph.D. diss., University of Toledo, 1981.

Kappler, Charles J. *Indian Affairs: Laws and Treaties.* Vol. 2. Washington, D.C.: U.S. Government Printing Office, 1904.

Kern, John. *A Short History of Michigan.* Lansing: Michigan Historical Division/Michigan Department of State, 1977.

Kerr, Merle L. *A History of Raisin Township from the Beginning to the Present.* Adrian, Mich.: Lenawee County Historical Society, 1976.

Kirkland, Caroline. *A New Home—Who'll Follow?* Ed. William S. Osborne. New Haven: College and University Press, 1965.

Kirkland, Edward Chase. *A History of American Economic Life.* 3d ed. New York: Appleton-Century-Crofts, 1951.

Knapp, John I., and R. I. Bonner. *Illustrated History and Biographical Record of Lenawee County.* Adrian, Mich.: Times Printing, 1903.

Kolodny, Annette. *The Land before Her: Fantasy and Experience of the American Frontiers, 1630–1860.* Chapel Hill: University of North Carolina Press, 1984.

Kunitz, Stanley J. and Howard Haycraft, eds. *American Authors: 1600–1900.* New York:

H. W. Wilson, 1938.

Kunze, Bonnelyn Young. *Margaret Fell and the Rise of Quakerism.* Basingstoke, Hampshire: Macmillan, 1994.

Landon, Fred. "Benjamin Lundy." *Dictionary of American Biography,* 11:506–7. New York: Scribner's, 1933.

Langer, William L., ed. *An Encyclopedia of World History.* Boston: Houghton Mifflin, 1946.

Larkin, Jack. *The Reshaping of Everyday Life, 1790–1840.* New York: Harper and Row, 1988.

Lerner, Gerda. *The Grimké Sisters from South Carolina: Pioneers for Woman's Rights and Abolition.* New York: Schocken, 1971.

Lewis, Kenneth E. *West to Far Michigan: Settling the Lower Penninsula, 1815–1860.* East Lansing: Michigan State University Press, 2002.

Lindquist, Charles N. *Lenawee County: A Harvest of Pride and Promise: An Illustrated History.* Chatsworth, Calif.: Windsor, 1990.

Lippincott, Horace Mather. *Early Philadelphia: Its People, Life, and Progress.* Philadelphia: Lippincott, 1917.

Lundy, Benjamin. *The Life, Travels, and Opinions of Benjamin Lundy.* Comp. Earle, Thomas. New York: Kelley, 1971.

Lutz, Alma. *Crusade for Freedom: Women of the Antislavery Movement.* Boston: Beacon, 1968.

Mack, Phyllis. *Visionary Women: Ecstatic Prophecy in Seventeenth-Century England.* Berkeley: University of California Press, 1992.

Martineau, Harriet. "Travels in Michigan." *Michigan History* 7 (January–April 1923): 43–51.

Matthews, Glenna. *Just a Housewife: The Rise and Fall of Domesticity in America.* New York: Oxford University Press, 1987.

McClellen, Elisabeth. *History of American Costume, 1607–1870.* New York: Tudor, 1937.

Merrill, Walter M. *Against Wind and Tide: A Biography of William Lloyd Garrison.* Cambridge: Harvard University Press, 1963.

Miller, William Lee. *Arguing about Slavery: John Quincy Adams and the Great Battle in the United States Congress.* New York: Random House, 1995.

Montgomery, Florence M. *Textiles in America, 1650–1870.* New York: Norton, 1984.

Morton, Patricia. *Discovering the Women in Slavery: Emancipating Perspectives on the American Past.* Athens: University of Georgia Press, 1996.

Myres, Sandra. *Westering Women and the Frontier Experience, 1800–1915.* Albuquerque: University of New Mexico Press, 1982.

Ndukwu, Maurice Dickson. "Antislavery in Michigan: A Study of Its Origin, Development, and Expression from Territorial Period to 1860." Ph.D. diss., Michigan State University, 1979.

Osterud, Nancy Grey. *Bonds of Community: The Lives of Farm Women in Nineteenth-Century New York.* Ithaca: Cornell University Press, 1991.

Pike, Nicolas. *A New and Complete System of Arithmetic, Composed for the Use of the Citizens of the United States.* Newburyport: Mycall, 1788.

Roberts, Warren E. "The Tools Used in Building Log Houses in Indiana." *Pioneer America* 9 (July 1977): 32–61.

Ruchames, Louis, ed. *The Letters of William Lloyd Garrison, 1836–1840.* Cambridge: Belknap Press of Harvard University Press, 1971.

Ryan, Mary P. *Women in Public: Between Banners and Ballots, 1825–1880.* Baltimore: Johns Hopkins University Press, 1990.

———. *Womanhood in America from Colonial Times to the Present.* New York: Watts, 1975.

Shade, William Gerald. *Banks or No Banks: The Money Issue in Western Politics, 1832–1865.* Detroit: Wayne State University Press, 1972.

Stewart, James Brewer. *Holy Warriors: The Abolitionists and American Slavery.* New York: Hill and Wang, 1976.

Thompson, Ralph. *American Literary Annuals and Gift Books, 1825–1865.* Hamden, Conn.: Archon, 1967.

Watson, John F. *Annals of Philadelphia and Pennsylvania in Olden Time: or, Memoirs, Anecdotes, and Incidents of Philadelphia and Its Inhabitants from the Days of the Founders.* 3 vols. Ed. Willis P. Hazard. 1830; Philadelphia: Stuart, 1884.

Webb, Samuel. *History of Pennsylvania Hall.* Philadelphia: Merrihew and Gunn, 1838.

Wells, Robert V. "Quaker Marriage Patterns in a Colonial Perspective." *William and Mary Quarterly,* 3d. ser., 29 (1972): 415–42.

Whitney, Daniel. *The Family Physician and Guide to Health.* Pen-Yan, N.Y.: Gilbert, 1833.

Whitney, W. A., and R. I. Bonner. *History and Biographical Record of Lenawee County, Michigan.* Vol. 1. Adrian, Mich.: Stearns, 1879.

Wolloch, Nancy. *Women and the American Experience.* New York: Knopf, 1984.

Woodford, Arthur M. *Detroit and Its Banks.* Detroit: Wayne State University Press, 1974.

Woodford, Frank B. *Parnassus on Main Street.* Detroit: Wayne State University Press, 1965.

Yellin, Jean Fagan. *Women and Sisters: The Antislavery Feminists in American Culture.* New Haven: Yale University Press, 1989.

Yellin, Jean Fagan, and John C. Van Horne, eds. *The Abolitionist Sisterhood: Women's Political Culture in Antebellum America.* Ithaca: Cornell University Press, 1994.

INDEX

I

J